Foundations of Inf

Why does information technology disappoint or enslave us? Why do so many information systems projects collapse? How can we do better? There are many technical, social, economic and other aspects to consider. How do we ensure we take all these into account as we research ITC or employ them? ICT affects our lives and world more profoundly than ever before. How may we understand it? This book employs philosophy to lay foundations for understanding the complexity of ICT in five areas:

- The nature of information and computers, and artificial intelligence;
- The use of ICT at work and home, for serious and less-serious use;
- The ICT features that annoy or delight us;
- Societal issues, such as surveillance, e-government, ICT in developing countries, climate change, what technological progress is and what is the role of ICT as a whole and of the information systems field;
- ICT development—including computer programming, knowledge engineering and project management.

The ideas in this book emerge from five decades of experience of the author with ICT, across industry, the professions and academic life. Information systems researchers will enjoy this book because it offers them new ideas and fresh perspectives.

On the 500th anniversary of the European Reformation, this book introduces and applies the Reformational Philosophy of mid-20th-century Dutch thinker, Herman Dooyeweerd to contemporary challenges of the 21st century. Excitingly, this accessible philosophy is grounded in everyday experience and yields a rich seedbed of ideas, which researchers and practitioners can develop to their advantage.

Andrew Basden is professor of human factors and philosophy in information systems at the University of Salford, Manchester, UK.

Routledge Studies in Innovation, Organization and Technology

For a full list of titles in this series, please visit www.routledge.com

36 **Low Cost, Low-Tech Innovation**
New Product Development in the Food Industry
Vijay Vyas

37 **The Entrepreneurial University**
Context and Institutional Change
Edited by Lene Foss and David V. Gibson

38 **Dynamics of Knowledge-Intensive Entrepreneurship**
Business Strategy and Public Policy
Edited by Franco Malerba, Yannis Caloghirou, Maureen McKelvey and Slavo Radosevic

39 **Collaborative Innovation**
Developing Health Support Ecosystems
Edited by Mitsuru Kodama

40 **Innovation Drivers and Regional Innovation Strategies**
Edited by Mario Davide Parrilli, Rune Dahl-Fitjar, and Andrés Rodríguez-Pose

41 **Information Theft Prevention**
Theory and Practice
Romanus Izuchukwu Okeke and Mahmood Hussain Shah

42 **The New Production of Users**
Changing Innovation Collectives and Involvement Strategies
Edited by Sampsa Hyysalo, Torben Elgaard Jensen, and Nelly Oudshoorn

43 **Foundations of Information Systems**
Research and Practice
Andrew Basden

Foundations of Information Systems

Research and Practice

Andrew Basden

LONDON AND NEW YORK

First published 2018
by Routledge

2 Park Square, Milton Park, Abingdon, Oxfordshire OX14 4RN
52 Vanderbilt Avenue, New York, NY 10017

Routledge is an imprint of the Taylor & Francis Group, an informa business

First issued in paperback 2019

Library of Congress Cataloging-in-Publication Data
Names: Basden, Andrew, 1948– author.
Title: Foundations of information systems : research and practice / by Andrew Basden.
Description: New York : Routledge, 2017. | Includes bibliographical references and index.
Identifiers: LCCN 2017009589 | ISBN 9781138797017 (hardback) | ISBN 9781315757483 (ebook)
Subjects: LCSH: Information technology. | Information behavior.
Classification: LCC T58.5 .B375 2017 | DDC 003/.54—dc23
LC record available at https://lccn.loc.gov/2017009589

ISBN: 978-1-138-79701-7 (hbk)
ISBN: 978-0-367-87030-0 (pbk)

Composed on Amiga 1200 with Protext and Pagestream.

Typeset in Sabon
by Apex CoVantage, LLC

Contents

Figures

Tables

Preface

My Journey

My intellectual journey has been from hard to soft. Starting in the tangibles of electronics in the 1960s, I ended up in the abstractions of social science and philosophy in the 2000s. Coming from Scotland, I have always sought the integration of theory and practice.

I started computer programming in the 1970s, first in computer-aided design and data structures for my PhD, then in business data and then to produce a database of medical records in primary healthcare. I learned much about the nature of data and that development of information systems is a combination of technical, human and social skills, in which attitudes and beliefs are as important as programming skill. In 1980 I joined a chemical company to work with expert systems and learned a lot about knowledge and eliciting it from experts and then representing it in computers. I strengthened my understanding that knowledge and ICT development are complex and unpredictable in which human relationships are vital, and gained an appreciation of the difference between experience and understanding. For some reason, the expert systems I was involved in creating became successful in real-life use—several in the chemical industry and one in the surveying profession.

After a dozen years in industry and public bodies, I returned to academic life in 1987 and wanted to understand my many experiences—about information, about programming, about knowledge and its elicitation and about human relationships and attitudes. For a decade, I engaged in research to try to do this and came up with some fresh approaches, especially in information systems development, in the realm of human-computer interaction and in data structures. I taught undergraduate and postgraduate students about databases, expert systems, business systems, HCI and multimedia.

"You're the only one who mentioned benefits," remarked someone after my presentation at a conference in the 1990s. 'Benefits' of ICT in use had been important in my work, but when I entered academia, I found little interest in it in the HCI and expert systems communities. (I had not discovered the Management Information Systems community then—and am glad

I did not because they were too fixated on management issues rather than down-to-earth issues of interest to users.)

All this time, I had had little interest in philosophy, thinking it was too abstract. I pictured a line, with philosophy at one end, with 'real life' at the other, and scientific theories in the middle. But bend the line into a circle, and philosophy ends up next to real life—and that is where I see it now. Good philosophy is immensely practical, because it recognises the diversity of meaning in life.

This changed when, around 1994, I discovered a philosophy that can speak to and listen to 'real life' (or as I shall call it in this book, 'everyday experience'). The philosophy is from a Dutch thinker, Herman Dooyeweerd. His work is little known in English, though well known in his native tongue. What first attracted me to his ideas was his suite of fifteen aspects that everyday experience exhibits. Recognising that this could help me understand the complex interplay of benefits and detriment (for example, a system might reduce costs but destroy families by requiring people to work longer hours: economic benefit, social harm), I began to study his ideas. This opened me to ideas of other philosophers and social theorists, such as Habermas, and I noticed parallel concerns between Dooyeweerd and the others, even though there were deep differences in approach. I found this intriguing.

When I became a professor in 2003, I was given a mandate to "explore this Dutch philosopher and how he applies to information systems." This is what I have tried to do ever since. I had begun a website to collect information and discussion about Dooyeweerd, *The Dooyeweerd Pages* (www.dooy.info), which is still running, and had discovered a small group of international academics who were likewise exploring his ideas in the areas of systems thinking, technology and social sciences.

Dooyeweerd in Academic Life

As I published papers on how Dooyeweerd's philosophy could be used in practice, I noticed that I could apply Dooyeweerd's ideas to all areas of the information systems field in which I had been involved. These form the five main areas discussed in this book and include both technical and social areas. This contrasted with other philosophers who I found could apply to only some of them. I also noticed that Dooyeweerd provided very practical ideas and guidance as well as philosophically sound theoretical ideas. This was exciting. Dooyeweerd provided an holistic and widely interdisciplinary view (Strijbos and Basden 2006) that was rare. Rarer still was that this did not sacrifice depth nor relevance to everyday life. The problem was that no journals seemed to be interested in publishing the broad depth or the deep breadth that Dooyeweerd afforded.

So I wrote a book, *Philosophical Frameworks for Understanding Information Systems* (Basden 2008), in which I tried to bring all these ideas together. In it I included two chapters that discuss Dooyeweerd's philosophy and five that discuss how it can apply to five main areas of interest in information systems and technology: Computer use, IS development, IT resources, societal factors and the nature of computers (see §1-4.1). Doing so helped me draw my ideas together, but I did not much engage with discourses then going on in the various areas.

At the turn of the millennium, I was asked at short notice to prepare and deliver a masters course on *Key Issues in Information Systems Development*. I decided to design it around my chapter on IS development and taught IS students Dooyeweerd's philosophy. *Despite* being mature students from professional practice in many countries, they loved Dooyeweerd's philosophy.

Or perhaps it was *because* they were: they appreciated an approach that was open to the diversity and complexity of 'real life'. Though Dooyeweerd was a Dutch Christian and had tried to create a philosophy that was commensurable with Christian belief, it was interesting that those who liked his ideas the most were from Hindu, Muslim or African Christian cultures rather than Western. They appreciated the dignity that Dooyeweerd gave to the faith and ethical aspects alongside the economic, social and technical, as all being part of the complexity of life.

This told me something important: Dooyeweerd's ideas need not be a specialist, personal interest, but could, indeed did, have value for others. That knowledge, and encouragement from the late Prof. Dr. Heinz Klein, one of the fathers of the information systems field and one of the highest-quality thinkers I have known, inspired me to engage with other philosophical thinkers alongside Dooyeweerd. Heinz encouraged me to explore Habermas, for example, and how Dooyeweerd could link with his thought; an outcome is in Basden (2002).

Likewise, my PhD students very much appreciated Dooyeweerd's ideas and made them central to their own research. They developed Dooyeweerd's ideas in ways that I could not, and some of their thinking is included in this book—and I would like to give credit to them.

Why This Book?

With this experience in teaching, applying and engaging Dooyeweerd, my ideas have developed, and I have seen how Dooyeweerd's ideas can engage with a wide range of thinkers, theories and ideas and be useful to many other kinds of people. I believe it is important that Dooyeweerd's ideas are taken seriously by mainstream practice and research, so I wanted to write a book that would encourage both researchers and practitioners in mainstream fields to consider, understand and apply Dooyeweerd.

This will do several things. It will hopefully bring benefit to both practice and research. In addition, it will also reveal where the weaknesses lie in his ideas. Thus far, his ideas have been taken up largely by narrow philosophical and theological communities, who have not been sufficiently critical. It is only when communities of thought and practice have seriously tried his ideas, found problems and tried to solve those problems that we will know what the pertinent problems in Dooyeweerd's thought are.

It has been a privilege to pioneer the application of Dooyeweerd in an interdisciplinary field like information systems, but I am nearing the end of my academic career. I hope others will take on the mantle. I wanted to collect together many of the relevant ideas and experiences from the past 40 years to make them available, so that others might be stimulated to research or apply them for themselves. Many of the ideas have yet to be researched or developed.

Aim of Book

The aim of this book is to:

- Offer foundational understanding of five areas of information technology and information systems.
- Introduce a philosophy (Dooyeweerd's) that can fruitfully apply across all five areas to provide a sound basis for bringing the five areas into harmony; usually a different philosophical basis is found for each area, and these different philosophies are incommensurate with each other.
- Demonstrate that Dooyeweerd's philosophy can suggest radical new paradigms (ways of thinking and working) in each of the areas, and thus new directions for research; in many cases, philosophy is used to bolster a status quo (whether those of affluent society or those of academia).
- Demonstrate how Dooyeweerd's philosophy helps us understand practice and the practice of research more deeply, and the relationship between them.
- Demonstrate Dooyeweerd's ability to engage well with a wide range of discourses across these five areas, often ones that seem to contradict each other, to affirm, critique and enrich them rather than reject or replace any.
- Provide researcher-friendly references to Dooyeweerd's ideas, to allow deeper exploration.

A richer interdisciplinary world awaits researchers, academics and project teams, and I hope this book will help them address complex, seemingly intractable issues across multiple aspects.

This is an ambitious aim for one book. Some of it was covered in Basden (2008) but here more deeply. Coverage of issues will, I hope, be deep enough to stimulate interest and point in a clear direction, but not deep enough to have answered all the questions that are raised, or even raise all that could be. I hope to stimulate readers to carry this work forward and explore the possibilities—including determining whether Dooyeweerd's philosophy lives up to the promises I make for it.

About This Book

To meet these aims, Dooyeweerd's philosophy is presented in Part I. In Part II, five areas of information systems are discussed in a way that provides foundations for, immanently critiques and enriches extant discourses. Examining these discourses brings out their fundamental issues, which are reinterpreted using Dooyeweerd's philosophy in order to build a foundational framework for understanding the area. The framework is then applied to the discourses to critically affirm and enrich them within a broader perspective.

This book is not a rearrangement of what I have already published in papers or Basden (2008) but is an attempt to develop new ideas. In an editorial in *MIS Quarterly*, Straub (2009) encouraged writing that moves us into "intellectual territory that is unexploited," where we find "exciting, blue ocean ideas". Applying Dooyeweerd's philosophy seems to cultivate 'blue-ocean' thinking.

I hope that the reader will find this book to be a rich spawning ground for blue-ocean ideas. The chapters are designed to be read in any order, just as you would with a collection of books. For example, readers interested in the artificial intelligence question could go directly to §5-6, or those interested in affordance, to §7-2.3 and §7-3.3. However, to do so, readers should be willing to follow the cross-references that are given there to sections where Dooyeweerd's ideas are explained. Though only few chapters might be of interest to readers initially, perhaps the links to other topics will stimulate them to consider other issues.

Influences on Me

Several influences have contributed to my thinking.

1. I have mild *Asperger syndrome* and dyslexia, so I have looked at the world in a different way from most people. This has generated a number of original ideas, some of which have been fruitless, but some—those in this book—have proven fruitful to some degree and, I trust, will be of benefit to others. Dyslexia has meant that I have had difficulty in trying to express the ideas. Part of the difficulty comes from just trying to express what I mean, which is often tangled, but part comes from my Aspergic inability to understand what others expect or find meaningful. Straub (2009, vi) recognised that "if the ideas are too radical and lie too far beyond the reviewers'/evaluators' experience, their comfort zones will be stretched beyond their limits and the sad result will be rejection of the paper." Two extra responsibilities are thus laid on an author like myself, not only to express my ideas, but also to work out how they might be relevant in the eyes of others, and to work out a strategy for introducing the ideas to those others.
2. *Christian faith*. Being a follower of Jesus Christ (with evangelical-charismatic-calvinistic-celtic influences) gives direction to the different

ideas. Though I think differently, I want to (a) understand the nature of reality, with joy, (b) bring good to the world, with wisdom and responsibility especially for the natural creation, (c) be open to the diversity of meaningfulness and to the potential of people and their ideas.

3. *Amiga computer*. Designed in the 1980s to be a platform for multimedia and games, the Amiga happened also to have a superbly elegant operating system that could run general purpose software efficiently. *This is a computer for life*, I immediately thought, and purchased an Amiga 500 around 1989. I still use an Amiga 1200 computer out of choice, which came out in 1992, though now upgraded with USB, Internet, etc., because of its smooth user interface, and the excellent word processor, *Protext*, which I have used for writing this book. With *Protext*, as soon as I think, the words are on screen. The Amiga has shaped what I believe ICT should be and do.
4. *IS community mindset*. I have never felt entirely comfortable in the information systems field, maybe because of my sojourn with industry. Many of the theories extant in the field have seemed to me rather distant from reality. Positivist approaches seemed too narrow and trivial and lack normative force. Socio-critical approaches have normative force, but their norm seems too narrow. Interpretivist approaches, though broader, seem too swayed by what seems fashionable at the time. Very few are the premier-journal papers that I find interesting or useful.

How I Wrote This Book

To write this book, I decided to cover five areas as I had with *Philosophical Frameworks for Understanding Information Systems*, and that an explanation of Dooyeweerd's philosophy should be included, so that readers did not have to search elsewhere. However, whereas in the main chapters of that work, I would first discuss a Dooyeweerdian framework for understanding, and then discuss just a few other authors, in this work, I begin in the usual way, by reviewing the discourses of each area.

The idea of focusing on discourses came from my students, Nick Breems and Sina Joneidy, who used them in their PhD research to identify the meaningful issues therein and analyse these using Dooyeweerd's aspects. It enabled distinctions to be made that are clearer than is usual in the IS field, especially in the area of ICT use, and to place discourses that are somewhat overlooked by the field. In all, about fifty discourses are reviewed.

This caused a problem. Whereas with some I was familiar, with others I was less so, and with a few I had to enter the discourse from scratch. With most, however, I had an intuitive understanding of their issues, built up over 40 years of working with ICT, and I let that guide me. In some areas, many sources are journal papers, in others, the Internet, because that is where most of the active discourse occurs, because I want to respect everyday experience. The depth of overview varies, is often shallower than I like and sometimes omits important thinkers or topics.

This variability might not matter, for two reasons: I am interested in disclosing meaningful issues rather than responding to arguments, and I go deeper than the level at which most arguments are carried out, examining their foundations—in order to lay foundations for information systems research and practice. That is what this book is about, and Dooyeweerd helps us lay those foundations and build frameworks for each on those foundations.

References

Basden A. 2002. The critical theory of Herman Dooyeweerd? *Journal of Information Technology*, 17, 257–269.

Basden A. 2008. *Philosophical Frameworks for Understanding Information Systems*. IGI Global Hershey, PA.

Straub, DW. 2009. Editor's comments: Why top journals accept your paper. *MIS Quarterly*, 33(3), iii–ix.

Strijbos S, Basden A. (Eds.). 2006. *In Search of an Integrative Vision for Technology: Interdisciplinary Studies in Information Systems*. Springer, New York.

Acknowledgements

If this book is useful, then most of the credit must go to those who have helped in the writing of it, each in different ways. Though the material is my own, it would not have been presentable within the tight timescales imposed by the publishers, if ever, had not others helped.

I am deeply indebted to my wife, Ruth. Throughout the years in which the book has been germinating and written, she has given me enormous love and sacrificial support. When I despaired, she provided calm redirection. When I became frustrated, she challenged me to rethink what I was trying to say, and to whom. As a result, Chapter 7 especially was reorientated more towards users, and this led all the others, and everything became clearer.

Much of the credit for this book must go to Stephen McGibbon. Stephen spent a considerable amount of time advising me on from which angle to present the material. His experience in the software industry helped me with all chapters of Part II, but especially by challenging and strengthening Chapters 7 and 9. His knowledge of Dooyeweerd's philosophy helped with Chapter 3 and those in Part III. That he shares my faith immanently helped when I began to despair that it would ever be completed or be of any value, in providing solid and challenging encouragement. Stephen advised me what to omit when the work was too long and when its argument was tortuous, or when there was too much padding. He helped me change my style of argument to something more gracious. He also took some of the load of proofreading.

I am very grateful to Dr. Roelien Goede (Northwest University, South Africa), who has contributed critical additions in Chapters 1, 6, 7, 8 and the final chapters, and helped with proofreading. Professor Helen Richardson (Sheffield Hallam University, UK) provided incisive comments from the perspective of information systems and identified missing topics, especially in Chapter 8. Professors Anita Mirijamdotter (Linnaeus University, Sweden), Sytse Strijbos and Henk Geertsema (ex Vrije Universiteit, Amsterdam, the Netherlands) have helped me understand Dooyeweerd and systems over the years, and challenged or encouraged me on direction of the book.

John Oikonomopoulos has devoted considerable effort to offering challenging critique. Not only did he help with proofreading, but he uncovered weaknesses that would annoy philosophers or undermine the arguments, especially in Chapters 2 and 3, and the Introduction. Jordan Chaney, CEO of a software company, provided encouragement and suggestions for enriching the work. He showed that the book would be of more value to practitioners than I had expected, so I oriented it more towards practice.

I would like to thank PhD students who have accompanied me on this journey with Dooyeweerd: Mike Winfield, Suzanne Kane, Kamaran Fathulla, Gareth Jones, Hawa Ahmad, Subrahmaniam Krishnan-Harihara, Nick Breems, Ghadah Khojah, Sina Joneidy, Karen Swannack, Opeoluwa Aiyenitaju-Adewolu and also Alex Kimani, for the research they have carried out, mostly using Dooyeweerd, which has developed my own ideas, and for allowing me to mention their ideas here.

Because the material in this book is wide-ranging, and some is from fields that I previously worked in and therefore am no longer up to date on, I am deeply indebted to the founders of and contributors to Wikipedia for allowing me access to much information, and to the creators of Google search for making it possible to find many relevant articles.

Trademarks

Part I

This part introduces the topic of the book (Chapter 1), the role that philosophy plays in laying foundations for information systems research and practice (Chapter 2), and the philosophy that will be employed in order to lay foundations (Chapter 3).

Since this philosophy, developed by Dooyeweerd, is not widely known, Chapter 3 offers a substantial explanation, and Chapter 4 prepares us for Part II by discussing how the philosophy can engage with discourses and research extant in the information systems field.

1 Introduction

At the time of writing this book, the future of the automotive company Volkswagen hangs in the balance because programmers installed a 'defeat device'. Vehicle pollution emissions are supposed to be controlled, but the emissions control system reduces driving performance. The Volkswagen defeat device software detected whether the car is undergoing emissions testing and if not, switched the control system off, so that in normal driving, the pollution emissions were between 15 and 30 times higher than they should be (Ford 2015), and drivers were unaware.

Upon disclosure of cheating, Volkswagen's shares worldwide plummeted by 30 per cent, and the trust that Volkswagen had built up as an ethical, environmentally aware company evaporated. Volkswagen was fined billions of dollars and is having to replace the software on 11 million cars worldwide. Readers will know the outcome.

The CEO of Volkswagen told the US Congress that the defeat device had been installed by "a couple of software engineers" and had not been company policy. The full story can be found on *Wikipedia* at https://en.wikipedia.org/wiki/Volkswagen_emissions_scandal.

Information systems (or 'information technology' or 'information and communications technology') like this can have serious, unexpected repercussions. Repercussions occur not only for embedded software like engine management systems, but also for large organizational systems, computer games, websites, individual mobile applications, and indeed all kinds of systems. The type of repercussion varies with the type of system and its context of use. For example, might the game *Pokemon Go* get screen-bound young people out walking? Some repercussions might be good, others bad.

> Note on terminology: Throughout this book, the terms, '*Information systems*' (IS), '*information technology*' (IT), '*information and communication technology*' (ICT), '*computers*', and '*digital media*' might all appear in this text and will signify almost the same thing (synonyms), namely the combination of technical artefacts and human context. Most discussion in this book will be relevant to all of them. No term is ideal. 'Information systems' connotes organizational systems, but

> we also consider individual and mobile use. 'Computers' and 'information technology' emphasise the technical side but we emphasise the human and informational sides too. 'Digital media' might prove a transient fashion. So '*information and communication technology*' *(*ICT*)* is preferred, often with 'information systems', to cover all the above. The others are used where connotation matters.

How may we understand what is going on or what might happen in the future? ICT is designed, developed and installed. ICT is used. Its use brings repercussions which, if widespread, can affect society's attitudes and beliefs.

Where does responsibility lie? In the Volkswagen case, does responsibility stop with software engineers? Does it not often extend to management, from whom attitudes diffuse through their organizations? It appears that the culture in Volkswagen had deteriorated over the years, to be one of fear and control rather than of honest innovation. That Volkswagen had made several versions of the 'defeat devices' suggests involvement by management (Cremer et al. 2015).

Does the responsibility stop with management? Does it not often extend to the (global) culture within which companies operate—the business culture that accepts as normal, competitive outsourcing, offshoring and body-shopping, which creates a precarious life for all?

1-1 About This Book

This book aims to lay foundations for understanding the phenomenon that is ICT in our lives. It takes a broad view across areas that are not usually considered together—its nature, use, design and development, through to its impact in society—and it seeks depth of understanding that will be helpful for both practice and research.

It will employ philosophy to lay these foundations but in a way that is sensitive to everyday experience, because the philosophy it uses (that of the Dutch thinker, Herman Dooyeweerd) is one that takes everyday experience as its starting point. As a result, it offers new ways of looking at a wide range of areas of interest in research and practice in information systems, suggesting new avenues of research. Throughout the book, a hundred suggestions are made for specific, promising pieces of research in the information systems field, which are gathered together in the final chapter.

Foundations. Information Systems. Research. Practice. In this chapter, these will be considered in reverse order, to address questions like: What are these? Why are they important to us? This chapter sets the scene for the others, explaining rather than discussing.

Chapter 2 discusses philosophy in general, and Chapters 3 and 4, Dooyeweerd's philosophy. Chapters 5 to 9, in Part II, develop foundational frameworks for understanding in five main areas to do with information systems and ICT, which are discussed in Section 1-4 below:

- The nature of ICT;
- ICT use;
- ICT features;
- ICT and society; and
- ICT development.

Chapters 10 to 12 draw this all together and make recommendations.

Most of the chapters have been written in a way that each can be read somewhat independently of others, without having to read through the chapters that precede them. Readers will find reading through rewarding, but those interested in benefits of ICT in use, for example, might jump immediately to Chapter 6 if they wish, or those interested in the artificial intelligence question, to Chapter 5. The danger of skipping is, of course, that concepts encountered might be misunderstood, having been explained earlier, so copious cross-references are included to where concepts are explained, indicated by "§". Later, if they wish, readers might read through chapters they skipped, in order to gain background understanding.

In fact, just perusing the tables might provide insight (e.g., try Table 6.2 to understand interaction with ICT).

1-2 Practice

This book is about how foundational understanding might contribute to practice around ICT, including the practice of research, by putting us in a position to offer good-quality guidance, including to those who offer guidance. To do this, there will be an emphasis on practice as everyday experience, though this is not always explicit.

1-2.1 What Is Practice?

Sadly, 'practice' has two misleading connotations, neither of which is intended in this book: (a) of professional activity, as for example in health's 'general practice', and (b) of learning a skill. In this book, its meaning is much wider, about everyday life around ICT.

'Practice' refers to everyday experience of *using ICT* (whether as emissions-tester, car-driver (indirectly), games-player or insurance clerk entering data; see §6-2.16). 'Practice' also refers to the everyday experience of *developing ICT*. Even when highly methodical, rational and technical, ICT development also involves: socializing, being creative, competing or collaborating, being generous or mean, cheating or refusing to cheat, even pressured by management—and for example stopping work to pray at certain times. When it comes to ICT in relation to *society*, 'practice' takes on a different form, as pervasive beliefs, assumptions and expectations, or infrastructure, which, lying unquestioned, affect all we do or aspire to.

Even *research* is practice: being polite while interviewing, being careful while analysing data, doing justice to the literature and also competing or collaborating, believing (or not) in the value of what we do, and so on.

Practice, as everyday experience, is therefore of many different kinds. Practice is action. We can almost always differentiate between better and worse practice, between good and bad.

1-2.2 *Everyday Experience*

Sometimes, 'everyday' has connotations of being second-class, mundane, unworthy of our attention. That is not what is intended here. Here, everyday experience is respected and adopted in an attempt to develop foundational understanding of information systems. The precise form this respect takes is explained in §3-1.1, but for now, it will suffice to list a number of concepts and terms that are associated with everyday experience and practice. Some have emerged from certain thinkers. (This list may be considered a long note on terminology on terms used here.)

- **Practice:** "actual performance or application of knowledge, as opposed to mere possession of knowledge", often as "the exercise of a profession" (Webster 1971, 1780). Contrasted with theory or academia.
- **Everyday life:** The total functioning, situation and being of people engaged in living, working, playing, etc. Example: using Twitter on a mobile phone while walking along.
- **Real life:** Everyday life, emphasising its complexity, richness and the unexpected, as in "Theoretically it's easy to use, but in real life it's frustrating."
- **Everyday experience:** Everyday life from the perspective of the experiencer, their experiencing and being experienced. Example: technical experience covers the technical aspect; everyday experience covers all aspects of life.
- **Everyday functioning or activity:** Functioning while directly engaged in living, working, playing, etc., without much abstraction. Contrasted with *theoretical thinking*.
- **Down-to-earth issues:** The kind of issues encountered in everyday life, which are important to those involved, 'on the ground' (Ahmad and Basden 2013). Example: clarity in health records. Contrasted with high-level issues, of interest to academia, management or ICT suppliers, who discuss power-relations, cost-effectiveness and object-oriented design.
- **Life domains:** Conceptually separated yet interwoven domains of life in which people fulfil various roles; see §6-2.17. Opposes the assumption that only the professional domain is meaningful.
- **Pre-theoretical attitude of thought or naïve attitude:** The attitude our thinking takes in most everyday life, when we accept and engage with things around us without critique of them. Contrasted with the

theoretical attitude of thought, which involves higher level abstraction (Clouser 2005); see §3-4.3.

- **Tacit knowledge:** Knowledge we possess that cannot (easily) be explained (Polanyi 1967), but on which we rely in everyday functioning. Contrasted with explicit knowledge. See §3-8.4.
- **Intuition:** "the act or process of coming to direct knowledge without reasoning or inferring" (Webster 1971, 1187), with which it is contrasted. Everyday life involves a mixture of intuition with reasoning. See §3-8.4. Instinct, as direct psychical knowing, is one component of intuition.
- **Lifeworld:** Shared background understanding, often tacit; see §3-1.1. Contrasted with the scientific worlds of, e.g., physics, which depend on the lifeworld (Husserl 1970). "The life-world is above all the province of practice, of action" (Schutz and Luckmann, 1973, 18).
- **Community of practice** (Wenger 1998): The group of people who engage together in an area of practice.
- **Interdisciplinarity:** Working in, or studying, multiple disciplines often depends on many of the above. Contrasted with working in a single professional or academic discipline.

We must give due respect to all of these in our attempts to understand ICT, if we are to properly understand it in its fulness. Everyday life around ICT is rich, diverse and full of surprises that delight or frustrate. In ICT development, for example,

> One needs to have as broad a knowledge base as possible. It is the outer parameters that one must have knowledge about.
>
> (Jacob and Ebrahimpur 2001, 78)

It is hard to capture these 'outer parameters' in theories or guidelines, yet if we misunderstand or overlook them, our ICT practice as well as our understanding will be undermined and often distorted.

> Example: The core value of the insurance sector is 'utmost good faith', so a brokerage ICT system that failed to include it remained unused; see §9-6.2.

1-2.3 Guiding and Understanding Everyday Practice

In order to improve everyday practice, or perhaps prevent problems like those in Volkswagen, guidance is needed, and to be worthy of being relied on, guidance requires that we understand what we are guiding. Understanding is philosophically discussed in §3-4.3 and so only an outline is given here.

The first germ of understanding is distinguishing relevant issues from irrelevant (cf. *gestalt* figure-ground) and among relevant issues, making distinctions (classifying types). When these are made explicit, we are in a *theoretical attitude of thought*; when not, or before making such distinctions, we are in the *pre-theoretical attitude of thought.*

Example: CMMI (Capability Maturity Model Integration) is a project management approach referred to in Chapter 9. Process is meaningful to it, which it classifies as levels to focus on: people, management, standards, measures and innovation.

Example: The Technology Acceptance Model (TAM), discussed in Chapter 6, separates out the concepts of acceptance of ICT, intention to use, perceived usefulness and ease of use, and relationships among them—suggesting that only these need be considered for acceptance.

The results of theoretical thought (*theories*) may be rules and principles, to guide, models and theories, to explain or describe, or frameworks for understanding, to situate and stimulate. CMMI offers principles by which processes at each level may be guided. TAM explains the influence that perceived ease of use and usefulness have on likelihood of ICT acceptance.

All three kinds can help us understand and guide everyday experience and think about alternatives, so this book concerns itself with all three kinds, but mostly with frameworks, from which the other two may be derived. For example, TAM, though called a theory, is generic enough to be a framework for understanding, and many have used to form explanatory theories. From TAM, two simple guiding principles might be generated, "To improve acceptance, improve perceptions of (a) ease of use, (b) usefulness."

Unfortunately, most theory is narrower in focus than everyday experience is. CMMI, for instance, is about process but gives little guidance about responsibility. All TAM's constructs are about what we will call the formative aspect and ignore issues like age, information quality and fun; see §6-4.8. Dooyeweerd (1955) argued that theory will always be narrower than everyday experience (see §3-4.3). The way theories get over this is either to fill themselves with detail, as CMMI does, or require their users to fill in the detail, as TAM does. Either way, there is a danger of much that is important in everyday experience being overlooked, by either the detail-collectors or the theory-users, because of their predispositions.

We want understanding that is sensitive to the entire diversity of everyday practice around ICT. Perhaps we want a theory of practice? Bourdieu (1977) outlined a theory of practice, in which he tried to uncover the conditions that make practice possible, and those that make knowledge possible. Unfortunately, though he recognised that practice precedes theory, he still presupposed that theory itself is sufficient to understand everyday practice. Dooyeweerd argued that it should be the other way round (§3-1.1); first we need to understand what makes theory possible from a pre-theoretical standpoint, and only then may we employ theory to understand the pre-theoretical.

Is it enough to accumulate a host of idiographic instances from everyday experience? This is what Collins and Porras (1998) did, drawing out some general principles from examples of "successful habits of visionary companies". Can we be sure they have given us all the principles we need? What might Collins and Porras have omitted? We do need generic knowledge that explains or guides or stimulates but that applies across a range of situations. The way to such knowledge is partly through research—research that is sensitive to the heterogeneity of everyday life practice.

1-3 Research

This section discusses what is meant by 'research', less in terms of methods and more in terms of its meaningfulness in life. The view of research here is intended to apply to all kinds of research or inquiry relevant in the information systems field. Deeper discussion of research is found in §4-2/3.

To simplify somewhat, *professional research* aims to understand a particular situation (e.g. "Why did our profits fall?"), whereas *academic research* aims more generally to formulate understanding that contributes to humanity's *bodies of knowledge*. This book is about academic research.

Academic research in the information systems field has been dominated by three main approaches—positivist (hypothesis-testing), interpretivist (insight-gathering) and socio-critical (emancipatory)—but here 'research' can also include others, such as action research, design research and also philosophical reflection, in which the findings are philosophic insights. The main three approaches are presumed to be incommensurable with each other, which prevents respect or communication between them, yet in practice, each contributes something different, and §4-2.2 shows that they are not necessarily incommensurable.

To contribute to bodies of knowledge requires four things: that the contribution (a) be made explicit, so that others can understand and use it, (b) be general, so that it applies across unforeseen situations, (c) be worthy of being relied on, so it may be built on, and (d) can help to improve the world, at least potentially, so it links with everyday practice.

What is included in the bodies of knowledge is not truths so much as beliefs about how the world functions in general, on which it is reasonable to rely to guide practice or as axioms for other theories. In positivist research, reliability is sought by rigorously testing hypotheses, in interpretive research, by recognising biases among both researcher and researched (principles 3, 5, 7 in Klein and Myers [1999]), and in socio-critical research, by resorting to self-critique (Myers and Klein 2011). In all types, reliability is enhanced by debate that critiques and refines proposed ideas or findings; willingness to be critiqued is crucial to all kinds of research.

The generalization that occurs in research involves taking a theoretical attitude to the world, in which aspects are abstracted therefrom, such as the technical, social and economic aspects. How this differs from, and relates to, the pre-theoretical attitude of thought is discussed in §3-4.3. In particular, compared with everyday practice, research outputs (theories, etc.) are narrow, in different ways in the three main approaches: in positivist approaches, narrowing occurs in the definition of hypotheses to be tested, in interpretivist approaches, by the lens through which the world is viewed and in socio-critical approaches, by the socio-critical theory employed (Myers and Klein 2011).

This means that world improvement by research tends to be aimed at one aspect (e.g., efficiency, communicability, emancipation) and ignores possible 'collateral damage' in other aspects. Practical improvement ('application of research') must consider all possible such hidden aspects ('outer parameters', mentioned earlier). The foundational understanding developed here provides research methods that can ameliorate this problem; see §4-4.

Not only are the *content* or *output* important but also the *doing* or practice of research. Whereas output (theories) is theoretical, the doing of research is a pre-theoretical human, social activity, concerned not only with methods but also with motivations, biases, justice and the like, which can have a serious effect on the output. These are discussed in Sections 3-4 and 4-3, but one element is mentioned here.

The whole edifice of research (in all fields)—journals, conferences and funding—can be flawed in three ways. 1. Many topics are ignored because reviewers and editors opt for fashionable ones—and so do researchers who want to advance their publication rates. Example: The IS field has traditionally ignored uses of ICT in computer games and home computing (§6-2.6), and geographic information systems and scientific computing (§6-2.17). 2. Reviewers don't understand and thus reject 'blue ocean' topics in favour of 'safe' ones. As Oliver Sacks (1973) once remarked, "I was struck by the irony, the paradox, of all this: when I had nothing much to say I could be published without difficulty; now I had something to say I was denied publication." (Thanks to Peter Kawalek for drawing this to my attention.) 3. The everyday experience of ICT is a mixture of good and evil, but academic literature is unbalanced towards the negative (pathological) so that 'healthy' ICT is not adequately researched. Simone Weil (1968) made an important observation that might reveal a cause, which I have not found elsewhere:

> Nothing is so beautiful and wonderful, nothing is so continually fresh and surprising, so full of sweet and perpetual ecstacy, as the good.
> No desert is so dreary, monotonous, and boring as evil.
> With fictional good and evil it is the other way round.
> Fictional good is boring and flat, while fictional evil is varied and intriguing, attractive, profound, and full of charm.

Therefore, our foundational understanding of research and ICT will encourage consideration of healthy as well as pathological ICT. It will encourage wider ranges of topics and provide a basis for understanding and critiquing 'blue ocean' ideas.

The need for articulation and critical refinement implies that we must be able to listen to the wide range of discourses that are occurring and others yet to occur. The flaws in the edifice of research imply, however, that we must not be limited to extant discourses but be open to the entire panoply of everyday experience. So, in the Chapters of Part II, a wide range of discourses will be briefly reviewed, bringing side-by-side ones that are often isolated from each other. For topics where discourse is sparse or absent, examples will be drawn from everyday experience, including that of this author.

1-4 Information Systems

There is an identity crisis in the information systems field (IS) (Benbasat and Zmud 2003); see §8-2.4.

Given birth by computing, the IS field went through a long adolescence of distancing itself from, and sometimes disparaging, its parents. One can detect this in various parallel but similar reactions, including soft versus hard systems thinking, social contructivism versus technological determinism and even interpretivism versus positivism. A social-constructivist mindset has treated the technical artefact as of little consequence in itself because its meaning can be limitlessly 'constructed'. Where the technical has been recognised at all (e.g., in the socio-technical movement), it is usually treated as a 'black box' (§6-2.15), the inner structure of which it is not necessary to understand.

Against this trend, interest has recently awakened in what is called the 'materiality' of ICT—that there is something 'solid' about ICT that is impervious to social-constructivist dismissal. This has led to interest in affordance (the possibilities that technology affords us). As will be seen in §7-2, §7-3, the IS discourse around these is still limited, not exploring the inner structures of ICT. The gulf between social and technical has not yet been successfully bridged. Though computer science, software engineering and human-computer interaction (HCI) can tell us something about the nature and development of ICT, too little dialogue occurs with them.

1-4.1 An Integrative View

This book tries a different approach. I came into the IS field from electronics, computer science, knowledge engineering and HCI, and brought with me a deep appreciation of the nature of ICT, as well as of the importance of the human and social aspects of its development and use. (See, for example, my attempt to discuss roles of ICT in Basden [1983] and to humanise development in Basden et al. [1995].) So, in my previous work (Basden 2008),

I suggested that we need to listen to, and tell, the *whole story that is IS* by considering five main areas of research and practice:

- Human use of computers,
- the nature of computers,
- IS development,
- IT resources (components) and
- IT as societal ecology.

The IS field studies use and society, often coalescing them into 'context', and occasionally development, but hardly ever the other two. Computer science and artificial intelligence study components and nature, software engineering studies development, and HCI studies use, development and resources. I argued that considering all five areas together provides a more holistic perspective, and developed a novel framework for understanding each based on Dooyeweerd's philosophy.

Leonardi and Barley (2008, 166) also pointed out the close link between use, development and ICT features, with continued development of ICT during and because of use and users' desire for changes to the features.

1-4.2 *The Approach Taken Here*

Since then, my understanding has matured, especially about how the frameworks can engage with extant ideas. The five areas have remained largely intact, so this book adopts them, discussing one in each chapter of Part II. The emphasis has shifted from IS and computers towards ICT, for the reasons explained earlier. The five areas are depicted in Figure 1.1.

In Basden (2008), each chapter presents the Dooyeweerdian framework first, and then discusses how it might engage with a few selected ideas in

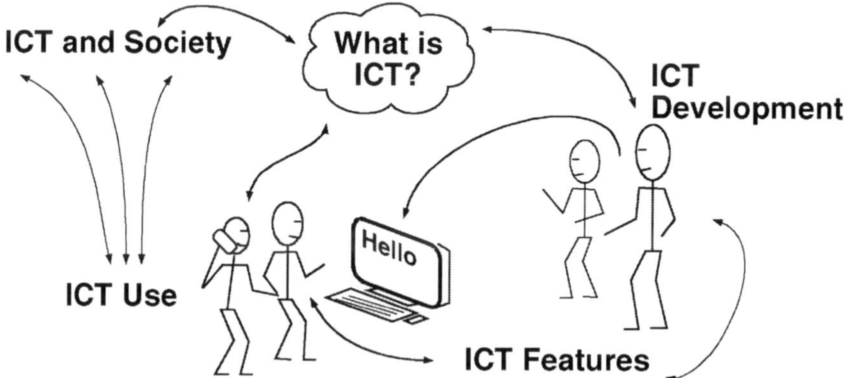

Figure 1.1 The Five Areas of Interest in the IS Field

its area. This book reverses this and engages more with extant ideas. In the chapter discussing each area, many discourses are briefly reviewed, to identify the different issues each discourse raises that are meaningful to the area as a whole. Then we discuss how a foundational understanding can be achieved that can embrace and enrich all the discourses and even the area as a whole. In each area, both research and practice are discussed, not separately but intertwined with each other.

Leonardi and Barley (2008) remark (p. 167), "Studying the interplay between . . . development, implementation and use will require modifications in typical research strategies" and suggest (p. 166) that whereas most studies are of one kind of ICT in a variety of contexts, the time has come to reverse this to compare radically different technologies in similar contexts. This is why many discourses are brought together in each area (seventeen for ICT use), rather than discussing each type of ICT separately.

1-4.3 Five Areas of Interest

The five areas are discussed in a different order from Basden (2008), and include:

- **The nature of ICT** (Chapter 5) is broadened from 'nature of computers' and is placed first in order to establish a foundational understanding of "What is ICT?" (though never a definition) via other questions: What are information, technology, documents, computers and programs? Can computers be like humans (the artificial intelligence question)? The foundational understanding is that the being of these is multi-aspectual with inherent normativity, which helps us understand them together and perhaps resolve the AI question.
- **ICT use** (Chapter 6) comes next because the 'being' of anything cannot be properly understood without reference to its meaningfulness in life (see §3-1.2). ICT use involves multi-aspectual engagements with the technology, with information, and repercussions in life that might be beneficial or detrimental, and maybe indirect and unexpected.
- **ICT features** (Chapter 7) are what users experience when using ICT; they influence what users can and cannot do. They include user interface objects, algorithms, protocols and computer languages. Two major issues are affordance and appropriateness. Whereas Basden (2008) took a developer's view, this book takes the users' view.
- **ICT and society** (Chapter 8) extends Basden's (2008) interest in ICT as an ecology in which we live, adding the other leg of structuration theory: impact of ICT on society, by widespread use and as infrastructure (including digital divide, surveillance and e-government and attitudes and beliefs). This chapter also discusses ICT as societal phenomenon, including progress, a 'liberating vision for technology' and the role of the information systems discipline.

- **ICT development** (Chapter 9) is treated, not as processes or methods, but as four multi-aspectual responsibilities for the future. It comes last because it is only after understanding the others that developers can fully take responsibility.

The Volkswagen case, with which this chapter opened, furnishes examples in all five areas. The nature of ICT is presumed to be that of intelligent automation, devoid of any normativity. ICT use occurs during driving and emissions testing, but indirectly, and the user's engagement is limited to the driving controls. The ICT features include not only those controls but also the algorithms for emissions control and defeating it. The societal view includes three things: the widespread use in 11 million vehicles causing unexpected pollution, the emissions testing infrastructure and the beliefs that the public held and hold about Volkswagen and what is acceptable. ICT development is, of course, the engineering of the software, but also includes multiple responsibilities for installing the defeat device.

No claim is intended that these five are the only areas. Rather, the discussions in Part II should be taken as exemplars of how such areas might be listened to, critiqued and provided with foundational understanding. No claim is intended that the foundations offered present any final or 'correct' view, but only views that are geared to everyday experience and are philosophically sound, offered as starters for discussion.

1-4.4 Some Cross-Area Issues

If we take an everyday-oriented approach, then we should understand what, if any, is everyday experience within each area. This is obvious for ICT use and development. Societal issues impact our everyday lives. ICT features and their affordance are part of the everyday experience of users, while their appropriateness is part of the everyday experience of developers who employ them as components. The nature of ICT, however, seems quite abstract. Nevertheless, in our everyday experience of ICT, we usually assume what ICT is and can do for us, at one of its levels described in Sections 5-3 and 5-4, like information or data. Moreover, we are usually aware in a pre-theoretical manner that other levels exist.

As recommended by Leonardi and Barley (2008), we bring radically different technologies together within each context, or area. So, ICT in businesses and organizations is brought alongside ICT for individuals and also global ICT. ICT in work and professional domains, is brought alongside ICT in other 'life domains', such as family and fun, home computing, art and music. ICT in developing countries is treated as fundamentally similar to ICT in Western economies. By bringing these together, and using the philosophical approach described in Chapter 3, it is hoped to find foundational understanding of all areas of ICT that, while it welcomes insights from sociology and management science, offers a core for the information systems field itself.

1-5 Foundations

Information systems (IS) researchers tend to be good at thinking about foundations, computer science researchers less so. Because the areas of interest span both fields, we need a foundational understanding that is useful to both. What makes a good foundation?

1-5.1 Current View of Foundations of IS

Unfortunately, the foundations that IS researchers discuss come mainly from sociology or management studies. These might provide valuable insights about the social and economic aspects of ICT, but they provide little core understanding of the informational aspect. Benbasat and Weber (1996) have argued that the information systems field lacked a sound and distinctive foundation, relying instead on reference disciplines like computer science, management science, cognitive science, organizational science, economics. This is "a fundamental strategic blunder" which "provides a short-term and relatively easy salve to the problems . . ." and "allows members . . . to abrogate responsibility for the hard task of identifying and building theories about those phenomena that make the discipline distinct" (p. 393). The "diversity which ensues under a reference-discipline regime distracts members of the discipline from the main game—namely, identifying whether there is a core to the discipline that gives it identity and, if so, articulating that core." Weber (2003), then the editor of *MIS Quarterly*, the top IS journal, wrote, "In the information systems discipline, *I searched in vain* for the powerful, general theories that underpinned research in disciplines like physics and economics" (p.iii, italics added).

Twenty years later, still no foundational understanding is in place. I hope that the foundations laid in this book will prove useful.

1-5.2 A Single Unitary Framework?

Should we seek a single over-arching framework for understanding? Some (e.g., Shaw and Garlan 1996) wish to define 'the' discipline of information systems as a single, unitary area of research and practice. Jones (2000) calls this "mission impossible". Lyytinen (2003) argues that it is "neither possible nor desirable to seek any ultimate foundation" for information systems. Pointing to the incommensurability between positivist and postpositivist approaches, he argues that such a quest is "hopeless", in that there is no agreement about what constitutes good theory nor about the appropriate criteria for progress in a field, so no ultimate foundation can be laid.

I argue against both his points. Section 4-2 argues that positivist can indeed be commensurable with other approaches. Section 8-6 proposes a philosophically strong understanding of progress and of a core aspect around which the whole of information systems coheres and finds its destiny.

Nevertheless, this book does not presuppose that we can find one 'ultimate foundation' for understanding ICT or information systems but rather seeks to lay foundations in the plural, one for each area. However, it will employ one philosophy as the ground in which those foundations are dug, and by which the foundations, and that which is built on them, can relate to each other.

On these foundations are constructed frameworks for understanding; the foundation is the concept-transcending *idea* of what is meaningful, the framework, a *conceptualization* thereof (Strauss 2009). Frameworks can support, for research, the generation of paradigms and of theories within these, and for practice, the erecting of scaffolding by which practical guidelines are constructed. (On the confusion about paradigms, see §3-5.2.2.) All these various levels constitute humanity's bodies of knowledge.

This provides a basis for understanding not only the relevant issues and the relationship between issues but also for expanding our understanding as new issues arrive and for understanding how issues in other areas and fields might be relevant.

Neither foundations nor frameworks, nor the choice of ground philosophy, can be proven either correct or incorrect, because they are held as pre-theoretical commitments, as sets of beliefs and assumptions about the area, to be adopted or not by those working in the area; see Section 3–4.

What we will aim for in the foundational frameworks that are developed in Part II is that each should be broad enough to enable the main issues to be addressed, be flexible enough to welcome new issues, be self-consistent and also consistent with each other, and both explain and guide, and that all these should be so for both research and practice.

The next chapter will look at philosophy and its role, briefly reviewing the range of philosophies that have been appealed to in information systems research and practice. It will explain why this book employs ideas from one radically different philosopher, the late Herman Dooyeweerd.

1-6 Contents of Book

Some characteristics of the writing in the following chapters deserve explanation.

1. A *Note on Terminology* explains how words and phrases are used in unusual ways, resolves ambiguity, gathers synonyms together or introduces terms. It is usually indented with protruding first line. Where not indented, it usually contains material that should be read.
2. Terms and concepts emphasised with bold or italics are ones that readers might wish to easily locate and refer back to.
3. Examples are inserted, often as indented paragraphs in which the first line protrudes. Sometimes these are in the main text, containing material to treat as main text.

4. Sometimes I refer to myself in the first person ("I") and sometimes in the third person ("this author", "Basden (2008)", etc.). I use "I" for personal experience and opinion or to show changes in my ideas, and third person when my experience or written work is to be treated as material as from any other thinker.
5. Citations in the present tense is to argument that pertains here. When authors are cited in the past tense, the emphasis is on the development of their thought, whether in past or recent present.

The book has three parts. Part I provides an overview of philosophy (Chapter 2), introduces Dooyeweerd's philosophy (Chapter 3) and discusses how Dooyeweerd may be used to form frameworks or undertake research (Chapter 4). Part II contains the five main chapters, one per area as enumerated above. Part III concludes the work, with three chapters addressing the questions "What?", "So what?" and "What now?" Chapter 10 reviews what has been achieved. Chapter 11 discusses limitations and possible contributions of the book. The final chapter, 12, makes suggestions for future action, including over 100 suggestions for research projects.

References

Ahmad H, Basden A. 2013. Down-to-Earth Issues in Information System Use. Proceedings of the Pacific Area Conference on Information Systems (PACIS). Paper 191.

Basden A. 1983. On the application of expert systems. *International Journal of Man-Machine Studies*, 19, 461–477.

Basden A. 2008. *Philosophical Frameworks for Understanding Information Systems*. IGI Global Hershey, PA.

Basden A, Watson ID, Brandon PS, 1995. *Client Centred: An Approach to Developing Knowledge Based Systems*. Council for the Central Laboratory of the Research Councils, London, UK.

Benbasat I, Weber R. 1996. Research commentary: Rethinking 'diversity' in information systems research. *Information Systems Research*, 7(4), 389–399.

Benbasat I, Zmud RW. 2003. The identity crisis within the IS discipline: Defining and communicating the discipline's core principles. *MIS Quarterly*, 27(2), 183–194.

Bourdieu P. 1977. *Outline of a Theory of Practice*, tr. R. Nice. Cambridge University Press, Cambridge, UK.

Clouser R. 2005. *The Myth of Religious Neutrality: An Essay on the Hidden Role of Religious Belief in Theories*. University of Notre Dame Press, Notre Dame, IN.

Collins JC, Porras JI. 1998. *Built to Last: Successful Habits of Visionary Companies*. Century, London, UK.

Cremer A, Wallace B, Lienert P. 2015. VW made several defeat devices to cheat emissions tests. *Reuters*, 17 October, accessed "www.reuters.com/article/us-volkswagen-emissions-software-idUSKCN0SB0PU20151017" 19 December 2015.

Dooyeweerd H. 1955. *A New Critique of Theoretical Thought* (Vols. I–IV 1975 ed.). Paideia Press, Jordan Station, Ontario, Canada.

Ford J. 2015. VW launches investigation into 'defeat device' allegations. *The Engineer*, 21 September, accessed "https://www.theengineer.co.uk/issues/sept-2015-online/vw-launches-investigation-into-defeat-device-allegations/" 19 December 2015.

Husserl E. 1970. *The Crisis of European Sciences and Transcendental Phenomenology*, tr. D. Carr. Northwestern University Press, Evanston, IL.

Jacob M, Ebrahimpur G. 2001. Experience vs. expertise: The role of implicit understanding of knowledge in determining the nature of knowledge transfer in two companies. *Journal of Intellectual Capital*, 2(1), 74–88.

Jones M. 2000. Mission impossible: Pluralism and 'multi-paradigm' IS research. *Information Systems Review*, 1(1), 217–232.

Klein HK, Myers MD. 1999. A set of principles for conducting and evaluating interpretive field studies in information systems. *MIS Quarterly*, 23(1), 67–93.

Leonardi PM, Barley SR. 2008. Materiality and change: Challenges to building better theory about technology and organizing. *Information and Organization*, 18, 59–76.

Lyytinen KJ. 2003. Information systems and philosophy: The hopeless search for ultimate foundations. In JI DeGross (Ed.), *Proceedings of the Americas Conference on Information Systems: AMCIS 2003*. Association for Information Systems, Atlanta, GA.

Myers MD, Klein HK. 2011. A set of principles for conducting critical research in information systems. *MIS Quarterly*, 35(1), 17–36.

Polanyi M. 1967. *The Tacit Dimension*. Routledge and Kegan Paul, London, UK.

Sacks O. 1973 *Awakenings*. Duckworth, London, UK.

Schutz A, Luckmann T. 1973. *Structures of the Life-World* (Vol. I). Northwestern University Press, Evanston, IL.

Shaw M, Garlan D. 1996. *Software Architectures—Perspectives on an Emerging Discipline*. Prentice-Hall, Upper Saddle River, NJ.

Strauss DFM. 2009. *Philosophy, Discipline of the Disciplines*. Paideia Press, Grand Rapids, MI.

Weber R. 2003. Editor's comments: Still desperately seeking the IT artifact. *MIS Quarterly*, 27(2), iii–xi.

Webster. 1971. *Webster's Third New International Dictionary of the English Language, Unabridged*. G. & C. Merriam & Co., Springfield, MA.

Weil S. 1968. *On Science, Necessity, and the Love of God*. Oxford University Press, Oxford, UK.

Wenger E. 1998. *Communities of Practice: Learning, Meaning and Identity*. Cambridge University Press, Cambridge, UK.

2 Philosophies

"One critical, but largely unrecognized aspect in these debates [about information systems]," wrote Lyytinen (2003), "is the necessity to draw upon philosophical studies as they relate to the nature of scientific knowledge and its foundations." This chapter discusses the role philosophy plays as 'ground' in which to dig and lay foundations for understanding.

During my tenure in professional life, I had found four aspects of knowledge (items & relationships, quantitative & qualitative values, spatiality, change; see Basden (2008, Chapter VII)); but what was the 'full set'? It would need philosophy to answer that. So upon returning to academic life in 1987, I approached a professorial colleague who knew some philosophy and innocently asked her what the full set was. She replied, "There aren't any. Your aspects are socially constructed."

I was stunned and left her determined not to show such ignorance again. However, two things told me she was wrong—my intuition and my experience of the errors and difficulties that arose from trying to reduce one aspect to another. Still privately curious, I continued to ponder what aspects of knowledge there might be, how to distinguish them, how to design suitable ways of representing each in software. Even though I agreed that human beings do socially construct their categories, I believed that there is a reality that transcends us and cannot be socially constructed. The recent interest in affordance and the materiality of ICT seems connected with my 1980s quest.

Though at the time I abandoned philosophy, I knew that I would nevertheless need philosophy to help me address this issue. It was only later that I found a philosophy which did not force me into either social constructivism or naïve realism or even critical realism—and which seemed provide a basis for thinking about the aspects of knowledge and many other issues at a fundamental level.

2-1 Why Philosophy Is Important

Philosophy is 'love of wisdom' (*philo*, *sophia*).

2-1.1 Roles and Types of Philosophy

Philosophy is important not only in research but also in practice, as Midgley (2000) explains well:

- Philosophical assumptions can be used to critique and justify practice.
- Philosophy can help us define alternatives and explain why each should be considered.
- Philosophy helps us select and defend guidelines for practice.
- Philosophical arguments inform debates about methodology.
- Philosophy can help justify intuitive notions and ethical stances.
- Philosophy provides different views of practice (frameworks for understanding it).
- Philosophy reveals why the reason for incompatibility between approaches so they cannot simply be 'compared'.

In relation to research, most of these apply directly because research is itself practice (see §4-3). However, the theoretical nature of research is also supported by philosophy:

- Philosophy helps to lay conceptual foundations on which to build theory (Hodges 1995).
- Philosophy is important in yielding unconventional and imaginative ideas (Courtney and Porra 2000), which is what will occur in the chapters in Part II.

Those nine reasons are all about philosophy helping process (critique, define, select, . . . build, yield), and they presume philosophy takes a neutral stance thereto. Yet, my experience with my colleague above suggests that philosophy is not neutral and is itself socially constructed. That philosophy *loves*, not just *discusses*, wisdom suggests that we need to re-admit some idea of the Good into the content of philosophy, and not just presume that we will seek the Good if our processes are helped.

Philosophy can be seen as having a number of main branches:

- Ontology: What is the nature of the world with which those who work in an area engage?
- Epistemology: How do we come to understand and know our area? What constitutes good research?
- Philosophical ethics: What is Good and Evil in the area: normative or anti-normative, problematic or to be aspired to?
- Methodology: What methods should we use in research and practice, and why?
- Anthropology: What is it to be human?
- Critical philosophy: What presuppositions lie at the root of our thinking>?

It is common in the fields of computer science and software engineering to elevate the role of ontology above all others, while in the information systems field, it is common to downplay the importance of ontology and elevate the role of epistemology.

Even that taxonomy of branches of philosophy does not meet with universal agreement, and I have never found it useful, having found they intermingle, especially in relation to wisdom. As will be discussed in §3-2.1, philosophy has long neglected everyday experience and long ignored the question of meaning, yet these will be central in all areas in discussing foundations in research and practice.

2-1.2 Views About Philosophy

Over the past 3,000 years, several views have been held about the nature and role of philosophy. To the pre-Socratic Greeks, philosophy linked religious belief with thinking about the principles of the natural world. Then it became moral and political theorizing, and under Plato and Aristotle, philosophy became vast metaphysical constructions. In the mediaeval period, dominated by Augustine, Aquinas and Anselm, Western philosophy concerned itself with the relationship between faith and reason, and was the 'handmaiden of theology'. After the Renaissance philosophy took up the task of exploring the foundations of the natural world, and then turned to examination of the human mind, and then the human condition more generally (Descartes, Hobbes, Locke, Hume).

To Kant, philosophy's role was to determine what reason can and cannot do. To Hegel, the philosopher's vocation was to approach the absolute through consciousness. Comte restricted his 'positive' philosophy to accepted rational, scientific methods. Bergson, in contrast, believed that the deepest and most important knowledge came from what he called philosophical intuition. For Whitehead, the duty of philosophy was primarily to "frame a coherent, logical, necessary system of general ideas in terms of which every element of our experience can be interpreted" (Levi 1975, 272). To the early Wittgenstein, "The object of philosophy is the logical clarification of thoughts." Marxism sees philosophy as a tool to further class interests and provides insight into how class interests affect worldviews. To Dewey, philosophy's role is to help us understand the unity and interrelatedness of all that is, including ethics and methodology.

This is, of course, a limited account of philosophy and its 2,500-year span, but it is not entirely unfair or inappropriate as an overall account, for reasons that will become apparent in the next chapter.

Philosophy is many-sided and can serve many purposes. "Part of what makes it difficult to find a consensus among philosophers about the definition of their discipline" suggests Levi (1975, 248) in *Encyclopedia Britannica*, "is precisely that they have frequently come to it from different fields, with different interests and concerns, and that they therefore have different areas of experience upon which they find it especially necessary or meaningful to reflect." He traces threads of meaningfulness that crop up repeatedly, for example:

- Aquinas, Berkeley and Kierkegaard all saw philosophy as a means to assert the truths of religion and to dispel the Materialistic or Rationalistic errors that, in their opinion, had led to its decline.
- Pythagoras, Descartes and Russell, all mathematicians, grounded everything in the concept of number and the method of deductive thinking.
- Plato, Hobbes and Mill were obsessed by problems of political arrangement and social living.
- The Milesians, Bacon and Whitehead began with an interest in the physical composition of the natural world, "so that their philosophies resemble more closely the generalizations of physical science than those of religion or sociology".

Each thread in philosophy seems centred on a way in which reality in its widest sense can be meaningful, a theme that arises repeatedly throughout this book. This makes us wonder whether many so-called philosophies are in fact philosophical thinking linked to particular spheres—the religious, quantitative, social, physical, etc.

Scientific thinking is also linked to similar spheres. The latter three are the core interests of mathematics, social science and physics or biology. If we take a broad view that allows science to extend beyond the natural sciences, to attempts to understand the 'laws', etc., by which each sphere of reality 'works', theology is the science of belief or religion. That view will be taken here. ('Laws' and 'works' receive clearer definition in Chapter 3, as does 'science'.) On this view, the science of information systems can be seen as having the informational sphere at its core (see §5-3.5, §8-6.1.1).

As *The Cambridge Dictionary of Philosophy* (Audi 1999) suggests, it is the role of science to find out what is true, but the role of philosophy to find out what truth is. 'Truth', however, is problematic (see §3-4.1.2) and in any case, foundations are concerned not only with truth but also with how we should live in each area (normativity), with presuppositions that are not 'true' so much as 'held', by a deep, often tacit, commitment, and with what it is meaningful to consider, discuss and research.

We still need a view of philosophy that can be valid and useful across all spheres and address the nature of truth and the Good in each, as love of wisdom.

Two great traditions in Western philosophy are opposed to each other by Lyytinen (2003). In North America, *Analytic Philosophy* has dominated, which sees philosophy as a branch of logic, to ensure we think clearly. It assumes, as Lyytinen put it, that "Philosophy should provide the ultimate language and a logic for the justification of IS knowledge". As such, some might see this as providing an "ultimate foundation" for understanding IS.

Lyytinen believes, however, that "Philosophy deconstructs any language and logic that has been developed for such purposes", as a "critical voice". This is the view arising from *Continental Philosophy* that has dominated in Europe, which Lyytinen calls it 'postpositivist'.

But just as the discussion of ICT should not be constrained by any analytic or positivist view, neither should it be constrained *a priori* by Lyytinen's (2003) Continental 'postpositivist' anti-foundationism. Deconstruction is indeed important, because many so-called foundations are inappropriate, but Lyytinen's language of "seeks to undermine any quest" speaks of a pre-theoretical dogma against 'ultimate foundations', and the need to adhere to such dogmas must be questioned.

From Lyytinen's article, it seems that his dogma arises from two things, a fear of unimaginative conceptual frameworks (often of an analytic-positivist kind) that are inappropriately forced on us, and a dislike of the battles that have raged between paradigms vying for supremacy over each other.

There is a third view of philosophy, which is adopted in this book, which might be called *Integrative Philosophy*. It sees philosophy as the "integrative discipline" (Hart 1984) or the "discipline of disciplines" (Strauss 2009), or as dealing with interrelatedness (Dewey). It takes a broad view of reality, being sensitive to all its aspects and their various rationalities, and thus able to assist us in interdisciplinary thinking across the boundaries of disciplines and sciences. It is particularly helpful in dealing with the diversity of everyday experience and will offer a common ground in which to lay foundations for each of the areas of the information systems field. Integrative Philosophy tries to understand the sciences to gain a wider, cross-disciplinary standpoint that enables us to understand all kinds of theoretical or scientific views in relation to each other.

The approach here is to employ one philosophy in an integrative way to provide the 'critical voice' that Lyytinen desired (indeed, it questions what it means to be critical), while recognising the importance of good reasoning (it sets reasoning within the ambit of the pre-theoretical). It should not arouse Lyytinen's fears.

Our response to any statement of what philosophy is must take account of the characteristics of the human being who philosophises—which is why I began this chapter with an experience. However, this raises the question of whether there is any philosophical thinking in its own right, whatever field it might be linked to. On what basis may we recognise philosophy?

2-2 Application of Philosophy in ICT and Information Systems

Philosophy has been applied within the field of information systems and in computer science for 50 years, either as a reference discipline to help solve particular problems, such as the artificial intelligence on whether computers can be like humans, or as a basis on which to develop ideas or methodologies.

2-2.1 Philosophical Discussions in Information Systems

This section briefly reviews the main types of philosophy that have been appealed to in the fields of ICT and information systems.

From the start, to address the question of whether computers can think, artificial intelligence has asked philosophical questions about what thinking and computers are. Newell (1982), for example, appealed to Dennett's idea of intentionality.

Winograd and Flores (1986) used Heidegger's philosophy to argue against the then-prevalent view that computers are surrogate humans with which we interact, as artificial intelligence assumed, and instead that computers are proximal tools of which we might not even be aware. Their now-classic work radically changed the direction of artificial intelligence and human-computer interaction.

Philosophy is applied more widely in *Philosophical Aspects of Information Systems* (Winder et al. 1997), which contains useful articles by a number of authors. However, the collection of issues discussed seems neither systematic nor comprehensive.

Mingers and Willcocks (2004) provide a more systematic discussion of *Social Theory and Philosophy for Information Systems*. Each chapter exposes a particular philosophical position in relation to IS, and is written by an acknowledged expert in that thinking. Table 2.1 lists the chapters, their authors, the topic of each and to which of the five areas identified in Chapter 1 its discussion is relevant.

Table 2.1 Philosophical Discussions of *Social Theory and Philosophy for Information Systems* (Mingers and Willcocks 2004)

Chapter, Authors	*Topic*	*Area*
1. Lee	Social theory and philosophy in general	All except FT
2. Markus	Functionalism and neo-functionalism	ISU
3. Introna, Ilharco	Phenomenology of Husserl and Heidegger	NIC
4. Myers	Hermeneutics	ISU, ISD
5. Probert	Adorno's critical theory	SOC
6. Huynh	Habermas' critical theory	SOC
7. Willcocks	Foucault's notion of power/ knowledge	SOC, ISU
8. Jones, Orlikowski, Munir	Structuration theory	SOC
9. Mitev, Wilson	Social shaping of technology	SOC
10. Mingers	Critical realism	ISD
11. Merali	Complexity and IS.	NIC

Key: ISU = ICT use, ISD = ICT development, FT = ICT features, SOC = ICT and society, NIC = nature of information and computers

This collection brings together several philosophical approaches to IS in a way that is systematic and very helpful to readers. Yet even this does not fulfil our requirements. It ignores FT and lets SOC dominate. It does not show how these philosophical approaches could work together to help us understand 'the whole story' and the work as a whole seems to reflect the tendency to downplay ontology. As the authors admit, many other philosophers were omitted, including Bourdieu, Luhmann, Merleau-Ponty, Maturana and American Pragmatism. Marxist philosophy is present only indirectly. Process philosophy, which is employed by Midgley (2000) to understand 'systemic intervention', pre-Kantian thought and Scholastic thought, such as of Lonergan are not discussed. The philosopher I am about to introduce is not mentioned.

Moreover, each philosophy or social theory is used to address a limited issue in the IS field. In this book, we could adopt a similar approach, appealing to different philosophers who seem to suit each area. There are disadvantages of doing this. 1. Most Western philosophers have tended to form their thoughts by reference to problems in others; while we might applaud their insights about specific issues, most have blind spots, which prevent a truly broad approach to laying foundations. 2. Western philosophy has tended to dichotomous views (Tarnas 1991), and opposing philosophers will most likely be referred to from different areas, which would prevent genuine dialogue between the areas, thus reinforcing the gulf between the IS field and computer science.

2-2.2 Philosophical Issues in ICT and Information Systems

We can see the need for a broader view by looking at the philosophical issues that pertain in each area of interest in information systems. Table 2.2 shows some of these.

Table 2.2 Some Philosophical Issues Raised by ICT and Information Systems

Area	*ICT Issue*	*Issue in Philosophy*
ICT Usage	User-computer relationships	Self and world
	Human activity with computer	Subject-object functioning
	Impact in use	Meaning and repercussions
	Benefit versus detriment	Good and evil
	Variety of impacts	Diversity
ICT Development	Teamwork	Social theory
	Development lifecycle	Process
	Guidelines	Normativity
	Human creativity	Freedom and intention
	Requirements analysis	Possibility, responsibility
	Knowledge elicitation	Knowledge, epistemology
	Conflict	Perspectives

(*Continued*)

Table 2.2 (Continued)

Area	*ICT Issue*	*Issue in Philosophy*
ICT Features	User-feature engagement	Subject-object relationship
	Affordance	Meaning
	Encapsulating reality	Ontology of diversity
ICT & Society	Widespread impact	Functioning and repercussions
	Ecological relationship	Structural relationships
	Structuration	Social philosophy
	Progress	Teleology
	The ICT project	Philosophical ethics
Nature of ICT	Nature of computer, info	Ontology
	Multiple levels	Philosophy of existence
	The AI question	Anthropology, ontology

It should be clear why (with Lyytinen) we do not seek a single, unitary framework to cover all areas. Because most extant philosophies, especially during the last 500 years, tend to focus on a subset of these issues, each area has appealed to a different type of philosophy in order to understand the issues it faces.

Since every area has some link with everyday experience (see §1-4.4), it means that we cannot presume that any of the philosophical issues may be ignored. This suggests that for a fully everyday approach, we need a philosophy that can address all the issues. One such is the philosophy pioneered by the late Herman Dooyeweerd (1894–1977).

2-3 Dooyeweerd's Philosophy

Dooyeweerd's thinking developed within the stream of ideas now called Reformational Philosophy. It has its roots in the Calvinistic outlook of the Netherlands, which might have been subjected also to some Celtic influence. Dooyeweerd was inspired by the Dutch statesman, Abraham Kuyper, who contended that each sphere of society should be free from domination by others, and, with Dirk Vollenhovan, developed this into a philosophical theory of the diverse nature of reality: there are many irreducibly distinct spheres of law and meaning. This is developed in Chapter 3.

He initially studied jurisprudence and politics but moved into philosophy when he realised that his field's problems were philosophical at root. From there, he realised that philosophy itself exhibits deep-rooted problems, which affect all disciplines, from mathematics and physics to sociology, jurisprudence and theology. "In the debate among philosophical schools," wrote Dooyeweerd (1955, I, 37), "one receives the impression that they are reasoning at cross-purposes, because they are not able to find a way to penetrate to each other's true starting-points." These starting-points, he continued, are "masked by the dogma concerning the autonomy of theoretic thought"—that theoretical thought is neutral, authoritative and self-dependent. The problem "touches the empirical sciences as well as philosophy, since both imply the theoretical attitude of thought."

Dooyeweerd sought something deeper than the difference between philosophies, something common to all—not a 'super-philosophy' but rather something grounded in everyday experience and the humanness of all philosophers.

Dooyeweerd did not consider the physical, technical, human, social and societal realms of the world to require fundamentally different philosophical treatment, but rather to be different aspects of one reality. This multi-aspectual view underpins all areas of ICT with the same scheme of thinking, and it provides a basis for understanding the relationships among areas.

He also offered radically different notions of subject and object, things, meaning, time, progress, the good and the self. In particular, he made a critique of theoretical thought that goes deeper than most philosophers did and can provide answers to the ultimate question, "How may we understand what enables us to understand?" With this, all the research approaches can be understood in relation to each other, as indicated earlier and discussed in §4-2.

These possibilities are inherent in his approach, rather than having to be added from outside. This is because his starting points were different: everyday experience, meaningfulness, diversity and coherence. Despite and because of his radically different starting point, his philosophy is able to engage with most others—over 100 in his *magnum opus* (Dooyeweerd 1955). Dooyeweerd might be a meta-philosopher, but I hesitate to claim such a grandiose title.

The next chapter offers a comprehensive summary of Dooyeweerd's thought, in which the above claims will be substantiated. It should be of sufficient depth to enable readers to understand how his thought enables us to lay foundations in all areas of information systems without needing to read elsewhere.

References

Audi R. (Ed.). 1999. *The Cambridge Dictionary of Philosophy* (2nd ed.). Cambridge University Press, Cambridge, UK.

Basden A. 2008. *Philosophical Frameworks for Understanding Information Systems*. IGI Global, Hershey, PA, USA.

Courtney JF, Porra J. 2000. Mini-track on the philosophical foundations of information systems. *Americas Conference on Information Systems, AMCIS 2000*, Long Beach, CA, USA.

Dooyeweerd H. 1955. *A New Critique of Theoretical Thought* (Vols. I–IV, 1975 ed.). Paideia Press, Jordan Station, Ontario, Canada.

Hart H. 1984. *Understanding Our World: An Integral Ontology*. University Press of America, Lanham, NY, USA.

Hodges WS. 1995. Five roles that philosophy can play in MIS research. *Proceedings of the 1995 Americas Conference on Information Systems, AMCIS 1995*, Pittsburgh, PA. Association for Information Systems, Atlanta, GA.

Levi AW. 1975. Philosophy, history of Western. In *Encyclopaedia Britannica*, 15th Edition (Vol. 14, pp. 247–275). Encyclopaedia Britannica, Chicago, USA.

Lyytinen KJ. 2003. Information systems and philosophy: The hopeless search for ultimate foundations. In JI DeGross (Ed.), *Proceedings of the Americas Conference on Information Systems: AMCIS 2003*. Association for Information Systems, Atlanta, GA.

Midgley G. 2000. *Systemic Intervention: Philosophy, Methodology and Practice*. Kluwer/Plenum, New York.

Mingers J, Willcocks LP. (Eds.). 2004. *Social Theory and Philosophy for Information Systems*. John Wiley & Sons, Chichester, UK.

Newell A. 1982. The knowledge level. *Artificial Intelligence*, 18, 87–127.

Strauss DFM. 2009. *Philosophy, Discipline of the Disciplines*. Paideia Press, Grand Rapids, MI.

Tarnas R. 1991. *The Passion of the Western Mind*. Pimlico, Random House, New York.

Winder RL, Probert SK, Beeson IA. (Eds.). 1997. *Philosophical Aspects of Information Systems*. Taylor and Francis, London, UK.

Winograd T, Flores F. 1986. *Understanding Computers and Cognition: A New Foundation for Design*. Addison-Wesley, Reading, MA.

3 Dooyeweerd's Philosophy

This chapter explains and discusses Dooyeweerd's philosophy, to enable readers to understand how philosophical foundations are laid the five areas of information systems that are discussed in Part II.

Dooyeweerd's philosophy is wide-ranging, comprehensive and deep, so this chapter is somewhat lengthy. A summary would have been shorter, but I wanted to provide readers with sufficient understanding so they could employ Dooyeweerd's ideas without needing other sources. The text is augmented with examples, brief reference to issues and thinkers in the field, and pointers for deeper study in Dooyeweerd's writings and elsewhere. What has been omitted is philosophical justification of Dooyeweerd's ideas, which may be found via those pointers, and should also be in a forthcoming book on Dooyeweerd's philosophy.

However, readers need not read through it unless they wish to. Instead they might read bits that interest them or that are referred to from elsewhere. The discussion largely follows Dooyeweerd's own structure—of introducing starting points, discussing the nature of philosophy and theoretical thought and then using that to understand diversity and coherence of the world and then of things—but readers may skip parts. For example, readers who do not wish to understand Dooyeweerd's ideas about theoretical thought might read Section 3-1, then §3-3.1 on Dooyeweerd's interesting subject-object relationship, then skip to §3-6 onwards to read about the most-used portion of Dooyeweerd's philosophy, aspects—then later read the rest to obtain background.

The chapter has nine main sections plus a conclusion: 1. Dooyeweerd's starting points in everyday experience and meaningfulness; 2. Challenges in and for philosophy, explaining why Dooyeweerd adopted a different approach; 3. Dooyeweerd's reinterpretation of subject-object and time; 4. Theoretical thought; 5. Ground ideas, philosophies, sciences and paradigms; 6. How to delineate aspects (the portion of Dooyeweerd's thought we use most); 7. What are aspects? 8. What aspects enable; 9. Things, types and relationships.

3-1 Everyday Experience and Meaningfulness: Dooyeweerd's Starting Points

This section outlines two important starting points of Dooyeweerd's philosophy, which are important in understanding information systems and ICT. All philosophy starts somewhere, and Dooyeweerd made his starting points clear: everyday experience and meaningfulness. This unusual starting point will provide many fresh insights in all five areas of the information systems field, and new avenues for research.

3-1.1 Starting-Point 1: Everyday Experience and the Pre-Theoretical Attitude of Thought

What we mean by 'everyday experience', 'pre-theoretical attitude of thought' and the related ideas is explained in the list in §1-2.2. It has no negative connotation (as in 'everyday clothes') but refers to 'real life' and engagement therein without standing back to analyse it, and the terms listed there are used almost synonymously here. Everyday experience does involve thinking, but that is always situated within the everyday.

As discussed there, we want to understand everyday practice. Unfortunately, for most of its life, philosophy has deemed everyday experience and the pre-theoretical attitude of thought inferior to the theoretical attitude, and unworthy of attention, except perhaps as an anthropological curiosity. This attitude continues to this day, for example in "Given the difficulty of doing philosophy (i.e. escaping from the natural attitude which constantly seeks to reassert itself) . . ." (Moran 2000, 146). The 'natural attitude' has been presumed to be biased, messy and unreliable, while the theoretical attitude is presumed neutral, clear and reliable.

Fortunately, in the past century or so, the everyday in its various forms has begun to attract interest among philosophers. There are three ways of according respect to everyday experience. In these, Dooyeweerd went further and deeper than most other thinkers did.

1. Interest in everyday experience. A number of lines of interest have developed, including American pragmatism (on achievement), Bergson (on intuition), Husserl's idea of lifeworld (shared background knowledge on which scientific work depends), developed subsequently by Schutz and Habermas (lifeworld as pre-given and characterised by meaningfulness and normativity and generated by communicative action), Heidegger's existentialism (engagement), some of Foucault's work, Bourdieu's (1977) notions of habitus and field, and de Certeau's (1984) study of everyday life.

It seems, however, that almost every philosophical study of everyday experience has tended inexorably towards seeing it through the lens of just one of its aspects: pragmatism towards functionalism, Bergson towards biology, Husserl towards knowledge, Foucault towards power, Bourdieu towards signification and de Certeau towards aesthetics (e.g., Ganguly 2002). Dooyeweerd argued that, by doing this, philosophy has fundamentally misunderstood the nature of everyday experience. Instead, he tried to be open to all the varied aspects of everyday experience equally. In this book, we will take Dooyeweerd's view of everyday experience as widely diverse; see below.

2. Appealing to everyday experience. Appeal to everyday experience is made when philosophers wish to argue that some aspect of reality has been overlooked and deserves consideration. For example, Kuhn (1962/1996) surveyed the 'real life' of doing science when he wished to introduce the idea of paradigm shifts. Dooyeweerd likewise frequently appealed to everyday experience, for example,

> To all of these speculative misunderstandings [made by philosophers] naïve experience implicitly takes exception by persisting in its pre-theoretical conception of things, events and social relationships.
>
> (Dooyeweerd 1955, III, 28)

('Naïve' is a term used by philosophers to refer to pre-theoretical or everyday experience.) We will appeal to everyday experience of ICT to highlight aspects or possibilities that have been hitherto overlooked.

3. Starting with everyday experience. Most philosophers presume that we may apply theoretical thought to understanding the pre-theoretical. Dooyeweerd reversed this, taking everyday experience or the pre-theoretical attitude of thought as a starting point from which to understand theoretical thought. To Bourdieu (1990) also, 'practice' precedes theoretical knowledge, but Dooyeweerd went deeper philosophically, in that he made the theoretical attitude itself a philosophical problem that deserves consideration; see §3-4. Thus his opening words in Volume I of his *magnum opus* (1955) are:

> If I consider reality as it is given in the naïve pre-theoretical experience, . . .

From there over the next 70 pages, he proceeded to understand the theoretical attitude of thought and its validity and role. Only then could he return to understand everyday experience theoretically, aware of theoretical thought's limitations. So Dooyeweerd's stance is no romantic reaction against earlier denigration of the everyday, nor an uncritical 'naive realism', but a strongly philosophical position. Dooyeweerd achieved this with a transcendental critique discussed in §3-4.3 onwards.

Dooyeweerd could then bring fresh insight to understanding how theoretical thought relates to everyday experience. While many thinkers presumed that everyday thought may be replaced (or destroyed or 'colonized') by theoretical thought, Dooyeweerd held that

> The naïve attitude cannot be destroyed by scientific thought. Its plastic horizon can only be opened and enlarged by the practical results of scientific research.
>
> (Dooyeweerd 1955, III, 31)

"Results" include telescopes for astronomy, microscopes in biology and debugging software in computer science, but also theoretical models.

Unfortunately, adequate philosophical tools for starting from the pre-theoretical attitude were just not available, so Dooyeweerd had to forge his own. His immanent and transcendental critiques of theoretical thought, outlined in Section 3-4, led to an understanding of the fundamental conditions that make theoretical thought possible. He then used this understanding as a sounder basis than mere presumption gives, to investigate philosophies and the nature of everyday reality. He came up with ideas that will stimulate fresh approaches to ICT in Part II.

3-1.2 Starting-Point 2: Meaningfulness

We may continue the very first words of Dooyeweerd's *magnum opus*:

> If I consider reality as it is given in the naïve pre-theoretical experience, and then confront it with a theoretical analysis through which reality appears to split up into various modal aspects, then the first thing that strikes me, is . . .
>
> (Dooyeweerd 1955, I, 3)

This splitting up is no random chopping. On what basis may we "split"? To do justice to what we encounter in everyday experience, splitting presupposes some meaningful distinction. It is not, Dooyeweerd said, a differentiation between types of thing but of meaning. Dooyeweerd made meaning his second starting point—a second radical departure from most philosophy.

3-1.2.1 Kinds of Meaning

But what is meaning? We can differentiate at least four meanings of 'meaning' that have been discussed (which might overlap):

- *Signification-meaning*, the meaning carried by words, phrases, etc.;
- *Interpretation-meaning*, the meaning we assign when we interpret something, e.g., a group of scattered feathers means a bird was killed;
- *Attribution-meaning*, the meaning we attribute to things, such as the vase my grandmother owned;
- *Life-meaning*, as in "What is the meaning of my career (or life)?".

Dooyeweerd used 'meaning' in a fifth way, which goes beyond these, is more fundamental and underlies them. While these four usually involve meaningfulness to me/us, Dooyeweerd's idea is meaningfulness as such, perhaps in spite of us.

- *Meaningfulness*, the idea that all things are meaningful whether or not we signify, interpret or attribute. Though Dooyeweerd called it

> 'meaning' along with the others, in order to emphasise its difference, I call it 'meaningfulness'.

(The above may be treated as a note on terminology.) Dooyeweerd's notion can incorporate the others.

3-1.2.2 Treatment of Meaning in Philosophy

Over the course of its history, philosophy has seldom discussed meaning, of any kind, and especially not meaningfulness of Dooyeweerd's kind. Where meaning has been discussed, it has usually been presumed that meaning derives from something more fundamental—from essence of things or final cause (Aristotle), from self-maintenance (Heidegger), from interpretation (Gadamer, Ricoeur), from discourses (Habermas). The meaning of life has attracted debate, but only within a relatively isolated silo, and has been presumed to consist of one of its aspects, like goodness or pleasure.

Most recent philosophers presuppose that meaning is purely subjective, generated *ex nihilo* (out of nothing) by humans (or sentient beings)—or maybe intersubjectively in groups. This implies that the kinds of meaning generated are essentially arbitrary and hence its diversity is not worth studying; only generative processes are worth studying.

3-1.2.3 Dooyeweerd's Understanding of Meaning, and the Metaphor of Ocean of Meaningfulness

There is an alternative view. Polanyi and Prosch (1975) suggest that we 'dwell' in meaning. Meaning(fulness) surrounds us and is already there prior to us, like the ocean in which fish swim.

To Dooyeweerd, not only does meaningfulness surround us, but it enables our very being and functioning. The ocean does not just surround fish but enables them to swim and even to be fish. So meaningfulness enables us to occur and exist. As Dooyeweerd continued (p. 4),

> *Meaning* is the *being* of all that has been *created* and the nature even of our selfhood.

So things *are* meaning; they don't *have* meaning as any kind of property (Dooyeweerd 1955, I, 3). This allowed Dooyeweerd to consider kinds of things without falling into essentialism (see §3-9.2).

> Note on terminology: Dooyeweerd himself did not employ the metaphor of an **ocean of meaningfulness** in which we 'swim' and which enables our 'swimming', but referred to it as a '*law-side*', in that all our occurring is constituted in responding to prior law (see §3-3.1 below). Though I will use that term when considering functioning, 'law' has

> unhelpful and misleading connotations of constraints and power-structures that are not intended. It is too narrow a concept in that, as I understand the whole of what Dooyeweerd was trying to say, we 'dwell' not only in law, but also in meaningfulness, in joy, goodness and the possibility of achievement, to name but a few. To express this wider notion of dwelling, the metaphor of *ocean of meaningfulness* will be used throughout this book to emphasise its prior and enabling nature, and of 'swimming' for our functioning and existence.

This 'dwelling' is also characteristic of the pre-theoretical attitude of thought; Dooyeweerd's two starting points are not unconnected.

All being, and the four other kinds of meaning, derive from meaningfulness, which is more fundamental. A bird's nest "is not a 'thing in itself', which *has* a specific meaning in the bird's life. It has *as such* no existence apart from this meaning" (Dooyeweerd 1955, III, 108). Dooyeweerd did not restrict this to humans or sentient beings but extended it to all beings, including physical. Rock exists, *qua* rock, by virtue of the physico-chemical sphere of meaningfulness. As we will see in §7-3.3, the rock has double existence; it is also a climbable-object for an animal who wants a vantage point and is so by virtue of the sensory-motor sphere.

Meaning "has the character of referring" (pp. 4, 110), and "constantly points without and beyond itself toward an origin, which itself is no longer meaning" (p. 9). This implies that nothing is self-sufficient. Inter-dependency pervades all, and all points beyond itself to an origin. Clouser (2005) uses the term 'divine' for this origin, as that self-dependent on which all else depends.

This implies that (1) in research and practice we cannot truly understand a thing by reference only to itself, but must understand its context (c.f. technology-in-context, §5-2), (2) nothing has meaning located in itself (c.f. Schuurman's idea of technology-as-servant §8-6.2). Dooyeweerd argued that when we treat something as meaningful-in-itself, it eventually loses its meaning and becomes harmful. This is worked out for ICT in Chapter 8.

On the other hand, by making meaningfulness and everyday experience his starting points, Dooyeweerd opened up new avenues of philosophy, which can provide new foundational understanding in fields of study like information systems. For example, starting with meaningfulness helps us understand the relationship between disparate discourses in each area of ICT, makes us alert to hidden and unexpected possibilities, throws light on the multi-level nature of computers and might resolve the artificial intelligence question.

3-1.2.4 The Diversity and Coherence of Meaningfulness

Dooyeweerd continued his opening words (1955, I, 3) with,

> then the first thing that strikes me, is the original *indissoluble interrelation* among these aspects . . . A[n] indissoluble inner coherence binds the

> numerical to the spatial aspect, the latter to the aspect of mathematical movement, the aspect of movement to that of physical energy, which itself is the necessary basis of the aspect of organic life. The aspect of organic life has an inner connection with that of psychical feeling, the latter refers in its logical anticipation . . . to the analytical-logical aspect. This in turn is connected with the historical, the linguistic, the aspect of social intercourse, the economic, the aesthetic, the jural, the moral aspects and that of faith.

Here is both diversity and coherence of meaning. The diversity is seen in that, for example, the social aspect cannot be reduced to the lingual, nor the formative ("historical"), nor any other, nor vice versa. Each is an irreducibly distinct sphere of meaningfulness or *aspect*. Dooyeweerd lists fifteen aspects there.

The coherence, which Dooyeweerd called "inter-modal cosmic coherence", is that no single aspect stands alone but each one "refers within and beyond itself to all the others", as the above passage indicates. As Dooyeweerd (1955, I, 4) put it, "We have been fitted into this coherence of meaning with all our modal functions". This coherence of meaning is the 'ocean' in which we 'swim', yet it is diverse. Three kinds of coherence are discussed in §3-7.4, of which inter-aspect dependency is most important to us (e.g., life depends on chemistry).

Reductionism refuses to recognise the diversity, in several ways (Clouser 2005), with two being most detrimental. (a) One aspect is treated as the only important one, leading us to ignore others; as in technological determinism (see §8-4.1) or treating economics as the 'science of human beings' (Leite 2010). (b) One aspect is presumed to be self-explanatory and able to explain all others; for example, trying to explain everything in terms of power, language, psychology, evolution or chemistry. Often both types occur together. Communities of thought infected with reductionism, of which we will meet several during our discussions, have little incentive to explore what aspects (kinds of meaningfulness) there might be. Anti-reductionism ignores the coherence—as seen in the in the dualistic arguments about whether computers can be like humans (§5-6).

Dooyeweerd recognised both diversity and coherence.

3-1.2.5 An Initial Look at Diversity

Thus meaningfulness is not uniform, but is a diverse "system of modal functions of meaning" (Dooyeweerd 1955, I, 5), which offers distinct ways of being meaningful as "modal speciality of meaning" (p. 7): *aspect*.

Looking through my bunch of keys, I notice the gleam on the metal of one, then select another with which to open my door. Discovering it is bent and will not work, I find a stone to hammer it back into shape, and then it works. (Thanks to Gareth Jones for this example.) My keys exhibit several aspects simultaneously. The main aspect is that of the purpose of keys, a

Table 3.1 Aspects of Running a Chemical Production Business

Aspect	Kernel	Management situations or issues
Quantitative	Amount	Figures, accounting
Spatial	Extension	Spatial layout of site and buildings
Kinematic	Movement	Movement around site and building; movement of product
Physical	Energy	Physical integrity of buildings and plant; chemical reactions
Organic-biotic	Life	Food hygiene in canteen; product safety
Psychic / Sensitive	Feeling	Use of eyes, ears in production; how employees feel
Analytical	Distinction	Clarity and logicality of instructions, goals and vision
Formative	Construction	Planning, Designing, Manufacturing
Lingual	Signification	Signage; records; trademarks; communication
Social	Togetherness	Team building; structure of organization
Economic	Frugality	Budgets, deadlines; waste, efficiency; resources
Aesthetic	Harmony, fun	Harmony of organization; enjoying work
Juridical	Due	Legal matters, contracts; responsibility
Ethical	Self-giving	Generosity, Ethicality of organization
Pistic / Faith	Belief	Vision and mission; loyalty; religious faiths

legal one (rightful access). A spatial aspect (shape) is important, a physical (the metal must not wear or bend), and an aspect of distinctness (each must be unique). The gleam suggests an aesthetic aspect, and that each key bears its maker's name (aspect of signification). All this is what being a key entails.

Situations likewise exhibit multiple aspects, but in a more complex manner. Table 3.1 shows aspects of a situation in chemical production. Column 1 names each aspect, column 2 describes its meaning, column 3 gives examples of issues that are meaningful in the aspect.

Columns 1 and 2 provisionally introduce Dooyeweerd's suite of fifteen aspects, which we shall use throughout this work; refer back to here. Dooyeweerd delineated these fifteen by a long process that is described in §3-6, and what the aspects entail is discussed from §3-7 onwards.

3-1.2.6 Overview

If we are to engage in interdisciplinary research and practice, as in the information systems field, then we must understand this diversity and coherence of meaningfulness. Research usually focuses on an aspect via a conceptual 'lens'. So what lenses are possible? Dooyeweerd recognised the need to self-critically think about the meaningfulness within which we dwell. But how can we do this?

To understand, we employ theoretical thought. How can we understand how we understand? Theoretical thought is itself a 'swimming in' the 'ocean' it is trying to theorise. Can fish understand the ocean? Dooyeweerd argued that most philosophy has presumed theoretical thought is neutral, authoritative and valid and hence has not properly challenged itself about it. He believed that, before we may investigate the diversity and coherence of everyday experience properly, we must challenge ourselves about our theoretical thinking. The next three sections outline his attempts to do this.

3-2 Challenges for, and in, Philosophy

This section provides material by which ideas will be critiqued in later chapters. It may be skipped by those who are currently more interested in understanding the nature and meaning of reality.

Long before I knew of Dooyeweerd, I valued everyday thinking and felt that no philosophy could really help me. Neither in technical activity of software development, nor the non-technical issues of IS development and use, nor in my wish to integrate them, did I find philosophy useful. I could not explain it. Intuitively, I felt that there was a deep problem in philosophy, which seemed concerned with narrow, abstract issues. It was only when I discovered Dooyeweerd that I could understand my concerns and have some confidence that they were well-founded.

3-2.1 Problems in Philosophy: The Immanence Standpoint

Dooyeweerd believed that philosophy was in need of radical 'inner' reformation. This is not according to criteria with philosophy (e.g., from economics or theology), but to those that philosophy itself should recognise and own. The implication for developing foundations of a field is that we can be more independent of conventional, contemporary philosophy.

Dooyeweerd identified several reasons why reformation is needed. He argued that most extant philosophies:

- have divorced meaningfulness from reality (Dooyeweerd 1955, II, 25,26), treating it as something not quite real, and thus lacking motivation to properly understand meaningfulness (see §3-1.2.2);
- have prevented a truly sensitive approach to understanding everyday experience, instead, always forcing us to take one sphere of meaning as our point of reference for all the others (Dooyeweerd 1955, I, 15) (see §3-1);
- have absolutised specific aspects or types of thing (Dooyeweerd 1955, III, 169), thereby generating competing and conflicting '-isms' (Dooyeweerd 1955, I, 46,169) (materialism, historicism, economism, aestheticism, etc.);
- have deeply presupposed a dualistic idea of what is meaningful (ground-motive; see §3-2.3), which has led philosophy into fruitless dialectic;

- have not adequately discussed the coherence or relationships between the aspects (Dooyeweerd 1955, II, 49), making a genuinely interdisciplinary research extremely difficult (§3-1.2);
- have posited the problem of concept formation incorrectly, as form-matter dualism, phenomenon-noumenon dualism (§3-4.1.1) or sensory input) (Dooyeweerd 1955, II, 50), all of which restrict our understanding of research;
- have not properly addressed the structure of things as encountered in everyday experience (Dooyeweerd 1955, III, 167), as multi-level beings (since Dooyeweerd passed away, systems thinking has tried to move towards this).

Some of these manifest themselves in the information systems field, as shall be seen later.

In a 3,000-year survey of philosophy (§3-4.2), Dooyeweerd traced the root of the problems in philosophy to what he called an *Immanence Standpoint.* Indeed, where I have written "most extant philosophies" above, Dooyeweerd wrote "immanence-philosophy".

Immanence-philosophy, argued Dooyeweerd, chooses an Archimedean Point (a fixed point on the basis of which to understand all else) from within temporal reality rather than beyond it, such as the *cogito* (Descartes) or existential thought (Heidegger) (Dooyeweerd 1955, IV, 88); this is why he called it 'immanence'. Dooyeweerd noted that,

> The age-old development of immanence-philosophy displays the most divergent nuances. It varies from metaphysical rationalism to modern logical positivism and the irrationalist philosophy of life. It is disclosed also in the form of modern existentialism. The latter has broken with the Cartesian (rationalistic) 'cogito' as Archimedean point and has replaced it by existential thought, conceived of in an immanent subjectivistic historical sense.
>
> (Dooyeweerd 1955, I, 13)

Strands of philosophy that we, in the 21st century, believe to be radically different—such as positivism and interpretivism, subjectivism and objectivism, Descartes and Heidegger—are all in the same camp.

This does not mean, however, that we should ignore all that has emerged from such thinkers. In his critique of theoretical thought outlined in §3-4, Dooyeweerd argued that it is not the insights themselves that are problematic, but the ways they are worked out under the influence of problematic presuppositions such as those of the Immanence Standpoint. Thus, for example, Foucault's insights on power and knowledge have considerable value, but they must always be used with critical caution to discern the malign influence of the Immanence Standpoint, rather than uncritically. See §6-2.13 for example.

3-2.2 Ground-Motives

Every era in philosophy has exhibited the problems inherent in the Immanence Standpoint, but in different ways. Each era has been dominated by dualistic (dialectical) *ground-motives*. A *ground-motive* is a "spiritual driving force that acts as the absolutely central mainspring of human society", which "not only places an indelible stamp on the culture, science, and social structure of a given period but determines profoundly one's whole world view" (Dooyeweerd 1979, 9). Ground-motives are deep supra-theoretical presuppositions about where to look to determine what is meaningful ('Origin of Meaning' in §3-4.3.6). They affect research and philosophy as well as practice.

Dooyeweerd made a penetrating survey of the history of philosophy, from the pre-Socratic Greeks right through to the 20th century. Reading original texts as far as possible, and sometimes reinterpreting thinkers like Aristotle, Kant and Heidegger, he exposed the presuppositions underlying each idea that might prevent it from achieving what originally motivated it. In this survey (Dooyeweerd 1979), he identified four major ground-motives that have driven Western thought over the past 2,500 years.

The **Greek Form-Matter ground-motive** (FMGM), discussed in pages 15–22, sees reality as a tension between form and matter. We can see its influence in dualities like mind vs. brain, mind vs. body, works-with-mind vs. works-with-hand, spiritual vs. material, online vs. 'bricks-and-mortar', and at the root of various philosophical positions like materialism.

The **biblical ground-motive of Creation, Fall, Redemption** (CFR), discussed in pages 28–39, sees reality as created by or from a divine origin ('God') that is not part of it, and yet provides the possibility of remedy for ills, which are seen as law transgression. Its influence is found more in everyday life than in academic life, and attempts to work out a theoretical approach based on it have been sparse. This is partly because, from 1500 to 500 years ago, another ground motive dominated European thought.

The **Scholastic Nature-Grace ground-motive** (NGGM), discussed in pages 111–149, arose from synthesis of FMGM and CFR. It sees reality as a tension between the sacred and the mundane. We can see its influence in dualities like reason vs. faith, secular vs. sacred, natural vs. supernatural, state vs. church, public affairs vs. private beliefs. The exclusion of the topic of the divine from modern academic discourse and its relegation to the silo that is theology is traceable to this ground-motive. It sparked two reactions: the Reformation and the Renaissance, from which the next ground-motive emerged.

The **Humanistic Nature-Freedom ground-motive** (NFGM), discussed in pages 148–206, sees reality as a tension between determinism or control and freedom, where freedom is the presumed human ability to interpret or choose. Its influence may be seen in dualities like constraint vs.

freedom, nature vs. human, management-by-control vs. management-by-facilitation, essentialism vs. social construction, positivism vs. interpretivism, objectivism vs. subjectivism, being vs. morality (Hume), natural science vs. humanities, which Dooyeweerd called the 'science ideal' vs. 'personality ideal'. Kant's 'Copernican revolution' in philosophy is seen by Dooyeweerd as the epitome of the Nature-Freedom ground-motive, in that it places human free consciousness rather than the world as the origin of our ability to know.

The historical emergence of the ground-motives is shown (simplified) in Figure 3.1. Only a tiny selection of typical philosophers is shown, but also the influences among them are more complex than depicted by the arrows, with NFGM also having some roots in FMGM. The cross represents the start of the Christianity, and the dotted arrow is discussed in §3-2.4.

These ground-motives are not unique to Dooyeweerd, being recognised also by Vollenhoven (1950), Heidegger (1971), Habermas (2002) and others. Dooyeweerd, however, provided a more systematic and penetrating understanding of them and how they relate to each other. This allowed him critical distance from the Nature-Freedom ground-motive that so dominates today's thought, as well as from the Scholasticism that is found even today in some religious academic circles.

Dooyeweerd did allow for others, mentioning that of the Zoroastrian religion (Dooyeweerd 1979, 112) and Choi (2000) has undertaken a similar exercise with Korean thought.

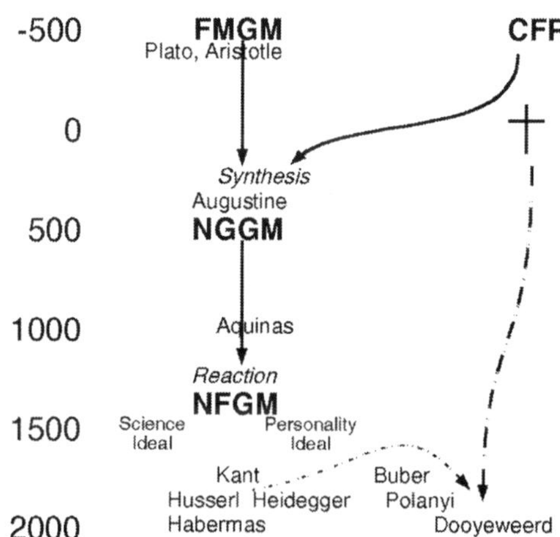

Figure 3.1 Development of Ground-motives of Western Thought

3-2.3 Problems with Dualistic Ground-Motives

Ground-motives dominate theoretical thinking of an era and, today, in the field of information systems, the Nature-Freedom ground-motive exerts far-reaching influence on the way ideas and paradigms develop by generating the lenses through which we view reality. Despite their dominance in their eras, ground-motives are not truths, but presuppositions of a 'religious' nature. We will see the narrowing influence of such lenses in ICT and IS.

Three of the ground-motives began as dualities but under the Immanence-Standpoint, they became oppositional dualisms, in which one pole is treated as absolute and good, while the other is either ignored or shunned. This is what Dooyeweerd called a religious antithesis, because of adherence and commitment, and all meaning finds its ultimate reference in the dualism. Thought influenced by dualistic ground-motives often locates a problem at one of its poles, and seek a solution at the opposing pole.

Example, FMGM: "We might have distinguished a system genus between biosystems and sociosystems, namely psychosystems. We have refrained from doing so from fear of encouraging the myth of disembodied minds." Bunge (1979, 257)

Example, NGGM: Contemporary thought e.g. in sustainability has forfeited valuable insights that come from Christian thinking (Basden 2017). Might a change be coming, however, with the increased visibility of Islam in, e.g., banking?

Example, NFGM: In the information systems field, it is rare for research to benefit from both positivist and interpretivist approaches together.

Such oppositional absolutizations occur more in research than in practice. Under their influence half of reality is ignored, as either worthless or to be explained away. For example, for decades, the information systems field has ignored the 'materiality' of ICT; see Chapter 7. Everyday experience does not recognise the dualistic oppositions, so (commenting on NFGM) "The ordinary man has always believed that there was such a thing as fate, but such a thing as free will also" (Chesterton 1908, 35).

Some thinkers have tried to bridge between poles, especially from the socio-critical approaches in IS, but ultimately have failed, because they presuppose the very opposition between them. (Examples: Hegel [Dooyeweerd 1955, I, 64–65]; §4-2.2, §8-3.)

Dooyeweerd believed that poles can be brought together, because he refused to accept any of the dualisms as 'true'. To do so requires transferring to the non-dualistic CFR ground-motive.

3-2.4 Dooyeweerd's Adoption of the Biblical Ground-Motive

> 'Does God exist?' is the most important question in systems thinking.
> (Churchman 1987, 139)

Dooyeweerd found that the biblical ground-motive, of Creation, Fall and Redemption (CFR), overcomes some of the problems generated by the Immanence-Standpoint. It is not dualistic but pluralistic. Under a dualistic ground-motive, humanity has seen itself at one pole and the rest of Creation at the other, seeing nature as to be feared or denigrated (FMGM), ignored (NGGM) or controlled (NFGM), whereas under the CFR motive, nature and humanity are both together Created and inter-dependent. (Note: Dooyeweerd's Creation presupposition is not fundamentalist Creationism; he criticised that [Clouser 2005].)

Thinkers are influenced in their choices of philosophical standpoint by their own deepest religious commitments, augmented by society's ground-motives, whether to materialism, Marxism, liberalism, Islam, Hinduism, Confucianism, Roman Catholic Christianity or, as Dooyeweerd was, Calvininian, with possibly a little Celtic, Christianity (Basden 2008). It was Calvin's belief in the importance of the secular side that prevented Dooyeweerd adhering to NGGM, but Dooyeweerd later criticised Calvin for not going far enough.

It must be admitted that Dooyeweerd's rejection of Immanence-philosophy was partly due to his own Christian belief, though he spent years within Immanence-philosophy before he made the break (Dooyeweerd 1955, I, v). Part of his motivation was to find a philosophy that was commensurable with his Christian belief in a way that most that he had experienced were not (and sometimes he saw his discussion as an attempt towards a 'Christian philosophy'), but part was genuinely philosophical in nature, a struggle with the growing awareness that Reason cannot be neutral, as many since him, including Habermas and Foucault, have also recognised.

Note on terminology: By '*Religion*' Dooyeweerd did not refer to creeds or rituals, but to "the innate impulse of human selfhood to direct itself toward . . . [an] absolute Origin of all temporal diversity of meaning" (Dooyeweerd 1955, I, 57). 'Religious' here means deep belief or commitment that motivates and directs what we do or think, our holding of paradigms. Our working within ground-motives is a religious functioning.

Mention of 'religion' or 'Christian' might alienate some readers, but I urge readers to continue, for three reasons.

1. *Type of Christian thought*. Dooyeweerd's kind of Christian thought differs radically from those which try to prove God exists, or to force Christian (or other) doctrines onto philosophical or scientific bodies of knowledge

(Dooyeweerd 1955, II, 40). Dooyeweerd believed one is impossible, the other improper, in principle. Though he personally believed Christ to be the Truth, the ultimate coherence of all, Dooyeweerd believed that in doing philosophy philosophical principles should be adhered to (Dooyeweerd 1955, I, v). Religious beliefs should be acknowledged and taken seriously, rather than ignored, but they should not be allowed to dominate in their content. Clouser (2005, 342) explains,

> Our claim is not that all theories are produced or forced on us by some divinity belief . . . The claim is that the nature of a theory's postulates is always *interpreted* in the light of what is presupposed as divine.

Dooyeweerd wanted to find a way in which radically different kinds of philosophy, including his own, could talk with each other, but because theoretical thought is not neutral he needed to explore its nature first in order to find a common framework for discussion; see §3-4, §3-5. He did not seek to promote Christian theological ideas but rather wanted to offer fruitful contributions

2. *Insights*. Dooyeweerd's philosophy might be able to ameliorate the problems mentioned earlier, so that everyday experience can be critically respected as it presents itself to us, meaningfulness need no longer be divorced from reality, and no longer need we be constrained by dualisms. His starting points (everyday experience and meaningfulness) are 'allowed' because of his rejection of the Immanence-standpoint.

Dooyeweerd broke with traditional (Scholastic) 'Christian' philosophy and explored the philosophical rather than theological implications of Creation, Fall, Redemption; this is an important contribution to philosophy because very seldom has this been tried before.

> Example: Some see meanings as emanating from a sovereign Creator's mind, or some kind of 'final cause'. Others see meanings as emanating from our own sovereign minds. Dooyeweerd does neither, instead seeing the Creator as providing the *possibility* of meaning by creating an ocean of meaningfulness within creation 'swims' (§3-1.2.3), but not the meanings themselves. This accounts better for the freedom we experience in attributing meanings to things without sinking into subjectivism—something we shall find important in several places in Part II.

Polanyi, Buber and a few others might be understood as guided by this ground-motive, but Dooyeweerd worked it out much more deeply, critically and systematically. It is too early to tell whether he succeeded, and whether the potential this ground-motive promises will be actualised, because it has not been sufficiently tried in a critical mainstream environment. In using Dooyeweerd's ideas to discuss foundations of information systems research and practice, this book is, perhaps, a contribution to that kind of philosophical research.

3. *Usefulness of Dooyeweerd's ideas.* Michael Faraday's idea that magnetism is a force rather than particles came about because, while the materialists refused to consider anything other than material causes, he was freed to consider forces by his strong biblical beliefs (Russell 2000). However, nobody suggests that only Christian believers may use or theorise about magnetism as a force. That Dooyeweerd's ideas about the diversity of meaningfulness and law in everyday experience arise partly from his Christian beliefs does not preclude those with different religious beliefs from benefiting from them.

Paradoxically, my experience has been that Hindus, Muslims and Humanists like Dooyeweerd's ideas more than Christians do. Maybe too many Christians are still trapped in the Scholastic ground-motive, which gave rise to the sacred-secular divide, locating mainstream scholarship at the pole opposite their religious beliefs. So I have not aimed this work at Christian thinkers but at those in the mainstream.

The importance of Dooyeweerd's (1955) *New Critique of Theoretical Thought* has been recognised by the Dutch National Library Archive as important Dutch literature and is available for free download from there; see end of final chapter for details.

Dooyeweerd's philosophy has also been called Cosmonomic Philosophy, Philosophy of the Law Idea, Reformational Philosophy, Calvinistic Philosophy or even Christian Philosophy (I believe, miscalled as 'Christian' because other philosophies also claim that title). I like his philosophy because of the new ways of thinking that are opened up by it.

Dooyeweerd himself was not arrogant. Yet he was courageous. He saw a new doorway and tried (in stumbling and not altogether clear ways) to push that door open and to clear the beginnings of a pathway through the thickets beyond. If his attempts still left some brambles and roots in the ground over which we might still trip, or if the path he clove is rather meandering, that is not a fault. Rather, he showed that there might be a way worth exploring.

Dooyeweerd's way encourages reconsideration of several major issues. Among these are the subject-object relationship and time, discussed next, then theoretical thought, aspects and things.

3-3 Reinterpreting Subject-Object and Time

Dooyeweerd's starting-points and independence of thought led to his reinterpreting a number of important philosophical themes. In this section, his novel understanding of the subject-object relationship and time are discussed, then, in later sections, theoretical thought, research, aspects and existence.

3-3.1 Law, Subject and Object

Dooyeweerd developed a very interesting notion of the subject-object relationship, which expresses everyday experience better than Descartes or Heidegger can, and overcomes problems that have troubled many fields, including IS. In this section, an example is used of an e-mail being sent that invites its recipient to a hike.

3-3.1.1 Law as Oceanic Enabler of Functioning

Though Dooyeweerd started with meaning, he wrote much about law and functioning in a way that suggests that law presupposes meaningfulness. (The nature of the link is not argued here.)

By 'law' Dooyeweerd does not mean humanly constructed rules, statutes or social norms, but like meaningfulness, something much deeper, which enables things to occur. While rules *constrain*, this kind of law *enables and guides*—an idea not unknown to Giddens (1993, 129ff). Law is diverse, each aspect offering a different kind of law. Example: Laws of the physical sphere (aspect), like gravity; laws of the lingual sphere, about signification. Dooyeweerd often called them '*law-spheres*, a term used here synonymously with 'aspects' and 'spheres of meaning'.

Law presupposes subject—in both senses of the English word: to be subject to law and to enact agency. One seems to connote constraint and the other, freedom, so under the influence of the Nature-Freedom ground-motive (see §3-2.2 above), these two meanings seem to oppose one another. Dooyeweerd, however, integrates them because of his different ground-motive.

Taken together, all the law-spheres form what Dooyeweerd called the *law-side* of reality. Law-side correlates with *subject-object-side*:

- The **law-side** refers to the law-character of what I have called the ocean of meaningfulness, comprising the framework that enables the entire subject-object-side cosmos to exist or occur, including enabling me to send e-mail.
- The **subject-object-side**, also called subject side, entity side or fact side, comprises all that actually occurs in the cosmos. Example: my sending of an email, and the email that is sent. It comprises both entities, processes and situations, and these are of many kinds, such as entities like numbers, rocks, plants, animals, thoughts, plans, computers, books, poems, social norms, statutes, beliefs and much more.

The distinction between law-side and subject-object-side is approximately recognised by other thinkers, for example, in the realm of linguistics, Ricoeur (1981) (language and discourse-as-event), de Saussure (*langue* and *parole*) and Hjelmslev (*schema* and *use*). On the Immanence-Standpoint, however, these are often confused, and law is often reduced to entity ("the first germ of law was an entity" [Peirce 1898]), or vice versa.

Generality, possibility and universality are found in the law-side; specificity, actuality and individuality, in the subject-object-side.

Law defines what is possible within a sphere of meaningfulness. Law gives meaningful *possibility*, especially of functioning. Example: "Square circle" might be meaningful to mention within the spatial aspect, but by the laws of that aspect, no square circle is possible. Example: Laws of the lingual aspect make e-mail (and other communications) possible.

Law has something of promise about it; contrast "Keep to the syntax and semantics!" and "If you keep to the syntax and semantics of your language, the recipient of your email will understand you better." Law enables and expresses meaningful *functioning* (activity) that has *repercussion*. Later Table 3.5 gives examples of functioning and repercussion meaningful in each aspect.

All *functioning* (activity) is therefore understood as a responding-to-aspectual-law, rather than as either free agency or determined behaviour, as in most philosophy. Just as a fish's swimming is constituted in responding to ocean water, so the entire cosmos, in functioning, is constituted in responding to the law-side. Law is thus not a compendium of rules to which subjects might refer when they function, but something that calls forth a response (Geertsema 2011). This is similar to Polanyi's 'dwelling' (Polanyi and Prosch 1975).

Wolters suggests (1985, 17) "the law-subject correlation . . . bears new and important philosophical fruit, pointing a way which can break through such dilemmas as natural law versus historicism and substance versus function." For example, whereas Descartes elevated thinking to a special position above all else, Dooyeweerd treated thinking as law-responsive functioning alongside all else.

3-3.1.2 A New Idea of Subject and Object

The idea of 'oceanic' law-side leads to a radically different notion of subject and object, which will find application, for example, in understanding IS affordance (§7-2.3, §7-3.3).

Dooyeweerd (1955, II, 367–369) identified four ways in which Immanence Philosophy has unhelpfully conceived of object:

- as generic 'thing' (as in the Object-oriented approach, §7-2.4.3);
- as metaphysical concept of substance;
- as that which is non-free over against the free (usually human) subject (Descartes);
- as that which is known or acted on by a subject (Descartes).

All four 'level out' the distinctions between the spheres of meaningfulness (aspects), e.g,. between lingual, social and economic objects. Descartes' view implies a gulf between subject and object, shown in Figure 3.2a, which Heidegger (1962) tried to bridge by his notion of 'being-in-the-world' and *Dasein* (a being for whom their own existence is an issue); see Figure 3.2b. But Heidegger dissolved the subject-object distinction. Everyday experience

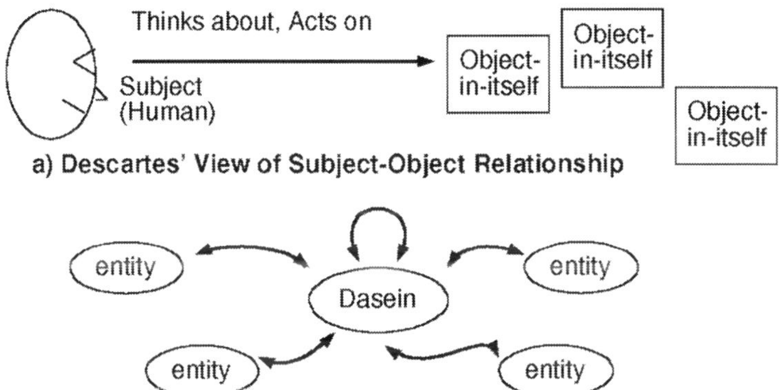

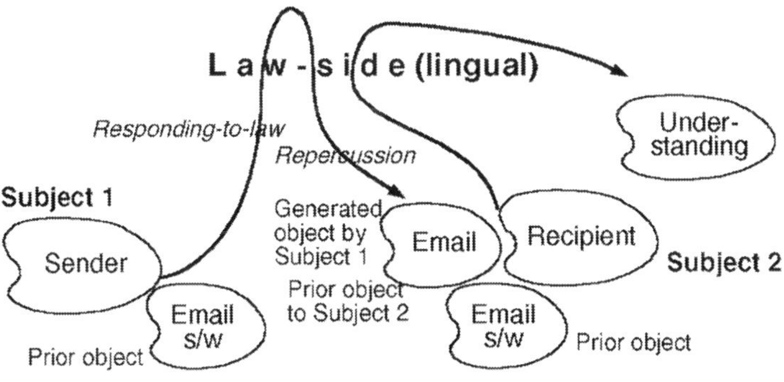

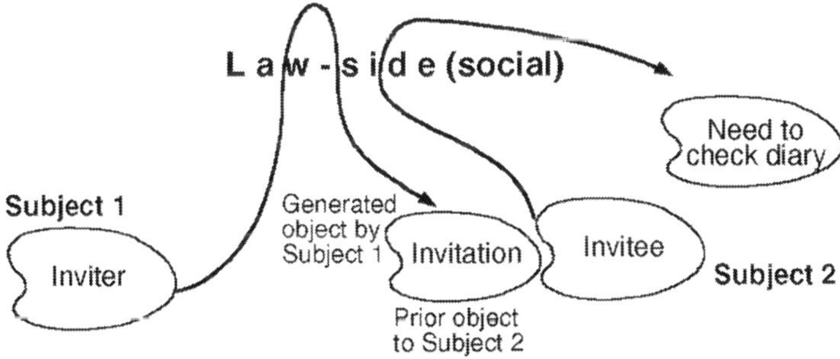

Figure 3.2 The Subject-object Relationship as Conceived by Descartes, Heidegger and Dooyeweerd

tells a different story from both: subject and object are often intimately, proximally engaged yet distinct.

Dooyeweerd's view radically differs from both. By making aspectual law central to the being and functioning of both subject and object, he proposed a fifth meaning:

- **Object** as partner with subject in responding to law.

This copes with diversity if we recognise different spheres of law. Figure 3.2c shows subjects and objects involved in sending and receiving e-mail, considered from the perspective of the lingual aspect. The sender's writing and the recipient's reading are both constituted in responding to the laws of the lingual aspect. The sender (lingual subject) makes use of e-mail software (lingual object) in responding to the laws of the lingual aspect to compose an email, which is also a lingual object. The recipient (lingual subject), using e-mail software (lingual object), responds to lingual laws to read the e-mail (lingual object) and thereby gains understanding (also a lingual object).

From the perspective of the social aspect, sender becomes inviter, recipient, invitee and e-mail, invitation, as seen in Figure 3.2d. The software is invisible, because it is socially meaningless.

Dooyeweerd (1955, II, 369) identified two ways in which something is object:

- **Prior object:** that with which a subject is engaged during their functioning, which pre-exists the functioning;
- **Generated objects:** that which is produced as a result of such functioning.

In Figure 3.2c, the email software is prior object to both sender and recipient, the email is generated by the sender and prior object to recipient, and the understanding is recipient-generated object.

Dooyeweerd's view not only retains the subject-object distinction and proximal engagement, but is richer and more precisely expresses the situation in all its aspects. It also accounts for *subject-subject relationships* (between sender and recipient).

3-3.1.3 On Limitations in Functioning

Not just humans, but the entire cosmos is subject to law—though each is subject in different ways. In Dooyeweerd's view, humans may function as subject in every aspect, animals up to the psychic aspect, plants up to the organic, and inert matter up to the physical. So animals climb (psychical aspect), but rocks cannot. All things may function as object in any aspect. So a rock might help the animal climb (psychical object).

Up to the physical aspect, all these kinds of thing can function as subject. So to Dooyeweerd, rocks function as physical *subjects*, not objects.

What about ICT? Basden (2008) argued that computers, as silicon, plastic, etc., can function as subject only up to the physical aspect, and function as active lingual objects when run by a user. Breems (2017) has suggested that computer systems might be seen as functioning as *subject-by-proxy* (e.g., a computer playing chess). Breems' idea is more helpful, and is discussed in §5-4.4, §7-3.3.1.

An entity may function as a subject in one aspect and object in another simultaneously. Consider a computer being used to compose an e-mail, from the perspective of two aspects:

- Physical aspect: Both computer and user function as subject (according to laws of physics).
- Lingual aspect: User functions as subject, computer (running software) as lingual object.

Such a view, elaborated in §5-4, breaks the logjam of the artificial intelligence question (§5-6). That subject and object are roles depending on aspect also helps understand affordance (§7-3.3).

Dooyeweerd's discussion of subject-object occupies pages 366–412 of Dooyeweerd (1955, II).

(The human self is subject, but much more than a subject, transcending temporality and even the law-side, and open to the divine, and it can never be theoretically understood; no discussion of this is needed here.)

3-3.2 Time and Progress

When we procrastinate (see §6-3.7) we suddenly find 'time' has flown past. Our sensory experience of time differs from clock time—Bergson's *duree*. Dooyeweerd recognised this as just two of the many aspects of time, psychical and physical. Time, to Dooyeweerd, has a subject-object-side, in duration and how we experience it, and a law-side in what necessarily comes after what. Examples: 55 after 54 (quantitative), cause-effect (physical), birth-growth-maturity-death (organic), premise-conclusion (analytic), reward or punishment after action (juridical).

Dooyeweerd called the coherence of all aspects of time, *cosmic time*, and discussed many issues related to time that do not concern us, such as eternity, end-of-time and the self, which are discussed more fully in Basden (2008), and one that does: progress.

What is the fundamental difference between *progress* and regress? Humanity—indeed the entire subject-object-side—opens up the potential of each aspect by its very functioning, occurring and living. Time is not like railroad tracks along which we travel, but is created by our functioning (as constituted in responding-to-aspectual-law and yielding repercussions). Responding-to-aspectual-law constitutes *time* in its actuality in each aspect. By functioning, the entire cosmos actualises, or opens up, or 'unfolds' the potential inherent in each aspect's possibility.

Progress is related to this. Example: *Technological progress* is an opening up of the potential of the formative aspect, and artistic progress, of the aesthetic aspect. The lingual aspect has been opened up by speaking, writing, drawing, printing, broadcasting, etc., and in §8-6.1, it is suggested that the advent of ICT and information systems may be seen as another important contribution to opening up the lingual aspect.

A major spur to aspectual opening is theoretical thought (science, philosophy), by which we gain good understanding of the laws of each aspect in ways that can be applied generally. The nature and operation of theoretical thought is discussed next.

3-4 Theoretical Thinking, Philosophy and Research

This section explains Dooyeweerd's understanding of theoretical thinking and its roles and limitations. It is referred to in most subsequent chapters when we discuss research. It may be skipped by those who are more interested in Dooyeweerd's positive view of everyday experience and meaningfulness via his aspects.

If we try to understand theoretical thought by a process of theoretical thinking, then we are already presupposing its possibility. Such circular understanding is suspect. It is better to try to understand theoretical thought by taking everyday experience as a starting-point because, as is now increasingly widely recognised, the life, experience and beliefs of the theoretical thinker all impinge on their theoretical thought. This makes Dooyeweerd's starting-point of everyday experience especially relevant in order to understand theoretical thought and all the concepts above.

> Note on terminology: '*Theory*' refers to beliefs about the way reality works, in any of its diverse aspects, that are general (can be applied to unforeseen situations), and are worthy of being relied upon. '*Theoretical thought*' is not just the activity of thinking theoretically but involves the mission of contributing good theory to humanity's bodies of knowledge. '*Body of knowledge*' is the collected knowledge of a field, usually general in nature, on which practitioners and researchers rely. '*Science*' develops theories in specific fields, whether mathematical, natural or social sciences (§3-5.2). Here, '*Research*' is not restricted to empirical scientific studies, but refers to any attempt to contribute reliable general beliefs (theories) to humanity's bodies of knowledge; almost synonymous with theoretical thought; includes philosophical reflection. So, '*thinker*' and '*researcher*' are almost synonymous, whether empirical or reflective.

3-4.1 The Nature of Theoretical Thought

Dooyeweerd argued, on the basis of his extensive survey in Volume I of Dooyeweerd (1955), that most philosophy, from an Immanence Standpoint

(§3-2.1), has presumed the possibility of theoretical thought rather than critically examined it. It has treated theoretical thought as autonomous, authoritative and neutral.

Though the *processes* and *methods* of theoretical thought have been studied by Kant, Husserl and more recent thinkers (e.g., Popper, Polanyi), they still presupposed the theoretical *attitude* of thought. In the very activity of studying, they presumed they could adopt a theoretical attitude of thought and that it would lead them to good understanding. Dooyeweerd believed they had not gone deep enough and that the very theoretical attitude of thought should first be examined from the perspective of the *pre-theoretical attitude of thought*—that is, taking everyday experience as a starting point. Whereas many treat the thinker as merely a thinker, focusing on their analytic aspect, "Over against this tradition Dooyeweerd emphasized that it is the human person who thinks, does scientific work, and theorizes" (Geertsema 2000, 96).

Dooyeweerd, ahead of his time, questioned this and faced the challenge of understanding what theoretical thought is, going philosophically deeper than others who now recognise it (e.g., Habermas' knowledge-interests, Foucault's knowledge-archaeology).

3-4.1.1 The Kantian Gulf

Before Immanuel Kant, knowledge was presupposed to depend on input from the world, with human consciousness as filter and reasoner. The main debate was over whether laws like gravity were genuine, or merely patterns detected in data. Kant's 'Copernican revolution' put human consciousness at the centre, as the autonomous interpreter of the world, sovereignly deciding what counts as data and rationality. Thought was divorced from thing (*'Kantian gulf'*). As a result, it is argued, we cannot ever know the *ding an sich* (thing in itself, noumenon) but only the phenomenon like its taste and shape.

This would seem to provide a basis for questioning the neutrality of theoretical thought, and indeed many recent thinkers have taken it to be so, but Kant did not wish to accept that conclusion, and tried to see reason, along with space and time, as 'built-in'.

The Kantian gulf expresses the Nature-freedom ground-motive (§3-2.2) and has been problematic for theoretical thought in both philosophy and sciences. It creates an absolute antithesis between subjective and objective, as we have in the IS field today. It presumes a world that 'hides' rather than 'reveals' itself, resulting in absolute 'secular skepticism', which engenders an infinite loneliness in the world (Tarnas 1991, 336), privileging opinion and power over curiosity, joy and humility. It distances theoretical thought from everyday experience, despite Kant's attempt at a critique of judgement.

In the information systems field, views like 'essentialism' are denigrated and ignored, and we find social privileged over technical, despite calls to recognise the latter.

Critical Realism, as expounded by Bhaskar (1975) and advocated by Mingers (2004), tries to bridge the Kantian gulf by taking a non-Kantian stance (Klein 2004). It posits three levels of reality (mechanisms, events and experiences); the reality of mechanisms transcends the others and echoes Dooyeweerd's notion of a law-side. However, Critical Realism ends up theorizing everyday experience (Dooyeweerd 1955, III, 44–47); Bhaskar begins with the scientific enterprise of finding out about reality theoretically rather than understanding theoretical thought from an everyday perspective as Dooyeweerd did. Though Bhaskar (2012) has 'everyday' in the book title, it is seldom mentioned in the text and not in its index. (Adequate comparison between Critical Realism and Dooyeweerd still awaits us: a research opportunity in philosophy.)

3-4.1.2 Theoretical Thought as Part of Reality

Instead of a gulf between knowing subject and known object, Dooyeweerd believed that,

> Knowledge and understanding do not start with the subject as if knowledge has to bridge an original gulf between the two. . . . There is no original gap that needs to be bridged. Knowledge presupposes that we are in a relationship already.
>
> (Geertsema 2000, 101)

He held that both knower and known occur within, and are subject to, the same oceanic law-side. This enabled Dooyeweerd to circumvent the Kantian gulf without any pre-Kantian essentialism, and to question the neutrality of theoretical thought without subjectivism. "There is no truth in itself" wrote Dooyeweerd (1955, III, 577). This is, however, not a subjectivist denial of truth, but a denial of in-itself, in that truth involves the whole 'ocean' and no one piece of it (pp. 561–577). No theory or statement can encompass all the meaningfulness that is truth.

It also enabled Dooyeweerd to penetrate more deeply than others did into what makes theoretical thought possible. He made both immanent critique of theoretical thinkers, and two transcendental critiques of the possibility of theoretical thought itself.

> Note on terminology: *Immanent critique* is critique of existing ideas 'from the inside', seeking to understand, in their own terms, what they see as meaningful or as problems with previous thought. Immanent critique was carried out by Habermas, Dooyeweerd and others. *Transcendent critique*, by contrast, is 'from the outside', ignoring what is meaningful to the ideas being critiqued, and is usually used as a weapon in battles (e.g. Marxism v. Capitalism). *Transcendental critique* (note 'al') attempts to critically discern "the universal,

necessary conditions that make a thing possible" (Clouser 2005), and was employed by Kant, Husserl, Bhaskar, Dooyeweerd and others. *Immanence Standpoint* is a perspective (see §3-2.1) and has nothing to do with immanent critique, which is an activity. Dooyeweerd employed immanent critique to show "always has been" and transcendental critique to show "cannot be otherwise"; see below.

3-4.2 Dooyeweerd's Immanent Critique of the History of Western Theoretical Thought

Dooyeweerd has written hundreds of pages on the history of theoretical thought (1955, I, II; 1979), mainly in Europe, with some in other cultures. His coverage of philosophers is vast: 14 ancient Greek, 14 Scholastic, 3 Reformational, 14 Renaissance, 25 19th-century and 34 20th-century philosophers, along with scores of legal theorists, political theorists and many in the sciences. (Many who discuss the history of theoretical thought skip the Scholastic period, e.g., Klein [2004].) A notable gap is absence of American Pragmatism.

As far as possible, he read these thinkers in their original languages, to ascertain what was meaningful to each thinker, what motivated them as problems in their fields. By immanent critique, Dooyeweerd tried to expose presuppositions on which their thought was based and discussed how these undermined what they were trying to achieve. An overall picture emerged that theoretical thought has never been neutral, never autonomous of the thinker's pre-theoretical experience.

> Immanence-philosophy in all its nuances stands or falls with the dogma of the autonomy of theoretical thought. . . . Not only traditional metaphysics, but also Kantian epistemology, modern phenomenology and phenomenological ontology in the style of Nicolai Hartmann continued in this respect to be involved in a theoretical dogmatism.
>
> (Dooyeweerd 1955, I, 28)

The picture revealed the problems listed in §3-2.1 as the result of the Immanence-standpoint. It showed that theoretical thought has never adequately addressed meaningfulness nor pre-theoretical, everyday experience, has tended to develop by swinging between poles of the ground-motive currently in force, and has always fostered 'isms' that elevate one aspect to which other aspects are reduced. These resulted in antinomy. Example: Xeno's paradox of Achilles and tortoise (see §3-6.2). Example in the information systems field: In the notion of emancipatory information systems development, Wilson (1997) detected sinister elements of "enforced emancipation".

These problems will not be addressed, let alone solved, Dooyeweerd believed, unless we recognise the deep religious (in Dooyeweerd's meaning) root of theoretical thought. Geertsema suggests (2000, 85), "The main aim of his philosophy has always been to show how the religious starting point controls philosophical and scientific thought, both in relation to humanistic and Scholastic thinking and in relation to his own reformational conviction."

That philosophy inescapably has religious roots might seem an abstruse point, irrelevant to ICT research, but when taken seriously, it has far-reaching and liberating consequences, opening doors onto many new fruitful avenues of research. These emerge from Dooyeweerd's transcendental critiques.

3-4.3 Dooyeweerd's Transcendental Critiques of Theoretical Thought

Dooyeweerd, however,

> is not satisfied with an argument that shows that in fact philosophy always has been influenced by religious convictions.
>
> (Geertsema 2000, 99).

Rather,

> He wants to show that it cannot be otherwise, because it is part of the nature of philosophy or theoretical thought. For that reason he called his critical analysis a transcendental critique.

Dooyeweerd employed two transcendental critiques to lay bare the fundamental conditions that make philosophy and theoretical thought possible. A transcendental critique aims to expose the 'transcendental' (universal, necessary) conditions that make something possible (Clouser 2005).

The first, discussed by Dooyeweerd in (1955, I, 22–33), explained in Kalsbeek (1975) and discussed in Chaplin (2011) and Basden (2008), does not much concern us because it was restricted to philosophy and has been criticised.

3-4.3.1 Dooyeweerd's Second Transcendental Critique of Theoretical Thought

Dooyeweerd's second transcendental critique of theoretical thought arose because of limitations with the first. Out of it comes an understanding of research that is highly serviceable in the information systems field. It tries to understand scientific as well as philosophical thought, and I have found it useful in the information systems field.

Dooyeweerd believed that Kant and others had asked right questions but had not asked sufficient questions or gone deep enough in their critique. He saw his second critique as "resuming" Kant's project (Dooyeweerd 1955, I, 36).

Dooyeweerd argued that three transcendental problems of theoretical thought must necessarily be addressed by any attempt to understand foundations, defend them and enable discourse between philosophies. Unfortunately, Dooyeweerd's exposition of this transcendental critique (1955, I, 4–60) is rambling and not easy to understand. This has led to criticism that it is not truly transcendental, but influenced by Dooyeweerd's own presuppositions (Chaplin 2011). There is some validity in that (since ultimate transcendental-ness lies only in the Divine) but it does not undermine the value of Dooyeweerd's critique. Combining that (philosophically oriented) exposition with Dooyeweerd's (1955, III, 168) briefer discussion of transcendental critique in the field of philosophical sociology, we may understand better. That is the basis of my interpretation that follows.

Several attempts to explain Dooyeweerd's transcendental critique are available. Clouser (2005) and Strauss (2009) give it an analytical twist. Geertsema (2000) reinterprets it hermeneutically. Chaplin (2011) interprets it in the light of Christian thinking and trying to understand the state. The reader might prefer those interpretations to my own, which is influenced by my desire to understand the confusions, conflicts and complexities of research, especially in interdisciplinary fields like ICT and information systems.

3-4.3.2 Preparing to Understand Three Transcendental Problems

Before outlining Dooyeweerd's three transcendental problems, it is necessary to discuss how they may be approached.

1. What is the role of theoretical thought? Is it not to contribute theoretical findings to humanity's bodies of knowledge? Theories are beliefs about the way reality works in general terms, on which it is reasonable to rely. This characterization of theories takes into account both their generality and also the rigour needed in research or thinking.
2. Dooyeweerd refused to de-personalise theoretical thought; it must always be understood in relation to the person who thinks.
3. What Dooyeweerd was talking about was theoretical thinking *in its completeness*. Complete theoretical thinking is "inter-individual" or *communal* (Dooyeweerd 1955, I, 59), and must include not only the individual's findings but also the community's critical debate about, and refinement of, their findings.
4. Remember Dooyeweerd's starting points, especially that in a pre-theoretical attitude we encounter diversity of meaningfulness which is yet somehow coherent. Those who begin by presupposing a theoretical attitude possibly cannot properly critique it.
5. Whereas Dooyeweerd was attempting a transcendental critique of *any* theoretical thought, whether philosophical or scientific, his main exposition in (1955, I, 4–60) was oriented mainly towards philosophical thought, and includes discussion of issues that are important in philosophy but less so in IS research. So we must also understand his shorter

exposition of transcendental critique oriented towards philosophical sociology (Dooyeweerd 1955, III, 168), where the way the three transcendental problems are expressed is different. We need also to take into account his lengthy discussion of the problem of epistemology, in Part II of his Volume II of Dooyeweerd (1955).
6. In an earlier article, Dooyeweerd (1947) actually posed four transcendental questions. The first of these questions leads to considering the three transcendental problems in Dooyeweerd (1955). This is considered first.

3-4.3.3 The Starting Question

"What is the difference between theoretical and pre-theoretical attitudes of thought?" Dooyeweerd remarked (1999, 6),

> Neither Kant, the founder of the so-called critical transcendental philosophy, nor Edmund Husserl, the founder of modern phenomenology, who called his phenomenological philosophy 'the most radical critique of knowledge', have made the theoretical attitude of thought into a critical problem. Both of them started from the autonomy of theoretical thinking as an axiom which needs no further justification.

Dooyeweerd's answer was that, whereas "naïve experience has an integral vision of the whole" (Dooyeweerd 1955, I, 84), theoretical thought necessarily involves abstraction from the empirical world. As Klein and Myers (1999) recognise in their principles of interpretive field studies, it is not enough to just collect idiographic data, but we must abstract and generalise therefrom, to provide findings for humanity's bodies of knowledge, which can be applied by others in different situations.

3-4.3.4 First Transcendental Problem (TP1): Abstraction, Thinker and World

What is it that we abstract from the total situation we study? Dooyeweerd's answer, expounded in (1955, I, 38–45), was that we abstract aspects (ways in which world is meaningful) from subject-object-side actuality. Such abstraction occurs in all kinds of research (positivist, interpretivist, socio-critical, design, action research). The aspect of interest is chosen by the researcher/thinker; for example, socio-critical research looks for social structures of domination.

Many (e.g., Aristotle, Russell, Bhaskar) presuppose that data comes to us ultimately via our senses; Dooyeweerd disagrees (1955, I, 50). He provides philosophical grounds for what we already experience as researchers, that data *qua* data comes directly to us, each kind intuited differently according to the aspect that makes it meaningful. For example, economists study costs and currencies. Even though senses are involved as part of the multi-aspectual functioning (see §3-8.3) that is data collection, data is not reducible to, nor wholly derivable from, sensory input.

Abstraction, Dooyeweerd argued, is not the proximal law-subject-object relationship of everyday thinking (see §3-3.1.2) but a more distal relationship that is fundamentally different, involving two 'oppositions'. One is between the thinker and the world being thought about, which he called *Gegenstand* (c.f. "A theory is other than myself" (Polanyi 1974, 4) and the phenomenon of the detached observer).

The other is between the aspects abstracted and those not abstracted, which are often ignored (example: economics research focusing on monetary mechanisms but ignoring political and religious forces). No abstraction can capture the full richness of reality. This opposition is not found in reality itself, which exhibits fundamental coherence and 'resists' being pulled apart in this manner by abstraction (Dooyeweerd 1955, I, 31). This leads to transcendental problem 2.

3-4.3.5 Second Transcendental Problem (TP2): Theoretical Synthesis and Multiple Rationalities

In order to generate findings from the data, which are new contributions to humanity's bodies of knowledge, rationalities must be activated. This is *theoretical synthesis* (Dooyeweerd 1955, I, 45–52).

As Dooyeweerd, Winch, Habermas and others argued, there are multiple rationalities, which are irreducibly distinct (what makes sense in one makes no sense in others). Example: "In science, for example, it would be illogical to refuse to be bound by the results of a properly carried out experiment; in religion it would be illogical to suppose that one could pit one's strength against God's" (Winch 1958). Different fields argue differently to generate new knowledge. Later Table 3.4 illustrates the rationality for each aspect.

On what grounds may multiple rationalities be synthesised? Dooyeweerd said this requires critical self-reflection. His argument is not entirely clear, but I understand it as follows. It is the responsibility of the thinker to ensure there are no antinomies, category errors, irrelevances or unwarranted reductions in the reasoning by which findings are generated. This, however, requires harmonizing irreducibly different rationalities for which activity there is no *a priori*, overarching law. This is a pre-theoretical rather than theoretical activity, involving all aspects of the person who is the thinker, especially his or her pistic aspect, of presuppositional beliefs. This brings us to the third transcendental problem.

3-4.3.6 Third Transcendental Problem (TP3): Grounds of Critical Self-Reflection

This question concerns how the findings from theoretical synthesis, as candidates for humanity's bodies of knowledge, are critically examined and refined. This requires recognition of the self of the researchers and thinkers involved—as exemplified in Klein and Myers' (1999) principles 3 and 5 of interpretive research (of researcher-researched interaction, and of dialogical reasoning). Though individual thinkers might be self-critical, it usually involves the community of thought (Dooyeweerd 1955, I, 59) and is carried out via its discourse.

Dooyeweerd's discussion on this, in (1955, I, 52–60), is tortuous and geared more to philosophy, so I use the following to exemplify it. Suppose the thinker/researcher has published their findings and the community begins to respond. A public conversation ensues (in print), going something like:

> Critic 1: "The author fails to consider X." (TP1)
> Critic 2, "The author has not analysed correctly, and should employ rationality R." (TP2)
> Rejoinder: "But X is not relevant, because Y. Rationality R is inappropriate because S." (On the basis of what is meaningful)
> Critic 3: "But S/Y are inappropriate in this field, because of T." (About paradigms)
> Rejoinder: "But T is the current paradigm and is not appropriate; what is being suggested is a new paradigm U." (Paradigm shift)
> Critic 4/5: "But the U must be resisted/welcomed because of O."

With such discourse, the findings are refined and enter the body of knowledge, as general and reasonably reliable beliefs.

All but the first two are about TP3. O refers to an *Origin of Meaning*. An Origin of Meaning that to which the community refers in order to determine the scope of what could be meaningful when judging ideas and paradigms. It is the community's belief about the coherence of meaning, or the totality of what is meaningful, and is determined by what it takes to be self-sufficient and on which all else depends—what Clouser (2005) calls a divinity belief.

The Origin of Meaning is usually the ground-motive under the influence of which the community operates to offer alternative paradigms. Western theoretical thought has usually operated under the three dualistic ground-motives. In his transcendental critique of theoretical thought in philosophical sociology (Dooyeweerd 1955, III, 168), Dooyeweerd's Origin of Meaning (the biblical ground-motive led him to reject all totalising or reductionist views of society that are based on any single aspectual view [such as family or state], because sociology needs a basis on which to relate to its "totality of meaning" of the social aspect of reality).

While the Humanistic ground-motive provides only two ways of being meaningful (freedom, determination), resulting in dialectical swings, the biblical ground-motive as expounded by Dooyeweerd provides a richer variety, within which new ideas can often fit more comfortably. Though some might react against such a claim, it deserves critical discussion, but not in this book.

3-4.4 Reflection on the Above

Dooyeweerd went further than other contemporary thinkers who agree that theoretical thought is neither autonomous nor neutral, by revealing transcendentally at least three places where non-autonomy is located:

- in choice of what it is meaningful to think about (TP1);
- in responsibility for harmonizing mutually irreducible rationalities during theoretical synthesis (TP2);
- in reference to a presumed Origin of Meaning during critique (TP3).

How do Dooyeweerd's questions relate to extant thought? Kant addressed the second transcendental question, Husserl addressed the first, but neither addressed the third. Foucault arguably began to address the third but was perhaps too absorbed in his understanding of power to provide a proper transcendental critique of theoretical thought. Only Dooyeweerd, as far as I know, has tackled all three.

In these three ways, theoretical thought, including philosophy, is treated as a (special) part of everyday experience, rather than standing against it in judgement. Theoretical thought is always-already limited and non-neutral, and inherently narrows and distorts whatever we think about, even though it might provide genuine generic insight.

3-5 Ground-Ideas, Philosophies, Sciences and Disciplines

This section provides material with which extant ideas and discourses may be critiqued. It may be skipped for now by those more interested in Dooyeweerd's understanding of aspects, especially in relation to everyday analysis, but should be returned to for full understanding.

Dooyeweerd developed his transcendental critique into a device to allow discourse and mutual understanding between disparate philosophies and paradigms of research: the three-part Ground Idea. After introducing this idea, it is used to help us understand sciences, disciplines and paradigms.

3-5.1 Dooyeweerd's Notion of Three-Part Ground-Idea

Three issues necessarily underlie all theoretical thought that aims to contribute general findings to humanity's bodies of knowledge:

- About **world**: aspects of the world that are selected,
- About **rationalities** or sense-making: responsibility for harmonizing rationalities, by which findings emerge that are general and valid;
- About **wider meaningfulness**: critique in relation to the potential body of knowledge in relation to an Origin of Meaning.

Dooyeweerd argued that any full philosophy that might act as underpinning for scientific research takes a position on these three transcendental problems. Philosophies may be characterised by reference to the positions they take, which together Dooyeweerd called the 'ground-idea' of the philosophy. This makes Dooyeweerd's transcendental critique of theoretical thought usable in several ways.

1. Dooyeweerd claimed (1955, I, 70,526) that explication of ground-ideas opens the way for mutual understanding and discourse among philosophies, even those apparently incommensurable. Section 4-2.2 contains an exemplar of how positivist, interpretivist, socio-critical and action research in information systems may be integrated in this way.
2. Philosophers may be brought together in novel combinations (e.g., Foucault with Calvin?) by reference to world, rationalities and meaningfulness. This is why, in this book, a wide range of thinkers is brought together.
3. This notion offers an exciting possibility of generating and evaluating new philosophies from 'reasonable' Ground-Ideas.
4. PhD students in the IS field are expected to identify the philosophy that underpins their research approach, but many struggle to do so. Perhaps, instead, they might identify their Ground-Idea, by identifying each component of world, rationalities and wider meaningfulness instead of named philosophies.

Dooyeweerd's notion of three-part Ground-Ideas has not yet been widely employed in such ways; these call for several avenues of philosophical research.

3-5.2 Sciences, Fields, Disciplines and Paradigms

To Dooyeweerd, *science* may be seen as the theoretical uncovering of the laws of a selected aspect, expressed in the form of theories. We will adopt Dooyeweerd's terminology because it places all fields of study on an equal footing as contributing to bodies of knowledge, which is important in interdisciplinary endeavours. A *discipline*, as "a subject that is taught: a branch of learning: a field of study" (Webster 1971), involves science, and a *field*, as "an area, category or division wherein a particular activity or pursuit is carried out", includes disciplinary activity and scientific pursuit. Both these definitions imply demarcation of what is meaningful from what is not—study of, teaching and learning revolving around, and activity meaningful in certain aspects that are selected, as in science.

3-5.2.1 Fields of Interest

Thus fields, disciplines and sciences may be seen as centring on one aspect of the world, or a few, with selected rationalities. The popular connotation, that 'science' tests theories by experimentation, is ignored.

Table 3.2 suggests broad sciences that centre on each aspect. Column 2 suggests sciences or disciplines, column 3 suggests research methods.

Notice how this applies equally across all kinds of science and research, without denying their differences. Cross-over sciences like physiology will, of course, have more than one core aspect.

Attempts to employ methods from other aspects usually result in problems that confuse the operation of its science. Critique of findings is first by reference to the core aspect of the science and its rationality (TP1, TP2), and

Table 3.2 Sciences and Disciplines, Appropriate Research Methods and Issues

Aspect	Science / discipline	Research methods / issues
Quantitative	Arithmetic, Algebra, Statistics	Deduction, theorem proof
Spatial	Geometry, Topology	Geometric proofs
Kinematic	Phoronomy, Kinematics, Dynamics	Infinitesimal calculus
Physical	Quantum physics, Physics, Chemistry, Materials science	Laboratory experiment, with physical reasoning
Organic-biotic	Physiology, Life sciences, Biology, Ecology, Taxonomy	Greenhouse experiments, field studies, dissection
Psychic / Sensitive	Psychology, Sensory sciences, Cognitive sciences	Stimulus-response trials, Control groups
Analytical	Logic, Analysis	Logical proof, cognitive methods
Formative	Design science, 'Sciences of the Artificial', History	Game playing, puzzle-solving, artefact-construction, model building, forensics
Lingual	Linguistics, Semiotics, Hermeneutics, Literature, Language studies – and Information Systems (§5-2.5)	Text analysis, discourse analysis; interview analysis, cognitive studies
Social	Social science / Sociology, Organizational studies	Surveys, questionnaires, interviews, model building
Economic	Economics, Management science	Statistics, model building, As social science
Aesthetic	Aesthetics, Art, Performance, Sport science, (Systems thinking?)	As social science + construction
Juridical	Legal science, Political Science	Review of cases and histories, Reflection, legal deduction
Ethical	Ethical theory	Attitude surveys, reflection
Pistic / Faith	Theology, Some anthropology	Reference to sacred writings, hermeneutics, anthropological studies, apologetics

then to *wider meaningfulness* of other aspects, which are selected by reference to an Origin of Meaning (TP3).

In the debate around the identity of disciplines like information systems, discussed in §8-2.4, this can shift attention away from static identity towards the more dynamic and normative dignity, destiny and responsibility. This possibility is discussed and deepened in relation to the information systems field in §8-6.3 and in Basden (2010), where neighbouring aspects also come into play. It offers an understanding of interdisciplinary research, not only as the bolting-together of originally separated interests, but also for sensitive inter-discourse among disciplines as advocated by Boden (1999).

Aspects are ordered by dependency, as discussed in §3-7.4.5, so sciences of later aspects depend on earlier ones to some extent (e.g. biology on chemistry).

3-5.2.2 Paradigms

Kuhn (1962/1996) argued that science moves forward by periods of normal science punctuated by revolutionary paradigm shifts. However, Kuhn's notion of paradigm is confused (Masterman 1970), and with his examples drawn mainly from the natural sciences, it is not clear how it may be applied to the social sciences. Burrell and Morgan (1979) have proposed sociological paradigms, but these have been criticised as too polarised (see §9-2.5) and not faithful to Kuhn. How, then, may we understand the notion of *paradigm* more clearly?

One is by reference to the three-part Ground-Idea: each paradigm finds a particular aspect of the world important, employs specific rationalities and relates to wider meaningfulness in certain ways, especially when paradigms take the form of epistemological approaches. This is applied to the positivist, interpretivist and socio-critical approaches found in the information systems field in §4-2.

Another was suggested by my PhD student, Sina Joneidy: that paradigms may be understood in relation to spheres of meaningfulness (aspects) (Joneidy 2015). He surveyed seminal papers that introduced new paradigms in the field of information systems use, and found that each was motivated by different aspects that hitherto had been overlooked. These aspects might be secondary to the core aspect of the field. This suggests that a paradigm is a perspective within a field that focuses on a different secondary aspect in relation to the core one. On this basis, most of the disparate significations of 'paradigm' found by Masterman (1970) can be situated within a wider picture of meaningfulness. This idea requires further development; Joneidy's work continues.

Both Hegel and Dooyeweerd understand development of thought as dialectic (thesis-antithesis-synthesis, ground-motive poles), but this fails to account for actual development, especially in interdisciplinary fields like environmental care and information systems. Basden (1999) suggests that development may instead be understood as a shift of attention from one dominant aspect to others that had previously been overlooked. To be sensitive to such aspectual dominance or aspectual ignorance will inform our discussions of discourses around ICT and its research approaches.

3-5.3 Reflection

We are halfway round the circle of understanding. We have followed Dooyeweerd in understanding the nature of theoretical thought, with very few presuppositions except the starting-points of everyday experience and meaningfulness, and commitment to respect their diversity and coherence. From these starting-points, theoretical thought is revealed as activity that can generate useful understanding for humanity's bodies of knowledge, without over-claiming, because it recognises that it involves pre-theoretical choices of what is relevant, responsibility for harmonizing aspects and deeply rooted beliefs about what is meaningful.

We are now in a position to employ that broad understanding of theoretical thought to understand everyday experience with a sensitive theoretical approach. This involves three things: to understand how we may delineate aspects (which were only provisional in §3-1.2.5), the nature of aspectuality and then of things. That will bring us full circle.

3-6 How to Delineate Spheres of Meaningfulness (Aspects)

This section enables us to understand the validity and limitations of Dooyeweerd's suite of aspects, which is used throughout this book.

Earlier (§3-1.2.5) Dooyeweerd's suite of fifteen aspects was introduced provisionally, and we have relied on it in our discussions. But how do we know whether we can rely on Dooyeweerd's delineation of aspects—spheres of meaningfulness?

§3-6.1 Comparison With Other Suites of Aspects

Many thinkers have come up with other suites of aspects; may we not use those? Table 3.3 compares them with Dooyeweerd's suite.

(Discussion of these may be found in www.dooy.info/compare-asp.html.)

Despite some combining or overlapping, three things stand out. 1. Most of the suites are subsets of Dooyeweerd's. 2. Only seldom is anything unplaceable, and this is usually because it is multi-aspectual. 3. In most suites, the order is similar. This implies that Dooyeweerd's suite is at least a reasonable one to use. The way Dooyeweerd delineated aspects, and his philosophical underpinning of them, makes it even more reasonable.

Table 3.3 Suites of Aspects Compared

Dooyeweerd aspects	*Maslow*	*Checkland Es*	*Hartmann levels*	*Bunge systems*	*Habermas action types*	*Giddens modalities*	*Wilenius*	*Boulding*	*Roget's Thesaurus*	*Encyc. Britan. Outline*
Quantitative									Abstract relations	Maths
Spatial									Space	
Kinematic									Space (motion)	
Physical			Inorganic	Physical			Physical	Mechanical	Matter	Matter, energy, Earth
Organic	Biological		Organic	Biological			Organic	Reproductive Evolutionary Ecological		Life
Psychic	Safety		Psychic				Mental-Psychical	Cybernetic	Affection (personal)	Life
Analytic	Enquiry	Efficacy						Human	Intellect	Logic science philosophy
Formative		Effectiveness	Historical	Technical	Instrumental	Power domination		Human?	Volition: personal, Intellect: idea form'n	Technology
Lingual	Expression				Communicative	Interpretive schemes, Signification			Intellect: communic'n	(Symbolism)
Social	Affiliation Esteem		Supra-individual	Social	Strategic?		Social	Social	Volition: intersocial, Affection: sympathetic	Society, History

Economic		Efficiency				Resources				Wealth
Aesthetic	Aesthetic	Elegance			Dramaturgical?		Aesthetic	Social?		Art
Juridical					Normatively regulated	Norms Legitimation	Truth	Social?		Law, politics
Ethical		Ethicality				Domination, Moral sanction?	Ethics		Affection: moral	
Pistic	Transcendence Self actualiz'n				Discursive?	Meaning	Religous belief	Transcendental Creodic Demographic?	Affection: religious	Religion

3-6.2 Delineation of Aspects

The challenge in knowing the aspects (theoretically) is that, with aspects, we cannot take the *Gegenstand* relationship that begins theoretical thought, because they are the very 'ocean' that enables our 'swimming' that is the thinking about aspects. So Dooyeweerd had to find other means. He used several tools together and iteratively to delineate aspects—and so may we.

1. His own intuition. Intuition expresses our very 'swimming' in the ocean that is the coherence of aspects—but it is shaped by our experience and culture.
2. Sensitive listening to others. Dooyeweerd sought immanent understanding of the reflections of others about aspects, over 3,000 years across a variety of cultures and in many disciplines—while taking into account the influence of their Origin of Meaning, how they saw the world and treated rationalities. Few aspect-delineators listen so sensitively or to such wide a range.
3. Clear philosophical understanding of the nature of aspects. To Dooyeweerd, aspects (law-side) cannot be conceptualised directly, but only indirectly via our engagement as part of the subject-object-side
4. Respect for everyday experience. This means recognising the full humanity and context of each thinker, including our own, and allowing pre-theoretical experience a voice in the discussions.
5. The method of antinomy (Dooyeweerd 1955, II, 37–41). If aspects are irreducibly distinct in their meaningfulness and laws, then antinomy ('against law') can arise from reducing one aspect to another.

   Example: Xeno's paradox of Achilles unable to overtake the tortoise who was given a start in a race arises from reducing the kinematic aspect (movement) to the spatial (sequence of positions).

   Example: Wilson's (1997) paradox of 'enforced emancipation' arises from conflating the formative and juridical aspects.

Part I of Dooyeweerd (1955, II) is 426 pages of discussion of the aspects. The treatment is variable, because Dooyeweerd's aim was not so much to argue for his suite as to demonstrate how discussion of aspect-delineation might proceed. Dooyeweerd warned that no suite of aspects, including his own, can ever be an absolute, final truth; it can be at best a good guess, arising from the presupposition that reality is fundamentally diverse.

> In fact the system of the law-spheres designed by us can never lay claim to material completion. A more penetrating examination may at any time bring new modal aspects of reality to the light not yet perceived before. And the discovery of new law-spheres will always require a revision and further development of our modal analyses. Theoretical thought has never finished its task. Any one who thinks he has devised

> a philosophical system that can be adopted unchanged by all later generations, shows his absolute lack of insight into the dependence of all theoretical thought on historical development.
>
> (Dooyeweerd 1955, II, 556)

Several Dooyeweerdian thinkers have suggested modifications to Dooyeweerd's suite, especially around the aesthetic aspect, but none is entirely convincing; see Basden (2008).

3-6.3 Advantages of Dooyeweerd's Suite

In discussing foundations of the information systems field, any suite of aspects could in principle be employed, but Dooyeweerd's suite:

- has wider coverage than other suites, including mathematical, pre-human, cognitive, social and societal aspects (§3-6.1);
- coheres (§3-7.4);
- was geared to everyday ('real life') experience, rather than specific interests (e.g. Bunge's systems, Maslow's needs);
- takes into account 3,000 years of reflection across several cultures—some, for example, skip the Scholastic period—and applies across all cultures;
- is grounded in a clear philosophical understanding of the nature of aspects;
- has been subjected to philosophical scrutiny by the method of antinomy.

At this point in time, Dooyeweerd's suite of aspects is the best suite available to us. So we use it here.

3-7 What Are Aspects? Philosophical Attributes of Aspects

This section provides an understanding of how Dooyeweerd understood what aspects are as such, and what their value is in our attempts to use them in discussing ICT and IS.

Webster's Dictionary (1971) defines aspect, in roughly the sense meant here, as "a particular status or phase in which anything appears or may be regarded", but Dooyeweerd gave the idea philosophical depth. This section discusses some philosophical 'attributes' of aspects-as-such, or *aspectuality*. It will help us affirm, critique and enrich the multifarious discourses in the field of information systems.

3-7.1 Aspects as Ocean of Meaningfulness

Dooyeweerd's aspects are spheres of meaningfulness that, together, constitute the ocean of meaningfulness within which we 'swim' (see §3-1.2.3).

Together, they enable all being and occurrence. Each aspect is a distinct sphere of meaningfulness, with a kernel meaning, around which revolves a constellation of meanings.

Each aspect is also a sphere of law, offering different laws that together constitutes a law-side, which enable functioning by the subject-object-side of temporal reality (§3-3.1). Each aspect provides a distinct kind of **possibility**, e.g., economic possibility, physical possibility, ethical possibility. It is aspectual law that defines what is possible in principle within what is meaningful.

The ocean is, therefore, a *social-spatial-juridical-lingual-physical-economic-organic-ethical-analytical-pistic-etc. law-side* that enables us and all temporal reality to be and function in all these ways. This implies that all the aspects are ubiquitous, intertwined and inter-dependent, and that all aspects are equally important; there is no 'higher' or 'over-arching' aspect, even though they are in sequence, as explained in §3-7.4.5. By understanding the aspects theoretically, we can begin to theoretically understand their diversity and coherence of meaning.

So no aspect is absolute, in three senses. (1) No aspect is self-sufficient; to function meaningfully in an aspect requires functioning in other aspects. (2) No aspect can be the foundation for enabling or explaining the others. (3) No aspect is able to do fully and entirely what it aims to; for example, in the lingual aspect, no word, phrase or utterance can ever contain the full meaning that we intend; c.f. Gödel's Theorem in mathematics. **Absolutization** of an aspect leads the research community to see everything as an extension of the meaning of that aspect, and try to justify everything in terms of that aspect, fostering reductionism and preventing a true interdisciplinary attitude.

3-7.2 Grasped by Intuition

"It is important to realize that in physics today, we have no knowledge of what energy *is*", wrote Feynman (1964), ". . . there are formulas for calculating some numerical quantity." But these do not "tell us the mechanisms or the *reasons* for the various formulas." We understand energy intuitively, but not theoretically. The same goes for the kernel meaning of every aspect. Each aspect has a kernel meaning than can be grasped by intuition, but not by theoretical thought. What are justice, amount, signification? We understand them intuitively, by 'dwelling' in their possibility, but not theoretically by the *Gegenstand* that is inescapable for theoretical thought (§3-4.3.4).

Beware, then, of assuming that any kernel meaning can be theorised, reasoned about or defined. Our deepest foundation is always a clutch of intuitions of meaningfulness, as of course Husserl (1970) was discovering in his *Krisis*. Words cannot fully express the kernel meaning of an aspect but can come near, as do those in Table 3.1. Several words might help us triangulate the kernel when they surround it; Dooyeweerd used several words for each aspect, such as belief and faith as well as pistic.

The benefit of this intuitive graspability is that categories based on aspects tend to be easy to understand by everyone, and they can cautiously inform analysis. Cautiously, we can expect this intuitive grasp of aspectual meaningfulness to transcend cultures, because cultures themselves arise from 'swimming' in the 'ocean' of meaningfulness. This can be helpful in cross-cultural situations, even though intuition itself is affected by cultural, experiential and religious modification (Dooyeweerd 1955, III, 29), because there is an intuition of the law-side that underlies subject-object-side intuition; see §3-8.4.

3-7.3 Aspectual Irreducibility and Categories

The aspects are irreducibly distinct in their meaning and laws; no aspect can be reduced to any others, even in combination. The economic aspect cannot be reduced to the social, nor the social to the economic. All aspects are equally important: none can be dismissed as less meaningful, less interesting, or deserving of less of our attention. So no aspect can be eliminated by declaring it to be a figment, nor can any aspect be treated as essentially the same as another, nor can any aspect 'cause' another (Clouser 2005). When we absolutise an aspect, as the Immanence Standpoint does (§3-2.1), we distort our view of reality.

Dooyeweerd sometimes called aspectual irreducibility, 'sphere sovereignty'.

Dooyeweerd's aspects have no *genus proximum* (Dooyeweerd 1955, II, 14), no super-aspects under which they can be grouped. While it can sometimes be pragmatically useful to group them, such as into mathematical, pre-human, cognitive, social and societal, such aspect-groups are not fundamental, but always based on our arbitrary choices.

Reducing one aspect to another gives rise, over a period, to major problems in philosophy, such as antinomy (§3-4.2), problems in science like reductionism (§3-1.2.4) and problems in practice like elevating some issues while ignoring others.

The irreducibility of aspects provides philosophical grounds for understanding diversity, categorizing, avoiding the overlooking of important factors and fostering interdisciplinary perspectives. This makes aspects useful for analysis and clarification, as employed many times in the main chapters in Part II, where many tables are indexed by aspect. They are also useful for creating categories. If categories are aligned with aspects, they are likely to be orthogonal to each other and avoid category errors. Example: Dahlbom and Mathiassen's (1993, 135) three types of quality, functional, aesthetic and symbolic, relate to the formative, aesthetic and lingual aspects. Many categorizations, such as in §3-6.1, may be seen as subsets of Dooyeweerd's suite of aspects. Do remember, however, that Dooyeweerd's suite of aspects is not a final truth (§3-6.2), but a best guess—though perhaps the best we have. Throughout Part II, Dooyeweerd's aspects are used to critically assess categories, and perhaps suggest additional ones.

Aspects, however, are more than categories. See §3-8.

3-7.4 *The Coherence of Aspects*

Giving too much emphasis to the irreducibility of aspects can lead to fragmented views. Dooyeweerd was clear (1997, 154):

> Sphere-sovereignty does not yield a watertight compartment or mechanical division among the areas of life. It is, as we have seen, an organically most deeply cohering principle . . .

There is a harmony among aspects, which Dooyeweerd called 'sphere universality' (1955, II, 331).

3-7.4.1 Aspectual Simultaneity

Though aspects are irreducibly distinct and may be differentiated conceptually, they pertain simultaneously in the being, functioning, etc., of things. That is, all actual things in the subject-object-side exhibit all aspects together (rather than just one, for instance), and function in all aspects simultaneously (rather than sequentially, for instance). Section §3-8.3 discusses this functioning; here we look at inherent coherence among aspects themselves. This is important in understanding, among other issues, the activity, repercussions and normativity of ICT use (§6-3.3), the responsibilities of ICT development (§9-3), the relationship between data, information and knowledge (§5-3). However, in any given situation, one aspect might be more evident than others; see also §3-9.4.

3-7.4.2 No Conflict Among Aspects

Dooyeweerd (1955, II, 3) held that there is no conflict among aspects and their laws, such as is implied by "Being too ethical jeopardises the success of business!" (presumed aspectual conflict between ethical and economic aspects). Dooyeweerd's position is being borne out in the business sector by authors like Collins and Porras (1998). Any apparent conflict occurs, argued Dooyeweerd (1955, II, 334ff), because of the Immanence Standpoint.

3-7.4.3 Inter-Aspect Analogy

Each aspect contain echoes of all the others. For example, causality is physical, but there is something that resembles it in all aspects, such as logical implication and formative (historical) repercussions (Geertsema 2002). See

Dooyeweerd's own account of many analogies (1955, II, 118ff.).

Inter-aspect analogy is not to be confused with the concrete analogies that we make between things, such as metaphors; rather, it provides the possibility of metaphor and is what enables metaphors to 'work'. The claim, "Everything is metaphor" (e.g., Murakami 2002) may be affirmed as expressing Dooyeweerd's idea of coherence of meaningfulness, but it may be critiqued for ignoring the difference between original and analogical meaningfulness and then enriched by each aspect offering different analogies.

Too much reliance on analogy can mislead because the laws of one aspect cannot be reduced to the analogical one. Example: Google's Material Design approach to user interfaces uses a physical metaphor, though bringing some uniformity, has sometimes reduced ease of use and creativity (Cousins 2015).

3-7.4.4 Inter-Aspect Dependency

Each aspect depends on other aspects, both earlier and later (Dooyeweerd, 1955, III, 91), but the two directions differ. **Retrocipatory dependency** means that the functioning in an aspect depends necessarily on good functioning in an earlier aspect. The earlier aspects provide a foundation or substratum, as in Hartmann's notion of lower strata 'bearing' higher ones.

> Example: Good writing and talking (lingual functioning) depends on good structuring (formative) and clarity (analytic). Good social activity depends on good talking and writing. See also the discussion of information and computer systems levels in Chapter 5.

Antecipatory dependency (or 'transcendental dependency') is the inverse. If aspect Y depends retrocipatorily on aspect X, then aspect X antecipates (and anticipates) aspect Y.

> Example: The lingual aspect strongly antecipates the social, and lingual functioning would be very limited (e.g. to setting up reminders for ourselves) if not used in communication with others. Irrational numbers (quantitative) antecipate spatiality, being mere speculative curiosities if spatial meaningfulness is ignored.

Antecipation is important in the opening-up of aspects that constitutes progress (§3-3.2).

> Note on terminology: An aspect *retrocipates* earlier aspects, which are its *substratum*. Retrocipatory dependency is sometimes called *foundational dependency*. An aspect *antecipates* those aspects later than it, its *superstratum*, those in what Dooyeweerd (1955, III, 108) sometimes called the *transcendental direction*. Dooyeweerd used

'anticipate' but, we use that for expectation by humans, and following Strauss (2009) we use 'antecipate' since 'ante' means 'before'.

Dependency does not imply reducibility. That is, the social might depend on, and require, the lingual, but it cannot be reduced to it, nor can the lingual be reduced to the social. The separation of inter-aspect dependency from reduction is a fruit of starting with meaningfulness and can help to clarify issues. Example: Giddens' reduction of power to inequalities of resources, discussed in §8-5.3, may be understood better by the foundational dependency of the juridical and ethical aspects on the economic.

Supervenience and emergence may be understood in terms of Dooyeweerd's antecipatory and retrocipatory dependency: properties meaningful in the later aspect supervene on those of the earlier, and emerge from the earlier; e.g., life from physics. But does most emergence theory 'smuggle in' meaning from the later aspect? Example: If we say that life functions emerge from physico-chemical functioning, on what basis may we recognise the emergent function, except by already having organic criteria on which to judge it? Might Dooyeweerd's suite of aspects help emergence theorists understand what meanings they are already presuming?

3-7.4.5 The Order of Aspects

The difference between retrocipatory and antecipatory dependency expresses an order among aspects, which is fundamental. Dooyeweerd called it the order of cosmic time. One of the very few diagrams that Dooyeweerd devised, reproduced in Figure 3.3, shows each aspect as a kernel with a constellation of meaning, half of which antecipates later aspects and half of which retrocipates earlier ones.

The order does not depend on subjective interpretation—though our fallible *knowledge of* the order does. Example: sentience (psychic aspect) depends on organic functioning, which depends in turn on chemistry and physics. Immanence Standpoint philosophy had never posed the problem of this order (Dooyeweerd 1955, II, 49) (though it is notable how most suites of aspects show similar ordering to Dooyeweerd's), and Dooyeweerd spent much of Volume II trying to understand it. Though he might not have gotten

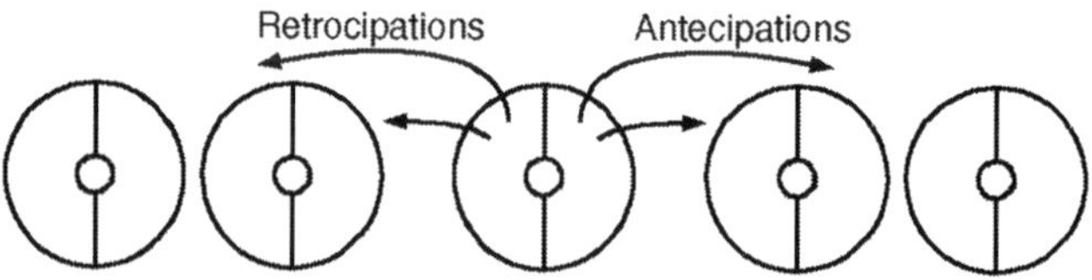

Figure 3.3 Spheres of Meaning in Sequence

everything right, and some have suggested different ordering, we will adopt his ordering here.

> Note on terminology: Dooyeweerd refused to call his aspects 'higher' and 'lower, because they are all equally important (§3-7.1). Instead, he referred to them as 'later' and 'earlier', and this terminology is used here.

The quantitative and pistic aspects are earliest and latest and are special, being terminal (Dooyeweerd 1955, II, 52–54).

3-7.4.6 Aspectual Targets and Reaching-Out

Our words can signify colours, costs, collaborations and so on; in doing so, the lingual aspect is targeting or 'reaching out' to the psychic, economic and social aspects respectively. Colours, costs and collaborations can be analysed, counted, judged and so on, in which case it is the analytic, quantitative and juridical aspects that are reaching out. The idea of aspectual reach-out is important, for example, in understanding information content (§6-3.5.2), where the lingual aspect targets multiple aspects. However, Dooyeweerd does not seem to have discussed it, and it does not seem to be a dependency or analogy. Philosophical research is needed.

3-7.5 Aspectual Normativity: Good and Evil

Truth-telling, justice, frugality and loyalty seem positive, while lying, injustice, waste and disloyalty seem negative. They are positive and negative in different ways, which can be understood by reference to different aspects, the lingual, juridical, economic and pistic. Each aspect defines the possibility of good of a different kind, and most aspects also define an opposite, kinds of harm and evil; this is aspectual normativity. Each aspect defines normativity in both functioning and in the repercussions of that functioning; see below.

> Note on terminology: As used here, *norm*, *normative* and *normativity* have no social connotation (as 'social norms' do) but denote a basic good, which contributes to overall flourishing, and often a corresponding evil, which jeopardises it. The words *good* and *evil* are used when describing functioning, and *beneficial* and *detrimental* when describing repercussions thereof.

"The purpose of norms [aspectual laws]" said the Dooyeweerdian economist Goudzwaard (1979, 243), "is to bring us to life in its fullness by pointing us to paths which safely lead us there. Norms are not straitjackets which squeeze the life out of us."

Aspectual normativity does not directly concern what ought (not) to be done or believed, but rather is a sphere of 'ought' within which we can decide what ought (not) to be done or believed—though the innate fruitfulness of aspectual normativity gives a strong steer in this. Social norms and structures may be seen as society's attempts to express which aspectual normativity is meaningful to them. Most structures express juridical and ethical normativity, but could express wider normativity, and "which . . . is meaningful to them" arises from society's pistic functioning. I am not aware that anyone has developed this correlation, and it calls for research.

Table 3.5 expresses the good each aspect might contribute, for example persistent being (physical), life (organic), enjoyment (aesthetic), justice (juridical). From the organic aspect onwards, it is meaningful to differentiate negative from positive.

Each aspectual Good is necessary as a foundation for the operation of later aspects, and hence is Good in at least that it makes it possible to actualise the meaningfulness of later aspects.

Freedom is reinterpreted by Dooyeweerd as the possibility of responding to laws of aspects in ways that are not determined, and is closely linked with responsibility. Each aspect offers a different kind of freedom, ranging from that at the quantum level of physics, through freedom of interpretation (analytic), economic freedom to pistic freedom of belief. At the macro level of physics and in all mathematical aspects, response to law is largely determined. (Some thinkers assign freedom from the analytic aspect onwards.) In all aspectual law there is some determination, not so much in the latitude of functioning as in the fact that we cannot escape the effects or repercussions of our functioning (the element of promise in aspectual law; see §3-3.1.1).

An agent can thus be free in some aspects and determined in others. This will be useful in considering responsibilities in ICT development (§9-3), benefits and ethics of ICT use (§6-4.10, §6-4.13). This aspectual view of freedom might replace the sterile conflicts between the poles of the Nature-freedom ground-motive.

3-8 Aspects Enabling Concrete Reality

This section summarises ways Dooyeweerd's aspects are important in helping us understand and discuss many of the issues meaningful in the discourses in the various areas of IS and ICT.

Aspects, as spheres of meaning and law, enable the cosmos to be and occur; they are a transcendental condition for it, the 'ocean' in which we dwell. This section summarises the philosophical roles that aspects fulfil. Aspects are modes of being, rationality, functioning, knowing and ethics, so Dooyeweerd called them *modal aspects*. (Dooyeweerd himself never set these out as systematically as is done here, so some of his views might be unwittingly misrepresented.)

3-8.1 Aspects as Modes of Being and Rationality

As a sphere of meaningfulness, each aspect provides a distinct way of existing. Things exhibit **multi-aspectual being**; all things exhibit all aspects, at least latently. Example: Praxiteles' sculpture, *Hermes and Dionysus*, is both a block of marble (physical aspect) and a work of art (aesthetic) (Dooyeweerd, 1955, III, 110–127). Chapter 5 uses this to understand the nature of information, documents and computer. Section 3-9 discusses Dooyeweerd's theory of beings in more detail.

Likewise, each aspect enables and defines distinct kinds of **property**, such as size, density, cost. In fact, Clouser (2005, 267) defines 'aspect' as "a basic kind of properties and laws". **Relationships** between things are also of different kinds, according to aspects, such as greater-than, causes, parent-of. Each aspect specifies a distinct way of making sense or nonsense, and hence **rationality**. Examples of types of thing, relationship and inference typical of each aspect are presented in Table 3.4.

Table 3.4 Some Examples of Things, Relationships and Rationalities (Inferences) Meaningful in Each Aspect

Aspect	*Some things*	*Some relationships*	*Some inferences*
Quantitative	Magnitudes (integers, fractions, proportions etc.)	Greater and less than, sets	Those of arithmetic
Spatial	Space itself, areas / volumes, shapes / lines, positions, sizes, dimensions	Proximity, touching, inside, crossing, overlapping, surrounding	Those of geometry and some topology
Kinematic	Movements, paths, flows, rotation, divergence	Faster/slower, forward/ back, moving together, diverging, curling	Differential and vector calculus
Physical	Energy, forces, fields; Particles, chemicals, gases, solids, solvents; Mechanical devices	Causes, attractions / repulsions, solutions	Those related to energy, entropy, chemistry, materials
Organic-biotic	Organisms (system/ whole), organs (parts), tissues, cells; Food, life, progeny, populations, species, environment; Diseases	Organism-environment, part-whole; Parent / child / mate, food chains, symbiosis, etc.	Those of life, health and ecological sciences

(*Continued*)

Table 3.4 (Continued)

Aspect	*Some things*	*Some relationships*	*Some inferences*
Psychic / Sensitive	Sensations / signals, senses (smell, sight, sound, etc.), mental / emotional states, motor actions; Neurones, receptors, ears / eyes	Stimulus-response, animal affordance	Psychological (behaviorist, ecological)
Analytical	Concepts, distinctions, 'objects', identities	Contradiction, logical entailment, figure-ground	Cognitive, analytical, logical
Formative	Structures, plans, modifications, techniques, tools, goals, purposes, intentions, power, etc.	Means-end, 'in-order-to', etc.; histories	Those of achievement, purpose, design, engineering
Lingual	Signs, words, diagrams, utterances, paragraphs, documents; Headings, bullets, quotations; Nouns, verbs, etc., vocabularies, languages	Synonym / antonym, cross reference, rhyme	Syntactic, semantic, hermeneutic, etc.
Social	People, groups, organizations, roles, titles, nicknames, etc.	Friendship / acquaintance / enmity; lead-follow, organizational hierarchy	Those of social norms (politeness etc.), or roles
Economic	Resources, limits, consumers, currencies, stocks, markets, currencies	Supplier / customer, exchange, relationship to limits, etc.	Those of economics and management
Aesthetic	Nuance, style; delight (interest, surprise, humour, fun), leisure / sport / art, orchestra	Harmony, situatedness, counterpoint, melody, allusion, etc.	Those of art or humour, etc.
Juridical	Responsibilities / rights, debt, owner; Laws, policies, government; Security measures, police, courts	Ownership, reward / punishment, contracts	Those of jurisprudence, proportionality (appropriateness)

Aspect	*Some things*	*Some relationships*	*Some inferences*
Ethical	Attitudes, gifts, sacrifices, etc.	Buber's *I-Thou* relationship; Benefactor; Marriage / troth	Those of self-giving and openness
Pistic / Faith	Commitment, belief, creed, ritual, religion / ideology; Axioms, assumptions; Visonaries, priests	Committed-to, believe-in, rely-on	Theological, apologetic; those of meaningfulness, commitment

The rationality of one aspect has no rational force in another (implied from aspectual irreducibility, §3-7.3). There is no over-arching super-rationality, so researchers must take responsibility for how rationalities are employed together, especially in theorizing (see §3-4.3.5).

3-8.2 Distinct Ways of Functioning

All activity (and seeming non-activity) is **aspectual functioning**, which is constituted in responding to the laws of aspects, within which we 'dwell' (see §3-1.2.3). Each aspect as law-sphere enables concrete existence to concretely function (occur, happen, behave) in a different mode. Figure 3.4 depicts aspectual functioning of plants, people and a computer. Subjects respond to law. This constitutes occurrence, and leads to repercussions.

Aspectual functioning is by subjects and objects (for example, both poet and poem function in the aesthetic aspect), but subjects are active agents. The figure depicts examples of functioning by an agent in more than one aspect: trees in organic-biotic and physical, and poets in aesthetic and juridical.

The computer, strictly, functions as subject only up to the physical aspect and as object thereafter, including in the lingual aspect. However, it makes sense to say that it functions as *subject-by-proxy* in the lingual aspect, which is shown by the dashed line. Subject-by-proxy, an idea being developed by Nick Breems, refers to something active, in which its functioning occurs when human users are involved, and is a useful concept especially when considering virtual reality (§5-5.3).

Because aspectual law has the characteristic of promise (§3-3.1.1), aspectual functioning has **repercussions**, a different kind for each aspect; the functioning-repercussion pair explains '*causality*', different in each aspect. Examples: force and its equal, opposite reaction (physical); squandering can 'cause' destitution (economic). Repercussions occur whether or not we recognise them, so there might be unexpected repercussions of our activity. This is useful in considering ICT use in Chapter 6.

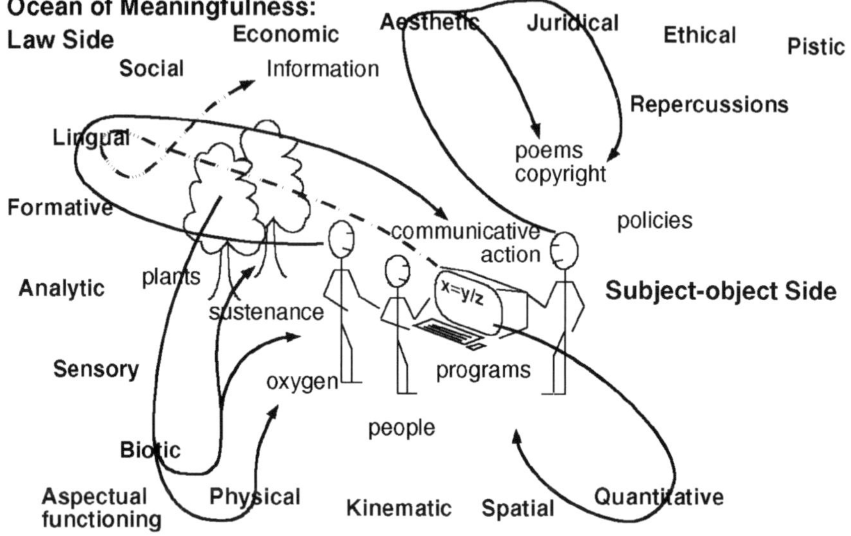

Figure 3.4 The Functioning of Things: Subjects Responding to Law, Generating Occurrence and Repercussions

Aspectual functioning has inbuilt normativity, can be good or evil and usually good functioning in an aspect is likely to yield beneficial repercussions. The timescale between functioning and (full) repercussion lengthens with the aspects, from almost immediate to centuries (Lonergan's [1992] 'longer cycles').

Table 3.5 shows examples of good and evil for each aspect, along with typical timescales of full development of repercussions. The first four aspects have no 'evil'.

The various kinds of (inter-)subjective meaning that were distinguished from what I called 'meaningfulness' in §3-1.2 may now be understood as arising from functioning in various aspects:

- *Signification-meaning*, carried by words like 'red', arises from functioning in the lingual aspect targeting another aspect (psychic for red);
- *Interpretation-meaning*, the assignment of subjective meaning when we interpret, arises from the analytic functioning of distinguishing targeting another aspect, e.g. scattered feathers means bird-kill (biotic);
- *Attribution-meaning*, is similar but might be more social in its target, as of my grandmother's vase;
- *Life-meaning*, as in "What did my career mean!", involves pistic functioning.

Using the metaphor of ocean of meaningfulness, just as fish take gulps of water to breathe or feed, so in these (inter-)subjective meanings we take 'gulps' of the ocean of meaningfulness. The lingual, analytic and pistic are different kinds of gulp-taking with the target aspects being what is gulped.

Table 3.5 Normativity of Each Aspect, With Typical Timescales

Aspect	*Good functioning*	*Evil functioning*	*Time*	*Beneficial repercussion*	*Detrimental repercussion*
Quantitative	As-given-amount	-	-	Reliability	-
Spatial	Simultaneous continuity	-	-	Space	-
Kinematic	Movement	-	-	Change (non-stasis)	-
Physical	Force, causality	-	pS	Persistence	-
Organic-biotic	Feeding, respiration, reproduction	Starvation, suffocation	μS	Vitality, survival	Disease, extinction
Psychic / Sensitive	Interaction	Insensitivity	mS	Sensory and emotional vitality	Sensory, emotional deprivation
Analytical	Distinction	Conflation	Sec	Clarity	Confusion
Formative	Industry, planning, construction	Laziness, destroying	Secs	Accomplishment, construction	Missed opportunities, destruction
Lingual	Expressing, signification	Deceiving	Mins	Information	Misinformation
Social	'We' rather than 'I, you'	Hatred, disdain	Hrs	Friendship, amplified activity	Enmity, undermining each other
Economic	Frugality	Squandering	Days	Prosperity	Waste, poverty
Aesthetic	Holism, harmonizing, allusion	Reductionism	Wks	Integrality, enjoyment, interest	Fragmentation, boredom
Juridical	Giving due, responsibility	Irresponsibility	Mths	Justice	Injustice
Ethical	Self-giving love, vulnerability, trust	Selfishness, self-protection	Yrs	Pervading attitude of goodwill, generosity	Competitive, harsh culture
Pistic / Faith	Belief, commitment, courage	Strong motivation for healthy vision throughout society	Dcds Cent	Disloyalty, cowardice, idolatry	Loss of meaning or morale

That account is oversimplified—and indeed, the nature of these types of meaning still needs to be explored philosophically—because all such functioning involves more aspects. For instance, intersubjective meanings involve also the social aspect. Indeed, all human activity is multi-aspectual functioning.

3-8.3 Multi-Aspectual Functioning

Though we might differentiate functioning in various aspects like that, all real activity involves all aspects, at least latently, and should always be understood as multi-aspectual functioning.

> Example: As I write, I am functioning lingually, but also and at the same time formatively (structuring my thoughts), anaytically (separating concepts to include and omit), psychically (mental activity), organically (alive), physically (brain chemistry), kinematically (both in brain fluid movement, and in movement of thought), and also in the post-lingual aspects, such as social (thinking about readership), economic (parsimony), aesthetic (style), juridical (doing justice), ethical (generosity or meanness), pistic (writing what I believe).

Multi-aspectual functioning is constituted in functioning in each aspect, but in the real situation (as opposed to our thinking about it) all aspects are intertwined in a coherence of meaningfulness that involves simultaneity, dependency, analogy and reach-out (see §3-7.4). Our real activity is not an integration-of-initially-distinct-functionings in each aspect, but rather an integrality-prior-to-separation-into-aspects; Dooyeweerd used the term *systasis* to denote this.

Commonly in the information systems field, social functioning is separated from individual. In Dooyeweerd's scheme, by contrast, social and individual functioning are inseparably interwoven, each depending on the other foundationally and antecipatorily. The notion of integrated multi-aspectual functioning will be very helpful in discussing all areas of the information systems field, especially with the integration of individual and social.

3-8.4 Ways of Knowing

To understand knowledge is especially important in knowledge management (§6-4.4) and knowledge engineering (§9-6). What is knowledge? Knowing may be understood as a form of multi-aspectual functioning in which a residue of that functioning remains in the subject and might affect their future functioning; this is knowledge. There are many aspects of knowing and knowledge. This is recognised by feminist writers like Adam (1998), who stress that knowing involves not just propositional knowledge but embodied skill. Thinkers like Polanyi, Bourdieu and Kuhn draw attention to the pertinence of yet other aspects. Polanyi (1967) differentiated tacit from explicit knowing and as his ideas have been developed, it seems there are different kinds of tacit knowledge.

Table 3.6 distinguishes the ways or aspects of this functioning that is knowing, some tacit and others explicit. Each supports the next (aspectual retrocipatory dependency; see §3-7.4.4); for example, the organic operation of nerve cells enables neural messaging.

Table 3.6 Aspects or Ways of Knowing

Aspect	*Ways of knowing*	*Tacit / Explicit*
Quantitative Spatial Kinematic	-	-
Physical	(Persistent change of physical state resulting from some functioning in the physical aspect)	Tacit 1
Organic-biotic	a) E.g. plant bent towards light 'knows' where the light is; muscles grow with exercise. b) Nerve cells grow and establish synapses.	Tacit 1
Psychic / Sensitive	a) Memory. Receiving stimuli and holding a memory of them in the nervous system b) Recognition of a pattern (seen or heard) c) Instinct	Tacit 1
Analytical	a) Being aware b) Holding concepts and 'facts' c) Categorization d) Knowing how to reason and theorize	Explicit 1
Formative	a) Skills: knowing how to achieve things b) 'Knowing my way around'	Tacit 2
Lingual	a) Expression of ideas that sharpens memory b) Discourse, debate that disseminates knowledge c) Books, libraries, knowledge bases (set down in symbolic form)	Explicit 2
Social	a) Shared cultural knowledge, assumptions; Lifeworld b) Buber's 'I-Thou' encounter (also ethical) c) Networks of knowledge	Tacit 3
Economic	Understanding limits on our knowledge e.g. assumptions.	Tacit 3

(*Continued*)

Table 3.6 (Continued)

Aspect	*Ways of knowing*	*Tacit / Explicit*
Aesthetic	a) Sense of the whole, of harmony. b) Art helping us understand reality. c) Wisdom as all the previous in context of the whole.	Tacit 3
Juridical	a) An informed sense of the essence of things b) Proportion and a sense of 'perspective'	Tacit 3
Ethical	a) Complete 'entering in' with the other (Bergson) requires self-giving. b) Buber's *I-Thou* relationship	Tacit 3
Pistic / Faith	a) Certainty b) Assumptions (about what is so) c) Presuppositions (about what is meaningful) d) Committing to a belief, whether large or tiny; perseverance, prejudice	Tacit 3

Analytical knowing is explicit because we are aware of concepts and distinctions. Lingual knowing is explicit because we externalise it by expressing it in symbolic form. Other forms are tacit knowing, in three ways. Tacit knowing type 3, post-lingual knowing, depends foundationally on, and usually involves, lingual functioning, and hence might contain something that is expressible. This is the type that Baumard (1999) seems to discuss as tacit knowledge in organizations, and which Nonaka and Takeuchi (1995) believe is expressible via their cycle of socialization, externalization, communication and internalization. Tacit type 2, pre-lingual but post-analytic knowing is unlikely to be explained because it retrocipates analytic but not lingual functioning, so might be conceptualizable but not expressible. Tacit type 1, pre-analytic knowing depends on neither, and probably can never be conceptualised or expressed fully. This is the kind of knowing to which Polanyi mainly refers (e.g., muscular and sensory-motor knowing involved in riding a bicycle), though he also refers to skills (Type 2). Nonaka and Takeuchi (1995, 63) give the example of knowing how to knead dough by stretching and twisting it. The feel of stretching is psychic knowing (Type 1), while knowing one must twist while stretching is formative knowing (skill, Type 2), which had not previously been articulated. They give an example of 'brain-storming camps' in which there was an unspoken rule that there should be no criticism without constructive suggestions; the rule would be explained at first, but then became tacit (Type 3). Alex Kimani is currently formulating a theory of tacit knowing based on Dooyeweerd's aspects.

Full knowing, which is everyday experience, involves every aspectual way of knowing in harmony. While Bergson contrasts intuition with analytical thought, Dooyeweerd maintained that they cannot be divorced from each other, and offers three accounts of what is often called intuition:

- multi-aspectual ways of knowing the *subject-object-side*, which are expressed in Table 3.6,
- an intuitive grasp of *law-side* aspectual meaning,
- the immediate experience of *self*.

It is the first that is most affected by culture and experience, while the second may be quite universal and cross-cultural. Distinguishing these might enrich our understanding of intuition.

3-8.5 Ethics

Dooyeweerd's understanding of the normativity of aspects might contribute to theories of ethics. Consequentialist ethics may be seen as focusing on aspectual repercussions and deontological ethics, on functioning in response to aspectual law. Virtue ethics may be understood as focusing on the subject that thus functions and must take account of that subject's dispositions (pistic functioning) and multi-aspectual knowledge. Discourse ethics stresses intersubjective agreement on what is good and evil (lingual and social functioning).

Each may be critiqued as being only part of the picture, but also for the narrow range of normativity recognised. Most emphasise juridical and ethical aspects and overlook others, such as lingual (lying).

Discourse ethics especially relies on having ways to understand diverse complexity; this may be provided by Dooyeweerd's aspects in that each incorporates its own normativity. All theories might be enriched by taking account of the normativity of every aspect. Dooyeweerd held that for full flourishing (*eudaimonia*, *shalom* or *salaam*) we must function well in every aspect and that negative functioning in even one aspect might jeopardise the whole. This is what Basden (2008) called the **Shalom Principle**, which will be used especially in considering ethics of ICT use in §6-4.13, social infrastructure §8-4.3 and responsibilities in ICT development in §9-3. It may be used to understand urban sustainability (Brandon and Lombardi 2005) and ecosystem values (Gunton et al. 2017).

One beauty of Dooyeweerd's scheme is that aspectual norms transcend cultures.

3-9 Dooyeweerd's Understanding of Existence and Things

This section summarises Dooyeweerd's understanding of 'thingness', types and relationships. His ideas of multi-aspectual being and enkapsis, especially, are referred to.

In our experience, we do not encounter aspects directly, but only indirectly by engaging with things, such as mobile phones, money or mountains. What is a thing? How does each type of thing differ? What of changes in things (the phone application that is upgraded)? What are reifications, counterfactuals, and why are some things impossible (square circle, the present King of France)? What are fictitious things (e.g., Gandalf) or avatars in games?

The answers given to, or assumed for, these questions deeply affect how we approach both research and practice. These questions are important when considering the materiality of ICT (§7-3.2) and design of features (§7-4), ICT development and the nature of ICT and society (chapters 9, 5, 8).

The following is drawn mainly from Dooyeweerd's penetrating discussion of thingness, in Volume III of (1955), *The Structures of Individuality of Temporal Reality*.

3-9.1 Everyday Experience of Things

"As far as I know," wrote Dooyeweerd (1955, III, 53), "immanence philosophy, including phenomenology, has never analysed the structure of a thing *as given in naïve experience*." Most philosophical discussion of thingness is already committed to a theoretical view (e.g., Plato's Ideas, Aristotle's substance concept, Heidegger's *Dasein*).

"In veritable naïve experience," wrote Dooyeweerd (1955, III, 54), "things are not experienced as completely separate entities." Though echoing Heidegger, Dooyeweerd offers a fresh approach, which accommodates insights from such thinkers but provides more.

Dooyeweerd began Volume III with the question of how do we account for changes in a thing. The book with pages torn or scribbled on is still the same book, but burn it in the fire, and it ceases to be the same thing (Dooyeweerd 1955, III, 3). In a short section headed 'Reality as a continuous process of realization' Dooyeweerd (1955, III, 109), poetically remarked:

> For the reality of a thing is indeed dynamic; it is a continuous realization in the transcendental temporal [i.e., antecipatory] direction. The inner restlessness of meaning, as the mode of being of created reality, reveals itself in the whole temporal world.

Does not this describe very well the frustrations and joys of ICT development and those of users encountering new features on their tablets? See Chapters 9 and 7.

3-9.2 Existence as Meaningfulness

As has already been discussed (§3-1.2), Dooyeweerd suggested that we can understand thingness (existence) by starting with meaningfulness. As already cited,

> *Meaning* is the *being* of all that has been *created* . . .
>
> (Dooyeweerd, 1955, I, 4, his italics)

The being of an organization is rooted in what it means to be organised (Smircich 1983). Similarly, money exists by reference to the economic sphere of meaningfulness and cannot be understood or engaged with, *qua* money, in any other way (not even the materials of its construction). This is true for all existence, even physical and mathematical: mountains exist, *qua* mountains, by reference to the physical aspect, and it is by laws of that aspect that they come into being, erode and cease to be.

The difference between kinds of being (organization, money, mountain, etc.) lies in the sphere of meaningfulness by which they exist—the social, economic and physical aspects in this case. The difference between a mountain and a hill involves a secondary aspect, the spatial (size). Similarly for different types of organization, such as business (economic) and church (pistic).

This view radically departs from the notions of substance or essence (essentialism), naive realism, existentialism and social constructivism, yet it can accommodate insights from all four. Philosophical comparison of these views may be found in Dooyeweerd (1955, III) and Basden (2008) but does not concern us here.

3-9.3 The Multi-Aspectual Structure of Things

The cohering simultaneity of aspects (§3-7.4) opens the way to understand existence as multi-level. Each type of thing is meaningful in every aspect, each a *mode of being* of that thing or, as I called them in Basden (2008), *aspectual beings*. However, usually a few aspects are particularly important in accounting for its existence as a certain type of thing. For example,

- money: economic and physical
- sculpture: aesthetic and physical
- poem: aesthetic and lingual
- a bunch of keys: juridical, physical and analytic
- mountains: physical and spatial
- a bird's nest: physical, organic-biotic and sensitive
- a speed limit: juridical and kinematic.

Also for events or processes:

- the race: kinematic, social, aesthetic
- the activity of programming: lingual, formative
- the war: juridical, social, formative, pistic.

It can cover non-entitary existence too:

- waves in the sea: physical, kinematic
- atmosphere: physical, kinematic and perhaps organic-biotic
- atmosphere: aesthetic, psychic, social (e.g., in a meeting).

Each is a combination of several aspectual beings. Situations, such as managing chemical plant as in the earlier table 3.1, tend to exhibit all aspects more clearly.

3-9.4 *Type Laws*

Dooyeweerd enables us to be more precise, however. He believed that the law-side contains not only aspectual laws that govern functioning but also laws that govern types of thing and how individuals of each type can be, become, change and cease to be. Dooyeweerd called these laws, '*individuality structures*', while Clouser (2005) called them '*type laws*', the terminology used here. Dooyeweerd (1955, III, 76–79) concluded a discussion of this with,

> In general we can establish that the factual temporal duration of a thing as an individual and identical whole is dependent on the preservation of its structure of individuality.

Type laws (individuality structures) comprise profiles of aspects that are important for the existence of things of that type. They specify certain roles for these aspects, of which Dooyeweerd discussed three:

- **Qualifying aspect** or function: The qualifying aspect governs the 'in-itself' of the thing and its main norm to guide its development, regardless of context. Examples: A tree is qualified by the organic-biotic aspect, a language by the lingual aspect, an organization by the social aspect.
- **Leading aspect** or function: The leading aspect governs how the thing presents itself to its context. Example: Businesses, sports clubs and churches are all qualified by the social aspect, but led by a different aspect: economic, aesthetic, pistic respectively.
- **Founding aspect** or function: The founding aspect governs the coming-into-being of the thing as a unique individual. Example: Though a tree is qualified by the organic-biotic aspect, physical conditions determine how one tree grows differently from others, so its founding aspect is the physical.

This can help us understand persistence during change. Books are qualified by the lingual aspect, and being torn does not destroy that, but burning in fire does. From the physical aspect tearing my book makes it a different thing, but from the lingual aspect (a thing to read) and the juridical aspect (my ownership of it) it remains the same. A thing may be both same and different without contradiction in different aspects. So can ICT as it is being developed.

The qualifying aspect can have normative force (from the innate normativity of aspects; §3-7.5). If a church turns into a money-making operation, we know something is wrong—and we can understand this in terms of disregarding its pistic leading aspect. Bergvall-Kåreborn (2006) has discussed the value of the notion of qualifying aspect.

3-9.5 Types of Thing

Table 3.7 shows examples of things qualified by each aspect in column 2 (c.f. column 2 in Table 3.4) and, in column 3, examples of organization by leading aspect within their social qualification:

Things are understood by their meaningfulness, which leads them freely towards a destiny. Dooyeweerd recognised that the leading meaningfulness of some things, '**semi-manufactured products**', such as planks of wood, has yet to be supplied (e.g., to be made into a chair or bridge) (Dooyeweerd 1955, III, 129). Software libraries may be understood this way; so might trees, blocks, planks, sticks used for axes in *Minecraft*!

3-9.6 Structural Relationships

Relationships may also be seen as things in Dooyeweerd, by identifying their qualifying and other aspects and are of two basis kinds. *Structural relationships* are germane to the structure of things, as part of their individuality structures. They contrast with *functional relationships*, which result non-germanely from subjects responding to aspectual law with the freedom made possible by each aspect. Two types of functional relationship have already been discussed, law-subject-object relationships in §3-3.1.2 and *Gegenstand* relationships in §3-4.3.4, so we now discuss two types of structural relationship, part-whole and enkapsis. In Chapter 5, these help us understand computers and information.

Table 3.7 Examples of Types of Thing Qualified by Each Aspect

Aspect	*Example types (qual.)*	*Example institutions (leading)*
Quantitative	Number	Statistical service
Spatial	Shape	Mapping
Kinematic	Path	Traffic routing service
Physical	Mineral	Chemistry lab
Organic-biotic	Plant	Farm; Family
Psychic / Sensitive	Animal	Ophthalmologist, psychiatrist
Analytical	Concept	Research centre
Formative	Tool	Factory; Lobby group
Lingual	Language	Library; Media; School
Social	Relationship	Club
Economic	Money	Business
Aesthetic	Art	Sports club; Artist collective
Juridical	Responsibility, law	Law courts; Parliament; State
Ethical	Love (self-giving)	Marriage
Pistic / Faith	Belief	Church, Mosque

3-9.6.1 The Part-Whole Relationship

The most-discussed structural relationship is the part-whole relationship. Dooyeweerd gave it a new twist, because he viewed it from the point of view of meaningfulness rather than being or process. Whereas in Systems Theory, parts and wholes are equivalent in principle, Dooyeweerd gave priority to wholes: it is not the brain that understands or feels but the person (c.f. Boden 1999).

Parts have no meaning as parts without reference to the whole (Clouser 2005, 287) and are qualified by the same aspect. But when parts are treated as whole, they lose that meaningfulness and are qualified by a different aspect, usually earlier. Example: In our bodies, a lung is organically qualified, but on a lab bench, it is merely a complicated air pump, physically qualified.

3-9.6.2 Enkaptic Relationships

In Praxiteles' sculpture, *Hermes and Dionysus* (Dooyeweerd 1955, III, 110–117), a part-whole relationship exists between the torso and the body, but it does not seem right to say that marble is part of the torso of Hermes, nor that the torso is part of the block of marble. Why not?

Dooyeweerd borrowed the word 'enkapsis' from biology to account for such relationships, giving it wider application. In an enkaptic relationship, two or more wholes are joined in a structural relationship in which all are necessary and usually yield another whole. He identified five types of enkapsis:

- **Foundational enkapsis** is that which occurs between meaningful wholes and the same thing viewed from a different aspect, such as the sculpture and the block of marble from which it is made—or between a character and a byte and the memory chip (§5-4.3).
- **Subject-object enkapsis** is exhibited by a hermit crab and its shell—or ICT in use (§6-3.3, §6-4.5).
- **Symbiotic enkapsis** is exhibited by clover and its nitrogen-fixing bacteria—and between ICT use scenarios that reinforce each other (§6-4.5).
- **Territorial enkapsis** is the relationship between, for example, a city and its university, orchestra or football team—or between an organization and its website (§6-4.5).
- **Correlative enkapsis** is the relationship that exists between an *Umwelt* (environment, such as a forest) and its trees, fungi, etc.—or between us and society (§8-5), computers and the Internet (§5-4.1) or ICT use and organizational culture (§6-4.5).

Enkapsis helps us avoid confusions between the distinct kinds of relationships that might occur between wholes. In Part II, enkapsis is encountered several times (e.g. §6-3.3, §7-3.1, §8-5.2, §9-8), including some that do not seem to fit those; might they contribute to Dooyeweerd's ideas?

Correlative enkapsis is the relationship between an *Umwelt* and its denizens. Just as a forest exists by virtue of its trees, insects, fungi, etc., which are themselves maintained by the forest, so the Internet exists by virtue of the computers connected to it, which themselves depend on the Internet.

An *Umwelt* is a different kind of being, which is constituted in the subject-functioning of others, which I will call '*denizens*'. Dooyeweerd discussed the biotically led *Umwelt* of the forest, but in §8-5.2, we discuss the socially led *Umwelt* of society, and elsewhere the formatively led and lingually led *Umwelten* of Internet and the worldwide Web.

An *Umwelt* is not static, nor pre-determined in its shape, (Dooyeweerd 1955, III, 648). Unlike an organization, an *Umwelt* has no parts, nor is constituted of aspectual layers. The notion requires research however; for example, Dooyeweerd did not discuss inter-*Umwelt* interactions, which we encounter in §8-5.4.

3-9.6.3 Social Relationships and Institutions

Dooyeweerd (1986) explored the different kinds of social relationships. He distinguished between intracommunal relationships within organizations and communities, intercommunal relationships between organizations or communities and interpersonal relationships between individuals.

The norms for one type do not carry over into others, and each type involves different kinds of consensus in order to function well. The intracommunal relationship requires the assumption of roles, with a tempered authority and deference. The intercommunal relationship requires giving due importance to the interests of each party and recognition of expertise. The personal relationship requires friendship and cooperation.

Power-relationships are meaningful in intracommunal relationships, which involve authority and subordination. but not in the interaction between individuals or communities. This might help enrich Foucault's blanket treatment of the power-nexus, and allow us to escape from the tendency to assign power to anti-freedom under the Nature-freedom ground-motive (§3-2.2). Power can be seen as enabling and freeing. For a good discussion, see Kalsbeek (1975, 199–200).

3-10 Conclusion

We have come full circle, following Dooyeweerd around it. Starting with everyday experience and its pre-theoretical attitude of thought, and with meaningfulness as that in which we 'dwell', we have understood something of the nature and limitations of theoretical thought, and with that understanding, come to a clearly delineated understanding of the aspects of everyday experience and meaningfulness in their diversity and coherence. We can now employ this understanding in thinking about foundations for information systems research and practice.

References

Adam A. 1998. *Artificial Knowing: Gender and the Thinking Machine.* Routledge, London, UK.
Basden A. 1999. Engines of dialectic. *Philosophia Reformata*, 64(1), 15–36.
Basden A. 2008. *Philosophical Frameworks for Understanding Information Systems*. IGI Global, Hershey, PA.
Basden A. 2010. On using spheres of meaning to define and dignify the IS discipline. *International Journal of Information Management*, 30, 13–20.
Basden A. 2017. Suggestions for future sustainability: Philosophical and practical. In P. Lombardi, G. Shen, P. Brandon (Eds.), *Future Challenges for Sustainable Development Within the Built Environment* (pp. 319–343). John Wiley & Sons, Chichester, UK.
Baumard P. 1999. *Tacit Knowledge in Organisations*. Sage, London, UK.
Bergvall-Kåreborn B. 2006. Reflecting on the use of the concept of qualifying function in system design. In S. Strijbos, A. Basden (Eds.), *In Search of an Integrative Vision for Technology: Interdisciplinary Studies in Information Systems* (pp. 39–62). Springer Science & Business Media, New York.
Bhaskar RA. 1975/2008. *A Realist Theory of Science* (2nd ed.). Verso, London, UK.
Bhaskar RA. 2012. *Reflections on Meta-Reality: Transcendence, Emancipation and Everyday Life. A Philosophy for the Present*. Routledge, London, UK.
Boden MA. 1999. What is interdisciplinarity? In R. Cunningham (Ed.), *Interdisciplinarity and the Organisation of Knowledge in Europe* (pp. 13–24). Office for Official Publications of the European Communities, Luxembourg.
Bourdieu P. 1977. *Outline of a Theory of Practice*. Cambridge University Press, Cambridge, UK.
Bourdieu P. 1990. *The Logic of Practice*, tr. R. Nice. Polity Press, Cambridge, UK.
Brandon PS, Lombardi P. 2005. *Evaluating Sustainable Development in the Built Environment*. Blackwell Publishing Ltd, Oxford, UK.
Breems N. 2017. Subject-by-proxy: A tool for reasoning about programmer responsibility in artificial agents. *Ethicomp*, 5–8 June 2017, De Montfort University, UK.
Bunge M. 1979. *Treatise on Basic Philosophy, Vol. 4: Ontology 2: A World of Systems*. Reidal, Boston, MA.
Burrell B, Morgan G. 1979. *Sociological Paradigms and Organisational Analysis. Heinemann*, London, UK.
Chaplin J. 2011. *Herman Dooyeweerd: Christian Philosopher of the State and Civil Society*. University of Notre Dame Press, Notre Dame, IN.
Chesterton GK. 1908. *Orthodoxy*. The Bodley Head, London, UK.
Choi Y-J. 2000. *Dialogue and Antithesis: A Philosophical Study of the Significance of Herman Dooyeweerd's Transcendental Critique Thesis*. Potchefstroom University, South Africa.
Churchman CW. 1987. Systems profile: Discoveries in an exploration into systems thinking. *Systems Research*, 4(22), 139–146.
Clouser R. 2005. *The Myth of Religious Neutrality: An Essay on the Hidden Role of Religious Belief in Theories*. University of Notre Dame Press, Notre Dame, IN.

Collins JC, Porras JI. 1998. *Built to Last: Successful Habits of Visionary Companies*, Century, London, UK.

Cousins C. 2015. Is Material Design Killing the Web? Accessed "http://webdesignde-opt.com/2015/10/is-material-design-killing-the-web" 15 September 2016.

Dahlbom B, Mathiassen L. 1993. *Computers in Context: The Philosophy and Practice of System Design*. Blackwell Publishing Ltd, Oxford, UK.

De Certeau M. 1984. *The Practice of Everyday Life*, tr. S. Rendall. University of California Press, Berkeley, CA.

Dooyeweerd H. 1947. Introduction to a transcendental criticism of philosophic thought. *Evangelical Quarterly*, XIX (1), January, 42–51.

Dooyeweerd H. 1955. *A New Critique of Theoretical Thought* (Vols. I–IV 1975 ed.). Paideia Press, Jordan Station, Ontario, Canada.

Dooyeweerd H. 1979. *Roots of Western Culture: Pagan, Secular and Christian Options*. Wedge Publishing Company, Toronto, Canada.

Dooyeweerd H. 1986. *A Christian Theory of Social Institutions*, tr. M Verbrugge. The Herman Dooyeweerd Foundation, La Jolla, CA.

Dooyeweerd H. 1997. *Essays in Legal, Social and Political Philosophy*. The Edwin Mellen Press, Lewiston, NY.

Dooyeweerd H. 1999. *In the Twilight of Western Thought: Studies in the Pretended Autonomy of Philosophical Thought*. The Edwin Mellen Press, Lewiston, NY.

Feynman R, Leighton R, Sands M. 1964. *The Feynman Lectures on Physics*. California Institute of Technology, CA, USA.

Ganguly K. 2002. Everyday life. *Cultural Critique*, 52, 1–9.

Geertsema HG. 2000. Dooyeweerd's transcendental critique: Transforming it hermeneutically. In DFM Strauss, M Botting (Eds.), *Contemporary Reflections on the Philosophy of Herman Dooyeweerd* (pp. 83–108). The Edwin Mellen Press, Lewiston, NY.

Geertsema HG. 2002. Which causality? Whose explanation? *Philosophia Reformata*, 67(2), 173–185.

Geertsema HG. 2011. Embodied freedom. *Koers*, 76(1), 33–57.

Giddens A. 1993. *New Rules of Sociological Method*. Polity Press, Cambridge, UK.

Goudzwaard B. 1979. *Capitalism and Progress: A Diagnosis of Western Society*, tr. and ed. Josina Van Nuis-Zijlstra. Wedge Publishing Foundation, Toronto, Canada; Grand Rapids, MI.

Gunton RM, van Asperen E, Basden A, Bookless D, Araya Y, Hanson DR, Goddard MA, Otieno G, Jones GO. 2017. Beyond ecosystem services: Valuing the invaluable. *Trends in Ecology and Evolution*, 32(4), 249-57.

Habermas J. 2002. *Religion and Rationality: Essays on Reason, God and Modernity*. Polity Press, Cambridge, UK.

Heidegger M. 1962/1927. *Being and Time*, tr. J Macquarrie, E Robinson. Blackwell Publishing Ltd, Oxford, UK.

Heidegger M. 1971. *Poetry, Language and Thought*, tr. A Hofstadter. HarperCollins Publishers, Inc., New York.

Husserl E. 1970/1954. *The Crisis of European Sciences and Transcendental Phenomenology*, tr. D Carr. Northwestern University Press, Evanston, IL.

Joneidy S. 2015. *Making Sense of the Information Systems Use Field*. PhD Thesis, University of Salford, Salford, UK.

Kalsbeek L. 1975. *Contours of a Christian Philosophy*. Wedge Publishing Company, Toronto, Ontario, Canada.

Klein HK. 2004. Seeking the new and the critical in critical realism: déjà vu? *Information and Organization*, 14, 123–144.

Klein HK, Myers MD. 1999. A set of principles for conducting and evaluating interpretive field studies in information systems. *MIS Quarterly*, 23(1), 67–93.

Kuhn TS. 1962/1996. *The Structure of Scientific Revolutions*. University of Chicago Press, Chicago.

Leite F. 2010. Economic Science and Theory: The Special, the Sublime, the Climax. Accessed via "www.marketoracle.co.uk/Article22190.html" 29 August 2015.

Lonergan B. 1992. *Insight: A Study of Human Understanding*. University of Toronto Press, Toronto, Ontario, Canada.

Masterman M. 1970. The nature of a paradigm. In I Lakatos A Musgrace (Eds.), *Criticism and the Growth of Knowledge* (pp. 59–89), Cambridge University Press, Cambridge.

Mingers J. 2004. Re-establishing the real: Critical realism and information systems. In J Mingers, L Willcocks (Eds.), *Social Theory and Philosophy for Information Systems* (pp. 372–406). John Wiley & Sons, Chichester, UK.

Moran D. 2000. *Introduction to Phenomenology*. Routledge, London, UK.

Murakami H. 2002. *Kafka at the Shore*, tr. P. Gabriel. Vintage International, Penguin Random House.

Nonaka I, Takeuchi H. 1995. *The Knowledge Creating Company*. Oxford University Press, Oxford, UK.

Peirce CS. 1898. *Reasoning and the Logic of Things*. Harvard University Press, Cambridge, MA.

Polanyi M. 1967. *The Tacit Dimension*. Routledge and Kegan Paul, London, UK.

Polanyi M. 1974. *Personal Knowledge*. University of Chicago Press, Chicago.

Polanyi M, Prosch H. 1975. *Meaning*. University of Chicago Press, Chicago.

Ricoeur P. 1981. *Hermeneutics & the Human Sciences*, tr. Jb. Thompson. Cambridge University Press, Cambridge, UK.

Russell CA. 2000. *Michael Faraday: Physics and Faith* (Oxford Portraits in Science Series), ed. O. Gingerich. Oxford University Press, New York.

Smircich L. 1983. Concepts of culture and organizational analysis. *Administrative Science Quarterly*, 28(3), 339–358.

Strauss DFM. 2009. *Philosophy, Discipline of the Disciplines*. Paideia Press, Grand Rapids, MI.

Tarnas R. 1991. *The Passion of the Western Mind*. Random House, London, UK.

Vollenhoven DHTh. 1950. *Geschiedenis der Wijsbegeerte. I. Inleiding en geschiedenis der Griekse wijsbegeerte voor Plato en Aristotles*. Wever, Franeker.

Webster. 1971. *Webster's Third New International Dictionary of the English Language, Unabridged*. G. & C. Merriam & Co., Springfield, MA.

Wilson FA. 1997. The truth is out there: The search for emancipatory principles in information systems design. *Information Technology and People*, 10(3), 187–204.

Winch P. 1958. *The Idea of a Social Science and Its Relation to Philosophy*. Routledge and Kegan Paul, London.

Wolters AM. 1985. The intellectual milieu of Herman Dooyeweerd. In CT McIntire(Ed.), *The Legacy of Herman Dooyeweerd: Reflections on Critical Philosophy in the Christian Tradition* (pp. 1–19). University Press of America, Lanham, NY.

4 Foundations, Research and Practice

This chapter discusses how Dooyeweerd's philosophy might help to (a) engage with extant thought in the information systems field, and (b) to undertake research in that field. This prepares for the discussions in Part II, which lay foundations for understanding five areas relevant to the field. What is discussed might be applicable to other fields, providing insights, guidance and exemplars for those who wish to lay foundations in other fields.

Since theoretical activity is not just for intellectual recreation but is part of a wider reality, everyday experience is important. What everyday experience means for each of the areas discussed in the next five chapters is different:

- Nature of ICT—which informs our everyday expectations in both research and practice, and the artificial intelligence questions that tantalise society;
- ICT use—in its diversity of functioning and repercussions, its technical, human and social aspects;
- ICT features—more technical perhaps, but recognising that features are what users encounter most directly, and should therefore resonate with the nature of the world in which users operate;
- ICT and society—an ecology in which we live and which we generate together over a longer-term;
- ICT development—looking to ICT's future emplantment in the world, hence responsibilities.

As with Dooyeweerd (§3-1.1), our discussions will respect everyday experience in three ways. Most chapters start with everyday experience, contain an attempt to understand the everyday experience of its area, and allow everyday experience a voice in our theoretical discussions.

In this mode, extant discourses must be engaged with, though often taking a different (Immanence) standpoint, so the next section discusses how our engagement might be fruitful. The later sections discuss how Dooyeweerd can help us in the practical activity of doing research.

4-1 Engaging With Extant Theory and Philosophy

Especially during research, we must engage with theories and philosophical foundations already extant. Since Dooyeweerd's starting-points, his standpoint and his ground-motive are so different from those which underpin most research in the five areas of IS (§3-2), how may we engage with the discourses that are occurring, in a way that is useful? In Basden (2008) my engagement was limited to a few examples, because I had to work out a Dooyeweerdian approach first. In this book, I not only update Dooyeweerdian ideas but try to engage with as wide a range of discourses as possible. This section explains my approach.

4-1.1 Why Kuyper's Antithesis Is Not Where I Started

(This section is mainly for Reformational thinkers; other readers might skip it.)

Dooyeweerd's rejection of the Immanence Standpoint has its roots in Abraham Kuyper's emphasis on a 'religious antithesis' between Christian and 'non-Christian' thought, but is a more nuanced, philosophical development thereof (Dooyeweerd spoke of "Christian" and "apostate" motives). Many Reformational thinkers have adopted Kuyper's antithetical stance towards mainstream philosophies; see Chaplin's (2011) discussion intended for Christian scholars.

Dooyeweerd did not (Dooyeweerd 1955, I, 524). (And in most places he used the term 'religious antithesis' differently, to refer to polar tension within dualistic ground-motives (e.g., ibid., 123).) Though there is indeed a "radical antithesis" (p. 522) between 'Christian' and 'apostate' motives, which is religious at root (see terminology explained in §3-2.4), Dooyeweerd believed that the Ground-Idea of the Biblical ground-motive (§3-2.2), "embraces" the Kuyperian 'antithesis' "between the apostasy of nature and its destiny according to creation", not by some dialectical synthesis but by grace and work of Jesus Christ, which acts in and on the whole person of the thinker and in the world.

I understand Dooyeweerd as saying that, while we should recognise the radical religious difference between Dooyeweerdian and Immanence thought, the two should not be antithetical to each other but can be 'gracious' to each other. Christian thought, at least, has very clear reasons for being gracious—but unfortunately is often ungracious. Therefore, instead of making radical antithesis the starting-point, we start as Dooyeweerd did, with everyday experience, meaningfulness and diversity. There are five reasons for doing so.

First, most readers of this book are not primarily interested in religion but about ICT, information systems and philosophy. Putting antithesis up front might unnecessarily alienate people. (Yet, if alienation is the price of truthfulness, should it not be paid? I believe that truthfulness may be procured and maintained in other ways.)

Second, perhaps more important, Dooyeweerd himself began with meaningfulness and the assumption of an everyday attitude, both encountered on his first page. Only after this did he mention some themes that might seem religious. This priority pervades his work, despite the importance of religion.

Third, everyday experience and cohering diversity of meaningfulness are common to the experience of both, and commensurate with Dooyeweerd's ground-motive.

Fourth, Dooyeweerd argued that even where there is deep religious division, there need not be theoretical division, and that the notion of Ground-idea (§3-5) applies to all kinds—so they can understand each other.

Fifth, and perhaps most important, Dooyeweerd wanted to connect with other thinkers as far as possible, rather than set up an isolated citadel of thought. Emphasising Kuyperian antithesis breeds an adversarial attitude. This has, I believe, prevented Dooyeweerd's thought attracting the mainstream interest and scrutiny that I believe it deserves.

I would like to suggest what I believe to be a more fruitful approach. It transplants extant thought from the sterile soil of the Immanence Standpoint (see §3-2.1) into Dooyeweerd's more fertile soil, without undermining the thought-plant's integrity.

4-1.2 Engaging With Thought that Takes a Contrary Standpoint

Dooyeweerd argued that even though there might be an antithesis in standpoint or ground-motive, there need not be an antithesis in the employment of philosophical thinking (Dooyeweerd 1955, I, 120ff.). Philosophy, he maintained, must always be undertaken in ways that are proper to philosophy itself, not theology. This includes criticality (not antipathy) towards everything, with sensitivity to what everyday experience tells us—and this is mandated whether one takes an Immanence or Dooyeweerd's standpoint. So not only should Dooyeweerdian thinkers engage with the mainstream, but mainstream thinkers should engage with Dooyeweerd.

As one reads through Dooyeweerd (1955), we see enormous respect for thinkers with whom he disagreed, and that he treated their ideas as genuine *insights*, even if not truths. (Apparently, Dooyeweerd read Heidegger's *Being and Time* thirteen times before he felt he understood it.) Such insights were often a corrective to previous thought that had become problematic, and thus may be understood as opening up aspectual reality. However, the way they were subsequently worked out within an Immanence Standpoint might have limited their fruitfulness. This, of course, is how good philosophy has always proceeded.

Example: Some in Reformational Philosophy circles believe that Dooyeweerd was too influenced by phenomenology and the linguistic turn in philosophy (e.g. Zuidervaart 2004; Strauss 2013). I disagree. Though

Dooyeweerd drew on insights these provided, he worked them out in his context of his own standpoint and Biblical ground-motive.

4-1.3 A More Fruitful Approach: Listening, Affirming, Critiquing, Enriching

The attitude to extant thought taken in this work is not adversarial but may be expressed as *Listen, Affirm, Critique, Enrich*. Because it might be useful more generally, it is expressed as guidance.

- **Listen** to the discourses intently and immanently, to discern what is primarily meaningful at their core, which explains the reason they occur and what their main contributions might be. Uncover their deepest assumptions and presuppositions. Respect for the diversity of meaningfulness is important here, assisted by intuitive grasp of Dooyeweerd's aspects (§3-7.2).
- **Affirm** what the other thought is aiming at by understanding immanently what it sees as problematic in previous thought. Refuse to get distracted by peripheral paraphernalia (e.g., connotative terminology). The lenses through which researchers view the world (§3-4.3.4) can be identified by reference to Dooyeweerd's aspects. His understanding of inter-aspect relationships (§3-7.4) can provide a basis for understanding the relationship among lenses.
- **Critique** the way the other thought has developed what motivated it. It is usually this element that has been constrained by an Immanence Standpoint or dualistic ground-motive; refer to problems listed in §3-2.1, especially absolutization of aspects. Expose foundational presuppositions, and work out if they prevent it achieving what it hoped. Examples: Critical systems thinking presupposes the dichotomy that it wishes to overcome (see §4-2.2); the artificial intelligence debate remains unresolved because of all three dualistic ground-motives (§5-6.2). Dooyeweerd's notion of Ground-Idea can assist this exposure.
- **Enrich** other thought, suggesting insights from Dooyeweerd. Especially, suggest aspects that have been overlooked. Example: Soft Systems Methodology has been enriched by Dooyeweerd's aspects (see §6-4.5).

Listening, affirming and critiquing often involve immanent critique, while critiquing and enriching, transcendental critique (§3-4.3). Transcendental critique (revealing necessary, universal conditions that make something possible) can reveal unexpected possibilities not currently discussed.

In the chapters in Part II, the discourses occuring in each area will be 'listened to', to understand what is centrally meaningful to the area, whether currently discussed or not. Then Dooyeweerd's ideas will be applied to affirm, critique and enrich the thinking in the area, both individual discourses and the area as a whole. This will suggest research that it may be beneficial to carry out in each area, including new avenues of research that are likely to be fruitful, which are collected together in Chapter 12. Section 4-2 demonstrates this approach.

4-2 Example: Information Systems Research Approaches

This section offers an example of applying that approach to an important part of information systems research: three research paradigms or approaches.

4-2.1 Listen: Discourses on Research Approaches

Positivist, interpretivist and socio-critical approaches are usually thought to be incommensurable with each other, though recent discourse has tried to integrate at least interpretive and socio-critical (Doolin and Mcleod 2005; Myers and Klein 2011).

Briefly, the **positivist approach** aims to test hypotheses for 'truth' by empirical research. Usually involving quantitative measures and statistical reasoning, it often constructs predictive models. However, as awareness of the complexity of the field increased, this proved unserviceable to gain rich understanding of ICT. Lee (1999) suggests that a fundamental tradeoff between rigour and relevance limits the positivist approach.

Many researchers turned to an **interpretivist approach**, the aim of which is not to test hypotheses but to gain insight about what is meaningful in situations, and harmonise the multiplicity of issues encountered. It welcomes opinions, as indicators of what is meaningful, and recognises these are shaped by *Weltanschauungen* (Checkland 1981). Klein and Myers (1999) drew together principles for interpretive study. Interpretive approaches draw heavily on phenomenology (e.g. Introna and Ilharco 2004) and hermeneutics (e.g., Myers 2004), and are frequently inspired by the idea of *social construction of reality* (Berger and Luckmann 1967).

Interpretivist approaches are criticised, however, for not adequately addressing issues of social structure, normativity and/or the pre-theoretical conceptual 'lenses' through which we view the world.

The **socio-critical approach** takes account of these and seeks to question prevailing assumptions. It presupposes that the situation in every discipline is dysfunctional, because of oppressive power structures. It contributes especially to the discourse on ICT and society and organizational ICT use, taking a strongly normative stance; §8-2.3.5 discusses it more deeply. ICT is seen as either as enforcing and reinforcing oppression or helping to accomplish emancipation. Emancipation might be either from oppressive life-conditions or from assumptions and biases, and conflict is welcomed as bringing these to the surface. Assumptions of both researcher and researched are challenged (Klein and Myers 1999). Myers and Klein (2011) have reviewed socio-critical IS research to propose a set of principles.

Note on terminology: Often called the 'critical approach', it can be confused with 'critical' in philosophy or in practical life. So we use *socio-critical approach* here, which emphasises its interest in social structures.

Positivist, interpretivist and socio-critical approaches are seen by many as radically incommensurable with each other because of the (presupposed) deep incompatibility between objective and subjective. The discourses around these three paradigms have tended to isolate themselves from each other.

Three problems with the socio-critical approach are identified in §8-2.3.5: tendency to ignore everyday experiences in favour of 'large' issues, to see everything in a terms of oppression/emancipation and thus distort reality and to disrupt and challenge rather than heal and build. These point to a deep antinomy at the heart of socio-critical approaches.

4-2.2 *Critique, Affirm: Paradigm Incommensurability*

The presumption of paradigm incommensurability arises from the dualistic Nature-freedom ground-motive. The relationship between positivism, interpretivism and socio-criticalism echoes that between hard, soft and critical systems thinking. Eriksson (2003) has argued that Hard and Soft Systems Thinking emerge from opposing poles of the Nature-freedom ground-motive and that Critical Systems Thinking tries to merge them but will ultimately be unsuccessful because it presupposes the gulf it is trying to bridge. Emancipation is simultaneously both of the freedom and nature poles, as desire and as constraining norm, leading to the antinomy of "enforced emancipation" (see §8-2.3.5).

However, if the underlying philosophies of these approaches are examined with Dooyeweerd's notion of Ground-Idea (§3-5), the apparent paradigm incommensurability evaporates, by asking,

- about **world:** Which aspects (spheres of meaningfulness) are selected for study, to provide data?
- about **rationalities:** How do researchers integrate the distinct rationalities by which we generate findings?
- about **wider meaningfulness**, with reference to **Origin of Meaning:** What is it meaningful for the research community to consider when critiquing findings offered as candidates for the bodies of knowledge?

4-2.3 *Affirm and Enrich: Integration*

Basden (2011) has undertaken an aspectual analysis of these three questions for positivist, interpretivist and socio-critical approaches, employing Dooyeweerd's suite of aspects (§3-7/8) as a taxonomy of meaningfulness.

The *positivist approach* presupposes that the world operates by invariant, causal, largely mechanical laws, as an analog of the physical aspect, and tries to minimise expressions of Freedom in both researcher and researched world; this is its ultimate meaningfulness. Of world, it seeks quantified 'facts' obtained by measurement or statistics. Of researcher, it demands detachment and suppression of opinion, belief and ethics, and a reduction to logical-statistical rationality in order to minimise free variability.

From the world, the *interpretivist approach* abstracts idiographic interpretations ("appreciations": Checkland [1981]) each distinguished from others by clearly articulating its detail and context ("social and historical background": Klein and Myers [1999]). Its rationality is aesthetic rather than logical, seeking harmony between detail and context (Klein and Myers 1999, 71): Gadamer's hermeneutic cycle. Interpretivism's wider meaningfulness is that beliefs, assumptions and *Weltanschauungen* (pistic aspect) are of primary importance. Since the Nature-Freedom ground-motive sees these as expressions of freedom, they go unquestioned, so interpretivist research fails to properly understand or challenge belief structures and norms (Hirschheim et al. 1995).

To the *socio-critical approach*, the world consists of social structures to be critiqued and transformed (hence its limited lens). The main rationality is pistic, involving apologetics in relation to socio-critical authors, whose writings are treated as revelatory. The wider meaningfulness that motivates critique and transformation is a presupposition of 'wrongness' (juridical aspect), from which emancipation is sought (hence negativity). The usual source authors, Habermas, Foucault and Bourdieu, exhibit differences that make the picture more complex and how these may be understood in relation to aspects of world, rationalities and meaning, is discussed in Basden (2011).

Here we also add *Action research*. As a "pursuit of worthwhile purposes" (Reason 2006), its wider meaningfulness is from the ethical aspect. It sees the world as full of conversations among the participants (lingual aspect), which are more than just for eliciting information. Its rationality is how to make changes (formative aspect).

Table 4.1 shows these aspects of the world, rationalities and origin of meaning that are most important to positivist (P), interpretivist (I) and socio-critical (C) approaches, and action research (A). It combines two tables from Basden's (2011).

Such an analysis of research approaches does three things. First, it shows that the approaches are not necessarily incommensurable, suggesting that an integration may be found between them, in which each makes its own unique contribution. Second, it provides spaces where other approaches may be located that need no longer to be squeezed into the main three, such as action research. Third, it replaces conflict with mutual cooperation as

Table 4.1 Main Aspects of Positivist (P), Interpretivist (I), Socio-critical (C) and Action (A) Research

Aspect	*World*	*Rationality*	*Meaning*
Quantitative	P: quantified 'facts'	P: quantitative methods	
Spatial			
Kinematic			
Physical			P: mechanistic causality
Organic-biotic			
Psychic/Sensitive			
Analytical	I: distinct cases (interpretations of detail and context)	P: logical (detached observer)	
Formative		A: how to make changes	
Lingual	A: conversations		
Social	C: social structures		
Economic			
Aesthetic		I: harmonising (researcher as sense-maker)	
Juridical			C: 'wrongness', 'unwarrantedness' of the structures from which emancipation is sought
Ethical			A: worthwhile purposes
Faith/Pistic		C: subversion, apologetics	I: beliefs, *Weltanschauung*, meaningfulness are to be accepted by researcher without question

part of the multi-aspectual activity that is research, which we consider next. A similar exercise might be carried out with Burrell and Morgan's (1979) sociological paradigms, which might address their inconsistencies.

4-3 The Activity of Research

Though the philosophical underpinnings of research may be characterised by three-part Ground-Ideas, actually carrying out research is multi-aspectual

Table 4.2 The Multi-aspectual Activity of Research

Aspect	*Activity*
Quantitative	Counting, statistics; scale
Spatial	Geographic distance between researchers
Kinematic	Movements of thought
Physical	Physical environment
Organic-biotic	Researcher health
Psychic / Sensitive	Sensory-motor activity of observation
Analytical	Abstract aspects; Clear thinking
Formative	Planning, techniques; Facilitation
Lingual	Writing, discussing, interviewing
Social	Networking: community of practice; Consensus; Researcher-researched relationship and co-construction of data
Economic	Managing resources (time, budget, skills)
Aesthetic	Harmonizing rationalities; Enjoying interesting work
Juridical	Research 'ethics', ethical approval
Ethical	Generous attitudes vs. 'walking over rivals'; Transparency, welcoming criticism
Pistic / Faith	Paradigms; Presuppositions; Commitment (to ideas/methods); Denial; Courage against or perseverance with accepted thought

functioning (§3-8.3), involving every aspect in principle. Table 4.2 contains examples of the activity of any kind of research for each aspect.

Understanding the contribution of every aspect might improve discussion of research methods. By the Shalom Principle (§3-8.5), the quality of research activity depends on functioning well in all aspects, so such a table, if worked out more fully, may be used to evaluate, guide or critically justify research activity of any kind.

This is why action research, for example, involves not just data collection, analysis and action, but such things as transparency, democracy, facilitation, errors of collusion, working against denial, taking time, power, politics and scale (Reason 2006).

4-4 Research and Reflective Practice Using Dooyeweerd

Research in information systems or other fields is seen as yielding findings that may be offered to humanity's bodies of knowledge, which are generally applicable and on which it is reasonable to rely (§3-5.1). Reflective practice is seen as reflecting on situations in some generality of meaningfulness. Dooyeweerd can help both.

4-4.1 Dooyeweerd-Oriented Research

In carrying out research or undertaking reflective practice, the above listen-affirm-critique-enrich can be useful when undertaken with a self-critical attitude. Portions of Dooyeweerd's philosophy can be useful at various points in research. Table 4.3 briefly suggests where each portion might be manifested in papers or PhD theses, based on my own experience.

These suggestions arise from observation. An important opportunity awaits those who will research them by reviewing research projects in various fields

Table 4.3 Employing Dooyeweerd's Ideas in Research

Research stage	*Aspects*	*Ground-Idea components*	*Ground-motive Standpoint*	*Other*
Introduction	Intuitive grasp of diverse aspectual meaningfulness helps situate, justify the research aim.	World, Origin of Meaning	Can reveal dialectic	Everyday experience; Meaningfulness
Literature Review	Which aspects studied, ignored; 'camps' often centred round aspects	World, Origin of Meaning	Expose ground-motives as root of conflicts; Immanence Standpoint as root of other problems (§3-2.1)	
Conceptual Frame-work	Dooyeweerd's aspects can help widen extant frameworks.	World, Ra-tionalities	Critique of extant frameworks	Meaningfulness, everyday experience; Law-subject-object; time, progress; multi-aspectual things; enkapsis
Research Methods	Aspectual analysis (§4-4.2); Appropriate methods (Table 3.2)	Rationalities	Non-neutrality of theoretical thought	
Results	Aspectual analysis	World		
Findings / Discussion	Aspectual analysis; Precise understanding of kernel meaning	Rationalities	Non-neutrality of theoretical thought	
Conclusion	Contribution of overlooked aspects	Origin of Meaning		Relate to everyday experience

and testing them in actual research projects. Experience has been gained, however, of one research activity, which is now discussed: aspectual analysis.

4-4.2 *Aspectual Analysis*

Aspectual analysis is analysis that employs Dooyeweerd's aspects to reveal what is meaningful during interviewing and/or while analysing transcripts of interviews or other texts. Readers might benefit from some of the forms it has taken, drawn from the experience of some of my research students.

Aspectual analysis directs our attention to the diversity of what is meaningful to interviewees or writers, rather than to things or processes, being particularly useful in interpretive research and interdisciplinary situations in practice. Aspectual analysis relies on the belief that all aspects are of equal importance (§3-7.1) and can take several forms.

4-4.2.1 *Using Aspects in Practical Situations*

When taking part in a discussion or observing a situation, intuitive grasp of aspects can make us aware of which aspects are being most discussed and which are being overlooked—often economic and formative are stressed and ethical, aesthetic and lingual ignored. We can then, in appropriate ways, introduce the overlooked aspects into the conversation.

When writing, aspectual self-critique is useful, being aware of which aspects most and least make issues meaningful about which one is writing. Sometimes it is appropriate to give some aspects more emphasis than others.

4-4.2.2 *Using Aspects While Interviewing*

Mike Winfield and Suzanne Kane both used Dooyeweerd's aspects during interviews. Both would start by introducing the interviewee to the meaning of each aspect.

Mike studied expertise. He would ask the interviewee, "Please can you name a couple of aspects that are most important to you"—for example, organic-biotic and economic for a vetinary surgeon. He would ask the interviewee to identify issues meaningful in those aspects and how they were related and plot this as a box-and-arrows diagram like that in Figure 4.1. As issues emerge that are meaningful in other aspects, the interviewee is asked to identify the aspects that make them meaningful, and the process continues until the interviewee is happy that all aspects he or she finds meaningful have been covered.

In this way, a record of meaningful issues is compiled, which, Mike found, covered almost every aspect. Participants are often surprised to find their expertise so rich. Mike called that, **Multi-aspectual Knowledge Elicitation (MAKE)** technique. For a full account, see Winfield and Basden (2006).

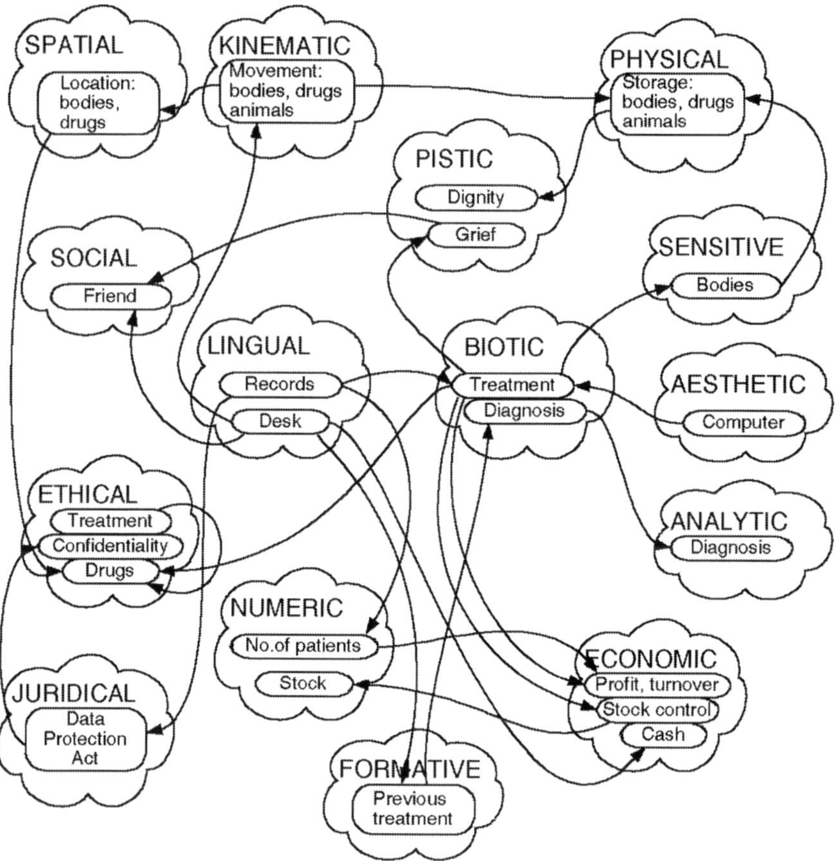

Figure 4.1 Aspect Map Generated in Multi-Aspectual Knowledge Elicitation

Suzanne Kane (2006) wanted to study the aspirations and concerns of those returning to education for ICT courses. She found MAKE too dependent on conceptual thinking, and devised **Multi-aspectual Interview Technique (MAIT)**. After introducing Dooyeweerd's aspects to the interviewees, instead of asking them which aspects were important, she would allow them to go through the aspects one by one, saying anything they wished that is meaningful in that aspect. Sometimes the interviewee might skip an aspect, perhaps returning to it later. At the end, she would ask the interviewees whether there was anything they would like to say that was not related to the aspects; very few did.

Several important benefits of employing Dooyeweerd's aspects in interviewees were found. (1) Both Mike and Suzanne found that the intuitive nature of aspects facilitated understanding and conversation and that presenting aspects to the interviewees gives them responsibility and freedom in interpreting aspectual meaning. (2) Both MAKE and MAIT have proven adept at eliciting tacit knowledge, especially knowledge that has become taken for granted. (3) Suzanne found that even those not experienced in conceptual thinking could employ aspects. Instead of constraining the interviewee, reference to aspects freed them to mention issues about which they might usually feel embarrassed (e.g. money, health) or which they assumed were too trivial or private to mention (e.g. feelings, faith). Participants in both MAKE and MAIT expressed appreciation at the end for the way the aspects had opened their awareness.

In both MAKE and MAIT, the interviewees' interpretation of what each aspect means is accepted without criticism, because the main reason for using Dooyeweerd's aspects is to encourage interviewees to open up and express things that are seldom mentioned or had become taken for granted.

4-4.2.3 Qualitative Aspectual Analysis

Hawa Ahmad employed Dooyeweerd's aspects during analysis, rather than during interviewing. In her study of 'down-to-earth' issues that users of ICT encounter (Ahmad and Basden 2013), she employed a conventional open interview technique, without aspects, and then undertook qualitative aspectual analysis of transcripts of the interviews to reveal issues that are meaningful to ICT users. She called them **'down-to-earth issues'**, which are meaningful to users 'on the ground' (e.g., (un)helpfulness of support staff), to distinguish them from 'high level' issues, which are of interest to management, ICT suppliers and academics (such as cost, technological sophistication and power-relations), which predominate in most literature. The phrase 'down-to-earth issues' will be used throughout this book.

Hawa would identify which aspects make each phrase or utterance in the interview meaningful. Example:

QUESTION: If you have more things to do at one time, how do you handle the pressure?

ANSWER: I know I have work to complete [*Formative*] and it is my responsibility, [*Juridical*] so I'll do it. I will do it by priority, which one needs to be completed first [*Analytic, Juridical*]. Then at a later stage I will do the rest [*Formative*].

In addition, meaningfulness might be deduced with the help of aspects by those who know the context, such as the background reasons for prioritizing tasks. Hawa deduced an aesthetic aspect (prioritizing helps completeness and work enjoyment), and a social aspect (prioritizing helps other staff).

From such analyses, Hawa collected together issues within each aspect, prior to conventional qualitative coding analysis that grouped issues within each aspect. Aspects are thus being treated, not as qualitative categories, but as spaces within which people can find meaningfulness. Several advantages of such aspectual pre-categorization were found. It mitigates some problems in standard qualitative analysis, including the influence of researcher's self and the danger of disregarding aspects (Denscombe 2003). Aspectual analysis very readily reveals multiple meanings, not just between different participants as Klein and Myers (1999) stress, but also within each participant.

This method was taken further by Ghadah Khojah's study of down-to-earth issues in use of electronic medical records (Khojah 2013), in two ways. First, using aspects, she distinguished direct answers to interviewer questions from extra information that is spontaneously volunteered, perhaps as opinions or stories. Aspects helped unearth what made them meaningful. Volunteered information more accurately indicates what the interviewee (rather than interviewer) finds meaningful and is therefore of more value in research, enhancing the reliability of findings that emerge. Second, hidden down-to-earth issues were uncovered because the aspectual findings *stimulated reflection*. Example: Why, in the juridical aspect, are nurses more concerned with working 'properly' while other staff are more concerned with staff responsibilities?

Both Hawa and Ghadah found that Dooyeweerd's aspects are helpful to understand meaningfulness in cross-cultural research, as suggested in §3-7.1. Opeoluwa Aiyenitaju-Adewolu, using Ghadah's method to study teachers' experience of ICT in classrooms, has studied the difference between direct and volunteered answers in more detail, to show the stark contrast between the two.

Sina Joneidy (Joneidy 2015) applied qualitative aspectual analysis to texts extracted from seminal papers in the field of information systems. Selecting passages that indicate motivations, he analysed which aspects made phrases meaningful, and found that each seminal paper focused on a different aspect. This reveals *why* new paradigms arise, to augment the usual discussions of *how*.

4-4.2.4 Quantitative Aspectual Analysis

Hawa, Ghadah and Opeoluwa not only looked at qualitative lists of issues but undertook quantitative aspectual analysis. Counting the number of issues within each aspect can generate *aspectual profiles*, which indicate which aspects are of most and least interest to interviewees or authors. Figure 4.2 contains two barcharts that show the aspectual profiles of down-to-earth issues of interest to users of medical records 'on the ground' and those discussed in the literature.

This reveals that while both found formative (technical) and juridical issues important, academics over-discuss social and economic issues and under-discuss pistic, lingual and early-aspect issues, compared with users. Consequently, literature is a poor guide to what needs to be taken into

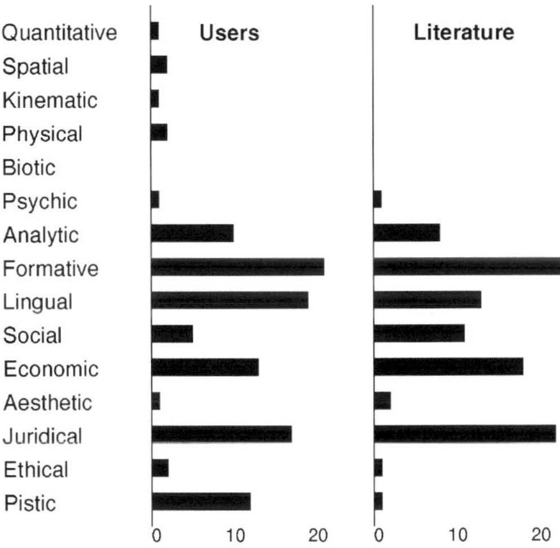

Figure 4.2 Aspect Profiles of Down-to-earth Issues Meaningful to Users and in Literature

account when evaluating or designing EMR systems! This difference was even more stark when qualitative aspectual analysis revealed different types of issues being discussed in the formative and juridical aspects. For example, in the formative aspect, users were considerably exercised about "achieving work", while the literature showed greater interest in malfunctions. Interestingly, from an IS perspective, Ghadah's research revealed that the meaningful down-to-earth issues did not differ between users of paper and electronic medical records as much as is conventionally assumed.

By a similar quantitative aspectual analysis, Opeoluwa has shown that the profile of spontaneously volunteered information is spread more evenly across all aspects from psychic to pistic, than that of direct answers to questions. This could have important implications for interview techniques.

Such quantitative aspectual analysis can also help compare benefits and harm of using ICT. Figure 4.3 shows the amount of benefit (right-pointing bars) and harm (left-pointing bars) found for an imaginary geographic information system. Immediately we see benefits occur in spatial, analytic and lingual aspects but harm in later aspects. Given the longer timescales of later aspects (Table 3.5), this would predict some immediate success for the GIS but long-term failure unless the later-aspect issues are taken seriously.

4-5 Conclusion

After coming to understand Dooyeweerd's approach and ideas in Chapter 3, this chapter has suggested how it might help us engage with extant

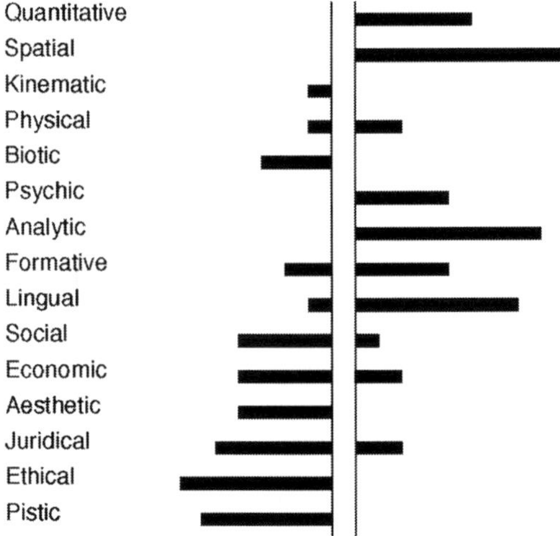

Figure 4.3 Depiction of Positive and Negative Impacts of GIS

literature, and might be employed directly in research and reflective practice, especially as aspectual analysis. We are now in a position to discuss each of the five areas of interest about ICT in the information systems field.

References

Ahmad H, Basden A. 2013. Down-to-Earth Issues in Information System Use. Proceedings of the Pacific Area Conference on Information Systems (PACIS). Paper 191.

Basden A. 2008. *Philosophical Frameworks for Understanding Information Systems*. IGI Global, Hershey, PA.

Basden A. 2011. Enabling a Kleinian integration of interpretivist and critical-social IS research: The contribution of Dooyeweerd's philosophy. *European Journal of Information Systems*, 20, 477–489.

Berger P, Luckmann T. 1967. *The Social Construction of Reality: A Treatise in the Sociology of Knowledge*. Penguin Books, London, UK.

Burrell B, Morgan G. 1979. *Sociological Paradigms and Organisational Analysis*. Heinemann, London, UK.

Chaplin J. 2011. *Herman Dooyeweerd: Christian Philosopher of the State and Civil Society*. University of Notre Dame Press, Notre Dame, IN.

Checkland P, 1981. *Systems Thinking, Systems Practice*, John Wiley & Sons, New York.

Denscombe M. 2003. *The Good Research Guide: For Small-Scale Social Research Projects* (2nd ed.). Open University/McGraw-Hill, Maidenhead, UK.

Doolin B, McLeod L. 2005. Towards critical interpretivism in IS research. Chapter 12 in D Howcroft, EM Trauth (Eds.) *Handbook of Critical Information*

Systems Research: Theory and Application. Edward Elgar, Cheltenham, UK, 244-71.

Dooyeweerd H. 1955. *A New Critique of Theoretical Thought* (Vols. I–IV). Paideia Press, Jordan Station, Ontario, Canada. (Original work published 1953–1958).

Eriksson D. 2003. Identification of normative sources for systems thinking: Inquiry into religious ground-motives for systems thinking paradigms. *Systems Research and Behavioral Science*, 20(6), 475–487.

Hirschhein R, Klein HK, Lyytinen K. 1995. *Information Systems Development and Data Modelling: Conceptual and Philosophical Foundations*. Cambridge University Press, Cambridge, UK.

Introna LD, Ilharco FM. 2004. Phenomenology, screens and the world: A journey with Husserl and Heidegger into phenomenology. In J Mingers, L Willcocks (Eds.), *Social Theory and Philosophy for Information Systems* (pp. 56–102). John Wiley & Sons, Chichester, UK.

Joneidy S. 2015. *Making Sense of the Information Systems Use Field*. PhD Thesis, University of Salford, Salford, UK.

Kane SC. 2006. *Multi-Aspectual Interview Technique (MAIT)*. Doctoral Thesis, University of Salford, Salford, UK.

Khojah GM. 2013. A new approach to the transition from paper to electronic medical records. In D Stacey, J Solé-Casais, H Gamboa (Eds.), *HEALTHINF 2013: Proceedings of the International Conference on Health Informatics, 11–14 February* (pp. 277–283). Barcelona, Spain.

Klein HK, Myers MD. 1999. A set of principles for conducting and evaluating interpretive field studies in information systems. *MIS Quarterly*, 23(1), 67–93.

Lee AS. 1999. Rigor and relevance in MIS research: Beyond the approach of positivism alone. *MIS Quarterly*, 23(1), 29–34.

Myers MD. 2004. Hermeneutics in information systems research. In J Mingers, L Willcocks (Eds.), *Social Theory and Philosophy for Information Systems* (pp. 103–128). John Wiley & Sons, Chichester, UK.

Myers MD, Klein HK. 2011. A set of principles for conducting critical research in information systems. *MIS Quarterly*, 35(1), 17–36.

Reason P. 2006. Choice and quality in action research practice. *Journal of Management Inquiry*, 15(2), 187–203.

Strauss D. 2013. Understanding the *Linguistic Turn* and the *Quest for Meaning*: Historical perspectives and systematic considerations. *South African Journal of Philosophy*, 32(1), 90–107.

Winfield MJ, Basden A. 2006. Elicitation of highly interdisciplinary knowledge. In S Strijbos, A Basden (Eds.), *In Search of an Integrated Vision for Technology; Interdisciplinary Studies in Information Systems* (pp. 63–78). Springer Science & Business Media, New York.

Zuidervaart L. 2004. The great turning point: Religion and rationality in Dooyeweerd's transcendental critique. *Faith and Philosophy*, 21, 65–89.

Part II

This part discusses how foundational understanding may be obtained in five main areas of interest in the information systems field, one chapter for each: the Nature of ICT, ICT Use, ICT Features, ICT and Society, ICT Development.

Each chapter, after reviewing a number of discourses that are occurring or could occur in its area to identify meaningful issues, proposes a foundational framework for understanding the area. This is built using Dooyeweerd's philosophy. The extant discourses are then discussed in relation to the framework, to affirm, critique and enrich them within an understanding of the area as a whole. Except for Chapter 5, each chapter begins with a diagram that depicts how the area is understood by the framework that will be built.

Each chapter demonstrates a different way in which readers might employ Dooyeweerd's philosophy; consequently each has a different structure.

These chapters may be read in any order, largely independently of each other, even though each area relates in complex ways to others. Where concepts or ideas are referred to that are introduced or discussed in other chapters, cross-references are given that readers can follow for explanation or deeper understanding.

5 On the Nature of Information and Communication Technology

This chapter considers questions like "What is technology?", "What is information?", "What is a computer?", What is a program?" and "Can computers be like humans?" It may be skipped if the reader is interested more in ICT use, features, society and development because, for anything here useful to those chapters, cross-references will be given.

Questions like these are also important in their own right, however, when we face claims like John Perry Barlow's (1996) *Declaration of the Independence of Cyberspace*, that cyberspace is a different type of reality, of mind, information, thought, in which body and matter are either not needed or irrelevant, and in which different social arrangements, ethics, views of what is considered criminal or legal, legislative frameworks and freedoms pertain, or the opposite claim by Donna Haraway's feminist *Cyborg Manifesto* (1991), that body is important and knowledge is not propositional. Both are polemics; not only do we not want to accept them uncritically, but we do not want them to set the agenda for debate. We need to understand the theories of reality on which they are based and gain a sound basis for understanding the nature of ICT.

Dooyeweerd argued that philosophy taking the Immanence Standpoint "has never analysed the structure of a thing *as given in naïve experience*" (Dooyeweerd 1955, III, 53). The nature of things has always been theorised according to favourite philosophical ideas. This chapter tries to get a little closer to understanding what ICT *is* as encountered in everyday experience. That does *not* entail reducing ICT to what users or developers take them to be, but it must offer a way to take those into account.

This chapter reviews several what-is discourses and discusses how Dooyeweerd's ideas might bring clarification to concepts, enrichment of frameworks and resolution of conflicts. The other chapters refer back to this one when they need to.

Note on terminology: In this chapter, 'ICT' (information and communication technology) will usually be used interchangeably with 'computer' even though ICT involves more.

5-1 Introduction: "What Is?"

What is "What is?" What do we mean by that question? What kind of answer do we seek? Extant philosophies offer several ways to answer that question, of which Dooyeweerd listed eight (see Basden [2008,179–80]). Two are of most interest here, in terms of *being-in-itself* or *being-in-the-world*.

The *being-in-itself* answer tries to find the essence of X, which can fully explain X, or from which all about it can be derived. Essence is usually seen as either given type (Plato's Ideas), substance (Aristotle) or process (Heraclitus, Whitehead). To say that a computer is a machine that processes bits, as in the Turing Machine model, is a being-in-itself kind of answer. Being-in-itself answers can sometimes help us understand the possibilities and limitations that a thing affords, but suffer from several serious shortcomings, especially in relation to computers. They take little account of the world around and as a result can become irrelevant in everyday experience. They make us rigid in our understanding, expectations and rules. They lead to interminable disputes about which is the 'true' essence (is a computer a Turing machine or a data processor?). They relegate ethical and normative issues to secondary place.

The *being-in-the-world* perspective, made famous by Heidegger, answers the question by looking at the context that forms the thing. To say "The system is my communication lifeline" is this kind of answer. Its strength is that it makes the "What is?" question more relevant. It led Winograd and Flores (1986) to focus on computers as proximal tools, especially for enabling conversation, an idea developed by Polanyi (1967) for artefacts in general. It suffers from several weaknesses. Being-in-the-world approaches do not answer "What is ICT?" questions but hollow them out, by reducing them to ICT use, ICT development and ICT in society. They mix together a plethora of disparate issues—technological, personal, societal—inviting confusion and myriads of possible category errors. Paradoxically, because the world is so diverse, to gain traction, whole ranges of issues can be ignored (for example, Winograd and Flores have been criticised for ignoring political issues [Suchman 1994]). Understanding possibilities becomes difficult. Both the being-in-itself and being-in-the-world perspectives tend to ignore normativity—a serious deficiency when claiming relevance—and must resort to bolting these on.

Dooyeweerd criticised both as taking an Immanence Standpoint (§3-2.1), which, among other things, divorces meaning and normativity from reality, and prevents deep analysis of the structures of existence. Dooyeweerd not only rejected both approaches, but he denied the implicit claim of both to set the agenda for answering "What is?" questions. Dooyeweerd sought an answer to "What is?" questions in meaningfulness (§3-1.2): a thing *is* insofar as it *means* (Dooyeweerd 1955, I, 4). Meaningfulness constitutes an 'oceanic' law-side that makes both being and dynamic becoming and functioning possible; see §3-1.2.3. The law-side comprises both aspects, which govern functioning, as aspectual laws (§3-3.1) and type laws or structures of individuality (§3-9.4), which govern the structure and becoming of things.

This can address the challenges. Normativity is built in. Category errors reduce because aspects separate issues out. Being-in-itself and being-in-the-world coalesce because both derive from meaningfulness, with both thing and world made possible by the same law-side. Being and change are understood together. The possibilities afforded by a thing can be more easily analysed, even taking into account the contingencies of the world. Relevance is easier to ensure. Essence disputes may be resolved by locating contenders in the aspects they emphasise and allowing the possibility of multi-level answers to the question, "What is X?"

In the following sections, a number of what-is questions are discussed—of technology, information, documents, computers and programs, and then the artificial intelligence question is tackled. In each, some extant discourses are reviewed, including 'philosophy of' discourses, which reveals some of the above problems, and then a Dooyeweerdian resolution of them is discussed.

5-2 What Is Technology?

The question "What is technology?" is addressed by discourses around the philosophy of technology.

5-2.1 Philosophy of Technology

Philosophy of technology has a long history, with the ancient Greeks seeing technology as imitation of nature, and the Scholastics moving towards technology as helping to improve human living conditions by controlling the ravages that nature make upon us, for example by medicine and shipping. About 150 years ago, technology became seen as an extension of human organs (Kapp 1877), being linked with the excitement of innovation in the new United States of America (Benjamin Franklin) or alternatively, seen as something used to oppress workers (Karl Marx).

During the 20th century, the latter two views especially have persisted as starting points for optimistic and pessimistic views of technology. A plethora of philosophers of technology have discussed the nature of technology in relation to society and its impact on society, notable among them being Heidegger ("What is technology as such, given its context?"), Ellul (tyranny of technology over humanity as a whole, technology as religion, and technology in the context of religion), Ihde (hermeneutics of technology) and Haraway (feminist accounts of technology).

Mitcham (1994) discusses many of these, distinguishing between an engineering approach, to which the practices of engineers and technologists and "the technological way of being-in-the-world" (p. 39) are meaningful, and a humanities approach, to which impacts of technology are meaningful. This book needs finer distinctions, in that, though this chapter takes what

Mitcham would call a technology approach, the issues discussed in Chapters 7 and 9 span Mitcham's two, and we distinguish individual from societal impacts (Chapters 6 and 8).

Moreover, most discussions in the philosophy of technology seem to be limited to higher-level issues, especially those that are abstract and of interest to academics, and seem unable to reach out to the wider range of issues that are important to ICT in all its manifestations, which we meet in other chapters.

One exception to this is Verkerk et al.'s (2015) excellent text on the philosophy of technology (Carl Mitcham's Foreword therein indicates its excellence). It works out a sequence of issues relating to technology, ranging from philosophical issues of the meaning of technology and the complexity and diversity that technologists face, across issues of its design and the management of its development, to issues of its use and its impact on society—several of the areas we have covered in this book. Each chapter seems to be informed by one portion of Dooyeweerd's thought—his ideas about meaning, aspects, norms, society, etc.—and brings in portions of thought from Heidegger, Mitcham, Simon, Latour, etc. In this way, Verkerk at al. demonstrate clear ways in which Dooyeweerdian thought can engage with extant thought.

Their work is, however, of only limited utility here because (a) its aim is not to advance new ideas but to present an understanding of philosophy of technology to Masters students with an overview of current thinking, (b) it discusses technology in general rather than ICT, and, as we shall see below, philosophy of technology is of only limited help to us.

One philosophy of technology will be examined more deeply here, as an example of how Dooyeweerd might advance their thought, that of Heidegger.

5-2.2 Heidegger's View of Technology

Heidegger, to whom several ICT thinkers refer (Winograd and Flores 1986; Dreyfus and Spinosa 1997; Introna and Ilharco 2004), broke new ground in attempting to understand 'what technology is'. Heidegger's (1978) *The Question Concerning Technology* employs etymological reflection on various Greek words and contains many valuable insights that resonate today. Technology is not just instrumental but *reveals* inherent potential of materials. When making a chalice, the silversmith should not be seen as wrestling with silver to force it into the chalice-form that the smith wants, but rather as enabling the potential of chaliceness already in the silver to 'arrive' in existence (p. 219). Technology is thus 'revealment' or 'arriving' of potential, a feature it shares with poetry. This imparts responsibility for bringing things into existence (c.f. Section 9-3). We might question, though, what constitutes this 'potential'; Heidegger does not adequately address that.

Modern technology distorts this, being a frame of mind ('enframing'), which sees the rest of reality as nothing more than raw materials to shape in order to serve humanity's ends; a 'standing reserve' of energy. Whereas the chalice has meaningfulness beyond the human, the many products of modern technology, such as the airplane, have meaningfulness only for the human. It does not seem to be a difference between craft and 'systemic' technologies that is at issue here, but the idea of serving the self of humanity rather than the rest of reality.

Paradoxically, this self-serving results in technology having sway over humankind. Ultimately, even humanity, according to Heidegger, is seen in this way: the woodcutter is seen as meaningless except in serving the interests of the pulping industry, which is itself seen as meaningless except in serving the interests of the printing industry, who also see readers as merely serving its own interests.

Humanity is being 'sent' towards a destiny, is itself 'arriving' or being revealed, and the destiny Heidegger saw with modern technology caused him much anxiety. He tried to argue that the destination is not fixed, and there is a choice: humanity can instead arrive at a destiny in which it is in harmony with the world, revealing the world's potential, through art—though when I read that I felt it was based more on Heidegger's wish than on his customary careful thinking. (His idea, however, sounds very like the biblical interpretation of humankind's role as opening up the potential of the rest of creation, not for humanity's sake but for the sake of the rest of creation (Basden 2017)—but Heidegger did not allow himself access to the biblical idea.)

5-2.3 Affirming, Critiquing and Enriching Heidegger's Ideas

While Heidegger (1978) grounds revealment and enframing largely in reflections on etymology, Dooyeweerd can provide deeper philosophical understanding.

Heidegger's suggestion that technology reveals the innate 'chaliceness' of silver (Heidegger 1978, 219) is matched by Dooyeweerd's (1955, III, 109–128) discussion of revealing the 'sculptureness' of marble. Dooyeweerd would explain such 'revealment' as formative human functioning governed by the pistic (chalice: "consecration") and aesthetic (sculpture) aspects. Whereas Heidegger tried to counter the 'instrumentalistic' view of technology, Dooyeweerd cautiously affirms it because it too is of the formative aspect, though critiques it when it is shorn of aesthetic or pistic functioning. Where Dooyeweerd agreed with Heidegger about the evils of instrumental*ism* is the absolutization of the formative, which should be treated as just one aspect among them all (see §3-7.1).

Heidegger did actually recognise some of the other aspects of the technological activity of revealment. His idea of 'giving' in the technological process, in which the world 'gives' itself to us, opens itself up to us, and humanity 'gives' the materials the opening-up of their potential, is very like Dooyeweerd's ethical aspect. Heidegger's idea of revealing strongly echoes Dooyeweerd's idea of aspectual opening (§3-3.2). The 'indebtedness' of the chalice to the silversmith for helping it to 'arrive', and the responsibility of the human who is in the 'driving seat' of technology, are juridical aspects of technological activity. Heidegger seems to have dwelt on these two, possibly because they are often overlooked in technological activity, but Dooyeweerd can also draw attention to others. Social aspects of technological activity might include agreements and cooperation, economic aspects, response to resource limitations, aesthetic aspects, not only in the beauty of the thing produced but also in the elegance of the activity itself, pistic aspects of technological activity, in the vision, assumptions and commitments underlying the activity. In such ways Dooyeweerd affirms Heidegger's view and then enriches it by taking it further.

As to what is revealed, however, Dooyeweerd would critique Heidegger and look for answers. Heidegger's idea of technology revealing the innate potential of the material, however, begs the question of what constitutes potential; whence the 'chaliceness'? There is something that "confines the chalice within the realm of consecration" (Heidegger 1978, 220), but Heidegger does not discuss whence the realm of consecration arises; he presupposes it.

Immediately Dooyeweerd's view comes to mind, of aspects as possibility (§3-7.1). All things function in all aspects of the 'ocean of meaningfulness', at least latently (§3-8.3)—the physical silver also functions in the pistic aspect. More precisely, the silversmith functions as subject in the physical and pistic aspects (and more), in which silver is a prior object (physical) and chalice is generated object (pistic) (§3-3.1). The chalice is silver, and the silver is chalice.

Heidegger does not resolve the conundrum of how to account for the meaningful-to-human potential inherent in non-human materials like silver, yet such questions are important if we are to understand ICT affordance (see §7-2.3, §6-2.15), and how ICT's potential is itself 'revealed' as 'informationness', and how it can reveal other potentials, such as 'socialness' (§8-6.1.1). Dooyeweerd's view of law-subject-object functioning is employed to understand affordance (§6-4.15, §7-3.3).

Insofar as Heidegger's idea of enframing is an attitude, then not only revealment but also it can be understood well by reference to Dooyeweerd's understanding of the ethical aspect. While in revealment, humanity functions positively in that aspect, in enframing it functions negatively in serving itself (ethical dysfunction of selfishness), and this results paradoxically in humanity's enslavement by technology. Thus enframing is not so separate a phenomenon from revealment as Heidegger's discussion seems to suggest, but merely a dysfunction in one aspect. This provides firmer grounding for Heidegger's idea that humanity has a choice of destination, than Heidegger seems to offer.

Dooyeweerd suggested that Heidegger "moves in the paths of immanence philosophy" (Dooyeweerd 1955, IV, 88); if this is so, then it might explain some of the struggles that Heidegger had. It forced him to treat meaning as separate from reality, yet in his notion of the potential of chaliceness in the silver, as in his discussion of poetry, Heidegger (1978; 1971) seems to have been calling for meaningfulness of pistic and aesthetic kinds that are already intrinsic in reality. Dooyeweerd's oceanic idea of meaningfulness directly answers that call and offers Heideggerian thought simpler accounts of revealment and enframing, and of the link between them. It also accounts for that which is revealed via the formatively qualified functioning of technology. In such ways, it may be that Dooyeweerd can affirm, critique and enrich this part of Heidegger's thought, and that dialogue between the two may be opened up.

5-2.4 Artefacts

Technology generates *artefacts*—humanly constructed things that have a function intended by their designers. Artefacts exhibit what Kroes and Meijers (2006) and others call a dual nature, as physical, tangible things, and as incorporating the intentions of people who use or design them.

Somehow the physical structure and the intentional function constrain each other. Little philosophical work has been carried out concerning this (Stanford 2013). "Up till now," Stanford continues, "there is no accepted general account of function that covers both the intentionality-based notion of artifact function and the non-intentional notion of biological function—not to speak of other areas where the concept plays a role, such as the social sciences." Some of this could be, but is not yet, within the discourse on affordance (§7-2.3).

From a Dooyeweerdian perspective, however, such an account may be developed by reference to aspectual functioning, and a suggestion is made in §7-3.3 for function and intention in affordance. Intention is a concept meaningful in the formative aspect, so the dual nature of artefacts refers to two aspects of a multi-level being, physical and formative. Function, despite its formative overtones, is a trans-aspectual idea, denoting the time-activity of being in each aspect, and hence biological, social and other function causes little problem except to recognise which aspect makes each meaningful (organic, social there).

The functioning of an artefact (including ICT artefact) may be understood from a Dooyeweerdian perspective as a complex subject-object relationship, in which the artefact is the object and its user, the subject. This can involve up to three different main aspects:

- main aspect of the functioning by which the artefact is created, which, as argued in the next section, is formative for pre-ICT artefacts and lingual for ICT artefacts;
- aspect that makes its intended function (purpose) meaningful, such as biotic for a seed drill, formative for a hammer, juridical for a judge's gavel (this is sometimes referred to as 'inscription' in the IS literature);
- aspects of its actual use, which is usually but not always as intended.

The difference between **malfunctions** and good functioning may be understood in relation to the innate normativity of these aspects (§3-7.5). The above suggests a foundation for differentiating kinds of malfunction, especially those of the creation from those of the use of the artefact (e.g. errors in manufacture, design or use), and in the case of ICT artefacts yet further differentiations, discussed in the next section.

Stanford (2013) identifies a set of questions that have yet to be addressed. Each can be addressed by Dooyeweerd as suggested in Table 5.1, but differently for pre-ICT and ICT artefacts, because of differences discussed in the next section (to which column 3 refers). These ideas must still be developed and refined, but are offered here in the hope that readers might be stimulated to do so.

Table 5.1 Challenges in Understanding Artefacts (Stanford 2013) and Dooyeweerdian Understanding Thereof

Challenge	*Understanding pre-ICT artefacts*	*Understanding ICT aftefacts*
Possibility and nature of malfunction	Dysfunction (§3-7.5) in the formative aspect of artefact-creation or in the target aspect (§3-7.4.6) of artefact-intention, both of which depend by retrocipation and antecipation on other aspects (§3-7.4.4).	See next section: Four dysfunctions, in lingual aspect of code-writing, in lingual aspect of user interpretation, in virtual law-side appropriateness and in affordances.
Co-existence of several functions in the use of an artefact	Several target intention-aspects.	Multi-aspectual virtual law-side (§5-5.2).
Accidental use	Later aspects retrocipatorily influencing formative functioning of use (§3-7.4.4).	Unexpected possibilities in virtual law-side.
Loss of original intention	Target intention-aspect changes over time (§3-9.1).	Some aspect of virtual law-side no longer meaningful.
Types or kinds of artefact and their classification	Dooyeweerd's aspectual theory of types (§3-9.5).	As pre-ICT.
Difference between "kinds of kinds" (e.g. between knife and cutter)	Aspectual structures of individuality (§3-9.3).	Aspectual affordances (§7-3.3).

Challenge	*Understanding pre-ICT artefacts*	*Understanding ICT aftefacts*
Relation of parts (e.g. pistons) to wholes (aircraft)	Dooyeweerdian part-whole and enkaptic relationships (§3-9.6).	several part-whole and enkaptic relationships among features (§7-3.1).
Difference between humanly-constructed artefacts and 'natural' things	Generated object of functioning in formative versus pre-analytic aspects (§3-3.1)	As pre-ICT.
Byproducts and waste products generated in the production of artefacts	Formative functioning depends on, but does not absolutely determine, physical functioning of material (§3-7.4.4).	n/a
Difference between end-products and the materials for making them (boards, screws, etc.)	Semi-manufactured products (§3-9.5).	As pre-ICT.
Process of design	Multi-aspectual functioning of designer (§3-8.3).	Four responsibilities of ICT developers (Chapter 9).
Difference between artefacts and works of art, both of which need to be creatively formed	Formative versus aesthetic aspects (§3-7, §3-8).	Lingual versus aesthetic aspects.

Three things may be noticed. 1. Every challenge may be directly addressed by some Dooyeweerdian idea; this implies that such an exercise would be well worth undertaking. 2. Most challenges are addressed by different Dooyeweerdian ideas; this implies (if Dooyeweerd is used as a yardstick) that the Stanford challenges cover a wide range of issues and its list contains few overlaps. 3. There are some missing challenges, which might be identified by reference to the subsections in Chapter 3, such as: What is artefact used for?: aspectual targets (§3-7.4.5); Ethics and normativity of artefacts: aspectual normativity (§3-7..5); Multi-layered structure of artefacts: aspects as modes of being (§3-9.3).

5-2.5 Information and Communication 'Technology' and Artefacts?

Most discussion about the philosophy of technology focuses on technology as a homogeneous, undifferentiated phenomenon, lumping together agricultural, chemical, power, electronic and many other technologies alongside ICT.

Certainly, there is a technology element common to them all, of a process of construction and of enabling people to achieve more than before (both formative aspect). It also leads people to assume and aspire to this 'more'. Agricultural technology enabled people to feed better, and assume a right to have as much food as they wish, despite the reduction in biodiversity that resulted. Chemical technology enabled people to create new materials, and assume that new materials are the norm despite the pollutions they cause unseen. Power technology enabled people to have electricity on demand, and assume a right to uninterrupted supply despite the climate change it causes. Electronic and electrical technology enabled people to have gadgets, and want to gather, own and use more and more gadgets, despite the impact on health. ICT enables people to do more with information, and we are discovering what changes in aspiration are occurring. Heidegger's concern about enframing is upheld.

However, information and communication technology (ICT) is different in several ways. In most technologies, engagement with the technology impacts directly on life, but in ICT there is a middle stage, discussed in Chapter 6, engaging with meaningful content (EMC), which is generated from engaging with the technical artefacts, and which in turn generates impacts on life. Example: social media. The difference may be depicted as:

Most technology — impact on life.
ICT — meaningful content — impact on life.

Whereas gadgets and buildings are *constructed*, programs and web pages (meaningful content) are *written*. The development, nature and impact of ICT is more like that of literature, journalism or some film-making than of electronic or construction technologies.

It will be suggested later (§5-5.2) that each ICT artefact contains a virtual law-side, which encapsulates in written form the known laws of the aspect(s) that afford possibilities that are relevant to the artefact's purpose (target aspect), together with those of aspects on which it depends. These determine the meaningful content with which the user engages, which is absent from pre-ICT artefacts, except in very rudimentary ways.

The answers to the Stanford questions differ from those for pre-ICT artefacts, as shown in column 3 of Table 5.1, and are usually more complex. In particular, malfunctions arise from at least four different kinds of aspectual dysfunction:

- dysfunction in the lingual process of writing the code: encapsulating the laws of target aspect(s) of its purpose to constitute the virtual law-side;
- dysfunction in the lingual engagement by the user with the artefact, often by user misinterpretation of the user interface (§6-3.4);
- dysfunction arising from errors in the virtual law-side, especially those of inappropriateness (§7-4.2.1), so that the ICT artefact behaves in ways that let the users down;
- dysfunction in its use, which is invited by inappropriate artefact affordances (§7-3.3).

These four malfunctions are bound together by enkapsis (§3-9.6.2). For each, there might also be similar dysfunction in the aspects on which each of these aspects depend by retrocipation or antecipation (§3-7.4.4).

These differences between ICT and pre-ICT artefacts are not adequately recognised by most discussion of the philosophy of technology. For example, Heidegger's idea of technology as revealment and enframing is centred on human productive potential, the ability of humans to shape things either to bring their potential into being or to serve ourselves. For example, the socio-technical approach (§6-2.3) tries to bridge between technology and life. Yet, as Lee (2004) argues, something is missing: "Information itself is a rich phenomenon that deserves its own separate focus no less than either information technology or organizations."

In Dooyeweerdian terms, we may express this difference as:

- *Technology* is a phenomenon qualified by the formative aspect.
- ICT, *information and communication technology*, is a phenomenon qualified by the lingual aspect.

The procurement and success of each is governed by different aspectual norms, even though lingual functioning depends on formative (§3-7.4.4). Therefore, the question, "What is ICT?" should be informed by the philosophy of information.

5-3 What Is Information?

"What is information?" is the "hardest and most central question in PI [philosophy of information]" says Floridi (2004, 560). There are several discourses around that question.

5-3.1 Some Theories of Information

The aim of the following very brief overview is to gain a broad rather than deep appreciation of how various communities have tried to understand the phenomenon of information.

Information is something communicated, and Shannon (1948) was particularly interested in the engineering challenge of how a message could be transmitted faithfully through a noisy medium. "The significant aspect," he wrote, "is that the actual message is one selected from a set of possible messages" and information is "produced" when the selection is made. In order to advance a mathematical theory of communication, he reduced the set of possible messages to two (Yes and No)—which is the possible states of one digital "bit". All messages may be reduced to bit patterns.

Since noise is random, Shannon and others recognised the link between this level of information theory and the physical thermodynamic notion of entropy. However, information cannot be reduced to matter and energy (Wiener 1948), who was interested in the role of information in controlling systems as well as in communication. Information is related to order, a capacity for useful work.

These theories provide some limited insight into the thing, information that is distinct from us, as something that can be transmitted. However, Shannon explicitly excluded semantic issues of "meaning", and they ignore the human originator and recipient of it. The science of hermeneutics is also concerned with problems in communication, but at the semantic level of the possibility of misunderstanding, and with human processes of interpretation. Gadamer (1966, 7) argued that we need to go deeper than miscommunication across a distance between originator and recipient, because "a common understanding always precedes these situations" (c.f. tacit knowledge [Polanyi 1967]). Hermeneutics, to Gadamer (1967), is a universal reflection. There are two problems with this. 1. He does not sufficiently distinguish between meaning-as-signification and the meaningfulness of all around us on which we may reflect; see §3-1.2. 2. He privileges the recipient over the originator of information, a tendency we find also in Ricoeur (1981), whose answer to the question, "What is text?" was that it is in reading that the destiny of text is fulfilled. Hermeneutics takes less interest in the information as transmittable thing distinct from originator and recipient. Nevertheless, its emphasis on the human interpreter is a useful corrective to those who might presuppose that we may understand information without reference to human agency.

Floridi (2004) remarks that "Information is still an elusive concept", which is a scandal because theoretical work in information relies on clear understanding. "The philosophy of information (PI) is a new area of research with its own field of investigation and methodology." So, following the footsteps of Hilbert's (1900) philosophy of mathematics, Floridi delinated 18 'Open Problems' for the philosophy of information, concerning what information is and how it operates, some of which address issues not covered by the above discourses, such as how data can acquire meaning and whether an informational approach can solve the mind-body problem. Few of his questions concern us, and no adequate answers are given. They revolve around intelligence and cognitive behaviour, making very little reference to the either human interpretation or to communication. Underlying his positing this set of questions seems to be a presupposition that information is stuff like matter or energy, being-in-itself rather than being-in-the-world. His view ignores tacit knowledge.

Fisher et al. (2005) have collected 70 views about information, ranging from information flow to archiving, covering information grounds, horizons, encountering, intents, etc. There are many views not contained in the above, and a full review should take them into account, but few, if any, of them address the question, "What is information?"—though locating them all might in a multi-dimensional space might show them circling some centre.

Except for Fisher's ad hoc collection, the above discourses seem to focus on one aspect of what information is: Shannon on the analytic (message selection), Wiener on the formative (useful work), hermeneutics on the lingual (interpretation), Floridi variously on the psychic, analytic and formative and a little on the lingual. None are oriented to the information systems field. Systems thinking offers a more holistic and useful view.

5-3.2 A Systems View of Information: Data, Information and Knowledge

The fields of information systems and computer science are faced with data, information and knowledge, for example 'contained' in a company's knowledge base. This raises the questions, "What are data, information and knowledge?", "What is the relationship between them?", "What is it to 'contain' them?" Such questions are important in, for instance, knowledge management, big data and data warehousing.

A typical answer to what these are is that "data is raw numbers and facts, information is processed data, and knowledge is authenticated information" (Alavi and Leidner 2001, 109). Langefors (1966) added 'capta', which denotes what is 'captured' from perceptions, which might be one place earlier in the sequence:

Capta — Data — Information — Knowledge.

Some would like to add Wisdom the right hand end. Dollar (2000, 58) places context there: "logical and physical structure, intellectual content, and context that were apparent at the time of creation or receipt", and Jennings (2000) suggests that the context is social.

> Note on terminology: '*Knowledge*' can mean two things. The usual meaning of 'knowledge' is what a person knows, knowledge as the product of knowing; see §3-8.4. In this chapter, however, we encounter '*knowledge*' referring to stocks of interpreted and processed 'information' that are 'held' somewhere, as in a repository, whether a library (a stock of knowledge) or a database (e.g., knowledge of the patients in a hospital). This 'holding' might be on paper or in electronic form or even stone tablets, but both are by way of representation in some language. 'Knowledge' in this sense refers to what symbols signify.

Engagement with capta, data, information and knowledge occurs at the user interface, when we see shapes on the screen (the capta), or when trying to decipher ancient manuscripts, as we see them as numbers or words (data), see these as part of a sentence or table (information) and understand what it is about. Similarly, graphics, animation, sound, especially the spoken voice. Similarly when we read a book or look at a poster.

From the perspective of data mining or of optical character recognition (OCR), this often denotes stages of processing: start with bit patterns or pixel patterns, discern lexical atoms (letters) therein, form these into words and sentences, and identify what these signify. In practice, results from later stages feed back into earlier stages of processing to refine the 'seeing' process. It is often treated as a process of attributing meaning to things that (it is presumed) exist without meaning.

5-3.3 Problems With a Sequential View

Four things, however, are ignored or presupposed by that sequential view.

1. *Prior meaning*. Checkland and Holwell (1998, 90) suggest "the attribution of meaning in context converts capta into something different, for which another word is appropriate: the word 'information'." Even though this is sequential, meaning and context is something we hold/have/are prior the act of interpretation, and without it no interpretation is possible. Even in OCR, prior meaning is built in, into the software as laws of OCR processing, into the collections of fonts used, and into semantic nets.
2. *Simultaneity*. In everyday experience of engaging with information, there is no chronological separation of stages. In most cases, we see shapes (hear sounds), discern letters (or phonemes or other meaningful atoms), recognise words and appreciate signification simultaneously. The 'capta' is already 'data', already 'information' and already 'knowledge.' In a computer game, the movement and shapes I see on screen are always-already a dragon and are a danger that I must counter (§6-3.1). In the field of knowledge management, Tuomi (1999) put forward an "iconoclastic argument" that "the often-assumed hierarchy from data to knowledge is actually inverse: knowledge must exist before information can be formulated and before data can be measured to form information." Capta-data-information-knowledge is all one whole.

   Note on terminology: The term, "capta-data-information-knowledge" is clumsy. So I will call it simply '*information*', and this will carry all four meanings, unless I make it plain otherwise. I choose 'information' rather than 'knowledge' because 'knowledge' is too easily confused with the more general result of human knowing, as it is employed in §3-8.4, and also because the word 'inform' carries with it connotations of signification.

   The usual sequential account comes from presupposing a distal relationship (*Gegenstand* §3-4.3.4) between the reader and the information. This occurs, for example, when the archaeologist is faced with marks on stone never seen before, or when a manager sees figures on screen and must expend effort to make sense of them, and when a novice is learning a new user interface, but it should not be expected to occur all the time. Though data on screen might not yet contribute to a manager's knowledge without distal processing, it itself is not 'just data': it is (say) a profit figure, which was at one time information and knowledge for an originator of the information.

3. *Originator*. The standard sequential view takes too little account of the originator of the information—that person who generated the sales figures for the manager to read. Tuomi's iconoclastic view re-establishes the dignity of, and interest in, the originator. Even in the case of deciphering ancient manuscripts, there is now recognition of the importance of understanding the originator and what they might have intended within their context.

   Example: Apache servers produce records of accesses to web pages. At least three human originators may be identified. One is the person who accessed the web pages: the record is knowledge of who accessed which page when. One is the developer of *Apache*, who decided what kinds of knowledge-about-access it should be possible to record. One is the system administrator, who set the *Apache* parameters to record this but not that. As an analyst of *Apache* records myself, I take all these into account during my interpretation.

4. *Mere data?* Can there be such a thing as 'mere data' that is not yet information or knowledge? If Tuomi is correct, there is no such thing as 'mere data', devoid of meaning. All data, *qua* data, already signifies something, even if particular readers or hearers do not yet know what that signification is.

What about artificial intelligence taking the place of any or all originators? Even there, a human being developed the artificial intelligence and set its runtime parameters. I suggest that, however many steps we take or branches we follow, we will find human input at the ends of the various branches. Artificial intelligence is discussed later.

5-3.4 A Dooyeweerdian Understanding of Information

Dooyeweerd's understanding of existence is rooted in meaningfulness rather than either being-in-itself (essence) or being-in-the-world, which arose because of the Immanence Standpoint in philosophy over the past 2,500 years (§3-2.1). To Dooyeweerd, "What is?" questions can be addressed by reference to meaningfulness.

Dooyeweerd would view capta, data, information and knowledge as aspects of one thing, or as things enkaptically bound into a whole (§3-9.6.2). Instead of trying to answer "What is data-in-itself? Information-in-itself? Knowledge-in-itself? Information-in-the-world?" Dooyeweerd would answer the question "What makes the concepts of data, information, knowledge and context meaningful?", by reference to the 'ocean of meaningfulness' which enables all to Be and Occur (see §3-1.2.3).

A full philosophical elaboration of a Dooyeweerdian account of the nature of information (as capta-data-information-knowledge) is still awaited. However, the following provides a systematic outline of what that account might entail, sufficient to address the issues above and make progress. Two questions are addressed: what is information, and what is signified by information? Since Dooyeweerd's suite of aspects is a taxonomy of spheres of meaningfulness, we employ it as a conceptual tool here.

5-3.5 What Is Information?

The following is a systematic outline of a possible Dooyeweerdian understanding of information and its possibilities (key concepts are emphasised); it may be elaborated by readers.

- Information, as in 'information systems' and data in computers, involves intended *signification* rather than just meaningfulness. Information is signification-meaning, which refers to selected aspects of the ocean of meaningfulness, as the target aspect of lingual functioning. Example: redness is psychical so "red" signifies something psychical. Information must be differentiated from 'information' that is not yet signified, such as quantum wave functions in physics (a physical analogy of the lingual) or analytically- or forensically-interpreted signs like animal tracks or a crime scene (an analytic analogy of the lingual). Both are meaningful but treating them as information conflates the various meanings of 'meaning' listed in §3-1.2.1. Including 'information' in discussion of information invites confusion.
- Information is a *lingual object*, i.e., an object of lingual subject functioning, which is governed by lingual aspectual law (§3-3.1.2).
  - Information might be one word, sign, symbol or token, or a sentence or much more. Examples: Exchange rate in a newspaper; Website.
  - In the case of computers, the object might be dynamic. Examples: Mature green dragon threatening me (§6-3.1); Patient notes entered by previous nurse.
  - It is the lingual object that may be transmitted.
- As a lingual object, its *normativity* is primarily lingual but as something within the entire ocean of meaningfulness it is also governed by the norms of all aspects. This lingual-led multi-aspectual normativity is manifested in two ways:
  - Normativity of informational functioning: e.g., be clear, truthful, parsimonious, lenient; see §6-3.5.3;
  - Normativity of information content, that of the world represented in the computer (§6-3.5.2), i.e., its virtual law-side (§5-5.2).

- Information implies a lingual subject-subject relationship. Two possible subjects relate to the lingual object in different ways: to the *originator*(s) (speaker, writer) information is a *generated object*; to the *recipient*(s) (hearer, reader) information is a *prior object* (see §3-3.1.2).
    - The main aspect of the subject-functioning, of which information is the object, is the *lingual aspect*: Originators *express*; recipients *interpret*.
    - Originator might be recipient. Example: memory aids to self. Usually, however, they are different.
    - ICT software is information, of which the ICT developer is the main originator and the users are recipients. In web pages or books, the author is the main originator and readers are recipients.
    - In interactive software the user is originator of the lingual objects (information) entered.
- On *signification*:
    - Signification is close to the kernel meaningfulness of the lingual aspect and thus cannot be precisely defined. Its reality is experienced in the doing, and may be grasped by intuition.
    - The lingual functioning of signification is supported by functioning in all other aspects (*multi-aspectual functioning*). Earlier aspects foundationally serve the lingual. Later aspects influence the lingual.
    - Information is therefore a *multi-aspectual being* (i.e., multi-layered; see §3-9.3), *qualified by the lingual aspect*.
    - Therefore capta, data, information, knowledge and social context are all aspects of information. They may be seen either as aspectual functioning that are linked by inter-aspect dependency (§3-7.4.4), or aspectual beings that are bound together as the whole that is information by foundational enkapsis (see §3-9.3, §3-9.6.2).
    - Therefore, these can never be separated from each other, except conceptually. The symbol or data has no existence *qua* symbol or data without content. Nor has content, *qua* content, without symbol.
    - Hence, there is no 'mere data' awaiting meaning. However, it might be yet to be interpreted by a recipient.
    - The syntax-semantics distinction is that of the formative-lingual dependency. The semantics-pragmatics distinctions may be two, (1) the lingual-social inter-aspect relationship, (2) pragmatics refers to the lingual functioning of making the utterance, and semantics, to its target aspect (aspect of content).
- Why *lingual* object? Why not *formative*? 'Inform' is lingual. ICT use, ICT development, ICT features and ICT and society all find signification, not just technology, important. Formative shaping is only meaningful insofar as it enables signification. Why not *social*? Because signification treats originator and recipient as individuals rather than

as 'we', and originator can be recipient, as in memory-aids. Though important, these aspects are not central.

Aspects of the lingual functioning, and the object that is information, are shown in Table 5.2. Column 1 is each aspect. Column 2 shows the phenomenon above made meaningful by that aspect (aspect of information). Columns 3 and 4 express the subject-functioning of recipient and originator. Column 5 is used later.

Table 5.2 Aspects of Information as Multi-layered Existence

Aspect	*Phenomenon*	*As received*	*As originated*	*Big Data*
Quantitative Spatial Kinematic		(Important in 'data' processing)		
Physical	Medium	That which makes the medium possible, e.g. stone, paper, silicon, air (carries sound).		
Organic-biotic	Components of medium	Organs function		
Psychic / Sensitive	Capta (Bits)	That which our senses detect: signals	The marks or sounds our motor or vocal organs emit	Disparate file formats
Analytical	Data	'Symbols' we recognise among signals, attend to and conceptualize as of a type (numbers, letters, words, icons)	The 'symbols' we write, draw or utter that signify for us.	Identifying the diverse contents
Formative	Information ("processed data")	The structure we detect among symbols	The structure we construct among symbols	Structuring, not just processing
Lingual	'Knowledge'	The signification we interpret the symbol structures to convey	The signification we intend when we structure the symbols	Interpretation of diverse meaningfulness of content
Social	Context (Dollar 2000)	Cultural context at creation or receipt; shared view of what is meaningful (power)		Cultural relevance

Aspect	*Phenomenon*	*As received*	*As originated*	*Big Data*
Economic	Resource	Wasteful writing, speaking	Information overload	Overcoming superfluity, not just processing volume
Aesthetic	'Wisdom'	Harmony within the conversation, and with other knowledge of both originator and recipient.		Harmonizing the disparate contents (not just media)
Juridical	"Authenticated information"	Authentication	Accuracy, provenance, prohibition of the nefarious	"accuracy or validity of Big Data predictions" require "impartial auditors" (Mayer-Schönberger & Cukier 2013)
Ethical		Forgiving attitude towards originator; vulnerability in trusting the information.	Awareness of limitations in one's information; willingness to be critiqued.	Trustworthiness of the findings (Davenport & Patil 2012)
Pistic		Assumptions, presuppositions		Being aware of limitations (deMauro et al. 2014)

Some aspect assignments need explaining. Medium components are organic-biotic insofar as they might interact with organs (e.g., pages of book turned by fingers and focused on by eyes) or work at an equivalent level (e.g., as brain neural cells operate by signals so do computer processor and memory). Though I earlier assigned the Shannonian bit to the analytic aspect, because it refers to distinction, bits here are seen as signals rather than distinctions and hence psychic; they do, however, antecipate distinction. Alavi and Leidner's (2001) "authenticated information" refers to whether the interpretation is 'true', doing-justice to its referent, rather than merely opinion, guess or one-off. To Dooyeweerd, this is a juridical aspect of information. 'Truth' is not a simple property but refers to all reality in all its aspects; see §3-4.1.2.

In a similar way, a **paper document** is a multi-aspectual whole in which the physical aspect is the medium, the organic aspect, its sheets of paper, binding, ink, etc., its psychic aspect, the visible marks on the paper, including both lettering and smudges, etc., its analytic aspect, the letters and other atomic symbols that the marks make, ignoring smudges, its formative aspect, the structure of those atomic symbols, including that expressed via spatial layout, its lingual aspect, the content, and its social aspect the background understanding shared between writer and readers; see Burke and Basden (2004) for a full discussion.

5-3.6 What Is Signified?

On what is signified in the lingual object that is information (its content):

- What information signifies is the *target* (§3-7.4.6) of the lingual signification. This may be any, several or all aspects, so information may be about amounts (quantitative), amounts of resource (quantitative, economic), faiths (pistic), texts (lingual), texts about religion in a community (lingual, pistic, social), and so on.
- Information usually signifies more *implicitly* than is *explicitly* signified, so information depends on *tacit knowledge*. Example: annual profits figure (quantitative, economic explicitly signified), also signifies implicitly the originator's decisions about what to include in incomings and outgoings that year (analytic), desired company image (pistic) in their annual report to stockholders (lingual, social), etc. If recipients share the same background knowledge as originators (common context [Dollar 2000] or lifeworld), they effectively augment the explicit signification with the implicit when they receive it.
    - Semantics and pragmatics might refer to explicit and implicit signification, but this is not explored here.
- *Cross-cultural understanding*. The recipient can usually understand some of the originator's implicit signification because both function within the same 'oceanic' law-side (§3-3.1.1). However, because of their different subject-object-side (cultural) contexts, what the information signifies to each might not fully coincide.
- Lingual signification targets meaningfulness rather than existence. This allows information to be about the fictional or even impossible (e.g., Gandalf or 'square circle') as well as the real. Impossibility breaks aspectual laws and is different in each aspect.
- *Limitations of information*. However, because no aspect is absolute, the signification cannot capture the full meaningfulness experienced and intended by the originator.

5-3.7 Existence and Persistence of Information

While I have been writing this book, the right to be forgotten on the Internet has become important, because of embarrassing material being disseminated.

In some jurisdictions, the law has been changed to allow people to demand that such material is removed from the Internet, and countervailing concerns have been raised about freedom of expression.

But what constitutes removal? When can it be said that something no longer exists on the Internet? This widens to other related questions, such as: What does it mean for information to 'exist' or be destroyed? (Ignore, here, the physical 'law' of the conservation of physical 'information'.) When is information changed? When is one copy similar to or different from another?

The aspectual understanding of information suggests a way to address such questions: What existence, destruction, sameness and difference are is different for each aspect, and differences that are meaningful in one aspect are not in others.

> Examples: File compression (non-lossy) is an operation solely on bit patterns (psychic aspect) so that data and structure do not change (analytic and formative aspects). File deletion involves tagging its filename (analytic aspect), but its bit pattern is still on disk (psychic aspect), and it can usually still be recovered.

To remove something from the Internet, we must decide in which aspect we want to remove it.

Existence (in a computer) in the *psychic aspect* is bit patterns, usually contained in a file, and each copy is a different existence. To cease to exist psychically involves blanking the bit pattern of every copy held in storage. This is the most secure but most arduous non-existence.

Existence in the *analytic aspect* is: being distinguished as a particular kind of data—as photograph, text, numbers, etc. This implies not just a stored bit pattern but also a means of interpreting it as that kind of data, i.e., a coding protocol like binary for numbers or JPEG for photographs. Analytic non-existence can be achieved in two ways: remove information about where to find the bit pattern, or remove the coding protocol, or knowledge thereof (e.g. remove the ".jpg" at the end of the file—not very secure). Also, over long periods codings become obsolete and eventually forgotten. To remove analytic existence fully, however, might be challenging.

Existence in the *formative aspect* concerns shaping and structure, which, on the Internet, involves links. Removal of all links means it ceases to exist in the formative aspect: it can never be found. Google's URL removal tool does this (and other things).

Existence in the *lingual aspect* concerns interpretation of the content. To cease to exist lingually means that the material no longer conveys the same meaning. Text can be changed, explanations given or apologies issued. For photographs, parts can be blanked out. This does not deal with memories, however.

Existence in the *social aspect* is concerned with expectations. etc. Example: Usually people look only at the first page returned by ranked searches, so Downey (2012) and others advise moving the offending material down the rankings, for example by swamping it with good material.

'Existence' in the *juridical aspect* concerns whether it is a legal issue, i.e., inappropriate. Removal might involve taking legal action.

It is useful to consider what happened to cause the problem, and from that determine the response. It is usually the social, aesthetic and juridical aspects, rather than earlier ones, that make the material problematic. However, it might be the *ethical aspect*, of attitude, that is most important overall: what attitude did the person who disseminated the offending material have? What attitude did those who sniggered, 'liked' and shared it have? What attitude did the embarrassed person have? What attitude did the hosting organization have? Sometimes attending to attitudes of various parties or even of society might be more effective than trying to enact laws about the keeping and deletion of data that curtail freedom of expression.

Thus, to understand the nature of information as a multi-aspectual entity is not just a philosophical but also a practical issue. The above discussion may be broadened to consider information in any medium, e.g., paper.

5-3.8 Example: Big Data and Data Mining

This understanding of data, information and knowledge can throw useful light on the idea of Big Data and suggest new avenues for research. We do not discuss algorithms, etc., here, but rather informational issues.

Organizations collect masses of data and sift through it to 'extract' knowledge by data-mining techniques. DeMauro et al. (2014) provide a useful overview of the topic, including research and definitions. The discourse around Big Data identifies volume, velocity and variety as its main characteristics—but is that all?

Characterizing big data with volume, velocity and variety tends to shift focus onto the mathematical aspects and associated number crunching, so that other aspects are ignored (Joneidy 2015), except perhaps the analytic and economic. Attention to other aspects will enrich research and practice.

'Variety' refers to number of types of sources of data (structured data from databases, etc., unstructured data like newsfeeds and non-textual data like audio and video); attention to qualifying aspects of sources (formative, analytic and psychic; c.f. §6-3.4) can widen the perspective and account for how and why each needs different treatment, and thus reduce confusion in meeting the challenge of integrating information from them. However, even this is not sufficient, because, as Table 5.2 shows, both originator and recipient function in all the other aspects too. Column 5 shows how each aspect is necessary to the success of big data. Research in Big Data should look at how each of those aspectual issues can improve the efficacy of the resulting knowledge, and the role of human wisdom in setting the parameters for processing.

Concerning content, the range of issues mined is limited to a few aspects. If information is multi-aspectual in content, as argued above, then much of value is likely to be overlooked. Section 6-3.5 shows how all aspects of content may be taken into account.

5-4 What Is a Computer?

Note on terminology: In this section 'computer' means not just the hardware but something that is running, or could run, useful software. It is the technical portion of the ICT artefact.

5-4.1 Four Views of the Nature of Computers

Four views about the nature of computers may be differentiated, each of which provides different insights, and each of which may be understood via a Dooyeweerdian foundation:

- The *computer-as-object* (proximal tool) view, which is informed by Polanyi (1967), may be understood more precisely as the user engaging with interface and technology (EIT): §6-3.4.
- The *computer-as-agent* view, which is held by many in artificial intelligence, sees the computer as distal from, and in conversation with, the human, or as avatars in virtual worlds.
- The *computer-in-the-world* view, emphasised by Winograd and Flores (1986) with reference to Heidegger, may be understood as the user engaging in life with ICT (ELI): §6-3.6.
- The *computer-as-world* view. When the user immersed in a (virtual) world like *Call of Duty*, neither the computer-as-object, nor computer-as-agent, nor computer-in-the-world understandings seem sufficient. Here the user is within the world that is the ICT, and the ICT is no longer a discrete 'being' but is itself an *Umwelt*. Computers connected to the Internet may also be seen as constituting an *Umwelt*, though a technical rather than informational one, made possible by correlative enkapsis (§3-9.6.2).

These possibilities are too often confused with each other but should not be. How Dooyeweerd might inform the ambit of each view, the relationships between them and when each is appropriate, calls for research. We need a foundational understanding that embraces them all.

5-4.2 Multi-Aspectual Structure of Computers

Dooyeweerd would direct us towards understanding computers as multi-aspectual beings (§3-9.3). Newell (1982) made a similar suggestion, a multi-level view of the nature of computers. He argued that computer systems could be described and understood at several levels, including: a device level, in which physical laws held sway, a circuit level, of electronic components, a logic level, of digital 'logic' or bits (bit patterns, bitmaps), a symbol level, in which the computer is seen as variables and algorithms, and a knowledge level, which is the semantic content ("The computer told me . . ."). This classic paper set the direction of research for many in AI, KBS and HCI for the next 20 years, because it expressed what people found intuitively true, especially the irreducible difference between various levels.

Basden (2008) argues that Newell's levels match almost exactly Dooyeweerd's physical to lingual aspects, and developed Newell's ideas into a multi-aspectual view of what a computer is.

As information and documents, so computers can be understood as multi-aspectual wholes, which appear to be different types of thing when viewed from different aspects. Just as a sculpture comprises a physical being (marble) and an aesthetic being (Praxiteles' Hermes: §3-9.6.2), so a computer with software comprises several aspectual beings. As various aspectual beings, the computer (including mobile device) is:

- a physical being: materials (scrap value),
- an organic being: electronic components,
- a psychic being: Turing Machine,
- an analytic being: data store,
- a formative being: information processor, and
- a lingual being: applications, knowledge base.

The computer is all these together, simultaneously, all bound together by foundational enkapsis (§3-9.6.2). Each aspectual being functions in a way governed by the laws of its aspect, and this functioning may be seen as the functioning in that aspect of the whole. The link with the multi-aspectual being of information, in Table 5.2, is obvious.

This, I believe, is what Newell (1982) was trying to express. Not only can Dooyeweerd inform Newell, but also Newell might inform Dooyeweerd's still incompletely formed ideas about enkapsis, in ways outlined in Basden (2008).

5-4.3 The Multi-aspectual Functioning of a Computer

For a relatively static thing like a sculpture, this is sufficient, but to understand a dynamic thing like a computer, it is useful to consider its functioning too in each aspect. In the physical aspect, and earlier, this is subject-functioning, in that the computer responds to physical and mathematical laws as subject. However, in all other aspects, it functions as object within the subject-functioning of human beings—usually the users and developers. In the physical and earlier aspects, the computer has a *subject-subject relationship* with the user, while in all later aspects it is a *subject-object relationship* (as Dooyeweerd rather than Descartes understood it; see §3-3.1). To developers it is a generated object, to the users, a prior object. Interactivity of the computer means that the user alters this prior object and might also generate new objects, such as new records in databases.

How the computer and its users function in each aspect is shown in Table 5.3, which shows how ICT (computer) functions in each aspect. Column 1 gives the aspect, column 2, examples of how the user functions,

Table 5.3 Aspectual Functioning of ICT and User; Also of ICT Design

Aspect	*of user* *Input / Output*	*Rel*	*of ICT* *Input / Output*	*of design* *(normative)*
Quantitative Spatial Kinematic	By retrocipation from physical (§6-3.4)			
Physical	Physico-chemical energy, fields, forces.	S-S	Physico-chemical energy, fields, forces.	Design electronic and mechanical components.
Organic-biotic	Muscle cells active / Nerve cells (eye, ear) stimulated.	S-O	Currents from mouse or touch-screen / Voltages that control screen. - **Hardware**	Design hardware to suit human body.
Psychic-sensitive	Hand or finger movements / See shapes, colours, spatial arrangements, hear sounds.	S-O	Receive mouse or touch-screen signals / Set bit-patterns, pixels to display shapes, fonts, colours, emit sounds.	Design lowest-level user interface routines for easy response.
Analytical	Choose what to ask computer to do / Differentiate figure from background, recognising its type as symbol.	S-O	Recognise tokens of command / Display or speak data (amounts, text, etc.).	Design low-level affordance (§7 3.3) for clarity of information-type.
Formative	Structure commands to computer to achieve intended goal / Intelligently respond to displayed or heard structure (e.g. follow links).	S-O	Recognise what user wants to achieve and take action (e.g. get linked page) / Arrange or emphasise display or sound elements to show information structure (e.g. links as blue underline).	Design the structure of user interface (higher-level affordance: §7-3.3).

(*Continued*)

Table 5.3 (Continued)

Aspect	*of user Input / Output*	*Rel*	*of ICT Input / Output*	*of design (normative)*
Lingual	Find, understand and engage with meaningful content.	S-O	Offer meaningful content to user. (Note: input, output combined.)	Design content for understandability.
Social	Understand cultural assumptions, connotations, idioms in the information.	S-O	Capitalize on cultural assumptions of user.	'User-friendliness': understand background assumptions and user-expectations in info, decide how to make explicit (esp. web sites: §9-2.7.2).
Economic	Efficiency of user interface (e.g. fast page loading) and of content (e.g. concise text)	S-O	Optimize searches, content and display.	Optimize search; Be frugal in content (e.g. what appears on small screens?) Chapter 7.
Aesthetic	Appreciate interface (e.g. colour scheme) and content (e.g. interest). Harmonize content with what known already.	S-O	Look good. Provide interesting content, which harmonizes with what users require.	Sensitively anticipate use (Section 9-5). Design aesthetics of user interface.
Juridical	Do justice to the content and other users.	S-O	Provide accurate, appropriate information (§7-3.4).	Do justice to domain knowledge (Section 9-6) and stakeholders (§9-5).
Ethical	Be patient and forgiving of content and developer; expend effort giving good information.	S-O	Awareness of possible limitations (e.g. *Wikipedia* includes page histories)	Design so users are fully aware of limitations (§9-5).
Pistic / Faith	Be critically aware of assumptions inscribed in the ICT.	S-O	Assumptions underlie the content and interface.	Be aware of assumptions being inscribed (§9-5.1).

column 4, examples of how the computer functions. Column 3 shows the relationship between user and computer. Column 5 suggests how that other subject (originator), the developer or designer, functions when creating the ICT artefact and the normativity it entails. The table should be treated more like a picture that can be reflected upon, than a piece of prose to read.

Notice how the relationship between user and computer is simultaneously subject-subject and subject-object in different aspects.

The table shows the wide range of issues that relate to computers and ICT. Earlier aspects provide a substratum on which the qualifying lingual functioning depends; later aspects provide its fuller meaningfulness as ICT. All aspects are important in both use and development of ICT and its features, so Chapters 6, 9 and 7 have links back to here. The Table can thus be used to guide research policy, and also in teaching to reduce inter-level confusions.

5-4.4 Some Implications

The aspectual view is more detailed and precise than the enkaptic view but can too easily lose the wholeness that the enkaptic view brings. Both views together are important. Both enable us to differentiate ICT from other types of existence and functioning.

The aspectual view reveals that Barlow's (1996) idea of cyberspace and Haraway's (1991) idea of cyborg and the importance of the body, both offer some insights but that neither can claim any superiority over the other. Their mutual opposition may now be seen as arising from reductionistic over-emphasis on certain aspects and ignoring others.

In all later aspects, ICT functions as object, but that does not imply it is passive (so Clouser's [2005] equivalencing of object-functioning with "passive" is problematic). The computer might be said to exhibit some agency, especially from an everyday perspective, which we experience in our smart mobile phones, which Latour (1987) emphasises in organizational ICT.

Nick Breems, who undertook an examination of the Dooyeweerdian understanding of ICT use (Chapter 6), has suggested that the computer displays a kind of functioning as *subject by proxy*. In the lingual aspect, for example, the computer 'communicates' with its user or with other computers. The range of the aspects is why it is now recognised that computer interoperability needs to consider semantic (lingual) as well as syntactic (analytic, formative) issues.

A perhaps more fundamental implication is for the philosophical ideas of *being-in-the-world* and *being-in-itself*. Bearing in mind that the Dooyeweerdian subject-object relationship is proximal, not the distal Cartesian one that Heidegger found so problematic, the table clarifies how Dooyeweerd can incorporate both approaches to being. The Being-in-the-world of the computer is primarily the relationship it makes with its user, as emphasised by Winograd and Flores (1986) and by Milewski's (1997) 'delegation', and could refer to columns 2, 3 and 4 merged together. This links with our discussion of ICT use in Chapter 6, and involves a relationship with developers, as shown in column 5 (see Chapters 9, 7). Being-in-itself can now refer, not just to the aspects in which the computer functions as subject, but also to the later aspects, antecipating them, in anticipation (*sic.*) of the running and use of the computer.

5-5 Programs, Virtual Worlds and Software

What is a computer program? To say that it is a statement in computer language of what we want the computer to do, though true, is not enough. Two views of program will be discussed, one metaphorical, one ontological.

5-5.1 Program as Performance Art

We may first notice the similarities between computer programs and performance art, like music or drama, where a score is performed.

Dooyeweerd's (1955, III, 110) philosophical discussion of performance art might inform our understanding of programs. (Remember that Dooyeweerd used 'subjective' and 'objective' in a special way; see §3-3.1.2.):

> Works of art belonging to the last category [performance art] lack the constant actual existence proper to things in the narrower sense. They can only become constantly objectified in the structure of scores, books, *etc.* . . . such things as scores and books, are, as such, symbolically qualified. They can only *signify* the aesthetic structure of a work of art in an *objective* way and cannot *actualise* it.
> This is why artistic works of these types are always in need of a subjective actualization lacking the objective constancy essential to works of plastic art. Because of this state of affairs they give rise to a separate kind of art, *viz.* that of *performance*, in which aesthetic objectification and actualization, though bound to the spirit and style of the work, remain in direct contact with the re-creating individual conception of the performance artist. The latter's conception, as such, cannot actualise itself in a constant form, though modern technical skill has succeeded in reproducing musical sound-waves by means of a phonograph.
>
> (his emphasis)

Much of this may be applied to programs being run:

- Creator: composer = programmer-designer.
- Creator's imagined idea: idea of music = conceptual design of program.
- Music score = written-program; both written in a formal language. But score is not the music; written program is not the running-program.
- Performer: player = user.

- Playing the music = running the program; both actualise the creator's idea.
- One performance of a piece of music differs from the next; one run of a program differs from the next.
- Players/users can be one or many.
- Score/written-program persists; performance/running is transient.
- Recording: on tape or, for example, keystroke recorder.

To take this outline suggestion further, refer to, and adapt, Dooyeweerd's discussion (1955, III, 109–117).

There are two differences between music and program. Music is usually qualified by the aesthetic aspect, programs by lingual aspect. Music is often intended to be performed for an audience; a program is usually run by the user for the user (and colleagues) but no audience.

The above insights are based on a metaphorical comparison, and further development thereof is left to the reflections and research of others. We will turn to a view that is less dependent on metaphor.

5-5.2 Program as Virtual Law-Side

A program—or a piece of music or a play—is a set of rules that govern how things occur during its running—or performance. The running of the programming and the performing of the music actualises their laws, just as the actual being and occurring of the cosmos actualises the cosmic law-side.

A program may therefore be seen as a law-side for a virtual world, a *virtual law-side*, which enables that virtual world to be and occur, a *virtual subject-object-side*, which is the virtual world. (See §3-3.1.1.) Virtual law-sides are designed and brought into being as programs by ICT developers.

> Note on terminology: *Virtual law-side* includes encapsulated information not only of imaginary worlds like games, but also of real worlds like patient or insurance records. In both cases, the program—its data structures and algorithms—determine what is meaningful and by what laws it operates.

The virtual subject-object-side includes both agents and contexts that are made possible by the virtual law-side, with which the user engages as meaningful content (see §6-3.5).

- Both (real) law-side and programs enable being and occurrence.
- Both subject-object-side and running program is what exists and occurs.
- Law-side and programs are universalia while both subject side and running-program are specific instantiations of this.
- Both law-side and programs define what is meaningful, possible and lawful.

- Both law-side and programs comprise distinct aspects of meaning-law.
- As law-side defines normativity of real world, so program defines normativity of virtual world.
- Just as in the law-side, aspects govern functioning and type laws govern types of thing that exist, so in programs, procedures govern activity and data classes, the types of thing that exist.

That is why we may treat programs (or ICT artefacts, as they are called elsewhere) as virtual law-sides.

> Examples: In a computer game, the game itself is the virtual law-side and the avatars and objects scattered around are the subject-object-side. An insurance claims system is a virtual law-side, in which the insurance records are the subject-object-side (§6-3.5.2).

But do self-modifying programs (e.g., neural nets) challenge this parallel, since our cosmic law-side does not get modified by the subject-object-side? The parallel is a little more complex: In the real world the aspects are the fundamental laws, but society creates and modifies rules and norms which also govern us and these can be changed. The modifiable parts are like society's rules; it is the laws that govern self-modification that are the aspects of the virtual law-side.

5-5.3 Virtual Worlds

What is the ontic status of beings we encounter in virtual worlds, including local games like *ZAngband*, MUDs (Multi-User Dungeon games) or Massively-Multiplayer Online Games) like *Call of Duty or Clash of Clans*?

The theory that these beings are 'only information' or 'pure mind' (Barlow 1996) does not accord with our everyday experience of virtual worlds. In ICT use (see Chapter 6) we find that engaging with meaningful content (EMC), i.e., the virtual beings, is intertwined with engaging in life with ICT (ELI); even the most absorbing virtual world affects, and is affected by, our 'real' life functioning.

Dooyeweerd (1955, III, 113–116) discussed the ontic status of the content of art that is creatively imagined by the artist (the bodies of Hermes and Dionysus as sculpted by Praxiteles and in computer games, the avatars, artefacts and contexts). However, his rather opaque discussion does not suit us because it about something passive (the artist's idea of the human body), whereas in computers the virtual world is dynamic.

Pacé Dooyeweerd, it is perhaps more useful to conceive of virtual characters and items as actually existing as the subject-object-side that has been enabled by the virtual law-side. This is illustrated in Table 5.4, which shows the aspects of functioning in the *ZAngband* dungeon-exploration game. Though they seem to function as subjects in their virtual world of

Table 5.4 Aspectual Functioning of Virtual Character in *ZAngband* (or Other Virtual World)

Aspect	*The virtual being . . .*
Quantitative	is one (or many if they "breed explosively").
Spatial	is at a location.
Kinematic	moves.
Physical	cannot walk through walls.
Organic-biotic	must eat to stay alive, and recovers health.
Psychic/Sensitive	sees, hears, sleeps.
Analytical	identifies things and enemies.
Formative	plans.
Lingual	communicates.
Social	can be gregarious.
Economic	has limited supplies, must conserve.
Aesthetic	does fun things.
Juridical	gains rewards, cheats other characters.
Ethical	is generous or mean.
Pistic/Faith	is committed to a deity.

the program or book, this is only as *subject by proxy* (see §5-4.4); their existence in the real world is purely as object-functioning, and occurs only in relation to users who run the software.

It is likely that the aspects of the virtual law-side, and their laws, will largely match those of a subset of the real law-side. This is important when the application is 'serious', but it also remains largely true in computer games; "there is no discourse so fictional that it does not connect up with reality" (Ricoeur 1981, 141). In computer games, however, the laws of some aspects will be deliberately modified (e.g., organic-biotic death is not the end). Yet, even so, most laws of most aspects will match our reality because otherwise how could players recognise or enjoy the game?

The creation in software of the laws of the law-side—its possible functioning, its rationalities, and its types of being—is discussed mainly in §7-4, as the development of modules for each aspect. The modification of the law-side will be by processes discussed in Chapter 9. A table like §5.4 could be useful during design, to ensure it is fully rounded.

5-5.4 Innards of a Computer

Most of the above concerns the way human beings engage with the computer via the user interface. But there is also program and data 'behind' the interface or 'inside' the computer, which I shall call '*innards*'. 'Innards' is a colloquial terms for that which is 'inside' an entity. We assume that bit, data or information are 'inside' the computer, yet when we open the box, we see not these but only electronic components.

Why do we believe that bits, data and information are 'in' the computer, when they are hidden from our sensory experience? How may the innards of a computer be understood? I cannot find much discussion of this, yet the idea is important when discussing ICT features (Chapter 7). The following outlines a possible understanding of innards.

First, we may see that each kind of innards exists by reference to certain aspects, as indicated in Table 5.2. Then, Dooyeweerd argued that even though it is through sensory functioning that most of our experience comes, "Naïve experience . . . is by no means restricted to the sensory aspect of its experiential world." (Dooyeweerd 1955, III, 102). That bits, data, information, etc., in a computer cannot be seen or heard does not exclude them from our everyday experience. Some thinkers, from Aristotle to Russell who recognise only the psychic and analytic aspects in theoretical thinking, have treated such things as theoretical abstractions from our senses; we need not do so because we recognise many aspects (c.f. §3-4.3.4).

How can we experience hidden innards? Dooyeweerd argued that our sensory function can be 'opened' by means of techniques and technological apparatus, such as microscopes, telescopes and models, to experience cells, galaxies and atoms respectively. Things are 'hidden' for various reasons, and different apparatus or theories answer the different reasons. The following apparatus allows us to experience the innards of the computer in each aspect. By reference to the aspects discussed above, the following examples may be delineated:

- Organic aspect: Oscilloscopes to see voltage variations.
- Psychic aspect: Memory (hex) dump software.
- Analytic aspect: To interpret this memory dump as data fields, a lot of memory-dump software also shows the bytes interpreted as ISO characters.
- Formative aspect: To interpret structure and purpose of this data, the user needs to know the structures of the program or features, or a tool that knows this (for example the amazingly useful program called *Amiga Structure Browser*, which allows me to move around the structures of the *Amiga* operating system).
- Lingual aspect: A program has meaning only insofar as the user knows what the parameters signify and what the program is supposed to do in terms of its application.

Though theories, techniques and technological apparatus are the product of the theoretical attitude, their concrete actualisation in life brings them into the sphere of our everyday experience and through them, our everyday experience of innards is proximal. It is no theoretical abstraction.

This offers a soundly philosophical way to underpin our intuitive belief that the computer 'contains' various things inside it, and these are meaningful at various different aspects. The idea is used extensively in Chapter 7.

5-6 The Artificial Intelligence Question: "Computer = Human?"

This section discusses an issue that has taxed us since computers arrived: the similarity and difference between computers and human beings—can computers think, understand, etc.? This is the central question of artificial intelligence (AI). Readers may skip it, unless they are interested in this question.

Supporters of 'strong AI' claim that computers can, in principle, be equivalent to human beings. Opponents argue that this is impossible, in principle. Boden (1990) collected views and summed up the debate as "What things does a machine (whether biological or not) need to be able to do in order to be able to understand?" (p. 103).

The debates over the past 50 years about this question have brought little resolution. The main difference today is whether computers might surpass, not just equal, humans, along with some ethical concerns, which seem 'bolted on'. It is not clear what practical value these debates have, except to sell books, tease us with puzzles and try to score points. Is there some value hidden in them? From an everyday perspective, it seems that the main fuel of the debates has been the arguments themselves, so is it time to go beyond them, rather than retreat from them or get sucked into them, and find something in them that is more meaningful to the world outside?

To clarify the foundations on which the question is debated is the contribution that Dooyeweerd might be able to make, and perhaps to suggest new foundations. This section briefly reviews the grounds on which debate has taken place and suggests new ground. An earlier but deeper version is in Chapter V of Basden (2008).

5-6.1 On Comparing Computer to Human Being

The famous Turing Test suggests we answer the AI question by comparing the behaviour of computer and human. Such behaviourist tests, however, offer little insight into why (on what grounds) computers can, or can never, be like humans. Moreover, the Turing Test restricts us to symbolic expressions, which privileges explicit over background knowledge and excludes whole ranges of tacit knowledge from the comparison.

So the debates have widened, and most may now be seen as about two properties, X and Y, which are exhibited fundamentally by humans and computers respectively. The AI question is to what extent and in what ways X = Y. Three main (X, Y) pairs may be detected, each of which takes the debate in a different direction.

1. *Debate about substance: Human is mind, computer is matter.* Proponents of strong AI argue that mind can be reduced to matter, as 'only' a label for matter functioning in particular ways. Opponents deny this.

Some look to emergence theory to bridge the gulf between them, but as mentioned in §3-7.4.4, emergence itself may be questioned. The debate based on matter and mind remains unresolved.

2. *Debate about causality: Humans operate biologically, computers, physically.* Searle (1990) argued that biological causality, which operates in humans, is fundamentally different from physical causality, by which computers operate. Biological causality enables genuine understanding and the processing of information; physical causality enables mere manipulation of formal symbols. But if we open up the (physical) case of a computer we find no "formal symbols" there being manipulated! On what grounds does Searle claim that symbols operate by physical causality? On what grounds does "information processing" require biological causality? Searle did not say; it remains a mystery. The debate is ideological in nature, as Colburn (2000, 80–81) put it, "If the idea that mental processing can be explained by computational models of symbol manipulation is an AI ideology, there seems to be a countervailing ideology, embodied by Searle and many others, that no matter what the behavior of a purely symbol manipulating system, it can *never* be said to understand, to have intentionality." Similar mystery is characteristic also of some Roman Catholic or other religious arguments, that human beings are animated by some kind of 'divine spark', which computers lack. The debate over mysteriously distinct causalities or divine sparks continues unresolved.
3. *Debate about determinacy: Human is free, computer is determined.* Some proponents of strong AI might hold as a dogma that all freedom is illusory, others, that even physical behaviour is non-determined. Newell (1982) tried a more sophisticated argument. He posited several levels of description at which human/computer agents operate (device, circuit, logic, symbol, knowledge levels; see §5-4.2), and that the agent's behaviour at the first four levels is determined but that at the knowledge is non-determined, because no agent can fully know what another agent knows and hence their responses to that agent can never be predicted on the basis of knowledge. Hence the behaviour of that agent cannot be predicted. Newell admitted (Newell 1993, 33) that his argument proved "rather hard to understand". Since Newell restricted his argument to ability of agents to predict, and ignored the issue of whether behaviour as such can be non-determined, his argument does not really address the AI question. Other problems with Newell's argument are found in Basden (2008). The debate around determinacy continues unresolved.

Supporters of Heidegger might immediately interject that the AI question can be answered by reference to 'being-in-the-world', with the world being its computer's users and developers (Winograd and Flores 1986). It might be irrelevant to discuss X and Y. Seemingly closer to an everyday perspective and containing important insights, it nevertheless might not truly address the AI question because it conflates subject with object (§3-3.1.2) and thus offers no foundation on which to explore the differences and similarities between computer and human.

(This simplified overview calls for further research.)

5-6.2 A Dooyeweerdian Critique of the AI Debates

In a short section on the dynamic nature of the reality of things, Dooyeweerd (1955, III, 109) sums up these approaches. The "X = Y?" debates seek "a supposed thing-reality", the other seeks a foundation in "the whole temporal world", both of which "seek it in a '*fata morgana*', a mirage". As an alternative to both, Dooyeweerd suggests grounding the being of the computer in meaningfulness (§3-1.2, §3-9).

Dooyeweerd (1979) argued that debates like these, which refer to fundamental ideas like mind, mysterious causalities or freedom, are driven by ground-motives that influence what the thinking community believes the alternatives are. The three "X = Y?" debates may be seen as aligned with the three dialectical ground-motives described in §3-2.2, as shown in Table 5.5, columns 1-4. Column 5 is used later.

Dooyeweerd argued that dialectical ground-motives constrain theoretical thought, at a deep level, because they treat the polar oppositions as inescapable 'truths', whereas they are only presuppositions shared by debaters. He argued that the religious nature of dialectical ground-motives prevents resolution of such debates. Proponents of strong AI may be seen as trying to ignore one pole or reduce it to the other, but this blinds them to wide ranges of issues that keep on emerging. Opponents of strong AI find the polar opposition convenient but then cannot allow for any relationship between them.

Table 5.5 Alignment of AI Debates With the Ground-motives

Humans	*Computers*	*Ground-motive*	*Typical author*	*Aspect pair*
Mind	Matter	Greek: Form-Matter	Many	Analytic Physical
Biological causality, semantics, understanding	Physical causality, syntax, symbol manipulation	Scholastic: Nature-Grace	Searle	Organic Physical
Free	Determined	Humanistic: Nature-Freedom	Newell	Lingual Physical
Aspectual functioning (S)	Aspectual functioning (O)	Biblical (Creation, Fall, Redemption)	Dooyeweerd	All aspects

If Dooyeweerd is correct, it is not surprising that this has led the AI debate over the past 50 years into blind alleys. This is why the debate remains unresolved.

5-6.3 A Dooyeweerdian Resolution of the AI Debates

From the Creation-Fall-Redemption ground-motive, both human and computer behaviour are seen as multi-aspectual functioning. X and Y may be treated, not as opposing poles but as aspects in which computers function. Each debate may be seen as discussing two aspects, shown in column 5 of Table 5.5. Since each aspect is irreducible to others, it can be tempting, when one wants to argue against strong AI, to set them in opposition to each other. Proponents of strong AI are tempted to try to reduce one aspect to the other, maybe appealing to emergence theory.

In Dooyeweerd's view, however, the aspects are not opposed but work together in mutual coherence, and yet are at the same time irreducibly distinct. Each aspect allows us to say something critically valid and interesting about both computers and humans. Seeing computers in terms of aspects allows us to capitalise on the multi-aspectual understanding developed in §5-4 above. Instead of monistically seeking a single ground for supporting strong AI, or a dualistic ground for opposing it, Dooyeweerd provides a pluralistic ground for understanding AI philosophically. In the irreducible distinctness of aspects he provides grounds for understanding differences between humans and computers, and in the coherence of aspects, he provides grounds for understanding similarities.

Table 5.3 shows how human and computer function in each aspect and what kind of relationship they have. In the physical aspect, both function as subject (subject-subject relationship), both responding as agents to the same laws, and that is the common basis for their interaction (§3-8.2). In later aspects, the human functions as subject, and computer as object (subject-object relationship). Yet that object-functioning is still meaningful, and it is valid to say, "The computer did X"—X being, e.g., "responded" (psychic aspect), "analysed" (analytic aspect), "searched semantically" (analytic, lingual), "informed me" (lingual), etc. The only proviso to this is that the computer does so only by virtue of humans who are functioning as subject (user and arguably programmer) and thus may be 'subject-by-proxy'. Moreover, all these things are true together.

We may now situate the debates. Each aspect enables a different type of 'causality' (repercussion), which accounts for the fundamental difference between physical and organic-biotic or pistic causalities—stressed by Searle and Roman Catholic thinkers—but also their coherence. Each aspect sees the agent in a different way, such as physical and psychical—stressed in the mind-matter debates. The determinism-freedom debate refers to the latitude that each aspect offers the agent, which is governed by the latest aspect in which they function as subject—physical for computer and all for human but where the lingual is most important in relation to ICT (§5-2.5). So Newell was not completely wrong in singling the knowledge level out when trying to argue for non-determinedness; where he fell short, perhaps, was in not understanding the law-subject-object relationship between aspects, humans and computers and the radical difference between object- and subject-functioning.

Finally, if computers and humans function in all aspects, then it is easy to see that the three debates are not really so separate, but are merely picking out three different aspects, in which there is a subject-object relationship, to pair with the physical subject-subject relationship. This not only brings the debates together but suggests that there might be yet other grounds for debating the AI question, such as "Humans are artistic; computers are plodding" (aesthetic aspect).

5-6.4 *Benefits of a Dooyeweerdian Approach to the AI Question*

Thus Dooyeweerd enables us to address the AI question, "Computer = Human?", not by discussing only "computer" and "human", but by discussing "=". We find it different for each aspect.

How might this benefit us? Each aspect opens up a different area for debate about whether computers might be equal to or surpass human beings. Reference to aspects can bring clarity to debates by separating out what is meaningful in each, so that we no longer "talk past each other" (Colburn 2000) nor need to score points. Dooyeweerd's law-subject-object idea lets us understand the computer in relation to users and developers without obscuring its own kind of reality; this leads us into Chapters 6, 7 and 9. Since each aspect contains innate normativity, Dooyeweerdian thought might underpin the current move to discuss ethical issues of AI, in a way more fundamental than mere 'bolting on' and which includes types of normativity beyond what is usually considered 'ethical'.

The possibility that computers might surpass us need not threaten human life, aspirations, responsibility, nor our mandate to open up the potential of the aspects (§8-6.1.1). Equaling or surpassing humans may be discussed with reference to specific aspects, for example the analytic and formative aspects are important in chess, which computers can do, but the aesthetic aspect is important in genuine artistry, which computers cannot. This can move debates about artificial intelligence closer to the everyday experience of users, developers and researchers.

Of course, this does not address the challenge of consciousness, only behaviour. To do so would involve understanding the 'self', which Dooyeweerd believed to be impossible in principle. That discussion is left for another time.

5-7 Testing Dooyeweerd's Philosophy?

Dennett (1998) suggested that artificial intelligence can provide new ways to test philosophy in general. The idea of program as virtual law-side, coupled with this Dooyeweerdian approach to the artificial intelligence question, could be used in testing Dooyeweerd's aspects, and perhaps even Dooyeweerd's whole notion of law- and subject-object-sides.

What I envisage is research that constructs programs with different virtual law-sides and see how they function over the long term. Alternatively, we might survey, examine and explore a wide variety of existing programs, especially perhaps computer games. In doing so, it should be remembered that programs are always run not only as EMC but as ELI (see Chapter 6), which might itself influence the results.

If it is objected that programs consist of statements and that these can never fully express meaning, we must remember that use adds meaningfulness from tacit or shared background knowledge (§5-3.5).

Interestingly from a philosophical point of view, Newell (1982) seems to have done what Dooyeweerd suggested had never been done from within an Immanence Standpoint (§3-2.1): he analysed the structure of a thing, the computer, from the point of view of naïve experience. What Newell arrived with, only five years after Dooyeweerd's death, is very similar to the Dooyeweerdian, multi-aspectual understanding of things. Systems thinkers like Checkland did similarly with information. Indeed this author owes a large debt to Newell and Checkland, because during the 1980s they both attuned him to Dooyeweerd's aspects when he first met them a decade later.

In view of the very easy way in which Dooyeweerd's philosophy accounts for these things (nature of artefact, information, documents, computers), I am surprised that philosophers of technology have such trouble with them.

5-8 Conclusion

This chapter has introduced a new approach to answering the question, "What is?" as it has been applied to technology, information, documents, computers and programs—various manifestations of ICT. Drawing on Dooyeweerd's idea that the being of something is constituted in its meaningfulness, and that this is multi-aspectual, this approach provides a view of these things that is multi-level. Information is data is knowledge, and the three cannot be separated from each other, except perhaps conceptually as distinct aspects of the one thing. Dooyeweerd's non-Cartesian idea of the subject-object relationship has opened up a way to bring together originator, recipient and information-as-object, while conventional discourses tend to consider one or the other. A new way of addressing the artificial intelligence question has been outlined, which might turn fruitless conflicts into fruitful discourse.

Affirmation. Dooyeweerdian philosophy has allowed us to affirm the relevance and validity of the various philosophical problems that have been raised. Those of the relationship between information, data and knowledge, and the various levels of the computer, have been seen as the perspectives from different aspects. The validity of the artificial intelligence question has been affirmed by reference to meaningfulness, but it has also been severely criticised.

Critique. The ways the artificial intelligence question has been addressed has been criticised for presupposing each of the three dualistic ground-motives identified by Dooyeweerd as leading theoretical thought into blind alleys (see §3-2). Theories of information have been criticised for focusing on too few aspects. The debate around data, information and knowledge has been criticised for presupposing a substance framework or the subject-object-conflating approach of Heidegger.

Enrichment. The multi-level nature of information, documents and computers has been recognised. Not only can this bring clarity to various discourses, and locate competing ideas within a wider picture, but it can also suggest other aspects that might play a role. Dooyeweerd's notion of law-subject-object relationships in all aspects has engendered an outline of a theory of what information is, which includes both the human beings and the information object without ignoring either of them.

Seldom does a new way of approaching the artificial intelligence question arise. Yet this is exactly what a Dooyeweerdian approach makes possible, by directing our gaze away from polar oppositions, towards multi-aspectual meaningfulness. It is an approach that can address more specific issues and escape the confines of ideological conflicts.

This approach has also enriched the whole area by drawing attention to two questions that have seldom been discussed. Two possible kinds of rich answer have been suggested to "What is a program?": as performance art, and as virtual law-side for a virtual world. "What are the innards of a computer?" has been answered by reference to Dooyeweerd's idea that everyday experience is not restricted to the psychic aspect but may include the realities of aspectual functionings that are not mediated directly via psychical functioning of the senses.

Thus the nature of ICT is revealed as a rich phenomenon that can be understood by Dooyeweerd as both in the light of human functioning and yet also as irreducible to human functioning and exhibiting its own separate existence. This understanding is commensurable with everyday experience yet is not itself a full everyday approach. The everyday Being of these things cannot be truly understood without their meaningful functioning in the world—their use and development. So the next four chapters will discuss that, and they in turn will make reference back to this ontological understanding.

References

Alavi M, Leidner DE. 2001. Review: Knowledge management and knowledge management systems: Conceptual foundations and research issues. *MIS Quarterly*, 25(1), 107–136.

Barlow JP. 1996. A Declaration of the Independence of Cyberspace. Accessed "http://homes.eff.org/~barlow/Declaration-Final.html" 16 March 2005.

Basden A. 2008. *Philosophical Frameworks for Understanding Information Systems.* IGI Global, Hershey, PA.

Basden A. 2017. Suggestions for future sustainability: Philosophical and practical. In P Lombardi, G Shen, P Brandon (Eds.), *Future Challenges for Sustainable Development Within the Built Environment* (pp. 319–343). John Wiley & Sons, Chichester, UK.

Boden, MA. 1990. Escaping from the Chinese room. In MA Boden (Ed.), *The Philosophy of Artificial Intelligence* (pp. 89–104). Oxford University Press, UK.

Burke M, Basden A. 2004. Towards a philosophical understanding of documentation: A Dooyeweerdian framework. *Journal of Documentation*, 60(4), 352–370.

Checkland P, Holwell S. 1998. *Information, Systems and Information Systems: Making Sense of the Field.* John Wiley & Sons, Chichester, UK.

Clouser R. 2005. *The Myth of Religious Neutrality: An Essay on the Hidden Role of Religious Belief in Theories.* University of Notre Dame Press, Notre Dame, IN.

Colburn TR. 2000. *Philosophy and Computer Science.* M.E. Sharpe, Armonk, NY.

Davenport TH, Patil DJ. 2012. Data scientists: The sexiest job of the 21st century. *Harvard Business* Review, 90(10), 70–76.

DeMauro A, Greco M, Grimaldi M. 2014. What is Big Data? A consensual definition and a review of key research topics. *Proceeding of International Conference on Integrated Information*, 97–104. AIP Publishing LLC, Melville, NY, USA.

Dennett DC. 1998. *The Intentional Stance.* Bradford Books/MIT Press, Cambridge, MA.

Dollar CM. 2000. *Authentic Electronic Records: Strategies for Long-Term Access.* Cohasset, Chicago.

Dooyeweerd H. 1955. *A New Critique of Theoretical Thought* Vols. I–IV. Paideia Press, Jordan Station, Ontario, Canada. (Original work published 1953–1958)

Dooyeweerd H. 1979. *Roots of Western Culture: Pagan, Secular and Christian Options.* Wedge Publishing Company, Toronto, Ontario, Canada.

Downey SA. 2012. How to Delete Things From the Internet: A Guide to Doing the Impossible. Accessed "https://www.abine.com/blog/2012/how-to-delete-things-from-the-internet/" 13 May 2016.

Dreyfus HJ, Spinosa C. 1997. Highway bridges and feasts: Heidegger and Borgmann on how to affirm technology. *Man and World*, 30, 159–177.

Fisher KE, Erdelez S, McKechnie L. 2005. *Theories of Information Behavior.* Information Today, Medford, NJ, USA.

Floridi L. 2004. Open problems in the philosophy of information. Metaphilosophy, 35(4), 554–582.

Gadamer H-G. 1966. The Universality of the Hermeneutical Problem. Chapter 1 in DE Linge (Ed.), *Philosophical Hermeneutics.* University of California Press, Berkeley, CA, USA. P. 3-17.

Gadamer H-G. 1967. On the scope and function of hermeneutical reflection. Chapter 2 in DE Linge (Ed.), *Philosophical Hermeneutics.* University of California Press, Berkeley, CA.

Haraway D. 1991. *Simians, Cyborgs and Women.* Routledge, New York.

Heidegger M. 1971. *Poetry, Language and Thought*, tr. A Hofstadter. HarperCollins, New York.

Heidegger M. 1978. *The Question Concerning Technology and Other Essays.* HarperCollins, New York.

Hilbert D. 1900. Mathematical problems. *Bulletin of the American Mathematical Society*, 8(1902), 437–479. Translated from the German original.

Introna LD, Ilharco FM. 2004. Phenomenology, screens and the world: A journey with Husserl and Heidegger Into phenomenology. In J Mingers, L Willcocks (Eds.), *Social Theory and Philosophy for Information Systems* (pp. 56–102). John Wiley & Sons, Chichester, UK.

Jennings NR. 2000. On agent-based software engineering. *Artificial Intelligence*, 117, 277–296.

Joneidy S. 2015. *Making Sense of the Information Systems Use Field*. PhD Thesis, University of Salford, Salford, UK.

Kapp E. 1877/1978. *Grundlinien einer Philosophie der Technik Zur Entstehungsgeschichte der Cultur aus neuen Gesichtspunkten*. Braunschweig, Chicago, USA.

Kroes P, Meijers A. 2006. The dual nature of technical artifacts. Special issue of *Studies in History and Philosophy of Science*, 37, 1–158.

Langefors B. 1966. *Theoretical Analysis of Information Systems*. Studentlitteratur, Lund, Sweden.

Latour B. 1987. *Science in Action*. Harvard University Press, Cambridge, MA.

Lee AS. 2004. Thinking about social theory and philosophy in information systems. In J Mingers, LP Willcocks (Eds.), *Social Theory and Philosophy for Information Systems* (pp. 1–26). John Wiley & Sons, Chichester, UK.

Mayer-Schönberger V, Cukier K. 2013. *Big Data: A Revolution That Will Transform How We Live, Work and Think*. John Murray, London, UK.

Milewski AE. 1997. Delegating to software agents. *International Journal of Human-Computer Studies*, 46, 485–500.

Mitcham C. 1994. *Thinking Through Technology: The Path Between Engineering and Philosophy*. The University of Chicago Press, Chicago, IL.

Newell A. 1982. The knowledge level. *Artificial Intelligence*, 18, 87–127.

Newell A. 1993. Reflections on the knowledge level. *Artificial Intelligence*, 59, 31–38.

Polanyi M. 1967. *The Tacit Dimension*. Routledge and Kegan Paul, London, UK.

Ricoeur P. 1981. *Hermeneutics & the Human Sciences*, tr. JB Thompson. Cambridge University Press, Cambridge, UK.

Searle JR. 1990. Minds, brains and programs. In MA Boden (Ed.), *The Philosophy of Artificial Intelligence* (pp. 67–88). Oxford University Press, Oxford, UK.

Shannon CE. 1948. A mathematical theory of communication. *Bell System Technical Journal*, 27(3,4), 379–423, 623–666.

Stanford. 2013. Philosophy of technology. In *Stanford Encyclopedia of Philosophy*. Accessed "http://plato.stanford.edu/entries/technology/#MetIssStaChaArt" 28 April 2015.

Suchman L. 1994. Do categories have politics? The language/action perspective reconsidered. *Computer Supported Cooperative Work*, 2(3), 177–190.

Tuomi I. 1999. Data is more than knowledge: Implications of the reversed hierarchy for knowledge management and organizational memory. *Journal of Management Information Systems*, 16(3), 103-117.

Verkerk MJ, Hoogland J, van der Stoep J, de Vries MJ. 2015. *Philosophy of Technology: An Introduction for Technology and Business Students*. Routledge, London, UK.

Wiener N. 1948. *Cybernetics: Or Control and Communication in the Animal and the Machine*. MIT Press, Cambridge, MA.

Winograd T, Flores F. 1986. *Understanding Computers and Cognition: A New Foundation for Design*. Addison-Wesley, Reading, MA.

6 Understanding ICT Use

This chapter lays a foundation for understanding use of information systems or ICT, especially as it occurs in the everyday experience of life or work. The foundation is laid in Dooyeweerd's philosophy as outlined in Chapter 3, and takes the form of a conceptual framework with which extant discourses about ICT use may be affirmed, critiqued and enriched.

The conceptual framework is depicted in Figure 6.1, where the user of ICT—whether old-style desktop or mobile device or anything else—is on the left, and 'everyday life' is shown on the right.

The conceptual framework recognises two main things. (a) In ICT use, the user (on left) engages with three things, with the technical artefact, with meaningful content and with life. The three engagements are shown by arrows, with acronyms EIT, EMC and ELI (Engaging: with Interface and Technology, with Meaningful Content and in Life with ICT) described in Section 6-3, where the framework is introduced. (b) ICT use is highly diverse, which may be tackled by employing Dooyeweerd's aspects, shown by the small sets of lines at each arrow. We might call it an '*aspectual engagements framework*'.

Figure 6.1 Three Multi-aspectual Engagements that Constitute ICT Use

6-1 Introduction

The conceptual framework developed in this chapter has two main elements that set it apart from others, in being able to study ICT use from an holistic, everyday perspective while being philosophically sound, and being able to engage with a wide range of discourses in the IS use field.

This, it is hoped, will enable us to understand the everyday experience of ICT use. 'Everyday' does not refer to particular domains of use but rather to the 'real life' of ICT use wherever it is and for whatever purpose. Even the most structured professional use has an everyday reality that impinges on it and determines how beneficial it is. A wide variety of kinds of application will be expected, in both work and wider living, across mobile, desktop and systemic use, including such technology as public information screens. Some are personal uses, some social and some organizational.

Many discourses have arisen around ICT use, which try to understand, for instance, what ease of use, usefulness and information quality are. In order to understand ICT use in its diversity, we need to understand what is meaningful to as wide a range of them as possible. So, nearly a score of discourses are briefly discussed in Section 6-2, to reveal what issues each finds important and what challenges each must address. They will be discussed without reference to the conceptual framework. It will be found that very few, if any, can do justice to the full diversity and reality of everyday experience of ICT use, and many foundational questions arise that do not seem to have been addressed.

In Section 6-3, we discuss foundations of ICT use, as seen from the everyday perspective, referring to Dooyeweerd's philosophy. The aspectual engagement framework is developed, and then demonstrated by applying it to one everyday problem, computer procrastination.

In Section 6-4, we apply the framework to the discourses outlined in Section 6-2, showing that it can affirm, critique and enrich each one, and suggest new avenues for research. It can also situate all the frameworks in a wider picture. Section 6-5 adds some concluding reflections.

Note on terminology: In this chapter, *IS (information systems)* is largely synonymous with *ICT*. Both involve both *technical artefact*, people and structures.

§6-2 Attempts to Understand ICT Use

Use of ICT has developed and changed over 50 years, with each decade bringing new issues to light, most of which remain salient today. Many discourses arose, in various communities of thought involving researchers and reflective practitioners. This section provides an overview of some main issues each discourse addresses that it finds centrally meaningful and normative.

I have included as many discourses as I have been aware of since I entered the field in the early 1970s, without using Dooyeweerd's ideas in the selection of them. Some were drawn to my attention by Joneidy and Basden (2012) and Breems and Basden (2014), others came from my experience. In the information systems field, some that are tangled together (e.g., acceptance and success) have been separated out because the foundational issues that inform them are different. The order is approximately chronological.

Three of our discourses began during the 1960s and 1970s, when ICT was expensive, isolated (mainframe computers), operated by specialists and used primarily for managerial purposes in large organizations and for intensive scientific calculations. They are still relevant today, though much evolved.

1. Ease of Use and Interactions with Technology
2. Organizational Issues in Information Systems
3. Effect of IT on Work

During the 1980s, the 'micro' or personal computer arrived, giving rise to new uses, and this stimulated a number of discourses:

4. Knowledge-Intensive Organizational Functions
5. ICT in its Wider Environment
6. Home Computing, Computer Games, Computer Music and Art
7. Information and Data Quality

During the 1990s, new perspectives on organizational ICT emerged, and the Internet and the Worldwide Web became important.

8. Acceptance of Technology
9. Information Systems Success
10. What Usefulness and Success Are
11. User, Technology and Task
12. Intensive or Innovative Use of ICT
13. Normativity in ICT Use
14. Non-use of ICT and Resistance

Since then, social media and mobile devices became a primary medium for social interaction. Computing power became widely available, even in developing countries. Most of the above discourses changed to accommodate these changes, and some new ones emerged.

15. Use of Features of ICT and Their Affordance
16. 'Meaningful' Use and Down-to-earth Issues
17. Applications and Everyday Life Domains Overlooked by the IS Field

This is a plethora. It shows how complex ICT use is in reality. Even so, some are missing. Some discourses that might be expected belong in other chapters: the data-information-knowledge relationship, to Chapter 5, societal issues, to Chapter 8, information systems development, to Chapter 9, and most of the discourse on ICT features, to Chapter 7. Some might belong in this chapter but are omitted because they pervade many other discourses (e.g., power relations), some because they are not centrally about ICT use (e.g., ICT strategy and the role of the Chief Information Officer), and some because they centre on a particular technology (e.g., Web 2.0, social media). Each technology can enable many things. Perhaps learning should be incorporated more strongly into the discourse on intensive use. Perhaps what Web 2.0 and social media enable should be included, such as 'democratization' of information so that previously suppressed topics can be aired, and new ways of socializing. Doing so is left to readers.

In the discussion of the discourses, our interest lies in what makes the issues they discuss meaningful, e.g., benefits or possibilities. Space limitations prevent comprehensive reviews of each discourse, and many important authors are neglected, so coverage is sparse and probably one-sided. The aim is to obtain an everyday perspective on what is important in each discourse, rather than a complete understanding of theory.

Readers may skim the discourses, or even skip them, if their main interest is in the foundational framework in §6-3. Readers who are interested in the discourses are invited to add discourses, or discuss the ones here in greater depth, taking them forward in the ways that are demonstrated in this chapter as we listen to them, and then affirm, critique and enrich them using Dooyeweerd's thought.

6-2.1 Discourses on Ease of Use and Interactions with Technology

With the move from centralised computing (mainframes) to interactive computing in the 1970s and personal computing in the 1980s, interest in human-computer interaction (HCI) and ergonomics rose. The focus of ergonomics is largely on hardware and our sensory-motor functioning with it, while that of HCI is largely at the conceptual level of structures and processes of information. These fields make use of findings from the fields of psychology, such as Miller's (1956) study of how many things people can be aware of at any one time. Look and feel is also much studied. Their main norm is ease of use, though this can involve several different levels (e.g., Card et al. 1983).

Various discourses occur within these two, around virtual reality, computer graphics, animation, learning to use computers, accessibility, ease of use and, with the advent of mobile devices, voice input. Interface design is a major discourse, which extends to design methods and into computer science, and is discussed more in Chapters 7 and 9.

Many findings from psychology tend to be rather low level. A higher-level attempt to understand HCI is found in Green and Petre's (1996) idea of *Cognitive Dimensions*, which are principles that contribute to ease of use in all its manifestations within the user's everyday experience of interaction. Example: viscosity refers to the feeling of resistance that some interfaces give the user. Green and Petre treat human-computer interaction as involving a 'notation' or 'language' that carries semantic meaning to/from users, explicitly or tacitly, similar to knowledge representation languages.

The field is often treated as a design science. Seldom has there been an attempt to provide philosophical grounding for HCI or ergonomics. One exception is the classic work of Winograd and Flores (1986), which argues for a picture of proximal human engagement with the technical artefact rather than distal command-and-response, which had characterised earlier work. They sought to understand this by reference to Heidegger's ideas of tools 'at-hand' or 'to-hand'. Their argument was so well-written and persuasive that it changed the mindset in much of the field of HCI and artificial intelligence.

While the discourse on interactions is wide-ranging and mature, it takes little account of the information content as such, which is mediated via the interactions. Issues like information quality, discussed below, are largely ignored, because HCI offers no conceptual framework for understanding it. Issues like realism in virtual reality are usually reduced to the physico-sensory phenomenon of immersiveness of the technology and ignore the quality of the virtual world itself.

While there has been some interest in such detrimental impacts as repetitive strain injury, the discourse on interactions takes very little account of their usefulness in life and work. It fell to the discourse in Management Information Systems to welcome this interest.

6-2.2 *Discourse on Organizational Issues in (Management) Information Systems*

During the 1970s and 1980s, computers were installed to increase productivity in organizations, often by automation to reduce labour costs (1970s) or by enhancing management activity (1980s). The field of Management Information Systems (MIS) was born.

The issues discussed are those that relate to ICT use in the organization and thereby are meaningful to management. They include productivity, cost savings, resource planning, profits, ICT policy and many more. Social media has extended some of these, such as marketing. The organizational context in which these are discussed is primarily business, government and service organizations, with occasional extension to voluntary organizations. Issues that relate to individuals that, in aggregation, impact the organization, like technology acceptance and IS success, could be of interest but are treated as separate discourses below because they raise issues beyond the interest of organizational management.

As cases started emerging during the 1980s where ICT decreased productivity, the Productivity Paradox became a popular theme (Landauer 1996). Vast spending in ICT "failed to yield significant productivity gains" (Pinsonneault and Rivard 1998). Many reasons were advanced to explain the paradox, and models and taxonomies of aspects were proposed to overcome it, e.g., product, process, participation, politics (P4) (Renkema 2000). Pinsonneault and Rivard explained the paradox by invoking the fable of Icarus, whose greatest asset (wings) was also his downfall (flying too close to the sun). Similarly with ICT: hubristic faith in ICT led to unquestioned committal of large spending, without wisdom (§8-2.2.4). In reaction, Carr (2003) argued that "IT doesn't matter", on the grounds that, by then, ICT no longer added competitive advantage because it had become a utility like drains and street lighting.

The main challenge in this discourse is to understand the real value of ICT to the organization and the diversity of kinds of issues that constitute the relationship between them.

These include such issues as mandatory use (versus voluntary [Venkatesh et al. 2003]), ICT infrastructure in the organization, system reliability, ICT strategy, ICT security, etc., especially with increasing use of mobile devices. Many of these are also relevant to non-organizational ICT use, such as e-shopping or e-government. They tend to be what discourse §6-2.16 calls 'high level' rather than 'down-to-earth' issues, and some overlap with those discussed in Chapter 8.

As computing spread to assist other workers, 'Management Information Systems' became just 'Information Systems' (IS). A number of other discourses arose that are outlined in the following sections, each finding different core issues meaningful. While many of the discourses below are of interest to organizations, they are also important in other 'life domains' (§6-2.17)—yet has the organizational origins of the field of Information Systems limited those discourses by instilling an unfortunate presupposition of organizational use? There are also discourses that have been rather neglected in the IS field until recently, but which should be included in any discourse on ICT use.

6-2.3 Discourse on the Effect of IT on Work and the Socio-Technical Approach

The discourse above is from the perspective of management; a parallel discourse developed from the perspective of the workforce. The effect of technology on work became a topic of interest during the 1960s. The discourse has a strong normative thrust.

Because of Marxist or socialist influences, some of the discourse, especially the 'Scandinavian approach', is about workers' rights and conditions of work in relation to ICT. Some of it is about possibilities for work. "Automation, new sources of energy and the growing use of the electronic calculating machine," wrote The British Labour Party in 1964 (Labour 1964), "are beginning to transform almost all branches of our economic and social life. As these trends develop, the importance of leisure will steadily increase." A more recent concern is about gender and ICT (Adam et al. 2004).

A more balanced 'socio-technical approach', originating in the 1950s, was applied to the field of Information Systems (IS) by Enid Mumford in a set of principles, under the acronym ETHICS (Mumford and Weir 1979), followed by published case studies of its use and subsequent refinement (Mumford 2006). Mumford's socio-technical approach focuses its interest on issues like job satisfaction when working with technology.

The notion of socio-technical struck a chord that extends beyond concerns about work conditions, especially to inform design approaches (see §9-2.5). However, it has become rather vague in its meaning. Many of the other discourses mentioned here claim to adopt a socio-technical orientation, but what is meant by this often seems to mean little more than recognising, as Wikipedia ('Sociotechnical Systems' accessed 7 February 2015) puts it, "the interaction between people and technology in workplaces" with "theory regarding the social aspects of people and society and technical aspects of organizational structure and processes." Some view socio-technical issues in terms of power (e.g., Markus 1983).

There seems to have been little critique of the socio-technical approach. As a motivation to recognise both people and technology, the approach is useful, and it shares with the issue of affordance a philosophical challenge with the Cartesian subject-object relationship; see §6-2.15 below. However, Mumford's ETHICS proposal declined for a variety of reasons, many of them to do with vision and belief and reluctance to change (Elbanna and Newman 2013). It has also tended to be influenced by seeing 'socio' and 'technical' as opposing poles of a dualism that must somehow be brought together.

One important exception is Lee (2004), who refuses to see socio-technical as a dualism, arguing that something is missing in it: "information itself is a rich phenomenon that deserves its own separate focus no less than either information technology or organizations" (p. 13). Where can we locate this "rich phenomenon"? Lee points hopefully in the direction of hermeneutics and systems theory, but only vaguely. A more precise suggestion is offered in §6-4.3.

A concern over the relationship between ICT and workforce would suggest an interest in what, in §6-2.16, are called down-to-earth issues. In practice, however, it has stayed largely at the abstract level of issues like rights, leisure and job satisfaction. Even at this level, the discourse has adopted, unconsciously, the perspective of workforces in the Affluent North rather than the Global South.

6-2.4 *Discourse on Knowledge-Intensive Organizational Functions*

During the 1970s, from work in Artificial Intelligence came Expert Systems (Knowledge-Based Systems). These were computer programs in which human knowledge was encapsulated, which then supposedly allowed the computer to undertake expert human tasks. Example: *MYCIN* (Shortliffe 1976) held expert knowledge of bacterial infections and proved more accurate in diagnosis than most physicians were. MYCIN never came into use, however. From what I was told by those involved at the time, though MYCIN could provide more accurate diagnoses, the main challenge was to decide what to do, and the physicians' accuracy was sufficient. The main issue was usefulness, not perfect accuracy, of the knowledge.

During the 1980s, as business in the Western world moved away from manufacturing towards services, knowledge-based technology was increasingly applied to supporting decision-making (Decision Support Systems). In Knowledge Management, which arose from a belief that an organization's knowledge is an asset that gives competitive advantage, organizational knowledge is held in data stores, documents, and also the minds of employees. Knowledge sharing is thus crucial. Knowledge is often tacit, either to the individual (Polanyi 1967) or to the organization as a whole (Baumard 1999), and Nonaka and Takeuchi (1995) devised the SECI model of how tacit knowledge is shared. Polanyi's and Nonaka-Takeuchi's views are dominant, which has reduced incentive to more deeply understand tacit knowledge, so there is confusion about the nature and possibility of explication of tacit knowledge.

ICT might facilitate some knowledge management. Eliciting knowledge to encapsulate in ICT for either expert systems or knowledge management proves challenging, partly because of tacit knowledge and partly because information can never fully express the entire meaningfulness of knowledge. Example: The supposedly precise fact, annual profits figure, might have been massaged (see §5-3.6). Information incorporates assumptions and pragmatic meanings.

Data Warehousing tries to address this, but it depends on selection of what data it is meaningful to store. Wixom and Watson (2001) empirically investigated data warehousing success, but the only factors they chose to investigate were about implementation, and their concept of data quality was too abstract and did not include such hidden assumptions. Their discussion exemplifies a more generic problem discussed in §6-2.16.

Big data tries to circumvent having to make difficult judgements about assumptions behind information sources, by looking for patterns. It cannot, however, escape from the arbitrariness of choosing what to look for and how to process it, nor the inconsistency between assumptions behind different sources; see §5-3.8.

The discourse on knowledge management (KM) has grown wide, covering kinds of KM (Earl 2001), processes (Alavi and Leidner 2001), 'tiers' (data-information-knowledge; see §5-3.2) (Hicks et al. 2006) and structural elements (Maier and Hädrich 2006). How may we integrate and understand all these views? The socio-technical approach, suggested by, e.g., Sajeva (2010), tends to dualistic over-simplification. Section 6-4.4 examines some of them in more detail.

What seems to be important in these discourses is engagement with the content of knowledge, so understanding the nature of knowledge, its quality and its usefulness become important. It is important, for an everyday perspective, to recognise that knowledge management, presumed to be confined to large commercial corporations, in fact can be operated by tiny non-commercial organizations, like Uganda Development Services, the founding vision of which was to enable small, especially indigenous, development organizations to share their knowledge.

6-2.5 Discourse on ICT in Its Wider Environment

To understand the relationships ICT use has with its wider environment requires discourse about structures. Two conceptual frameworks are considered: Systems Thinking and Actor Network Theory.

Systems thinking treats ICT-with-its-users as a system within an environment, with which it interacts. The environment is usually the organization. Systems thinking is based on a biological metaphor of part-whole hierarchy (cells, organs, organisms, environment). This basic idea has been extended by many: Viable Systems Model (Beer 1984), Soft Systems Thinking about human activity systems (Checkland 1981), Critical Systems Heuristics about the 'uninvolved affecteds' (Ulrich 1983), Critical Systems Thinking about systemic constraints (Jackson 1991), holistic Systemic Intervention (Midgley 2000), disclosure of appropriate norms (Disclosive systems thinking) (Strijbos 2000) and others. Systems thinking often takes a societal perspective, discussed in Chapter 8.

Systems thinking has, however, been criticised for not adequately handling complexity and innovation (Stacey et al. 2000). Apart from Disclosive Systems Thinking, which treats norms as to-be-discovered, and Critical Systems Thinking, which elevates one norm, emancipation, most versions lack inherent normative thrust, so normativity must be 'bolted on'. Systems thinking also gives little help in addressing diversity, so much can be neglected. Part of the root of the problem is the biological metaphor on which systems thinking is grounded (Habermas 1987).

Actor-Network Theory (ANT) (Latour 1987) has a significant following. Instead of seeing the information system as an entity within an environment, ANT sees ICT as an actor within a network of actors. Networks might be organizations or communities of practice. ANT treats ICT artefacts as 'actants' of equal status with human beings, recognising that ICT sometimes seems to take its own actions and have its own impact (the doctrine of technology-human symmetry). However, it is in danger of suppressing the fact, encountered in everyday experience, that computers are not the same as humans even though they act.

As with systems thinking, Actor Network Theory has trouble with normativity and offers no foundation to understand diversity of kinds of actant, activity or relationship that we encounter in everyday experience.

6-2.6 *Lack of Discourse on Home Computing, Computer Games and Computer Music and Art*

As 'micro computers' became cheaply available during the 1980s, home computing (e.g., amateur programming) and computer games, music and art emerged and gained momentum. The academic IS community, however, showed little interest and largely overlooked these applications until recently.

Many such applications are *hedonic* rather than utilitarian in their meaningfulness, but it was not until 20 years had passed by that hedonic use began to be discussed (van der Heijden 2004; Lin and Bhattarcharjee 2010). Venkatesh and Brown (2001) did recognise hedonic alongside utilitarian and social uses (they ignored amateur programming) but were interested only in broad brush categories of adoption and use, and not in understanding home/amateur use as such. Most papers on computer games or home computing take an outsider's, theoretical view from perspectives of psychology, sociology or dysfunctional use (see §6-2.13 below), rather than understanding them immanently. Example: Verenikina et al. (2003) reviewed psychological theories on the effect of computer games on children's playing and cognitive development, but did not discuss gaming as such.

Computer gaming is usually treated as a means to an end, like helping children learn. Liu et al. (2013) is one of the few articles that discusses games in the premier information systems journal, yet even they restrict their discussion to 'serious games' as used for business purposes like motivation or marketing.

To this day, there is little direct interest, within the field of information systems, in computer gaming or amateur computing as topics to be understood in their own terms. Hsu and Lu (2004) argue that standard constructs like usefulness and ease of use do not apply.

Paradoxically, lack of theory, instead of slowing home computing and games development in the 1980s, allowed new ideas and innovative applications (some of which belatedly attracted commercial and academic interest). As a result, confusions occur. For example, Rambusch and Susi (2008) conflate the activity of the avatar (the player in the game's world) with the activity of the user in hitting arrow keys; they need a theoretical basis on which to differentiate them.

Theoretical understanding of games, music and other amateur computing needs to be developed immanently, i.e., 'from the inside'. Virtual world developer Richard Bartle (2004) has attempted an immanent theory of virtual worlds, but this has not been noticed within the IS field—and it has its own limitations, as discussed in Chapter 9.

6-2.7 Discourse on Information and Data Quality

Good decisions depend on good quality information. With volumes of data coming across the Internet during the 1990s, concern about data quality or information quality grew. Information quality is often characterised by a few dimensions, such as accuracy, reliability and completeness (Lin 2010).

Wang and Strong (1996), whose study has served as a reference point for this discourse, reviewed the criteria believed to constitute data quality. The 179 criteria they collected were reduced to 20 in a second survey. Feeling that 20 was impractically many, they grouped them into four categories. Those categories were initially based on a metaphor of data as manufactured product and data-user as consumer, eventually relabelled to reflect better the issues attached to them. Five of the 20 criteria were eliminated as not clearly fitting into these categories, which suggests that researcher preconceptions are not altogether absent from their findings. It is to Wang and Strong's credit that they so transparently describe their method of analysis, but their presupposition of manufacturing metaphor for data might be problematic. The source of their 179 criteria is limited to business people and university MBA students. Their grouping is problematic, in that several criteria could be in several groups. Section §6-4.7 discusses the criteria.

Wang and Strong sought criteria; the notions of information fulfilment (Burke 2006) and information satisfaction (Ives et al. 1983; Ang and Soh 1997) located information quality more in the needs of the user, implying a norm of involving users in development (c.f. §9-5.1), but they do not provide such a usable set of criteria.

The discourse around information quality is usually restricted to the organizational work context and seldom extends to other areas like computer games or geographic information systems. It is somewhat isolated from other IS discourses.

6-2.8 Discourse on the Acceptance of Technology

As personal computers became widespread, decisions on their adoption became influenced more directly by the perceptions of individuals who use them. Davis' (1989) famous Technology Acceptance Model (TAM) says that acceptance of technology depends on perceived ease of use and perceived usefulness. By introducing a parsimonious model of acceptance, which was apparently well-tested, TAM struck a chord, becoming a reference point for much subsequent work.

Criticisms stimulated modifications and alternatives. For example TAM2 (Venkatesh and Davis 2000) recognises mandatory as well as voluntary use, while TAM3 (Venkatesh and Bala 2008) makes ease of use more precise. Venkatesh et al. (2003) discovered rather poor predictability in TAM and other models and constructed the UTAUT model, which adds factors like age, gender and experience. The emphasis in all these lies in being able to predict acceptance of ICT, by measuring perceived ease of use and usefulness.

What comprises usefulness and ease of use, however, Davis did not specify, but suggested that they be interpreted as tangible 'external variables', according to the situation and preferences of the analyst, to be posed as questions in surveys, such as 'Work more quickly' and 'Job performance' (Davis 1989). Subsequent models incorporated some external variables explicitly. Yousafzai et al. (2007) found over 80 external variables in subsequent studies (listed in §6-4.10). Having to choose external variables undermines the apparent ease of using TAM, and the possibility of using inappropriate variables undermines the validity of TAM studies (e.g., standard ideas do not apply in computer games (Hsu and Lu 2004)). Moreover, the measures of *perceived* usefulness or ease of use do not capture the full engagement of users with ICT in its tacit dimensions (Polanyi 1967) but privileges that which can be expressed in surveys. The TAM family of models is no longer parsimonious!

6-2.9 Discourse on Information Systems Success

The discourse on IS success is closely associated with that on acceptance, both seeking quantitative measures. Whereas discourse on acceptance measures subjective perceptions, that on success must consider factors that influence success without being perceived.

Delone and McLean (1992) proposed an Information Systems Success Model (ISSM) with which the potential for success could be measured. This was criticised for combining process and causal relationships (Seddon 1997) and Delone and McLean (2003) updated their model. Six factors constitute IS success, which affect each other in a circular fashion—system quality, information quality, service quality, intention to use, user satisfaction and net benefits. Thus, the theory.

But consider the following:

> Olive Cook was a charity worker in the UK, who took her own life in 2015. She liked to give to charity whenever asked, but had become bombarded with requests for donations, and this overwhelmed her. Computer-controlled mailing systems adopted by charities would not only repeatedly solicit donations from those who showed any willingness, but the amounts solicited would be 'tailored' to what the person had previously given, each time suggesting an increased amount. Since news of this case broke, trust in charities and tendency to donate to them has reduced.

Were the mailing systems a success or failure? How can we tell?
As with TAM, the constructs are broad and must be operationalised by similar kinds of external variables. Example: in Delone and McLean's (2004) study of e-commerce success, 'system quality' involves: usability, availability, reliability, adaptability, response time. But why were, for example, trustworthiness or enjoyment not included? As TAM, so ISSM offers no grounds for selecting meaningful variables.

What is 'net benefit'? The next discourse addresses this.

6-2.10 *Discourse on What Usefulness and Net Benefit Are*

There was a second reason why Davis' (1989) TAM struck a chord. Since the 1970s, ease of use had been extensively studied, but as computers became more widely used in the 1980s, and people were affected by this use, beneficially or detrimentally, several authors began to discuss usefulness in various guises, including 'performance' (Robey 1979), 'role' (Basden 1983), 'user information satisfaction' (Barki and Huff 1985) and 'value' (Swanson 1987). It was Davis (1989) who clearly placed usefulness alongside ease of use, followed by Delone and McLean's (1992; 2003) net benefit alongside system quality.

But what constitutes usefulness or net benefit? I treat them as similar, and want, not definitions like "enhance . . . job performance" (Davis 1989, 320), but to understand what constitutes them.

Before these models can be used, the intuitive nature of usefulness and net benefit must be conceptualised as variables expressed as questions for surveys. Paradoxically, supposedly rigorous research has, at its heart, the analyst's interpretation of what variables mean (see §3-4.3). What is problematic is that this has seldom been recognised as problematic; the choice of variables is seldom examined critically.

One exception is Yousafzai et al. (2007), who collected over 80 external variables that researchers had used to measure perceptions of usefulness and ease of use, 70 of them influencing usefulness and 64 of them, ease of use. They grouped the variables as: Organizational characteristics (17), System characteristics (29), Personal characteristics (25), Other (12). The three categories are too abstract, however, to provide much insight into the nature of usefulness or ease of use, and it is disappointing that there is so much in the 'Other' category. The full list is analysed in Section 6-4.10.

We need a foundation for understanding what usefulness and net benefit are, and how they relate to such variables.

6-2.11 *Discourse on User, Artefact and Task*

As experience of ICT use became richer during the 1990s, ICT artefacts increasingly did not quite fit the tasks their users wanted to perform.

Goodhue and Thompson (1995) developed a model of *Task-Technology Fit (TTF)*, which enables calculations of fit from eight factors. It was modified for group tasks by Zigurs and Buckland (1998).

Instead of identifying constructs, Burton-Jones and Straub (2006) discussed the ontological structure of the ICT usage situation. TTF is concerned with task and technology, and TAM is primarily concerned with the user's perceptions; Burton-Jones and Straub argue the need to take all three into account—user, system and task. They argued that much previous work was partial manifestations of this triad. Because of its intuitive appropriateness and generality, their triad is increasingly becoming a reference point for work since then.

What might be missing from user-system-task, however, is information. Neither Task-Technology-Fit nor User-System-Task provide a basis for understanding the dynamics of how a task occurs with the artefact, nor how 'fit' emerges.

6-2.12 Discourse on Intensive or Innovative Use of ICT

Learning to use ICT is a topic of interest to the HCI community, and during the 1980s, there was a significant discourse on how people learn to interact with technological features, much of it drawing on the field of psychology. That is only part of the story.

Learning goes through stages of initiation, adoption, adaptation, acceptance (routinization) to infusion, where ICT is used to its fullest potential to enhance organization effectiveness (Cooper and Zmud 1990). Others have developed similar ideas (McLean et al. 2011; Bagayogo et al. 2014; Jain and Kanungo 2005). Most of the discourse is around organizational use, but Fadel (2006) and Tennant et al. (2011) apply the idea of infusion to individuals. But what actually is infusion? What makes each of the stages important?

Users find new tasks and versions of task—"using more features to accomplish a more comprehensive set of work tasks" (Fadel 2006, 279). Innovative use, whereby features are used in ways not expected by their designers, has been celebrated as an expression of freedom of users from technological or organizational constraints. Singletary et al. (2002) Linked innovative use to perceived usefulness and ease of use, echoing the structure of Davis' (1989) TAM, but this merely quantifies it and provides little extra understanding.

6-2.13 Discourses on ICT Ethics and Normativity

Most of the above discourses are about things or processes; there are also important discourses on normativity (good and evil) in IS use (e.g., 'ICT ethics'). Several are considered here, some of which are loosely linked: dysfunctional use, technology ethics, and emancipation.

Dysfunctional Use of ICT

Use of the Internet has exacerbated problems like addiction, fraud and bullying, or "cyberloafing" (Lim 2002). Some studies focus on causes, some on impact and some on ways to prevent dysfunction (Breems and Basden 2014). This discourse has a negative focus on dysfunction and pathology (Young and de Abreu 2011), and is often viewed from the perspective of psychology, yet it is multidimensional (Caplan et al. 2009).

Consider the following vignette:

> Paul was prosecuted with many pornographic pictures of underage girls on his computer. Paul was an ordinary family man, but began to look at a few legal pornographic pictures. After a time, popups appeared which tempted him with 'barely legal pictures', of girls aged 15–17. Curious, he looked. Later, he was tempted with 14 year-olds, then 13, then 12, and gradually was looking at pornographic pictures of even younger girls. In the interview Paul seemed genuinely remorseful for what he had done.
>
> (Forethought 2015)

Where should the dysfunction (evil) be located—in Paul, in software design, in graduality of temptation, in society—and on what basis? Only by asking that can we understand what to do.

Technology Ethics

Discourses on ethics of technology discuss the positive as well as negative. To bio-ethics, cloning, nuclear weapons, etc., has now been added ICT issues like privacy and security. Often the discourse merges with that of the philosophy of technology, but it then loses its orientation to ICT (§5-2.5). Of the three main philosophical theories of ethics, consequentialist ethics can consider outcomes of ICT use, deontological ethics, the norms that govern use, and virtue ethics, the user. Mingers and Walsham (2010) claim that little of this discourse is found in the field of information systems and attempt to introduce it, but argue that these three kinds of ethics are insufficient. Because of the importance of information, they advocate Habermasian discourse ethics, which requires discussion among all those affected (as wide a set of stakeholders as possible) to define ethical rightness. This recognises that, in the real world, many kinds of issues emerge and it specifies, not ethicality as such, but methods for agreeing it in practical situations. That, however, makes ethics dependent on method; on what basis may we believe that the outcome is not wholly prejudiced by the methods used or the presuppositions underlying them? How does discourse ethics avoid Groupthink?

Emancipation

Socio-critical approaches are founded on the norm of *emancipation*. ICT can either impose unwarranted constraints or emancipate us therefrom (Walsham 2001; Walsham and Sahay 1999). Emancipation is often associated with, and seen in terms of, *power relations*. However, when one norm is emphasised, it can become a lens that distorts instead of enlightening.

Example, from Basden (2008, 159–165): Walsham (2001), in an otherwise excellent discussion, interprets an engineer's use of their computer system as a way of "leveraging power over" (p. 91) his company, whereas in fact the text shows him motivated by its very opposite: generously going beyond the call of duty. Though power is present in all situations, power-oriented discourse can miss the good and beauty in everyday experience.

Seldom do these discourses on normativity interact with each other; we need a philosophical foundation that encourages them to. There are other normative issues, often overlapping with societal issues (Chapter 8).

Example: Bridge-players decided, after playing over the Internet, to fly across the world for a 'real' game. The climate change emissions from three such return flights to one meeting, totalling over 30,000 air miles, exceed those from three people driving to play bridge locally every week for 10 years. ICT use contributed to climate change indirectly. (Basden 2008)

Seidel et al. (2013) is the only paper I have encountered that recognises that ICT can change climate-irresponsible behaviour of individuals. Even that one is concerned mainly with how organizational ICT infrastructure might change individual behaviour, rather than tackling the issue of responsibility directly.

Normativity imparts responsibility, which overlaps with ICT development (Chapter 9). While responsibility of ICT use towards fellow human beings is widely discussed, our responsibility for animals, biodiversity and planet is not (see §8-2.1). Why not? On what basis may we consider human and non-human together?

6-2.14 Discourses on Non-use of ICT and Resistance

Most discourses above assume that ICT use is, or should be, inherently beneficial (c.f. 'life without ICT', §8-2.2.1). In some situations, non-use of ICT might be appropriate.

Resistance to ICT use has attracted interest in the socio-critical research community (below), which celebrates it as an expression of power relations (Markus 1983). Alternatively resistance is seen as something to overcome (e.g., Jiang et al. 2000). Lapointe and Rivard (2005) review the literature on resistance to gain a broader perspective on what needs to be taken into account when understanding resistance, such as triggers and interaction. They conclude that resistance is under-researched, with many antecedents that cannot be reduced to the mental.

Resistance is not the only kind of non-use. Selwyn (2003) reviews explanations of non-use (including economic, psychological, phobic, ideological and diffusional) and suggests that we need to cease seeing non-use pejoratively as an aberration, extend beyond mono-causal explanations and recognise both individual and collective issues. People might alternate between use and non-use. He emphasises meaningfulness especially in everyday life, where people 'read' ICTs from several perspectives, within which use or non-use may be seen as equally normal.

6-2.15 Discourse on Use of Features of ICT and Their Affordance

As discussed in Chapter 7, ICT features, such as the photosphere facility in *Google Earth*, affect what users do and cannot do as they use ICT. Yet the information systems field has, until recently, showed little interest in ICT features, treating the technical artefact as a 'black box'. Jasperson et al. (2005) and others wanted to open up this black box, to be able to discuss the features that constitute it. This discourse is about what to expect of ICT features, and why. How does the make-up of ICT features constrain and enable us, both in the past and as future possibility? This has obvious links with the design of ICT, discussed in Chapter 9.

Some call this issue '*materiality of ICT*' (Orlikowski 2007), others call it '*affordance*', the word preferred here because ICT features afford users possibilities for action. The issue of affordance, originated in the field of ecological psychology, then aroused interest in the human-computer interaction (HCI) field during the 1990s and in the IS field since 2000. Affordance provides concepts and vocabulary with which to study agents engaging with their environment, in which properties meaningful to the environment enable properties meaningful to the agent; in the HCI and IS fields, environment is ICT and agent is the users. Most of our discussion of affordance is in Chapter 7, where the nature of features is explored.

The discourses in HCI and IS around affordance are aimed at: (a) promoting the idea (Norman 1988; Zammuto et al. 2007), (b) using it as a lens through which to gain insight (Rambusch and Susi 2008; Seidel et al. 2013), (c) assembling taxonomies of affordances (Hartson 2003; Majchrzak et al. 2013; Zammuto et al. 2007). So far, in these fields, there is little discussion about the nature of affordance. There is some discussion in the field of ecological psychology, but how to bring the insights they offer across the IS field has not been discussed, and we do not know in what ways it should be amended or extended. One possible extension is to add normativity, i.e., affordances that bring detriment as well as benefit, as Conole and Dyke (2004) and Majchrzak et al. (2013) do, but there is little discussion on the relationship between benefit and detriment.

We face several challenges, which are discussed in §7-2.3:

1. *Taxonomies*. The taxonomies compiled so far reveal very different kinds and types of affordance, ranging from, e.g., editability (afforded by ICT in general) to network-informed associating (afforded by social media). Taxonomies sometimes overlap but usually contain entries that cannot exist alongside others. Most of the taxonomies do not claim completeness, so on what grounds may we critique them and identify and judge additional types of affordance? On what basis may we differentiate negative from positive affordances?
2. *Subject-object Relationship*. The agent-environment relationship is a subject-object relationship, yet there is a conundrum that neither Descartes nor Heidegger can solve: properties that are meaningful to agent are located in the environment, even when there is no agent present (§7-2.3.3). How may we understand this? Seidel et al. (2013) suggests a model of how affordances arise, but this is only about process and not the foundational question of how such process is possible.
3. *Confusion*. Rambusch and Susi (2008) discuss affordances in a computer game. However they mix together the affordances in the virtual world (avatar seeing door handle, which affords opening) and the real world (user pressing keys affords action). That feels like a category error—but on what basis? They also neglect the affordance of fun by the game itself to the user.

We need a philosophical foundation on which to address such questions. Section §6-4.15 suggests one, which is discussed more deeply in §7-3.3.

6-2.16 Discourse on 'Meaningful' Use and Down-to-earth Issues

Most of the discourse in the field of Information Systems has centred on issues of interest to management, such as productivity, to ICT suppliers, such as acceptance, or to academics, such as power-relations. However, in arenas like health informatics, this is not enough. There, ICT must be specifically aimed at improving patient care. The issues that are important are those of ICT users 'on the ground', such as nurses and physicians who use electronic health records (EHR) systems, and clerks that keep those records. However, because most of the discourse is around issues of interest to management, ICT suppliers or academics, this influences the design of systems and they fail to meet the needs of their users. Only 28 per cent of ambulatory commercial systems detected critically problematic drug-drug interactions (Classen and Bates 2011).

The US government published the HITECH act, which emphasises what they call '*meaningful use*' in health informatics. We need not get embroiled in American political debates to recognise the significance of this idea, because it has much wider application than health.

To achieve 'meaningful use' is not simple and is proving harder than expected (Classen and Bates 2011; Vest and Jasperson 2010). Though success has been achieved in some mature, bespoke EHR systems, which have been refined for "decades", less-mature commercial systems have demonstrated very little 'meaningful' benefits. Most measures in the IS field do not reflect the complexity, multiple levels and expected uses in health systems.

'Meaningful use' is perhaps a slight misnomer, in that all use is meaningful to someone, including management or academics. So Ahmad and Basden (2013) suggest the term '*down-to-earth issues*', for the kinds of issue that ICT users 'on the ground' find meaningful to their work or life tasks. By contrast, 'high level' issues are meaningful to management, ICT suppliers and academics and tend to be more abstract and of narrower scope.

Down-to-earth issues are diverse but may be found in Wenger's classic discourse on Communities of Practice (1998). In his vignette of a day in the life of Ariel, a medical insurance claims clerk, we find (pp. 18–34),

> She ignores a number of caution messages and moves to the next screen where she checks the address. It is important to make sure the address is correct so the check will reach its destination properly. You definitely will get a void if the address is wrong [which is a penalty and means she would have to enter all the data again].
>
> (p. 22)

Knowing which caution messages to ignore, and what to be careful about, are down-to-earth issues. This this might be classified as quality of information (§6-2.7), but that is rather a static notion that belies the sense of active responsibility that Ariel feels, and about which she learns what is 'reasonable' (p. 33). Such 'down-to-earth' are richer and more dynamic than can be fitted into many of the categories found in the IS literature.

But how can we study down-to-earth issues without robbing them of richness? What constitutes them? Unfortunately, 'everydayness' is often disdained by those interested in power and structural issues (Thomas and James 2006), so discussion of such questions is rare. Ahmad and Basden (2013) present five challenges for studying down-to-earth issues:

- Perspective: Consider everyday issues meaningful to those working 'on the ground' with ICT, rather than those of interest to cohorts like management, ICT suppliers, academics.
- Focus: Be open to issues beyond organizational or work tasks.
- Indirectness: Be sensitive to indirect impacts of ICT use.
- Hiddenness: Seek to disclose tacit meaningful issues, of which even ICT users might not be aware.
- Plethora: Find a way of managing the myriad of issues encountered.

To meet these challenges requires a philosophical foundation that values everyday experience and offers a way to respect diversity and what is hidden.

6-2.17 *Discourse on Applications and Life Domains Overlooked by the IS Field*

It has already been noted (§6-2.6) that conventional information systems (IS) discourses long overlooked home computing and computer gaming, art and music. There are other ICT applications outwith conventional organizational management, which are likewise largely overlooked in the IS literatures. Each has generated its own silo of discourse, which might benefit the information systems field by raising neglected issues, including . . .

Geographic Information Systems (GIS) manage spatially referenced information, as found in maps. GIS are important in ecological analysis, mineral exploration, logistics, government planning, etc., but have seldom been discussed in mainstream IS journals (one notable exception being Walsham and Sahay [1999]). GIS applications face different challenges in that spatiality is a world, not a commodity or artefact, and cannot be reduced to concepts or text. The spatial world is important in everyday life, which might explain why *Google Earth* and *Google Maps* are widely used.

Computer Aided Design (CAD) also finds spatiality important, but deals with small areas and in greater precision, in electronic circuit layout, architecture, etc. Whereas GIS deals with a given spatial world, CAD deals with creating a spatial world.

Scientific computing makes massive calculations about physical phenomena for applications like astronomy, fluid flow and climate modelling. These ICT systems require considerable computer power, so either expensive centralised computers are used, or the problem is distributed to computers around the Internet.

Health informatics has some links with the IS field, drawing on some of its theories, but it faces issues that are not widely discussed in the IS field itself. One of these is 'meaningful use' (§6-2.16).

There are also many *life domains* in which ICT is used, but which have different norms and issues from professional, organizational use that has been presupposed by most IS discourses today, such as: education, family, friend, consumer, finance, leisure, social, self and community (Techatassanasoontorn and Tanvisuth 2010). In such applications and domains, concepts like usefulness and success take on different meanings (Hsu and Lu 2004), which need to be included for a full understanding of ICT use. Domains 'spillover' into each other (e.g., friend, social and community). The challenge is to find a basis for identifying such domains and then understand what is unique about ICT use in each.

Given their importance, it is curious that the information systems field has not given these domains and applications the attention they deserve. It might be time for the IS field to leave behind its management-organizational origins and take account of all such applications and domains. But on what basis may it do so, and still retain its core?

6-2.18 Reflections on the Discourses

Does not near a score of discourses in the area of ICT use indicate a wide variety of issues and concerns for both research and practice in the information systems field? Most of the discourses contribute a different understanding of the everyday reality of ICT use. An holistic perspective needs to take account of them all and also provide a way to incorporate other issues and concerns as we encounter them.

Issues range over interaction with the technology, engagement with information, to living or working with ICT. Some are normative, others merely descriptive. Nevertheless, the human experience of ICT is not of separated independent issues, but of ICT use as a whole, even if this is too complex and amorphous to be defined precisely. A number of uses and domains were identified that the IS field does not yet adequately address, in §6-2.6 and §6-2.17.

It is interesting that the earlier discourses tend to focus narrowly on certain aspects or structures, while later discourses recognise wider issues of everyday experience and meaningfulness. It is as though, as the field of information systems matured, it left behind its functionalistic, narrow interests in technical and organizational issues and became gradually more open to experience and wisdom in ever richer arrays of discourses. And yet, as becomes clear later, none offers a full holistic view, which we try to develop in the next section.

As explained in Section §3-1, everyday experience and meaningfulness are precisely the two main starting points of Dooyeweerd's philosophy. This invites us to explore how Dooyeweerd's philosophy can help us understand ICT use, in Section 6-3, and then apply this understanding back to these discourses, in Section 6-4, to see how they might be not only 'listened to' as we have tried to in this section, but also affirmed, critiqued, and enriched (§4-1.3).

6-3 An Aspectual Engagements Framework for Understanding ICT Use

This section discusses foundations of ICT use and develops a conceptual framework based on Dooyeweerd's ideas, which aims to be applicable to any kind of ICT (mobile, desktop or systemic) in any domain of use, and to be able to speak to all the discourses above, contributing fresh insights in each.

As we proceed, three main examples of use will be referred to, all from an everyday perspective: (a) a typical day in the life of Ariel, a medical insurance data-entry clerk, described in a vignette by Wenger (1998), (b) my use of ICT to write this book, (c) playing computer games, especially fighting a mature green dragon in *ZAngband*. The first is organizational use, the other two, personal; the first two are 'serious' uses, the third, 'hedonic'.

6-3.1 Origins of the Framework

In Basden (2008), I argued that information systems or ICT use (then called 'computer use') may be seen as three intertwined multi-aspectual functionings (§3-8.3):

- **HCI**, human-computer interaction (e.g., moving the mouse, reading a screen),
- **ERC**, engaging with represented content (e.g., reading or editing text),
- **HLC**, human living with computers, in which computer use is part of life (e.g., writing a book).

In everyday experience of ICT use, each aspect applies to each of those functionings.

This conceptual framework was able to make sense of playing computer games just as easily as 'serious' ICT use. Distinguishing ERC from both HCI and HLC is helpful in that it allows us to see game-playing, as, for example, 'fighting a mature green dragon', rather than as merely 'interacting with shapes on the screen' (viewed as HCI) or as 'wasting time' (viewed as HLC).

None of the three functionings occurs without the others. HCI is needed in order to engage with content, which occurs for the sake of HLC: Pressing keys and seeing shapes on screen enables me to fight the dragon, which results in my having fun and wasting time. Pressing keys enables me to edit this text, which results in improving my book. However, they do not occur in sequence, but simultaneously. My seeing shapes and pressing keys *is* fighting the dragon, which *is* my having fun. I am simultaneously technology-wielder, avatar and player-user. In writing my book, I am simultaneously technology-wielder, writer/editor and author.

Each functioning is multi-aspectual, but in different ways. HCI involves organic-biotic functioning (fingers), psychic (see screen, respond), analytic (discern shapes as significant), formative (process them), lingual (understand content). ERC involves analytically interpreting the situation (dragon or text), formatively deciding what to do with the content (fight, edit), juridically doing justice (to the game rules, to the meaning of the text). HLC of game-playing involves fun (aesthetic) and time-wasting (economic). The innate normativity of each aspect occurs in all three functionings, and may be positive in one and negative in another (e.g., fun and time-wasting).

6-3.2 A New Aspectual Engagements Framework

Nick Breems employed this framework, of three functionings with fifteen aspects, to understand computer procrastination, as described in §6-3.7. In doing so, he demonstrated that the framework provides a more satisfactory and fruitful account than was available via extant theories in the HCI or psychology fields or theories of technology acceptance or dysfunctional ICT use.

He found, however, that the framework needed some modification. ERC, engagement with represented content, involves more than content that is explicitly represented in the computer, in program, database or symbols in the user interface. It involves also behaviours (e.g., whether the mature green dragon is moving aggressively towards me), and also tacit meanings, often in shared background knowledge (e.g. the game *ZAngband* is based on Tolkien [1977]). So he suggested calling it 'engaging with meaningful content (EMC)'. A similar distinction may be found in Ricoeur (1981, 141), between first-order reference (ostensive information) and second-order reference (lifeworld, tacit interpretation or Heidegger's 'being-in-the-world'). Ricoeur, however, claims that abolition of the first is necessary for the second, while Dooyeweerd allows all to occur together. The nature of these deserves research.

Likewise, HCI is only part of our everyday experience of the technical artefact. Examples: The battery in my tablet becomes empty, or loose connections disrupt a presentation, as do incompatibilities in versions of software. These are not user interface issues, but problems with the technology (hardware, software). So, HCI is widened to be 'engaging with interface and technology (EIT)'.

HLC is widened to 'engaging in life with ICT (ELI)', on the grounds that it is with Internet as well as computers (hence information and *communication* technology, ICT), along with other things essential to ICT and IS, such as training and support services.

Each is not just a functioning, but an *engagement with something*. Hereinafter our discussion will be of the following three engagements, three distinct things that the user engages with while using ICT:

- **EIT**: Engaging with interface and technology, the user interface mediating information, and the technology including such things as cables and battery level;
- **EMC**: Engaging with meaningful content (in the computer game, such engagement is immersive and engrossing);
- **ELI**: Engaging in life with ICT, which includes both work and non-work life.

Whether there are any other engagements that are necessary in ICT use is a possibility that awaits future discussion and research.

Each engagement is guided or evaluated by a different norm—*ease of use* for EIT and *usefulness* or *benefit* for ELI. But what is the norm of EMC? This has not been adequately discussed, but we may tentatively suggest *veracity*, which combines understandability of the content with its appropriateness (accuracy or 'truth').

Of the discourses outlined in Section 6-2, most concern ELI, and the extensive discourse around HCI (§6-2.1) explores EIT. Some recognise ELI and EIT together, including socio-technical approaches and discourses on acceptance and success.

EMC has been the Cinderella among the discourses, with no discourse devoted to it. EMC has been either ignored, studied in isolation or conflated with EIT or ELI. The only discourses that clearly recognise it are those around knowledge-intensive applications (§6-2.4), data and information quality (§6-2.7) and some of the applications, such as games. Some allude to it, like Delone and McLean's (2003) ISSM and ICT features (§6-2.9, §6-2.15). There is little understanding of EMC, or of its difference from and links with EIT and ELI. This is why Lee's (2004) observation is so important that, between technical and social (aligning with EIT and ELI), is "rich phenomenon" which is information (aligning with EMC). A full account of the discourses follows in Section 6-4.

Davis' (1989) Technology Acceptance Model and Burton-Jones and Straub's (2006) triad recognise EIT and ELI but not EMC. Suggestion: Why not incorporate veracity and meaningful content respectively? ISSM recognises all three, as system, information and service quality, but only in general terms.

How each discourse may be enriched is discussed in Section 6-4. Before we do so, however, we need to establish a more detailed philosophical foundation for understanding of ICT use and elaborate the nature of these three engagements.

6-3.3 ICT Use as Dooyeweerdian Law-subject-object Functioning

To Dooyeweerd, all activity is a functioning by subjects with objects in response to laws of multiple aspects of the 'ocean of meaningfulness'—a law-subject-object relationship in each aspect (§3-8.2). ('Ocean of meaningfulness' refers to the idea that both we and ICT exist and occur—'swim'—by meaningfulness, shared at the deepest level; see §3-1.2.3.) So the three engagements, EIT, EMC and ELI, may each be treated as a law-subject-object relationship(s). Each has different functioning, subject role, and objects, prior and generated (see §3-3.1.2), as shown in Table 6.1. The overall norm is in brackets under functioning.

The three engagements are intertwined with each other, in a relationship that is not causal, nor sequential, nor even one of dependency, but is rather a form of *enkapsis* (§3-9.6.2). Each is necessary and does not occur without the other two (though they might be latent). It does not seem to be precisely any of the kinds of enkapsis recognised by Dooyeweerd and might thus contribute to his ideas (§3-9.6.2). The intertwinement of the three occurs by a generated object of one being the prior object of the next. This does *not* imply they occur one after the other, because such generation is not necessarily a chronological process (shift in time) but can be a shift in meaningfulness (aspect). Instead, the human activity of engaging with meaningful

Table 6.1 The Three Engagements as Law-Subject-Object Relationships

Engagement	*Subject role*	*Functioning (Overall norm)*	*Prior object(s)*	*Generated object(s)*
EIT, Engaging with interface and technology	Technology-wielder	Using as 'wielding' (Ease of use)	Interface: Shapes or text on screen, sounds from speakers, etc. ('Interface objects' in HCI); Technology: cables, screens, power sources	New interface objects; For EMC: Meaningful content (e.g. Mature Green Dragon, Ariel's insurance records)
EMC, Engaging with meaningful content	Information-user (Games: player or user-as-avatar)	Interpretation & expression (Veracity)	Meaningful content	New content; For ELI: Knowledge, attitudes, intentions, etc.
ELI, Engaging in life with ICT	ICT-user	Life and work with ICT (usefulness, benefit)	Knowledge, attitudes, intentions, etc.	Repercussions in life

content is simultaneous with engaging with interface. (Sometimes it might be chronological, especially in the repercussions of ELI, as discussed in §6-3.6.)

Though they have different functioning, objects and main norm, the three engagements are all multi-aspectual, sharing the same set of 'oceanic' aspectual laws. Each is diverse in its full functioning, repercussions and normativity.

The multi-aspectual nature of each engagement is discussed in the three next sections. Since Dooyeweerd's suite includes aspects that govern individuals, organizations and societal structures, as well as pre-human activity, they can all be considered together within the one conceptual framework, rather than being separated into different discourses. The usefulness of this *Aspectual Engagements Framework* becomes clear when the discourses are discussed.

6-3.4 Aspects of Engaging with Interface and Technology (EIT)

This section discusses use of Dooyeweerd's suite of aspects to provide a foundational understanding of engaging with interface and technology (EIT) in everyday experience of ICT use. It offers a conceptual framework for evaluating and designing the user interface and the technology, which can inform the fields of human-computer interaction and ergonomics.

Note on terminology: The user *interface* (noun) cannot be separated from the user's *engagement* with it (verb), and the two will usually be used synonymously. The interface has no other existence, *qua* interface, apart from the engagement, whether actual or potential (§3-1.2, §3-9). Likewise, things like *interface objects* will be synonymous with the engagement by which they exist.

Note on terminology: '*Interface*' refers to the user interface; '*technology*' includes the non-interface parts such as cables, operating system, connection to the Internet, etc.

The role of each aspect is briefly discussed, then Table 6.2 offers some detail in the form of examples. Readers may skip to 'reading' the table if they wish, returning to the text for deeper understanding. Compare Table 5.3.

The **mathematical aspects** are relevant in two ways. All physical functioning of the technology depends on them. They are more directly relevant when coupled with another aspect, such as number of items on screen (quantitative aspect with analytic), screen layout (spatial aspect with psychic and formative) or animation (kinematic aspect with lingual).

The physical and organic aspects are those of *hardware* of ICT, the materials and components. The **physical aspect** makes materials, energy and forces important, and is normative insofar as these (fail to) support later aspects of EIT; see examples in Table. The **organic aspect** is relevant in the relationship between the user's bodily organs (fingers, eyes, ears, etc., and nervous system) and the hardware components, as studied in ergonomics.

It is with the organic aspect that the distinction between *input and output* emerges. They remain distinguishable until the formative aspect. It is in the organic and psychic aspects that visual, aural, haptic and motor *interface channels* differ most clearly.

The **psychic aspect** of engaging with the interface includes the user's sensory-motor responding (hearing, seeing, feeling) and pre-analytic mental activity (pattern recognition, short- and long-term memory, spreading activation, etc.). The user interface is treated as shapes and sounds. Fitts' Law (Fitts 1954), about time it takes to respond to stimuli appearing on screen, is a psychical finding. It is the psychic aspect that makes such issues as screen resolution and pixels important and, internally, bit arrays (§5-5.4).

The psychic to lingual aspects of interface parallel those of information and computers (see Sections 5-3, 5-4), except that the visual and haptic channels especially harbour a "complicated spatial analogy in the psychical aspect" with an "indirect foundation" (Dooyeweerd 1955, II, 168). To understand the workings of the visual user interface and motor responses, including 3D, involves psychical feeling of space via the organic analogy of space around the body, and then via physical and kinematic analogies of space. What feels directly spatial is, Dooyeweerd claims, complex. This can explain how, in animation, we sense movement in space, even though movement is meaningless to the spatial aspect.

The relevance of the **analytic aspect** ranges from identifying which cable plugs into which socket (the technology) to distinguishing things on screen or sounds from the speakers (interface). My Amiga's simple, variably-sized icons are easier to detect and select than the intricate, uni-sized icons in neat grids (Windows, iOS, Android) (Byrne 1993). The interface is treated as a collection of *interface objects*—it matters not whether visual, aural, haptic or motor—to which the user gives attention. A typical research finding is that the number of things a human can give attention to is "the magic number 7, plus or minus 2" (Miller 1956). The analytic norm is clarity of distinction; this can be reversed in computer games to hide things.

The **formative aspect** governs the structure and processing of that which is analytically distinguished at the interface or in the technology. In the visual channel, the structure is often expressed spatially and in the aural (e.g., speech), kinematically. Its norm is ease of achievement—getting the technology to work (!) and doing things via the user interface. Cognitive effort is a formative issue, with proximal user interfaces, of which the user is almost unaware, requiring less effort than distal interfaces do (Polanyi 1967; Winograd and Flores 1986). Example: HSV (Hue, Saturation, Value) sliders are easier than RGB (Red, Green, Blue) for adjusting colour hue. Example: It is easier if knobs controlling cooker hotplates are arranged spatially like the hotplates rather than in a neat line, as on most cookers (Eberts 1994, 171). A typical concept in this aspect is Norman and Draper's (1986) gulfs of evaluation and execution: analytic and formative. A typical formative theory is Card et al.'s (1983) classic GOMS model (goals, operators, methods and selection rules); interestingly, some of the criticisms of GOMS refer to other aspects than the formative (e.g., psychic aspects of tiredness or visual impairment). User flexibility, in how to achieve things, is also a formative issue. Sometimes, however, as for dangerous things, the formative norm of ease of engagement should be reversed. The formative aspect of structure and processing is in the service of information (lingual aspect).

The **lingual aspect** of the interface is the meaningful content that is mediated via the formative structure and processing together. The lingual aspect of EIT is thus the primary link with engaging with meaningful content EMC, discussed below. The meaningful content is not restricted to static, explicitly signified information, but includes also tacit interpretation of something dynamic: for example, not only the mature green dragon but also the way it behaves.

The norm of the lingual aspect of EIT is understanding what the originator of the meaningful content intended (output interpreted by user), and what the user intends (input expressed by user). User interface objects (visual, aural, tactile) should be designed primarily to evoke signified-meaning that contributes to meaningful content, because that is their reason-for-being:

both its explicit signification and its tacit interpretation. Animations, pictorial backgrounds and music should usually convey meaningful content (lingual purpose) rather than being just for decoration (aesthetic purpose), a rule that many websites break, and as a result evoke wrong or misleading main messages (Flanders 2002).

Interface wording is particularly important. Example (Spolsky 2001): When the user hits the 'exit' button, the *Juno* package asks:

> Thanks for using Juno. Are you sure you want to exit? Yes. No.

but a much simpler exit question would be preferable:

> Exit now? Yes. No.

Spolsky comments: (a) Since there are no detrimental impacts of exiting Juno, it should not ask "are you sure". (b) The 'Thanks' is superfluous. (c) Making the user question whether they wish to exit is inappropriate. But why? In addition to the lingual aspect of asking users for confirmation, the Juno question weaves in other aspects misleadingly: (a) juridical aspect of danger, (b) social aspect of politeness, (c) pistic aspect of belief. Aspectual analysis can help designers see which phrases are appropriate and which are not.

The technology's 'meaningful content' is, e.g., labels on the case.

The **social aspect** of engaging with the interface is primarily found in the cultural expectations of what interface objects mean or the standards to which they adhere. Both standards and cultural expectations often function tacitly as the shared background knowledge (lifeworld) by which a community operates. Software settings are often a social function that allows individual users to differentiate themselves from the standard.

From the social aspect onwards, engaging with the technology often overlaps with engaging in life with ICT (ELI). See Table for examples.

The **economic aspect** concerns limited resources of the interface (such as screen space, user time and user patience). Its norm is frugality: e.g., remove superfluous information from screen or spoken interface, reduce download, startup and shutdown times. (My *Amiga* starts up in 20 seconds and shuts down in zero!) When using a distant system, such as in e-government, issues of availability (access, downtime, etc.) are economic issues related to the technology.

The **aesthetic aspect** concerns harmony, enjoyment and style. Apple Computer products have historically emphasised the aesthetic aspect of EIT—not only their pleasant user interface, but even the technology in the form of its solder joints (Young and Simon 2005, 48). Letting aesthetics dominate when designing web pages causes problems, as Flanders (2002) copiously and humorously illustrates.

The **juridical aspect** gives us norms of appropriateness or due—to users, to content and to designers. See Table.

The **ethical aspect** is probably most relevant to EIT in generosity or considerateness during the engagement with the interface, in two ways. 1.

Designers go to extra trouble to make it a good experience for the users, or contrariwise, "couldn't care". Example: Many menus and websites are hierarchical in structure, which makes them more arduous to navigate than those with multiple cross-linking (generosity in ways of reaching the features desired). More seriously, what real sacrifices are demanded or expected of users? 2. Users are forgiving rather than overly critical about design flaws.

The **pistic aspect** is relevant in at least two ways. 1. What assumptions does user (need to) make that helps or hinders their engagement? This is often determined by. . . 2. What vision underlies the design of the user interface (e.g., Apple Computer's emphasis on aesthetics or *Google's* Material Design)?

Table 6.2 gives examples of aspects of engaging with interface and technology, in columns 2 and 3. Column 4 shows examples of normative issues that reduce ease of use or hinder EIT.

Table 6.2 Examples of Aspects of Engaging With Interface and Technology (EIT)

Aspect	*Engaging with technology*	*Engaging with interface*	*Normative issues*
Quantitative	Number of components	Number of things on screen, of pixels	-
Spatial	Shape of components	Screen layout	-
Kinematic	Moving the mouse	Animation	-
Physical	Touch-screen glass, plastic of case, mouse-ball friction	Light and sound emission, wavelengths, transmission to user	Loose connections, loss of battery power, much-used flash disk becomes unreliable.
Organic-biotic	Emissions from screen	Engagement of user's organs (eyes, ears, fingers, etc.) with mouse, keyboard, screen, speakers, switches, etc.	Too small or large for hand, finger? Repetitive strain injury
Psychic / Sensitive	Seeing screen, hearing speakers	Colours (hue etc.), sounds (volume, pitch, decay, etc.); Hitting keys, moving mouse	Visible, hearable, tactile; dimpled, tactile keys on keyboard
Analytical	"Which socket do I plug this into?"	Text, numbers, etc.; Emphasis (bold, italics); Icons	Easy detect icons, text, speech etc.; Distractions, clutter

Aspect	*Engaging with technology*	*Engaging with interface*	*Normative issues*
Formative	Visiting lecturer can't get laptop working with our display!	Screen structure (main area, toolbars); Control (HSV sliders better than RGB)	Ease of achievement (proximal not distal interface)
Lingual	Labelling; user manual	Signification of icons, menus, pictures, etc.; Message of whole screen	Ease of understanding what author / designer intended
Social	Technology as status symbol	Shared assumptions; User interface standards (e.g. OK, Cancel buttons left or right?);	Ease of use enhanced by cultural expectations
Economic	Desk-space taken up, power consumption, running costs, downtime	Limited screen space; Download time	Use UI resources wisely
Aesthetic	Pretty phone covers	*Apple*'s user interface; *Amiga*'s smoothness	Decide on pleasant rather than ugly (but don't let aesthetics get in way of user)
Juridical	Technology patents	Accessibility, appropriateness (§7-3.4); Patents	Due to user, designer and content
Ethical		Several ways to achieve things; User is patient with annoyances	Generosity in both designer and user
Pistic / Faith	Loyalty to operating systems, brands, etc.	Interface assumptions. Vision that drives design of interface.	Remember: underlying vision might not be true to world.

This brief overview of how each aspect is relevant to engaging with interface and technology is by no means exhaustive, but it has brought issues from all aspects together into the one picture, which is rare in HCI literature. It aims to illustrate and stimulate thinking about EIT and its design and evaluation, by showing the variety of norms that pertain, some of which are seldom mentioned in books on interface design, such as generosity or battery power, but pertain in everyday use. As the *Shalom Principle* (§3-8.5) states, every aspect is important.

Engaging with interface and technology (EIT) is usually meaningful only when enabling engagement with meaningful content (EMC), which is discussed next.

6-3.5 Engaging With Meaningful Content (EMC)

This section discusses how Dooyeweerd's aspects can provide a foundational understanding of the user engaging with meaningful content (EMC) in the everyday experience of ICT use. EMC is discussed in more detail than EIT or ELI here because the literature on it is sparser.

EMC is important to both virtual reality and 'real' reality, including in professional applications. It has been suggested above that the main quality norm of EMC is *veracity*, a combination of understandability and appropriateness to what users would reasonably expect of the content, but this takes different forms in different applications. In serious applications, users usually expect accuracy and often completeness as a representation of the real world, while in games some imaginative departure from this is expected.

The meaningful content with which the user engages is conveyed not only by explicitly represented data (insurance claim numbers, dragon-shapes) but also by behaviour (e.g., how the dragon fights) and with interpretation, often from background tacit knowledge.

> Note on terminology. '*Information*' will usually be synonymous with '*meaningful content*', i.e., including non-explicit and dynamic meaning, but occasionally, in some extant theories, it will refer only to explicitly signified meaning. See also Section 5-2.5.

6-3.5.1 The Diversity of Engaging With Meaningful Content

Dooyeweerd's aspects can be useful in analysing and evaluating this norm by separating out what is important in engaging with the meaningful content. As an example of EMC in a serious application, consider Ariel's entering an insurance claim into the system found in the following, with aspect-abbreviations added in brackets:

> She now comes [kin] to the 'paylines,' [anl] the screen on which she will enter information about the charges [eco] so that benefits can be calculated [qtv]. She starts [kin] with the office visit. She enters [lng] first the type of service [anl], then the name of the service provider [anl, soc], which leads her [kin] into the providers file [lng]: there she makes sure she checks that the provider's address [spa] is correct [jur] since the insured has 'assigned' the benefits to be disbursed directly [fmv] to the doctor [soc]. Then she enters the date of service [fmv] and the charges [eco]. In this case, she must also enter a deduction [eco] because the provider happens to have a special contract with Alinsu [soc, jur]. She

> uses a calculation sheet [lng] to figure out [qtv] what the deduction is, looking up [lng] the standard [soc] charge for this type [anl] of office visit in a ring binder [pcl], entering the amount [lng] on her calculator to compute a reduction of 15% [qtv], and choosing the larger amount [fmv] of the two. It has occurred to her [psy] that it would be more advantageous for Alinsu [eth] to take the smaller one, but the procedure says [lng, soc] to take the larger one [qtv].
>
> (Wenger 1998, 22)

Ariel's engagement with meaningful content is replete with diversity of aspectual meaning, twelve of Dooyeweerd's fifteen aspects occurring there.

However, astute readers might have noticed that the aspect sometimes refers to the meaningful content (information) with which she engages, and sometimes to Ariel's functioning in the engagement. Indeed, two sets of issues in EMC must be distinguished, about the content that is engaged with, and the quality of engaging with that content. Dooyeweerd's ideas are useful for both, as discussed in the following sections.

6-3.5.2 *Aspects of the Meaningful Content Engaged With*

Taking the user's perspective, the *meaningful content* with which they engage is a 'world' represented inside the ICT ('innards': §5-5.4). Taking the ontological perspective of Section 5-5.2, this world is the virtual law-side (a constructed 'ocean of meaningfulness'), and a virtual subject-object-side governed by it.

The Aspectual Engagements Framework proposes that the veracity of a world is enhanced as more aspects are represented in the virtual law-side by the designers, as laws, norms, types, possibilities, rationalities, etc. So Dooyeweerd's aspects offer a useful conceptual tool by which to evaluate or design the meaningful content with which the user engages.

This applies whether the meaningful content (world) is a representation of our *real world*, as in Ariel's claims processing, or of fictitious *virtual worlds*, as in computer games, where veracity is often called 'realism'. In serious applications, especially in business, all these (laws, possibilities, types, etc.) must be as close as possible to those of the real world—though some flexibility should be built into the design to allow for new types in future. In fictitious virtual worlds, especially computer games, however, many types can occur not found in the real world. Example: *ZAngband* has dragons, hobbits, cyberdemons, magic staffs, etc. The laws that govern the virtual world may depart slightly from those of the real world (for example, some creatures in *ZAngband* travel through rock), but the vast majority of the laws should be recognisable; for example, most creatures have limited resources which run out (economic law), the stronger the creature, the harder they can hit (psychic, physical), the more intelligent, the more creatures can track you (formative law), and so on.

Table 6.3 compares how each aspect is catered for in four worlds, a serious application, a puzzle pastime, an old-style game and a more recent game, giving examples of how each aspect might be present in the meaningful content that is engaged with.

Column 2 contains phrases that indicate the kinds of information that Ariel engages with in processing insurance claims, from the excerpt above.

Table 6.3 Aspects of Several Information Worlds

Aspect	*Ariel*	*Yahzee*	*ZAngband*	*Clash of Clans*
Quantitative	"benefits can be calculated" "reduction of 15%" "the larger amount"	Five dice; score [Note].	User keeps track of the game: amount of strength, hit-points, objects, enemies; number of turns.	Number of buildings, of defenders, Amount of gold, elixir, trophies, etc.
Spatial	"provider's address"	-	Layout of passages, caves; Proximity of monsters. Without spatial aspect, this game would just not exist.	Layout of village; Area defended by weapons.
Kinematic		-	Exploring, fleeing monsters; Route to object; Dexterity. Movement is crucial to the game.	Attackers move through village; Villagers move about in interesting ways.
Physical		-	Cannot move through walls, must dig. Frost shatters potions, fire burns scrolls.	Buildings take time to be destroyed.
Organic-biotic		-	Must eat. Wounds, healing. Death when Hit Points reach zero.	-
Psychic/ Sensitive		-	Seeing, blindness, infravision, hearing, confusion, memory; Potions can cure or inflict these.	(Sounds, music as decoration.)

Aspect	*Ariel*	*Yahzee*	*ZAngband*	*Clash of Clans*
Analytical	"paylines" "type of service" "name of the service provider" "provider's address"	Distinct patterns on dice.	Identifying objects is crucial to game.	Buildings distinguished.
Formative	"the insured has 'assigned' the benefits to be disbursed directly" "date of service"	Goal: maximum score. Plan in which box to record each throw.	Intelligent creatures. Achievements include: exploration, finding special objects, defeating powerful enemies, quests.	Achievement is everything in this game. Achieving quests; Upgrading buildings; Train troops; Attacking other players' villages; Defending against attacks. Clan wars.
Lingual		-	Read scrolls to achieve things; Labels in unknown language. 'Scrolls of rumour' give tips.	Messages from Chief's deputy; Inter-player communication.
Social	"name of the service provider" "the doctor" "special contract" "standard charge"	-	Weak: Some NPCs are friendly not hostile.	Players can join clans, working together in clan wars.
Economic	"charges" (x2) "deduction"	Core of the game: carefully manage filling of limited number of boxes.	Can carry only limited amount; Limited Hit Points etc.; Can trade in shops.	Central to game: Mining, storing resources to upgrade buildings, train troops, etc.

(*Continued*)

Table 6.3 (Continued)

Aspect	*Ariel*	*Yahzee*	*ZAngband*	*Clash of Clans*
Aesthetic		- [Note]	Messages are often fun; Fun tricks built into game. Incongrous unique characters appear (Robin Hood with Gollum!) Player charisma.	Realistic-looking scenery, buildings; Villagers move around cutely (of no importance in game); Can buy decorative features.
Juridical	"special contract"	-	Weak: Some creatures have price on their head, being outlaws.	There are some gang rules. Fairness: can attack only those at similar level.
Ethical		-	-	Can donate troops to help fellow clan members.
Pistic/Faith		-	Vision of game: explore, gain experience, defeat Serpent of Chaos; Can be aided by a deity, who has capricious power to help or hinder.	Vision of game: powerful village.

Note (Yahtzee): Aesthetic aspect of fun occurs in ELI, but there is little aesthetic in virtual world itself, except that some versions have decorated dice. Numbers on the dice are analytical more than quantitative, because it is the pattern rather than amount that is important.

Column 3 shows aspects of the world that is *Yahtzee*, where five dice are thrown and certain patterns score for the player. These patterns are recorded in boxes of a form, and the challenge is to decide in which box to place each throw so as to maximise the final total.

Column 4 contains examples of the *ZAngband* world in each aspect. It is an old game but it has rich gameplay, and it is important to stand back from the fashion-dominated scene of games. In *ZAngband*, which I play on my *Amiga* computer with the keyboard, I (as avatar) find my way around a labyrinth of passages and caves, encountering non-player characters (NPCs), such as mature green dragons or hobbits, most of which I have to battle, or objects, which I can pick up and use if I think they are useful, but I must identify them first using staffs of perception or scrolls of identify. Quaffing a potion of augmentation, for example, increases strength, constitution, intelligence, wisdom, dexterity and charisma, whereas quaffing a potion of poison might kill me. The screen shows the map of where I am, with the passages and caves I have already visited, and the objects I remember encountering there. When I fight a mature green dragon, it fires acid to burn me. Fighting gives me experience and equipment, which will help me towards my eventual goal of killing the Serpent of Chaos.

Column 5 shows aspects of *Clash of Clans*, a currently fashionable multiplayer game played across the Internet. The user plays the role of designer and chief of a village, deciding which kinds of buildings should be where, and where protective walls should be. The number available of each is limited. Most of the buildings either generate resources, train troops or protect the village. Resources like gold and elixir are required for both building construction and troop training. Each building takes time to build, leading to anticipation and planning which building to construct next with limited resources. Other villages can be attacked, and one's own village is regularly attacked by others, to steal resources and gain victories, which are measured by number of trophies. Some villages are controlled by the game; humanly controlled villages can group together in clans, to help each other. Non-participation in clan activity leads to expulsion. The overall aim of the game is to increase the strength and prowess of your village, in both defence and attack, as measured by number of trophies. There are several modes of playing, with emphasis on attacking, defending or building. *Clash* has an explicit link with ELI, in that players can purchase game resources using real money.

Each aspect offers distinct laws, norms, possibilities, rationalities, etc. (§3-7), and these are encapsulated in software by designers, as discussed in Section 7-4. In general, in serious applications, the more aspects of content engaged with, the more appropriate to the 'real life' of the usage of the application, and the more robust the application will be in future expansions. Likewise, the more aspects expressed in a website, the more satisfying or useful it is. Ariel's system seems reasonable but might lack some types of information that would be included now, such as religion (pistic aspect).

We may extend this proposal to data mining and big data. Those discourses show a tendency to focus only on aspects of immediate interest to those in management for whom data is mined, especially the economic, but if Dooyeweerd is correct in believing that all other aspects are relevant, and they impact and influence the focused aspects, it would be wise to deliberately consider the relevance of data in each and every aspect; see §5-3.8.

In computer games, the richer the virtual law-side, i.e., the more aspects encoded into it, the more satisfying the game for longer to more types of players. The content in Yahtzee is meaningful in only a few aspects, which is common among puzzle games. Of the richer games, *ZAangband* has a more balanced profile of aspects than *Clash of Clans*, and this explains why it has been satisfying to play for fifteen years, and the playing itself at any level is satisfying. *Clash* is oriented towards the formative aspect of achievement, which gives a different and more compelling kind of satisfaction. I find *Clash* more addictive but *ZAangband* more fun. *Yahzee* is relaxing.

There is potential for research into (a) operationalizing this aspectual engagements framework for the design of software content (websites, serious applications, games), (b) how far one can depart from the laws of the real aspects in a rich game and (c) what happens when the assumptions of Western cultures that are usually built into post-social aspects of the virtual world are removed.

6-3.5.3 *Quality of Engagement With Meaningful Content*

As discussed above, the actual engagement with this multi-aspectual content is itself multi-aspectual functioning (§3-8.3). Its quality is governed by the *Shalom Principle* (§3-8.5), which says that for the best engagement, functioning in all normative aspects should be positive. Quality of content (information, data) may be measured by reference to each aspect.

The quantitative to organic-biotic aspects play little part, except as a foundation for later aspects. All kinds of application are considered, from serious to games. Since the norms are similar to those of reading a book, the user might be called a reader. The following are examples of how each aspect is relevant to the quality of engagement with meaningful content. A deeper investigation (research) is needed.

- **Psychic:** Does the content arouse apprehension in a game, or when Ariel has to take extreme care?
- **Analytic:** Are the concepts in the content clear or confused? Are arguments and reasoning rational?
- **Formative:** Is the content structured or random? How easily can its reader formulate ideas from it?
- **Lingual:** Can the reader understand what is signified?
- **Social:** Do cultural expectations interpret the information in certain ways? What if readers do not share the background knowledge (life-world) that developers had?
- **Economic:** Is the content succinct or is much superfluous, with unnecessary repetition?
- **Aesthetic:** Is the content interesting or boring, delightful or disgusting? Is there harmony in it, or is it fragmented?
- **Juridical:** Is the content accurate? Is it timely? It is appropriate? Does it give its sources and readers their due? Does it do or incite injustice to any, or does it encourage us towards rectifying injustices?

- **Ethical:** Is the content generous, merciful to the reader, such as to the novice, or is it mean-spirited or written with disdain?
- **Pistic:** Is the content believable? How important is it? Believability takes us to the quality of the world being engaged with.

Notice how this combines into one framework structural issues along with social and cognitive and even pre-cognitive issues, dissolving the barriers that have grown up between discourses.

6-3.6 Engaging in Life with ICT (ELI)

This section discusses how Dooyeweerd's philosophy can provide a foundation for understanding engaging in life with ICT (ELI), as everyday experience. For example, how does Ariel's processing insurance claims (Wenger 1998) or playing *Pokemon Go* on a mobile phone affect or become affected by people's lives?

Philosophically, Dooyeweerd notions of meaningful multi-aspectual functioning (§3-8.3) and intimate law-subject-object relationship (§3-3.1.2) are particularly useful. In ELI, user is subject, ICT artefact or features, prior object(s), with subjects and objects governed by a common 'ocean of meaningfulness' or law-side. Dooyeweerd's aspects are very useful in understanding ELI.

Some ELI occurs because of engagement with meaningful content (EMC), some just because ICT is being used (e.g. headaches from mandatory use), and some without ICT at all (non-use §6-2.14) in an ICT-oriented context. It is the first we primarily wish to understand because, in the other two, ICT could be replaced by anything else, in principle.

Whereas in EIT and EMC, we can identify roles that each aspect plays, in ELI this is not possible, because ELI is highly diverse and unbounded except for the specific facts of the actuality of ICT and the current context (the subject-object-side). So, no table or list of aspects is given here, only examples that demonstrates how we might think about it using aspects.

Wenger (1998, 23) describes the following ELI of processing insurance claims:

> Since the patient went to such a 'preferred' doctor, Ariel must remember to increase the rate of reimbursement from 80% to 85%. But this means she will have to split the claim in two since the other charges are to be reimburses at 80%, and cannot be included in the payment. She likes the idea of having this claim generate two 'batches' that will count toward her production . . .

However,

> You will get into trouble for splitting claims unnecessarily.

This shows a link between EMC and ELI, and possible repercussions in life. We may understand this by reference to aspects of EMC (world) and ELI as follows:

- The information was such as to require splitting, resulting in two claims (analytic functioning and generated object in EMC). Two claims rather than one is prior object in her ELI formative functioning of 'making production', measured quantitatively (a quantitative repercussion in ELI).
- Had she split the claim inappropriately (analytic repercussion but juridically dysfunction in EMC), the same object of two claims is generated. However, if the juridical dysfunction is picked up, she would be punished (juridical repercussion in ELI).

This demonstrates some **benefits of aspectual analysis**. It not only *separates out issues*, but *opens our thinking* by reasonable deductions so that things not explicit in the original statements are *revealed*, such as possible juridical dysfunction of inappropriatcly splitting claims.

The generated objects or repercussions of such ELI are usually many and either positive, negative or a mix of both in different aspects. In Ariel's case, these include: the healthcare provider receiving their due (juridical), the patient receiving treatment (organic-biotic), Ariel's production figures increasing (formative, quantitative), some satisfaction (psychic), the possibility of a check on the splitting of claims (analytic) and the possibility of 'trouble' (juridical).

In general, we might classify repercussions of ICT use as:

- *direct or indirect repercussions*, the latter usually because a repercussion affects someone else, who then acts differently—often involving the social aspect;
- *expected or unexpected repercussions*, the latter usually because we have overlooked an aspect;
- *short-term and long-term repercussions*, the latter usually in the juridical, ethical and pistic aspects because of longer timescales (Table 3.5).

An example of these in combination might be that, after installing a system, some find themselves aspiring (pistic aspect) to use the system for more and more tasks or, after purchasing one application for their mobile device, aspiring to more and more applications.

This links ELI with societal issues of ICT, discussed in Chapter 8. There can be at least three ways in which individual or local ICT use can affect societal structures (§8-4.3): (a) the ICT user is in a position of leadership in society (politicians, media, etc.), (b) a courageous person used ICT to influence leaders, maybe by mass campaign, (c) ICT use is multiplied by millions (§8-4.2).

6-3.7 *Understanding Full ICT Use; The Example of Computer Procrastination*

ICT use, therefore, is seen by this framework as three multi-aspectual engagements that are intertwined. This implies that, to understand ICT use properly, we must give attention to all aspects of every engagement. Sometimes certain aspects or certain engagements might be less relevant than others, but their exclusion should be for good reasons rather than just being overlooked.

As an example of how this might be done, consider the complex problem of computer procrastination, discussed in Breems and Basden (2014). Procrastination itself, in which we put off a task by engaging in some more enjoyable activity, is common in everyday life. ICT, however, seems to make it easier to procrastinate, tempting us with computer games or social media. What is it about ICT that makes computer procrastination so prevalent? Nick Breems set out to study this. He reviewed the discourses of Psychology, Human-Computer Interaction, Technology Acceptance, Problematic Internet Use and Non-Work-Related Internet Use, but found that the problem of computer procrastination does not seem to have been studied. Why not?

Employing the original version of the framework, described in §6-3.1, of three multi-aspectual engagements, he reflected on his own experience of computer procrastination by introspection and generalizing sensitively, analysed how important each aspect is in each engagement. He then reviewed literature in the five discourses similarly. The results were plotted using six aspectual heatmap diagrams, in which each cell represents one aspect of one engagement, the darker the cell, the more important the aspect. The heatmaps for the five discourses are to the left, and that for computer procrastination, to the right.

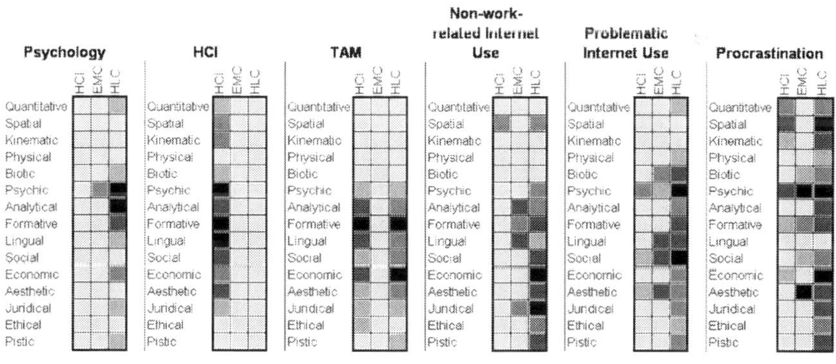

Figure 6.2 Six Heatmap Diagrams Showing Aspects and the Three Engagements of ICT Use

Reproduced by kind permission of Elsevier Publishers.

Insofar as his reflection may be generalised, the procrastination heatmap shows the spatial and psychic aspects being particularly important in HCI (EIT), the aesthetic and formative aspects being particularly important in EMC and the spatial, psychic and economic aspects being particularly important in HLC (ELI), with several other aspects being moderately important. For example, the juridical aspect of HLC refers to the guilt that is felt after wasting time in procrastination.

The other five heatmaps show immediately that none of the discourses cover all the aspects or engagements that are important in computer procrastination. This might explain why the problem of computer procrastination has not yet been adequately studied in any field. Nick Breems used his own experience; the aspects of each engagement of computer procrastination call for wider empirical research.

The heatmaps can suggest (a) in which aspects each discourse might contribute some useful insight to the understanding of computer procrastination, (b) how they might be extended. For example, if the field of Non-work-related Internet use were to take HCI and EMC more seriously, particularly the psychic and aesthetic aspects, then it might be in a position to address the problem of computer procrastination. See Breems and Basden (2014) for more.

This application of the aspectual engagements framework demonstrates that it might affirm, critique and enrich discourses in relation to everyday experience of ICT use. In the next section, each of the discourses examined in Section 6-2 is discussed from the perspective of the framework, along with some other portions of Dooyeweerd's thought occasionally.

6-4 Enriching and Integrating the Discourses on ICT Use

The aim of this section is to briefly indicate how the aspectual engagements framework and Dooyeweerd's ideas in general might address a range of ICT usage issues by discussing how it can affirm, critique and enrich each of the discourses that we 'listened to' in Section 6-2 in a way that indicates avenues for fruitful research and enhanced practice. It might also affirm, critique and enrich our understanding of the whole area of ICT use now and in the future.

Each section here corresponds to one in Section 6-2, with similar numbering; it might be helpful to refer back. These sections offer outline rather detailed suggestions. It is hoped that readers' imagination might be stimulated. Abbreviations introduced above are used for the three engagements:

- EIT: engaging with interface and technology,
- EMC: engaging with meaningful content,
- ELI: engaging in life with ICT.

6-4.1 Discourse on Ease of Use and Interactions with Technology

The discourse on interaction with the computer, in the fields of human-computer interaction (HCI) and ergonomics, whose main norm is ease of use, are concerned with aspects of EIT as discussed in §6-3.4, especially the organic-biotic to lingual, as they became recognised over the past 40 years of this discourse. Guidelines for design reflect the normativity of each of the aspects. Green and Petre's (1996) Cognitive Dimensions may be seen as trying to obtain an everyday perspective that recognises that the reason-for-being of HCI is to support EMC.

See §6-3.4 for a discussion of the importance of each of Dooyeweerd's aspects to HCI. The aspects in which there has been less interest to date, such as juridical and ethical, might indicate new areas of research.

6-4.2 *Discourse on Organizational Issues in Information Systems*

This discourse focuses on ELI—both its aspectual functioning and its repercussions (§6-3.6). It is often the indirect, unexpected repercussions that are of most importance. The diversity of organizational issues that affect ICT use in organizations invites us to employ Dooyeweerd's aspects to help understand them.

However, much of this discourse tends to be limited to aspects that are meaningful to management (usually the economic and social), at the expense of others (c.f. Renkema's [2000] P4). Mandatory use is meaningful in the formative aspect. By socio-critical researchers, the juridical aspect is emphasised above others (see Table 4.1). Carr's (2003) provocative article entitled "IT Doesn't Matter" may now be understood as interest restricted to the economic aspect, which ignores the meaningfulness of the lingual aspect that qualifies ICT (§5-3.5), despite the economic aspect depending foundationally on the lingual, which makes ICT important.

Since every aspect should be treated as equally important (§3-7.1), we may both affirm the validity of these aspects, and critique the lack of interest in others. For example, the pistic aspect helps us understand senior management's frequent unquestioning and sometimes hubristic commitment to ICT, which might lie unrecognised at the root of the Productivity Paradox. In such ways, Dooyeweerd's suite might enrich this discourse by widening it and critiquing taxonomies and models that are proffered.

The discourse may also be enriched by Dooyeweerd's (1986) theory of social institutions (§3-9.6.3) to help understand what constitutes the organization, and by his theory of enkapsis (§3-9.6.2), to understand how organizations relates to individuals, to ICT and to the wider world.

6-4.3 *Discourse on the Effect of ICT on Workforce and Socio-Technical Approaches*

The discourse on the effect of ICT on the workforce is concerned primarily with ELI, and its indirect repercussions at the individual and organizational levels. Aspectual normativity infuses the discourse, whether about how ICT has harmed the workplace or has positive potential. The aspects of interest are different from those in management, being mainly the juridical aspect, about what is due to the workforce. However, what is due, i.e., the target (§3-7.4.6) of the juridical aspect, may be meaningful in any aspect. Mumford (1995) may be seen as emphasising the aesthetic (leisure, job satisfaction). That the aspects pertain across all cultures (§3-1.2.3) makes it relatively easy to extend the consideration beyond those aspects meaningful to workforces in the Affluent North, to those in the Two-thirds world.

The oversimplifying dualism of the socio-technical approach is sometimes understood as a presupposition of the Nature-freedom ground-motive, but it is more fruitful to see it in terms of elevating the social and formative aspects. Then Lee's (2004) rejection of dualism, seeking to locate information 'between' the social and the technical, is affirmed as the lingual aspect, lying between the social and formative (see also §8-6.3).

6-4.4 *Discourse on Knowledge-Intensive Organizational Functions*

The importance of engagement with knowledge content and of its usefulness in knowledge management and knowledge-based systems makes EMC, ELI and the link between them important. Various portions of Dooyeweerd's philosophy can affirm, critique and/or enrich this discourse.

Alavi and Leidner's (2001) emphasis on a process perspective on knowledge may be closely paralleled by Dooyeweerd's theory of knowledge as aspectual functioning (§3-8.4). Maier and Hädrich's (2006) view that participants, goals and instruments are also important emerges quite naturally from Dooyeweerd's idea that the aspectual functioning that is knowing involves people as subjects and various prior and generated objects (§3-3.1.2).

Issues like accuracy, completeness and timeliness of content (or data or information) are made more complex, than in the discourse on information quality, by tacit knowledge, hidden assumptions and cultural connotation.

According to the theory of knowing as multi-aspectual functioning, in most aspects, knowing is tacit, but for different reasons (§3-8.4). Polanyi (1967) contended that tacit knowledge *cannot* be explicated and Nonaka and Takeuchi (1995) that it *can* be: both can be correct if we consider different aspects. Polanyi's tacit knowledge is pre-analytic, hence does not involve conceptualization, and Nonaka-Tackeuchi's is post lingual, often involving both conceptualization and expression. Research to understand tacit knowledge in this way is being carried out by Alex Kimani, to be published in a forthcoming paper. He is situating the variety of views about tacit knowledge in a wider understanding of aspectual knowing. For two analysis techniques that elicit tacit knowledge, based on Dooyeweerd's aspects, see §4-4.2.2.

Some extant views in knowledge management can be affirmed using Dooyeweerd's aspects. Earl's (2001) kinds of knowledge management align with seven aspects:

- Systems approach: codify all knowledge—lingual aspect;
- Cartographic approach: locate knowledge-holders—social aspect; spatial analogy of location;

- Engineering approach: 'capabilise' employees—formative aspect;
- Commercial approach: make money out of knowledge—economic aspect;
- Organization approach: encourage collaboration—social aspect;
- Spatial approach: provide spaces where knowledge may be shared informally—spatial, kinematic aspect;
- Strategic approach: believe knowledge is important and implement the above—pistic aspect, with its retrocipatory effect on all other aspects (§3-7.4.4).

Hicks et al.'s (2006) tiers of knowledge may be affirmed with aspects: psychic ("in the mind of the person"), analytic ("atomic attribute values about the domain"), formative (data processed), lingual ("clear instructions and authority to perform a task"), and economic ("exploitation of knowledge-based resources"). It may be critiqued by asking why the social aspect is missing, and enriched by suggesting that the aesthetic, juridical and other aspects might also be important; see Table 3.6.

These suggestions need to be critically explored in more detail by research.

6-4.5 Discourse on ICT in Its Wider Environment

The discourse on ICT in its wider environment by systems thinking mainly centres on ELI, and usually at the organizational or societal level. Different versions may be seen as interested in different aspects. Hard, soft and critical systems thinking find the formative, analytical and juridical aspects important, respectively. Systemic intervention finds the aesthetic, juridical, ethical and pistic aspects important. Disclosive systems thinking tries to find all aspects important, because it explicitly wishes to disclose all meaningful norms; it can explicitly make use of Dooyeweerd's aspects to achieve this (Goede et al. 2011).

Actor-Network Theory (ANT) is interested in the lingual and social aspects, as seen in its concepts like inscription, translation and delegation. It recognises both the functioning of actants and the repercussions (direct, indirect) mediated through the network. Its idea of symmetry may be affirmed by Dooyeweerd's idea that objects, like subjects, respond to aspectual law. Its conflation of subject and object does not occur in Dooyeweerd, so Dooyeweerd's law-subject-object idea (§3-3.1.2) might offer a useful philosophical underpinning for ANT that overcomes this.

The reason why both systems thinking and ANT have difficulties with normativity may be that both presuppose that existence (system, actant) is the most fundamental construct: then normativity becomes secondary and must be 'bolted on'. Their difficulty with diversity arises because they first theorise the structure of thing-reality and only secondarily consider diversity. Both problems arise from the Immanence Standpoint (§3-2.1).

By contrast, since Dooyeweerd started with meaningfulness, normativity is inherent (§3-1.2.3), and since he started with everyday experience

(§3-1.1), which presents us with diversity from the start, questions of diversity are addressed by him before questions of structure (aspects before thingness: §3-9.2).

I suggest that both systems thinking and Actor-Network Theory might be 'transplanted' from the barren soil of the Immanence Standpoint to the more fertile soil of Dooyeweerd's philosophy without jeopardising the insights they yield. For example, Basden and Wood-Harper (2006) have grounded Checkland's (1981) idea of CATWOE in Dooyeweerd's aspects. The narrow emancipatory norm in Critical Systems Thinking may be widened to include the normativity of every aspect.

ANT's idea of actant may be reinterpreted as multi-aspectual beings, engaged in multi-aspectual functioning in multi-aspectual subject-object relationships, opening up multi-aspectual possibility. Example: a nurse might interact with the patient record (subject-object) in the lingual aspect, and with the patient (subject-subject) in the social and ethical aspects. Might ANT benefit from an idea of multi-layered networks, each meaningful in a different aspect (lingual network, economic network, ethical network, etc.)?

Might the part-whole relationships of systems thinking and the simple networks of ANT benefit from Dooyeweerd's idea of *enkapsis*? From §3-9.6.2, for ICT use, these might include:

- Correlative enkapsis: the ICT artefact in use within, and affecting, organizational culture;
- Subject-object enkapsis: A planner and the technical tools s/he depends on;
- Symbiotic enkapsis: Two ICT-in-use scenarios that reinforce or undermine each other;
- Territorial enkpasis: The organization and its website;

as well as others yet to be discovered.

This outline suggestion, of how Dooyeweerd's philosophy can affirm, critique and enrich systems thinking and ANT, calls for research.

6-4.6 *Lack of Discourse on Home Computing, Computer Games and Computer Music and Art*

The poverty of the discourse about home computing and computer games, art and music can be explained by the inadequate treatment of everyday experience, with consequent focus on professional life. What does occur is mainly about repercussions of such use from psychological, sociological, educational or societal perspectives. Dooyeweerd would critique that situation for focusing on aspects that are peripheral (psychic, social, lingual and juridical aspects) while ignoring their core aspect that primarily makes computer games, art and music (hedonic use) meaningful, the *aesthetic aspect*.

The conflation of avatar with user by Rambusch and Susi may be explained by the conflation of EMC with either EIT or ELI.

By contrast, the understanding of ICT use introduced above recognises all engagements and all aspects. All aspects of EIT occur more richly than in professional use. All aspects of EMC are important in the content of computer games; see Table 6.3. All aspects of ELI are active in home computing, the aesthetic aspect of fun, the formative aspect of achievement (especially in amateur programming), the social aspect of relating and so on.

6-4.7 Discourse on Information and Data Quality

The discourse on information and data quality (§6-2.7) is the one that most centres on engaging with meaningful content (EMC). Its isolation from other IS discourses confirms the latter's misunderstanding and neglect of EMC. It is the aspectual norms that pertain for meaningful content that can underpin discussions about information fulfilment and satisfaction. A discussion of the relevance of each aspect can be found in §6-3.5.

Wang and Strong's (1997) quality criteria may be understood as aspectual norms, as follows, the final five being those that did not easily fit into their pre-chosen categories.

- accuracy: juridical
- believability: pistic
- objectivity: pistic
- reputation of its source: social
- relevancy: juridical
- timeliness: economic
- completeness: aesthetic
- value-added: economic
- appropriateness of amount: quantitative and juridical
- interpretability: lingual
- ease of understanding: lingual
- consistency: analytic
- conciseness: economic
- accessibility: economic
- security: juridical

- traceability: social, pistic
- variety of data sources: social, aesthetic
- ease of operation: formative
- flexibility: ethical, formative
- cost-effectiveness: economic.

This shows a reasonably healthy distribution across many aspects, but with emphasis on economic and juridical aspects being explained by a business-oriented sample. It is gratifying to see recognition of pistic issues. To critique and enrich their categories, we might refer to under-represented aspects, such as ethical and early aspects.

However, their four final categories (intrinsic, contextual, representational and accessibility data qualities), which excluded five criteria, are problematic. Not only are they derived from a metaphor (instead of, for instance, from philosophy) but they are categories of structure, which, being orthogonal to aspectual categories, will each include several aspectual criteria. Usually, aspects make better categories than do theories about structure.

6-4.8 Discourse on the Acceptance of Technology

Foundationally, what is acceptance of technology (§6-2.8), and why is it important? We may affirm its importance by seeing acceptance as a pistic issue and technology, as formative. Davis' (1989) other constructs (ease of use, usefulness, intention to use) are primarily meaningful in the formative aspect.

That the external variables are not predetermined suggests that Davis recognised the possibility of multiple aspects of his independent variables; Table 6.4 (next section) confirms this. This provides a foundation for research into why each aspect is relevant, both as depended on by the pistic (acceptance) and as retrocipation and antecipation (§3-7.4.4) by the formative (usefulness, ease of use).

Table 6.4 Yousafzai et al.'s Grouping of External Variables of TAM

Aspect	*Organizational characteristics*	*System characteristic*	*Personal characteristics*	*Other characteristics*
Quantitative				
Spatial				
Kinematic		Navigation		
Physical				
Organic-biotic			Age, gender	
Psychic/ Sensitive		Interface, response time	Personality	
Analytical		Perceived complexity, visibility	Awareness, cognitive absorption	Task characteristics
Formative	Internal computing training, peer usage, training, transitional support	Convenience, objective usability, perceived risk, screen design, trialability	Educational level, experience, personal innovativeness, self-efficacy, skills and knowledge	External computing training, facilitating conditions

Aspect	*Organizational characteristics*	*System characteristic*	*Personal characteristics*	*Other characteristics*
Lingual		Information quality, output quality, result demonstrability, terminology	Computer literacy	Argument for change
Social	Image, end-user support, internal computing support, management support, organizational support, organizational structure	Social presence	Involvement, perceived developer's responsiveness, role with technology	Cultural affinity, external computing support, situational normality, social influence, social pressure, vendor's co-operation
Economic		Accessibility, access cost, response time	Perceived resources, tenure in workforce	
Aesthetic	Implementation gap	Compatibility, media style, perceived attractiveness	Perceived enjoyment, perceived playfulness	
Juridical	Organizational policies	Confirmation mechanism, perceived software correctness, relevance with job, accuracy, system quality, Web security		Subjective norms, task technology fit
Ethical	Competitive environment		Computer attitude, voluntariness	
Pistic/Faith	Group's innovativeness norm, job insecurity, organizational usage, peer influence	Perceived importance, reliability	Computer anxiety, intrinsic motivation, shopping orientation, trust	

Ease of use concerns EIT; usefulness concerns ELI. Critique: There is no recognition of EMC. Enrichment: Might EMC also be present as a construct (e.g., as 'veracity')?

Our understanding of ICT use might explain the longevity of Davis's TAM: it parsimoniously incorporates all aspects at least tacitly, and recognises two of the engagements, which had hitherto been occupied separate discourses. It might also suggest that research would be fruitful into incorporating EMC and using aspects to guiding the choice of external variables (e.g., few in ethical aspect).

6-4.9 Discourse on Information Systems Success

Delone and McLean's (2003) six constructs may be largely affirmed by our framework. *System quality*, *information quality* and *service quality* seem to cleanly relate to EIT, EMC and ELI, and are all multi-aspectual. *Net benefit* may be understood as multi-aspectual ELI (see §6-2.10). *Intention to use* and *user satisfaction*, however, privilege certain aspects (formative, pistic, psychic). This might indicate where the most fruitful critique and enrichment might lie.

If 'success' is only in relation to goals, achieved by using the IS as a tool, the privileging might be defended, but perhaps we should consider success more widely, especially in the light of the case of Olive Cook, cited in §6-2.9. 'Intention to use' and 'user satisfaction' must be reinterpreted as something more directly related to the everyday life of victims like Olive Cook (or beneficiaries), in ways discussed in §6-4.10, §6-4.13. The ethical aspect is particularly important, yet easily overlooked.

6-4.10 Discourse on the Usefulness and Benefit of ICT Use

From a Dooyeweerdian perspective, usefulness and net benefit refer to the multi-aspectual *shalom* (§3-8.5), a harmony of positive repercussions in each aspect of ELI. It indludes direct and indirect, individual and organizational repercussions. The discourses on acceptance and success contribute to understanding usefulness and benefit.

Davis' (1989) external variables may be seen as aspectual statements of the potential *shalom* that is usefulness. Yousafzai et al. (2007) collected over 80 from several studies; Table 6.4 shows the aspects that make them meaningful. Columns 2-5 are Yousafzai et al.'s grouping.

Such an aspectual analysis (§4-4.2) has several benefits. 1. It reveals the breadth of coverage by the community, but also imbalances and gaps via empty cells. 2. It can bring together similar issues (e.g. under formative, all the trainings). 3. It stimulates reflections on: (a) the salience of each construct (e.g., why does a competitive environment make ICT more or less useful?), (b) how constructs might affect each other (e.g., Is there a link between Individual voluntariness and competitive environment, both ethical aspect?)

Because Dooyeweerd's aspects are spheres of law, invoking negative as well as positive in each aspect (normativity), we can analyse complex situations. Benefit and detriment coexist (Shalom Principle; §3-8.5). Often these are in different aspects, such as economic benefit but social disbenefit, by which Eriksson (2001) explained unexpectedly reduced profits after installing an ordering system.

6-4.11 *Discourse on User, Artefact and Task*

Burton-Jones and Straub's (2006) user-system-task triad involves subject-object relationships (user-system, user-task) with meaningfulness (task purpose). Goodhue and Thompson's (1995) Task-Technology Fit (TTF) tries to provide norms by which the fit to this meaningfulness may be analysed. Dooyeweerd's law-subject-object idea very readily offers a philosophical foundation for both, in that aspectual law not only defines the subject-object roles and enables the task, but also provides its meaningfulness and deepest norms. Therefore, we may examine TTF's constructs aspectually:

- Quality: juridical
- Locatability: actually formative in what they intend
- Authorization: juridical
- Compatibility: aesthetic (harmony)
- Ease of use/training: formative
- Timeliness: economic
- System reliability: partly pistic
- Relationship with users: social.

Immediately we can see that the analytic and ethical aspects might be missing. Incorporating them might enrich TTF.

To critique Burton-Jones and Straub's triad, we refer to the three engagements that constitute ICT use. The user-system and user-task relationships may be seen as the engagements EIT and ELI. These can be enriched by making them multi-aspectual. But where is engagement with meaningful content, EMC? It is the user-information relationship that is missing from the triad; so the triad may be enriched by adding it.

This suggests several new avenues for research.

6-4.12 *Discourse on Intensive and Innovative Use of ICT*

The discourse on intensive use of ICT (§6-2.12) focuses on the individual and his or her functioning with ICT. This can, in principle, cover learning in all of EIT, EMC and ELI. Intensive use ('infusion' [Cooper and Zmud 1990]) may be seen as ICT being used proximally and beneficial in many aspects of ELI, served by EMC and EIT.

Cooper and Zmud's stages may be affirmed, critiqued and enriched by Dooyeweerd's aspects:

- initiation (matching): analytic—EIT,
- adoption (decision): analytic-formative—EMC?,
- adaptation (training, availability): lingual-economic,
- acceptance (role in organization): social,
- routinization (adjustment of work): economic-aesthetic,
- infusion (integration, support 'higher' activities, trust): aesthetic-ethical.

Affirmation: The order of stages roughly matches that of Dooyeweerd's aspects, which is defined by foundational inter-aspect dependency (§3-7.4.4). Critique: The juridical aspect is missing. Enrichment: Might this suggest that an extra stage occurs in practice, in which we check on the appropriateness of routinised use, for example?

Innovative use may be understood, not just celebrated or measured. Dooyeweerd (1955, I, 105) recognised the possibility of what we call innovative use:

> Everything that has real existence, has many more potentialities than are actualized. Potentiality itself resides in the factual subject-side; its *principle*, on the contrary, in the cosmonomic-side [law-side] of time. The factual subject-side is always connected with individuality (actual as well as potential), which can never be reduced to a general rule. But it remains bound to its structural laws, which determine its margin or latitude of possibilities.

The oceanic law-side provides the basic aspectual possibilities that transcend the known purposes of the designers and users (§3-8.2), and frequently it is an overlooked aspect that opens the way to innovative use. It is the actuality of the subject-object-side (such as the design of ICT features and their affordance; see §7-3.3) that provides actual potential.

6-4.13 Discourses on ICT Ethics and Normativity

> Note on terminology: '*Ethics*' of ICT is usually about right and wrong, and thus juridical. This differs from 'ethics' as Dooyeweerd understood it, which is about self-centred or self-giving *attitude*.

Most of the normativity discourses reviewed in §6-2.13 revolve around repercussions of ICT use in life and are thus almost wholly about ELI, rather than EMC or EIT. This immediately suggests the discourses might be enriched by considering the normativity of EIT and especially EMC (content).

If this is done, we must be careful about the laws by which the normativity is judged. Should the normativity of EMC be judged by those of the real law-side, which governs us, or by those of the virtual law-side encapsulated in the software, which governs the virtual world (§5-5.2) and generates meaningful content? What happens when the two normativities clash, as in some computer games where violence is part of the game?

Simple answers are likely to fail. Since EMC affects ELI, their law-sides can never be entirely separated, but they are conceptually distinct. So the first thing is to explore the link between EMC and ELI in each case. In computer games this might be more tenuous than in, for example *Wikipedia*. In the case of pornography, the link between EMC and ELI is strong. Consider the vignette of Paul and pornography in §6-2.13:

> Example: The evil in objectification of a girl's body is of the *juridical* aspect (grossly inappropriate), and *pistic* (beliefs about the meaningfulness of girls). Disloyalty to Paul's wife is also *pistic*. Self-gratification is evil by reference to the *ethical aspect*, not the psychic (so it is usually hidden from psychology). Analysis of the designers' evil concerns decisions over content, to include planned graduality (*formative*, *kinematic*) and frissance (*aesthetic*). The evil lies, not in these, but in what they were towards, which is the juridical, ethical and pistic evils just discussed.

This reveals why punishing Paul through the judicial system of courts might be ineffective: it does nothing to solve the problem of inner pistic and ethical evils, and it completely misses the evil in the designers. The evils related to design are found as Paul engages with the content (EMC) while his own evil is found in his ELI.

Without such nuanced understanding of complex evil, dysfunctional ICT use will not be successfully tackled, because several aspectual evils reinforce each other. The *Shalom Principle* (§3-8.5), which understands overall benefit or goodness as emerging from positive adherence to the laws of all aspects, and conversely evil, can provide a manageable view of this plethora of aspectual normativities. By separating them out conceptually with aspectual analysis, we can introduce some clarity, to help us understand *why* things are evil (or in other cases, good) and *how* reinforcement occurs. Dooyeweerd's aspects bring to light kinds of issues that are usually overlooked.

This is the basis on which Nick Breems was able to throw light on the complex, under-researched issue of computer procrastination; see §6-3.7 above. With a multi-aspectual approach, normativity of ICT use may be extended to the issues like climate change and biodiversity, as just two other aspects; see §8-4.2.2 for a discussion of these at the societal level. Responsibility is important and may be more deeply understood as the juridical aspect.

The norm of emancipation is narrower than *shalom*, being strongly meaningful in the juridical aspect. Power relations also have a formative aspect of achieving, and an ethical aspect of attitude behind that achieving: self-interest or generosity. Walsham's mistake (§6-2.13) was to presume self-interest rather than generosity while he was focusing on the formative aspect. Dooyeweerd can thus disclose the assumptions or presuppositions that lurk at the roots of a topic like power or emancipation.

The four philosophical theories of ethics mentioned in §6-2.13 may be recognised, integrated and enriched as follows: by the idea of law-side 'ocean of meaningfulness' (§3-1.2) to which we respond as subjects and objects as we function and as normatively characterizing both functioning and repercussions as good or bad.

- *Consequentialist ethics*: Functioning in each aspect of each engagement has repercussions relevant to the aspect. The notion of inter-aspect dependency (§3-7.4.4) can help us understand multi-level consequences. The 'oceanic' nature of normativity accounts for unexpected consequences.
- *Deontological ethics*: Each aspect offers norms to follow, but their 'oceanic' givenness implies deeper laws than the humanly created norms or rules, which are of the subject-object-side.
- *Virtue ethics*: The acting subject may by normatively characterised by reference to aspectual law, and their strengths and weaknesses in each aspect and tendency to fulfil or resist each aspectual law.
- *Discourse ethics* involves lingual functioning that targets various aspectual norms (§3-7.4.6). It can escape Groupthink if it focuses on oceanic aspectual norms rather than constructed norms.

Thus Dooyeweerd might provide a foundation on which to understand the complexities of the normativity of ICT use, both good and evil, and situate the various normativity discourses so they may be brought into contact with each other and contribute to a richer picture. Much research is needed to develop this approach.

6-4.14 Discourses on Non-use of ICT and Resistance

The discourses on non-use of ICT and resistance to ICT focus on ELI: engaging in life—*with or without ICT*. From Dooyeweerd's perspective, ELI is multi-aspectual subject-object functioning, and whether its prior objects (§3-3.1.2) include ICT or not is immaterial. Neither use nor non-use are privileged; c.f. life without ICT, §8-6.1.1. This affirms Selwyn's (2003) conclusion, without either celebrating or denigrating resistance.

Various reasons for non-use may be accounted for by Dooyeweerd's aspects:

- Resistance to ICT use of an ideological nature is pistic. So is the countervailing presumption that resistance should be overcome.

- Resistance of a functional nature is formative aspect.
- Peer pressure for either use or non-use is social.
- Not being able to afford ICT is economic.
- Not understanding ICT is analytic.
- Being denied ICT is juridical.
- Reasons of style are aesthetic.

Since aspects pertain simultaneously, Dooyeweerd makes it easy to allow for multiple reasons.

Both Selwyn and Dooyeweerd treat meaningfulness of the user's life as the starting point for considering non-use, and consider it multi-aspectual. However, Selwyn (2003) fears essentialism, and fear distorts understanding. Dooyeweerd does not, because he has strong philosophical grounds for rejecting essentialism (§3-9.2), and can afford to identify aspects as spheres of meaningfulness, hence offering a firmer foundation for considering non-use than Selwyn can.

6-4.15 Discourse on ICT Features and Affordance

The main discussion of how Dooyeweerd might provide foundational understanding of ICT features and affordance is found in §7-3.3. This section summarises how the challenges issued in §6-2.15 might be addressed.

1. Kinds of affordance may be characterised by two aspects, agent and environment aspects, and types within kinds, by adding a third aspect, a specific purpose aspect; see Table 7.1 in Chapter 7.
2. With Dooyeweerd, affordance comes from a law-subject-object relationship (§3-3.1.2), in which users function as subject (agent) and ICT features as object (environment). The meaningful possibility that features afford may be accounted for by both user and features functioning in the same 'ocean of meaningfulness' or law-side. Normativity of affordance, which is mainly appropriateness, is innate if seen as aspects. See §7-3.
3. Confusion was found in Rambusch and Susi (2008) (see §6-2.15), between user as technology-wielder, as avatar, and as game-player. These may be distinguished be the three engagements, EIT, EMC, ELI.

6-4.16 Discourse on 'Meaningful' Use and Down-to-Earth Issues

What health informatics calls 'meaningful use', and Ahmad and Basden (2013) call 'down-to-earth issues', refer to the everyday experience of the person 'on the ground' who uses ICT. Instead of simplifying its complexity by reference to IS theories, which might misinterpret it, Dooyeweerd offers aspects and their irreducibility and coherence (Section 3-7). All three engagements (EIT, EMC, ELI) might be involved because we are considering the everyday experience of ICT users.

Ahmad and Basden's five challenges can be partly met in open interviews with aspectual analysis as described in §4-4.2. Perspective: Dooyeweerd's respect for everyday experience ensures 'on-the-ground' users are listened to, eschewing both previous academic literature that might theorise issues, and management and ICT suppliers' concerns. Focus, Indirectness: During interviews, intuitive awareness of aspects makes the interviewer sensitive to issues beyond work and professional life, and to indirect impacts of ICT use. Hiddenness: Aspectual analysis is useful to uncover tacit issues hidden even from the interviewee, because aspects can highlight meaningfulness that appears trivial at first. Plethora: Aspects distinguish issues according to main meaningfulness, which then simplifies qualitative grouping processes.

Hawa Ahmad developed a method for systematically using Dooyeweerd's aspects to analyse excerpts from interviews, which is now being employed by two of my students to explore down-to-earth issues in electronic health records and in ICT in teaching (Khojah 2013; Aiyenitaju and Basden 2016).

6-4.17 Silos of Discourse on Applications Overlooked by the IS Field and in Everyday Life Domains

Applications overlooked by the IS field, and everyday life domains, may be readily understood as different application areas in which different aspects are particularly meaningful. Of the applications the aspects are (including two from the IS field, and computer games):

- Geographic Information Systems: spatial and kinematic aspects;
- Computer-Aided Design: spatial and formative;
- scientific computing: physical transduced to the quantitative aspect;
- medical computing: organic-biotic and psychic aspects;
- organizational IS: social, formative;
- managerial IS: economic, formative, social;
- computer games: aesthetic, formative.

These are aspects of ELI (life of application) and EMC (kind of content)—and thus might be useful cases for understanding the link between EMC and ELI.

Techatassanasoontorn and Tanvisuth's (2010) life domains, with the domain of work added, may be characterised as follows:

- education: lingual, social;
- family: social, organic-biotic (health), ethical (care);
- friendships: social, ethical (giving);
- consumers: economic;
- finance: economic, quantitative;
- leisure: aesthetic, social;
- social: social, lingual (conversation);

- self: pistic;
- community: social, juridical;
- work: formative, economic.

Identifying aspects important in each domain can help us think about domains and the part they play in the whole of life. The aspects assigned to family are those Dooyeweerd believed qualified the family and the marriage (which is what the authors meant) combined with the social, but family life has an everyday, pre-theoretical character that involves every aspect. So do all life domains. Because the aspects shown are the main but not the only important ones, thinking about life domains should always be flexible. The aspects also might suggest new applications or domains, such as for theatre or engaging with the natural world, which are missing from the above list.

Discourse about interaction between domains (overlaps, 'spillovers') might start by identifying common aspects among them (friends, social, community, family are all social). Then Dooyeweerd's idea of the coherence of the aspects, especially as expressed in inter-aspect dependency and the *Shalom Principle* (§3-7.4) might enable more precise understanding.

What is the common thread among all these for the information systems field? In all applications of ICT in all domains, their aspects are the target aspects of the lingual (§3-7.4.6), which is the aspect that qualifies ICT and IS (§5-3.5, §8-6.1). So the discourses around application of ICT in each life domain must take account, in their engaging with meaningful content (EMC), of the main aspects, secondary aspects and shalomic dependency of one domain on the other (example: successful family leisure depends on mutual care among family members).

The overall norms of ELI and EMC, usefulness and veracity, take on different forms in different applications, depending on their target and other aspects. In an insurance claims database, for instance, accuracy and completeness of data are paramount. In *Google Earth* the topographic data must be accurate and complete, but if the attached photographs are not accurate it is more a nuisance than a catastrophe. In computer games and virtual worlds, these norms require reinterpretation (Hsu and Lu 2004). Usefulness might be reinterpreted as enjoyment. Veracity might be reinterpreted as *realism*, in that, though we find creatures that do not exist in the real world, they operate according to laws we recognise as reasonable even if not identical to those we function in.

So, the challenge issued in §6-2.17 may be reinterpreted as: It is time for the information systems field to target the whole range of aspects in principle, not just the social and economic.

6-4.18 *Affirming, Critiquing and Enriching Discourses on ICT Use*

Figure 6.3 shows which aspects of which engagements each of the discourses finds important, by an aspectual heatmap for each discourse, as used by Nick Breems (§6-3.7). Each heatmap has one column of cells for each engagement, those for EIT, EMC, ELI left to right. Each of the 15 cells in a column represents an aspect of that engagement, with quantitative at the top and pistic at the bottom. The darker the cell, the more important the aspect in the discourse.

Because the information systems field has neglected certain applications and computer games (§6-4.17, §6-4.6), heatmaps 17 and 6 are treated differently. Heatmap 17, for domains and applications overlooked by the IS community, shows aspects of neglect, and the striped cells indicate target aspects of some applications mentioned in §6-4.17. Heatmap 6, for computer games and home computing, shows what seems important to the applications themselves; the EMC column shows the importance of aspects of engagement rather than aspects of any game world.

The interpretation of each discourse is from my own intuition, taking account not only of what is discussed above, but also a wider literature in, and experience of, each; readers might like to undertake a more systematic analysis.

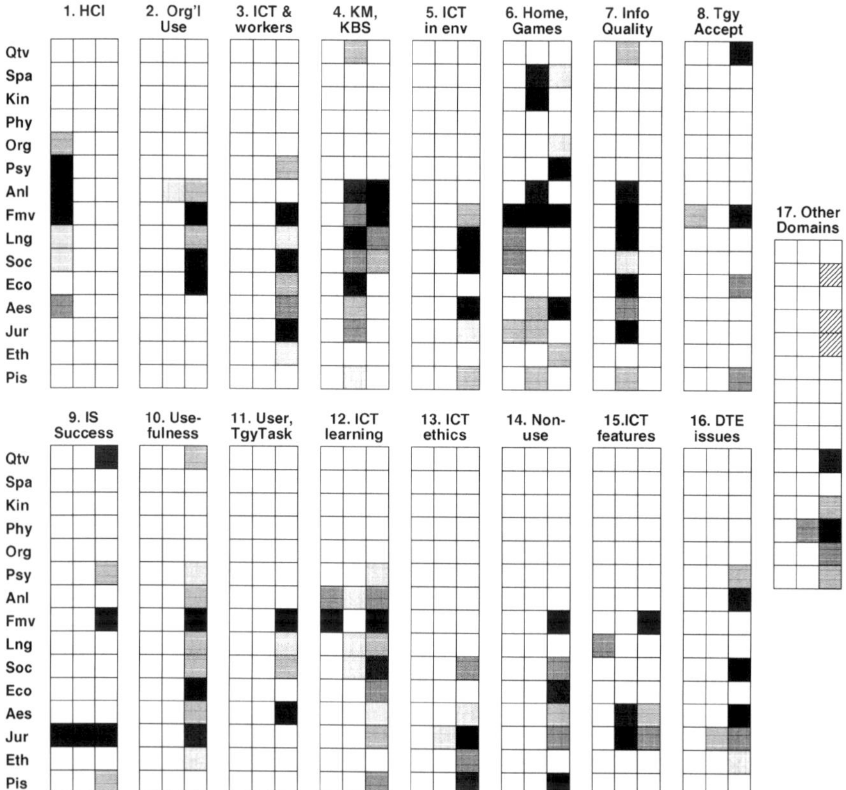

Figure 6.3 The Interests of ISU Discourses

Regarding aspects, such an analysis helps us listen to the discourses and affirm their interest in certain aspects. It is also clear that even in ELI certain aspects are given much more attention than others—the formative and juridical, especially. This can also critique each discourse, by pointing to its limited ranges of aspects, and suggest that other aspects be considered. For example, the discourse on dysfunctional ICT use tends to focus on the juridical aspect, but by recognising more aspects of ELI, then inter-aspect dependency might offer deeper understanding of causes. The limited ranges of aspects also suggests that there is scope for new discourses that will address other aspects of ELI and which will research aspects of EMC and EIT. For example, there is little on the ethical aspect, as the aspect of goodwill, generosity and self-giving love, the dysfunction of which is isolation, self-protection and self-interest. Several suggestions have been made for how it may be incorporated. Suggestions are given in Chapter 12.

Regarding engagements, it can be seen that most of the discourses are interested in ELI. Only HCI, learning and games seem interested in EIT, and only information quality, knowledge management take EMC seriously, with games and features showing some interest. The lack of interest in EIT and EMC is worrying, reinforcing concern about many discourses treating the ICT artefact as a black box (§6-2.15), about which nothing need be understood. Even discourses that pride themselves on being holistic, such as systems thinking, are shown to be quite limited within this wider picture (§6-4.5). However, signs of an opening-up are appearing in the field, with an interest in the materiality of ICT, and in affordance, as discussed in Chapter 7.

The discourses might be enriched by considering three things: new aspects (as above), other engagements if appropriate and other portions of Dooyeweerd's philosophy. For example, the discourse on dysfunctional ICT use tends to focus on repercussions, paying insufficient regard to functioning. By incorporating functioning as well as repercussions, it might offer clearer solutions. The following is a list of portions that are relevant to each discourse.

1. Ease of use and interactions with technology—Aspects, Law-subject-object
2. Organizational issues in IS—Aspects, Theory of social institutions, Enkapsis
3. Effect of ICT on Work, Socio-technical approach—Aspects, Normative repercussions, Pluralism rather than dualism
4. Knowledge-intensive organizational functions—Theory of knowing, Aspects, Diversity of meaningfulness
5. ICT in its Wider Environment—Theory of being, Aspects, Immanence Standpoint, Law-subject-object, Enkapsis
6. Home computing, computer games and computer music and art—Aspects, Importance of everyday experience, Pre-theoretical attitude

7. Information and data quality—Aspectual normativity
8. Technology acceptance—Norms of engagements, Attitudes, Diversity
9. Information systems success—Aspectual normativity
10. Usefulness and benefit—Shalom principle, Aspectual normativity
11. User, technology and task—Law-subject-object relationship
12. Intensive, innovative use of ICT—Aspects, Everyday experience, Theory of knowing
13. Normativity in ICT use: Dysfunctional use, Power and Ethics—Aspectual normativity, functioning & repercussions, especially later aspects
14. Discourses on non-use of ICT, resistance—ICT as object within multi-aspectual human functioning; Everyday experience
15. Use of features of ICT, Affordance—Aspects, Law-subject-object
16. 'Meaningful' use, Down-to-earth issues—Pre-theoretical attitude of thought, Everyday life, Aspectual analysis, Three engagements
17. Applications and domains overlooked by the IS field—Target aspects, Meaningfulness of each aspect

The list can indicate which parts of Dooyeweerd's philosophy might be most fruitful to consider in enriching discourses. For example, the discourse on affordance might benefit from adopting a Dooyeweerdian view of the subject-object relationship, as discussed in §7-3.3.

Possible research avenues in each discourse are listed in Chapter 12.

6-5 Concluding Remarks

In this chapter we have reviewed nearly twenty discourses that are going on in the area of interest that is ICT usage, including some discourses that as yet are not very audible in the field of information systems. Then we proposed a conceptual *aspectual engagements framework* that can provide foundations on which ICT use and the issues important in the discourses around it may be understood. Then we explored the application of this framework and portions of Dooyeweerd's philosophy to each discourse, in a way that affirms, critiques and enriches the discourses and the area as a whole. What we found is depicted in Table 6.5 and the above list.

Affirmation. All discourses were affirmed as being valid and important, as part of a wider picture. All are about human engagement, but with three distinct things, sometimes in combination: about engaging with the technology and interface, about engaging with meaningful content and about engaging in life with ICT. Each of these may be understood in terms of Dooyeweerd's non-Cartesian subject-object relationship. The wide diversity of meaningfulness, normativity and functioning in what each discourse concerns itself with may be usefully considered by reference to Dooyeweerd's suite of aspects. Most discourses tend to focus on certain aspects.

Critique. (1) Most discourses are too narrowly focused on certain aspects. While it is valid to focus on certain aspects, it is preferable if all others are also considered as meaning context. This critique is especially relevant to discourses that focus on either the technical, the personal, the organizational or societal issues to the exclusion of others. Adopting Dooyeweerd's suite of aspects, which cover the whole range, might help to ameliorate this. (2) Too few discourses take EMC into account. (3) Ethics and other normative issues are currently isolated from most of the others, and there is a tendency to see normative concern as unwarrantedly constraining freedom or 'innovation'; this false dichotomy may be understood as a deep, unquestioned presupposition arising from Nature-freedom ground-motive. Instead, should not every single discourse consider the difference between good and evil, between benefit and detriment, and integrate these with considerations of freedom and innovation? (4) Several other troublesome dichotomies may also be critiqued by reference to the Nature-freedom ground-motive. (5) In many discourses there is, perhaps, too much theorizing and too little recognition of everyday experience.

Enrichment. (1) Overall, a Dooyeweerdian approach can move all discourses, research and practice in the entire area of ICT usage towards a more everyday perspective, which will enhance consideration of 'real life' without sacrificing theoretical depth. (2) Each discourse and research activity can be widened in its mindset so that, even though focusing on a limited range of issues, it can be always taking all other aspects into account as a meaning-context. (3) Engagement with meaningful content, usually overlooked, becomes integrated with engagement with interface and technology, and in life with ICT. Each discourse can now take all three engagements into account. (4) By this means, many discourses currently fixed on organizational issues can both take into account, and also provide insights for, computer gaming, home computing and the various application silos. (5) The framework provides a basis for stimulating inter-discourse, on the grounds of aspects (spheres of meaningfulness) they share. (6) The normativity inherent in aspects motivates each discourse and research to consider good and evil within its main focus, not as bolted-on constraints so much as inherent responsibility and opportunity, alongside considerations of aspectual possibility that makes innovation possible. No longer do these have to be considered separately, and then forced together artificially.

Dooyeweerd's suite of aspects has been offered as a practical conceptual tool for throwing fresh light on all issues of ICT usage raised by the discourses, including many that are often overlooked. It provides a basis for developing discourses that have yet to be opened up.

I doubt whether this picture, offered by seeing ICT use as three intertwined multi-aspectual human engagements, can ever be precisely modelled in the manner in which positivistic researchers prefer, because the interlinkings are too dynamic, but Dooyeweerd's philosophy can perhaps provide more clarity than hitherto, and help us explore the relationships among discourses and how each can benefit others.

What I do know is that I used the aspectual engagements framework to structure teaching of several undergraduate modules on HCI and Humans and Computers over a number of years, and that both students and colleagues found it very useful, because it separated out various issues and ensured that we covered a lot more than most such modules did.

References

Adam A, Howcroft D, Richardson H. 2004. A decade of neglect: Reflecting on the gender and IS field. *New Technology, Work and Employment*, 19(3), 222–240.

Ahmad H, Basden A. 2013. Down-to-Earth Issues in Information System Use. Proceedings of the Pacific Area Conference on Information Systems (PACIS). Paper 191.

Aiyenitaju OT, Basden A. 2016. Applying Dooyeweerd philosophy in an empirical project. Presented at *Christianity and the Future of our Societies, CFS2016*, Evangelical Theoligische Faculteit, Leuven, Belgium.

Alavi M, Leidner DE. 2001. Knowledge management and knowledge management systems: Conceptual foundations and research issues. *MIS Quarterly*, 25(1), 107–136.

Ang J, Soh PH. 1997. User information satisfaction, job satisfaction and computer background: An exploratory study. *Information & Management*, 32, 255–266.

Bagayogo FF, Lapointe L, Bassellier G. 2014. Enhanced use of IT: A new perspective on post-adoption phase. *Journal of the Association for Information Systems*, 15(7), 361–387.

Barki H, Huff S. 1985. Change, attitude to change and decision support system success. *Information and Management*, 9(5), 261–268.

Bartle RR. 2004. *Designing Virtual Worlds*. New Riders, Berkeley, CA.

Basden A. 1983. On the application of expert systems. *International Journal of Man-Machine Studies*, 19, 461–477.

Basden A. 2008. *Philosophical Frameworks for Understanding Information Systems*. IGI Global, Hershey, PA.

Basden A, Wood-Harper AT. 2006. A philosophical discussion of the root definition in soft systems thinking: An enrichment of CATWOE. *Systems Research and Behavioral Science*, 23, 61–87.

Baumard P. 1999. *Tacit Knowledge in Organisations*. Sage, London, UK.

Beer S. 1984. The viable system model: Its provenance, development, methodology and pathology. *Journal of the Operational Research Society*, 35, 7–25.

Breems N, Basden A. 2014. Understanding of computers and procrastination: A philosophical approach. *Computers in Human Behavior*, 31, 211–223.

Burke ME. 2006. Achieving 'Information Fulfilment' in the networked society: Part 1: Introducing new concepts. *New Library World*, 107(1228/1229), 444–449.

Burton-Jones A, Straub DW. 2006. Reconceptualizing System Usage: An Approach and Empirical Test. *Information Systems Research*, 17(3), 228–246.

Byrne MD. 1993. Using icons to find documents: Simplicity is critical. *Proceedings of the InterCHI '93*, April, 446–453, ACM, USA.

Caplan S, Williams D, Yee N. 2009. Problematic internet use and psychosocial well-being among MMO players. *Computers in Human Behavior*, 25, 1312–1319.

Card S, Moran TP, Newell A. 1983. *The Psychology of Human Computer Interaction*. Lawrence Erlbaum Associates, Hove, Sussex, UK.

Carr N. 2003. IT doesn't matter. *Harvard Business Review* (May), 1–10.

Checkland P. 1981. *Systems Thinking, Systems Practice*. John Wiley & Sons, New York.

Classen DC, Bates DW. 2011. Finding the meaning in meaningful use. *New England Journal of Medicine*, 365(9), 855–858.

Conole G, Dyke M. 2004. What are the affordances of information and communication technologies? *Alt-J, Research in Learning Technology*, 12(2), 114–124.

Cooper RB, Zmud RW. 1990. Information technology implementation research: A technological diffusion approach. *Management Science*, 36(2), 123–139.

Davis FD. 1989. Perceived usefulness, perceived ease of use, and user acceptance of information technology. *MIS Quarterly*, 13(3), 319–340.

DeLone WH, McLean ER. 1992. Information systems success: The quest for the dependent variable. *Information Systems Research*, 3(1), 60–95.

DeLone WH, McLean ER. 2003. The DeLone and McLean model of information systems success: A ten-year update, *Journal of Management Information Systems*, 19(4), 9–30.

DeLone WH, McLean ER. 2004. Measuring e-commerce success: Applying the deLone & McLean Information Systems Success Model. *International Journal of Electronic Commerce*, 9(1), 31–47.

Dooyeweerd H. 1955. *A New Critique of Theoretical Thought* (Vols. I–IV). Paideia Press, Jordan Station, Ontario, Canada. (Original work published 1953–1958).

Dooyeweerd H. 1986. *A Christian Theory of Social Institutions*, tr. M Verbrugge, The Herman Dooyeweerd Foundation, La Jolla, CA.

Earl M. 2001. Knowledge management approaches: Toward a taxonomy. *Journal of Management Information Systems*, 18(1), 215–233.

Eberts R. 1994. *User Interface Design*. Prentice-Hall, Englewood Cliffs, NJ.

Elbanna A, Newman M. 2013. The rise and decline of the ETHICS methodology of systems implementation: Lessons for IS research. *Journal of Information Technology*, 28, 124–136.

Eriksson DM. 2001. Multi-modal investigation of a business process and information system redesign: A post-implementation case study. *Systems Research and Behavioral Science* 18, 181–196.

Fadel K. 2006. Individual Infusion of Information Systems: The Role of Adaptation and Individual Cognitions. Proceedings of the Twelfth Americas Conference on Information Systems, Acapulco, Mexico August 2006, Paper 38.

Fitts PM. 1954. The information capacity of the human motor system in controlling the amplitude of movement. *Journal of Experimental Psychology*, 47, 381–391.

Flanders V. 2002. *Son of Web Pages That Suck*. Sybex, San Francisco.

Forethought. 2015. BBC Radio 4, broadcast 20:45 hrs on 15 April 2015.

Goede R, Basden A, Ingram R. 2011. Disclosing disclosive systems thinking: Towards a methodology. In J van der Stoep and S Strijbos (Eds.), *From Technology Transfer to Intercultural Development* (pp. 29–40). Rozenberg Publishers, Amsterdam, Netherlands.

Goodhue DL, Thompson RL. 1995. Task-technology fit and individual performance, *MISQuarterly*, 19(2), 213–236.

Green TRG, Petre M. 1996. Usability analysis of visual programming environments: A cognitive dimensions framework. *Journal of Visual Languages and Computing*, 7, 131–174.

Habermas J. 1987. *The Theory of Communicative Action; Volume Two: The Critique of Functionalist Reason*, tr. T McCarthy, Polity Press, Cambridge, UK.

Hartson HR. 2003. Cognitive, physical, sensory, and functional affordances in interaction design. *Behavior & Information Technology*, 22(5), 315–338.

Heijden H. van der. 2004. User acceptance of hedonic information systems. *MIS Quarterly*, 28(4), 694–704.

Hicks RC, Dattero R, Galup SD. 2006. The five-tier knowledge management hierarchy. *Journal of Knowledge Management*, 10(1), 19–31.

Hsu C-L, Lu H-P. 2004. Why do people play on-line games? An extended TAM with social influences and flow experience. *Information & Management*, 41, 853–868.

Ives B, Olson M, Baroudi JJ. 1983. The measurement of user information satisfaction. *Communications of the ACM*, 26(10), 785–793.

Jackson MC. 1991. *Systems Methodology for the Management Sciences*. Plenum Press, New York and London.

Jain V, Kanung S. 2005. Beyond perceptions and usage: Impact of information system use on information system-enabled productivity. *International Journal of Human-Computer Interaction*, 19(1), 113–113.

Jasperson JS, Carter PE, Zmud RW. 2005. A comprehensive conceptualization of the post-adoptive behaviors associated with IT-enabled work systems. *MIS Quarterly*, 29(3), 525–557.

Jiang JJ, Muhanna WA, Klein G. 2000. User resistance and strategies or promoting acceptance across system types. *Information & Management*, 37, 25–36.

Joneidy S, Basden A. 2012. An exploration of the paradigms of information systems use. In LN Lindile, DM Haftor, S Strijbos (Eds.), *The Role of Education in Economy and Society: Proceedings of the 18th Annual Working Conference of the IIDE* (pp. 15–32), 16–20 April. Maarssen, the Netherlands.

Khojah GM. 2013. A new approach to the transition from paper to electronic medical records. In D Stacey, J Solé-Casais, H Gamboa (Eds.), *HEALTHINF 2013: Proceedings of the International Conference on Health Informatics* (pp. 277–283), 11–14 February. Barcelona, Spain.

Labour. 1964. *Election Manifesto*. Labour Party, London, UK.

Landauer TK. 1996. *The Trouble With Computers: Usefulness, Usability and Productivity*. Bradford Books, MIT Press, Cambridge, MA.

Lapointe L, Rivard S. 2005. A multilevel model of resistance to information technology implementation. *MIS Quarterly*, 29(3), 461–491.

Latour B. 1987. *Science in Action*. Harvard University Press, Cambridge, MA.

Lee AS. 2004. Thinking about social theory and philosophy in information systems. In J Mingers, LP Willcocks (Eds.), *Social Theory and Philosophy for Information Systems* (pp. 1–26). John Wiley & Sons, Chichester, UK.

Lim VKG. 2002. The IT way of loafing on the job: Cyberloafing, neutralizing and organizational justice. *Journal of Organizational Behavior*, 23, 675–694.

Lin C-P, Bhattacherjee A. 2010. Extending technology usage models to interactive hedonic technologies: A theoretical model and empirical test. *Information Systems Journal*, 20, 163–181.

Lin H-F. 2010. An investigation into the effects of IS quality and top management support on ERP system usage total quality management & business excellence, 21(3), 335–349.

Liu D, Li X, Santhanam R. 2013. Digital games and beyond: What happens when players compete? *MIS Quarterly*, 37(1), 111–124.

Mclean ER, Sedera D, Tan FTC. 2011. Reconceptualizing System Use For Contemporary Information Systems. 2011 Proceedings of the Pacific Area Conference on Information Systems (PACIS).

Maier R, Hädrich T. 2006. Centralized versus peer-to-peer knowledge management systems. *Knowledge and Process Management*, 13, 47–61.

Majchrzak A, Faraj S, Kane GC, Azad B. 2013. The contradictory influence of social media affordances on online communal knowledge sharing. *Journal of Computer-Mediated Communication*, 19, 38–55.

Markus L. 1983. Power, politics and MIS implementation. *Communications of the ACM*, 26(6), 430–444.

Midgley G. 2000. *Systemic Intervention: Philosophy, Methodology and Practice.* Kluwer/Plenum, New York.

Miller GA. 1956. The magic number seven plus or minus two: Some limits of our capacity for information processing. *Psychological Review*, 63(2), 81–87.

Mingers J, Walsham G. 2010. Toward ethical information systems: The contribution of discourse ethics. *MIS Quarterly*, 34(4), 833–854.

Mumford E. 1995. *Effective Systems Design and Requirements Analysis: The ETHICS Approach.* Palgrave Macmillan, Basingstoke, UK.

Mumford E. 2006. The story of socio-technical design: Reflections on its successes, failures and potential. *Information System Journal*, 16, 317–342.

Mumford E, Weir M. 1979. *Computer Systems in Work Design—the ETHICS Method.* Associated Business Press, London, UK.

Nonaka I, Takeuchi H. 1995. The knowledge creating company. Oxford, UK: Oxford University Press.

Norman DA. 1988. *The Psychology of Everyday Things.* Basic Books, New York.

Norman DA, Draper SW. 1986. *User Centred System Design: New Perspectives on Human Computer Interaction.* Lawrence Erlbaum Associates, Hove, Sussex, UK.

Orlikowski WJ. 2007. Sociomaterial practices: Exploring technology at work. *Organization Studies*, 28(9), 1435–1448.

Pinsonneault A, Rivard S. 1998. Information technology and the nature of managerial work: From the productivity paradox to the Icarus paradox. *MIS Quarterly*, 22(3), 287–311.

Polanyi M. 1967. *The Tacit Dimension.* Routledge and Kegan Paul, London, UK.

Rambusch J, Susi T. 2008. The challenge of managing affordances in computer game play. *HUMAN IT* (publ. University College of Borås), 9(3), 83–108.

Renkema TJW. 2000. *The IT Value Quest: How to Capture the Business Value of IT-Based Infrastructure.* John Wiley & Sons, Chichester, UK.

Ricoeur P. 1981. *Hermeneutics and the Human Sciences.* Cambridge University Press, Cambridge, UK.

Robey D. 1979. User attitudes and management information system use. *Academy of Management Journal*, 22(3), 527–538.

Sajeva S. 2010. The analysis of key elements of socio-technical knowledge management system. *Economics and Management*, 15, 765–774.

Seddon PB. 1997. A respecification and extension of the Delone and McLean model of IS success. *Information Systems Research*, 8(3), 240–253.

Seidel S, Recker J, vomBrocke J. 2013. Sensemaking and sustainable practicing: Functional affordances of information systems in Green transformations. *MIS Quarterly*, 37(4), 1275–1299.

Selwyn N. 2003. Apart from technology: Understanding people's non-use of information and communication technologies in everyday life. *Technology in Society*, 25, 99–116.

Shortliffe EH. 1976. *Computer-Based Medical Consultations: MYCIN.* Elsevier, New York.

Singletary LLA, Akbulut AY, Houston AL. 2002. Innovative Software Use After Mandatory Adoption. Paper presented at the Proceeding of 8th Americas on Information Systems (AMCIS), 1135–1138.

Spolsky J. 2001. *User Interface Design for Programmers*. Apress, New York.

Stacey RD, Griffin D, Shaw P. 2000. *Complexity and Management: Fad or Radical Challenge to Systems Thinking?* Routledge, London, UK.

Strijbos S. 2000. System methodologies for managing our technological society: Towards a 'Disclosive' Systems Thinking. *Journal of Applied Systems Studies*, 1(2), 159–181.

Swanson EB. 1987. Information channel disposition and use. *Decision Sciences*, 18(1), 131–145.

Techatassanasoontorn AA, Tanvisuth A. 2010. IS use and quality of life: A conceptualization and empirical investigation. *AIS Transactions on Human-Computer Interaction*, 2(2), 26–54.

Tennant V, Mills A, Chin W. 2011. *Investigating Information System Infusion at the Individual Level: Re-Conceptualisation and Operationalisation, Pacific Asia Conference on Information Systems (PACIS) Proceedings*. Published by AIS Electronic Library (AISeL).

Thomas G, James D. 2006. Reinventing grounded theory: Some questions about theory, ground and discovery. *British Educational Research Journal*, 32(6), 767–795.

Tolkien JRR. 1977. *The Silmarillion*. George Allen & Unwin, London, UK.

Ulrich W. 1983. *Critical Heuristics of Social Planning: A New Approach to Practical Philosophy*. John Wiley & Sons, Chichester, UK.

Venkatesh V, Bala H. 2008. Technology Acceptance Model 3 and a Research Agenda on Interventions. *Decision Sciences*, 39(2), 273–315.

Venkatesh V, Brown SA. 2001. A longitudinal investigation of personal computers in homes: Adoption determinants and emerging challenges. *MIS Quarterly*, 25(1), 71–102.

Venkatesh V, Davis FD. 2000. A theoretical extension of the technology acceptance model: Four longitudinal field studies. *Management Science*, 46(2), 186–204.

Venkatesh V, Morris MG, Davis GB, Davis FD. 2003. User acceptance of information technology: Toward a unified view. *MIS Quarterly*, 27(3), 425–478.

Verenikina L, Harris P, Lysaght P. 2003. Child's play: Computer games, theories or play and children's development. In J Wright, A McDougall, J Murname, J Lowe (Eds.) *Young Children and Learning Technology. Conference in Research and Practice in Information Technology* (Vol. 34, pp. 99–107). Australian Computer Society, Sydney, Australia.

Vest J, Jasperson J. 2010. What should we measure? Conceptualizing usage in health information exchange. *I. American Medical Informatics Association*, 17(3), 302–307.

Walsham G. 2001. *Making a World of Difference: IT in a Global Context*. John Wiley & Sons, Chichester, UK.

Walsham G, Sahay S. 1999. GIS for district-level administration in India: Problems and opportunities. *MIS Quarterly*, 23(1), 39–66.

Wang RY, Strong DM. 1997. Beyond accuracy: What data quality means to data consumers. *Journal of Management Information Systems*, 12(4), 5–34.

Wenger E. 1998. *Communities of Practice: Learning, Meaning and Identity*. Cambridge University Press, Cambridge, UK.

Winograd T, Flores F. 1986. *Understanding Computers and Cognition: A New Foundation for Design*. Addison-Wesley, Reading, MA.

Wixom BH, Watson HJ. 2001. An empirical investigation of the factors affecting data warehousing success. *MIS Quarterly*, 25(1), 17–41.

Young JS, Simon WL. 2005. *iCon, Steve Jobs: The Greatest Second Act in the History of Business*. John Wiley & Sons, New York.

Young KS, de Abreu CN. 2011. *Internet Addiction: A Handbook and Guide to Evaluation and Treatment*. John Wiley & Sons, New York.

Yousafzai SY, Foxall GR, Pallister JG. 2007. Technology acceptance: A meta-analysis of the TAM: Part 1. *Journal of Modelling in Management*, 2(3), 251–280.

Zammuto RF, Griffin TL, Majchrzak A, Dougherty DJ, Faraj S. 2007. Information technology and the changing fabric of organization. *Organization Science*, 8(5), 749–762.

Zigurs I, Buckland BK. 1998. A theory of task/technology fit and group support systems effectiveness. *MIS Quarterly*, 22(3), 313–334.

7 Understanding ICT Features

What is it about ICT and its features that affects the way we live and work? Take Nick Breems' recorded experience (c.f. §6-3.7):

> Feeling unengaged in the blog writing, you switch to a new browser window, navigate to a game site and play an online version of the old dice game Yahtzee. An hour later, you are still playing, trying to better your high-score, and feel guilty about the waste of time. No matter how mightily you steel your will to the contrary, and no matter the feelings of guilt and stress that result, this kind of online procrastination continually sneaks into your life and disrupts your productivity.
>
> (Breems and Basden 2014, 211)

Such problems (and opportunities) are discussed from the users' perspective in Chapter 6; this chapter looks at similar problems from the perspective of ICT itself. What it is about ICT that affects the way we live and work. It suggests several things, as depicted in Figure 7.1.

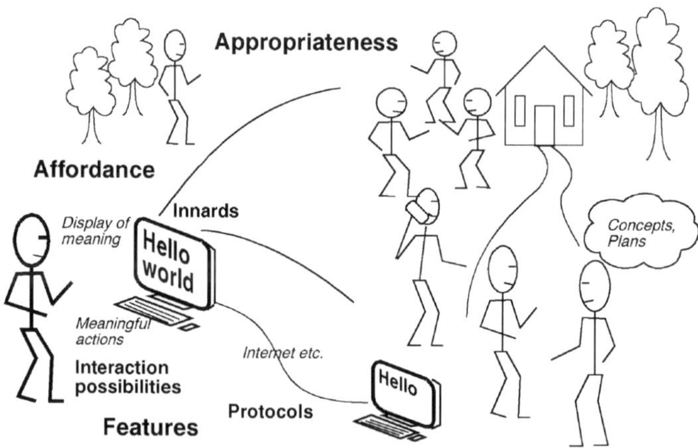

Figure 7.1 ICT Features

Depicted in the figure are: ICT features afford possibilities to users, which arise from 'innards' (§5-5.4), are mediated via interactions and widened by connections with other ICT via protocols. ICT features are to be seen as part of the world, rather than as mere constructs of developers with which users must cope, so ICT features should harmonise 'naturally' with the world. This provides two main issues: affordance (which is important in discourses about the 'materiality' of ICT) and appropriateness (which is a major part of the normativity of affordance). All involve every aspect.

7-1 Introduction: Why Features of ICT Are Important

Chapter VII of Basden (2008) discussed ICT features from the developer's perspective, as components or ICT resources that developers employ in creating the ICT artefact, and therefore from a computer science perspective. This chapter looks at ICT features in a way that is more relevant to users and the information systems (IS) field, as the nether end of the three engagements that users make with ICT as discussed in Section 6-3: engaging with the interface and technology (EIT), engaging with meaningful content (EMC) and engaging in life with ICT (ELI).

ICT features are not atomic. On one hand, they form hierarchies, in which several features together constitute another (example: a screen keyboard on a mobile device, a feature in itself, might comprise other features like voice-recognition, predictive typing and user-defined layout). On the other hand, ICT features will be treated as involving three things shown in Figure 7.1: possibilities that enable interaction via user interfaces, 'innards', which are the algorithms and data structures 'behind' the interface, and protocols, by which a computer interoperates with others especially across the Internet, and the appropriateness of each will be discussed.

> Note on terminology: '*Feature*' is the thing with which the user engages in ICT. Here, 'feature' carries no negative or humorous connotation, such as of being a software bug.

Examples are given that will be referred to later.

7-1.1 Examples of Interaction Possibilities

Interaction possibilities are what allow users to interact with the ICT features of a user interface. They are called this to emphasise an ICT-centred perspective that is user-oriented rather than developer-oriented. They refer

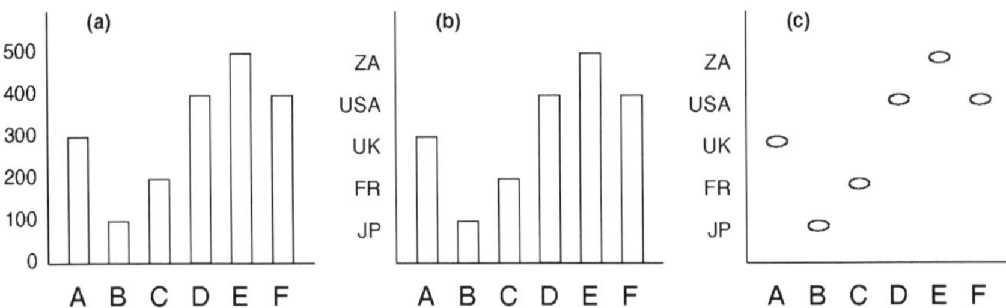

Figure 7.2 A Typical Bar Chart

to both input from user and output to user, involving visual, aural, haptic or other channels. Consider the following examples.

Barcharts. A barchart presents information about several things as a set of rectangles arranged side by side so that comparisons may be made. A simple one is shown in Figure 7.2, which presents information about six kinds of thing, A-F (kinds of food, automative manufacturers, etc.). Barcharts are most naturally interpreted by the user as a set of quantities, such as sales (all data fictitious), as in (a). Version (b) disrupts this assumption, by placing qualitative information about country of origin on the Y axis, and feels somehow unnatural. To link automotive businesses with country of origin, it is better to replace the bars by symbols where their top was, as in (c). There is something about bar length that more naturally expresses quantitative than qualitative information. When information is presented in unnatural ways, it is easy to be misled or confused.

Interactions. There are several ways to enter quantitative information like sales figures: enter digits via a keyboard, move a slider with mouse or finger, touch or mouse-click increase/decrease arrows and several more. Why does digit entry allow greater precision, and why are sliders quicker and more dynamic?

7-1.2 Examples of Innards

What I call 'innards' of a computer in §5-5.4 applies to ICT features. Innards comprise the data structures and algorithms 'inside' or 'behind' the user interface. The user experiences innards only indirectly via the interaction that occurs. Innards approximate to Model in Model-View-Controller and to Schema in the Service-Oriented Architecture, except that innards also include the algorithms by which the data is displayed, since those too are experienced by the user only indirectly. Innards can be interacted within several ways, e.g. barchart spoken to blind people. Consider the following.

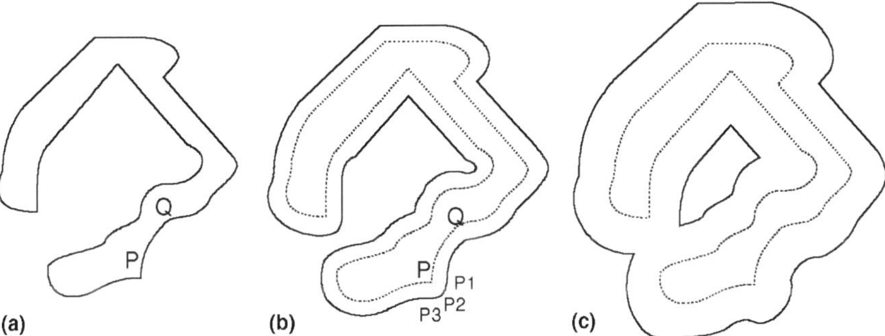

Figure 7.3 A Complex Shape (Woodland) and Its Extensions

Innards of barcharts. The innards must hold all the information expressed in the barchart or the means to calculate it, including: the quantities to be displayed, the list of things (and their labels, A-F), style of display (empty bar), etc. along with algorithms to display and alter these.

Complex shape. This will be discussed in detail so as to reveal what happens internally, for later. A complex shape, such as a boundary of woodland shown in Figure 7.3a, will usually be represented as a sequence of points, typically held internally as a list of coordinate pairs (x,y) that measure the position of each point.

Suppose we wish to expand the boundary by a fixed amount all round (e.g., predators roam up to 200m from the wood, and we wish to know in what surrounding area their prey is vulnerable), as in Figure 7.3b. (Note: This is boundary-expansion, not shape-magnification.) The new shape is also held internally as a list of coordinate-pairs and would be calculated from the boundary list by complex trigonometry. Extra points might be added (e.g., P1, P2, P3 from P) or points might disappear (none from Q). The innards for this would contain: (a) correct trigonometric algorithms, (b) list-handling algorithms, (c) the data structures for the two lists. Errors in any of these would give a wrong result. Now, suppose we extend the boundary farther, as in Figure 7.3c. The ends of the shape coalesce, and a hole appears. This cannot be held as a single list; it requires two, along with a way to link them. In the general case, a complex shape might have any number of holes and within each hole there may be 'islands' of the shape, which might themselves have holes. Complex indeed! Most shape-handling algorithms do not cater for shapes with holes (are they seen as exceptional cases by developers?). So, when the ICT in use encounters holed shapes, it will usually fail without warning and let the user down.

License revoked. Massachusetts Registry of Motor Vehicles revoked the license of a faultless driver because the face recognition feature found similarity between his face and a criminal's, *and* the algorithm that decided to revoke was too simple. (https://www.wired.com/2014/11/algorithms-great-can-also-ruin-lives/ accessed 19 December 2016)

Shooting down the Iranian Airliner. An air traffic monitoring system identified an Iranian passenger airliner with the code TN4474, but it then changed this to TN4131 because the system was designed to recycle codes. Because of this change, the airliner was not recognised and was shot down (Fisher and Kingma 2001). While human functioning was partly to blame, so was the way the software was designed on which the humans relied.

In these examples, something unexpected and deleterious occurs, from minor nuisance to fatality. This is part of the reality of ICT features, and we need a foundational understanding to enable us to understand what happens and why.

7-1.3 Examples of Protocols

Protocols are the rules and structures by which programs (or individual features) store information for later use or transmit it to others. Much of the Internet operates because of protocols like HTTP, or to send photographs to friends. Good protocols are required for interoperability and poor ones jeopardise it.

Text protocols. With *Adobe Reader* for reading *PDF* (the 2015 version), try searching for a phrase that happens to continue from the bottom of one page to the top of the next. It will not find it. So the individual user might miss an important piece of information. Data mining depends crucially on good text search features, and so in this case could miss data.

The problem lies not just in the reader application, but in the PDF protocol itself. Surprisingly PDF was not designed for text but for layout, as explained in §7-2.4.2. By contrast, the *HTML* protocol was designed from the start according to the nature of text rather than of layouts, with concept like emphasis, lists, paragraphs, headings, cross-references built-in.

Picture protocols. GIF (Graphics Interchange Format) stores a diagram as an array of index-numbers, each of which indexes a colour lookup table to find the colour of a pixel; the array of pixel colours creates the diagram when displayed. JPEG (Joint Picture Expert Group) stores a picture as an array of tuples, each of which indicates the colour of a pixel directly. It is designed for photographs, in which colours change subtly. Colours must be faithful but some blurring is acceptable, which allows very efficient data-compression. GIF is better for diagrams, where colour differentiation and sharp edges are more important than faithful colour, JPEG for photographs.

The foundational 'idea' on which a protocol is built—layouts or text, diagrams or photographs—radically influences its limitations and what it enables.

7-1.4 Example of Whole Features

The three work together, with innards and protocols 'behind' interactions. The feature of *photospheres* (360-degree photograph of the surrounding hemisphere), illustrates this:

- Interaction possibilities for photospheres: The user takes a number of pictures, aiming of the camera for each being guided by dots that appear on the screen. This feature ensures that all necessary photographs are taken from which the photosphere will be compiled.
- Innards of the photosphere feature: A complex algorithm combines all the individual pictures into one that contains all the information about the view within the hemisphere around and above. Since camera aim is not precise, it must work out the common edges between them, adjust brightness and hue to remove banding, and then distort each picture in appropriate ways to fit a sphere.
- Protocols for sending photospheres: Normally a JPEG protocol is used to store and send the composite picture, but extra information is needed to ensure that it is displayed properly, namely information about precisely how distortion occurs at every point in the picture. Also, information about geographic location at which the photographs were taken must be included if it is to be included on Google Maps.

Without all three of these, the photospheres feature would not be effective.

7-1.5 This Chapter

Whereas the *activity* of designing ICT is discussed in chapter 9, this chapter is concerned with the *object* of design. What constitutes ICT features to make them work well rather than badly, while recognising both the user's experience of them and the developer's responsibilities in creating them? We need a foundation for understanding the nature or shape of ICT features, their impact on ICT use and their design, from the point of view of the features themselves rather than of the user or designer, but in the context of both.

Section 7-2 reviews extant discourses around the themes of affordance and appropriateness. Section 7-3 suggests how Dooyeweerd's philosophy can provide a foundational understanding of these. Section 7-4 applies this in detail to the three elements of features in order to show how practical design might be guided.

7-2 Extant Discourses on Technological Features

Traditionally in the information systems field, ICT has been either ignored or treated as a 'black box' (Jasperson et al. 2005), so that its impact has not been sufficiently understood from the perspective of ICT itself. This section briefly reviews some IS discourses that treat ICT with more respect, to identify two foundational issues, affordance and appropriateness. The selection of discourses here is not intended to be authoritative or exhaustive, and there will be overlaps.

7-2.1 Features Rather Than Products

It is tempting to assume that we are discussing ICT products or applications as a whole, such as databases, social networking packages, geographic information systems, as in Chapter 6. Though ICT vendors, procurement and management might view ICT in this way, as a 'black box', Faraj and Azad (2012) argue that 'black box' does not accurately represent the user's experience, who see each software package as providing a distinctive "bundle of possibilities". Users' everyday experience of ICT—their annoyances, frustrations, achievements, satisfactions—is more about *ICT features* than ICT products. Jasperson et al. (2005), and others want to open up the black box and discuss the features that constitute the ICT artefact.

Many features are found across products, such as messaging or search, or at lower level, predictive text entry or zoom, and they help or hinder the user in similar ways regardless of product. So there is a generality about features, as features, that needs to be understood.

ICT features might range from small, atomic 'interface objects' like the search box on a browser, right up to large, almost systemic things, like the entire capability of *Google search* on which the box calls. Features seem to nest within each other, lower-level ones serving as 'parts' of higher-level ones—but maybe oversimplified: the huge Internet-wide feature of *Google search* serves my wee search box! Sometimes a whole application, such as Google Maps, might be treated as a feature.

7-2.2 The 'Materiality' of ICT

Until the 1980s or so, technological determinism dominated the discourse about the role of ICT in human life and society: technology would determine how we live; all we can do is learn to adapt to it (see §8-2.3.1). This was questioned by social constructivism, which emphasises the freedom people have to design, use and interpret technology as they wish (c.f. innovative use, §6-2.12, and resistance, §6-2.14). Social constructivism became a dominant paradigm.

However, this led to a tendency to ignore what has become known as *materiality* of ICT, a reality of which we must take account, something we stub our toes on. Freedom in use is not infinite; there is something inherent in the examples in §7-1 above that cannot be explained away by social constructivism. Hutchby (2001) argued that we need to recover an interest in the materiality of ICT, without falling back into technological determinism.

There is a growing recognition that we need to understand both the nature or shape of ICT, alongside human freedom in using it, and how the two interact.

Latour (1987) emphasised something similar when discussing the place of technical and other artefacts in human activity, proposing 'symmetry' between human actors and technological devices, calling them both 'actants' because ICT has some agency among users.

A major work on materiality is Orlikowski's (2007) essay, which argues that we should take both the human/social side and the material/technological side equally seriously. Traditionally, the discourse of sociologists, and of the IS people who followed them, "largely disregards, downplays, or takes for granted" the material/technological side (p. 1436), or it completely separates the technological from the social. In the field of organizational life, she points out, things like "bodies, clothes, rooms, desks, chairs, tables, buildings, vehicles, phones, computers, books, documents, pens, and utensils—to the less visible flows—such as data and voice networks, water and sewage infrastructures, electricity, and air systems" (p. 1436) are important, yet largely ignored. Her essay is a call to study the relationship between the two sides, a relationship she labels *sociomateriality*, and may be seen as representing many who are concerned about the same imbalance, a number who are listed by Orlikowski.

'Material' does not refer to 'matter' in its physical sense alone, but rather to the fact that there is something 'there' in ICT that is beyond social or even individual construction. Though Orlikowski (2007) lists examples of things with materiality, she does not clearly define materiality as such, leaving it to our intuition to understand it. No clear picture has emerged yet of what materiality is or how it functions.

Leonardi and Barley (2008, 163) believe that materiality has been "understudied", and lay the blame for this on the "stigma of determinism" which "gravitates" attention away from the technical features towards the "voluntaristic" field of the social. They observe that technology is reduced to "an abstract cause" in much of the discourse. What is meant by technological and social varies among authors. They wish to refocus attention on features "without resorting to determinism". "To integrate materiality with a more voluntaristic stance" (p. 164) requires attention to how the features of artefacts "become entangled in" people's work, by attending "to what a technology lets users do, what it does not let them do, and to the workarounds that they develop to address the latter". These need to be classified, which requires suitable 'language'. While these are useful suggestions, especially referencing everyday experience, they do not argue convincingly why voluntarism or social construction cannot explain this. We need a stronger understanding of the relationship between material, technological, human and social aspects, as well as a sound basis for classification.

7-2.3 Discourse on Affordance

One major recognition of this 'materiality' is the notion of *affordance*, by which ICT features 'afford' the user certain capabilities, which thus change human and organizational activity. Hutchby (2001) suggests that the notion of affordance might enable us to escape social constructivism and pose questions about the 'objective' reality of ICT without falling back into technological determinism.

7-2.3.1 Affordance in the Field of Information Systems

In the IS field, several authors have recently proffered lists of types of affordances (i.e., capabilities that ICT features offer, enable or encourage). Conole and Dyke (2004) look at how Internet-connected ICT affords new possibilities in educational practice, discussing the following:

- accessibility to information,
- speedy change of information,
- diversity,
- communication & collaboration,
- reflection,
- multi-modal non-linear learning,
- risk, fragility and uncertainty,
- immediacy,
- monopolization, and
- surveillance.

Treem and Leonardi (2012) argue that "social media are of important consequence to organizational communication processes because they afford behaviours that were difficult or impossible to achieve in combination before", and suggest the following four affordances are relatively stable:

- visibility of content,
- persistence of content,
- editability of content, and
- association.

Zammuto et al. (2007), suggest that ICT in businesses affords:

- visualization of entire work processes,
- real-time/flexible product and service creation,
- virtual collaboration,

- mass collaboration, and
- simulation.

Seidel et al. (2013) suggests four affordances that might enable environmentally sensitive organizational functioning:

- reflective disclosure, to change beliefs,
- information democratization, for participation,
- output management,
- delocalization.

Majckzrak et al. (2013) suggest that social media afford the following for "publicly visible conversations" in organizations:

- metavoicing (ability to comment on the presence rather than content, e.g., by voting 'Like'),
- triggered attending (setting emails or blogs to alert us to certain topics so we don't need to keep watching),
- network-informed associating, and
- generative role-taking.

The idea of affordance begins to answer Nick Breems' question about computer procrastination with which this chapter began.

7-2.3.2 Kinds of Affordance

The idea of *affordance* was coined by J.J. Gibson in the field of ecological psychology in order to understand how animals respond to their environment. "The affordances of the environment," explained Gibson (1979, 127), "are what it offers the animal, what it provides or furnishes." A running animal sees rocks and leaps up, stops and looks around, then continues climbing. To the animal, the rocks afford climbability and a vantage point. This is made possible by the physical and spatial properties of the rocks—flat, rigid, having friction, extended, at a certain height and so on—but these are not the properties the animal is thinking about.

This proved an attractive idea and generated considerable debate (see below), which continues to this day. It has been adopted in other fields. In the human environment of hardware artefacts like door handles, Norman (1988) used the idea of affordance to explain why certain things are easy to use or 'natural', while others are difficult. For example, Norman shows a picture of doors handles that at first sight look like plates to be pushed, but in fact should be pulled, so a prominent label, "PULL", was necessary.

The field of human-computer interaction (HCI) faces similar issues (Norman 1988; Hartson 2003). The visual, aural and tactile features of the user interface afford information of various types rather than others.

Naturalness of user interfaces may be explained by appropriate or inappropriate affordance.

> Example: The barcharts in §7-1.1 illustrate how the length or size of an object on screen affords display of quantitative but not qualitative information. Qualitative 3relationships are afforded better by spatial relationships like same-row and same-column.

In this field, affordance has a normative quality (Rietveld 2008). Affordance can be perceptible, hidden or false, with the hidden ones allowing novel uses (Gaver 1991) and false ones being used in games to challenge players. HCI affordance is discussed from the user's point of view in §6-2.1 and §6-4.1.

In the information systems field, the features of ICT afford benefits in human (work) life, such as have been listed above. Normativity becomes even more important in IS affordance, where ICT features might constrain or harm the user's activity as well as enable and benefit it. Though most authors discuss only the positives, Conole and Dyke (2004) explicitly list include some negatives, while Majchrzak et al. (2013) discuss the negative correlates of each positive. Example: Network-informed association can encourage blind preferential attachment ("rich get richer"). IS affordances are discussed from the user's point of view in in §6-2.15 and §6-4.15.

7-2.3.3 Foundational Understanding of Affordance

Thus we have various kinds of affordance, with a number of types as listed above within each kind. For a foundational understanding of IS affordances, we need to understand what affordance is across all kinds (or that there is no common thread). The discussion that follows is a summary of one that should soon be published.

In all kinds, there is an *agent* acting in, or engaging with, an *environment* in ways that are meaningful to both. In IS, the environment consists of ICT features. Just as a rock affords climbability to an animal, so ICT features afford editability, network-informed association, etc., to ICT users.

However, questions remain. How complete are the lists in each kind of affordance? On what basis may affordances be identified (Seidel et al. 2013)? How do the lists relate to each other, some seemingly 'lower level' than others? "At present," wrote Leonardi and Barley (2008, 166), "we have no language for making clear distinctions between types of constraints and affordances" and this seems still true. Treem and Leonardi's (2012) classification four years later is not final; Mansour et al. (2013) modified it.

Though most of the IS discussions have *drawn attention* to affordances and *catalogued* them, few have *explored* the underlying mechanism. Leonardi and Barley (2008) believe the lack of ability to classify may be "in part, because we have paid little attention to technologies' material properties and, in part, because we have examined a relatively small set of information technologies."

To address such questions requires an understanding of what affordance is and how affordance is possible. Might we capitalise on the discussions in ecological psychology, as reviewed in Chemero (2003) and elsewhere, about: Are affordances events, features, properties, situations, abilities or dispositions? Do affordances enable, invite or constrain? Are they perceived, observed or acted on unreflectively? Are they with or without mental representation? Are affordances real? That the debate shows little sign of resolution suggests that foundational philosophical issues remain unresolved.

There is indeed a philosophical conundrum at the heart of the notion of affordance, which Gibson recognised and struggled with, but which some of his followers have simply avoided: *the meaning of the feature to the agent is actually a property of the environment itself*. It is the rock itself that is climbable (a psychical property) and would remain so, even though no animal ever climbed it. It is the text in the computer that is editable, and would remain so even though no user ever edited it. This foundational problem occurs in all other kinds of affordance, but has not been widely discussed in the IS field.

It raises two philosophical challenges, that of the *subject-object relationship* (agent as subject, environment feature as object), and that of *meaning*.

Ecological psychologists have debated the former by reference to Descartes' notion of active subject and passive object, but this cannot satisfactorily account for how 'subjective' properties like climbability and vantage are enabled by 'objective' properties like rigidity, horizontality and friction. Some have turned to Heidegger or Merleau-Ponty, for whom the agent must be understood within an environment, and who offer an understanding of being-in-the-world, the active nature of perception and the importance of the body. But that is unsatisfactory for two reasons. One is that asymmetry between subject and object is dissolved rather than explained. In particular, it does not account for the directed dependency which Gibson (1979, 129) pointed out:

> The organism depends on the environment for its life, but the environment does not depend on the organism for its existence.

Likewise in information systems, the 'life' of mass collaboration (Zammuto et al. 2007) depends on features like address lists, internet connectivity and databases of social relationships, but the existence of these does not depend on mass collaboration.

The other reason is that Merleau-Ponty's emphasis on the body hinders a full appreciation of the aspects of IS features that do not primarily involve the body; such as editability (Treem and Leonardi 2012). Though some use the body as a metaphor, and metaphor can be inspirational, it is preferable to understand affordance directly.

To his credit, Gibson would not allow his findings to be forced into either Cartesian or Heideggerian straitjackets.

> An important fact about the affordances of the environment is that they are in a sense objective, real, and physical, unlike values and meanings, which are often supposed to be subjective, phenomenal and mental. But actually an affordance is neither an objective property nor a subjective property, or it is both if you like. An affordance cuts across the dichotomy of subjective-objective and helps us to understand its inadequacy. It is equally a fact of the environment and a fact of behavior. It is both physical and psychical, and yet neither.
>
> (Gibson 1979, 129)

The psychical meaning-to-the-agent of the environment is already 'built into' the environment as a possibility, before any agent is present. "Gibson's concept of affordances was an attempt to undermine the traditional dualism of the objective and subjective" (Costall 2012).

However, Gibson's own attempts to provide a theoretical foundation for this were "sketchy and confused" (Costall 2012) and hence generate controversy and confusion. Withagen et al. (2012) concluded that a full-blown account of affordance still awaits us; it still does.

The fact that, in IS, the environment of ICT features has been manufactured by ICT developers might provide some insights, but it cannot fully account for IS affordance. Does not the phenomenon of innovative use (§6-2.12) indicate that features offer affordances that developers did not anticipate?

The second philosophical challenge is that of *meaning*. Gibson and others have recognised that meaning is foundational in affordance. In all affordance, properties meaningful to the agent are located in an environment "infused with meaning" (Gibson 1979, 128). Gibson's ideas are "an ecological theory of meaning" (Schmidt 2007). In the 1950s, meaning was not a concept that psychologists liked to use, so it is the more significant that, in a 1954 paper, Gibson refers to meaning-concepts. According to Costall (2012, 87), Gibson had written "a remarkable, though largely forgotten, chapter on meaning, in his first book, The perception of the visual world (1950)", which "anticipated the concept [of affordance] in several important ways".

However, across the fields, much discussion of affordance ignores the issue of meaning in favour of other issues, or disguises it by other words, or refers to meaning implicitly rather than grappling with it explicitly. In §7-3.3 we explore how Dooyeweerd's radical understanding of subject-object and meaning might provide foundational understanding of affordance in all fields.

7-2.4 Discourse on Normativity of Features

Affordance can account for the *fact* of 'materiality' of ICT features and if suitably understood, the *mechanism*. There is another important discourse, about *normativity*. Compare:

- a speech-recognition feature, and
- a speech-recognition feature that can deal with stutter.

Both have the same kind of affordance, but one is better than the other. What makes a good ICT feature? What norms are there?

7-2.4.1 *The Norms of Ease of Use and Information Quality*

One norm is ease of use. There has been extensive discourse about what ease of use is and how to achieve it, within the human-computer interaction (HCI) community since the 1970s. Details change as technology changes, but there are generic principles or theoretical understandings that remain valid throughout, such as:

- Norman's distinction of the gulfs of evaluation and execution has provided architectural guidance to fulfilling the norm.
- Accessibility for those visually challenged has long been recognised.
- Norman's (1990) seven criteria for good interaction or Shneiderman's (1992) eight 'golden rules' (consistency, shortcuts for frequent users, information feedback, dialog closure, error-handling, action-reversal, internal locus of control, and short-term memory load) provided normative guidelines, and are still used today.
- Green and Petre's (1996) 'Cognitive Dimensions' determine the quality of an interface at a higher level.
- Interfaces should be 'proximal' rather than 'distal' (Winograd and Flores 1986; Basden and Hibberd 1996).
- The interface as a whole rather than its parts (e.g., 'findability' [Findlater and McGrenere 2007]).

Sutcliffe (2000) made two observations about such discourses. The area draws heavily on findings from psychology, but frequently these do not scale up or are too simplified in other ways to be of much value. Second, there are few new ideas and little overall theory. Much of the practical advice that is being promulgated today, such as on YouTube, refers back to material that was developed in the 1980s. Sutcliffe argued that new perspectives would be needed on using theory in design of features, in which design must be better linked with theory without confusing design.

A third observation is that most of these discourses are about the *activity* rather than *content* of the interaction. Yet, from an IS perspective, and as the examples in §7-1.1 show, content is important. Ease of use for amending textual and spatial information is different.

A second norm is quality of information. Data and information quality have usually been discussed from the users' perspective (see §6-2.7), but the same normativity applies to an ICT features perspective. Wang and Strong's (1997) classic list of criteria (accuracy, believability, consistency, etc.; see §6-4.7) is typical of many understandings of information quality. These are rather general norms, and do not take account of kind of information. Yet accuracy, for instance, takes different forms for financial amounts, maps, reports, photographs, etc. The issue of 'fake news' has become prominent while this book was being written, with discussion of the need for correction thereof on global social media.

Both norms differ for different kinds of information. Both need a third norm to take content into account: appropriateness.

7-2.4.2 The Norm of Appropriateness

Appropriateness means being sensitive to the kind of information or meaningful content of ICT features—quantitative, qualitative, spatial, textual, etc. (Basden 1993). Appropriateness sees ICT features as part of the (information) world and thus they should fit the way the world works and is, rather than being merely the outcome of a design process or human construction. The world is diverse; so must features be. Whereas ease of use applies mainly to interaction possibilities, and information quality applies mainly to innards, appropriateness applies to interaction possibilities, innards and protocols.

Appropriateness of interaction possibilities is the main normativity associated with affordance. It has already been illustrated with the example of barcharts (§7-1.1): bar length affords expression of quantitative amount but not of relationships; spatial relationships express relationships. If interaction possibilities are not appropriate to the type of content, then ICT users will misinterpret or mishandle them or will find them cumbersome to use to get things right. Norman (1988) provides many striking examples of inappropriate affordances; see Basden (2008).

Appropriateness of innards is about the potential to cause problems or benefits because of the contents of algorithms and data. If innards are not appropriate, then errors will occur in use that are unexpected and will let users down, because what they believed or assumed is not how the ICT functioned. As examples in §7-1.2 show, the results of inappropriate innards can range from mild nuisance to fatality. Whereas Chapter 6 is interested in the problems (or benefit) as such, here we are interested in why this is so in terms of what the ICT features are about. Examples in §7-1 include:

- The barchart is about quantitative information and analysis.
- The complex shape is spatial.
- The license-revoking is juridical.
- The airliner identification problem is analytic.

Appropriateness of protocols is illustrated in §7-1.3. Relying on GIF to send a photograph or JPEG to store a diagram is not ideal. Relying on PDF to store text can result in relevant data being missed by searches. The latter is because the core idea of PDF is not text but spatial layout and visual appearance. Text is seen as glyphs contained in boxes, each page being a separate box, with text stopping at the end of the page, so cross-page phrases are not recognised. If protocols are inappropriate, then it will prove either impossible to store or transmit the necessary information content or it will be at least error-prone, cumbersome and inefficient. This could seriously jeopardise interoperability, on which the entire edifice of ICT today depends.

7-2.4.3 Discourses on Appropriateness

There is, as far as I know, only one book that touches on appropriateness, published nearly 40 years ago. William Kent's (1978) *Data and Reality* is a classic work that is only now beginning to be appreciated. It discusses the link between reality and its representation in computers as conceptual models that shape the data, stressing the importance of them fitting reality in all its complexity. Since ICT features incorporate such models in all their elements, they too should 'fit' reality.

While many formal notations and formalisms for representing knowledge have been proposed, culminating, perhaps, in Wand and Weber (1995)'s attempt at a general domain ontology based on Bunge (see Basden [2008] for critical discussion), Kent (1978) had already argued that the relationship between reality and conceptual modelling is very complex and 'amorphous', more than even Wand and Weber allowed. He looked forward to a time when "data processing technology will move toward handling information in ways that are natural to the people who use it." This resonates with our idea that ICT features should be treated as part of reality rather than as constructs.

"It follows then" continued Kent "that a durable conceptual model should be based on constructs as close as possible to the human way of perceiving information" and he started along the path of subjectivism, seeking a solution. Linking data structuring with human perception might resonate with the interest in HCI affordance, but both leave unanswered the question of what is "the human way of perceiving information" and whether it does indeed "follow" from the need for "ways that are natural". Is not perception often deceived, by illusion or social structures and expectations? Was Kent too uncritical of the subjectivism then starting to become popular as a reaction against objectivism? His insights about the challenges of appropriateness of conceptual models remain unsurpassed, but we may question his attempt at explanation, and offer an alternative, which distinguishes "natural" from "human way".

Though Kent (1978) has still not been adequately discussed, since then a number of things have happened that bear out his call for natural ways to handle the relationship between data and reality. *Object-orientation*, seeing reality as objects of defined types (classes), each with attributes and activities appropriate to its type, has become dominant. *Design patterns* recognises that reality contains not isolated objects but whole patterns of them, which themselves should be designed (Gamma et al. 1995). *Cross-cutting concerns* are meaningful facilities that cut across all software code, which traditionally makes code-modification difficult and error-prone. *Aspect-oriented programming* (Kiczales et al. 1997) has arisen to tackle this; see §7-4.2.3.

Such developments all point to there being something about the world that calls for "natural ways" or appropriateness. I tried to discuss this in Basden (1993) and Basden (2008), but those thoughts were perhaps not sufficiently well-formed. Foundational understanding of appropriateness is still required.

It seems that appropriateness is hard to define or theorize. Appropriateness of interaction possibilities has been discussed within the discourse of HCI affordance, with copious examples from Norman (1988), but its nature has been seldom discussed. Appropriateness of innards and protocols has been discussed by Kent (1978) but only indirectly by others via domain ontologies. Otherwise, inappropriateness has either been tolerated or avoided rather than understood.

We need a more precise understanding of appropriateness and inappropriateness, which can help guide design, and which takes account of what is 'natural' without succumbing to subjectivism.

7-2.5 Overview

In this section, it has been suggested that we need to understand the nature of ICT features, and that extant discourses have not gone that far. Two main issues have been identified as important: *affordance*, which helps to account for the 'materiality' of ICT, and *appropriateness*, which is its main normativity. Each feature affords different possibilities and is appropriate in different ways. Both affordance and appropriateness are complex issues, which depend on the kind of meaningful content encapsulated in the ICT features. This links to both the interactions with the user and the benefits or detriments of using the ICT. Whereas Chapter 6 discusses these from the user's perspective, this chapter does so from the perspective of ICT features.

Neither affordance nor appropriateness are well understood. The next section discusses how Dooyeweerd's philosophy might prove useful in providing a foundational understanding of ICT features.

7-3 Towards an Understanding of ICT Features

This section draws on some of Dooyeweerd's philosophy, as outlined in Chapter 3, to make a basic proposal, then discusses how this works out in relation to affordance and appropriateness. Section 7-4 will then apply this in detail. An important idea is that users, developers and ICT all 'swim' in the same diverse '*ocean of meaningfulness*' (or 'law-side'), which provides deep connection between everything; see §3-1.2.3.

7-3.1 The Basic Proposal

The proposal has two main parts: (a) to understand the relationship among features and between features and ICT artefact via Dooyeweerd's theory of thingness, outlined in Section 3-9, and (b) to understand the relationship between features and humans (users, developers) in terms of multi-aspectual engagement as discussed in Chapter 6.

The relationship among ICT features and with the ICT artefact might be part-whole, but most are enkaptic (§3-9.6), for example:

- Part-whole: voice-recognition feature with stutter-handling;
- Foundational enkapsis: features at several levels, each a different aspectual being that constitute the whole, such as social networking, social databases and record-handling;
- Correlative enkapsis: ICT artefact/system as a 'forest' of features.

The relationship between humans and features is subject-object. According to §3-3.1.2, ICT users and developers are subject, ICT features are object, prior object to users and generated object to developers. Subject and object are bound together by multi-aspectual law, which governs both and makes subjectness, objectness and the relationship between them possible as proximal rather than distal engagement. This provides a foundation for understanding 'materiality' and affordance, and also the appropriateness and quality of features.

Together, both parts of the proposal enable us to consider all three elements differentiated in §7-1 (interaction possibilities, innards, protocols). We first discuss how it helps us understand affordance and appropriateness, and then this is used to understand the design of each element.

7-3.2 A Dooyeweerdian Understanding of Materiality of ICT

The reason the materiality of ICT has been "understudied" for decades is traced by Leonardi and Barley (2008, 171) to a conflation of "determinism with the material and voluntarism with the social." This is a clear manifestation of the stultifying effect of the dialectical Nature-freedom ground-motive (§3-2.3), which drives theoretical thinkers to see determination and freedom as absolute opposites. Let us move to Dooyeweerd's ground-motive that is more sensitive to aspectual diversity.

Materiality is a metaphor from the physical to "opportunities for or constraints on action" (Leonardi and Barley 2008, 162). Metaphors arise, Dooyeweerd argues, from inter-aspect analogies. So analogical echoes of physical causality, forces and persistence are found in the later aspects (see §3-7.4.3), for example:

- Formative aspect: ICT 'causes' repercussions, ICT offers resistance to 'forces' we impose on it in our use, and ICT persists in the sense that it remains there however and whether people use it, like a rock over which people might trip.
- Social aspect: ICT 'causes' (enables) relationships and roles, which 'persist' as organizational structures, and ICT 'forces' the social milieu towards certain kinds of relationship or role and away from others (e.g., transient versus long-lasting; c.f. societal issues, Chapter 8).
- Lingual aspect: ICT 'causes' (evokes) responses to information or answers to questions, knowledge persists in mind and in store of recorded material, and ICT 'forces' people towards certain kinds of information (c.f. Foucauldian 'power is knowledge').

Metaphors can inspire but also mislead. After being inspired, we are wise to consider the aspects directly that contain the analogies. Dooyeweerd's notion of inter-aspect analogy thus provides a useful and philosophically sound 'language' in which to begin a deeper understand, and perhaps classify, 'materiality' of ICT. Research into physical analogies in the various aspects in which ICT functions would be fruitful, as a start. However, we must understand features as such, not just materiality as a general concept.

Looking directly at aspects of features as they present themselves to us from an everyday perspective might provide a vocabulary for the 'language' for the discourse around materiality, which Leonardi and Barley say is lacking. This is what we do with affordance and appropriateness.

7-3.3 A Dooyeweerdian Account of Affordance

The conundrum in affordance, that meaning-to-agent is located in the environment feature, is readily explained by the notion of 'ocean of meaningfulness' (§3-1.2.3): both agent and environment function in the same aspects. We may understand this more precisely . . .

7-3.3.1 Affordance as Law-subject-object Relationship

We can understand affordance as a Dooyeweerdian law-subject-object relationship (§3-3.1.2), in which agent and environment-feature both function in all aspects, in some as subject, in others as object. There are thus two main aspects involved in affordance:

- An **agent affordance aspect**, in which agent functions as subject while environment-feature functions as object: a subject-object relationship;
- An **environment affordance aspect**, in which both agent and environment-feature function as subject: a subject-subject relationship, by which interaction obtains.

This constitutes affordance.

In saying that animal affordance is "both psychical and physical, and yet neither", Gibson (1979, 129) expresses the Dooyeweerdian understanding directly, even using Dooyeweerd's names for the two aspects. In the physical aspect, animal and rock function as subjects (e.g., force and equal-and-opposite reaction); in the psychical aspect, animal functions as subject (climbing) and rock as object (allowing-climbing); see §3-3.1. Space does not permit full discussion of how Dooyeweerd can fully satisfy Gibson in his search for meaning and to "undermine the traditional dualism of the objective and subjective" (Costall 2012).

In the case of information systems, the same account is appropriate, but the subject-functioning of the ICT feature is Nick Breems' notion, subject-by-proxy (§5-4.4).

(If we prefer not to use 'by-proxy' and hold computers as functioning as subject only up to the physical aspect, as in Table 5.3, §5-4.3, we may still account for affordance but more complexly. The lingual proxy-subject-functioning of the ICT is constituted in the engagement of user with computer (EIT in §6-3.3) by virtue of users and developers functioning in the lingual aspect. However, to understand affordance, I prefer to use the shorthand of 'subject-by-proxy', in which ICT functions as subject in the lingual aspect (§5-2.5, §5-3.5).)

Usually (always?) the environment aspect is earlier than the agent aspect, because it makes the agent functioning possible by inter-aspect dependency (§3-7.4.4).

In human functioning all aspects usually operate, so a full account of affordance must accommodate these. We will find a third aspect useful in distinguishing types of affordance:

- A **secondary affordance aspect**, which is one of the other aspects of affordance functioning.

This can refer to one of the other aspects on which the main ones depend in retrocipation or antecipation, or to a target aspect. Example: analytic detectability (Hartson 2003).

7-3.3.2 Classifying Affordances

Affordance is possibility; these three aspects (agent, environment, secondary) define which possibility. This offers a principled way of classifying aspects, by triple-aspect analysis. *Kinds* of affordance may be differentiated by pairs of agent and environment aspects, and *types* within each kind may be differentiated by the secondary aspect. Table 7.1 applies triple-aspect analysis to the various kinds and types of affordance listed in §7-2.

Each taxonomy is characterised by a pair of aspects, linked by inter-aspect dependency, and in most IS affordances, the lingual is the environment aspect, the aspect that qualifies ICT (§5-2.5). These lead the use of the

Table 7.1 Aspects of Various Types and Kinds of Affordance

Affordance Kind or Type	*Environment Aspect*	*Agent Aspect*	*Secondary Aspect*
Animal affordances (Gibson 1979)	Physical	Psychical	
		Climbability	Physical
		Eatability	Organic-biotic
Artefact affordances (Norman 1988)	Physical	Formative	
		e.g., Door handle	Kinematic (go through door)
HCI affordances (Norman 1988)	Psychical	Lingual	
ICT 'physical' affordances (Hartson 2003)	Psychic	Analytic	
		Clicking an object	Analytic
		Shape of objects	Spatial, Analytic
		21 others	Various
ICT 'sensory' affordances (Hartson 2003)	Psychic	Analytic, Formative	
		Detectability	Analytic
		Distinguishability of sound	Analytic
		Findability	Formative
		17 others	
ICT cognitive affordances (Hartson 2003)	Analytic	Lingual	
		Legibility	Analytic
		Predictability of meaning	Lingual
		Error avoidance	Juridical
		32 others	
ICT functional affordances (Hartson 2003)	Formative	Lingual	
		e.g., Automatic typing corrections	Formative
		Various unspecified	
IS affordances (Conole and Dyke 2004)	Formative	Lingual	
		Accessibility to information	Economic
		Speedy change of information	Formative
		Diversity	Aesthetic

Affordance Kind or Type	*Environment Aspect*	*Agent Aspect*	*Secondary Aspect*
		Communication & collaboration	Social
		Reflection	Analytic
		Multi-modal non-linear learning	Aesthetic
		Risk, fragility and uncertainty	Juridical
		Immediacy	Psychic
		Monopolization	Economic
		Surveillance	Juridical
IS affordances (Zammuto et al. 2007)	Lingual	Economic, Social	
		Visualization of entire work processes	Analytic, aesthetic
		Real-time/flexible product and service creation	Formative
		Virtual collaboration	Lingual
		Mass collaboration	Socia
		Simulation	Analytic
IS affordances (Treem and Leonardi 2012)	Lingual	Social	
		Visibility of content	Analytic
		Persistence of content	Economic
		Editability of content	Lingual
		Association	Formative
IS affordances (Seidel et al. 2013)	Lingual	Social	
		Reflective disclosure	Pistic
		Information democratization	Social juridical
		Output management	Economic
		Delocalization	Social-spatial
IS affordances (Majchrzak et al. 2013)	Lingual	Social	
		Metavoicing (e.g., voting 'Like')	Analytic
		Triggered attending (setting alerts in conversations)	Analytic
		Network-informed associating	Social
		Generative role-taking	Social

ICT artefact as a whole. Secondary aspects express different aspects of the multi-aspectual functioning of user with the ICT artefact, and might each be enabled by a different ICT feature.

It may be noticed, for instance, that both Treem and Leonardi's and Majchrzak et al.'s affordances have the lingual-social pair but are very different. It cannot be explained just by difference in technology. It seems that Treem and Leonardi's affordance types (editability, etc.) are of the lingual functioning with the ICT content, while Majchrzak et al.'s (network-informed associating, etc.) are of the social functioning. It may be that one is the ICT-feature-end of aspects of engaging with meaningful content and the other of engaging in life with ICT (EMC, ELI in §6-3.3).

Indeed, whole kinds of ICT/IS affordance seem to be variously of ELI, EMC and of EIT (engaging with the interface and technology). The links between this view of affordance and the framework developed in Chapter 6 is still to be explored.

7-3.3.3 Benefits of This View

This provides a framework within which all kinds of affordance may be situated. It provides a principled way of differentiating kinds of affordance, as agent and environment aspects, and understanding types within each kind, as other aspects of the user's engagement with ICT.

This view can account for how several kinds of affordance work together. Where the agent aspect of one kind is the environment aspect of another (as with HCI, IS), it is likely that one serves the other. Indeed, we might also refer to the three engagements discussed in §6-3.3, with interface and technology, with meaningful content and in life with ICT.

Such aspectual analysis offers a basis for critiquing taxonomies. It can force clarification of what is meaningfulness to agent and environment-features, and can help differentiate overlapping issues (such as 'association', which in Majchrzak et al.'s case is definitely social but in Treem and Leonardi's case seems a mixture of lingual and social).

It can also provide a basis for suggesting new types and kinds, by identifying aspects missing in a taxonomy and new aspect-pairs.

Example, *New types*: None of the cited authors have entries in the ethical and pistic aspects. Yet knowledge conversations (Majchrzak et al. 2013) might be expected to be of higher quality with a more generous, self-giving attitude pervades them (ethical aspect) rather than self-centredness, also when participants believe in what they are saying (pistic aspect) rather than for amusement. So we might challenge Majchrzak et al. to consider whether there is something about social media that affords the ethical or pistic in either positive or negative ways.

Example, *New kind*: The aesthetic-lingual pairing might provide an understanding of some of the affordances of computer games, with its multi-aspectual functioning in all aspects indicating affordance types (example, challenge: formative aspect).

It might be useful for further understanding and designing ICT features. For example, in computer games, false affordances might occur (e.g., virtual door handle does not open virtual door). False affordances should usually be used only in EMC, where the meaningful content is the virtual world of the game. In EIT and ELI, false affordances are usually detrimental. Such differentiations might help inform and enrich the process of creating the virtual law-side that is the program (§5-5.2).

Thus, Dooyeweerd's notions of law-subject-object relationships and oceanic meaningfulness provide a much-needed foundational understanding of how affordance is possible in all its kinds. IS affordance involves the lingual aspect, and Dooyeweerd's suite of aspects can help us account for types of affordance within each kind. It might not provide clear-cut answers but does at least help us raise questions.

This outline of a Dooyeweerdian theory of affordance calls for research.

7-3.4 A Dooyeweerdian Account of Appropriateness

This section provides a foundational understanding of the norm of appropriateness, which itself is a foundation for understanding ease of use and ICT feature quality.

The reason appropriateness is hard to define (see §7-2.4.3) is readily understood by Dooyeweerd: Appropriateness is near the kernel of the juridical aspect (see Table 3.4). It may be grasped with intuition and actualised in practice but cannot be defined or theorised. Kent (1978) sought a 'natural' link between conceptualizations and reality and believed that following human ways of perceiving will yield this, despite the possibility of perception being deceived. The Dooyeweerdian idea of 'oceanic' meaningfulness (§3-1.2.3) provides harmony between them, insofar as both reality and human perceiving alike are made possible within the same ocean of meaningfulness.

Appropriateness of ICT, then, is constituted in respecting the laws and meaningfulness of this ocean, to take account of them in all we think, do, decide, construct, etc. Though we grasp oceanic meaningfulness by intuition, separating out the spheres of meaningfulness and law (aspects) helps us untangle our intuitions, so they may be explicitly referred to, and unwarranted reductions may be avoided. Appropriateness, then, is respecting the meaningfulness and laws of each aspect as we develop and use ICT features.

In Chapter VII of Basden (2008), taking a developer's perspective, I used this approach to understand appropriateness of knowledge representation formalisms and of the ICT resources (modules of software libraries) that developers employ, to suggest how redundancy, omissions and confusion could be reduced during development, and thus build better ICT artefacts. In this book, taking the users' perspective, we use a similar approach to understanding the normativity or quality of the three elements of features, and what they afford ICT users.

- *Appropriateness of interaction possibilities* involves the interactions (output and input) affording something meaningful in the aspect in which the user wishes to function (the agent affordance aspect). Inappropriateness is when the aspects clash. This applies to both intended and unintended possibilities of use.
- *Appropriateness of innards* is when the laws and meaningfulness of the aspects, in which the feature is to function with the user, are encapsulated in the innards of the features. This includes those depended on by retrocipation and antecipation (§3-7.4.4). The veracity with which each aspect is encapsulated in the innards gives a *profile of possibilities*, on which ICT developers might capitalise (§9-3.3). This is made more tractable if ICT features are composed of aspectual modules (in each of which one aspect is encapsulated), as discussed in Basden (2008).
- *Appropriateness of protocols* implies that all that is meaningful in the aspect(s) of the kind of content for which the protocol is intended can be easily expressed therein, and that the rules of the protocol match the laws of the aspect(s). (Other aspects, on which the main ones depend foundationally or anticipatorily, will also need to be taken into account.)

How these proposals work is discussed and demonstrated in Section 7-4.

Usually a feature will have one aspect of primary importance, which qualifies it, and this aspect should also be the primary one for each of its elements. Of course, it is impossible to capture the entire lawfulness and meaningfulness of an aspect in any software, so the discussions above and below refer, by "all", to all that of each aspect which it is relevant and reasonable to capture.

7-3.5 Conclusion

This section has discussed how Dooyeweerd's philosophy can help understand what affordance and appropriateness are and what makes them possible, a discussion that seems to be lacking in extant discourses. The next section discusses these ideas in more detail, concerning the three elements of good features in a way that may be applied in research and practice.

7-4 The Design and Composition of Good ICT Features

The previous section developed a general understanding of affordance and appropriateness using Dooyeweerd's philosophy. This section is more down-to-earth: how to understand the elements of features—interaction possibilities, innards and protocols—in a way that allows us to design or evaluate them in practice.

Evaluation and design of these might be from the perspective of the professional or technical designer, or from that of the user who is frustrated (or delighted) by the ICT features and wants to understand why, and perhaps seek workarounds.

Features make things possible when users use ICT, by their innards, protocols and interaction possibilities. Since Dooyeweerd's aspects enable distinct kinds of possibility (§3-8.2), Dooyeweerd's suite of aspects is a useful conceptual tool to separate out the issues that might face us as users or developers, about interaction possibilities, innards and protocols.

7-4.1 Aspectual Interaction Possibilities

The appropriateness of interactions, whether visual, aural or tactile, may be understood by reference to aspects.

The examples in §7-1.1 illustrate how visual phenomena and motor behaviour can express some things more naturally than others. Aspects may readily explain why this is so. The primary visual property of the bars in Figure 7.2 is length, which is a spatial retrocipation to the quantitative aspect. When the bars are replaced by a dot positioned at their ends, the primary visual feature is the presence and position of the dot rather than a length, as antecipation of the analytic aspect of distinction. The spatial row-and-column positioning, with which most of us are familiar, can indicate a category labelled on the axes.

Table 7.2 shows (examples of) appropriate user interface objects for expressing information from each aspect to the user, in visual display and in

Table 7.2 Appropriate User Interface and Interactions to Express Meaningful Content in Each Aspect

Aspect	*Visual display*	*Sound*	*Input*
Quantitative amount	Precise: Digits; Imprecise: bar length, bar/pie charts, darkness	Volume, pitch	Hit keys, drag slider, etc.
Spatial extension	Maps, spatial arrangements	Quad sound	Drag to relocate / reorientate
Kinematic movement	Animation, paths	Musical rhythm	Joystick to control direction, speed
Physical energy / matter	Light / 3-D perspective of terrain	?	Haptic devices
Organic-biotic organisms	Boundary (org-env); Hierarchy charts for progeny	?	'Soft' haptic devices

(*Continued*)

Table 7.2 (Continued)

Aspect	*Visual display*	*Sound*	*Input*
Psychic / Sensitive sensing, emotion	Colour, texture	Textured sound	Sliders to control e.g. HSV; Camera, microphone
Analytical distinction	Icons, menus, tick boxes, Venn charts	Distinct sounds	Click to select
Formative achievement	Structure diagrams, lists, graphs, etc.	Music that evokes progress	Click to activate, drag to manipulate
Lingual signification	Text, diagrams, etc.	Speech, warning sounds	Keyboard typing, speech recognition; 'Reply' facility invites lingual functioning
Social together	Photo of person, box-arrows diagrams showing relationships, etc.	Speaking names etc.	'Share', 'Follow', etc.
Economic resources	Double-entry tables, "10 out of 12", part-filled box	(Only speech)	Prevent deleting a resource (law of conservation). 'Add-to-cart' facility, etc.
Aesthetic harmony, fun	Decoration Show things in relation to the whole	Music	Fine control of psychic phenomena; 'Like' facility
Juridical due	Explanations with cross-references help get appropriate information; 'Terms & conditions'	Speech with those	Easy ability to correct information, e.g. fake news
Ethical love	?	?	Wikis encourage people to give information for free
Pistic / Faith belief, commitment	Persuasive argument	Persuasive argument	Opportunity to commit (e.g. 'Pay' facility)

sound, and also appropriate input actions the user might take to manipulate that kind of information. The examples selected cover most user interfaces known today, and new ones can be added. The standard user interface elements are good at engaging with information of the first six or eight aspects, but new ones need to be invented for post-lingual aspects.

Notice how this approach brings together the traditional user interface issues like mouse versus keyboard and direct manipulation versus command line styles, with facilities that have become commonplace on mobile devices. This contrasts with conventional perspectives, which see the various types as very different, studied in different fields. This could provide a basis for understanding new kinds of interface possibilities, but of course the table should be expanded to include, e.g., haptic and tactile media.

Interaction possibilities are not, however, identical with engaging with the interface and technology (EIT) as discussed in §6-3.4. They also include engagement with meaningful content and in life with ICT (EMC, ELI), and how EIT affords EMC and both afford ELI, as the table above shows. Moreover, the meaningful content is mediated not only via the symbols of the interface but also by their behaviour. Their behaviour is governed by the innards and protocols, to which we now turn.

7-4.2 Aspectual Innards and Aspect-Oriented Programming

Innards are the data structures and algorithms of which features and indeed all software is constructed. They give shape to the virtual law-side that is the program, the running ICT, which itself enables the virtual subject-object-side that is the 'world' in the computer (§5-5.2: remember that virtual law-side refers to encapsulation of real as well as imaginary worlds).

A virtual law-side incorporates most of what aspects make possible—things, properties, possibilities, constraints, rationalities, relationships and functioning (§3-7 to §3-9)—as constructs like objects, attributes, variables to instantiate, value-ranges, if-then conditions, references and procedures respectively.

7-4.2.1 Innards of Each Aspect

For each aspect, a set of these may be identified, as shown in Tables 7.3a and 7.3b, which contain examples of each—not all positive. Each has somehow to be encapsulated in the virtual law-side that is the software, via appropriate languages. The table has two parts, with the things in Table 7.3a often implemented in data structures and types (objects, classes, etc.) and those in Table 7.3b, in algorithms and procedures. The aspect is in the left-hand column in Table 7.3a, and in the right-hand column in Table 7.3b, because they were originally intended to be printed on facing pages. Fuller wisdom about these may be helped by perusing Tables 3.4 and 3.5 in Chapter 3.

Most features of any size will have innards that encapsulate these for a *primary aspect* and also, to a lesser extent, for some *secondary aspects* on which it depends.

Table 7.3a Examples of What Innards Should Support for Each Aspect

Aspect	*Example Things*	*Example Properties*	*Example Relationships*
Quantitative	Integers, ratios, fractions, proportions; reals (antecipate spatial)	Many / few, precise / approximate; prime	Greater, less; factors
Spatial	Shape, line, area, volume, boundary; scale; dimensions	Long / short, wide / narrow, straight / curved, large / small, orientation	Proximity, surrounding, touching, overlap, in, out, left, right
Kinematic	Movement, route, flow, centre of rotation, (animation)	Fast, slow, turning, diverging, curling, backwards / forwards, duration of movement	Faster / slower, travel together, crossing
Physical	Waves, particles, forces, fields, impacts, causes; chemicals, solutions, liquids, gases, solids, crystals	Mass, energy, charge, frequency, intensity, rigidity, etc.	Attracts / repels, causes
Organic-biotic	Organism (system), organ (part), tissue, cell; food, excreta, population, species, environment	Health (integrity of system), dysfunction, stamina, age, etc.	Parent / child / mate, food chains, symbiosis, system-environment
Psychic / Sensitive	Stimulus (sound, sight, smell), signal response (e.g. motor action), channel (aural, visual, etc.), states (esp. emotional), memory	Colour (hue, saturation, value), pitch, loudness; fear, hunger	Stimulus-response
Analytical	Concepts, objects, identities	Clarity / confusion, distinctness, type	Different / same, contradiction, logical entailment
Formative	Structure, process, plan, goal, technique, tool, technology, intention	Feasibility, efficacy	Means-end, manipulation, histories,

Aspect	*Example Things*	*Example Properties*	*Example Relationships*
Lingual	Words, phrases, sentences, utterances, etc.; nouns, verbs, etc.; headings, lists, quotations, indices, etc.; argument, story	Tense, case, emphasis, understandability	Synonym / antonym, cross-reference, rhyme, thesaurus relationship, flow of argument or narrative
Social	Person, group, organization, role, status; title, name, nickname	Status, leadership, formal / informal	Friend / enemy / acquaintance, respect for, membership, hierarchy
Economic	Resource, product, stocks, limit (budget, etc.), consumer, labour, market, currency	Value, stock level	Supplier-customer, 'within budget', exchange rates
Aesthetic	Style, fun, leisure, sport, art (Many aesthetic existences are relationships.)	Harmony, holism, situatedness, enjoyability, elegance, beauty	Nuance, allusion, surprises, humour
Juridical	Due, rights, responsibilities, contracts, policies, laws, ownership, security measures, etc.	(In)appropriate, (un)just, (dis) proportionate	Debt, reward / punishment
Ethical	Sacrifices, gifts, attitudes	Selfish / self-giving, generous / mean, etc.	Troth, Buber's I-Thou relationship
Pistic / Faith	Belief, vision, commitment, confidence; rituals	Certain, meaningful, loyal	Committed-to, belief-in, rely-on

Example: The innards to cope with a complex shape (§7-1.2) will have the following for its spatial aspect:

- Existences: shapes and their extents, boundaries, points, locations, lines;
- Properties: position, length, angle, curvature, size, area, connectedness;
- Relationships: order of positions, proximity, connected, surrounding;

Table 7.3b More Examples of Innards Supporting Each Aspect

Example Constraints	*Example Inferences*	*Example Activities*	*Aspect*
A given quantity remains that quantity until changed by functioning not of this aspect	Those of arithmetic	Increment, subtract, scale, factor out; those of statistics (count, average, etc.)	Quantitative
e.g. Boundaries have no gaps	Those of geometry and some topology	Stretch, join, split, overlap	Spatial
e.g. Achilles beats Tortoise	Those of mechanics, e.g. s = v * t Some from topology	Start / stop, rotate, follow a path, meet; Animation	Kinematic
State at a location determined by surroundings. Energy conservation.	Causality	Physical interaction, material and chemical processes,	Physical
Integrity of organism	e.g. parent implies child	Grow, ingest, excrete, reproduce, autopoiesis, repair, die	Organic-biotic
Sense organ sensitivity or frequency range	Stimulus and response imply each other	Feel, respond, remember / forget	Psychic-sensitive
Principle of non-contradiction	Logic	Distinguish, deduce	Analytical
Formative action is constrained by nature of materials. Degeneration.	Ends imply means; inferences of structure; historical 'causality'	Form, link together, compose, manufacture, create, revise, undo, plan	Formative
Vocabulary, grammar of the language being used, pragmatic context.	Those of syntax, semantics	Write, draw, speak, sign; understand, translate	Lingual
Deference, peer pressure	Deductions from role, status, relationship	Relate (befriend, etc.), agree, work together, lead / follow	Social

Example Constraints	*Example Inferences*	*Example Activities*	*Aspect*
Conservation of resources	e.g. Scarcity increases value	Reuse, recycle, produce, distribute, exchange, fix price	Economic
e.g. "Less is more in art"	Gestalt?	Harmonise (e.g. music), perform, joke	Aesthetic
Appropriateness and due depend on recipient-type (person, animal, etc.); jurisdictions codify this.	Evidential judgements	Make judgements, ensure proper retribution, contract	Juridical
Self-giving must be genuine: no hidden agendas	Both self-giving and self-centredness affect surrounding attitudes and rebound unexpectedly	Give, forgive	Ethical
Commitments should be kept	Confidence enhances commitment	Make a commitment; worship	Pistic / Faith

- Constraints: the shape is closed, expansion is perpendicular;
- Inferences: whether a location is inside or outside a boundary; trigonometry;
- Activities: create the expanded shape.

Its foundational secondary aspect is the quantitative, as exhibited in treating positions as pairs of numbers and lengths and angles as numbers. An anticipated aspect is its application (organic-biotic, of predators and prey). It will also have a similar set of things for its formative aspect of list-handling, but this need not be the entire formative aspect.

7-4.2.2 How This helps ICT Developers

To ICT developers, this can clarify the criteria on which software libraries may be assessed and can guide designing. The incorporation of secondary aspects is usually by

- For earlier, foundation aspects (retrocipation): encapsulated objects or called functions whose innards are not visible to the caller and are virtual law-sides for that earlier aspect;
- For later aspects (antecipation): function hooks with parameters, to functions supplied by the antecipated aspects; knowledge of antecipated aspects might not be available, the hooks must be general-purpose.

By considering Dooyeweerd's aspects, the relationship the primary aspect has with others can be more systematically considered, rather than developing the primary aspect in isolation. This might reduce problems in refactoring of code, because it provides guidance as to which distinct kinds of issue are meaningful. Methods for aspectual refactoring await development.

This might furnish guidance for generating software libraries, but it is also a perspective on what software libraries are. They are not just routines and classes to use to do certain things, but are expressions of the way the world is believed to work in its various aspects. There is a responsibility here to be fully faithful to the way reality works, in all its aspects, and Section 7-1 contains examples of why that is important.

7-4.2.3 Aspect-Oriented Programming (AOP)

Aspect-Oriented Programming (AOP) (Kiczales et al. 1997) originated independently of Dooyeweerd's aspects, but some deep similarities in the use of 'aspect' are evident.

An AOP aspect is a 'cross-cutting concern', some meaningful issue that cuts across all software code (innards) in a system, such as logging or security authentication. Under a standard programming approach, to add features for logging to existing programs requires modifying code in many places, which results in tangled code, that (a) distracts the reader of the code from its main meaning, and (b) makes modifying code difficult and error-prone. The AOP approach is to make the insertion and subsequent maintenance of such concerns easier and less error-prone. It introduces the idea of 'join points', which are defined in existing code as places where it will allow itself to be modified. Then an 'aspect' is written (e.g., for logging) that provides 'advice' to all the code that it wishes to modify.

Black and Harman (2006) have suggested that Dooyeweerd's aspects can provide a philosophical foundation for AOP, in the way that Bunge was employed by Wand and Weber (1995).

The 'cross-cutting' nature of AOP aspects of this kind is very close to the oceanic pervasiveness of Dooyeweerd's aspects. Just as Dooyeweerd expected that every aspect is at least potentially active in each situation, and it can become manifest over time, so we might expect that every aspect is potentially active in the running of software, and that this will become manifest as the software continues in use. Hence cross-cutting concerns should be expected.

Dooyeweerd's suite of aspects can define the kinds of concerns that might cut across existing code: for example, logging is a lingual cross-cutting concern, security is juridical. A cross-cutting concern often speaks of generic domain knowledge, i.e., of the laws of a Dooyeweerdian aspect, and code tangles may be seen as resulting from inappropriate mixing together of aspectual knowledge. In this way, Dooyeweerd affirms the underlying motivation for AOP, and our approach would strongly advise that code that encapsulated different aspects should be separated into different software libraries.

The mechanism that AOP advocates for implementing cross-cutting concerns, i.e., join-points, at which 'advice' may be given, may be affirmed by the idea of aspectual antecipation (§3-7.4.4). It was suggested above that knowledge of antecipated aspects might not be available, so awareness of such inter-aspect relationships can help us anticipate (*sic*) it, as AOP's mechanism does.

Dooyeweerd not only affirms AOP but can also help with issues that challenge it. With join-points, program code can become less understandable and more difficult to maintain or evolve because, whereas human everyday experience of aspects is of them together, in the AOP code they are separated without any indication of how the cross-cutting aspects work. Without a prior understanding of what aspects (kinds of cross-cutting concern) might be possible, developers have little idea of what the joining 'advice' might offer; Dooyeweerd's suite can provide some prior understanding.

Another concern that might materialise is inefficient running. Not knowing how long the advice code will take to return a result, makes it dangerous to invite 'advice' in time-critical procedures. Example: The intensive trigonometric calculations for shape expansion (§7-1.2) need to run fast and logging to a file might slow it down. However, an awareness of typical timescales of aspects (Table 3.5) might help make judgements about this: the spatial aspect has extremely short times. This suggests that it might be advisable for every join-point to pass a 'speed-required' parameter.

In such ways, Dooyeweerd offers a philosophical foundation for AOP that can affirm and enrich it, and perhaps also critique it in future. These ideas await full development and research.

7-4.3 Understanding Transmission Protocols and File Formats

Just as there is appropriateness and inappropriateness in user interactions and innards, so there is appropriateness and inappropriateness in protocols. Inappropriateness leads to errors, often undetected, and especially jeopardises interoperability of software.

7-4.3.1 Aspects of Protocols

A good protocol will deal with two things: the activity of storing or transmitting, and its appropriateness to the kind of information being stored or transmitted. Table 7.4 shows three things for most aspects. Column 2 contains examples of issues of the activity of storing or transmitting, column 3 contains examples of protocols designed to transmit or store information governed by that aspect, and column 4, some challenges that the protocol is designed to meet.

The examples in column 2 show how complex storage or transmission can be. The design of good protocols involves taking all these into account, and an aspectual separation of issues can help ensure that none are overlooked.

Column 3 surprised me at first, showing such a wide range of kinds of information-content for which protocols have been devised. However, considering that computers have been storing and transmitting information for over 50 years, perhaps it is not surprising.

Table 7.4 Examples of Transmission Issues Meaningful in, and Protocols Appropriate to, Each Aspect

Aspect	*Transmission issues*	*Example protocols*	*Protocol challenges*
Quantitative	Record counts	Binary, floating point, BCD (Binary-Coded Decimal)	Rounding errors, overflow
Spatial	Proximity	SDTS (Spatial Data Transfer Standard)	Representing continuity
Kinematic	Transmission speed	MP3 (Motion Picture 3), UDP (User Datagram Protocol)	Timestamps
Physical	Media	JCAMP-DX (for spectroscopy)	Huge volumes of data
Organic-biotic	Hardware	XDF (exchange of biological datasets)	
Psychic / Sensitive	Noise	S/PDIF (Sony / Phillips Digital Interconnect Format) CMYK, RGB (Cyan-Magenta-Yellow-Black, Red-Green-Blue)	Streaming (aural) Representing colour (visual)
Analytical	Unambiguous separation of fields	CSV (Comma Separated Values)	Field and domains
Formative	Syntax of protocol	BNF (Backus-Naur Form)	Structure
Lingual	Semantics of protocol	HTML, SGML (Hypertext / Standard Graphics Markup Language)	Signification
Social	Standardization		People
Economic	Data compression		Conservation of resources

Aspect	*Transmission issues*	*Example protocols*	*Protocol challenges*
Aesthetic	Ensure harmony of data		Nuances, allusion, resonance
Juridical	Ensuring accuracy (e.g. checksums) and security (encryption); Appropriateness of protocol.		
Ethical	Extensibility		
Pistic / Faith	Trustworthiness of data; Commitment (e.g. in transaction processing)		Dependence on all other aspects

7-4.3.2 Primary, Secondary and Tertiary Aspects of a Protocol

The differences between HTML and PDF, or between GIF and JPEG (see §7-1.3), can now be clearly understood by identifying the aspects that make their core ideas meaningful.

- PDF: spatial (layout), psychic (visual appearance);
- HTML: lingual;
- GIF: analytic (differentiation by colour and shape);
- JPEG: aesthetic, economic (efficient compression).

This suggests that we might understand their limitations and strengths by aspectual analysis of them.

However, protocol design must be more complex and nuanced than this, because they will be used in a 'real' and very challenging world. To illustrate how Dooyeweerd's aspects might help us, let us look at one type of information content in more detail—text (which includes spoken as well as written).

In addition to a *primary aspect* of the kind of information for which the protocol must be designed, lingual for text, there are secondary and tertiary ones. The *secondary aspects* are those on which the primary one depends (in both retrocipatory and antecipatory directions: §3-7.4.4) for the full, rich functioning in the primary aspect, for example the tokens and vocabulary (analytic aspect), structure (formative), and the cultural assumptions employed by the author in writing, drawing or speaking (social). The *tertiary aspects* are those that govern special manifestations of the primary functioning, for example the printing of text or laying it out on screen, or reading out loud.

The secondary and tertiary should not gain prominence over the primary; however, they do need to be considered carefully in the design of any protocol. As mentioned earlier, PDF is primarily geared to the spatial and psychic aspect, which are those of layout and visual appearance. These are both tertiary aspects as far as text is concerned, and would not apply, for example, to reading out loud for visually challenged people. So, we might surprise some readers in suggesting that PDF is actually a poor protocol for storage and transmission of text, *qua* text, but a good one for printing and display. This explains why text-search on PDF can sometimes miss important data: Example in §7-1.3.

One protocol that is good for text is HTML. As originally conceived (before Cascading Style Sheets (CSS) was added), it would leave layout to the local browser, so as to suit the needs of reader, rather than author. However, CSS was added in order to provide spatial control by authors, and now has come to dominate web page design. Much of the original reader-control is, sadly, now impossible.

The richness of text is shown in Table 7.5. Column 1 shows some of the characteristics encountered in the lingual functioning of text. Column 2 shows which (secondary or tertiary; primary is lingual) aspects make them meaningful. Column 3 shows to what extent they are supported in ICT as a whole, especially word-processors, in protocols, search engines, word processors, etc. Column 4 shows which HTML facilities or tags can be used to support the text characteristic. Note that 'text' here includes images as tokens within it.

Table 7.5 The Rich Complexity of Our Textual Functioning

Text characteristic	*Secondary / tertiary aspect*	*Supported in WPs and other ICT*	*HTML tag / facility*
Words, images as tokens	Analytic	Yes	White space, IMG
Abbreviations	Economic	(Clumsy via autocorrect)	(DL, DT, DD)
Wrapping, Hyphenation	Spatial (margins)	Poorly (esp. in searching)	(Occurs in the browser)
Phrases, sentences	Formative	Rarely	
Paragraphs, sections, etc.	Formative	Yes, by newline, heading styles, etc.	P, H3 etc.
Listing	Formative	Only by bullets; inline listing not usually supported	UL, LI
Quotations	Social, juridical	No, except for quotation marks. (Different language rules should apply inside quotations)	BLOCKQUOTE, CITE
Cross-referencing	Lingual (meaning has character of referring (Dooyeweerd 1955,I,4)), formative	Seldom	HREF

Text characteristic	*Secondary / tertiary aspect*	*Supported in WPs and other ICT*	*HTML tag / facility*
Indices, contents	Analytic, economic (speed)	Yes	index.html
Layout	Spatial, aesthetic	Yes	(TABLE), CSS
Emphasis	Analytic	Yes, by italics, bold, etc.	EM, STRONG, I, B, BIG, SMALL, etc.
Change-tracking	Formative	Yes	STRIKE
Pagination	Spatial	Yes	
Text search	Formative, juridical	Incompletely	(In browsers); ISINDEX
Vocabulary	Analytic, juridical	Yes, via dictionaries, spell-checking	DD, DFN
Grammar	Formative	Sometimes	
Semantics	Lingual	In Semantic Web and search by alternative words	SUB, SUPER, CAPTION; Via cross references esp within document; IMG, MAP
Cultural or background knowledge	Social, pistic	No	Via cross references
Copyright	Juridical	In Amiga IFF	Maybe via META
Aesthetics	Aesthetic	Plenty	STYLE, FONT, IMG; CSS

On one hand, it is gratifying to see how many of the characteristics are supported to some extent by the facilities offered by the HTML protocol. It may be partly this wide recognition of the characteristics of lingual functioning that accounts for its success and the success of the World Wide Web as a whole.

On the other hand, it is disappointing to see how many characteristics of text, even in this incomplete table, are not well supported, given text processing and transmission has developed for over forty years.

The richness of textual information has been examined in detail. All other kinds of information are equally rich, when their everyday use is taken into account. So the above aspectual analysis should be seen as an exemplar on how to proceed with other kinds of information related to other primary aspects, and the protocols designed for them. Aspectual analysis can be useful in separating out issues for critique, enabling us to ask why each is important, and for guiding design.

7-5 Conclusion

It has been suggested that the ICT features, as experienced by users and designed by developers, may be understood via the lens of Dooyeweerd's philosophy. It provides a foundational understanding of what affordance is and what constitutes the main normativity of ICT features: appropriateness. Dooyeweerd's aspects can be useful for categorizing, critiquing and enriching extant categories of kinds and types of affordance, for understanding appropriateness of all three elements of ICT features in detail, interaction possibilities, innards and protocols.

Affirmation. The relationship between ICT features and users is treated as a non-Cartesian Dooyeweerdian subject-object relationship, which is multi-aspectual and proximal rather than uni-aspect and distal. This, together with Dooyeweerd's treating of oceanic meaningfulness as governing both subject and object together, provides a sound philosophical foundation for the notion of affordance, which has always been troubled by the agent-meaning being located in the environment feature. Dooyeweerd's aspects can be used to affirm all kinds of affordance, from psychological to social, along with taxonomies of types in each. The normativity and especially appropriateness of features is seen as encapsulating, not just how users wish to use them (subject side context), but knowledge of the law-side, to express potential and constraint in their most fundamental form.

Critique. The 'materiality' of ICT has been long-ignored by the information systems field, perhaps because of the stultifying influence of the nature-freedom ground-motive (§3-2.3), but is now being explored. The main hindrance in both developing the discourse around affordance and integrating it with other discourses, is the presupposition of either the Cartesian subject-object relationship or the Heideggerian reaction against it. Neither of these match our everyday experience. Discourses around normativity of ICT features (ease of use and information quality) have tended to ignore the diversity of types of content.

Enrichment. Dooyeweerd's suite of aspects can help understand affordance and materiality of ICT features as aspect triples, and thereby suggest new kinds of affordance and new types in each kind. The aspects can also form the foundation for understanding the appropriateness of ICT features and their elements (interaction possibilities, innards and protocols) in a detail that was not available hitherto.

The possibility of using Dooyeweerd as a foundation for aspect-oriented programming (AOP) has been briefly discussed.

It is through a detailed understanding of aspectual possibility and normativity as contained in the tables in Section 7-4, that we can begin to appreciate the complexity of each feature and see why ICT can no longer be treated as a 'black box'. Dooyeweerd opens a door to a way of tackling 'materiality' of ICT with wisdom, joy and hope, rather than as reaction, reluctantly and aimlesslessly. The wisdom is from the idea that all aspects cohere, the joy comes from the possibility of a practical analytic tool (namely Dooyeweerd's aspects as illustrated in the tables) and hope comes insofar as both users and ICT function in the same aspects of an 'ocean of meaningfulness' (§3-1.2.3).

Despite the detail in the tables, this is not meant to be a prescriptive approach, but rather to show how a whole long-term research activity is likely to be fruitful, along with some ideas that can bring immediate benefit to the practice of ICT development and use.

The ideas in this chapter should never be separated from awareness of human creativity in use (Chapter 6) nor the potential impacts arising from widespread use of ICT features (Chapter 8).

References

Basden A. 1993. Appropriateness. In MA Bramer, AL Macintosh (Eds.), *Research and Development in Expert Systems X* (pp. 315–328). Proc. Expert Systems 93, BHR Group, UK.

Basden A. 2008. *Philosophical Frameworks for Understanding Information Systems*. IGI Global, Hershey, PA.

Basden A, Hibberd PR. 1996. User interface issues raised by knowledge refinement. *International Journal of Human Computer Studies*, 45, 135–155.

Black S, Harman M. 2006. *Aspect Oriented Software Development: Towards a Philosophical Basis*. Technical Report TR-06-01, Department of Computer Science, King's College London, UK.

Breems N, Basden A. 2014. Understanding of computers and procrastination: A philosophical approach. *Computers in Human Behavior*, 31, 211–223.

Chemero A. 2003. An outline of a theory of affordances. *Ecological Psychology*, 15(2), 181–195.

Conole G, Dyke M. 2004. What are the affordances of information and communication technologies? *Alt-J, Research in Learning Technology*, 12(2), 114–124.

Costall A. 2012. Canonical affordances in context. *AVANT*, III(2), 86–93.

Dooyeweerd H. 1955. *A New Critique of Theoretical Thought* (Vol. I–IV, 1975 ed.). Paideia Press, Jordan Station, Ontario, Canada.

Faraj S, Azad B. 2012. The materiality of technology: An affordance perspective. In PM Leonardi, BA Nardi, J Kallinikos (Eds.) *Materiality and Organizing: Social Interaction in a Technological World*. Oxford University Press, Oxford, UK, 237-58.

Findlater L, McGrenere J. 2007. Evaluating reduced-functionality interfaces according to feature findability and awareness. *Proceedings of INTERACT2007*, Rio de Janeiro, Brazil.

Fisher CW, Kingma BR. 2001. Criticality of data quality as exemplified in two disasters. *Information & Management*, 39, 109–116.

Gamma E, Helm R, Johnson R, Vlissides J. 1995. *Design Patterns: Elements of Reusable Object-Oriented Software*. Addison-Wesley, Reading, MA.

Gaver WW. 1991. Technology affordances. *Proceedings of the CHI'91*, 79–84. ACM New York, USA.

Gibson JJ. 1979. *The Ecological Approach to Visual Perception*. Houghton Mifflin, Boston, MA.

Green TRG, Petre M. 1996. Usability analysis of visual programming environments: A cognitive dimensions framework. *Journal of Visual Languages and Computing*, 7, 131–174.

Hartson HR. 2003. Cognitive, physical, sensory, and functional affordances in interaction design. *Behavior & Information Technology*, 22(5), 315–338.

Hutchby I. 2001. Technologies, texts and affordances. *Sociology*, 35(2), 441–456.

Jasperson JS, Carter, PE, Zmud RW. 2005. A comprehensive conceptualization of the post-adoptive behaviors associated with IT-enabled work systems. *MIS Quarterly* 29(3), 525–557.

Kent W. 1978. *Data and Reality: Basic Assumptions in Data Processing Reconsidered*. North Holland, Amsterdam, the Netherlands.

Kiczales G, Lamping J, Mendhekar A, Maeda C, Lopes CV, Loingtier J-M, Irwin J. 1997. Aspect-oriented programming. *Proceedings of the European Conference on Object-Oriented Programming, ECOOP'97*, Springer-Verlag, Germany.

Latour B. 1987. *Science in Action*. Harvard University Press, Cambridge, MA.

Leonardi PM, Barley SR. 2008. Materiality and change: Challenges to building better theory about technology and organizing. *Information and Organization*, 18, 59–76.

Majchrzak A, Faraj S, Kane GC, Azad B. 2013. The contradictory influence of social media affordances on online communal knowledge sharing. *Journal of Computer-Mediated Communication*, 19, 38–55.

Mansour O, Askenäs L, Ghazawneh A. 2013. Social media and organizing: An empirical analysis of the role of Wiki affordances in organizing practices. *Thirty Fourth International Conference on Information Systems*, Milan, Italy.

Norman DA. 1988. *The Psychology of Everyday Things*. Basic Books, New York.

Norman DA. 1990. Why interfaces don't work. In B Laurel (Ed.), *The Art of Human-Computer Interface Design* (pp. 209–219). Addison-Wesley, Reading, MA.

Orlikowski WJ. 2007. Sociomaterial practices: Exploring technology at work. *Organization Studies*, 28(9), 1435–1448.

Rietveld E. 2008. Situated normativity: The normative aspect of embodied cognition in unreflective action. *Mind*, New Series, 117(468), 973–1001.

Schmidt RC. 2007. Scaffolds for social meaning. *Ecological Psychology*, 19(2), 137–151.

Seidel S, Recker J, vomBrocke J. 2013. Sensemaking and sustainable practicing: Functional affordances of information systems in Green transformations. *MIS Quarterly*, 37(4), 1275–1299.

Shneiderman B. 1992. *Designing the User Interface: Strategies for Effective Human-Computer Interaction*, Addison-Wesley, Reading, MA.

Sutcliffe A. 2000. On the effective use and reuse of HCI knowledge. *ACM Transactions on Computer-Human Interaction*, 7(2), 197–221.

Treem JW, Leonardi PM. 2012. Social media use in organizations: Exploring the affordances of visibility, editability, persistence and association. *Communication Yearbook*, 36, 143-89.

Wand Y, Weber R. 1995. On the deep structure of information systems. *Information Systems Journal*, 5(3), 203–224.

Wang RY, Strong DM. 1997. Beyond accuracy: What data quality means to data consumers. *Journal of Management Information Systems*, 12(4), 5–34.

Winograd T, Flores F. 1986. *Understanding Computers and Cognition: A New Foundation for Design*. Addison-Wesley, Reading, MA.

Withagen R, dePoela HJ, Arafijob D, Pepping G-J. 2012. Affordances can invite behavior: Reconsidering the relationship between affordances and agency. *New Ideas in Psychology*, 30, 230–258.

Zammuto RF, Griffin TL, Majchrzak A, Dougherty DJ, Faraj S. 2007. Information technology and the changing fabric of organization. *Organization Science*, 8(5), 749–762.

8 Understanding ICT and Society

This chapter explores the complex relationship between ICT and society.

Information and computer technology (ICT) has changed not only human activity, as discussed in Chapter 6, but also society as a whole; and society has influenced what kinds of ICT have emerged. ICT has widespread impacts (e.g., contributing to climate change or changing society's expectations). ICT has become an *Umwelt*, an environment, in which we live and work—as a forest is for trees, fungi and insects—an *Umwelt* that we ourselves generate.

This chapter tries to offer a way to understand what is going on. Figure 8.1 portrays some ideas that will be developed in this chapter.

There are several cycles of influence here, as depicted by the arrows. The trees can be seen as representing either the non-human environment, which must not be forgotten, especially climate change, or as figurative of societal and technological *Umwelten* or environments within which we work and live.

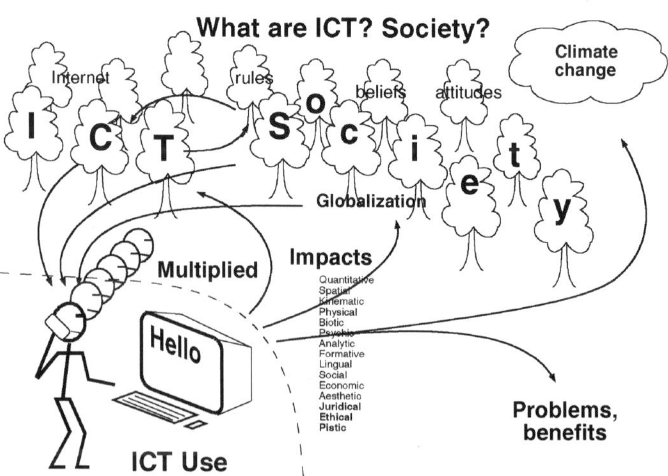

Figure 8.1 A Global View of ICT

8-1 Overview of Chapter

Many and varied are the types of discourse around the topic of ICT and society, but this chapter brings some of them together. Its coverage of each is perhaps partial and simplified, yet it aims to bring together a wider range of discourses than is normal, discourses that seldom interact. Dooyeweerd's ideas will be employed to help us understand this wider picture.

Whereas, in the other chapters, the human being relates to ICT from 'outside' it, as its original conceiver (Chapter 5), its creator (Chapter 7), its applier (Chapter 9) and its user (Chapter 6), in this chapter the human being is seen as 'inside' the ICT, just as we are in society. ICT is like an *ecology* or *Umwelt* in which we live, but which we ourselves form, just as society is to us. In addition to the cycles between us and ICT, and us and society, there is also a cycle between ICT-as-societal-phenomenon and society itself. Behind all this is the question of what ICT and society are as such, and what role or mandate ICT has as global historical phenomenon.

Section 8-2 reviews some of the discourses around ICT and society, identifying some challenges and meaningful core issues. Each subsequent section explores how a portion of Dooyeweerd's thought can make sense of ICT and society and address the challenges: Dooyeweerd's critique of philosophical presuppositions to examine roots (§8-3), aspects to separate out the various kinds of impact (§8-4), Dooyeweerd's theory of existence to understand ICT and society as interacting infrastructures (§8-5) and Dooyeweerd's theory of progress to understand technological advance and the mandate of the Information Systems Discipline (§8-6). Section 8-7 summarises how they are addressed. In the process, suggestions are made for how various discourses or theories might be enriched.

Note on terminology: To this author, '*society*' means that cultural milieu in which we live as: (1) the community of thought, belief and practice within which ICT and its widespread use is to be considered, (2) the society of a nation, (3) the dominant culture (affluent, Western?) and its values, meanings and norms that are mediated and pushed via the media and ICT and to which many in non-Western cultures aspire, and (4) global society, which recognises non-Western mindsets and cultures and beliefs as, in principle, of equal importance with Western.

8-2 Extant Discourses on ICT and Society

This section reviews some of the main discourses relevant to ICT as a societal phenomenon: widespread impact of ICT, ICT as infrastructure for life and work, the importance of attitudes and aspirations, how ICT and society impact each other, information and society, the role of the information systems field and technological progress. Within each, a number of challenges are identified.

How were the discourses chosen? Rather than defining them according to thinkers or theories, as some do (e.g., Webster 2006), I have tried to choose a variety of discourses that might represent the diversity of ways of addressing ICT and society. Whereas Webster, for example, addresses the narrow question, "How does the information society differ from previous ones?" this section asks a wider question: "What constitutes the dynamic relationship between ICT, society, us and the world?" Taking a pre-theoretical stance, the discourses I have chosen come from my intuitive reflections within and outwith academia since the 1960s. My choice is incomplete (for example, discourses on organizational ICT are not included) but aims for variety rather than completeness.

8-2.1 Discourses about the Widespread Impacts of ICT: Problems and Benefits

As discussed in Chapter 6, ICT brings with it the potential for new kinds of beneficial and detrimental repercussions. When myriads of people use ICT, these repercussions are multiplied to become widespread impact of ICT across society. Some are existing impacts amplified, while others are new kinds that were not possible before the advent of ICT and social media.

Crowdfunding and mass collaboration (Zammuto et al. 2007), for example, are made easier by social media, because of the number of people connected via the Internet, running similar software that makes assent to the collaboration easy and capitalises intelligently on lists of contacts. Such behaviour is seldom entirely new; did not the distribution of pamphlets during the Scottish Reformation (Whitley 1972) constitute mass collaboration? What is at issue is not whether the changes in behaviour are new, but to understand why and how individual actions are amplified by ICT.

Many impacts cause concern, such as cyberloafing, cyberbullying (Lim 2002), Internet fraud, breaches of privacy and confidentiality, addictive gambling and pornography. Some are less discussed, such as decline in map-reading skills occasioned by the widespread dependence on SatNavs (Copping 2012).

Discourses about negative and positive impacts tend to be isolated from each other, however, being either too critical or too uncritical of ICT, so that integrated views are rare.

Amplified impact of the use of ICT is not restricted to social aspects. ICT contributes to increased or decreased **Climate change emissions**, both directly and indirectly. Around 7.19 billion mobile phones (Boren 2014) consume gigawatts of power. The necessary telecommunications infrastructure required for the Internet and mobile phones to work consumes more than thrice as much power (Kumar and Mieritz 2007). Many articles discuss making ICT itself more energy-efficient, and some, how ICT can be applied in climate-related infrastructure, for example, to water management (e.g., Finlay and Adera 2012).

Few, however, discuss how ICT increases or decreases climate change emissions indirectly by changing our behaviour. The United Nations Environment Programme (UNEP undated) suggests that ICT has "an opportunity to play a leadership role in the reduction of energy consumption and greenhouse gas emissions" not only by increasing energy efficiency of ICT infrastructure and using renewable energy, but also applying ICT to stimulate flexible working and conferencing, and reducing transport-related emissions by encouraging e-commerce. These, however, are more hope than actuality, and might be undermined by changes in aspiration. In Basden (2008) I mention four online bridge players who flew across the world to meet for a 'proper' game of bridge—generating huge, unnecessary climate change emissions in so doing. ICT use can change values, attitudes or aspirations, which (Scultze 2002) calls 'habits of the heart'.

On what foundation may we understand positive and negative, visible with less-visible, physical and social, multiplication, changed behaviour, changes in infrastructure and changes in aspirations?

8-2.2 *ICT as Infrastructure*

ICT as technology becomes an infrastructure for computing and communication, the main example today being the Internet and the wide supply of personal computers, tablets and mobile phones. That in turn makes possible, and encourages, other kinds of infrastructure in society that were not possible or were different before, such as e-commerce, e-government or surveillance. In this section, we are less interested in ICT infrastructure as such than in the societal issues that relate to it.

Three examples will be discussed, in order to see the shape and trajectory of discourses around infrastructure, an issue arising from the presence of ICT (digital divide), an issue that has been transformed by ICT (surveillance) and an infrastructure made possible by ICT (e-government). Then we discuss what needs to be considered as infrastructure.

> Note on terminology: '*Infrastructure*' denotes a *societal structure* within and by which we live and work, and which supports, enables and guides or constrains that living. It might have been deliberately constructed, as with the transport infrastructure, of roads, fuelling points, etc., or it might not have, as with pervading attitudes. Infrastructure can be usefully be seen as an *Umwelt* viewed from the perspective of one of its aspects. '*ICT infrastructure*' includes not only the technical equipment but also skills, education and other social arrangements for living in relation to it.

8-2.2.1 The Digital Divide

The provision of ICT infrastructure is not uniform,. There is a *digital divide* between different nations, (especially) between so-called developed and developing nations), between kinds of organization (e.g., large and small businesses) and between different cohorts of people (Brown et al. 1995). The digital divide refers to inequalities in provision of or access to ICT resource (computer technology or fast communications), in level of ICT education and skills and in levels of use (Crawford 2013).

It is sometimes difficult to distinguish cause from effect in the digital divide because there is a cyclical relationship among the factors, so much of the discourse is about factors that correlate with it. Korupp and Szydlik (2005), for example, found that three sets of factors correlate with digital divide in Germany between East Germans, West Germans and Turks: human capital (education, use of a PC at work), family context (household composition and income) and social context (generation, ethnic background, religion, gender—German women used the Internet 60 per cent less than men in 2003). Hilbert (2010) tries to simplify such correlata into four 'dimensions', who connects, characteristics, degrees of ICT use, and type of technology. These are very general concepts, little more than convenient groupings that provide little understanding. Identification of correlata might help measure the digital divide, but success in getting an agreed measure has been limited because of the diversity of factors and their interaction with context.

Life without ICT does not seem adequately treated as a valid option, being either ignored or disparaged. Though European farmers must use the Internet to claim subsidies, many would prefer other means that work better. In 58 per cent of households surveyed, who did not have Internet access in the UK in 2014, the reason was "Do not need Internet, not useful, not interesting, etc." (ONS 2014). The number of academic articles on life without ICT, that I found in ICT or socio-technical journals, was zero.

Exactly why is the digital divide a problem? Kasperkevic (2014) interviewed a young woman at school who had no computer at home. Though the interviewer directed the discussion towards how difficult she found this, it is clear from the interview that the problem was caused, not by lack of ICT as such, but because the school assumed that all had good access over the Internet and demanded students should do all their work on computer. The root of the problem was not a digital divide as such, but attitude and policy, and that the online services has been designed accordingly. In much discourse about the digital divide, are the wrong things being blamed?

The discourse about the digital divide seems not yet self-critical enough.

8-2.2.2 Surveillance

ICT now enables vast quantities of information about us to be collected, stored and analysed, resulting in the surveillance society (Lyon 2001; 2007). Surveillance is ubiquitous in Western societies, collecting data via electronic tags, cameras, phone and email meta-data, location sensing and analysing such 'big data' by data mining and pattern recognition technologies.

Surveillance is perpetrated by government, military, police, employers and businesses, so the distinction between public and private enterprise is largely irrelevant. It is usually seen as an evil by those surveilled, invading privacy, or leading to corruption, "skewed visions of power", inappropriate social exclusion and creation of "a world where we know we're not really trusted" (Wood 2006). Yet sometimes it is seen as a good, protecting us against terrorism, especially after 9/11 (Lyon 2003), or irrelevant advertisements. It seems reasonable for the location-sensing in our phones to provide us with 'relevant' information about restaurants or car parking facilities near us. But consider the following:

> No one suggests that the store manager wishing to lure only the most creditworthy customers is devious in obtaining credit check services from Experian. It simply makes sense in the quest for greater profitability. But the results—the unintended consequences—of sifting through records to create a profitable clientele is that certain groups obtain treatment, based on ability to pay, and others fall by the wayside.
>
> (Wood 2006, 3)

But on what grounds may we find deeper understanding of surveillance and decide whether such things are acceptable?

Lyon (2007) provides a useful, critical overview of the field of surveillance studies—one of the best available so far, so I will rely largely on it to characterise the discourses around surveillance. A number of theories of surveillance are reviewed. One major discourse comes from Bentham's Panopticon and Foucault's appropriation of this: the metaphor of a central tower allows watching of all the inmates of a prison without the watchers being themselves watched. Yet, Lyon criticises Foucault as "studiously omitted any mention of the role of computers or of mass media, and its promotion of 'spectacle', in contributing to the kinds of discipline and bio-power into which he had otherwise demonstrated such insight" (p. 58). Foucault's ideas presuppose context of enclosed spaces where people cannot escape surveillance, which is not always true of the ICT society.

Lyon discusses five ways in which the discourse around surveillance has moved on, or should move on, from Foucault's too-widely-accepted metaphor. 1. Today, we are not just subjected to surveillance but also active, willing participants. Surveillance involves societal attitudes and values, which are usually assumed, and also contributes to those attitudes and values. "Surveillance fosters suspicion" (Lyon 2003) and breeds a "society of strangers" (Lyon 2007, 50) where trust is lost. 2. Surveillance today generates its own countervailing resistance, which range from the tiny non-compliances that ordinary people invoke to anti-surveillance movements and 'susveillance' where the many watch the watchers.

3. Drawing on Baumann, Boyne, Agamben and Deleuze, Lyon (2007) sees consumer seduction as making the panopticon redundant, in that people surveill themselves and accept surveillance unquestioningly. 4. Bentham's and Foucault's idea of 'gaze' must be extended beyond the visual to include 'social sorting' (categorizaton) of collected data. This allows predictive surveillance, which detects 'suspicious' patterns of behaviour before a crime has been committed, or selects 'promising' customers for marketing. For example, after 9/11, Muslims were singled out for particular surveillance. 5. Surveillance is no longer centralised (Foucault) but 'rhizomic' (Deleuze), with local nodes spreading and networked together.

All this is made possible by how ICT developed over the past 20 years or so. Lyon (2007) tries to go beyond both Foucauldian and Deleuzian presuppositions. He points out that sometimes surveillance is not always sinister, sometimes being for, e.g., health care rather than control. Surveillance is a convenience—not only to governments who want to stay in power, or corporations who want to tempt us ever more strongly, but also to health care providers who (for 'good' reasons) want to avoid the work of sorting information, and we, who wield loyalty cards. Desire for convenience puts all of us at risk, even when the intention is good, and breeds a "society of strangers" (Lyon 2007, 50) where trust is lost. Lyon's own view (2007, 68, 197) is that the "very vulnerable", the genuinely marginalised and those most at risk need to be taken into account more than they have been. The question is no longer "who watches the watchers?" but "who determines the categories?".

Lyon's (2001; 2003; 2007) discussion of surveillance is one of the best available, in its breadth with depth, in its holistic understanding of the entire field and of the discourse around it, and it its recognition of many issues, especially normative stances that others overlook. This might be no coincidence, because he was influenced by Dooyeweerdian thinking in his early days, and has perhaps internalised the ideas of the importance of everyday life, of diversity of factors, of normativity and from his Christian faith, the idea of concern for the disadvantaged. In his discussion of the impacts and functioning of surveillance in society, we can find almost every aspect covered in Lyon's work, ranging from the pistic aspect of belief, the ethical aspect of trust, the juridical aspect of regulations, the aesthetic aspect of fun, the economic aspect of resources and its motivation in commerce, the social aspect of participation, the lingual aspect of information, the formative aspect of technology and so on.

The question remains, however, why are we willing active participants in surveillance? This does not seem to be well discussed by Lyon (2007), and his solution seems to focus on only two aspects: the juridical aspect of justice, "strong safeguards" (2007, 187), legislation and politics and the lingual aspect of data, information and ensuring that people who are surveilled can find out the categories under which this occurs. Though he does mention surveillance based on trust, he does not develop this. In §8-4.3, we suggest how it might be taken further.

8-2.2.3 E-government (Electronic Government)

Electronic government (e-government) is an infrastructure for governance, whereby government business is carried out by computer and the Internet rather than by paper and personal contact. Some e-government services aim at enhancing the efficiency of internal activity, and some are designed to give citizens enhanced satisfaction and convenience. Both 'developed' and 'developing' nations are committed to e-government.

Gartner (2003) suggests there are four 'levels' or 'stages' of adoption of e-government: (1) presence, where ICT, and usually websites, are used to provide information; (2) interaction, where government interacts with citizens, and departments interact with each other, online; (3) transaction, where such things as paying taxes or licenses are carried out online; (4) transformation, which involves a reinvention of government functions and how they operate. This fourth stage, 'transformational government', is one to which most governments aspire, and hailed as a weapon with which to attack corruption. It is, however, the hardest to achieve successfully, and many e-government projects have ended in failure.

Most e-government discourse gravitates around benefits, opportunities, technologies and measurement. Heeks (2002) summarised some of the benefits for Africa in the areas of administration, connecting citizens with services, and building better societies. Since the recession began, discourse tends to focus on economic issues like costs, efficiency and availability (e.g., Alshomrani 2013).

Apart from occasional abstract critique of the idea of e-government in academic circles, problems are seen as challenges to be overcome rather than as an opportunity to understand where e-government is, and is not, suitable (Heeks 2002). Later, Heeks (2008) estimated that, of e-government projects in developing countries,

- 15 per cent were successful,
- 50 per cent were partial failures,
- 35 per cent were complete failures.

Sometimes e-government delivers the opposite of what it promises (e.g., greater enfranchisement for some becomes disenfrachisement of those without effective access to ICT [Bertot and Jaeger 2006]).

The reasons for widespread failure are many technical, economic, social, educational, etc.—but under them seems to lie deeper problems of vision and motivation. The phrase 'transformational government' often speaks less about what needs to be transformed, and more about an unquestioned faith in ICT as 'saviour'.

An example from a 'developed' nation: In the UK government's initiative in e-government,

> The strategy, 'Transformational Government—Enabled by Technology', is about transforming public services as citizens receive them and

> demonstrating how technology can improve the corporate services of government so more resources can be released to deliver 'frontline' services.
>
> (eGU 2006)

"Demonstrating how" assumes that it will do so, despite evidence to the contrary. The explicitly stated motivation, that government "keeps up with the private sector in delivering good, efficient services driven by information technology", reveals both an unquestioned faith in the ability of ICT to 'deliver' and a distorted vision of government as merely delivering services rather than maintaining just structures and policies in society—a shift in vision that has not been democratically debated.

Developing nations might aspire to "leapfrog underdevelopment and attain a final governance configuration that is similar to the one of developed countries" (Ciborra 2005, 269). The title of one government report is "How to Leapfrog: St Vincent & The Grenadines experience" (Thompson 2007). This aspiration is often hidden behind ostensive reasons like "enhance sustainable socio-economic development and accelerated poverty reduction both nationally and globally" (Saebo 2012).

Unquestioned adulation of ICT by government officials and members alike, often supported by public excitement about technology, and impelled by the desire for the prestige of being seen as a globally 'advanced' country, have led to unwise commitment to e-government projects without sufficient analysis, planning and scrutiny of what is needed. Heeks (2006) and Gauld and Goldfinch (2006) call it "idolization".

Idolization has not been widely researched, because it is often hidden behind overt reasons and arguments, and neither Heeks nor Gauld and Goldfinch explore it. Krishnan-Harihara and Basden (2009; 2010) have begun to do so, based on a description of the dynamics of idolization in Goudzwaard (1984), which is expounded later.

8-2.2.4 *What Is ICT as Infrastructure?*

Infrastructure is the "underlying foundation or basic framework" (Webster 1971, II, 1161) that enables or constrains what we do and how we live. ICT does both and hence may be treated as infrastructure. This section discusses what we should consider in order to understand ICT as infrastructure, drawing on the previous examples and elsewhere.

ICT as infrastructure obviously has a technical component of computers and networks, along with manufacturing, software engineering, training, etc. This was a core issue in the digital divide. There is also an economic aspect to ICT as infrastructure, in that technological advance depends on a thriving economy, which is itself supported by ICT. Surveillance raises the issue of legal and political infrastructure—the policies and laws that must be in place to ensure that the role ICT plays in society and our lives in not inappropriate. Two things, however, which constrain and enable what we do, deserve special mention since they are seldom recognised as infrastructure: societal attitudes and beliefs.

Together these form '*values*', and "Under some circumstances a technology incorporates the values of the society for which it was invented to such a degree that these values become dominant in every society which applies that technology" (Illich 1978).

Internet trust is increasingly important. Many facilities (e-government, shopping on Ebay, etc.) could not work without trust. Before the Internet, human beings trusted each other face-to-face, but the Internet (a) made this too expensive, (b) depersonalised trust by relying on certificates that supposedly guarantee that the computer we connect to is the one we expect. However, the real reason we trust Ebay is because we have experienced it to be trustworthy. Trust in e-government applications is decreasing because they are increasingly letting people down, partly because easy real-time access leads people to try more often and hence expose themselves more often to the possibility of being let down (Krishnan-Harihara and Kesar 2015). The discourse on Internet trust confuses the state of trusting—an attitude of willingness to commit—with having-confidence—a rational mix of competence and risk.

Surveillance, e-government and the digital divide all point to the importance of **societal attitude** (attitude that pervades society or community). Attitude determines whether we question our assumptions (e.g., that all school students have computers at home) and how we respond to unusual cases (ensure systems are designed for them, or "can't be bothered!"). If these are individual attitudes, they are shaped by pervading societal attitude.

Attitude is closely linked with ethics, and Schultze (2002, 36) warns of "layers of digital promiscuity that encourage selfishness and stifle moral responsibility at all levels of society", in which the '*digirati*' value personal freedom over responsibility and that "overdependence on informational knowing makes our relationships superficial, transitory and ultimately selfish" (p. 34). Paradoxically, sharing on Facebook breeds narcissism (Connell 2014; Alloway et al. 2014). Because of ICT and especially social media, the engine of the Westernized global economy becomes increasingly fuelled by attention-seeking (Beller 2006).

Attitude has also a positive side, in generosity and humility. "Humility," suggests Schultz (2002, 107), "asks us to justify our technological decisions not on the basis of what they do for our egos but on the basis of caring for others as responsible stewards of the gift of creation." On the other hand, "If we lack humility, our technological activities will express merely our own selfish contempt for the world." With humility, we consider what *not* to do with technology as well as what to do. Unfortunately, "Humility is so countercultural today that embracing it will threaten many of the powers of the information age. Humble people are often the truth tellers in a technological community."

Societal attitude is seldom discussed in the information literature. Attitude is recognised in psychology, as a measurable individual personality construct like narcissism or empathy, and in human resources, where the discourse is about employee attitudes and how to manage them, but neither provide what we need. Here, attitude is societal, not individual, and we want to understand the attitude of two groups other than employees—of those who shape society (managers, politicians, opinion-formers and other leaders) and of us all in everyday life.

The case of e-government especially draws attention to **beliefs and commitments**. Idolization of technology is rife, ranging from low-level 'holy wars' over favourite platforms or operating systems, to idolization of technology as such, as conferring prestige on nations (see above). The nature and mechanisms of idolatry are discussed more deeply in §8-4.3. Idols other than technology abound, such as the economy (Goudzwaard 1984) or Castells' (1996, 199) 'spirit of informationalism'.

Not only are there negative (harmful) forms of belief and commitment, as idolatry, there are also positive forms, including vision, courage and perseverance. Noble (1997) bemoans the fact that over the past 1,000 years technological advance has been inspired and motivated mainly by religion or ideology. It is belief that motivates, both to explore new ideas and to resist new fashions when they are hollow, and societal beliefs influence those of individuals.

Prevailing beliefs and commitments (including idolatry) are about what society finds meaningful. They are often hidden and only manifested indirectly via the shape of our behaviour or lifestyles or, in research, by what factors are chosen for investigation or inclusion in models. For example, Alshomrani and Qamarz (2013) discuss the benefits and challenges of cloud computing for e-government—cost savings, efficiency, flexibility and scalability. These are all economic issues. Three non-economic issues (privacy, security and lack of user control) are present, but only as challenges that might jeopardise economic success. Since it is written from the perspective of the kingdom of Saudi Arabia, one might have expected issues of religion, history and culture to have been discussed, but they are not.

ICT infrastructure, therefore, needs to be understood in its diversity, in its many aspects, taking due account of the role of the everyday experience of ordinary people as well as those of leaders in society. This is what we discuss in §8-4.3.

8-2.3 Discourse on the Impact ICT and Society Have on Each Other

Several discourses have emerged around how ICT and society interact with each other, five of which are outlined here—about freedom and determination, systems thinking, gender, structuration theory and socio-critical theory.

8-2.3.1 Freedom and Determination

Discourse in the information systems field on how ICT and society affect each other reads like a four-decade story with several narrators, each dialectical reacting to the others. The first narration saw computer and communications technology as advancing inexorably, so that all we can do is adapt to it. Its advance is predetermined by the very nature of technology itself. This view was later dubbed (by its critics [Dafoe 2005]) 'technological determinism' (TD).

Within this narration, optimists welcomed the advance and discussed the benefits of ICT, especially to corporations, national economies and individual fulfilment, while pessimists discussed the dangers to democracy, rights, privacy, world stability, climate, etc. All that pessimists could offer was retreat from the story, but they, as with Amish communities in the USA, were dismissed as romantics.

Rogers' (1962) classic Diffusion of Innovations (DoI) theory was enlisted, which explains how an innovation spreads throughout a social network. With four constructs (the innovation itself, communication channels, social system and time) and with five categories of people (innovators, early adopters, early majority, late majority and laggards), it is intuitively attractive and applies not just to diffusion of technology but also of ideas and policy (Mintrom 1997). It is criticised for assuming one-way communication channels without feedback (Robertson et al. 1996), but this detail does not explain the element of disdain with which later narrators held DoI. DoI is seen by later thinkers as within the TD narration, despite its recognising social system.

The second narration is that of Social Construction of Technology (SCOT) (Bijker et al. 1987). This argues that, far from technological advance being predetermined by the nature of technology itself, it is society that shapes or constructs technology. Technology is seen as a bundle of meanings, attributed by society. For example, though the World Wide Web was originally seen as globally interconnected information, has not commercial pressure turned it into a delivery mechanism? SCOT is an interpretive approach, which argues that technology is socially constructed by 'relevant social groups' within 'technological frames' (Howcroft et al. 2004).

Dafoe (2005) tried to integrate SCOT with DoI by arguing that categories like 'technological' and 'social' are abstractions, and that both SCOT and DoI are subject to the laws of competitive selection—but his argument is rather oversimplified.

The third narration was Actor-Network Theory (ANT) (Latour 1987), which criticised SCOT for replacing technological with social determinism. As mentioned in §6-2.5, ANT advocates symmetry between technological and human actants, treating human and non-human as essentially the same insofar as organizational and societal situations are concerned, and offers a set of conceptual tools for analysing such situations.

Both SCOT and ANT were criticised by the Social Shaping of Technology (SST) narration (MacKenzie and Wajcman 1999). Like ANT it argues for interaction between technological and social functionings in society, but at a societal rather than individual or organizational level. Example: The algorithms to select creditworthy customers inscribe underlying assumptions of a political nature about the meaningfulness of 'creditworthy' (c.f. §8-2.2.2). SST criticises both ANT and SCOT for taking an amoral, apolitical stance that supports the status quo and ignores the gendered content of ICT (Howcroft et al. 2004). It does not seek to incorporate SCOT with TD but rather replace both.

The phases of the TD-SCOT-ANT-SST (sometimes just TD-SCOT-SST) narrative of the development of ideas about how technology interacts with society each offer insights, but by and large, each narrator talks past the others and seldom tries to truly recognise the insights of the others.

8-2.3.2 Modernity and the Systematization of Society

In Chapter 6 (§6-2.5), systems thinking is applied to understand the artefact functioning in its user in a wider environment. Here, 'system' takes on a different meaning, as that set of structures that constrain and guide our activity, and which operate by mechanical rules, and is etymologically related to 'systemic'. Weber (1994) and Parsons (1971) used 'system' in this way.

The rules are mechanical insofar as they are designed to be obeyed without question, so people in 'the system'—whether an organization, the state or society—are supposedly absolved of responsibility ("We had to do this because the system tells us to!"). In 'the system' life becomes meaningless and devoid of normativity.

This is modernity, and it dehumanises. And from the 1970s, ICT has reinforced this by encapsulating ('inscribing') such rules and enforcing them.

Systemic life is contrasted with the lifeworld by Habermas (1987), which is replete with meaning and normativity. Habermas softened Weber's view by arguing that meaningfulness and normativity remain, but in modernity are generated within people's discourse by rational critique of validity claims (a version of *ex nihilo* discussed in §3-1.2.2). Since the 1980s, ICT has supported this (e.g., Decision Support Systems). It is found still to be dehumanizing, though in different ways.

Geertsema (1992) argues that the Weberian-Habermasian view is flawed in that even within the most draconian mechanical system, life and work can still have some meaning and normativity. Geertsema, informed by Dooyeweerd, has taken note of the everyday life of people within the system, while Weber and Habermas were theorizing it. Even the supposed mechanical following of rules only occurs because people tacitly agree do so.

8-2.3.3 Gender and Information Systems

The issue of gender and information systems is meaningful across several of our areas: ICT use (e.g., gender effects in ICT acceptance in §6-2.8), ICT features (inscribing gendered assumptions) and ICT development (influenced by gender stereotypes), but most of the discourse sees itself as a societal issue and takes a feminist stance.

The seminal article by Adam, Howcroft and Richardson (2004) is still a reasonably good overview of these discourses. The authors address two questions (a) to what extent gender issues are considered?, (b) how they have been theorised? They found a dearth of literature about both. To answer the first, they surveyed quantitative and qualitative research. In quantitative research they found a desire to study male-female differences, but that (a) many important papers on gender were ignored, (b) the issue was oversimplified because (c) usually only psychological and perhaps biological factors were considered, and social issues of gender were neglected. Qualitative research tended to focus more widely, but only on the workplace and issues like status and career progression.

Both types of empirical research treated both gender and technology as fixed and determined and ignored what Dooyeweerd would see as the multi-aspectual nature of gender. Some reduced gender to biology. Others made a dichotomy between 'masculine' interests (achievement, rationality, economics and juridification) and 'feminine' ones (feeling, sociality, aesthetics, values, ethics).

Attempts to theorise gender are few. One attempts to construct a model of gender-meaningful characteristics and such things as likely career progression, and another suggests that the field of computer ethics may be enriched if feminist ethics is incorporated.

Throughout the paper, an anti-essentialist, anti-determinist attitude is evident, both unquestioningly treated as to-be-escaped-from and even defeated. As such, might this be self-defeating, as self-performatively incoherent (Clouser 2005, 85), in that the very discourse presupposes some 'essence' and 'determination' centred on feminist ideals. A more nuanced picture emerges, however, from more closely examining what they find problematic in essentialism: not the notion of essences as such, but oversimplification of the issue by reduction to biological or psychological factors, so the deeper motivation might be the problem of reductionism. This is indeed what is found in some feminist literature, as discussed at greater length in Basden (2008, 325–326).

8-2.3.4 Structuration Theory

Giddens' (1984; 1979) Structuration Theory has become widely cited as a framework with which to understand the relationship between society and individuals ('macro' and 'micro'). In the information systems field, to understand the relationship between individual ICT use and society, and especially organizational structures (treated as society). Widespread use and acceptance of ICT changes the structures of society, while conversely those structures themselves influence ICT development and use.

Giddens saw problems in a subjectivist pole, which celebrates freedom of the individual actor and ignores structures and constraints, opposing an objectivist pole, which draws too heavily on the natural sciences and does not adequately address freedom. He posited a 'duality of structure', in which both can be taken into account with neither seen as primary, with a cyclical relationship, in which societal structures influence the agency of the individuals, while agency results in reconstituting the structures.

Giddens explored the nature of the structuration cycle. He discerned three 'dimensions' of structure: structures of signification, domination and legitimation (or meaning, power and norms). These operate via three modalities of interpretive schemes, facilities or resources, and norms. They are found in three kinds of agency interactions, as communication, power and sanction (1984; 'morality' in 1979). The three dimensions interleave each other, and cannot be separated in reality but only conceptually separated; for example, language use is itself sanctioned. Thus Giddens goes beyond the hermeneutic turn, which is too attached to signification to do justice to domination and legitimation. 'Signification' to Giddens, refers not only to the semiotic meaning of words (as I use 'signification' here), which occurs in agency, but also to what society as a whole finds meaningful, which constitutes structures of meaning. It is mediated via interpretive schemes, like language and 'stocks of knowledge' (lifeworld).

Giddens warned that his inclusion of power "does not mean that the concept of power is more essential than any other, as is supposed in those versions of social science which have come under a Nietzschean influence." With Parsons, he points out that power is not only negative or inappropriate but has a positive side, of achievement via "transformative capacity . . . intent . . . will". With Foucault, Giddens recognises that power is also "a property of society or the social community" (Giddens 1984, 15).

Giddens then, however, seems to limit power to allocation of resources (allocative goods and life choices). Resources, he says, are focused by legitimation and signification, into something that knowledgeable people can transform. Giddens' introduction of resources is sudden, with no warning nor any prior justification of why power should be thus limited.

Giddens' Structuration Theory has limitations. It is mainly descriptive, with no normativity to differentiate good from bad power, (Myers and Klein 2011). It treats the structures of society as beyond reproach or critique. When considering the impact of ICT on society, do we not need a normative basis on which to critique the structures that ICT is reconstituting?

Even his notion of structure itself has come in for criticism, as "vaporous" (Healy 1998): "important distinctions between structure (as rules and resources), systems (as products of structures) and agents (as mediating producers) all seem to collapse into one another" (Healy 1998, 510). The duality of structure and agency does not reflect all kinds of reality. For example, it is unrealistic to say that lower-status workers in a large car corporation can affect the structures of the corporation. To be fair, Giddens (1984, 263) did acknowledge that structural principles offer only one kind of constraint, but Healy believes Giddens' idea of structure as rules and resources is deeply problematic, though he does not explain why.

Though it is a framework for understanding society, Structuration Theory has been adapted to understand ICT in organizations.

For example, one of my students, Karen Swannack, employed Structuration Theory to study the use of virtual learning environments in universities, by seeing them as both providing structure and enabling agency. Faculty staff can upload lecture and other material, while students can communicate and discuss. She studied cultural differences between what students expect and lecturers offer, and how such tensions are resolved by discussions. She discovered that conflict and reflexivity generate new structures, which are then subsumed into 'structure' as a whole, thus adding a chronological element to the structuration cycle.

DeSanctis and Poole (1994) suggested an Adaptive Structuration Theory, to theorise the fact that societal or organizational structures are incorporated into ICT, and thus force or encourage ICT users to work in certain ways. Structures of domination and signification are incorporated explicitly, while structures of legitimation are the values or 'spirit' that underlie these.

Orlikowski (1992) was interested in the unintended repercussions of ICT use, and in unexpected ways in which it is used, sabotaged or avoided (cf §6-2.14), in relation to assumptions held by the organization about ICT. She adds 'interpretive flexibility' of technology alongside structure and agency, whereby human agents design, develop, appropriate and modify technology. However, she does not sufficiently distinguish between repercussions of ICT use (example: adoption of email in an organization increases communication as expected but also reduces status barriers (p. 406)) and structurational influence (example: use of spreadsheet reaffirmed rules established by the accountancy profession), nor between users and shapers of ICT. While both Orlikowski and DeSanctis and Poole recognise ICT as conveyor of societal structures, neither discuss ICT as an infrastructure in its own right, nor sufficiently explore the relationship between ICT as conveyor of structures and ICT as artefact in use.

Despite problems, Structuration Theory, with its variants, opens up important insights, especially of the cyclical and dynamic nature of the relationships between agency and structure, and that this has several distinct 'dimensions'. Later I attempt to place it on a firmer foundation than the opposition between subjective and objective that motivated Giddens.

8-2.3.5 Socio-Critical Theory, Emancipation and the Status Quo

Critical theory, which I call 'socio-critical theory' to differentiate it from philosophical criticality, is concerned to critique the structures of society and advocate emancipation. Kincheloe and McLaren (2002) provide a useful historical overview. Early 'critical theorists' of the Frankfurt School, Horkheimer, Adorno and Marcuse, engaged in conversation around Marx, Kant, Hegel and Weber and developed a deep belief that the world is shaped by injustice and subjugation. Leaving Germany for the USA during the Nazi era, these mainly Jewish thinkers were shocked by both the inconsistency between American rhetoric about egalitarianism and the reality of discrimination, and also the reigning assumption that social science could accurately measure all aspects of life. They produced material that stimulated the emancipatory ethos of the 1960s left-wing scholars, fostering critique of both capitalism and deterministic versions of Marxian thought. In Europe, Habermas developed this thought more systematically as a theory of knowledge interests (1972) and then a theory of communicative action (1986; 1987).

Socio-critical theorists particularly dislike "privileged groups" and the status quo, including management in business, which they saw as working to protect their privileges. Subjugated cohorts or peoples could be stimulated towards "critical empowerment" by questioning their conditions and disrupting and challenging the status quo.

There is a second side to subjugation, revealed in the writings of Gramsci: acculturation, in which "individuals. . . have been acculturated to feel comfortable in relations of domination and subordination rather than equality and independence" (Kincheloe and McLaren 2002, 90). People consent to domination through cultural institutions (media, educational system, family, church, etc.), often because of tacit assumptions and rules. So people should be made unhappy and their assumptions challenged. (How much are socio-critical thinkers acculturated into their own assumptions? In fact, socio-critical researchers tend to be more open than most about their own biases; c.f. Myers and Klein [2011].)

From a socio-critical perspective, society and culture are viewed as domains of struggle. Conflict is seen as inescapable, and some turn conflict in discourse into a good, in that it forces assumptions to the surface. In common with the social constructivists, socio-critical theorists see language as constructing the world not just describing it, but also as part of the apparatus of domination.

Several who are not of the Frankfurt School are also seen as socio-critical thinkers. Bourdieu is concerned about symbol violence. Since many see most of the above in terms of power, Foucault, who explored the nature of power, is seen as a socio-critical thinker—though also postmodern. Foucault argued that power is not restricted to certain cohorts, but pervades all we do and are, even determining what is counted, in society, as knowledge (power-knowledge nexus, power relations). Baudrillard (2007), however, suggests that this is too broad and that power is "collapsing" (p. 50), and that Foucault is discussing a theorization of power rather than actual power.

Thus the core idea of socio-critical approaches is a normative one: emancipation is sought from oppressive regimes, acculturation, determination of knowledge, language violence and one's own assumptions. This is why Table 4.1 sees socio-critical approaches as seeing the world in terms of the juridical aspect.

To ICT, socio-critical approaches are strongly normative, for example as seen in Social Shaping of Technology (§8-2.3.1). ICT is seen as either oppressing or emancipating people, reinforcing or subverting power relations and the status quo, contributing to or reducing 'symbol violence'—depending on whether the researcher takes Habermas, Foucault or Bourdieu as their starting-point. Critique of ICT was initially directed at ICT systems installed in large organizations, which forced people to work in certain ways, but is now directed more generally at the way in which ICT dominates our lives by acculturation (c.f. Lyon's (2007) concern about our being willing participants in surveillance, §8-2.2.2).

Four weaknesses of the socio-critical approach interest us. One is that it overlooks the everyday experience of people in favour of 'large', societal, often abstract issues of domination, thus ignoring wide ranges of issues. Another is to view all reality through a lens of power and oppression, which results in distorted intepretations (see example in §6-2.13). As Giddens (1984, 283) recognises, we need a basis on which to affirm power as one issue among many, even when it pervades them all. A third is that the notion of 'oppressive', is seldom critically examined, and depends largely on shared intuition of self-evident 'wrongness'.

A fourth weakness is a fondness for disrupting and challenging rather than seeking solutions and rectifying the problems they reveal (Kincheloe and McLaren 2002), a "tendency of critical research to demolish without rebuilding" (Brooke 2002, 274), who cites Thompson and McHugh (2002, 395), "in which everything it deconstructed or problematised, while solving nothing, is ultimately arid and self-defeating". (Walsham and Sahay's [1999] discussion of how ICT might emancipate Indian workers is a rare exception.) Though ICT might be used to emancipate, is there nothing about the status quo that is valuable? If "individuals . . . have been acculturated to feel comfortable . . ." (Kincheloe and McLaren 2002, 90), when is it right for socio-critical intellectuals to make them feel uncomfortable? Wilson (1997) suggests that such thinking can lead to the paradox of a rather sinister "enforced emancipation". Socio-critical theory offers very little basis for discussing and resolving such internal antinomy.

As a result of these weaknesses, Brooke (2002) reports a widespread doubt about the practical benefit of socio-critical research, which is seen as too abstract and not serviceable in empirical studies.

What is needed is a more nuanced view of good and evil than is provided by the simplistic absolutization of emancipation and demonization of power or acculturation.

8-2.4 Discourse about the Information Systems Discipline

What is the role of the field of information systems (IS) as a whole in society? This question is important for a number of reasons discussed by Benbasat and Zmud (2003), Hirschheim and Klein (2012) and others, for instance, for editors of journals deciding whether a paper is within scope, for citation indices, for political reasons in wider society, for inspiring vision among, and to attract, students, practitioners and researchers, as well as to have an idea of the field's responsibility and dignity in the world and its destiny (Basden 2010). (In this discussion the terms 'discipline' and 'field' are used with considerable overlap.)

The field of Information Systems grew out of the field of Management Information Systems (MIS), addressing issues of ICT use, IS development and ICT in society. After capitalizing on our technical roots in the 1970s, we began to distance ourselves from them (example: ignoring Bartle's theory of games; see §9-2.6), joining schools of business and management rather than computer science. We found ourselves undervalued by those we aspired to join, a symptom of which was Carr's (2003) provocative "IT doesn't matter", in which he argued that ICT is no longer seen as of strategic importance in business, because it brings little competitive advantage nowadays; ICT is like drains and street lights, necessary but unexciting. However we could not even agree on what defines our discipline, far less convince others what our contribution is (Agarwal and Lucas 2005). Proposed definitions have seldom captured the excitement and diversity that should characterise the discipline (Elliot and Avison, 2005), and the questions "Are we a real discipline? What is our identity?" have been debated for years, resulting in an inward rather than outward focus. (See a longer summary in Basden [2010].)

Several better questions arise. What is the intellectual core of the IS discipline? In what directions should it develop in future? How does IS relate to other disciplines, and how is it to be distinguished from them as unique or distinct?

Benbasat and Weber (1996) reviewed to which other disciplines reference is made in IS papers, arguing, as we saw in §1-5.1, that the IS field should have its own distinct theoretical core. In response to this, Baskerville and Myers (2002) sought to identify where the field of IS is referenced by others, finding a list of issues they believed to be "somewhat unique" to this field. They urged IS researchers to engage with other disciplines. However, Weber (2003) argued that if, after identifying issues, other disciplines have provided theories that can be adapted to these issues, then the information systems field would have no core of its own.

Surely, however, it depends on which issues. If we can clearly understand our theoretical core then we can still allow other fields to provide theories relevant to peripheral issues. Yet, because of a too-widespread aspiration to join the business fields, IS researchers have over-researched management aspects and under-researched others, especially information (Benbasat and Zmud 2003). To understand our core requires foundational frameworks for understanding, frameworks that are not derived from reference disciplines but from the nature of ICT, and yet which can be meaningful in other disciplines.

Two main approaches have been tried: historical analysis and theoretical identification of issues. Perhaps the best history-based attempt so far is by Hirshcheim and Klein (2012), with a wide-ranging review of the infancy, pre-pubescence, adolescence and adulthood of the field. They charted research themes, institutions and research methods, finding support for IS being a genuine discipline in the emergence of high-quality journals, institutions with 'political voice' and standards. They concluded that two things should be done for the future, (a) to build a common body of knowledge, despite a strong pluralistic interdisciplinarity and the danger of this constraining future research freedom, (b) to identify its mission(s) and 'customers', even though up to now IS has not led practice but has merely followed that in other fields, employing theories and frameworks from sociology, business or psychology rather than developing its own theories and frameworks.

Hirschheim and Klein (2012) do not, however, give any indication of on what basis customers or missions may be identified, nor how the danger of constraining research freedom may be overcome. Their history, though wide-ranging, is nevertheless narrower than the range of ICT use discourses outlined in Chapter 6. They mention the field of human-computer interaction only cursorily, and largely ignore ICT features, affordance, computer games, geographic information systems, etc. History-based analyses tend to be idiographic and also rather conservative, in that they offer no basis on which to identify new possibilities or judge innovative directions.

These limitations might be overcome by an approach that tries to think out the intellectual core of the IS discipline. Trajectories and new possibilities might then be identified and critiqued by reference to such cores. Several authors have taken this approach. Grover (2012) made four studies, treating the field as an aggregator of terms, a complex adaptive system, a knowledge market and an evolving biological system, and concluded that the IS field shows some maturity. However, most of his studies were backward-looking and at least two are based on metaphors.

Benbasat and Zmud (2003) proposed a model of relationships between main issues of the discipline: the ICT artefact, usage, impact, practices and capabilities. From their model, which is a semi-causal 'nomological net', they suggest rules of thumb for judging whether research is within the IS discipline or not. Their model recognises the ICT artefact as important (many discourses gloss over it), and that its use in the world is what primarily makes it meaningful (rather than its technical characteristics), and it allows critique of the current situation.

However, Benbasat and Zmud's proposal also illustrates some problems with the core-characteristics approach. First, they employ one theoretical lens (from a biological metaphor) to understand what a discipline is, rather than being open to everyday experience within disciplines. Using a single lens seems to be a common failing among model-based approaches. Second, they presuppose what they want to argue for: the distinctness of the IS discipline centred on the ICT artefact. Third, despite warning against doing so, they tend to treat the IT artefact as a 'black box', only giving only brief attention to the composition of the artefact and its conception, construction, implementation. By contrast, this book devotes two major chapters to this, alongside two on what Benhasat and Zmud would recognise, and recognises multiple aspects or cores and thus has multiple lenses.

An interdisciplinary field might have several cores, or parts to its core. The socio-technical approach, discussed in §6-2.3, defines itself by reference to two cores, social and technical, and Mumford (1995) provided ground-breaking ideas on attitudes to ICT in the workplace. However, the core aspects of social and technical are not enough, Lee (2004) argued that something is missing even when these are combined into the socio-technical approach: information itself (c.f. Benbasat and Zmud's [2003] comment above).

Discourses usually arise and grow because something that seems meaningful and important was previously overlooked (see §3-5.2.2). What is centrally meaningful to the field of Information Systems—or any other field—can help define its intellectual core, which directions it might take in future, and how it relates to other disciplines. In §8-6.3 Dooyeweerd's idea of meaningfulness will be used to address these.

8-2.5 Discourses about Technological Progress

Is it the destiny of humankind to be forever entrapped in ICT? How avidly should ICT be marketed to the non-Western, developing, Two-Thirds world? Technology in general and Information and Communication Technology in particular are harnessed to the idea of progress. Yet the idea of progress is so deeply rooted in the modern, Western mindset, from within which ICT arose, that it is taken for granted, with a strong normative component of improvement and betterment of humanity's condition or capability (Webster 1971, II, 1813). This immediately raises the philosophical question of what constitutes 'improvement', and imbues progress with an inescapable normativity.

But what is progress? How do we distinguish progressive from regressive? With many cultures of the world believing in a cyclical view of time, the idea of progress is not universal. Bury (1920/2013) offers an historical overview of ideas. To many ancient Greek thinkers, like Parmenides, time and change were seen as illusory or as an enemy. To others, like Plato, humanity had progressed from a state of Nature to a 'higher' state of Culture and Civilisation (from Matter to Form). In mediaeval Europe, progress was seen, especially by Augustine, as moving from a state of Nature to a state of Grace, guided by a Divine plan, interventions and revelations, which were ultimately inscrutable, so our only valid response was trust and obedience.

The Enlightenment view of progress was stimulated by scientific advances, based on developing reliable bodies of knowledge, held in encyclopedias, which freed later ages from having to rediscover what had been accomplished in previous ages. Voltaire believed this advances society. The American Revolution sought progress in the structuring of society and re-ignited hopes of progress by suggesting that history was not exhausted. Both the French and American revolutions saw progress as moving towards ever-increasing Freedom. Spencer saw progress as moving from military to industrial societies. Technology, including ICT, has been harnessed to serve this Enlightenment idea of progress, because they enable humanity to achieve more, more quickly and easily.

Thus each view of progress seems to be a different kind of improvement in humanity: personal, social, knowledge, society, economy, technology and the like.

These optimistic views ignored both the possibility of evil and error, and the pain that Kant believed to be inevitable in the processes of progress. Progress was seen as inevitable, and to be aspired to, but few explored why, except to refer to individual aspects listed above. Nisbet (1980) identified five presuppositions: that the past has little value, that Western civilisation is noble, that economic and technological growth in innately good, that reason, and its accompaniments of science and scholarship, is the way to knowledge, and that (human) life on earth is intrinsically good. Such presuppositions need critical examination.

Progress of the enlightenment kind does not have an unblemished track record. Its desirability has been questioned by many, including Nietzsche—though his own legacy has been far from universally positive. As early as 1932 Eder argued that it has led to increasing unhappiness and environmental problems. Sale (2007) powerfully argues that:

- progress benefits less than one-sixth of the world's population, at severe cost to the other five-sixths, and
- at the cost of '*affluenza*' within that one-sixth (heart disease, stress, overwork, family dysfunction, etc.);
- that progress demands ever-increasing sacrifices from the biosphere as every life support system becomes severely threatened;
- that progress consumes an unsustainable amount of the world's resources;
- that "on a larger scale, almost all that Progress was supposed to achieve has failed to come about, despite the immense amount of money and technology devoted to its cause."

Though Sale's essay is a polemic in which some of what he says might be overstated, much of what he says needs to be considered carefully. ICT threatens to exacerbate some of these trends, because it amplifies problems (§8-2.1) and allows infrastructures to be imposed (§8-2.2).

Rather than trying to either idolise or demonise progress, we need a clearer view of the relationship between the different kinds of improvement, with a basis for differentiating progress from regress, and to question assumptions that progress is inevitable or should be modeled on Western, Enlightenment views. After reviewing two sets of thinking about technology, some pessimistic about technology (Jünger, Heidegger, Ellul, Meyer), some optimistic (Wiener, Steinbuch, Klaus, Habermas), Schuurman (1980) criticised both sets as implying an "unpromising, somber future" (p. 314), and for their "inability to indicate a way of escape from the real problems that modern technology entails." The root of this, he argued, is a 'religious' presupposition (in the Dooyeweerdian sense §3-4.2), that theoretical thought is autonomous. We pick up his ideas again §8-6.2.

8-2.6 Drawing This Together

Understanding the global and longer-term impact of ICT and information systems, and what is good and what, evil, demands that we embrace all the discourses above, but our deliberations about this have not reached maturity. We now accept that the impact of tobacco is largely evil, and that of oil is a mix of evil and good, but we have not discussed what proportion of human effort (or of global spend) around ICT and IS goes to doing evil, preventing evil and doing good. For example, I might classify Mark Zuckerberg's *Facematch*, the precursor of *Facebook*, as directed towards doing evil, in that it treated girls as objects of fun and resulted in arrogance and depresssion, I might see security as directed towards preventing evil, and crowdfunding as directed towards doing new kinds of good, in that it makes 'ordinary people' more effective. Others will disagree. On what grounds may we discuss this?

Most of the discourses above began more than two decades ago. Since then, the dot-com bubble has burst, social media has become dominant, mobile devices proliferate, and expectations have changed about the nature of information. Even the relatively poor in the Two-Thirds world have access to some of that technology. Extant ideas like social constructivism, socio-critical approaches and Structuration Theory have been applied to these new situations and technologies but are still motivated by what seemed important or exciting decades ago. How many new insights of practical value do they still provide?

I believe that each discourse does contain important insights that are still relevant, but how can they be made more appropriate for today and tomorrow? How can the various discourses interact? To cope with new global situations, to foster interaction among discourses, and to address such questions, we need a foundational understanding that can respect the diversity of issues as all meaningful. We need a foundational understanding of technological progress that transcends yesterday, today and tomorrow, situates the discourses, and which is 'transcendental' insofar as it can reveal what makes ICT possible as a societal phenomenon. It needs to affirm the insights handed down from the past, yet provide a basis for critique and enrichment. Only this can provide a foundation for future-oriented research and practice.

Dooyeweerd's philosophy is explored as a possible provider of such a foundation. With its 'oceanic' idea of meaningfulness and normativity, it might be more future-proof, and be able to affirm yet critically enrich each of the discourses.

Instead of constructing a framework for understanding the theme of ICT and society and applying it to discourses, as is done in Chapter 6, this chapter discusses separately how four major portions of Dooyeweerd's philosophy described in Chapter 3 might throw light on various issues and discourses. Section 8-3 discusses Dooyeweerd's critique of philosophy, Section 8-4 explores how Dooyeweerd's aspects might help us, Section 8-5 applies Dooyeweerd's notion of enkapsis, and Section 8-6, Dooyeweerd's theory of progress. Section 8-7 then summarises this by discourse. Some of the above discourses are wholly addressed within one section, but some cut across several sections.

8-3 Applying Dooyeweerd's Critique of Immanence Philosophy to Discourses about ICT and Society

As discussed in §3-2.1, Dooyeweerd located the main problems of philosophy and theoretical thinking in the Immanence Standpoint and its presupposition of dualistic ground-motives. Most of the problems listed there can be readily detected in the above discourses on ICT and society.

1. *Separation of meaningfulness from reality.* Meaningfulness separated from reality is especially evident in Weber's suggestion that 'the system' is devoid of meaning and normativity, and also in Habermas' version, where meaning is generated *ex nihilo* by critique of validity claims. Meaning is seen as secondary or inessential to understanding society. This can blind some sociologists to the everyday meaningfulness that people experience. The separation can also be seen in the lack of normativity in Structuration Theory (§8-2.3.4).

Understanding the normative difference between progress and regress (§8-2.5), and the dignity of the information systems field (§8-2.4), presuppose a meaningful normativity that transcends us—so discourses around these topics, if meaningfulness is presumed inessential, will be limited to techniques, methods and paraphernalia like professional institutions. However, the discussions of reference disciplines might indicate that the discourse on the information systems field is reaching for the idea of an 'ocean of meaningfulness', which is not separate from reality. ('Ocean of meaningfulness' refers to the idea that both we, ICT and society exist and are enabled by meaningfulness, which is shared at the deepest level; see §3-1.2.3.)

2. *Treatment of everyday experience.* That the Immanence Standpoint prevents sensitive treatment of everyday experience is seen throughout most discourses, in that, when considering ICT and society, everyday experience is presumed to be largely about individual living. Not only is everyday experience of limited interest in academic investigation, but it becomes a distant phenomenon, and researchers do not even question its absence from their discourses. As a result, the diversity of everyday experience is often reduced to a small number of 'large' issues like government, economy and power, often seen in abstract terms. This is especially true of socio-critical approaches (§8-2.3.5).

3. *Absolutization of aspects and types of thing.* Absolutization, or at least elevation, of aspects is clearly seen in the approaches to technology discussed in §8-2.3.1. Technological Determinism elevates the formative aspect in several mutually reinforcing ways: it is concerned with technology, is interested in what we achieve or do with technology, and believes the human response is adaptation. Social Construction of Technology elevates the social aspect. Social Shaping of Technology elevates the juridical aspect ("regulations, legal duties, political strategies . . ." (Howcroft et al. 2004, 351)). Though other aspects are acknowledged (pistic aspect in "interests" (p. 351) or "ideological constraints" (p. 353), ethical aspect in critique of amorality), they are treated cursorily. Socio-critical approaches also focus on juridical evils of oppression, subjugation and inappropriate acculturation and assumptions (§8-2.3.5). Elevation of other aspects may be seen throughout the discourses, such as the economic in most discourses. As a result, in almost all discourses, many aspects are overlooked, and analyses in research and practice are distorted (§3-7.3).

Absolutization of types of things can be detected in the discourses around infrastructure (§8-2.2), for example of e-government, or of ICT itself so that life without ICT infrastructure is seen as a disabling deficiency rather than a valid option.

4. *Dualistic ground-motives.* The dualistic Nature-freedom ground-motive helps account for the TD-SCOT-SST sequence described in §8-2.3.1. Technological Determinism is aligned with the nature pole and Social Construction of Technology with the freedom pole. Because of the religious nature of the ground-motive, the relationship between them is one of antipathy. Social Shaping of Technology tries to accommodate some 'unfreedom' of societal structures and a strong normativity, but because it keeps hold onto freedom as a norm, this generates an internal antinomy (c.f. "enforced emancipation" §8-2.3.5).

5. *Coherence between aspects.* The relationship between aspects is especially important when trying to understand widespread impact of ICT use (§8-2.1), because of its rich diversity of factors. Though the social aspect is obviously important in widespread impact, it is often given undue predominance, as self-dependent, on which all else depends (§3-1.2.3). The role of societal beliefs and attitudes in infrastructure (§8-2.2.4), such as idolatry,

self-interest or self-protection seen in the e-government, digital divide and surveillance, and how they relate to all other aspects (e.g., social, lingual and economic) needs more attention.

Two discourses, however, seem to buck this trend. Feminist thought seems, at least partly, to recognise a variety of currently overlooked aspects (§8-2.3.3), but it tends towards ground-motive-driven reaction rather than healing. Giddens' Structuration Theory tries to understand the relationships between at least six aspects, as discussed later (§8-4.5).

6. *Problems in concept formation* are present in these discourses only in general ways found in any area and have been discussed in §4-2.

7. *The structure of things*. Most discourses on ICT and society presume that the 'thingness' of society, infrastructure or ICT is unproblematic. However Giddens (1984) does seem to have tried to explore the structure of the thing that is society, in positing a structure-agency duality with three dimensions. That he did so, and also took seriously the diversity and coherence of aspects, suggests that he was breaking away from an Immanence Standpoint. Is that why Structuration Theory has proven attractive, despite its shortcomings?

That Dooyeweerd's philosophy did not take an Immanence Standpoint (§3-2.4) opened up novel philosophical ideas about aspects, things and progress. The next three sections explore how they may be applied to offer a foundational understanding of ICT and society in a way that affirms, critiques and enriches extant discourses.

8-4 Applying Dooyeweerd's Notion and Suite of Aspects

In this section, we explore the potential of Dooyeweerd's suite of aspects to help make sense of ICT as a societal phenomenon. It includes several aspects that make societal issues possible, alongside aspects of individuals and pre-human aspects, so it offers the potential to integrate the societal with the personal. In this section, we look at discourses, widespread use and infrastructure.

8-4.1 Using Aspects to Situate Discourses

Earlier it was suggested that each of the paradigms of Technological Determinism, Social Construction of Technology and Social Shaping of Technology elevate a particular aspect. Dooyeweerd's understanding of aspects can provide a nuanced account, because he maintains that all aspects are of equal importance, all pertain and all are exhibited, even if some are latent.

- Thus Technological Determinism (TD) not only finds the *formative aspect* of technology of central interest (world), but in practice also finds the *economic aspect* of interest (because of close links to business and industry), and models itself on the rationality of the *physical aspect*, for which forces and causes are directly meaningful. However, might not other aspects also be detected in the everyday life of a technological determinist, such as commitment (pistic), some concern for justice (juridical) and enjoyment (aesthetic)?

- Social Construction of Technology (SCOT) finds the *social aspect* of central interest. However, social functioning relies on the *lingual aspect* of meaning-attribution and the *analytical aspect*, by which people freely conceptualise, both of which are recognised within SCOT. Its main rationality is social. Moreover, does not 'construction' indicate some importance of the formative aspect? As with actual technological determinists, do not social constructivists also give some importance to pistic, ethical, juridical and aesthetic aspects too?
- Social Shaping of Technology (SST) finds the *juridical aspect* of right and wrong, of domination and emancipation, a central driving motivator, but it also recognises the importance of beliefs and assumptions in all their forms (*pistic aspect*), and it also recognises the *social and formative aspects*, and what they depend on. It also tries to recognise multiple aspects to which this right and wrong are directed: injustice (juridical), gender (organic-biotic—but also more), power (ethical), distribution of resources (economic) and so on.

Recognition of the range of aspects involved provides grounds for common interest. Each aspect will be manifested somewhat differently within each paradigm, because of the inter-aspect analogies and dependencies that pertain (§3-7.4), but at least each may speak meaningfully with others. Following Basden's (2011) aspectual analysis of what is meaningful to positivism, interpretivism and criticalism, as outlined in §4-2, Dooyeweerd's notion of Ground-idea may be recommended as grounds for dialogue between TD, SCOT and SST.

This outline is only indicative, offering an opportunity for fruitful research.

8-4.2 Aspects of Widespread Use of ICT

Widespread use is ICT use multiplied or amplified by myriads.

This suggests that we should take account of the understanding of ICT use developed in Chapter 6. ICT use is seen as the intertwining of three distinct multi-aspectual engagements of humans with ICT:

- engaging with interface and technology (EIT) (§6-3.4)—the impact of technology itself is amplified;
- engaging with meaningful content (EMC) (§6-3.5)—the effect of content is amplified;
- engaging in life with ICT (ELI) (§6-3.6)—the repercussions in life are amplified.

Each one exhibits all fifteen aspects in principle, as a functioning with repercussions. It is these aspectual functioning and repercussions that are amplified, usually because of the *social aspect* of people working together.

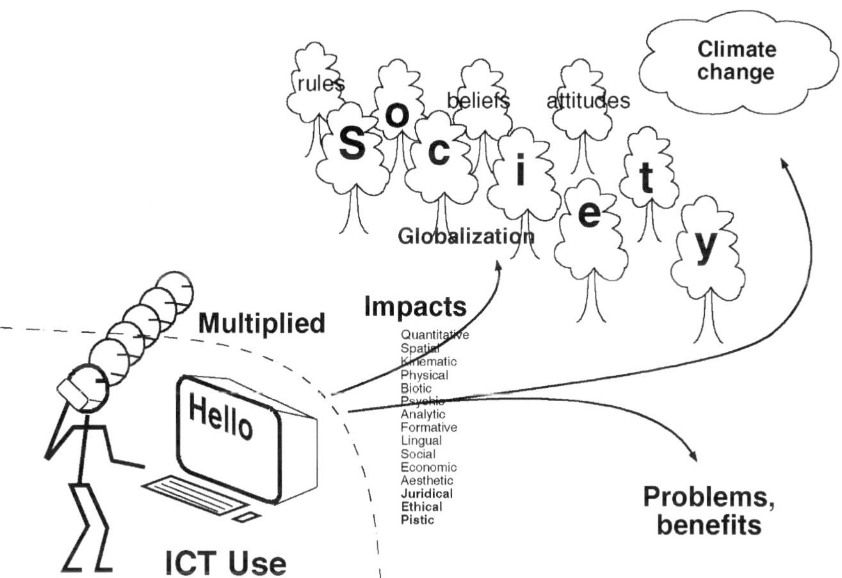

Figure 8.2 Widespread Impacts of Using ICT

8-4.2.1 Identifying and Relating the Various Issues of Widespread Impact

This suggests we may analyse and understand the issues of widespread use of ICT by identifying which engagement and which aspects are most important in characterizing it. For example:

- Crowdfunding: economic aspect, EMC (money as content);
- Cyberbullying: ethical, EMC;
- Cyberloafing: economic, ELI;
- Mobile phone use: lingual, EIT;
- Climate change 1: physical, EIT (power consumed);
- Climate change 2: pistic, EMC (changing beliefs, commitments);
- Climate change 3: various, ELI (lifestyles and behaviour);

Such an analysis offers a common foundation for understanding many apparently dissimilar issues, situating them and relating them to each other, rather than each being discussed in isolation from the others.

Amplification of each engagement needs to be judged differently, to attend to technology and user interface when the problem is EIT, to content when the problem is EMC and to the behaviour or attitudes when the problem is ELI.

8-4.2.2 *Aspects of Functioning That Leads to Widespread Impact; the Example of Climate Change*

To gain an overall picture of any one issue of widespread ICT use, such as computer procrastination or climate change, it is useful to understand the dynamics of amplification or multiplication, aspect-by-aspect. This can stimulate consideration of factors that might have been neglected. Remembering the innate normativity of aspects (§3-7.5) directs us to consider both positive and negative factors in each.

Table 8.1 shows aspects in column 1, and possible amplification mechanisms that are to do with technology or content in column 2 and those to do with human behaviour in column 3. Those in the table are not exhaustive, and further research is called for, to obtain a more complete picture.

Table 8.1 Aspects of Widespread Use of ICT and Its Impact

Aspect	*EMC / some EIT*	*ELI*	*Example: Climate Change*
Quantitative	Many users (EIT)	Multiplication of all below	Jevon's Paradox
Spatial	Global ICT network (Internet) (EIT)	Distances shrunk in all below	
Kinematic	Movement of data (EIT)		
Physical	Power consumption (EIT)	e.g. Bridge players (§8-2.1)	Climate change emissions from power generation.
Organic-biotic			Rainforest destruction (see economic)
Psychic / Sensitive	Dissemination of emotions (e.g. picture of Aylan Kurdi)	Collective desire	Desire to good or evil
Analytical	Easier comparison e.g. on price	Fixation on the given criteria, e.g. price . . .	. . . rather than ecological responsibility (part pistic)
Formative	Technical equipment and infrastructure; More power to achieve things.	Fixation on achievement . . .	. . . rather than ecological responsibility
Lingual	More information and opinion (websites, blogs); Information storage (Cloud).	Confusion or enlightenment	The debate about climate change was confused by a barrage of skeptical opinion

Aspect	*EMC / some EIT*	*ELI*	*Example: Climate Change*
Social	Contact with distant people; Widespread agreement, sharing.	Wider circles of friends, acquaintances.	Sharing transport reduces CC, stimulating travel increases CC (§8-2.1).
Economic	Low cost of ICT (EIT); Better information on resources, faster financial and bartering transactions	More people with ICT; Better linking supply, demand; Large corporations more efficient.	More efficient reuse, recycling (e.g. *Freecycle*); Resource-destruction by large corporations (see also ethical, pistic)
Aesthetic	Harmonizing many individual activities; More exposure to fashions	Global phenomena Greater game-addiction.	e.g. Avaaz orchestrating COP21 marches in December 2015.
Juridical	Privacy concerns (EIT); Dissemination of anger about injustices	Anger leads to policy and laws being hastily changed, leading to greater injustices.	International laws and treaties.
Ethical	Focus on individual likes or dislikes r.t. focus on good to others	Spreads attitude of self-centredness vs. generosity	National self-interest undermines CC treaties.
Pistic / Faith	Faster, wider dissemination of aspirations, expectations, assumptions, worldview; Dominant beliefs inscribed in ICT (EIT).	Changes aspirations, prevailing beliefs	Increases or decreases perceived importance of climate change, compared with other issues (idolatry, sacrifice: see below)

Note: *Jevon's Paradox* is that sometimes, when resource consumed by an artefact is known to have been reduced, overall consumption increases because people use them more. Example: Believing that mobile phones consume little power, we tend to keep them switched on more than we need to, and the multiplied effect of this is to increase overall power consumption.

Having identified such mechanisms of amplification, we can then apply them to a particular issue. A result of doing this for climate change is shown in column 4 (the entries are from initial analysis).

Attitude and aspirations are often impacted via EMC, engaging with meaningful content: Blogs are often written to convince, while Twitter feeds convince more subtly by drawing attention to a single aspect per message.

Climate change is offered as an exemplar, but other issues can be considered, such as problems like online gambling. Research is needed to critique, refine and fully operationalise the suggestion.

8-4.3 The Role of Aspects in Societal Infrastructure

We may gain a foundational understanding of ICT as infrastructure by reference to Dooyeweerd's aspects. A number of points will be discussed.

1. *The Being of infrastructure.* The Being and Occurring of infrastructure is constituted in the world's functioning in all the aspects in certain ways (§3-9.2). The two central aspects are the social and lingual. Infrastructure necessarily requires agreement and collaboration, which is social aspect. Social functioning depends on the lingual (§3-7.4.4), and thus, if the lingual aspect is ICT's qualifying aspect (§3-9.4), then ICT will be very important in all infrastructures today.
2. *Types of infrastructure.* We may use aspects in a simple way: to differentiate the various infrastructures within which we live. By identifying the main or qualifying aspect of our functioning within each kind of infrastructure, we can separate out issues and more clearly understand the dynamics and relationships of ICT and society. For example:

   - formative infrastructure: technology with its manufacture and training,
   - lingual infrastructure: language and libraries—and Internet,
   - social infrastructure: institutions,
   - economic infrastructure: the economy, money, banks,
   - aesthetic infrastructure: fashion,
   - juridical infrastructure: the systems of laws, policies and the state,
   - ethical infrastructure: pervading attitudes,
   - pistic infrastructure: prevailing beliefs, aspirations and expectations.

   Each constrains and enables our functioning in certain ways rather than others. None determines them, because we can choose to use a different language, question the prevailing beliefs, etc. With this we may conceptualise simultaneously *multiple infrastructures*.
3. *New kinds of infrastructure.* If ICT represents humanity's opening up of new potential of the lingual aspect, then ICT will enable new kinds of social activity (see §8-6.1) and thus new kinds of infrastructure. Research is needed to explore the role of all aspects.

Example: *Freecycle* provides an economy based on information, within which people pass on (and recycle, reuse) their unwanted articles free, thus creating a different economic infrastructure.

4. *Aspects of an infrastructure*. We may also use aspects, more deeply, to understand the issues around a single kind of infrastructure. Table 8.2 contains issues and problems relevant to surveillance, derived from lists in the Surveillance Studies Network Report (Wood 2006) (see §8-2.2.2),

Table 8.2 Aspectual Issues in SSN Report on Surveillance; Issues of e-government, Digital Divide

Aspect	*SSN Surveillance process*	*SSN Surveillance issue*	*E-government issue (examples)*	*Digital divide (examples)*
Quantitative			Population count	
Spatial			Geographic spread	Geographic divide
Kinematic			Movement of information	
Physical			Terrain challenges	
Organic-biotic				Health differences
Psychic/Sensitive	Data flow		Data flow	Mental health
Analytical	(Social) sorting			'Divide'
Formative	Function creep; 'technologies'	Choice	Technology for e-government; Training citizenry	(Access to) technology
Lingual		Transparency	Information available and accepted	(Access to) information
Social	Social sorting	Social exclusion	Roles (citizen, government); Collaboration	Status differences
Economic			Delivery of services; Costs	Access to ICT; Financial differences
Aesthetic			'Join the dots'	'Divide'
Juridical		Privacy, 'ethics', human rights; (social) exclusion; accountability	(Dis) enfranchisement	Equality, rights
Ethical		Domination; power	Pervading attitudes	Pervading attitudes
Pistic/Faith		Empowerment ?	Vision (idolatrous or valid)	Vision: what is ICT for? Religious backgrounds

and of e-government. The tangled issues of the digital divide might also be separated out in a similar way, with examples in column 5.

Each issue has been assigned to the aspect(s) that are most important in seeing it as problematic or meaningful, even though each also involves other aspects.

5. *Over-emphasis on aspects in infrastructure discourse.* If we examine the SSN's (Wood 2006) attempts to provide a comprehensive view of surveillance, we find certain aspects overplayed and others largely ignored. The juridical aspect is strongly emphasised. ('Ethics' there refers to some infringement of what is appropriate or just.) This raises the question: Is the juridical aspect really more important in surveillance, or is it merely because the SSN report was aimed at a government body?
6. *Missing aspects of infrastructure discourse.* The analysis reveals aspectual gaps, which prompts us to ask in what ways any of the missing aspects might be important. Consider an unlikely aspect, the aesthetic. Might aesthetic motivations, such as fun, make surveillance more problematic? Should we differentiate cynical from enjoyable fun, especially among hackers, and on what basis? Two neglected aspects of infrastructure are discussed in more depth: ethical, pistic. These constitute what are often loosely called 'values'.
7. *The ethical aspect of infrastructure.* The ethical aspect is manifested in trust and goodwill, both of which are essential for infrastructure to operate. Lyon (2007, 58) makes a radical suggestion: surveillance could be designed around a vision of trust instead of suspicion—perhaps even trust in the Creator's care. By contrast, consider the citation in §8-2.2.2, "No one suggests that the store manager wishing to lure only the most creditworthy customers is devious. . . It simply makes sense in the quest for greater profitability" (Wood 2006). Though this expresses concern that "others fall by the wayside" (which is meaningful in the juridical aspect), there is a deeper concern in the ethical aspect: it betrays an unquestioned acceptance of self-interest by society. Consumer surveillance seems motivated largely by self-interest, while military, government, policing and workplace surveillance seem motivated by self-protection. If Dooyeweerd is correct in thinking that the aspects bring *shalom* (§3-8.5) and that aspectual dysfunction (which self-protection and self-interest are) jeopardises this ("society of strangers" and suspicion of all; §8-2.2.2), then, despite understandable fears to the contrary, a surveillance designed around generosity and self-giving could be more effective in the long term. Indeed, my PhD student, Stephen McGibbon, who is exploring the nature of Internet trust, has suggested that trust is of the ethical aspect rather than pistic, in that when we trust we voluntarily put ourselves at risk. This suggests that a healthy (information) society arises not from ever more vigilant security but at least partly from its opposite, a generous attitude.

Remember the long time-scales of ethical repercussions (Table 3.5). To avoid mere idealism, and enact this radical suggestion, we must wisely take account of all other aspects too; this might help Lyon (2007) develop his radical idea.

8. *The pistic aspect of infrastructure.* The pistic aspect is about society's vision about what is ultimately meaningful and important and self-sufficient or self-justifying, and about commitment to that, usually at a subconscious level. It is about what vision our infrastructures serve and as in the case of e-government, this is often idolatrous. The idea of pistic infrastructure raises visional questions like, "Are luxury goods for the 'creditworthy' more important than equality of access?"—not just around a local store, but equivalent questions on a global basis, in the divergence of the rich from the impoverished nations and the well-resourced from the under-resourced. Perhaps the fundamental problem of the *digital divide* is pistic rather than economic in nature? It may be that the pistic rationality and insights of the socio-critical theorists (see §4-2.2) and also today's anti-capitalist movement can be seriously acknowledged here, without accepting their fundamental presuppositions. (Pistic infrastructure might resemble and even enrich Gramsci's idea of acquiescence by acculturation, a structure of belief that 'constrains', at unawares, how myriads of people function, but that is not explored here.)
9. *A study of idolatry.* As mentioned in §8-2.2.3, idolatry may be a significant factor in the high failure rate of e-government, especially in the attractive vision of 'transformational government. This is not surprising since idolatry is pistically dysfunctional and undermines the functioning in almost every other aspect. So does demonization. Though mentioned by Heeks (2006) and Gauld & Goldfinnch (2006), idolatry has not been sufficiently researched, until Subrahmanian Krishnan-Harihara expanded a small characterization of idolatry of Goudzwaard's (1984) essay on *Idols of Our Time*, which was written in response to what he felt was idolatry in Dutch politics of the time, of technology, of economism, of nationalism and of defence. Unlike his more considered, later works, which rationalize the notion, this essay is valuable because it expresses his intuitive view of how idolatry occurs.

   Subrahmaniam developed this seed-idea into a substantial model of how idolatry operates to undermine e-government projects. Goudzwaard (1984) suggests that idolatry begins when "people sever something from their immediate environment, refashion it and erect it on its own feet in a special place". Likewise, the idea of government is severed from its historical and social context, and refashioned as ICT-enabled 'transformational government'. It occupies a special place in government thinking, often given a separate department. Just as worshippers "kneel before" the idol and see it "as a thing that has life in itself", so e-government receives adulation and determines its own course of development. Just as worshippers "bring sacrifices", so much is sacrificed to install e-government, and the poor become increasingly disenfranchised. The full analysis can be found in (Krishnan-Harihara and Basden (2009).

He then went further, arguing that each of these has a positive as well as harmful possibility, which may be understood in relation to Dooyeweerd's aspects (Krishnan-Harihara & Basden 2010). Do not all innovations involve some 'severing' and 'refashioning', in that changes occur? Do not governments have to shift resources from some areas to others? These are analytic, formative and economic functionings, which need not be wrong. The difference between idolatrous and valid versions lies in the retrocipatory influence (§3-7.4.4) of the pistic aspect, of being committed either to good or to serving an idol.

10. *A call.* If Dooyeweerd is correct, that infrastructure involves all aspects, and that dysfunction in two important societal aspects, the ethical and the pistic, brings about serious unintended long-term consequences, which Lonergan (1992) called longer cycles of decline, then it matters that today's infrastructures have this twin dysfunction at their roots. The positive side of the pistic aspect is courage and faithfulness. For those with academic and political courage, to understand the ethical and pistic aspects of our ICT infrastructures, is an area of research and action that awaits exploration. It was, after all, attention to these aspects that was effective in abolishing that heinous infrastructure of the slave trade (Basden 2017).

8-4.4 Gender and Information Systems

Since feminist discourse on gender and information systems is admirably aware of its basic assumptions and theoretical lenses, its Ground-Idea is readily discerned. To the kind of feminist discourse espoused by Adam, Howcroft and Richardson (2004) (§8-2.3.3), the aspects abstracted from the *world* are the organic-biotic, social, aesthetic and ethical, in contrast to the 'masculine' aspects (analytic, formative, economic, juridical), which have been unduly emphasised. It seems that feminist thinkers are, in effect, calling for a wider range of aspects (Basden 2008, 325)—so they and Dooyeweerd's multi-aspectuality affirm each other (an interpretation confirmed by Alison Adam personally). However, this may be critiqued in that, while Dooyeweerd treats every aspect as equally important, feminist thought has a tendency to denigrate the aspects of 'masculine' thought. Such denigration might be useful in specific circumstances of historical domination but is limiting when made absolute.

The main style of *rationality* in this discourse, shared with socio-critical approaches of which this is a branch (§4-2), concerns beliefs, commitments, standpoints, etc. It is thus a pistic rationality. Since the fields of apologetics and some theology share this rationality, gender discourses might benefit from listening to some of the self-critical discussions in those fields.

Gender discourses revolve around the wrongness of the 'masculine' status quo. Though sometimes conceived in a juridical way as one among many aspects (a pluralistic Origin of Meaning), this is more often conceived in terms of the Nature-freedom ground-motive, a dualistic *Origin of Meaning*. This determines how new paradigms within the discourse are judged, and the dualistic tendency may be seen in how Adam et al. (2004) refer to 'essentialism' and 'determinism' as unquestionably to-be-escaped-from, rather than as allowing that they might offer a modicum of insight (which is possible under with pluralistic Origins).

8-4.5 Possible Contributions to Structuration Theory

Dooyeweerd can affirm Giddens' Structuration Theory, outlined in §8-2.3.4, and then allow us to critique and enrich it.

The most basic affirmation is that agency is seen as multi-aspectual functioning, which has repercussions in all aspects (§3-8.3), which, in some of the later aspects, constitute the alteration of societal structures, which also affect that functioning. Thus, the structuration cycle.

Aspectual repercussion echoes, and provides philosophical grounding for, Giddens' idea of causation. That multi-aspectual functioning is both governed by aspectual law and shaped by the subject-object-side context, which includes the societal structures, echoes Giddens' idea that structure is not just the "matrix" of things, and not just the set rules, beliefs, etc., that happen to be held by society at any given time, but the deeper laws that enable that holding. It may be that Giddens recognised something of the Dooyeweerdian idea of oceanic law-side, the aspects of which enable things to function and come into existence, and which also defines what is basically good, even if he did not so clearly distinguish it from subject-object-side actuality in the way Dooyeweerd did (§3-3.1).

Dooyeweerd can then critique and enrich Giddens' ideas in two ways, to enrich or to replace them.

Replacement is revealed as necessary by the roots of structure-agency duality being in the presumed subjective-objective dualism, which is an expression of the Nature-Freedom ground-motive. Dooyeweerd held this to be false and liable to mislead thinkers. Instead, Dooyeweerd could argue that simply speaking of functioning in different aspects of human functioning, including the post-social ones, is enough, and that reifying these aspects as 'things' is counterproductive. This would explain why Healy (1998) found Giddens' idea of structure to be 'vaporous'.

Then both structure and agency are aspectual functioning, different aspects in different dimensions. The structures of signification, domination and legitimation may be seen as functioning in three later aspects and the agency thereof in three earlier ones.

By structures of legitimation, Giddens means society's collective functioning about what is right and wrong, appropriate and inappropriate, a view of what it is or might be appropriate to hold as social norms or sanctions. Clearly, this is primarily a *juridical aspect*. The actual sanctioning that occurs among agents bespeaks social agreement (functioning in the *social aspect*).

Structures of signification are society treating certain things as of ultimate meaningfulness, a background to which reference is made without much question. This is functioning in the *pistic aspect*. In the meaning dimension, the agency of communication is obviously our functioning in the *lingual aspect*.

The power dimension is complex because, as Giddens complained, we have been too influenced by Nietzsche to absolutise power, thus preventing critical examination thereof. Giddens tried valiantly to reverse this absolutization by recognising two aspects of power and situating it alongside other things. Giddens (1984, 15) identifies agency of the power dimension as "transformative capacity . . . intent . . . will", which are clearly meaningful in the *formative aspect*. The meaning of structures of domination are clearly of the *ethical aspect* when we see that he used the negatively connoted word 'domination' rather than the more neutral 'dominion': Power can be employed, either in selfish pursuit of one's own agenda, or in order to enable and empower others, often with some sacrifice ('giving-away') by the self.

Table 8.3 summarises this.

The structuration cycle is then not so much a cycle as the interwoven coherence of aspects functioning simultaneously—which supports Giddens' contention that his three dimensions are interleaved. This turns a supposed weakness of Structuration Theory into a strength.

Seeing Structuration Theory in terms of aspects can also reduce the confusion about resources, which, as yet another aspect (economic), need have no special connection with power, but are merely one more

Table 8.3 Aspectual Understanding of Giddens' Dimensions of Structure

DIMENSIONS:	*Meanings*	*Power*	*Norms*
Structure Aspect	Pistic	Ethical	Juridical
STRUCTURE	Signification	Domination	Legitimation
MODALITY	Interpretive scheme	Facility	Norms
INTERACTION	Communication	Power	Sanction
Interaction Aspect	Lingual	Formative	Social

aspectual functioning alongside the others. Dooyeweerd (1955, IV, 88) might comment that Giddens does not understand how the economic aspect provides a substratum for the aspects that provide the main norms, the juridical and ethical, because the Immanence Standpoint hindered his attempt to tackle the problem of the relationship between the aspects (see §3-2.1).

If this interpretation of structuration is valid, and Dooyeweerd's suite of aspects is valid, then we can see a missing aspect, the aesthetic. The coherence of aspects (§3-7.4) suggests it might be brought into the theory, perhaps seeing it as a fourth dimension, in which the structure is fashionability or style. This requires thinking out.

That points the way to replacing the agency-structure duality with something more pluralistic. The normativity of aspects brings into Structuration Theory the possibility of normativity that it currently lacks, in a natural way.

However, the duality generated many insights that should not be lost. This may be retained and enriched by reference to Dooyeweerd's theory of existence. The discussion continues in §8-5.3.

8-5 Applying Dooyeweerd's Notion of Meaningful Existence, *Umwelt* and Correlative Enkapsis

In this section the structures and infrastructures of ICT and society are investigated, not in terms of their functioning, but in terms of their existence and relationships. Dooyeweerd's approach to existence (§3-9) is that Being and relationships are diverse and multi-levelled (multi-aspectual), because they are founded on meaningfulness.

The discussion in this section is tentative, possibly inconsistent and unfinished, but is offered in hope that it will stimulate.

8-5.1 Organizations and Society

It is important to differentiate, at least conceptually, between artefacts, organizations and society. In widespread use, ICT is seen as a lingually qualified artefact, an entity which, when used, brings repercussions. Organizations are socially qualified entities for which a leading aspect can identify the kind of organization. In all organizations, social functioning is important, but it serves the functioning of the leading aspect. The business is led by the economic aspect, the charity by the ethical and the state by the juridical. This is why Dooyeweerd criticised Weber for treating the state as a business (1955, III, 386) and Laski for treating it like a Miner's Federation. Even though there might be analogies between them, it is important to clearly understand the juridical leading aspect of the state.

Society, however, is a different kind of existence, an *Umwelt*, and involves a correlative enkapsis. So is the Internet.

8-5.2 Infrastructure as Umwelt and Correlative Enkapsis

As §3-9.6.2 explains, an *Umwelt* is an environment that is constituted of the very things that are its denizens. Its denizens exist and function (live, work, flourish) because of the *Umwelt,* yet it comes into being by virtue of its denizens functioning in several aspects. Its coming-into-being and its continued existence as an environment involves a cyclical functioning reminiscent of Giddens' structuration. An *Umwelt* should not be treated as any kind of organization, but is a completely different kind of Being, which is constituted in the subject-functioning of its denizens (Dooyeweerd 1955, III, 648).

Dooyeweerd discussed the organically led *Umwelt* of the forest, but here we discuss the socially, formatively and lingually led *Umwelten* of society, the Internet and the Worldwide Web. The difference between them is summarised in Table 8.4.

Each Umwelt can thus be identified with different aspects and as mentioned earlier, might be seen as an aspectual infrastructure. Thus, Dooyeweerd's notion of correlative enkapsis enables us to give *Umwelten* dignity that the use of the word 'reification' might deny and provides a basis for clearer foundational thinking.

These examples are not exhaustive, are an initial suggestion for deploying Dooyeweerd's idea and are likely to require modification. For instance, for a society to survive over a long period, all aspects are important; many 'societies' have perished because they disregarded the organic-biotic, lingual or economic aspects. Society and culture overlap considerably; the difference and overlap between them might be discussed in terms of aspects. Such issues are not discussed here and more work is needed, but must be kept at the back of the mind.

However, as discussed in §8-4.5, the juridical, ethical and pistic aspects are particularly important for the structures of society, and their longer timescales (Table 3.5) can inform our expectations about the causal-like relationships involved in structuration cycles.

Table 8.4 Kinds of *Umwelt*

Umwelt	*Aspects*	*Denizens*
Forest	Physical, Organic-biotic, Psychic	Trees, plants, fungi, insects, birds
Internet	Psychic, Analytic, Formative	Computers, routers, etc. Data packets
Worldwide Web	Analytic, Formative, Lingual	Web page content; User interactions (Web 2.0)
Culture	Lingual, social, aesthetic	People
Society	Social, Juridical, Ethical, Pistic	People, organizations, attitudes, beliefs
The economy	Lingual, social, economic	Producers, customers, currency, banks

Organizations, including states, can host a 'society' in the sense of organizational culture, which forms and flourish by virtue of the member of the organization or citizens of the state functioning in all aspects. Especially larger organizations exhibit juridical, ethical and pistic aspects in a structural form: its view of what is appropriate and lawful, its pervading attitude, and the beliefs and vision that prevail, some of which might be made explicit as rules or vision statements. But the society is not the organization.

Other aspects, not shown in the table, can affect the type of *Umwelt* of a given kind. For example, the ethical aspect plays an important role in the sharing economy and the social and formative aspects in the so-called Gig economy, which are attracting interest today. Such aspectual analysis can perhaps contribute something that traditional economic theories cannot. That Dooyeweerd saw the meaningfulness of the economic aspect as frugality rather than monetary value assists such understanding.

8-5.3 Further Contributions to Structuration Theory

Dooyeweerd's notion of *Umwelt* and correlative enkapsis can be employed to affirm and enrich the current form of Structuration Theory, even though it may be been motivated into existence by the Nature-freedom groundmotive. Giddens' structures may be seen as the *Umwelt* and agents, its denizens, with each contributing to the being and functioning of the other in all aspects.

This cyclical relationship may be seen as multi-aspectual. All the aspects discussed in §8-4.5 are still relevant, but within the context of correlative enkapsis. Giddens' three dimensions may be understood as the different ways in which the *Umwelt* is meaningful or as distinct aspectually defined *Umwelten*.

Then the detailed insights that Structuration Theory and its derivatives offer may be understood in terms of aspects of correlative enkapsis, and given philosophical grounding that is stronger than a mere attempt to overcome the subjective-objective divide.

Dooyeweerd does not allow us to consider the correlative relationship in isolation from other enkaptic relationships. In (1955, III, 652) he gives the example of a farm, in which cows form various organic-biotic enkaptic relationships with each other (copulation, mother-with-young, etc.) while at the same time relating correlatively with their natural environment, and in yet other ways to human structures such as the economic, social and aesthetic functions of the farm. Thus the correlative cyclical relationship in Structuration Theory is not the only player on the stage and should not be considered in isolation. How it works with other kinds of enkaptic relationship calls for research.

Finally, Dooyeweerd opens up something that I do not think has been discussed, a way to understand not only the intertwinement of each dimension-as-*Umwelt* with others, but also the interaction between them, which is discussed next.

8-5.4 Inter-Umwelt Interaction

How might ICT-as-*Umwelt*, economy-as-*Umwelt*, society-as-*Umwelt* and so on, interact with each other? Though they might show different ranges of aspects, they cannot be completely distinct. We may think of their interlinking in two ways, by inter-aspect dependency, and by multi-aspectual functioning, which form cyclical relationship between the *Umwelten*, as shown in Figure 8.3.

Inter-aspect dependency (§3-7.4.4) can account for how infrastructure of an earlier aspect makes possible infrastructure of a later; for example ICT-as-*Umwelt* has changed the social *Umwelt* and the economy.

Inter-aspect dependency does not, however, explain the role of the economy in ICT. Only in an advanced economy, it is said, can the technology be developed for today's ICT—technical developments including reduced size and power consumption in integrated circuits, could not, it is assumed, have occurred without the massive investments needed in specialised manufacturing plant, nor the billions of person-hours of software development and research. Both investment and person-hours are economic issues. The later-aspect *Umwelt*, the economic, seems to play a necessary role in that of the earlier aspect, the lingual, in a way that inter-aspect dependency cannot understand.

Dooyeweerd provides the conceptual tools to understand this: the two relationships are different. While the link from lingual to economic is inter-aspect dependency, that from economic to lingual (where ICT is today) is more of a functional relationship. Such functional relationships can involve any aspect. Has not the emergence of ICT to where it is now has also been driven by faith, excitement and sacrifice (pistic, aesthetic and ethical issues)

Figure 8.3 Cycle Between *Umwelten*

and by the development of law frameworks to support it, especially the Internet?

Finally, notice the "it is said" and "it is assumed" above. Perhaps an 'advanced', growing economy might not be absolutely necessary for ICT to have developed in the way it has. Hypothetically, at least, might it have been possible to get here without it, albeit at a slower rate, as for example Jackson (2009) argues (c.f. §8-6.1.3)? In order to explore such possibilities, research is needed into the relationship between *Umwelten* and between types of infrastructure.

This shows how Dooyeweerd can enable us to envisage different kinds of society and give philosophical grounding for doing so, with philosophical tools to employ. This leads to the question of what is 'advanced', and what is needed for any given future, which is the topic of the next section, on progress and destiny.

8-6 Applying Dooyeweerd's Views of Progress: Destiny of ICT

What is progress, especially as manifested in ICT? What is good and bad about progress? Is progress inevitable? Dooyeweerd's understanding of progress as aspectual opening (§3-3.2) provides a nuanced view, which can help us with some of these questions.

8-6.1 Progress as the Opening up the Potential of Aspects

Humanity, Dooyeweerd argued, has the mandate to 'open up' the potential of the aspects. Over the broad sweep of history, aspects have been opened up, more or less in their order of dependency (Dooyeweerd 1979). Consider the order in which aspect-centred sciences (Table 3.2) and infrastructures became established: the quantitative and spatial disciplines by the ancient Greeks, the physical and organic-biotic shortly after the Renaissance, then psychology, then sociology and so on. Detailed examination, however, reveals something more intricate, with some of the potential of later aspects opened earlier, forming cycles. Money depends on opening of the lingual as writing, yet money helped to open up the lingual aspect further in making printing more feasible, which made paper money possible, which made debt easier, which sped up investment to develop the ICT we see today. Just as with infrastructures (§8-5.4), there is a circularity here of which inter-aspect dependency can explain only half, and multi-aspectual functioning the other half.

8-6.1.1 ICT as Opening up the Lingual Aspect

The proposal here is that *ICT may be seen as opening up the lingual aspect.* This corresponds with ICT as qualified by the lingual aspect (§5-2.5) and is argued in Basden (2008), and we may briefly understand its implications as follows.

This lingual opening up that is ICT has been made possible by the opening up of the analytic and formative aspects in computer science and software engineering and it in turn enables further opening up of the social, economic, aesthetic and later aspects. Example: *Freecycle* (§8-4.3).

In earlier ages, the lingual aspect had been opened up by writing/drawing ("fixation", "distanciation" [Ricoeur 1981, 139]), printing, the telephone, film and broadcasting—as persistence of signification, dissemination, interaction at a distance, animation and real-time dissemination. ICT makes these more convenient or powerful: with paper the only way to correct errors was clumsily, using an eraser.

However, the importance of ICT is that it opens up two further potentials, interactive signification and globalised signification, which in turn contributes new possibilities in other aspects.

Interactive signification, made possible by computing technology, means that the user interacts with the content (e.g., spell-checkers, expert systems, computer games). Interactive signification opens up the economic aspect with 'what-if' models, the aesthetic by removal of mechanical chores, and so on.

Globalised signification means that the content with which the user engages is linked to the entire corpus of signification globally (c.f. "globally signifying" [Ricoeur 1981, 136]). The meaning of any given word or phrase cannot be fully understood without, in principle, reference to all related meaning (c.f. oceanic meaningfulness), and previously, this was only available clumsily via reference books. Nowadays, it is made possible by Internet technology, especially the Worldwide Web. Globalised signification opens up other aspects in turn, such as the formative aspect of finding information and the social aspect of distantly relating.

Might understanding these two contributions give us a wiser outlook? For example, is *life without ICT* merely impoverishment, or just a reaction against overweening ICT, or might it be a valid multi-aspectual lifestyle in which those two benefits are achieved in different ways? Separating out the benefits offered by ICT by aspect reveals that they might still be available without it, albeit less conveniently and at a slower pace. Choices are made more carefully. ("Do I really need to send that message, or is doing so merely tickling my desire for control or craving to be noticed?")

> A question for research into the philosophy of meaning: Does the globalization and interactivity of information, that ICT makes possible, tacitly and partially affirm Dooyeweerd's idea that meaning(fulness) is something within which we and whole reality occurs, rather than something we create *ex nihilo* and control?

This, of course, echoes Heidegger's idea of technology as revealment (§5-2.2), but Dooyeweerd provides more precision about the revealment, and gives ICT a *double mandate*, to open up the lingual aspect and explore how the opened-up lingual aspect may help to open up the other aspects, bringing new good to the world.

8-6.1.2 On Modernity

Klapwijk (1987) warned that Dooyeweerd's view of history is too optimistic, too close to modern Western culture. Such a criticism must be taken seriously, but Klapwijk ignores Dooyeweerd's belief that the way aspects have in fact been opened up is often far from good, as we have constantly seen above.

Habermas (1987) saw no fundamental incompatibility between modernity and lifeworld, and Dooyeweerd might agree. However, whereas Habermas located lifeworld meaning and normativity in critique of validity claims and limited such critique to three aspects, Dooyeweerd located meaning and normativity in an oceanic law-side, which has a much wider diversity and normative force.

Habermas drew on Weber's (1994) idea that bureaucratic systems advance their own logic to the detriment of human freedom, to understand 'colonization' of the lifeworld by systematization, juridification and rationalization. In Dooyeweerdian terms, systematization is an institutional functioning in the formative aspect, juridification, in the juridical, and rationalization, in the analytic and economic aspects—those aspects that feminist thought denigrates as 'masculine' (§8-4.4). For Dooyeweerd, the problem arises, not from these aspects as such, but from Humanist, Western society's elevation, almost absolutization, of them. When absolutization occurs, other aspects are 'closed down', such as the 'feminine' ones. 'Closing down' does not necessarily mean that functioning in that aspect ceases, but that society no longer values its proper functioning, so they can no longer blossom. Example: The ethical aspect of self-giving and generosity has been closed down in modern affluent society (though still prevalent in Sub-Saharan Africa).

Whereas Weber believed that 'the system' is devoid of meaningfulness and normativity, and Habermas rationalised it (§8-2.3.2), Dooyeweerd saw that even in the most structured work, there is still meaningfulness and normativity, because all is 'swimming' in the ocean of meaningfulness (c.f. Geertsema [1992]). It is just that society functions idolatrously and self-centredly in absolutizing some aspects, and this brings harm to many.

Strijbos (1996) struggled with the ethics of systemic life, suggesting that there are three possible approaches: an ethics of adaptation, an ethics of liberation and an ethics of transformation. Drawing on Dooyeweerd's idea of ground-motives (§3-2.2), he sees the first two as aligned with the nature and freedom poles of the Nature-freedom ground-motive, and their battle blinds us to the third option, which expresses itself when we abandon that ground-motive. Though that might explain the problem, it does not offer any solution.

8-6.1.3 Normative Direction of Progress

Dooyeweerd's idea of normativity of progress can be richer than either Weber's, Habermas' or Strijbos'. Mandates are normative, not just something-that-happens; Dooyeweerd believed that aspectual opening is good in principle and yet, because each aspect also defines evil, progress can have a serious downside.

With Dooyeweerd we can find two causes of the downside of progress, which are linked. One is that much opening up of aspects has been motivated by competitive self-interest, pride or idolatry (ethical or pistic dysfunction), and is thereby distorted and often self-defeating, and it breeds injustice. This links with widespread use of ICT, discussed in §8-4.2. The other cause is that aspects have been idolised (absolutised) while other aspects have been 'closed down', as mentioned above.

Our criticism of Western thought, life and culture, which has pervaded this book, is not an outright rejection, but is more nuanced. We can affirm the benefits it has brought in opening up the potential of certain aspects. But it can be critiqued because it evinces both these causes. Economic and formative (technological) aspects have been absolutized and ethical and pistic aspects, sidelined in public life of policy and academia. Pistic and ethical aspects still function beneath, however, as idolatry and self-interest, which have harmful retrocipatory impacts on all other functioning, so that even those which have been opened up increasingly serve idols rather than global and local good, and planet and future generations are sacrificed to its desires (§8-4.3). In its hubris, the Western outlook foists itself on the entire world. (Was the election of Donald Trump in the USA, which occurred during writing of this book, a symptom of this?)

Is it too much to suggest that, when Western culture was influenced by Christian ideas of responsibility to God and of self-giving love, some of these tendencies were curbed but, now that its influence has abated, they have full rein, so that economy, *Umwelt*, security and nationalism become idols that enslave us (Goudzwaard 1984)?

Sale's (2007) polemic against progress (§8-2.5) may now be critically understood as insight rather than unquestioningly welcomed or rejected. Each problem he mentions is rooted in ethical and pistic dysfunction by those who are well-resourced and lead the world, as retrocipatory repercussions in earlier aspects, of selfish disregard of others and idolatrous commitment to prestige, economic growth and technology; see discussion of ethical and pistic aspects of infrastructure (§8-4.3). Cost to five-sixths of humanity is juridical detrimental repercussion, affluenza is organic-biotic and psychic detriment, harm to life support systems is organic-biotic detriment, overconsumption of resources is economic detriment and the overall failure to achieve is a result of idolatry. Is this what God meant via the prophet Ezekiel, that the deepest evil is "affluence, arrogance and unconcern" (Bible, Ezekiel 16:49)?

To conclude: with Dooyeweerd we can escape the taking of sides for and against progress, technology and modernity. Each aspect offers its own potential for the good of all—not just for the one-sixth of the world that constitute the progressive wealthy, but for all humanity, not just for humanity, but for all Creation.

8-6.2 A Liberating Vision for Technology

Egbert Schuurman (1980) expanded Dooyeweerd's notion of aspectual opening to propose a 'liberating vision for technology'. He calls it technological 'meaning-*dynamis*', seeing meaning as oceanic. (Schuurman's later writings, e.g., (2003), clarify and simplify (1980) but since the latter is his PhD dissertation and contains more depth, it is used here.) It contains an extensive survey of thinkers in the philosophy of technology, about what technology is, and about its potential and problems. Schuurman was not content to simply bemoan the disruption to society, environment and individuals occasioned by technology, nor to make merely general visional points. He developed seven principles to follow in order that "the lopsided and crooked condition into which things have fallen can be straightened out" (p. 363); they are discussed at greater length in Basden (2008).

Though Schuurman's vision, born in the 1970s, speaks of "technology" and "engineer", it can readily be reinterpreted for ICT and information systems by a simple shift in aspectual focus, from formative to lingual. In no way does this undermine his proposal. The principles can take account of the special contributions of ICT opening up the lingual aspect, namely interactive and globalised signification.

1. Humankind's project of technology is to contribute to the opening up of the aspects. Technology is *meaning-disclosure*.
2. Technological development of itself is utterly insufficient. Likewise ICT. It must be led, not by its own inner meaning and dynamic, but by that of other aspects. Schuurman discussed especially the following:

    - **Aesthetic disclosure** by technology should result in harmony among all persons and authorities, in selection of materials and between nature and technology.
    - **Juridical disclosure**, so that technology and technological infrastructure enhances rather than detracts from what is due to all (including non-human). It implies judgements: making compromises among the various stakeholders.
    - **Ethical disclosure**—love—"will express itself in a good choice and a proper use of available materials and objects and in a good, artisan like finishing of technological products" and write ICT that promotes self-giving more than self-interest.
    - **Pistic disclosure** means that "humanity is called to the task of technology, and that people are obliged to accept this mission as a

> responsibility before God [i.e., not just to themselves, their accountants, shareholders or peers]" (p. 365).

This echoes some of the concerns of the Social Shaping of Technology, discussed earlier.

3. When this occurs, we can expect a deepening and enrichment of meaning as it is experienced within society and cosmos. Technology can bring 'existential joy' (Pacey 1996, 80–81). The reason technology is often a curse is largely because we ignore or distort aspects.
4. "The future of technology is in fact not determined, but open" (Schuurman 1980, 361). Humanity has responsibility for the way technology is developed, a multi-aspectual responsibility, in which all aspects are opened up in and by ICT, rather than closed down, and the relationships between them are respected and enjoyed.
5. "The key to modern technological activity is to be found in designing . . . in the engineer who does the designing. The engineer designs—or rather, projects—laws that are related to the fashioning of technological things and facts" (Schuurman 1980, 362). Such projection of laws is important in the design of ICT features (Section 7-4).
6. Such development is better when designers themselves are "finely attuned... to the meaning-*dynamis*" (p. 362). All four ICT development activities discussed in Chapter 9 are better when functioning well in all aspects.
7. Disruption of the vision. "Should the engineer fail to attain a correct insight, either because he surrenders, self-sufficiently, to absolutizations and thus shuts the whole process off, or because of shortcomings or shortsightedness, then meaning-disruption will arise and . . . prevail" (Schuurman 1980, 362). Five assumptions disrupt this vision: technology seen as applied science, as handmaiden of economic life, as neutral instrument, as the will to power and as technology for its own sake.

Schuurman's normative insight is important. He provides a vision for the whole of technology, however, rather than of separate areas of interest as in this work. More recently, Verkerk et al. (2015) have applied Schuurman's vision to several of the areas; see §5-2.1. Moreover, both discuss technology in general rather than information and communication technology, which, as argued in §5-2.5, has a different core aspect, as will now be discussed.

8-6.3 The Dignity, Destiny and Responsibility of the Information Systems Discipline

In §8-2.4, the key challenge concerning the information systems field or discipline was to discern its core, so that it might contribute to the world with confidence. The narrow interest in managerial affairs during the 1970s and 1980s seemed too weak to be its core, and some fear it still might be (Benbasat and Zmud 2003; Weber 2003), in that, after identifying phenomena of interest, theories from other fields might adequately explain them. Two attempts to identify the core were outlined, historical and theoretical, but one is backward-looking and provides no grounds for critique or innovation, while the other tends to look through lenses of narrow focus.

Dooyeweerd encourages us to start with meaningfulness, rather than methods, models, etc. Dooyeweerd's transcendental critique of theoretical thought, however, reveals that identifying phenomena of interest presupposes spheres of meaningfulness (§3-4.3.4), so the question is not whether other fields provide theories but whether there is a kind of phenomenon for which other fields do not provide adequate theories (Clouser 2005).

In Basden (2010) I argued that each discipline has a central aspect of interest, which most makes issues meaningful in its body of knowledge, to both researchers and practitioners. This is depicted in Figure 8.4, where the disciplines of information systems, computer science, jurisprudence and agriculture have the lingual, formative, juridical and organic-biotic aspects at their core.

The field's body of knowledge will be aware of issues meaningful in the *neighbouring aspects*, because those aspects most closely retrocipate and antecipate the central one (§3-7.4.4), less intensely. In the case of information systems, these are primarily the formative and social aspects, which are

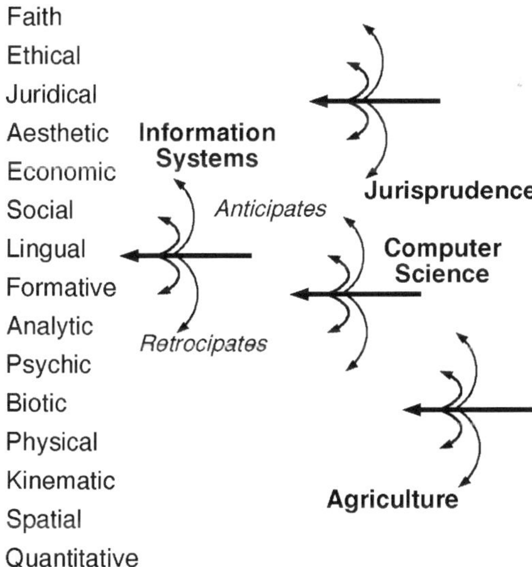

Figure 8.4 Disciplines With Central Aspect and Neighbours

the core of computer science and organizational/social science, and secondarily and more weakly the analytic and economic aspects. The formative and analytic aspects provide a foundation (hence this book's chapter on ICT features) while social and economic aspects are antecipated.

This undergirds Lee's (2004, 13) contention that "information itself is a rich phenomenon that deserves its own separate focus no less than either information technology or organizations." The lingual aspect provides a clear location for this. Lee's vague suggestion of considering hermeneutics is strengthened, in that hermeneutics, as a science of the lingual aspect (Table 3.2), can contribute to this opening process by research in interactive and globalised signification as such.

What about applications? Here, the functioning in the central lingual aspect targets the aspect of the application (see §3-7.4.6) as meaningful content—any aspect—thus contributing to functioning, discourse and practice in that aspect. Carr's (2003) provocative dismissal of ICT may now be ignored, because his core interest is the economic aspect, not the lingual.

Basden (2010) suggests that questions about identity of the discipline are replaced by questions about dignity, destiny and responsibility, located in its core aspect. This anchors our relationships with other disciplines. The problems with historical and theoretical attempts to identify the core are overcome by Dooyeweerd's respect for everyday experience, which makes us sensitive to a wide diversity of issues, and his idea of oceanic law-side aspects provides solid grounds for critique and future-orientation.

8-7 Summary and Conclusion: The Meaningfulness of ICT

This chapter has considered ICT and society by reference to several discourses that have continued over the past few decades. As Section 8-2 showed, each discourse raises various challenges. Sections 8-3 to 8-6 have explored how four main portions of Dooyeweerd's philosophy—his critique of Immanence Philosophy, his idea of aspects, his theory of things, and his understanding of progress—might provide foundational understanding of ICT in its manifestation as *Umwelt.*

In Chapters 6, 7, and 9, each discourse was reviewed, and then reinterpreted in the same order, with Dooyeweerdian ideas, so it was easy to see how Dooyeweerd might affirm, critique or enrich each discourse. This chapter has a more complex structure, where contributions are less easy to discern. So Table 8.5 summarises how each discourse about ICT and society might be affirmed, critiqued or enriched by Dooyeweerd. Column 1 indexes the table by discourse and topic within that. Column 2 summarises on what basis Dooyeweerd might affirm the topic, Column 3, how Dooyeweerd might critique it or support extant critiques, and Column 4, enrichments that Dooyeweerd might offer. They are grouped according to Section 8-2, with how Dooyeweerd might understand it overall.

Table 8.5 How Dooyeweerd Might Affirm, Critique and Enrich Extant Discourses

Discourse or Challenge	*Dooyeweerd affirms*	*Dooyeweerd critiques*	*Dooyeweerd enriches*
	§8-2.1: On Widespread Impacts of ICT. *§8-4.2: Aspectual functioning multiplied by social functioning.*		
Visible, less-visible and unexpected impacts (§8-4.2)	Aspects as ocean in which we 'swim', so we might be unaware of some (§3-1.2.3, §3-8.2); Post-social aspects have indirect impacts	Focus is on single aspects, ignoring especially long-term aspects.	Understand every aspect to stimulate consideration of all kinds of issues (§4-4.2).
Positive, negative impacts (§8-4.2)	Aspectual normativity (§3-7.5)	Idolatry and demonization	Each aspect has both + and –, of different kinds.
Variety of mechanisms (§8-4.2)	Aspectual functioning of many kinds; *shalom* (§3-8.5).	Isolation of aspects (§3-2.1)	Consider effect of each aspect, especially ethical, pistic (§3-8.3).
Fragmented picture	Identify aspects meaningful to each discourse; relate to all other aspects (§8-4)	Elevation of single aspects (§3-2.1)	Aspectual suite situates everything that is meaningful.
Climate change (§8-4.2.2)	All aspects together have repercussion that impact climate change.	Separation of natural from social sciences (§3-2.2).	Consider EIT, EMC, ELI and every aspect (Table 8.1).
	§8-2.2: Infrastructure *§8-5: Correlative enkapsis, Umwelt.*		
Digital divide (§8-4.3)	Multi-aspectual functioning, in which pistic, ethical are primary drivers, with formative (technical) aspect as focus (Table 8.2)	Little on causes and what makes DD detrimental.	Multi-aspectual normativity (§3-8.5). Understand life without ICT (§8-6.1.1).
Surveillance (§8-4.3)	Multi-aspectual functioning, in which juridical and analytical are primary (Table 8.2)	Why we willingly accept surveillance? Narrow solutions.	Importance of ethical and pistic aspects.
E-government (§8-4.3)	Multi-aspectual functioning, in which pistic, economic and juridical are primary (Table 8.2)	Little understanding of idolization.	Opens way to deeper understanding of idolization (§8-4.3).
Kinds of infrastructure (§8-4.3)	Use aspects to identify each kind.		Multiple infrastructures (§8-4.3)

(*Continued*)

Table 8.5 (Continued)

Discourse or Challenge	*Dooyeweerd affirms*	*Dooyeweerd critiques*	*Dooyeweerd enriches*
Normativity	Aspects: different kinds of good and evil, benefit and detriment (§3-7.5).	Separate discourses on good and evil.	Good and evil in each aspect, with multiple aspects.
Values (§8-4.3)	Ethical and pistic aspects, across society	Vague.	Distinct values as target aspects of pistic (§3-7.5).
Motivations	Motivation is pistic aspect targeting an aspect.		Understanding attitudes and aspirations by reference to all aspects.
Ordinary people involved (§8-3)	Dooyeweerd's starting point of everyday life (§3-1.1)		Everyday life given dignity.
	§8-2.3: Relationship between ICT and society *§8-5.4: Inter-umwelt relationships, enkapsis.*		
Dialectical sequence TD-SCOT-SST (§8-4.1)	Each emphasises different aspects	Trapped in dualistic ground-motive (§3-2.3)	Think in terms of aspects and *shalom* (§3-8.5).
Systematization of life (§8-6.1.2)	Meaningfulness and normativity as aspectual ocean	Isolation from everyday experience; Autonomy presupposition (§3-2.1).	Lifeworld and system both occur with ocean of meaningfulness (§3-1.2.3).
Structuration theory: meaning, power, norms (§8-4.5)	Correlative enkapsis: *Umwelt* = structure, denizens = agency. Pistic, ethical and juridical structures, lingual, formative and social agency	Confusion from Immanence Standpoint; economic aspect smuggled in.	Other structure-agency dimensions, e.g. aesthetic, economic.
Socio-critical approaches (§8-3)	Normativity of aspects, especially the juridical (§3-7.5)	Over-emphasis on one aspect (power); Too negative; Trapped in Nature-freedom ground-motive (§3-2.3)	Multiple aspectual normativities; consider the good (*Shalom* §3-8.5).

Discourse or Challenge	*Dooyeweerd affirms*	*Dooyeweerd critiques*	*Dooyeweerd enriches*
	§8-2.4: The IS field *§8-6: Core aspect is lingual, with neighbours.*		
Why does ICT matter? (§8-6.1.1)	To open up lingual aspect and, with it, others	Inter-subjectivism, historicist, idiographic descriptions look to past.	Dignity, destiny and responsibility not just identity.
How to circumscribe the field of IS? (§8-6.3)	Lingual core aspect with neighbouring aspects (formative and social, analytic and economic).	Socio-technical ignores lingual aspect.	Fully understand inter-aspect dependency between core, neighbour aspects, and how lingual targets all aspects (§3-7.4).
	§8-2.5: Technological progress *§8-6.2: Progress as opening up the potential of aspects (§3-3.2).*		
Beneficial, detrimental progress (§8-6.2)	Each aspect defines both positive and negative (§3-7.5).	Idolization + demonization	*Shalom* of all aspectual norms working together (§3-8.5).
Technology for technology's sake (§8-6.2)	Aspectual opening guided by norms of all other aspects (§8-6.2).	Idolization of technology (or ICT).	Multi-aspectual view enriches the opening of core aspect.

Dooyeweerd's insights do not match one-for-one with the discourses but rather cut across them.

Table 8.5 shows ways in which individual discourses might be enriched. A major enrichment, however, might arise from the ability of the Dooyeweerdian approach to collect the discourses together, by offering a basis on which we can respect the insights uniquely provided by each, and understand the relationships between them.

This chapter has shown how Dooyeweerd can help us envisage a different kind of society and a different role and dignity for ICT as a societal phenomenon, to do so in a less idealistic or ideological way and bring more good and less harm. It is neither idealism nor realism, as they are called. Rather, it digs down to the foundations on which both idealism and realism rest—the oceanic law-side that enables both idealism and realism, and also ICT and society, in the first place. The use of Dooyeweerd's suite of aspects should make this approach highly practical as well as philosophically sound.

References

Adam A, Howcroft D, Richardson H. 2004. A decade of neglect: Reflecting on the gender and IS field. *New Technology, Work and Employment*, 19(3), 222–240.

Agarwal R, Lucas Jr HC. 2005. The information systems identity crisis: Focusing on high-visibility and high-impact research. *MIS Quarterly*, 29(3), 381–398.

Alloway T, Runac R, Qureshi M, Kemp G. 2014. Is Facebook linked to selfishness? Investigating the relationships among social media use, empathy and narcissism. *Social Networking*, 3, 150–158.

Alshomrani S, Qamarz S. 2013. Cloud based e-government: Benefits and challenges. *International Journal of Multidisciplinary Sciences and Engineering*, 4(6), July, 15–19.

Basden A. 2008. *Philosophical Frameworks for Understanding Information Systems*. IGI Global, Hershey, PA.

Basden A. 2010. On using spheres of meaning to define and dignify the IS discipline. *International Journal of Information Management*, 30, 13–20.

Basden A. 2011. Enabling a Kleinian integration of interpretivist and critical-social IS research: The contribution of Dooyeweerd's philosophy. *European Journal of Information Systems*, 20, 477–489.

Basden A. 2017. Suggestions for future sustainability: Philosophical and practical. In P Lombardi, G Shen, P Brandon (Eds.), *Future Challenges for Sustainable Development Within the Built Environment* (pp. 319–343). John Wiley & Sons, Chichester, UK.

Baskerville RL, Myers MD. 2002. Information systems as a reference discipline. *MIS Quarterly*, 26(1), 1–14.

Baudrillard J. 2007. *Forget Foucault*, tr. N. Dufresne. Semiotext(e), Los Angeles, CA.

Beller J. 2006. *The Cinematic Mode of Production: Attention Economy and the Society of Spectacle*. Dartmouth College Press, Lebanon NH, USA.

Benbasat I, Weber R. 1996. Research commentary: Rethinking 'diversity' in information systems research. *Information Systems Research*, 7(4), 389–399.

Benbasat I, Zmud RW. 2003. The identity crisis within the IS discipline: Defining and communicating the discipline's core principles. *MIS Quarterly*, 27(2), 183–194.

Bertot JC, Jaeger PT. 2006. User-centered e-government: Challenges and benefits for government web sites. *Government Information Quarterly*, 23(2), 163–168.

Bible. New International Version, Hodder & Stoughton, New York.

Bijker WE, Hughes PT, Pinch TJ. (Eds.). 1987. *The Social Construction of Technological Systems: New Directions in the Sociology and History of Technology*. MIT Press, Cambridge, MA.

Boren ZD. 2014. There are officially more mobile phones than people in the world. *The Independent*, UK, 7 October 2014.

Brooke C 2002. Critical perspectives on information systems: An impression of the research landscape. *Journal of Information Technology*, 17, 271–283.

Brown RH, Barram DJ, Irving L. 1995. *Falling Through the Net: A Survey of the 'Have Nots' in Rural and Urban America*. National Telecommunications and Information Administration, United States Department of Commerce, Washington, DC, USA.

Bury JB. 2013/1920. *The Idea of Progress: An Inquiry Into Its Origin and Growth*. The Gutenberg Project EBook #4557.

Carr N. 2003. IT doesn't matter. *Harvard Business Review* (May), 1–10.

Castells M. 1996. *The Information Age: Economy, Society, and Culture, Volume 1, The Rise of the Network Society*. Blackwell, Oxford, UK.

Ciborra C. 2005. Interpreting e-government and development: Efficiency, transparency or governance at a distance? *Information Technology and People*, 18(3), 260–279.

Clouser R. 2005. *The Myth of Religious Neutrality: An Essay on the Hidden Role of Religious Belief in Theories*. University of Notre Dame Press, Notre Dame, IN.

Connell K. 2014. The shallow selfishness of social media sharing. *The Federalist*, 25 April,. accessed "http://thefederalist.com/2014/04/25/the-shallow-selfishness-of-social-media-sharing/" 24 December 2014.

Copping J. 2012. Warning over decline in map skills as ramblers rely on sat navs. *The Daily Telegraph*, London, UK, accessed "www.telegraph.co.uk/news/earth/countryside/9090729/Warning-over-decline-in-map-skills-as-ramblers-rely-on-sat-navs.html" 1 May 2015.

Crawford S. 2013. Dissolving the digital divide. *Impatient Optimists*. Bill & Melinda Gates Foundation, accessed "www.impatientoptimists.org/Posts/2013/03/Dissolving-the-Digital-Divide" 18 April 2015.

Dafoe A. 2005. Theoretical reconciliation: Selectionism in the social construction of technology and the diffusion of (military) innovations. *Dynamics of Industry and Innovation: Organizations, Networks and Systems, The DRUID Tenth Anniversary Summer Conference, Copenhagen Business School*, Copenhagen, Denmark, 27 June.

DeSanctis G, Poole MS. 1994. Capturing the complexity in advanced technology use: Adaptive structuration theory. *Organization Science*, 5(2), 121–147.

Dooyeweerd H. 1955. *A New Critique of Theoretical Thought* (Vols. I–IV). Paideia Press, Jordan Station, Ontario, Canada.

Dooyeweerd H. 1979. *Roots of Western Culture: Pagan, Secular and Christian Options*. Wedge Publishing Company, Toronto, Ontario, Canada.

Elliot S, Avison D. 2005. Discipline of information systems. In DE Avison, J Pries-Heje (Eds.), *Research in Information Systems: A Handbook for Research Supervisors and Their Students*. Elsevier, New York, 185-206.

eGU. 2006. *Transformational Government—Enabled by Technology*. U.K. Government, e-Government Unit, London, UK.

Finlay A, Adrea E. 2012. *Application of ICTs for Climate Change Adaptation in the Water Sector: Developing Country Experiences and Emerging Research Priorities*. Association for Progressive Communications & International Development Research Centre, South Africa.

Gartner Research. 2003. Traditional ROI Measures Will Fail in Government, accessed "www.gartner.com/resources/116100/116131/traditional roi.pdf" 13 April 2015.

Gauld R. and Goldfinch S. 2006. *Dangerous Enthusiasms: E-Government, Computer Failure and Information System Development*. Otago University Press, New Zealand.

Geertsema H 1992. *He Menselijk Karakter van ons Kennen* (The Human Character of Our Knowing). Buijten en Schipperheign, the Netherlands.

Giddens A. 1979. *Central Problems in Social Theory: Action, Structure and Contradiction in Social Analysis*. University of California Press, Berkeley, CA.

Giddens A. 1984. *The Constitution of Society: Outline of the Theory of Structuration*. University of California Press, Berkeley, CA.

Goudzwaard B. 1984. *Idols of Our Time*. Inter-Varsity Press, Downers Grove, IL.

Grover V. 2012. The information systems field: Making a case for maturity and contribution. *Journal of the Association for Information Systems*, 13, 254–272.

Habermas J. 1972. *Knowledge and Human Interests*, tr. JJ Shapiro. Heinemann, London.

Habermas J. 1986. *The Theory of Communicative Action: Volume One: Reason and the Rationalization of Society*, tr. T McCarthy. Polity Press, Cambridge, UK.

Habermas J. 1987. *The Theory of Communicative Action: Volume Two: The Critique of Functionalist Reason*, tr. T McCarthy. Polity Press, Cambridge, UK.

Healy M. 1998. Conceptualising constrains: Mouzelis, Archer and the concept of social structure. *Sociology*, 32(3), 509–522.

Heeks R. 2002. *e-Government in Africa: Promise and Practice*. IDPM, Manchester, UK.

Heeks R. 2006. *Implementing and Managing eGovernment*. Sage, London, UK.

Heeks R. 2008. Success and failure rates of e-government in developing/transitional countries: Overview. *eGovernment for Development*, accessed "http://egov4dev.org/success/sfrates.shtml" 26 October 2016.

Hilbert M. 2010. Technological information inequality as an incessantly moving target: The redistribution of information and communication capacities between 1986 and 2010. *Journal of the Association for Information Science and Technology*, 65(4), 821–835.

Hirschheim R, Klein HK. 2012. A glorious and not-so-short history of the information systems field. *Journal of the Association for Information Systems*, 13(4), 188–235.

Howcroft D, Mitev N, Wilson M. 2004. What may we learn from the social shaping of technology approach. In J Mingers, L Willcocks (Eds.), *Social Theory and Philosophy for Information Systems* (pp. 329–371). John Wiley & Sons, Chichester, UK.

Illich I. 1978. *Towards a History of Needs*. Pantheon Books, New York.

Jackson T. 2009. *Prosperity Without Growth: Economics for a Finite Planet*. Earthscan, London, UK.

Kasperkevic J. 2014. The unconnected life: An interview about growing up without internet. *The Guardian*, Monday 6 January, accessed 6 May 2017, "www.theguardian.com/money/2014/jan/06/life-without-internet-access-computer-interview" 2016.

Kincheloe JL, McLaren P. 2002. Rethinking critical theory and qualitative research. Chapter 5 in Y Zou, ET Trueba (Eds.), *Ethnography and Schools: Qualitative Approaches to the Study of Education*. Rowman and Littlefield Publishers, Lanham, MD.

Klapwijk J. 1987. Reformational philosophy on the boundary between the past and the future. *Philosophia Reformata*, 52, 101–134.

Korupp SE, Szydlik M. 2005. Causes and trends of the digital divide. *European Sociological Review*, 21(4), 409–422.

Krishnan Harihara S, Basden A. 2009. Understanding failures in e-government: Idolatry as a lens. In A Basden, D Eriksson, A Strijbos (Eds.), *The Problem of System Improvement: Proceedings of the 13th and 14th Annual Working Conference of the CPTS*. Maarssen, the Netherlands. ISBN: 978-90-807718-6-4.

Krishnan Harihara S, Basden A. 2010. Is idolatry a suitable tool to test e-government? In R Goede, L Grobler, DE Haftor (Eds.), *Interdisciplinary Research for Practices of Social Change. Proceedings of 16th Annual Working Conference of the Centre for Philosophy, Technology and Social Systems (CPTS)* (pp. 107–125), 13–16 April. CPTS, Maarssen, the Netherlands. ISBN/EAN: 978-90-807718-8-8.

Krishnan-Harihara S, Kesar S. 2015. Trust in mobile government projects in developing countries: The case of India. *ETHICOMP 2015*, 7–9 September, De Montfort University, Leicester, UK.

Kumar R, Mieritz L. 2007. *Conceptualizing 'Green IT' and Data Center Power and Cooling Issues*. Gartner Research Paper G00150322, September 2007, The Gartner Group, Stamford, CT.

Latour B. 1987. *Science in Action*. Harvard University Press, Cambridge, MA.

Lee AS. 2004. Thinking about social theory and philosophy in information systems. In J Mingers, LP Willcocks (Eds.), *Social Theory and Philosophy for Information Systems* (pp. 1–26). John Wiley & Sons, Chichester, UK.

Lim VKG. 2002. The IT way of loafing on the job: Cyberloafing, neutralizing and organizational justice. *Journal of Organizational Behavior*, 23, 675–694.

Lonergan B. 1992. *Insight: A Study of Human Understanding*. University of Toronto Press, Toronto, Canada.

Lyon D. 2001. *Surveillance Society*. Open University Press, Milton Keynes, UK.

Lyon D. 2003. *Surveillance After September 11*. Polity Press, Cambridge UK.

Lyon D. 2007. *Surveillance Studies*. Polity Press, Cambridge, UK.

MacKenzie D, Wajcman J. 1999. *The Social Shaping of Technology* (2nd ed.). Open University Press, Milton Keynes, UK.

Mintrom M. 1997. Policy entrepreneurs and the diffusion of innovation. *American Journal of Political Science*, 41(3), 738–770.

Mumford E. 1995. *Effective Systems Design and Requirements Analysis: The Ethics Approach*. Palgrave Macmillan, Basingstoke, UK.

Myers MD, Klein HK. 2011. A set of principles for conducting critical research in information systems. *MIS Quarterly*, 35(1), 17–36.

Nisbet R. 1980. *History of the Idea of Progress*. Basic Books, New York.

Noble DF. 1997. *The Religion of Technology: The Divinity of Man and the Spirit of Invention*. Alfred A. Knopf, New York.

ONS. 2014. *Internet Access—Households and Individuals 2014*. Office for National Statistics, Newport, South Wales, UK.

Orlikowski W. 1992. The duality of technology: Rethinking the concept of technology in organizations. *Organization Science*, 3(3), 398–427.

Pacey A. 1996. *The Culture of Technology*. MIT Press, Cambridge, MA, USA.

Parsons T. 1971. *The System of Modern Societies*. Prentice-Hall, Englewood Cliff, NJ, USA.

Ricoeur P. 1981. *Hermeneutics and the Human Sciences*. Cambridge University Press, Cambridge, UK.

Robertson M, Swan J, Newell S. 1996. The role of networks in the diffusion of technological innovation. *Journal of Management Studies*, 33(3), 333–359.

Rogers E. 1962. *Diffusion of Innovations*. Simon & Schuster, New York.

Saebo O. 2012. E-government in Tanzania: Current status and future challenges. In HJ Scholl, M Janssen, MA Wimmer, CE Moe, LS Flak (Eds.), *EGOV 2012* (pp. 198–209). LINCS 7443, International Federation for Information Processing, Laxenburg, Austria.

Sale K. 2007. Five facets of a myth. *Non-Fides*, 18 April, accessed "www.non-fides.fr/?Five-Facets-of-a-Myth" and "www.primitivism.com/facets-myth.htm" 21 May 2015.

Schultze QJ. 2002. *Habits of the High-Tech Heart: Living Virtuously in the Information Age*. Baker Academic, Grand Rapids, MI.

Schuurman E. 1980. *Technology and the Future: A Philosophical Challenge*. Wedge Publishing, Toronto, Ontario, Canada.

Strijbos S. 1996. Ethics for an age of social transformation; I: Framework for an interpretation; II: The idea of a systems ethics. *World Futures*, 46(3), 133–155.

Thompson, Hon. DJC. 2007. How to Leapfrog: St Vincent & The Grenadines Experience. Presentation by Minister of Telecommunications, Science, Technology & Industry, Government of S. Vincent & The Grenadines, accessed "www.finance.gov.vc/finance/images/stories/carcip/svg%20ict%20strategy-final.pdf" 17 February 2016.

Thompson P, McHugh D. 2002. *Work Organisations: A Critical Introduction*. Palgrave, Basingstoke, UK.

UNEP, United Nations Environment Programme. Undated. ICT and Climate Change, accessed "www.unep.org/resourceefficiency/Home/Business/SectoralActivities/ICT/ICTClimateChange/tabid/78948/Default.aspx" 11 March 2016.

Verkerk MJ, Hoogland J, van der Stoep J, de Vries MJ. 2015. *Philosophy of Technology: An Introduction for Technology and Business Students*. Routledge, London, UK.

Walsham G, Sahay S. 1999. GIS for district-level administration in India: Problems and opportunities. *MIS Quarterly*, 23(1), 39–66.

Weber M. 1994. *Political Writings*. Cambridge University Press, Cambridge, UK.

Weber R. 2003. Editor's comments: Still desperately seeking the IT artifact. *MIS Quarterly*, 27(2), iii–xi.

Webster. 1971. *Webster's Third New International Dictionary of the English Language, Unabridged*. G. & C. Merriam & Co., Springfield, MA.

Webster F. 2006. *Theories of the Information Society*. Routledge, London, UK.

Whitley E. 1972. *Plain Mr. Knox*. Scottish Reformation Society, Edinburgh, UK.

Wilson FA 1997. The truth is out there: The search for emancipatory principles in information systems design. *Information Technology and People*, 10(3), 187–204.

Wood DM. (Ed.). 2006. *A Report on the Surveillance Society for the Information Commissioner: Full Report*. The Surveillance Studies Network, Sheffield, UK.

Zammuto RF, Griffin TL, Majchrzak A, Dougherty DJ, Faraj S. 2007. Information technology and the changing fabric of organization. *Organization Science*, 8(5), 749–762.

9 Understanding ICT Development

Having discussed the nature, use, features and societal issues of ICT, we are now in a position to consider the responsibilities and activities involved in ICT development. Four main responsibilities are discussed in this chapter, depicted in Figure 9.1. Seldom are all four discussed together, as is done in this chapter.

The development of ICT artefacts involves four responsible human activities, as expressed by the four main people. The bars denote the diverse aspects of each. The names given here try to express the nuanced nature of each, but conventional names are included underneath. The closed line denotes the development project. 'Users' include other stakeholders. That the ICT artefact encapsulates knowledge of the way the world works is shown on the right.

> Note on terminology: *Information systems development* (ISD), *software engineering* (SE) and *computer programming* are the terms often

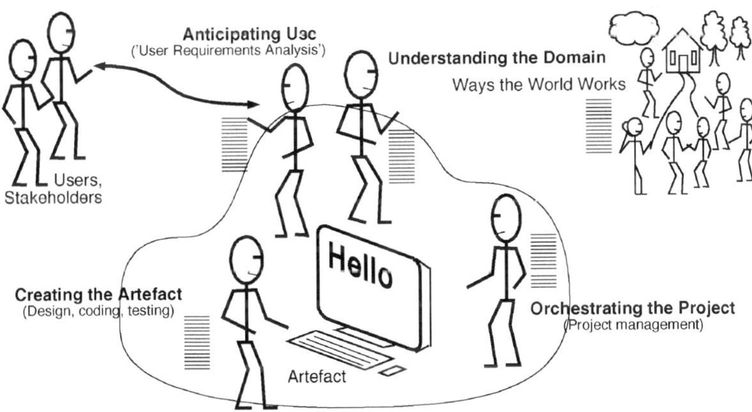

Figure 9.1 Responsibilities and Activities ICT Development

used, but seldom together. Because this chapter brings these activities together, it needs a term that can cover them all. The term '*ICT development*' will be used, covering technical, personal, organizational and social aspects.

9-1 Introduction

The ICT we use has to be developed. Its usability, content and repercussions depend on the quality of the processes of its development. So does the quality of the software library components from which it is built. We need to understand the nature of ICT development, and to find a basis for providing good guidance towards high-quality development. Given the many incidents of ICT project failure, ICT development is still a pressing issue.

Whereas ICT use, discussed in Chapter 6, looks to the present or past, *ICT development looks to the future*; it looks to possibilities in the light of what is.

Note on terminology: '*ICT artefact*', or just '*artefact*' refers to working software running on computer hardware. Here, it is used almost synonymously with '*program*', '*software*' and '*System*'. '*ICT developer*' is a person who contributes to developing the artefact. ICT artefacts can cover a wide range, including applications for mobile devices, computer games, websites, large systems like enterprise resource planning, or public systems like train announcement boards, as well as including generic *software libraries* (collections of generic components that are used by other ICT developers when constructing artefacts for '*end-users*').

ICT artefact implies its documentation, and the various protocols and rules that govern its use and future development must also be developed, and they are assumed to be included in the development project here.

Different methodologies have evolved to guide development of each kind of ICT artefact, along with a variety of views of what is important. What is common between them? How can we understand the differences? How might we situate new kinds of development as they emerge? How may we develop better methodologies and guidelines?

This chapter presents a foundational understanding of ICT development based on Dooyeweerd's philosophy, upon which answers to such questions may be built.

Section 9-2 surveys discourses related to ICT development, all of which encounter issues important in development but that are seldom brought together. Section 9-3 discusses the nature of ICT development, arguing for the four responsibilities depicted above, and discusses in general how Dooyeweerd's philosophy provides insight. Sections 9-4 to 9-7 discuss each of the four responsibilities in detail. The final sections draw this together and provide concluding remarks.

The review of discourses is brief and might be skewed by my own experience in ICT development—developing computer-aided design software, developing a medical record system in the 1970s, developing expert systems within the chemical industry and the surveying profession in the 1980s, developing software libraries for data structuring and inference in the 1990s and developing websites and multimedia since then. Reflecting on this experience resulted in a 'client-centred' approach to expert systems (Basden et al. 1995) and reflection on Dooyeweerdian foundations of ICT development in Basden (2002).

9-2 Discourses about Development of ICT and Information Systems

ICT development involves encapsulating knowledge of the world in ICT for use in real situations. Example: The world of physics (in Husserl's sense of a body of knowledge) might be encapsulated in a weather-forecasting program to be used by mountaineers on their mobile devices.

This section reviews a number of discourses that have arisen in ICT development in order to reveal issues that are important in principle. Whereas in ICT use, discourses revolve around issues, in this chapter, I have chosen discourses around the whole development activity that delivers ICT into use. There are many types of ICT, many types of use situations and many types of methodology that have emerged to guide the activity, yet they are all ICT development, and there are issues common to all types. It is the purpose of the reviews to reveal issues, rather than simply to critique methodologies.

As with other chapters, an everyday perspective is adopted, with some critical depth so as to reveal issues that have been overlooked. The treatment will be brief and is influenced by my experience of ISD from the early 1970s to this day. The order in which discourses are discussed is approximately that of when they first emerged. Some more recent ideas are not properly addressed, and readers are invited to add to the picture.

9-2.1 Discourses on Computer Programming and Software Engineering

The discourse on software engineering and computer programming is huge, yet a number of issues recur. Some are seldom discussed today, being taken for granted, but they are still important. The following are some important ones of which I have been aware, summarised for those in the information systems field; a fuller review should be carried out by those more deeply involved.

One issue is *computer languages* and what we hope to achieve by them. Originally, computers were programmed by entering bit patterns as machine code. To make this easier, assembler languages were produced, consisting of meaningful mnemonics for the instructions that were translated into the bit patterns. Since *program errors* were easily made, higher-level languages like *FORTRAN*, *COBOL*, *ALGOL* and *Pascal* were devised, which translated symbolic expressions into assembler code, checking that the kind of action expressed suits the type of data being processed. Much discourse in the 1970s was about the structure of such languages in order to promote flexibility and *expressive power*, which were required in order to write system software—languages like *BCPL* and C.

Software reuse became important, to reduce the waste and confusion that arises from duplication of effort or code; see below for software libraries.

In the 1980s the idea became popular that the world can be represented, not only as instructions and data variables, but as objects with properties and procedures meaningful to that class of object. The Object-oriented approach was born. This made the *representation of knowledge* about the world easier, and object-oriented languages emerged (C++, *Java*, etc.). Other ideas built on this. Design Patterns sees the world as architects do—not as discrete objects but as whole patterns of things and behaviours. See Basden (2008) for a discussion. The aspect-oriented approach (Kiczales et al. 1997) recognises '*cross-cutting concerns*' like logging, which are responsible for much of the 'boilerplate code' that clogs up programs, making them less understandable and less maintainable.

Right from the start, *testing of programs* became important, and elaborate test regimes have been developed to ease this very demanding, effort-consuming task. Testing is often seen as a stage to be managed, especially when engineering large systems; project management issues are discussed in §9-2.3.

Maintenance and *software upgrade*, to correct bugs or enhance functionality, have become perennial challenges. The programmers must ensure that the changes made are in full harmony with all the rest of the program and if possible, its situations of use. This requires an holistic understanding of the program—which is very difficult to achieve in large systems, and even more so when those who maintain or upgrade it are not those who originally programmed it.

So *documentation* is important—both within the program code as comments, which explain its 'what, how and why', and as external reference manuals. Documentation to help users of the software must also be written. The challenge here is that much of the original programmer's knowledge—the reason why they chose to write the code this way rather than that way—is tacit, and not verbalised.

Programmed ICT artefacts presupposes users. The *attitude of programmers* towards users is sometimes less than generous (Wood-Harper et al. 1998). The field of software engineering involves a wide range of human issues, beyond the analytical and technical. Programming and software engineering have become part of the human condition and must relate to the rest of reality. Some issues might surprise us. In a little monographs, *Things a Computer Scientist Rarely Talks About* Donald Knuth (2001, 130), one of the fathers of the field of computer science, recalls,

> I got hold of a program from IBM called SOAP, written by Stan Poley. That program was absolutely beautiful. Reading it was just like hearing a symphony, because every instruction was sort of doing two things and everything came together gracefully. I also read the code of a compiler that was written by . . . : that code was plodding and excruciating to read, because it just didn't possess any wit whatsoever. It got the job done, but its use of the computer was very disappointing. So I was encouraged to rewrite that program in a way that would approach the style of Stan Poley. In fact, that's how I got into software.

9-2.2 Discourses on Development of Software Libraries

Software libraries are components of software (e.g., object classes) that other ICT developers employ and rely on to perform general or specialised functions in the computer that are repeatedly needed (examples: statistical analysis, geometry, database access). Many of the issues important above pertain here, but modified to ensure good quality generality. Evans (2004) is an acknowledged authority on developing software libraries, but others, like Smith (2016), augment this with 'everyday' observations and principles. The following briefly distils some of the main concerns in discourses around development of libraries for those in the information systems community:

- Domains. Each library encapsulates knowledge about a particular domain of reality, such as statistics.
- Generality. The components in the library should work across a wide and unforeseen variety of situations of use.
- APIs (Application Program Interfaces). Other ICT developers need a clear definition of what each library component does and what parameters are passed to and from it, and an understanding of why and how, and its limitations. Otherwise the API becomes 'magic' or 'mysterious' (Smith 2016).
- Completeness. The knowledge encapsulated about the domain must be complete. Otherwise ICT artefacts developed using the library will cease to work sometimes.
- Exceptions. There are also exceptional conditions in the domain that it is easy for library developers to overlook but are important to remember. Otherwise the library is 'leaky' (Smith 2016).
- Extensibility. Future extensions of the library must harmonise with what is already there. Otherwise applications that use it might begin failing.

9-2.3 Discourses on Management of ICT Development Projects

Developing any kind of ICT artefact is a project that needs some measure of project management, to plan its schedule, resources and liaison with external stakeholders. This became a major issue in the 1970s and 1980s. The larger and more complicated the artefact (system) being developed, the more intensive this becomes. Three major families of project structure have emerged: sequential, iterative and agile.

Sequential methods, like the *Waterfall Model*, see the ICT development project as stages to be managed: analysis, design, specification, coding, testing, delivery. Each stage could be undertaken by a different team, as long as a good specification is developed to define the intended artefact. Project management schemes like PRINCE2 and CMMI (Ahern et al. 2004) are used to manage large projects. Emphasis is on rational analysis, control and management of resources, but in practice, these benefits often fail to materialise.

Its disadvantage is inflexibility. Once exposed to what the software might do, potential users change their minds about what they want, and this disrupts plans and extends schedules and budgets. Though often treated as a nuisance (Wood-Harper et al. 1998), user-mind-changing is (a) to be expected, since seeing what a technology can do for them opens up new ideas, (b) to be welcomed, since it increases the likelihood that the artefact will better fit the future (Basden et al. 1995). (User-mind-changing should be ignored when it is either about trivial preferences or especially about 'political' infighting in the organization.)

To cope with this, *iterative methods* were devised, in which software development is cyclical rather than sequential. Partridge and Wilks (1987) argued that prior specification is neither necessary nor desirable, because the artefact, as it develops in response to user participation, is its own specification. User requirements can be responded to quickly, but project times lengthen. Boehm's (1988) Spiral Model is an attempt to combine cyclical with sequential, as was the Client-Centred Approach (Basden et al. 1995). The Rational Unified Process (RUP) is somewhat suited to iterative projects.

The problem with both waterfall (sequential) and some iterative methods is their dependency on planning and documentation designed to ensure collaboration between teams of developers and with external stakeholders. In response to this, *agile methods* emerged that are 'lightweight'. Developers work in small teams in ways that minimise the need for management-oriented documentation and yet ensure that the client's requirements are quickly responded to and errors are kept minimal. Developers, especially programmers, are treated, not as resources to control (Waterfall Model) nor as free agents (iterative), but as responsible human beings.

Agile methods may be seen as recognition of the 'down-to-earth' issues of ICT development, after a focus on higher-level issues, especially in sequential approaches. Issues range from trust in the developer and with customer, communication and self-critique between developers, to fun and creativity of ICT development (Agile 2001; Beck 2000). Agile methods are characterised as being more 'meaningful' for the creators of the artefact.

Agile methods have proven successful for smaller projects but less so for larger ones. They can be difficult to tailor to specific situations (Karlsson and Agerfalk 2009) and are thought not suitable for critical software, nor where development effort is distributed across a number of teams in different places (Abrahamsson et al. 2009). The cohesiveness of agile teams might impair decision making because of groupthink or the Abiline Paradox (everyone seeming to agree) (McAvoy and Butler 2009).

Abrahamsson et al. (2009) suggests that we also need a more fundamental discussion of what constitutes agility. Agile seems to have grown up as practice without any understanding of its foundations.

A key challenge for all methods is the *post-adoption stage* of ICT development for maintenance or upgrade while it is in use, to correct bugs or extend its functionality. With new software, developers have freedom to choose which facilities and features to include and how to implement them, but with software in use, much of that freedom disappears and the current modes and styles of use need to be taken into account. Changes to the artefact might have unintended and unforeseen repercussions elsewhere, which lengthy testing might or might not reveal. Unfortunately, post-adoption development is often seen as a separate issue, to be considered later; even agile methods do not seem to have taken this seriously yet (Abrahamsson et al. 2009).

9-2.4 *Discourses on the Development of Expert Systems*

Concern with language expressiveness in representing worlds was taken up by the artificial intelligence community in the 1970s, who developed knowledge representation languages in which it was easy to express knowledge, either as statements in logic or as statements about items and relationships in a precursor of object-orientation, the semantic net. The generality and expressive power of such languages gave birth to expert systems (knowledge-based systems, in the development of which I was closely involved during the 1980s, as explained in Basden (1983), Attarwala and Basden (1985), Basden et al. (1995) and Chapter VI of Basden (2008)).

Typically, to obtain knowledge to represent using these languages, a 'knowledge engineer' would interview experts in the field. Unfortunately, much of the knowledge or expertise that should be represented was difficult to elicit (Bainbridge 1986), because some of their knowledge was tacit, in the form of unspoken assumptions or background (Collins 1974; Ngwenyama and Klein 1994). Much that was acquired was in story form, at the wrong level or irrelevant. Getting domain experts to cooperate fully required good social skills.

Techniques to overcome these problems vary. The one I found most effective was to seek understanding that underlies expert experience (Steels 1985; Attarwala and Basden 1985; Silvestro 1988; Premkumar 1989), practical details of which are in Basden et al. (1995).

The construction of expert systems sharpens the distinction between two kinds of knowledge that must be elicited and encapsulated:

- Domain knowledge: knowledge of the domain, such as stress corrosion cracking or crop protection, which is generic, and resides in domain experts;
- Usage knowledge: Knowledge about use and the needs, characteristics and context of the user, which resides in potential users.

In expert systems both are important, and both are complex. Domain experts and potential users require different elicitation techniques, though they overlap. For both, knowledge emerges gradually in fragments and must be harmonised by the knowledge engineer. We found we had to develop a different project structure, neither sequential nor iterative but governed by what needed to be achieved and centred on responsibility (Basden et al. 1995).

Many assumed that expert systems would be used in automation or to give advice. However, these are not the only roles for expert systems. While in industry in the 1980s, I discovered other roles were often more important and tractable (Basden 1983). In three expert systems in which I was involved, the Stress-corrosion-cracking system (Hines and Basden 1986), the Wheat Counsellor system for advising farmers on pesticide use (Jones and Crates 1985) and the ELSIE expert system for help quantity surveyors set budgets and plan projects (Brandon et al. 1988), two important roles were to ensure nothing had been overlooked, and to stimulate and refine human thinking by posing relevant questions on the basis of the encapsulated expertise. This makes the expert system a proximal aid to thinking. Eight roles are discussed in Basden (1983) (I know of no more recent discussion) and are important to consider when designing for use. Many ICT artefacts also fulfil these roles, especially in decision-support systems and later in some approaches to knowledge management (see §6-4.4).

Knowledge elicitation is an intensive process. Data mining and neural nets might bypass it by mechanical processing of knowledge and patterns, but the knowledge they encapsulate cannot be understood, and it usually cannot deal with the unexpected, unusual situations. For reliable, accurate and understandable knowledge, knowledge elicitation is still required.

9-2.5 Discourses on Information Systems Development

In the information systems field, it has been mainly the organizational aspects that are meaningful in discourses about ICT development. Rather than trying to understand ICT development in its own terms, the IS community has applied sociological or organizational theories, which generates useful insights from those perspectives. For example, Cao et al. (2009) apply adaptive structuration theory to Extreme Programming. Two discourses are examined here as typical.

9-2.5.1 *Hirshheim, Klein and Lyytinen: Conceptual and Philosophical Foundations*

Hirschheim et al. (1995) attempted to lay conceptual foundations for ICT development from an information systems perspective. Though 20 years old, and omitting games development and of course, the more recent agile development, their work provides insights that are still valuable.

First, they reviewed a number of approaches to ICT development then extant, identifying issues they believed to be meaningful to each, all of which are relevant to ICT development: control of project activity (formal life-cycle approaches), productivity and reduction of incompleteness, unstructuredness and inconsistency of specification (structured approaches), discovery of user requirements (evolutionary approaches), participation (socio-technical approaches), learning, with explication of Weltanschauungen that make situations meaningful as 'problem' (sense-making approaches), changes in the workplace (trades union approaches), how ICT is used to either oppress or emancipate people (emancipatory approaches). Their treatment is useful in revealing the diversity of normative issues involved in IS development. Their discussion of methodologies available up to the mid-1990s, SDLC, CASE, ETHICS, Soft-Systems, Multiview and Scandinavian approaches, and so on, is worth studying.

Hirschheim et al. then try to reduce the diversity by grouping them into Burrell and Morgan's (1979) four sociological paradigms (functionalist, social relativist, radical structuralist and radical humanist) which arise from the interaction of two dialectical oppositions, subjective-objective and consensus-conflict. They assign various practical ISD methods to each of the four.

Burrell and Morgan's paradigms have been criticised as reductionist and the presumed incommensurability not only does not match everyday experience, but "unnecessarily constrains the process of theory development" because of "polarized sets of assumptions about science and society" (Willmott 1993, 682) and most philosophical traditions are not mutually exclusive (Chua 1986). A more pluralistic approach is considered next.

9-2.5.2 *Towards Pluralism: The Example of Multiview*

Avison and Wood-Harper's (1990) *Multiview* approach to ICT development is more nuanced than many frameworks, having developed as a result of its authors applying it and learning lessons. *Multiview* arose by reaction against "technical rationalities" (Vidgen 2002) embodied in the Waterfall Model and a lack of interest in the goodness of fit of ICT. *Multiview* is a contingent approach, designed to encourage flexibility in the sequence in which the activities it recommends are undertaken: analyse human activity context, analyse information, analyse and design socio-technical aspects, design technical solution, design the user interface. These are more geared to actual IS development than are Hirsccheim et al.'s four.

Avison and Wood-Harper argue that the first four emerge theoretically from the interaction of two dualities: socio-technical and reductionist-systemic. Because of this, design of the user interface feels out of place, bolted-on. However, as someone steeped in practical ICT development, I know the importance of the user interface, and applaud the authors for originally refusing to be constrained by a 2-by-2 theorization. I prefer to question the theoretical assumption that all relevant issues can emerge from interaction of just two dualities.

The lessons learned from application of original *Multiview* are discussed in Avison et al. (1998) to yield *Multiview2*. They included: that each ISD situation is unique, the development process is understood differently from different perspectives, methodologies evolve, system definition is a social process and ethics is important. The authors began to see similarities between ICT development and research, and by reference to other theories, such as Habermas' (1972) idea of knowledge interests, Giddens' (1984) Structuration Theory and Latour's (1993) Actor-Network Theory, expanded the scope of *Multivew2*, to include the relationship between analyst, methodology and situation. Analysts as well as users have multiple perspectives, and the organizational constraints on development can be altered. The four activities based on two dualities were slightly changed and renamed, and the role of mediator between them is added. Sadly, design of the user interface disappeared, being reduced to 'software development', but then it was reinstated by Vidgen (2002), albeit squeezed between the social and technical and inexplicably limited to the reductionist side.

9-2.5.3 The Importance of Down-to-Earth Issues

Evidently, there is a tension between a desire for theoretical neatness and plurality of issues encountered in the everyday experience of ICT development. Hirschheim et al. (1995) sought plurality by accepting two dualisms and theorizing how they interact, squeezing seven approaches into 2-by-2. The academics involved in developing *Multiview*, though trying to be sensitive to the realities of actual ICT development, found themselves prioritising 2-by-2 issues and treating others as add-ons.

If we give priority to everyday experience over theorization, then we cannot accept being constrained by dualisms or even dualities. Lee (2004) sought plurality in a different way, by questioning whether two should be three, with the socio-technical duality having something in between them. We might ask: should there be more than three? See §6-2.3.

To determine what is needed and meet the needs of ICT in use is challenging, because of "expectation-perception gaps" (Wood-Harper et al. 1998): between what users need and what they think they need, between what users (say they) need and how developers understand this, between what developers understand and what they write in the specification, between what is specified and what is delivered and between what is delivered and what is useful.

Many of these gaps have opened up because the down-to-earth issues that are of importance to users and developers 'on the ground' (Ahmad and Basden 2013) are being ignored, in favour of higher-level issues that are of interest to management, ICT suppliers or academics—for example, human resources, technology infrastructure and empowerment, respectively. Examples of down-to-earth issues: "Users keep changing their minds!", "Time for next meeting", "My children are sick", "I'll help this newcomer understand the process". Such issues radically affect the quality and success of ICT and need to be considered during ICT development.

What I experienced outwith academia was more nuanced and pluralistic than the theories and dualisms suggest. Even issues like environmental responsibility impinged on what we did, though seldom seriously considered within ICT development discourses. In theory, participatory approaches might offer techniques to allow such issues to surface, but in practice this is hindered by (a) the participatory discussion revolving around higher-level or abstract issues, (b) 'groupthink' suppressing some important issues, (c) stifling of individual creativity and imagination, which are important, for instance, in developing computer games.

9-2.6 Discourses on the Development of Computer Games and Virtual Worlds

Computer games come in many kinds, from small pastimes for the individual, like *Yahtzee*, through individual games of adventure or creativity like *Minecraft*, to large multiplayer games like *Clash of Clans* or *Call of Duty*. The games sector is driven to-and-fro by fashion, so we need to stand back from the current scene in order to understand games development in a way that will still be valid in the future. So, while I refer to current games, I draw examples from older games that have rich gameplay.

There are several major differences between development of computer games and other kinds of software, and our foundational understanding of ICT development should have place for them. The content of the virtual world of the game is of supreme importance for gameplay, though stunning graphics and sound might help sell it. Experienced games developer Richard Bartle (2004) suggests that "the first duty of a virtual world [is] to be fun" (p. 629). 'Users' are players, and 'user requirements' become less of a straitjacket than in IS development, and more a wise courtesy (without which potential players might be put off). Echoing Donald Knuth (2001), Bartle (2004) sees designing more as art than engineering.

In contrast to most kinds of ICT artefact, the inexperienced user assumes importance. 'Newbies' are catered for, not only as yet-to-be-experts but as part of the game itself. Bartle (2004) points out that, once a game includes socialisation, some players enjoy helping newbies learn the game, a role which had not previously been expected. (Why not?) Therefore, in games development, flexibility to allow the unexpected is very important.

Challenges of post-adoption development become extreme in multiplayer online games. Not only must the game continue to play well during upgrade, but if a bug appears that players either complain about or take advantage of, it must be fixed very quickly, and this mitigates against careful checking that the change does not have unforeseen effects elsewhere. Formal proof of algorithms is sometimes employed.

9-2.6.1 Principles of Computer Games Development

Most of the principles of computer game development are gleaned from experience, and published on the World Wide Web rather than in books or papers. Long-experienced game designer, Matt Allmer published 13 principles of game design as a blog (Allmer 2009), which go beyond obvious principles like "Know your audience". Most are to do with game content with which the user engages ('EMC' in §6-3.5), such as "Anticipation: Inform the player that something is about to happen", some concern the interface and technology ('EIT', §6-3.4), such as "Sound: Ask yourself, 'Is the sound appropriate? necessary?' ", and some, how the development project is organised, such as "Plan components carefully, but in such a way that you can respond quickly to late 'must have' requested by publisher." His 13 principles are discussed in §9-6.4. They are mixed together, with no attempt at delineating different kinds, and so are slightly confused, and Allmer invites additions to the list.

Allmer's principles are for 'standard' games and might need reinterpreting for other kinds, for example pastimes or games where the player is invited to be creative, e.g., *Minecraft*. *LPMUD* allow players to alter the game itself; its author, Lars Pensjö, believed that players can design better than he could himself.

In view of all this, it is necessary to develop a foundational understanding by which principles can be scrutinised to find out why they are important, can be classified, can be added to without confused repetition, and can be reinterpreted for other kinds of games, some yet to emerge.

9-2.6.2 Theory of Computer Games Development

Theoretical understanding of games development is sparse and fragmented. Most comes from other fields like psychology or learning theory (see §6-2.6) or from a sociological or managerial perspective in information systems. Example: Furtado and Santos (2006) argue that game development is being "systematically industrialized", and offer a domain-specific language to assist this systematization. They validate the language, not by giving it to actual developers but by imagining a game-development scenario, which is reminiscent of the games of the 1980s! Though such theories offer some disparate insights, they do not constitute a theory of games development.

Bartle (2004), however, does attempt a theory, as an experienced designer. He usefully reviews the history of virtual worlds to show causalities and missed opportunities that reveal important issues. He offers reflections on players, world design and how various disciplines are relevant to developing world content. He ends with an attempt at an overall theoretical 'critical aesthetic' and some ethical considerations.

Bartle's main belief is that the designer has a covenant with the players, that the virtual world will:

- have value,
- have meaning and
- make sense (both text and subtext).

Bartle's theory is composed of three classifications of issues that are important: of types of player, based on his own experience, of types of storyline, drawn from Koster and Vogel (2002) and dualities drawn from film studies.

However, some of its foundations might be shaky, and might not apply to all kinds of games, nor to future kinds. Its empirical basis is weak, being from a self-selected survey taken in the 1990s, or else not specified, and it changes throughout his book. He focuses largely on multi-player worlds, ignoring single-player worlds and pastime games with limited worlds. Bartle admits that dimensions drawn from film studies might be rendered less valid by differences between film and games (in film, directors make the choice of viewpoint and artists generate the aesthetic; in games the players can make this choice, and the artistic endeavour is shared between the designer and players).

Nevertheless, Bartle's attempt at a theory contains many important insights and should be applauded, not least because it emerges from reflected-upon experience rather than other theories, and it is open to what is meaningful in neighbouring fields. What would be useful is not to test Bartle's theory by psychology or sociology, but to set it on a philosophical foundation that recognises the diversity of dimensions of everyday experience of games players and developers and can make his ideas more robust.

'*Gamification*' refers to use of features of games and play in serious ICT artefacts to further some serious purpose. Examples: to make learning 'enjoyable', as an exercise for students (Owston et al. 2009), as a tool to enhance students' perceptions (Eow et al. 2010) or to promote or test some theory, tool or conceptual model Furtado and Santos (2006). However, many who 'gamify' their artefacts do so without immanently understanding what gaming is about and produce material that is boring, dated and often inauthentic, and which undermines usability. The difference between games and gamified artefacts needs to be understood more deeply in order to avoid such dangers and ensure that game features actually enhance the purpose of serious artefacts.

9-2.7 Discourses on the Development of Websites

Websites exhibit characteristics different from those of other ICT artefacts, so their development is different. As with games, both content and look and feel (functionality and aesthetics) are of supreme importance, but games and websites are different.

9-2.7.1 The Character of Websites

In two ways, websites differ from games: in kind of content and in type of user ('reader' or 'client'). Unlike games, where the primary duty is fun, the primary duty of websites is information—information to inform, as in *Wikipedia*, provide resources as in *eBay* or ticket-booking sites, promote ideas, as in *blogs*, network, as in *LinkedIn*, etc. So classic knowledge elicitation is important for websites while imagination is important for games.

Unlike most other kinds of ICT artefact, including games, the users (readers) can be anybody across the world. Global reach means that language use, especially of idioms and humour, is more important than in most kinds of ICT, and legal issues are wider but less visible than in most software. In principle, once a web page has been published, it should remain in place forever, since it might be referred to, whereas in other software, functionality and content can be removed.

Post-implementation development becomes especially important; websites grow. It is the nature of information to change and grow, in ways more radical and voluminous than mere changes in functionality. Internal harmony is harder to achieve.

9-2.7.2 Discourses on Web Development

Several discourses about website development have emerged. One discourse is about specific technical challenges encountered during web development, such as effects of hanging pages (Kumar et al. 2015), adapting autonomously to changing conditions without human intervention (Berkane et al. 2015) or enabling users with no programming experience to create web mashups (Guo and Han 2014).

A second discourse is around web development methodologies, of which the following are typical (and found on the web, not in journals). The Web Site Design Method (WSDM) reinterprets Waterfall model stages and adds 'audience modelling', in order to understand readers—but it gives little guidance on phases beyond implementation. The IconMatrix adds a Transition phase, where the website is published and development is continued. Some methodologies give more attention to continual development after transition (Production: "Let's keep the system going") and its use of "Let's" seems oriented to participative development. Even this, however, does not do full justice to post-implementation development: systems do not just keep *going*; they keep *growing*.

What guides this growing? Little discourse on this occurs, possibly because it is to do with domain knowledge, for which few methodologies are available.

A third discourse is about how extant approaches in software engineering can be applied to creating the artefact that is the website. Berkane et al. (2015) propose design patterns for web design. Zhang and Hölzl (2015) propose an aspect-oriented development approach, HiLA, in order to ease the encoding of cross-cutting features like landmarks, access control, adaptation or rich user interface, which are difficult to implement with most approaches.

A fourth discourse occurs within the information systems field, raising general human or organizational issues like "problems associated with representative teams", "blurred boundaries" (Standing 2002), how users are treated, flexibility of methodology and importance of business strategy (Vidgen 2002). Some distinct characteristics of websites are recognised, such as the importance of language (Standing), the need for aesthetics and that user will be customer rather than employee (Vidgen), but neither seem to be aware of how radically different websites are in respect of content, growth and the plethora of unknown users. Most discourse in IS seems to treat websites as just generic IS with a few small differences. Though these authors propose their own methodology for web development, it is not clear how intensely they have been involved in actual web development.

A fifth kind of discourse applies insights from the perspectives of various sciences. Beer and Burrows (2007) discuss how sociologists should react to Web 2.0. Psychological theories like Gestalt theories and operant conditioning are often used.

Despite these discourses, there seems to be little discourse about the most important responsibility: designing website content. Each offers its own insights, like leaves on a tree, but they do not enable us to understand the whole tree. There seems to be little foundational understanding of website development as such, starting from the specific character of websites and taking into account everyday practice and the wide range of issues that could be meaningful. So there is no basis on which to bring the various discourses together, nor to provide direction for the future nor judge innovative ideas.

9-2.8 *Overview*

ICT development failures are still rife, even though half a century has passed since it became a recognised issue in need of research and practical development. The development project still overruns or exceeds budget. Project teams still do not work well together, perhaps because of mistrust, competition or lack of coherent vision, or key people leave. Designing, writing the code and testing still prove more challenging than originally allowed for. Bugs sill remain in the delivered artefact or system, or it proves clumsy in use. Or artefacts are still delivered that do not match the users' real needs. Or they have unexpected deleterious repercussions or wider impact when in use, which could and should have been foreseen.

ICT development raises a diverse plethora of issues, all of which have to be engaged with in practice and grasped and understood by researchers. Many approaches to ICT development have arisen, and methods and guidelines abound, which practitioners and researchers have been seeking ways to classify. Some classifications are by methodology, some by paradigm or historical stages, and some by type of artefact. It has been noted, however, how theoretical thought tends to gravitate to dualisms for its deepest spheres of meaningfulness. It would be useful to find a way to understand more generally the ways in which ICT development issues can be meaningful, without such reduction, respecting the issues that everyday experience of development encounters.

What is needed is a philosophically grounded understanding of the foundations on which development of ICT and information systems rests. In the next section, I explore how Dooyeweerd can provide this, from his starting points of everyday experience and meaningfulness.

9-3 Responsibilities in ICT Development

A foundational understanding of ICT development (or information systems development) must be able to afford theory about what ICT development is and principles to guide it. It should cover all kinds of development and the plethora of issues that are meaningful therein, and accommodate and situate all extant theory and methodology in the discourses discussed above.

Conventionally, the most fundamental distinctions made in the discourses are by type of developer (individual, small group or large team), type of artefact (small applications, large systems, etc.) or type of development activity (analysis, design, coding, testing, project management, etc.), but the considerable overlap within each distinction that we find in practice (e.g., one person might analyse, design, code and manage simultaneously) urges us to question their validity.

To Dooyeweerd, these distinctions are not the most fundamental; meaningfulness and normativity are more so (§3-1.2) and provide a foundation by which to understand types of developer, artefact and activity. An initial version of a Dooyeweerdian framework for understanding ICT development, presented in Chapter VI of Basden (2008) as four functionings, is here reoriented towards possibility and responsibility.

9-3.1 Possibility and Responsibility

We start from the pre-theoretical observation that the ICT artefact that is developed opens up possibilities for users that were not there before and closes down other possibilities—it alters the *profile of possibilities*. (This echoes Heidegger's idea of technology as revealment (§5-2.2) and Dooyeweerd's idea of opening up of aspects (§8-6.1).) Possibility is *future-oriented*, actualised as repercussions of ICT in use, so implies inherent *responsibility*—responsibility for both expected and unexpected possibilities. Developers bear responsibility, even though users also bear some responsibility for actualization of possibilities, and society, for possibility-expectations that it endorses. As Nils Löwe (2015) put it, in an article entitled *Our Responsibility as Software Developers*,

> In the recent past, there have been some incidents that showed us the problems and dangers latent in the use of software. Incredibly large amounts of customer data were stolen from eBay and Sony, among others. . . . During the last few years, I realized one fact: We software developers make these scandals possible. Our software influences the life of most people on this planet. Our systems get hacked and exploited. Our employers and customers use our software to change the world for good or ill. And, in the end, we are the people who build this software.

ICT developers see themselves as agents of change (Vidgen 2002), for 'systems intervention' (Churchman 1970; Midgley 2000). A key principle of Extreme Programming is "Accept responsibility" (Beck 2000). Bartle's (2004) idea of developers having a covenant with the players (§9-2.6.2) implies responsibility.

But what can we say about possibility and responsibility? Figure 9.2 depicts our main arguments, with thinner arrows showing how Dooyeweerd's philosophy is used.

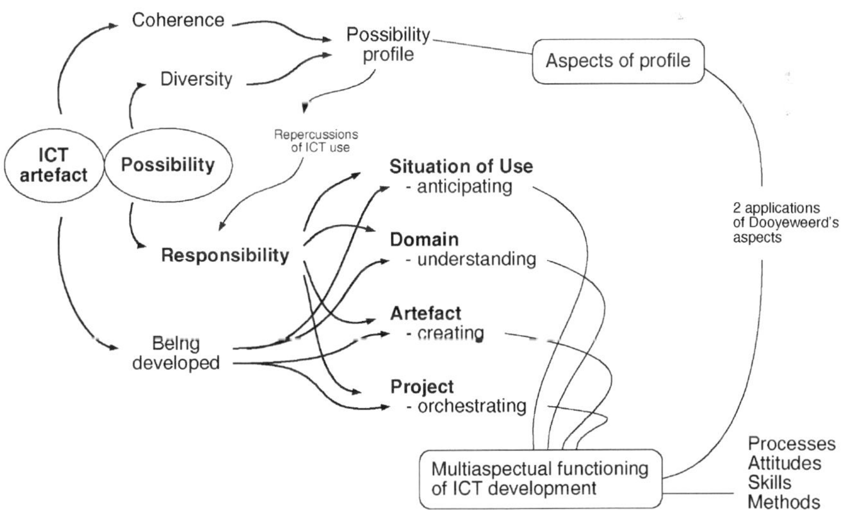

Figure 9.2 Towards a Foundational Understanding of ICT Development

As the top half of the diagram shows, the possibilities that the *ICT artefact* offers (or curbs) are *diverse* in kind, and the ICT artefact that is developed is an expression of a *coherence* in the diversity, a bringing-together around what we might call a *possibility profile*. The profile is linked to the purposes intended by the developers and other stakeholders, but not limited to them, and might include possibilities that encourage innovative use or yield unexpected repercussions (see §6-4.12). The features incorporated in the ICT artefact are, to a greater or lesser extent, appropriate to the profile, as discussed in Chapter 7.

The lower half of the diagram deals with the implications of possibility and the development of the artefact. The responsibilities associated with these possibilities are also diverse and cohere around the artefact but have at least four components, which in Basden (2008) were seen as four functionings that compose that of ICT development:

- Responsibility for *anticipating use*: To anticipate the kinds of situation in which the ICT artefact will be active;
- Responsibility for *understanding the domain*: To understand the way reality functions in general, its 'laws' that pertain regardless of situation;
- Responsibility for *creating the artefact*: To encapsulate this understanding in the artefact;
- Responsibility for *orchestrating the project*: To hold it all together, to harmonise.

Anticipating use is often referred to as 'user requirements analysis' and project orchestration as 'project management', but both are wider in their responsibility and activity. Creating the artefact is usually referred to as 'programming' or design, coding and testing, but is given a wider emphasis here. Understanding the domain is often called 'knowledge engineering'. Other responsibilities might come to mind, but these four are sufficient to cover most of what has occupied the discourses so far, and to demonstrate how others might be investigated.

Though often discussed as four distinct activities, they are closely intertwined in practice and need to be considered together, as parallel responsibilities rather than sequential processes or stages.

Use-anticipation and domain-understanding together provide knowledge from which the artefact is created, but there are two differences. Use-anticipating seeks knowledge of situations in which the artefact will be used—its context, users and other 'stakeholders'—and looks to the future. Domain-understanding seeks knowledge of the general laws by which the relevant spheres of reality work, in which the ICT artefact and its situation are themselves situated, and looks to what already exists and is known. They often mix.

Note on terminology: *Knowledge acquisition* will usually refer to gaining knowledge about use; *Knowledge elicitation*, to gaining knowledge of the domain.

Example: *Google Earth* is the artefact, its domains are primarily geography photography and tourism and its situations of use include viewing terrain, adding photographs and seeing where friends live.

It is the need to express knowledge in some programming or knowledge representation language that differentiates ICT development from other technological development, which is based only on design and construction (§5-2.5).

9-3.2 The Discourses

All actual ICT development involves all these responsibilities, but the reflective discourses on them summarised in Section 9-2 usually concentrate on certain ones:

- Software engineering: Artefact
- Software library development: Artefact, domain
- Project management: Project
- Agile development: Artefact, project
- Expert systems: Domain, situations of use, artefact
- Information systems field: Use, project
- Games: Artefact, domain, use
- Websites: Domain, use, artefact.

No discourse recognises all equally, though in practical principles we find elements of the ones not mentioned creeping in. Allmer's (2009) principles of games design, for instance, include two about project orchestration. That the responsibilities in games development show little overlap with those of the IS field might explain lack of cross-fertilization.

What is needed is a foundation that enables us to consider all four responsibilities equally, in which the discourses may all be situated, regardless of type of artefact, development team or activity. We now briefly outline how and why Dooyeweerd's philosophy is able to provide this, and then discuss each responsibility in detail.

9-3.3 A Dooyeweerdian Understanding of ICT Development

Dooyeweerd's philosophy can help us because, unlike the Immanence Standpoint (§3-2.1), which divorces the meaningfulness of responsibility from reality and demands that it be 'bolted on', he held that normative law is the foundation that enables all activity, process, principles, etc. Within the Nature-freedom ground-motive, which governs much thinking in the information systems field, possibility is treated as either freedom or the causal result of determinative laws, but in everyday experience, possibility is both. Dooyeweerd sees possibility as the potential afforded by the aspectual laws ('ocean of meaningfulness'). (Ocean of meaningfulness refers to meaningfulness that transcends us—both developers, users, society and ICT—and pertains to all alike at a deep level; see §3-1.2.3.) His philosophy can help developers in two main ways—to think about the profile of possibilities and guide the multi-aspectual functioning that is the ICT development activity, by reference to the shalom principle (§3-8.5). Using Dooyeweerd's aspects to gear an artefact and its features to a profile of possibilities is discussed mainly in Chapter 7; this chapter concentrates on aspects of the functioning of ICT development.

Each of the four activities that make up the overall activity of ICT development is a different multi-aspectual functioning, and the responsibility associated with each is a multi-aspectual responsibility. Though use-anticipation and domain-understanding both glean knowledge by which the artefact is created, domain-understanding seeks knowledge of the law-side (aspectual laws and type laws; §3-7.1, §3-9.4), while use-anticipation seeks knowledge of the subject-object-side.

Knowledge of both domains (law-side) and situations of use (subject-object-side) is expressed in a computer language to create the ICT artefact. It is suggested in §5-5.2 that a program or ICT artefact is a virtual law-side. We can easily understand that domain knowledge may contribute thereto, yet how can knowledge of subject-object-side situations contribute to a virtual law-side? The answer is that it is not knowledge of actual situations that is expressed, but of types of situations; such knowledge is generic, like domain knowledge. In the following example from the physical domain of heating, (A), the heat loss calculation, is generic domain knowledge, (B), U-values of types of wall, is generic situational knowledge:

A) Heat loss through wall = U-value * Area * Temperature-difference.
B) U-values for types of wall:
   Cavity wall, open cavity: 1.4
   Cavity wall, 50mm mineral wool insulation: 0.6

While the main responsibility in anticipating use is to stakeholders or their various situations (e.g., to ensure correct U-values for their types of wall), the main responsibility in understanding domains is to the domain itself (e.g., the heat calculation), for faithful elicitation of its knowledge, so that the artefacts created from it are not let down by incompleteness, error or inconsistency.

In terms of Dooyeweerd's theory of Being (Section 3-9), the situations of use and the domains are *Umwelten* in which users and ICT artefact are denizens, the artefact is a (complex) generated object (§3-3.1.2), and the project is a generated object that becomes an *Umwelt* for the developers. Any ICT systems used during development are prior objects within the developers' subject-functioning.

Each of the responsibilities is discussed in Dooyeweerdian terms in the next four sections, to inform both research and practice.

9-4 Responsibility for Creating the Artefact

The responsibility for creating the artefact is to produce the artefact(s) or system that can be used in meaningful ways to make beneficial repercussions possible. The main discussion of this section is how all aspects of the developers' functioning contribute to this responsibility.

'Responsibilities' does not refer to activities or roles but to their meaningfulness and normativity. The primary activities and roles within this responsibility are well known, as designing, coding, documenting and testing—which together are often referred to as 'programming'. In large development projects, these might involve different skills and people, but in practice there is much overlap between them. Each has its own norms and hence responsibilities, but together they constitute responsibility for artefact creation.

9-4.1 Extant Discourse on Responsibility for Artefact Creation

Unfortunately, extant discourse on responsibilities for creating the artefact is very limited. I googled (24 November 2016) "responsibilities of programmers" and "responsibilities of system developers". No scholarly articles were offered, suggesting there are very few, but I received 28 entries on jobs and careers, 10 on tasks and roles, three Wikipedia pages on computer ethics and system development and only one that actually discussed responsibilities: "Responsibilities of Programmers" (C2 2016).

That one is compiled from experience and provides a list of lists of fifteen responsibilities, which are allocated to five cohorts to whom the responsibilities are due: 'stakeholders' (who pay for the ICT artefact or system), 'customers' (end-users), society, peers and "ourselves and our families". In its broad coverage the list exhibits some practical wisdom and it is discussed below, and listed in Table 9.1.

On what basis may we judge such offerings or extend them? Since discussion of actual responsibilities seems to be sparse, we will proceed from philosophical reflection on experience rather than from extant theories or rules.

Since responsibility is normative and implies both functioning and outcomes (§3-8.2), and each aspect defines a distinct norm, we may use Dooyeweerd's aspects of the functioning that is creating the ICT artefact as a foundation on which to construct guidance about responsibility.

Much was made earlier about the importance of the user interface. In Chapter 7 it is suggested that user interface, innards and protocols should all be designed together with an eye to which aspect qualified each feature. Each feature involves a user interface element. Separating design of user interface from innards can risk elevating one above the other, leading to either poor or overly elaborate interfaces and 'political' conflict between programmers and graphic designers.

9-4.2 Aspects of Creating the ICT Artefact

Since ICT artefact-creation is multi-aspectual functioning (§3-8.3), the norms of all aspects of that functioning indicate distinct kinds of responsibility within the overall responsibility.

Table 9.1 summarises, in column 2, some issues meaningful in each aspect for which the artefact-creator is responsible. The issues are from reflection on 40 years' experience, informed by what has been written by both researchers and practitioners during that time, separated by semicolons. The list is neither complete nor balanced, but rather aims to place

Table 9.1 Some Aspects of the Responsibilities of Creating the Artefact

Aspect	*. . . of artefact-creation (Examples)*	*C2's responsibilities*
Quantitative	Much of the code is to do with numbers.	
Spatial	Laying out screens.	
Kinematic	Creating animations and wipes.	
Physical	Hardware issues: materials, battery power	
Organic-biotic	Hardware issues: components (e.g. loose connections!).	
Psychic / Sensitive	Visual, aural, haptic user interface channels.	
Analytical	Crisply conceptualize domain and use, select relevant, fully understand, separate concerns; Choose language, libraries, methods; Isolate errors.	
Formative	Construct idea of artefact (**Design**); Craft the code, with imagination; Plan, execute testing; Craft the documentation.	To keep up-to-date with latest tools and techniques of our craft (O). To assist the development of requirements; offer any technical expertise needed that we are able to provide (K). To strive to advance the state of the art (P,S).
Lingual	Communicate with use-anticipators and domain-knowledge-eliciters; **Write code**; Write documentation for users, other developers. Log activities.	To implement what is required (K).

Aspect	*. . . of artefact-creation (Examples)*	*C2's responsibilities*
Social	Relationship with use-anticipators, etc., 'participatory design'; Team programming; Consider future coders in in-code documentation; Consider users.	To not besmirch the profession by shoddy work or misconduct (P).
Economic	Efficiency of code: work within limited screen space, minimize user waiting time (e.g. downloads), 'boilerplate code'; software reuse.	To develop and produce accurate and reasonable schedules and estimates of cost, then deliver according to those estimates (K).
Aesthetic	Harmonize knowledge into artefact idea; Keep aware of usage context; User interaction style; Write "beautiful code" (Knuth 2001, 130); Ensure technical integration; Writing style in documentation; **Maintenance and upgrade**	To ensure that work is enjoyable and self-fulfilling (O). To provide good works which may be enjoyed (and built upon) by others (S).
Juridical	Do justice to reality, intended situation and users; Be faithful in translating idea into code, and in documentation; Understand inappropriateness of languages and software libraries. **Testing**	To obey the laws in how we do our work (assuming laws are just) (S). To produce work which meets reasonable quality expectations (S,U).
Ethical	Egoless programming (Weinberg 1999); attitude to users; trust users' expertise; design for flexibility; be aware users' technology might be slower.	To decline a job if it cannot be performed in good conscience (K,O). To produce work which is safe and which will not make the situation worse (U,S).
Pistic / Faith	Vision for meaningfulness (profile of aspectual possibilities) of the artefact; importance of users and of future maintainers.	To keep the customer in mind at all times (U).

issues that are taken for granted or not often considered alongside those that are.

Each of the roles above is qualified by a different main aspect, design by the formative (construction of an idea), coding by the lingual with formative (representing knowledge as structured language), documentation by the lingual with the social (documentation is for others), testing by the juridical and maintenance by the aesthetic (harmonising the new with what is already there). These are shown in bold in the lists.

Column 3 contains C2's (2016) fifteen responsibilities, with an indication of to whom or what they apply (K=stakeholders, U=users, S=society, P=peers, O=ourselves and families). One is omitted, as not germane to artefact-creation: "To earn an income to provide for ourselves and our families".

It can be seen that C2's responsibilities differ markedly from what aspectual responsibilities might predict. Reasons for this should be explored.

9-4.3 Discussion of Aspects of Artefact Creation

The feeling of wisdom in C2's list might arise from the fact that the fifteen responsibilities are spread across most human aspects, including two ethical-aspect issues. However, some gaps might be detected. The lack of responsibility for early aspects (e.g., organic-biotic) suggests that little consideration has been given to issues like climate change—though these might be included in an expanded 'society' cohort.

Responsibility towards the domain of the application—such as physics, psychology or music—is also missing. Domain knowledge is not just a resource but should be treated with respect (see §9-6), and the artefact-creator should ensure it is represented as fully and accurately as reasonably possible, especially when writing software libraries. It is tempting, early in artefact-creation, to implement simplified versions of domain knowledge that ignore exceptional conditions, but if we do that, it is easy to forget to add them in before delivery, and so our artefacts will let 'customers' down sometime in the future, when their situations of use include those exceptional conditions; see §9-6.2.

In such ways, this aspectual reflection can be used to critique and enrich extant *guidelines*, many of which are weaker than C2's.

More generally, seeing artefact-creation as multi-aspectual functioning suggests that the responsibilities for design, coding, testing and documentation are not as simple as is sometimes assumed.

While the core responsibility in *design* is to produce an idea of the artefact based on information acquired about situations of use and the domain, the designer should also actively consider other options, such as non-use (§6-2.14) and that sometimes "it may not be necessary to convert this information" (West 1992), because the *experience of user* can be capitalised upon when using the artefact. Consider the following from §6-2.16:

> [The user] ignores a number of caution messages and moves to the next screen where she checks the address. It is important to make sure the address is correct so the check will reach its destination properly. . . .
>
> (Wenger (1998, 22)

The user knows which warnings are more important than others.

While the core responsibility of coding is to faithfully express the design idea in a formal programming language or knowledge representation language, employing suitable software libraries, and thereby generate the ICT artefact, there is also a responsibility to be critically aware of the limitations of the languages and libraries available, and to either choose appropriate ones or, if that is impossible, to ensure enough time is allocated to creating additional code to overcome the limitations. This implies that the coder must liaise with designers and with those engaged in project orchestration (Section 9-7).

Responsibility for documentation is to convey understanding, not just information, of the artefact, so should explain why as well as what and how. Responsibility for testing is to ensure the artefact works as it should—and not just as a possibly flawed specification dictates.

This aspectual approach to creating the artefact is intended to apply to all kinds of artefact, whether large systems, mobile applications, websites, games, embedded systems and so on, though some of the responsibilities in Table 9.1 might apply more to some kinds than others. The main difference between them, however, lies not in artefact-creation, but in the three other responsibilities. For example, for large systems, project orchestration becomes more important. For websites, expert systems, games and software libraries, domain elicitation is important and for websites, organizational systems and bespoke software, anticipating use is particularly important.

These responsibilities will now be discussed. It is usual for artefact-creators to take on some of them, especially in agile approaches.

9-5 Responsibility for Anticipating Situations of Use

This section discusses the responsibility for *anticipating use* of the ICT artefact, and the role Dooyeweerd's aspects can play in providing a foundational understanding of it, which can help in practical development.

The responsibility for anticipating use is to gain a clear understanding of the entire potential situation in which the ICT will be used. It is a responsibility to understand not only current users but future ones too, not only what users want but what is needed, not only what users believe they need but what is really meaningful and beneficial in their situation (c.f. Wood-Harper et al.'s (1998) gaps).

> Note on terminology: '*Anticipating use*' is a term used here for what is sometimes called '*user requirements analysis*' or '*requirements engineering and management*', but here it is conceived more widely.

Whereas, conventionally, this involves project documentation, conformance to documentation guidelines, quality assurance, approvals and configuration management (Chemuturi 2013, 67), here attitudes, assumptions, harmonization, etc., are recognised as important too. Debates like whether needs rather than requirements should be analysed (Patnaik and Becker 1999) become less important.

9-5.1 The Complexity of Anticipating Use

The artefact in use has many meaningful possibilities, and anticipating them is a challenge. It is likely to be used in a variety of types of situation, by different types of users in different ways, sometimes unexpected, with a mix of beneficial and detrimental repercussions (see §6-3.6). The very activity of anticipating use can change perceptions among stakeholders of which possibilities should be targeted, so 'requirements' will change. If such changes are not taken into account, "the project may suffer from cost or schedule overruns . . . we may have a wrong product on our hands at the end of the project" (Chemuturi 2013).

The responsibility of anticipating use may be broken down into a number of others, all reinforcing each other.

1. Responsibility towards the *situations of use* is to ensure that the understanding thereof is broad enough. While most methods focus on problems to be solved (the negative), the positive can be given attention too, which instils more 'life-giving' changes (Norum 2001). Understanding of the situations of use can be broadened by involving many different stakeholders, to each of whom different things will be meaningful—those who will use the artefact (end-users), those who procure the artefact, operate it, regulate it, oppose it or technically interface with it, and also those aware of community, society and planet. This is why what is called *user participation* is so important, as argued by Midgley (2000) and Basden et al. (1995). Identifying stakeholders and what stake(s) they have can be assisted by Dooyeweerd's aspects. Yet even so, issues can be overlooked, so using Dooyeweerd's aspects to consider issues directly with imagination, can reveal more; see Table 9.2 below for examples.
2. The artefact will have *repercussions in use* in the lives of individuals or organizations, positive or negative, some of which are indirect (see §6-3.6). While users might bear most responsibility for these, developers also bear some responsibility, because how the artefact is designed influences its use; see Chapter 7.
3. Repercussions arise from user functioning, which in turn is influenced by the meaningful content with which users engage (see §6-3.5). It is developers who encapsulate this content in ICT artefacts.
4. There are several responsibilities towards *stakeholders*. It is important to expose assumptions and encourage stakeholders to question them.

   Example: As developer of the *Wheat Counsellor* system (Jones and Crates

1985), which advised farmers on use of fungicides, the author took on himself a responsibility for challenging the assumption, held by the agronomists, of ever higher crop yields, because he realised that British agriculture was then too heavily dependent on chemicals and that the pendulum would soon begin to swing away from this. After some initial resistance, the agronomists divulged the advice quite readily, and *Wheat Counsellor* became not only a better product but also more trusted.

This is an example of what Hirschheim et al. (1995, 49) called the warrior role of the developer, their others being expert, catalyst and emancipator. It is the responsibility of the analyst also to help stakeholders, and especially end-users, to actively consider all three engagements that constitute ICT use that are discussed in Chapter 6: engaging in life with ICT (ELI: §6-3.6), engaging with meaningful content (EMC, §6-3.5) and engaging with interface and technology (EIT, §6-3.4). While ELI concerns the more important beneficial and detrimental repercussions, the content and the interface and technology also have important effects; inadequate information, or difficulty in accessing it, could lead to wrong decisions. The artefact might change the situation in which it is used. Unexpected, innovative ways might be found of using the artefact, especially generic software, such as mobile applications.

5. The use-anticipator has responsibility towards the knowledge and *experience of users* (and other stakeholders) to (a) respect it, especially in understanding how it can be capitalised upon (see §9-4.3), (b) ensure it expands to properly understand how the artefact might benefit or constrain them. How annoying that website and application developers assume that my Android tablet should be treated as a mobile phone with small screen, and that my use is for entertainment rather than for serious purposes!
6. Those who anticipate use have responsibility toward society and world. They should consider possible impact of widespread use (§8-4.2), and on the structures of society, including attitudes (§8-4.3). The change of attitudes by social media should have been more thoughtfully considered than it has been. Though such impacts can never be precisely *predicted* they should be *seriously considered*. Some academic discourse has highlighted structural issues like power, which are too frequently overlooked in practical development, but even they missed attitude change. So the use-anticipator should be always aware of societal issues of ICT discussed in Chapter 8.

This has revealed something to the richness of anticipating use beyond the scope of traditional user requirements analysis. Aspectual analysis can help disclose it.

9-5.2 Aspects of Use That is Anticipated

Dooyeweerd's aspects can prove useful in several ways to help us think about the use that is anticipated: to construct profiles of meaningfulness of types of situation anticipated, to stimulate thinking about functioning and repercussions therein, both expected and unexpected, to identify stakeholders by aspect (e.g., juridical aspect: lawyers). Gareth Jones found a good way to employ Dooyeweerd's aspects in engaging stakeholders (Jones and Basden, 2004).

Table 9.2 gives some examples of some of these, the richness of use-functioning and its repercussions, to serve as exemplars for how anticipations of use might be approached. Column 1 gives the aspect. The other columns cite some examples of: expectations what artefact affords users (column 2), possible repercussions (column 3), responsibilities of developer (column 4), actual ICT features, of which I have experienced and which help afford these possibilities (column 5). The stakeholders are undefined; in a formal methodology the consideration of stakeholders would be more systematic.

These are only examples. In formal practice, a more systematic analysis would be carried out. To operationalise this calls for research to establish methods for each that a wide range of people can employ. Design of features is discussed in Section 7-4.

Because the aspects transcend the situations for which ICT might be developed, they can also be used to consider the possibility of non-use of ICT; see §6-4.14. Rather than seeing non-use of ICT under the blanket idea of 'resistance', aspects separate out distinct reasons for non-use.

> Example: Concerning the restoration of a Victorian swing bridge over a canal in the UK, Fuller (2015) commented, "Most interesting was the decision to retain the original reliable operating system and not replace it with a computer controlled system. With the original system, they can feel the workings of the bridge and know if a problem exists, something not possible with a pushbutton system." ICT was not used because of the psychic aspect of feeling.

9-5.3 Aspects of the Activity of Anticipating Use

The knowledge acquired about potential situations of use can be voluminous, so, if analysts are to clarify the target meaningful possibilities that the ICT artefact will enable, then the knowledge must be selected, summarised and harmonised. Only then can the analyst identify and conceptualise an idea of the artefact, which is the aim and responsibility.

The primary aspect of anticipating use is the analytic, in that its main purpose is to identify and conceptualise an idea of the artefact, and many extant methodologies recognise this, for example, Joint Requirements Development and Checkland's (1981) Soft Systems Methodology and CATWOE

Table 9.2 Examples of Issues Developers Might Consider in Each Aspect When Anticipating Use

Aspect	*Users expect to . . .*	*Possible repercussions*	*Responsibilities*	*ICT features*
Quantitative	make calculations.		Quantities, numbers	
Spatial			Spatial arrangements in life, on screen	
Kinematic			Movements in life, in content, on screen	
Physical			Consider climate-change emissions from widespread use (see §8-4.2.2)	Stress-corrosion-cracking system (§9-2.4) calculates risk of SCC.
Organic-biotic		Effects on health	Consider effects on ecology from widespread use	(*Wheat Counsellor* (§9-2.4) might privilege chemical farming)
Psychic / Sensitive		Emotions	Consider effect on emotions; consider sensorily-impaired users	Screen-readers
Analytical	make relevant distinctions.	Will features / content clarify or confuse user?	Build in transparency of content, structures and limitations of the system.	Expert systems: explanation facility.
Formative	plan or achieve (with ease of use).	Will features / content help or hinder planning or achievement?	Build in easy control of meaningful things.	ELSIE expert system (§9-2.4): users can override its assumptions.
Lingual	obtain and communicate information.	Will specified features / content assist or prevent users' information fulfilment?	Write specification with domain-elicitors.	*Adobe Acrobat*: Note-making.
Social	To relate to others, to fulfil roles better.	Will features / content help or prevent relating	Build in social information and ability to share and relate.	Social media: Follow, Share.

(*Continued*)

Table 9.2 (Continued)

Aspect	*Users expect to . . .*	*Possible repercussions*	*Responsibilities*	*ICT features*
Economic	save or manage resources.	Will features / content encourage frugality or waste?	Include features to evaluate resource implications and compare alternative scenarios . . .	. . . as in ELSIE expert system's 'What if' feature.
Aesthetic	have fun. harmonize things.	Will features / content be fun or boring? Will they help towards harmonization or fragmentation?	Ensure content is enjoyable. Ensure users can obtain broad multi-aspectual views of their situation.	Most computer games.
Juridical	meet needs appropriately.	Will use of the system emancipate, or increase dependency?	Ensure appropriate content. Try to reduce dependency on the features. Might any stakeholder be treated unjustly when the artefact is used?	The client of one expert system I helped build wanted users to be encouraged to question its results.
Ethical	bring benefit.	Will use of system make users more selfish and competitive or more self-giving, generous, collaborative?	Ensure that self-giving user-behaviour is not penalised. Make content, features 'generous'; Trust users' expertise. Be willing to take other project responsibilities.	*Facebook*: makes people more selfish? more self-giving?
Pistic / Faith	believe the information.	"we ask whether a faithful inquiring system is better than a faithless one." (Churchman 1971, 240) 'Sacred' and 'profane' stakeholders and issues (Midgley, 2000)	Ensure that users can determine how far they can rely on the content.	*Wikipedia*: Edit History.

analysis. However, a brief reflection throws up examples of how the other aspects are important in making that successful. The activity that is anticipating use is multi-aspectual functioning (§3-8.3), and its quality depends on fulfilling the norms of all aspects (§3-8.5). So it is useful to be guided by awareness of the aspects.

- Analytic aspect: Clearly conceptualise, separate out issues;
- Formative aspect: Be systematic, structure the information;
- Lingual aspect: Communication, reporting, specification;
- Social aspect: Maintain good relationships with stakeholders, in team;
- Economic aspect: Don't waste stakeholder's time or patience;
- Aesthetic aspect: Harmonise the knowledge gleaned, imagine alternatives;
- Juridical aspect: Do justice to every and each stakeholder and their concerns, and to wider issues;
- Ethical aspect: Deal with all stakeholders generously (including users who keep changing minds! [Wood-Harper et al. 1998]!), look for flexibility, expend extra effort to fulfil the above aspects;
- Pistic aspect: Keep seeking core meaningfulness, *Weltanschauungen*, question assumptions.

Even a brief reflection like this provides an holistic understanding of the activity and responsibility of anticipating use, which can be used to understand, affirm, critique and enrich extant approaches.

One good method to assist this is *Multi-aspectual Interview Technique (MAIT)*, which provides sensitive and supportive interviewing of people about their aspirations related to ICT, that frees interviewees to talk about things they would not usually mention. See §4-4.2.2 for more details.

9-6 Responsibility for Understanding the Domain

This section discusses responsibility for understanding the domain, how it may be known and how elicitation of domain knowledge may be guided by Dooyeweerd's ideas. Domains are, for instance, materials science, medicine or ethics. This main responsibility is to the domain itself, for faithful elicitation of its knowledge, so that the artefacts created from it are not let down by incompleteness, error or inconsistency. This embraces responsibilities for domains themselves, for their knowledge and for eliciting that knowledge.

9-6.1 Domains

At their most general, domains involve meaningful kinds of functioning and being, and to understand them from Dooyeweerd's perspective involves both aspectual law and type laws. Most domains centre on one aspect perhaps with secondary aspects.

Example: The *MYCIN* expert system (Shortliffe 1976), which diagnosed bacterial infections, functioned within (a tiny part of) the organic-biotic domain and the analytic domain. This means it had, encapsulated within it both organic-biotic laws relating to bacterial infections and analytic laws of logic, two domains linked together. This combination proved more accurate than the physicians' own 'encapsulation' of them in the form of their diagnostic skill.

Just as the aspects relate to each other by dependency, analogy and targeting (§3-7.4), so the ICT artefact will have encapsulated within it not only knowledge of those domains but knowledge of their inter-aspect relationships. In *MYCIN*'s case, the encapsulated relationship is that the analytic *aspect targets* the organic-biotic, in that *MYCIN* reasons *about* bacterial infections. In the computer game *Clash of Clans*, the aesthetic aspect of fun depends foundationally on the formative aspect of achievement (building or fighting), so it incorporates both those domains, and also *inter-aspect dependency*.

In the ICT artefact, the several aspectual domains might be implemented in various ways, either as explicitly separated domain ontologies, or with one domain as inference engine and another as knowledge base, or only implicitly and tangled together in the code. Obviously the first two are preferable.

The first responsibility, therefore, is to identify the domains that are relevant and the types of inter-aspect relationship between them, so that knowledge about them may be elicited.

9-6.2 Knowledge of Domains

The second responsibility is about conceptualization of the laws of the relevant domains as knowledge, so that it may be expressed in a computer language to create the ICT artefact. This provides a *domain ontology*.

What is discussed here is from the perspective of knowledge bases. However, much is important in developing software libraries, especially about completeness.

Guarino et al. (1999) defined a domain ontology as a computer-processible statement of "a set of things whose existence is acknowledged by a particular theory or system of thought", but this definition lacks the norm of completeness and cannot easily allow tacit knowledge. A Dooyeweerdian understanding, which might be more flexible, be more precise and allow tacit knowledge, would be: a domain ontology faithfully conceptualises the aspectual laws of the domain's aspect(s) and its type laws (§3-9.4) in a suitable computer language. (Type laws are often expressed as object-oriented classes: properties and actions an object can possess that are meaningful in various aspects.)

A host of domain ontologies have appeared, for example, in the medical field, SNOMED, OpenCyc, WordNet, GALEN, UMLS (Bodenreider and Burgun 2005). Types of thing are treated very differently in them; for example, blood is variously treated as mere liquid, as body substance, body fluid, etc., some focusing on its physical aspect, some on its organic anatomy, but few on its organic functions. The challenge of inter-ontology compatibility is widely recognised but not yet solved. To design ontologies by reference to Dooyeweerd's aspects offers a fruitful research opportunity.

All knowledge that is to be run on the computer as program, as distinct from merely delivered via the user interface, must be unambiguous, properly structured and accurately complete.

Unambiguity implies a theoretical attitude towards the domain, so Dooyeweerd's transcendental critique of theoretical thought (§3-4.3) may be directly applied to domain understanding. That a theoretical attitude abstracts aspects from among the rest (§3-4.3.4) implies that domain knowledge is best if separated out by aspect. That theoretical thought involves the orchestration of multiple aspectual rationalities (§3-4.3.5) implies that no rationality may be reduced to another. That theoretical thought is criticised by reference to what the community takes to be meaningful (§3-4.3.6) implies that critique of domains should be by reference to meaningfulness, or to an origin of meaning when assumptions are being questioned or 'blue-ocean' applications, are being developed. I find Dooyeweerd's pluralistic ground-motive (§3-2.4) preferable to the traditional dualistic Nature-freedom ground-motive, because it helps me uncover aspects that are often ignored and escape the dichotomy between "ICT must control" and "ICT must free".

Much domain knowledge is tacit knowledge ("we know more than we can tell" [Polanyi 1967]), which makes it hard to conceptualise. Dooyeweerd's theory of knowing (§3-8.4) can help us decide how to treat tacit knowledge. Collins (1974) gave the example of how one construction activity failed because "short" was interpreted differently by different groups (social knowing). Because this was post-lingual knowing, it could readily be explicated under appropriate conditions. Pre-lingual knowing is harder to elicit; see below.

Completeness covers at least four things.

- Every relevant domain must be known. Example, insurance domain: The core value of the insurance sector, by which it works, is 'utmost good faith'; Walsham (2001) describes a brokerage ICT system that remained unused because it omitted this domain. This is centred on the ethical aspect but was omitted, perhaps because it seemed rather nebulous to those eliciting knowledge. It is useful to ask carefully, how each aspect in turn might be relevant.
- The inter-domain relationships must be clearly understood, along with an idea of how to implement them. Aspectual targeting might be appropriately

implemented as one domain in an inference engine, the other as knowledge base (as in many expert systems including *MYCIN* above). Inter-aspect dependency might be better implemented as two distinct domain ontologies (as in *Clash of Clans* above) that call upon each other.

- Think about types of things qualified by the domain's main aspect. Example: In the domain of two-dimensional shapes, include not only lines, rectangles and ellipses but also many-sided shapes.
- What we think of as exceptions (rare conditions) occur, which it is tempting to ignore, especially in early stages of development. Later, often once the artefacts incorporating the domain knowledge are running, a situation of use hits the exception conditions and the artefact fails without warning. Example: Remember that two-dimensional shapes can have holes; see §7-1.2. Exceptions can often be detected by thinking about another domain in the same aspect, in this case, topology as well as geometry.

Three approaches have been taken to the conceptualization of knowledge of domains. The first, arising in early artificial intelligence, is to express everything as logical statements, and submit this to a universal reasoner like Newell et al.'s (1959) *General Problem Solver* or today's *LISP* and *PROLOG*. This assumes that all rationalities may be reduced to analytic rationality—which Dooyeweerd and other philosophers now reject. It proves inefficient and makes knowledge of the domain hard to understand.

From the 1970s, knowledge expressed as heuristics—rules of thumb that practitioners use when solving problems—was used for building expert systems. The heuristics were expressed as if-then production rules. Example: If organism is anaerobic, rod, and its stain is gramneg, then it may be enterobacteriaceae (Shortliffe 1976). The production-rule formalism can 'intelligently' question users and explain to them why the question is being asked.

Systems based on heuristics, however, tended to be brittle (suddenly collapsing into giving erroneous information) and their explanations were too mechanical. Instead, *Second-generation expert systems* (Steels 1985) based their knowledge on *understanding* rather than heuristics. Understanding is generic knowledge that is distinguished from context and problem-solving strategies (Attarwala and Basden 1985). This is the approach I took when building the expert systems listed earlier (§9-2.4), and the separation of generic understanding from specific context is one reason that most of them proved useful. Understanding need not be a theory or causal model, nor quantitative, but can be qualitative, as in Hayes' (1978) *Naive Physics Manifesto*, which reasons with qualitative 'common sense' knowledge about the physical domain.

In serious applications, the domain ontology should be as close to the real world as possible, and is elicited. In games, imaginative but judicious departures are expected as long as they keep the Barltean covenant with the players of making sense and being meaningful, and the domain ontology is created with imagination. The responsibility for these is discussed in the next two sections.

9-6.3 Eliciting Domain Knowledge

The responsibility in the activity of eliciting domain knowledge is to ensure, by appropriate techniques, that the relevant aspectual domains are identified and that appropriately complete and accurate knowledge is elicited of the laws and types of each, and to harmonise the domains.

Interviews with domain experts, augmented by books and (videos of) observation of actual practice, are usually how domain knowledge is elicited. Much of what is important in acquiring knowledge about anticipated use applies here (e.g. sensitive interviewing techniques, need to maintain good relationships with those who provide knowledge; see §9-5.3). However, whereas we can analyse situations of use because we can adopt a *Gegenstand* relationship with subject-object-side things, we cannot do so directly with domains, because they are law-side, the 'ocean of meaningfulness' within which we 'swim' (§3-1.2.3; §3-6.2). Instead, we have to either accept the ready-explicated theories experts offer us, and/or detect the relevant aspects in the stories and descriptions they tell us.

Between knowledge engineers and experts is a multi-aspectual subject-subject relationship, in which experts take an active role in explaining knowledge, rather than passively having nuggets of knowledge extracted from them. For example, the activity of elicitation sometimes refines the expert's knowledge (Fiol and Huff 1992; Basden and Hibberd 1996).

Identification of relevant domains may be achieved by Mike Winfield's *Multi-aspectual Knowledge Elicitiation* (MAKE), described in §4-4.2.2. It provides a mid-level view of issues in each aspect and is good for explicating tacit knowledge.

Elicitation of good, complete knowledge within a domain is best achieved, in my experience, by asking experts "Why?", "What else?" and "When not?", related to each aspect. Doing this uncovers understanding, separates it from experience and stimulates thinking about exceptions (Attarwala and Basden 1985). To each question, several answers might be offered, meaningful in different aspects.

> Example. Question: "Why do web pages not get hits?" Answer (formative aspect): "Because it's poorly linked." Answer (lingual): "Because it's poorly written."

Sometimes conflicts occur in the knowledge that is elicited, which many assume is problematic. It might, however, lead to the surfacing of assumptions, as some in the socio-critical field have recognised.

> Example, physical domain: When I was building the Stress Corrosion Cracking Expert System (Hines and Basden 1986), I discovered that the knowledge gleaned from two major experts conflicted. It turned out that one expert worked at temperatures less than 300 Celcius and the other at higher temperatures, where much of the chemistry is different. Both had taken their own temperature range for granted.

Knowledge elicitation is intensive work, and some try to avoid it. Data mining, and training neural nets can encapsulate domain laws but not in a way that provides understanding or separation of aspects, and they cannot disclose exceptional cases. Crowd-sourcing might provide understanding, but exceptional cases might be overlooked.

Though Dooyeweerd's aspects are helpful in analysing and separating things out during conceptualization, caution should be exercised because Dooyeweerd maintained that in actuality aspects can never be torn asunder from each other (Dooyeweerd 1955, I, 27). So a balance must be struck: one should never sacrifice intuitiveness of principles on the altar of aspectual separation, nor should one call confused thinking 'intuitiveness'.

9-6.4 Creating New Worlds

The domain knowledge for virtual worlds (especially computer games) comprises not just elicited but also imagined laws. The imagined laws provide some well-chosen departures from real-world laws. As §6-3.5.2 argues and Table 6.3 shows, virtual worlds are more satisfying if they encapsulate all aspects richly.

To design a game requires attention to all three engagements with users (players) discussed in Chapter 6, engagement with the interface and technology ('EIT', §6-3.4), engagement in life with ICT ('ELI', §6-3.6) and especially engagement with meaningful content ('EMC', §6-3.5). To illustrate this, Allmer's (2009) principles of game design, gleaned from experience, are analysed by aspect and engagement in Table 9.3. Columns 1,2 give the principle, column 3 the aspects that make it meaningful, and column 4 which engagement it is. (If 'P.O.' the principle is not about user engagement but about project orchestration.)

Table 9.3 Allmer's (2009) Principles for Games Design Analysed by Aspect

Principle	*Description*	*Aspect(s)*	*Notes*
1. Focal Point	Provide the primary focus at all times.	Analytic	EMC
2. Anticipation	Inform the player that something is about to happen.	Lingual about Pistic	EMC
3. Announce Change	Provide information about all changes to the player.	Lingual about Formative	ELI?
4. Believable Events and Behavior	Every event or behavior must occur according to the logic and expectations of the player.	Juridical	EMC

Principle	*Description*	*Aspect(s)*	*Notes*
5. Overlapping Events and Behavior	Dynamic is lost if only one change occurs at a time.	Aesthetic	EMC
6. Physics	Keep in mind gravity, weight, mass, density, force, buoyancy, elasticity, etc., as the starting point, but do not be limited by it.	Juridical tempered by Aesthetic	EMC
7. Sound	Ask yourself, "Is the sound appropriate? Necessary?"	Juridical concerning Psychic	EIT
8. Pacing	Spread out the moments of high concentration, mix up the sense of urgency, etc.	Kinematic tempered by Aesthetic	EMC
9. Spacing	Understand how much space is available on-screen and recognise the spatial relationship in the world.	Spatial	EMC and EIT
10. Linear Design versus Component Breakdown	Plan components carefully, but in such a way that you can respond quickly to late "must have" requested by publisher.	Formative	P.O.
11. Player	Address how the player and their interactions contribute to the experience.	Social and perhaps a little Ethical	EMC
12. Communication	Are appropriate team members correctly aware of the objectives and the solutions? Provide visual cues so the player learns when to punch rather than kick, jump rather than strafe, etc.	(a) Analytic (b) Psychic enabling Formative	P.O. EMC
13. Appeal	Does this draw the audience in?	Aspectually complex	EMC

Such an analysis provides the foundation called for in §9-2.6 for Allmer's principles: Classify by engagement and aspect, which assists clarification of why each is important and normative. Then place new principles and check overlaps checked by reference to aspects.

Bartle's (2004) theory of games development may be affirmed, critiqued and enriched. His idea of covenant with the players (§9-2.6.2) echoes our idea of responsibility and the emphasis on meaningfulness strongly suggests that Dooyeweerd's philosophy would comfortably underpin his ideas. His types of player and storyline might be analysed and made more robust by identifying which aspect governs each type and makes it meaningful.

These suggestions call for research.

9-6.5 Gamification

In 'gamified' artefacts, fun features are employed for serious purposes, but how do we avoid the dangers discussed in §9-2.6.2? How can fun features harmonise with and support, rather than undermine, the main purpose? I am unaware of any discussion addressing such questions, so I offer the following foundational understanding drawn from Chapter 6.

In computer games, the engagement in life with ICT ('ELI') is led by the aesthetic aspect (fun), and the features, both content and interface, are also fun. Engagement with the content and interface ('EMC', 'EIT') depends on functioning in earlier aspects, such as the formative (challenge) and the analytic (revealing or hiding things). (See §6-3, §3-9.4, §3-7.4.4.)

In gamification, however, the ELI is led by a different aspect, and much of the meaningful content is also led by that aspect. The fun features that have been added are still led by the aesthetic aspect, however, and it might be this difference in aspects (§3-7.3) that contributes to the inauthenticity that is often felt by users. It might be possible to overcome this by careful design of the aspectual functioning on which the fun features depend, to be meaningful to the main ELI aspect. For example:

- Analytic: Which content should be hidden to generate surprise?
- Formative: What should and should not be challenging?
- Lingual: When are jokes inappropriate?
- Social: Is the user learner or player?
- Economic: Parsimony.

Readers might like to develop this suggestion, that aspects can help clarify our thinking about gamification.

9-7 Responsibility for Orchestrating the Project

ICT development involves a project. If the overall responsibility of ICT development is to enable and encourage benefit, the primary responsibility for orchestrating the project is for making things come together to achieve that. This section discusses how a foundational understanding of it may be laid using Dooyeweerd's aspects, which can support all kinds of project discussed especially in Section 9-2.3.

Project-orchestration responsibility is a responsibility for coherence. It is both *outward-looking* and *inward-looking*. Outward-looking responsibility covers coherence of the artefact in its usage situations for all stakeholders, including such things as not only needs, processes and resources, but also mindset, attitude and justice. Inward-looking responsibility is for the project itself, to deliver a good ICT artefact. Most extant project management methodologies, like CMMI and PRINCE2, give more attention to the project processes and resources and see the outward as expressed only in what is communicated from external stakeholders.

Project-orchestration is the responsibility of all involved in the project (as is implied by discourses around team working and user participation); all have responsibility to ensure that all that happens in the project harmonises towards fulfilling the overall meaningfulness of the development. This is why we call it '*project orchestration*' rather than 'project management'; the latter tends to elevate the economic aspect of resources over the aesthetic aspect of orchestration and overemphasise the convenience of separating out defined roles.

How may structured project management approaches like CMMI be understood alongside approaches that criticise them, such as agile approaches, Scandinavian approaches and critical approaches encountered in academia? On what foundation may we stand to appreciate, critique and perhaps enrich both?

9-7.1 Aspects Important in Project-Orchestration

In Basden (2008) I discussed how each aspect is important in everyday experience of project-orchestration, in a way that reveals neglected issues. The following summarises that, adding some new material. The aesthetic is discussed first, being the aspect of orchestration, then the social, because it is a project, and then going backwards, then forwards from there. Various approaches are mentioned; how the aspects apply to agile development is discussed in §9-7.2.

The **aesthetic aspect** of harmonizing is the primary aspect of project-orchestration, to which all these other aspects contribute. This is recognised in Avison and Wood-Harper's (1990) Multiview and in CMMI's concept of integrated process improvement, which includes harmonizing with existing situations. Harmony in large and small projects is likely to be very different.

Internally, the development project may be likened to a symphony, and the team of people involved, to an orchestra. String, wind, percussion and brass sections together contribute to the whole (aesthetic aspect), with occasional emphasis on one or another. Each plays to the best of their ability (formative antecipating the juridical aspect), serving and supporting the others instead of seeking glory (ethical aspect). The playing has a certain overall plan but there also improvisation (formative aspect), which is seen, not as regrettable deviation but as making the whole even more meaningful (pistic). Yet improvisation is the minor element, so best used sparingly (economic aspect). The symphony beautifies and enhances the surrounding pieces, bringing out their own beauty and integrity (ethical aspect).

The importance of the **social aspect** in project orchestration is already widely recognised, but Dooyeweerd (1986) can perhaps bring fresh insight by differentiating three levels of the social: intercommunal, intracommunal and interpersonal (§3-9.6.3). In project-orchestration, these are: external relationships, team structures and social friendships of all participants. CMMI emphasises the first and second, and participative decision-making (Ives and Olson 1984) and agile approaches, the first and third. Power relationships are problematic in intercommunal and interpersonal relationships, but valid in intracommunal because; within a true social institution, relationships of 'authority and subordination' (Kalsbeek 1975, 199–200) are valid. The negative connotation of these comes from the Nature-freedom ground-motive, and they are not inherently so. To its credit, Emancipatory Development (Hirschheim and Klein 1994) does not reject authority structures, as is often assumed, but rather that they should be tempered with ethical and juridical norms.

The **lingual aspect** of project orchestrating is manifested in communication and documentation (reports, records, manuals). Waterfall and spiral approaches depend heavily on such documentation while agile approaches try to minimise it. Many approaches take the lingual aspect for granted, stipulating *how* communication or documentation should be done but not discussing *what* nor *why*, which are crucial for understandability. CMMI merely specifies format and forms, and Agile (2001) recommends merely that information conveyance should be face-to-face (social aspect). Even the Crystal family of agile development (Cockburn 2004), which makes overcoming barriers to communication its core aim, focuses on 'how'.

The **formative aspect** of project orchestration is manifested in goals, planning and techniques, in skills and training, and in the history of the project. The Waterfall model and Boehm's (1988) Spiral Model make this formal, while in iterative and agile development it is less formal. CMMI emphasises processes, planning and training.

The **analytic aspect** of project orchestration involves analysing and choosing: objectives, stakeholders, resources, paths to completion, etc. CMMI emphasises business needs, Soft Systems Methodology emphasises reflection and Midgley's (2000) Systemic Intervention emphasises boundary critique.

The **economic aspect** is exhibited in management of the limited resources available to the project—time, budget, expertise, access to participants, etc. Most development approaches emphasise this aspect, because of a resource-oriented mindset.

The **juridical aspect** of project orchestration is responsibility for repercussions and wider impact when the system is in use, and thus towards all stakeholders, whether acknowledged or not. It is the main reason why anticipating use is so important. It is recognised, for instance, in CMMI, as implied or actual contracts of delivery between the parties, in emancipatory development (Hirschheim and Klein 1994), as justice and emancipatory potential and as "accept responsibility" (Beck 2000).

Dooyeweerd's **ethical aspect** is specifically centred on self-giving (in contrast to traditional approaches to ethics), implying an attitude of generosity rather than competitive self-interest among those involved in the project—artefact-creators, use-anticipators, knowledge engineers and project-orchestrators (including management). Attitude is seldom discussed explicitly, neither in academic nor professional circles, though is recognised in agile approaches (see below). Stakeholder power/interest grids, while somewhat useful, are in danger of exacerbating self-interest.

The **pistic aspect** of project orchestration concerns, externally, prevailing beliefs (*Weltanschauungen* [Checkland 1981]) by participants, especially of why the ICT artefact being developed is meaningful and good ('vision'). Internally, the pistic aspect is exhibited, for example, in (dis)loyalty or motivation of team members. Conflicts that undermine the project are often pistic at root.

9-7.2 Principles of Agile Development

With this we can listen to, affirm, critique and enrich extant ideas about project orchestration (§4-1.3). Listening and affirming means understanding what is meaningful in the ideas, and why, and the irreducibility and normativity of aspects respectively can help this. Critique uncovers limitations. Enrichment suggests how to overcome them.

As an example, the 'Principles behind the Agile Manifesto' (Agile 2001) are analysed by aspect. The word 'agile' suggests the kinematic aspect as key issue, but it is usually unwise to make an early aspect the most important, because they antecipate and gain full meaningfulness from most others (§3-7.4.5). Perhaps the label 'agile' arises from reaction against neglect of the kinematic by previous approaches, rather than actually being most important. Aspectual examination of the principles might reveal more richly what actually is important.

- "Our highest priority is to satisfy the customer through early and continuous delivery of valuable software."—"Valuable" suggests normative meaningfulness of the kind Dooyeweerd envisaged that constitute aspects. "Early, continuous" implies kinematic. Critique: "Customer" and "delivery" suggests an unwise adherence to the economic aspect.
- "Welcome changing requirements, even late in development. Agile processes harness change for the customer's competitive advantage."—Ethical

aspect of generosity towards inconvenient changes is placed first. "Harness" suggests either formative achievement or aesthetic harmonizing. Critique: "customer's competitive advantage" limits this to a distortion of the economic aspect and dysfunction in the ethical aspect (self-interest of 'customer). Enrich: Replace "customer's competitive advantage" with "benefit of users and all stakeholders".

- "Deliver working software frequently, from a couple of weeks to a couple of months, with a preference to the shorter timescale."—"frequently", though kinematic-economic, is in order to stimulate recipient into understanding the software and its possibilities (analytic, lingual).
- "Business people and developers must work together daily throughout the project."—Emphasises harmonizing of two distinct roles (aesthetic, social) and frequency (kinematic).
- "Build projects around motivated individuals. Give them the environment and support they need, and trust them to get the job done."—Two important aspects of the development process: pistic aspect (motivation) with ethical (trust) attitude of management towards developers.
- "The most efficient and effective method of conveying information to and within a development team is face-to-face conversation."—About lingual aspect of team functioning, enhanced by social, couched in economic-formative terms. Critique: Does "face-to-face" include *Skype* by today's 'digital nomads'? Enrich: Aspects would allow this, and my own experience suggests so.
- "Working software is the primary measure of progress."—Quantitative functioning of project. Critique: It targets formative (working, progress); should that be the main thing to measure? Why?
- "Agile processes promote sustainable development. The sponsors, developers, and users should be able to maintain a constant pace indefinitely." Does "sustainable development" refer to contributing to wider sustainability, as it does in the construction industry? Unfortunately not. It means 'sustained': "constant pace" refers to kinematic (Strauss 2009, 13) of the project itself, rather than harmony (aesthetic) with environment. This suggests some unfortunate self-centredness. Enrich: Use aspects to help identify and affirm the deepest issue here: Is it that developers should not be overworked: juridical?
- "Continuous attention to technical excellence and good design enhances agility."—Formative aspect in service of agility.
- "Simplicity—the art of maximizing the amount of work not done—is essential."—Work-minimization is meaningful as formative-economic. Critique: Is simplicity important only in these aspects? Enrich: What about lingual simplicity in code, comments and documentation?
- "The best architectures, requirements, and designs emerge from self-organizing teams."—Social aspect, in its interpersonal rather than intracommunal form (§3-9.6.3).

- "At regular intervals, the team reflects on how to become more effective, then tunes and adjusts its behavior accordingly."—Self-critical reflection is ethical vulnerability targeting pistic beliefs and formative techniques.

In addition to the expected awareness of formative and economic aspects, because it is development for business, and of the kinematic aspect, because of its label 'agile', this shows an emphasis on the ethical aspect of self-giving in agile development. This is unusual among project-orchestration approaches. It is an attitude directed in three ways: developers towards users or clients, management towards developers in the team and developers towards themselves (vulnerability). Most of the impact of the ethical aspect is by retrocipation on all earlier aspects, so it is a hidden contributor to success. Is it this aspect, even more than the kinematic reaction against inertia, that has led to the success of the agile movement? Does this suggest that the core aspect of agile approaches is the ethical? Beck's (2000) use of "embrace" (change) suggests so.

However, might we see self-subversion of the agile approach in the narrow business orientation, in that it has introduced a dysfunction in the ethical aspect: competitive advantage?

Two human aspects are almost entirely missing. One is the juridical. There is no consideration of due here. Motivation and trust can be undermined by injustice. Another is the analytic aspect. Though this might be implied in reflection by teams, there is little about clarity of understanding of the application or domain. It might be that these aspects are taken for granted, but might it be because of reaction against earlier approaches that over-emphasised the juridical (managerial approaches emphasised contracts, and socio-critical, emphasised rights) and analytic, in making everything too formal? Despite this, would it be useful to recognise the situated importance of these two aspects? If agile approaches currently seem inappropriate to large projects (Abrahamsson et al. 2009), might this limitation be overcome by exploration of the importance of attitude, of justice and due, and of clarity of understanding?

In such ways we might critically examine project-orchestration approaches. The reflections above suggest avenues for new research.

9-8 Drawing This Together

To draw these discussions together, it is useful to identify one overall qualifying aspect that they all share, which qualifies ICT development as a whole, and a leading aspect for each that distinguishes them (§3-9.4). Which qualifying aspect we choose is determined by what we deem most important about development. The formative aspect emphasises technical construction, the social, agreements, the lingual, languages and communication.

We have chosen the juridical aspect of responsibility, because of the future orientation of ICT development. This can account for the importance of contracts in large projects.

From what is meaningful in each, the leading aspects are as follows:

- Creating the artefact: lingual (writing, expressing)
- Anticipating use: analytic (analysing)
- Understanding the domain: juridical (doing justice to the domain)
- Project orchestration: aesthetic (harmonizing).

Each is multi-aspectual in its activity and responsibility, with antecipatory and retrocipatory dependency of these aspects on others. Table 9.4 summarizes the major ways in which each aspect is important in each of the four main responsibilities discussed above, in order to reveal the diversity of each in the realities of ICT development. Most entries show examples of aspects of functioning responsibly but those of the quantitative to psychic aspects show what developers are responsible for (i.e. target aspect). Emboldened text indicates the main or leading aspect of the responsibility.

Table 9.4 Examples of Aspects of Each of the Four Main Responsibilities of ICT Development

Aspect	*Artefact Creation*	*Anticipating Use*	*Domain Understanding*	*Project Orchestration*
Quantitative	Number processing			
Spatial	Screen layout	Space in use		
Kinematic	Movements, animations	Dynamism of artefact		
Physical	Hardware issues	Climate repercussions		
Organic-biotic	Hardware component issues	Health repercussions		
Psychic/ Sensitive	User interface channels	Users' sensory needs		
Analytical	Analyse and select for design, coding, testing	**Analyse and clearly conceptualise usage issues**	Analyse domain laws; identify important aspects	Analyse and choose project objectives, stakeholders, etc.
Formative	Structure the artefact	Structure the information	Structure the knowledge	Plan project, ensure training
Lingual	**Write the code,** incl. documentation	Communicate with stakeholders; write specification	Elicit and express generic knowledge	Report, record, communicate about project

Aspect	*Artefact Creation*	*Anticipating Use*	*Domain Understanding*	*Project Orchestration*
Social	Design participatorily, ensure others will understand code; team working	Relate well with stakeholders; team working	Relate well with experts; team working	Ensure team working, maintain good relationships with stakeholders, use power appropriately
Economic	Ensure speed, frugally use screen space	Don't waste stakeholder time	Don't waste experts' time	Manage resources of all kinds
Aesthetic	Write elegant code, style the UI, maintain holistic awareness	Imagine alternatives; harmonise usage knowledge	Maintain coherence of the domain	**Harmonise internally and externally**
Juridical	Accurate code, errors	Give every stakeholder their due (including marginal ones like planet)	**Faithfully elicit laws of domain**	Maintain awareness for overall responsibility for repercussions of artefact in use
Ethical	'Egoless programming', design in flexibility	Allow users to change minds	Hunt out rare exceptions	Model and spread good attitude
Pistic/Faith	Vision for coding	Seek core meaningfulness; understand *Weltanschauungen*	Believe in the domain	Maintain vision, ensure commitment

The relationship between the four responsibilities is neither causality nor sequence, nor is it part-whole; it is enkapsis, in that each responsible activity is a whole (§3-9.6.2). Though project orchestration takes on a concern for the whole project, it is dangerous to see it as the 'whole' of which the others are 'parts'. The type of enkapsis is not foundational, as in a marble sculpture, because none of the responsibilities is the 'marble', nor subject-object enkapsis, as with the hermit crab and its chosen shell, nor correlative enkapsis, in that the development is not an *Umwelt*. It might be slightly similar to symbiotic and territorial enkapsis, but it might be a sixth kind of enkapsis that Dooyeweerd did not discuss. Philosophical research is called for.

This responsibility-oriented approach allows flexibility: the four associated activities may occur either in chronological sequence or in parallel, and roles may be allocated to certain people or shared among them.

Responsibility is not just juridical, it is an attitude—of sensitivity to the potential usage situation, of respect for the complexity of the domain, of artefact-creators being willing to challenge wrong, of adopting an holistic awareness of the entire project.

Example: We began this book with the case of Volkswagen, which admitted cheating emissions testing regimes by incorporating a software feature in its cars that switched off pollution control when driving on the road. The CEO of Volkswagen claimed that the feature had been installed by "a couple of software engineers", without being company policy, but subsequent actions suggest otherwise. The unethical, unwise activity, which cost the company reputation and many billions of dollars, might have been carried out by ICT developers, in their responsibilities of artefact creation and perhaps anticipating use. As such, we developers are in a position of trust and should never betray that trust, but should stand against all kinds of evil, including that of cheating.

However, that several versions of the cheat were developed suggests project orchestration responsibility. It seems a decision was made to prioritise the internal stakeholders of the company over external stakeholders who would suffer the pollution. This decision comes from a self-serving attitude within the company.

On a more positive note, readers might like to watch the Youtube video of the development of the game Runescape on "https://m.youtube.com/watch?v=7RNK0YBdwko". Runescape has been serving the community since 2002, growing with little commercial-style marketing and without large-corporation support to be, currently, the largest free massively multiplayer online roleplay game. This is because gameplay, community, fun and loyalty (aesthetic, social, pistic aspects) were important. The hour-long account shows all four responsibilities discussed here and many aspects of each, all fascinatingly interwoven. Failures as well as successes are shown, along with what was learned, to give a rich symphony of ICT development.

9-9 Concluding Remarks

This chapter has developed a foundational understanding of ICT development (information systems development) as four responsibilities and their corresponding activities, which function in coherence with each other. The diversity of each may be understood by Dooyeweerd's aspects. That aspects are spheres of law ensures a rich understanding of both responsibility and possibility, and thus a supports the future-orientation of ICT development. That Dooyeweerd's aspects are of everyday experience implies that principles can be composed and refined that will resonate with the practice of ICT development. Figure 9.2 depicts this.

The discussion in this chapter may be summed up as follows, using the scheme in §4-1.3.

Listening. A number of very different discourses that are not usually brought together have been briefly surveyed to expose issues that are important in ICT development. Readers might like to undertake a fuller review.

Affirmation. All types of development activity mentioned are affirmed as multi-aspectual human functioning that is normative, carrying not only project-centred responsibility towards the project and its known stakeholders, but also some longer-term shared responsibility for the eventual repercussions of ICT use. Four main responsibilities have been considered that relate, in extant discourses, to project management, user requirements analysis, knowledge elicitation and software development, but the remit of each has been expanded, in ways that are relevant to all kinds of ICT development. Philosophical grounds for distinguishing each responsibility from others is established. No discourse or research finding has been found irrelevant; all contribute useful insight into an overall picture.

Critique. There has been too little intercourse between the discourses, so there has been no way to recognise new issues. Dooyeweerd's aspects have been used to alert us to kinds of issues that have been overlooked. His penchant for everyday experience has provided a background against which to understand some of the deficiencies of extant approaches.

Enrichment is possible at several levels. In some places it has been shown how individual theories or professional practices may be enriched, by seriously considering overlooked aspects. Project management has been enriched into *orchestrating the project*, user requirements analysis, into *anticipating use*, which has also been differentiated from *understanding the domain*, and design-coding-testing, into *creating the artefact*. The discourse of ICT development as a whole has been enriched by bringing all four together as part of a wider picture, under the banner of responsibility, with managerial/social and technical concerns both present. It applies to all kinds of ICT discussed. Some integration and mutual understanding might be possible among discourses that seldom meet each other, each of the discourses might offer some insight that can be recognised as meaningful by others, and each might be enriched by others if the aspects are borne in mind.

One of the most popular courses I ever taught was that on *Key Issues in Information Systems Development*. Masters students from many different cultures learned about every aspect of each of the four responsibilities. The course was based on, and helped to develop, the ideas in this chapter. Its popularity was partly because it recognised aspects like those of faith and attitude alongside the more usual technical, informational and economic aspects, and partly because it was easy to bring in practical illustrations. The following is typical of many appreciative comments I received from students:

> The study of Aspects as specified in Dooyeweerd's philosophy completely revolutionised my thinking of Information Systems, in general and inculcated positive curiosity. The most valuable element that I gained from this module was the creative and efficient problem solving ability with the application of Aspects.
>
> (Mohammad Ali, Somalia, used with permission)

References

Abrahamsson P, Conboy K, Wang X. 2009. 'Lots done, more to do': The current state of agile systems development research. *European Journal of Information Systems*, 18, 281–284, doi:10.1057/ejis.2009.27.

Agile. 2001. The Agile Manifesto. Accessed 4th August 2015 "http://agilemanifesto.org" and "www.agilemanifesto.org/principles.html"

Ahern DM, Clouse A, Turner R. 2004. *CMMI Distilled, Second Edition: A Practical Introduction to Integrated Process Improvement*. Addison-Wesley, Reading, MA.

Ahmad H, Basden A. 2013. Down-to-Earth Issues in Information System Use. Proceedings of the Pacific Area Conference on Information Systems (PACIS). Paper 191.

Allmer M. 2009. The 13 Basic Principles of Gameplay Design. accessed "www.gamasutra.com/view/feature/132341/the_13_basic_principles_of_.php" March 2016.

Attarwala FT, Basden A. 1985. A methodology for constructing expert systems. *R&D Management*, 15(2), 141–149.

Avison DE, Wood-Harper AT. 1990. *Multiview: An Exploration in Information Systems Development*. Alfred Walker, Henley-on-Thames, UK.

Avison DE, Wood-Harper AT, Vidgen RT, Wood JRG. 1998. A further exploration into information systems development: The evolution of Multiview2. *Information, Technology and People*, 11(2), 124–139.

Bainbridge L. 1986. Asking questions and accessing knowledge. *Future Computing Systems*, 1(2), 143–149.

Bartle RR. 2004. *Designing Virtual Worlds*. New Riders, Berkeley, CA.

Basden A. 1983. On the application of expert systems. *International Journal of Man-Machine Studies*, 19, 461–477.

Basden A. 2002. A philosophical underpinning for I.S. development. In S Wrycza (Ed.), *Proceedings of the Xth European Conference on Information Systems, ECIS2002: Information Systems and the Future of the Digital Economy* (pp. 68–78). University of Gdansk, Poland, 5–10 June 2002.

Basden A. 2008. *Philosophical Frameworks for Understanding Information Systems*. IGI Global, Hershey, PA.

Basden A, Hibberd PR. 1996. User interface issues raised by knowledge refinement. *International Journal of Human-Computer Studies*, 45, 135–155.

Basden A, Watson ID, Brandon PS. 1995. *Client Centred: An Approach to Developing Knowledge Based Systems*. Council for the Central Laboratory of the Research Councils, London, UK.

Beck K. 2000. *Extreme Programming Explained: Embrace Change*. Addison-Wesley, Boston, MA.

Beer D, Burrows R. 2007. Sociology and, of and in Web 2.0: Some initial considerations. *Sociological Research Online*, 12(5), 30 September.

Berkane ML, Seinturier L, Boufaida M. 2015. Using variability modelling and design patterns for self-adaptive system engineering: Application to smart-home. *International Journal of Web Engineering and Technology*, 10(1), 65–93.

Bodenreider O, Burgun A. 2005. *Biomedical Ontologies*. Springer-Verlag, Germany.

Boehm BW. 1988. A spiral model of software development and enhancement. *IEEE Computer*, 21(5), May, 61–72.

Brandon PS, Basden A, Hamilton I, Stockley J. 1988. *Application of Expert Systems to Quantity Surveying*. Royal Institution of Chartered Surveyors, London.

Burrell G, Morgan G. 1979. *Sociological Paradigms and Organizational Analysis*. Heinemann, London, UK.

C2. 2016. The Responsibilities of Programmers. Web page accessed "http://wiki.c2.com/?ResponsibilitiesOfProgrammers", 24 November 2016.

Cao L, Mohan K, Xu P, Ramesh B. 2009. A framework for adapting agile development methodologies. *European Journal of Information Systems*, 18, 332–343, doi:10.1057/ejis.2009.26; published online 18 August 2009.

Checkland P. 1981. *Systems Thinking, Systems Practice*. John Wiley & Sons, New York.

Chemuturi M. 2013. *Requirements Engineering and Management for Software Development Projects*. Springer Science +Business Media, New York.

Chua WF. 1986. Radical developments in accounting thought. *The Accounting Review*, 61, 601–632.

Churchman CW. 1970. Operations research as a profession. *Management Science*, 17, 337–353.

Churchman CW. 1971. The religion of inquiring systems. In CW Churchman, *The Design of Inquiring Systems: Basic Concepts of Systems and Organization* (pp. 237–246). Basic Books, New York.

Cockburn A. 2004. *Crystal Clear: A Human-Powered Methodology for Small Teams*. Addison-Wesley, Boston, MA.

Collins HM. 1974. The Tea-Set: Tacit knowledge and scientific networks. *Science Studies*, 4, 165–186.

Dooyeweerd H. 1955. *A New Critique of Theoretical Thought* (Vols. I–IV, 1975 ed.). Paideia Press, Jordan Station, Ontario, Canada.

Dooyeweerd H. 1986. *A Christian Theory of Social Institutions*, tr. M Verbrugge. The Herman Dooyeweerd Foundation, La Jolla, CA.

Eow YL, Ali WZbW, Mahmud Rb. 2010. Computer games development and appreciative learning approach in enhancing students' creative perception. *Computers & Education*, 54, 146–161.

Evans E. 2004. *Domain-Driven Design: Tackling Complexity in the Heart of Software*. Addison-Wesley, Reading, MA.

Fiol CM, Huff AS. 1992. Maps for managers: Where are we, where do we go from here? *Journal of Management Studies*, 29, 267–286.

Fuller M. 2015. National accolade for restoration of bridge. *The Chester Chronicle*, Chester, UK, 29 October, 3.

Furtado AWB, Santos ALM. 2006. Using domain-specific modeling towards computer games development industrialization. In J Gray, J-P Tolvanen, J Sprinkle

(Eds.), *6th OOPSLA Workshop on Domain-Specific Modeling (DSM'06)* (pp. 1–14), 22 October. University of Jyväskylä, Finland, Portland, Oregon.

Giddens A. 1984. *The Constitution of Society: Outline of the Theory of Structuration*. University of California Press, Berkeley, CA.

Guarino N, Masolo C, Verere G. 1999. OntoSeek: Content-based access to the Web. *IEEE Intelligent Systems*, 14(3), 70–80.

Guo J, Han H. 2014. A method for facilitating end-user mashup based on description. *International Journal of Web Engineering and Technology*, 9(2), 99–124.

Habermas J. 1972. *Knowledge and Human Interests*, tr. JJ Shapiro. Heinemann, London, UK.

Hayes PJ. 1978. The naive physics manifesto. In D. Michie (Ed.), *Expert Systems in the Micro Electronic Age* (pp. 242–270). Edinburgh University Press, Edinburgh, UK.

Hines JG, Basden A. 1986. Experience with use of computers to handle corrosion knowledge. *British Corrosion Journal*, 21(3), 151–156.

Hirschheim R, Klein HK. 1994. Realizing emancipatory principles in information systems development: The case for ETHICS. *MIS Quarterly*, 18(1), 85–109.

Hirschheim R, Klein HK, Lyytinen K. 1995. *Information Systems Development and Data Modeling: Conceptual and Philosophical Foundations*. Cambridge University Press, London, UK.

Ives B, Olson M. 1984. User involvement and MIS success: A review of research. *Management Science*, 30(5), 586–603.

Jones GO, Basden A. 2004. Using Dooyeweerd's philosophy to guide the process of stakeholder engagement in ISD. In MJ de Vries, B Bergvall-Kåreborn, S Strijbos (Eds.), *Interdisciplinarity and the Integration of Knowledge: Proceedings of 10th Annual Working Conference of CPTS* (pp. 1–19), 19–24 April, CPTS'2004. Centre for Philosophy, Technology and Social Systems, Amersfoort, the Netherlands. ISBN 90-807718-3-X.

Jones MJ, Crates DT. 1985. Expert systems and videotext: An application in the marketing of agrochemicals. In MA Bramer (Ed.), *Research and Development in Expert Systems: Proceedings of the Fourth Technical Conference of the British Computer Society Specialist Group for Expert Systems*. Cambridge University Press, Cambridge, UK.

Kalsbeek L. 1975. *Contours of a Christian Philosophy*. Wedge Publishing, Toronto, Ontario, Canada.

Karlsson F, Ãgerfalk P. 2009. Exploring agile values in method configuration. *European Journal of Information Systems*, 18, 300–316, doi:10.1057/ejis.2009.20; published online 21 July 2009.

Kiczales G, Lamping J, Mendhekar A, Maeda C, Lopes CV, Loingtier J-M, Irwin J. 1997. Aspect-Oriented Programming. *Proceedings of the European Conference on Object-Oriented Programming, ECOOP'97*, Springer-Verlag, Germany.

Knuth D. 2001. *Things a Computer Scientist Rarely Talks About*. CSLI, Stanford, CA.

Koster R, Vogel R. 2002. Story-telling in the online medium. *Proceedings of Game Deevelopers Conference*, San Jose, CA, accessed "www.legendmud.org/raph/gaming/gdc_2002_Storytelling_files/frame.htm/".

Kumar PR, Singh AK, Mohan A. 2015. Efficient methodologies to overcome the effects of hanging pages in search engine optimisation. *International Journal of Web Engineering and Technology*, 10(2), 129–151.

Latour B. 1993. *We Have Never Been Modern*. Pearson Education Ltd., Harlow, UK.

Lee AS. 2004. Thinking about social theory and philosophy in information systems. In J Mingers, LP Willcocks (Eds.), *Social Theory and Philosophy for Information Systems* (pp. 1–26). John Wiley & Sons, Chichester, UK.

Löwe (LÃwe) N. 2015. Our Responsibility as Software Developers. InfoQ, posted by Nils LÃwe on 15 July, accessed "www.infoq.com/articles/Responsible-Software-Development" 24 March 2016.

McAvoy J, Butler T. 2009. The role of project management in ineffective decision making within agile software development projects. *European Journal of Information Systems*, 18, 372–383, doi:10.1057/ejis.2009.22; published online 28 July 2009.

Midgley G. 2000. *Systemic Intervention: Philosophy, Methodology and Practice*. Kluwer/Plenum, New York.

Newell A, Shaw JC, Simon HA. 1959. Report on a General Problem-Solving Program. *Proceedings of the International Conference on Information Processing*, 256–264.

Ngwenyama OK, Klein HK. 1994. An exploration of expertise of knowledge workers: Towards a definition of the universe of discourse for knowledge acquisition. *Information Systems Journal*, 4, 129–140.

Norum KE. 2001. Appreciative design. *Systems Research and Behavioral Science*, 18, 323–333.

Owston R, Wideman H, Ronda NS, Brown C. 2009. Computer game development as a literacy activity. *Computers & Education*, 53, 977–989.

Partridge D, Wilks Y. 1987. Does AI have a methodology different from software engineering? *AI Review*, Special Edition on Foundations of AI, 1(2), 111–120.

Patnaik D, Becker R. 1999. Needfinding: The why and how of uncovering people's needs. *Design Management Journal*, 10(2), 37–43.

Polanyi M. 1967. *The Tacit Dimension*. Routledge and Kegan Paul, London, UK.

Premkumar G. 1989. A cognitive study of the decision making process in a business context: Implications for design of expert systems. *International Journal of Man-Machine Studies*, 31, 557–572.

Shortliffe EH. 1976. *Computer Based Medical Consultation: MYCIN*. Elsevier, New York.

Silvestro K. 1988. Using explanations for knowledge-base acquisition. *International Journal of Man-Machine Studies*, 29(2), 159.

Smith J. 2016. What Makes a Good Software Library, accessed "www.thereformed-programmer.net/what-makes-a-good-software-library/" 1 December 2016.

Standing C. 2002. Methodologies for developing web applications. *Information and Software Technology*, 44, 151–159.

Steels L. 1985. Second generation expert systems. *Future Generation Computer Systems*, 1(4), 213–221.

Strauss DFM. 2009. *Philosophy: Discipline of Disciplines*. Paideia Press, Reformational Publishing Project, Grand Rapids, MI, USA.

Vidgen R. 2002. Constructing a web information system development methodology. *Information Systems Journal*, 12, 247–261.

Walsham G. 2001. *Making a World of Difference: IT in a Global Context*. John Wiley & Sons, Chichester, UK.

Weinberg GM. 1999. Egoless programming. *IEEE Software*, 16(1), 118–120.

Wenger E. 1998. *Communities of Practice: Learning, Meaning and Identity*. Cambridge University Press, Cambridge, UK.

West D. 1992. Knowledge elicitation as an inquiring system: Towards a 'subjective' knowledge elicitation methodology. *Journal of Info Systems*, 2, 31–44.

Willmott H. 1993. Breaking the paradigm mentality. *Organization Studies*, 14(5), 681–719.

Wood-Harper T, Jayaratna N, Wood B. 1998. *Methodologies for Developing and Managing Emerging Technology Based Information Systems: Information Systems Methodologies. Sixth International Conference on Information Systems Methodologies*. Springer Science & Business Media, New York.

Zhang G, Hölzl M. 2015. Improving the modularity of web-application models with aspects. *International Journal of Web Engineering and Technology*, 10(2), 98–128.

Part III

This part brings the discussions of Parts I and II together, to draw conclusions and make suggestions for action.

It reflects on the five areas as a whole and some cross-cutting concerns (Chapter 10), discusses possible contributions and limitations of the foundational approach using Dooyeweerd's philosophy that has been adopted (Chapter 11), and then collects together over a hundred suggestions for research projects and for improving practice that were mentioned in previous chapters (Chapter 12). It ends with a call to take the approach forward.

10 Overview and Reflection

When we try to understand ICT and information systems as a whole, we are faced with phenomenon vast, complex, powerful and fascinating. In Part II we looked at what ICT is, its use, its features, its relationship with society and its development, and laid foundations of understanding each area within the ground that is Dooyeweerd's philosophy (Dooyeweerd 1955). But the areas belong together, each affecting the other, and none exists without the others as meaningful in reality. The areas are shown in Figure 10.1.

The foundational understanding of each area is very briefly summarised, including its normativity, and some of the main relationships between them. Developers create artefacts out of features, which are engaged with in use, which affects and is affected by societal beliefs and attitudes, which also influence our view of what ICT is, which influences use and development. We can go into deeper relationships, for instance that society influences which features are expected and fashionable.

In Part III we bring the discussions together, to draw conclusions and spot opportunities for the future. This chapter discusses the foundational frameworks that have been developed and how they work together. It discusses a

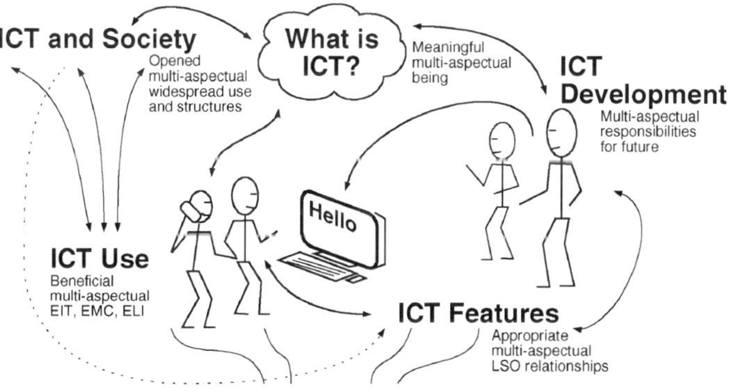

Figure 10.1 The Five Areas Covered in Part II

number of concerns that cut across all areas studied and then discusses how the frameworks might be extended into other fields. Chapter 11 discusses contributions and limitations of this work, and Chapter 12 makes recommendations for action.

10-1 Reflection on Foundations

Each of the chapters in Part II may be read independently of the others, even though they are best understood together. To what extent has Dooyeweerd's philosophy contributed to the revealing and establishing of good foundations in each of the areas related to ICT? The implications of these will be discussed in Chapter 12. Here we consider issues that pertain across all five areas together.

10-1.1 On Foundations for ICT and Information Systems as Such

As we saw in §1-5.1, Benbasat and Weber (1996) argued that the field of information systems (IS) lacked a sound and distinctive foundation, and Weber (2003) found that still true. Our discussions have sought to rectify that situation by laying a foundation for each of the five areas, in the one soil that is Dooyeweerd's philosophy. We have sought to construct these foundations, not by reference to neighbouring disciplines (Baskerville and Myers 2002), but by reference to the core meaningfulness of ICT itself, which is meaningful in all the discourses in each of the areas.

It has suggested frameworks that may serve as a foundational understanding for each based on a Dooyeweerdian understanding of what ICT is in its various realities. Since aspects, as spheres of oceanic meaningfulness and law, are also modes of being, functioning, rationality, possibility, normativity, etc., as discussed in §3-8, this provides foundations on which discussion of issues relevant to research and practice in each of the areas may rest. It has been discussed how foundational frameworks address the problems identified in the extant discourses, sometimes how they might help immanently critique those discourses, and how they might suggest enrichments. Research themes have been suggested, which are discussed again in Chapter 12.

Instead of trying to find the *identity* of the field of information systems and ICT, as Benbasat and Weber and others wish, they suggest the *dignity*, the *destiny* and the *responsibility* of the field (§8-6.3; Basden 2010), which are met in everyday experience.

As argued in §5-2.5, §8-6.1.1, these are centred on the *lingual aspect*. The lingual centre has informed and pervaded every one of the five areas, with retrocipation and antecipation to earlier and later aspects, and reaching out to all aspects as aspectual targets (§3-7.4). As discussed in §8-6.1.1, recognising the lingual foundation gives ICT a 'double mandate', to open up the lingual aspect and, because of new possibilities with information, to contribute to opening up other aspects too.

10-1.2 The Frameworks

The foundational frameworks may be summarised as follows (also in Figure 10.1):

- The *nature of ICT* (Chapter 5: information, computers and documents) is grounded in meaningfulness and understood as multi-aspectual being. This provides a way to break the stalemate that surrounds the artificial intelligence question. It also brings to the fore questions that are seldom asked.
- *ICT Use* (Chapter 6) is seen as subject-object and subject-subject engagements of three kinds, each of which exhibits all aspects and should be beneficial in each. The aspects identify key issues that are important and weave ethics into all considerations.
- *ICT Features* (Chapter 7) are seen as objects with which the user engages, composed of user interaction possibilities, innards or protocols. They work well for users to the extent that they appropriately encapsulate aspectual law. This provides deeper understanding of affordance and materiality.
- *ICT and Society* (Chapter 8) is seen as the interaction of two *Umwelten*, which may be understood as a multi-aspectual correlative enkapsis. This fruitfully addresses widespread use, structuration and progress as 'opening'. The information systems field was discussed.
- *ICT Development* (Chapter 9) is seen as at least four multi-aspectual responsibilities for the future potential use, which are enkaptically bound to each other. Each implies associated multi-aspectual development activity.

We aimed for certain characteristics that frameworks should exhibit. Breadth of each is assured by the use of Dooyeweerd's suite of aspects insofar as it is indeed comprehensive, flexibility, by Dooyeweerd's idea that aspects are spheres of law that make things possible, consistency, by the extent that Dooyeweerd's aspects and his whole philosophy are self-consistent, ability to both explain and guide, by the aspects being spheres of both meaningfulness and law, and relevance to both research and practice, by the aspects being those of everyday life rather than being derived from any specific theory, and by both 'dwelling within' the same ocean of meaningfulness.

10-1.3 On Multiple Frameworks and a Single Philosophy

In Chapter 1 we noted Weber's (2003) perplexity at the lack of "powerful, general theories" in the field of information systems and ICT and, against this, Lyytinen's (2003) belief that it is 'hopeless' to seek any 'ultimate foundation' and Jones' (2000) that this is "mission impossible". Have we proven Lyytinen wrong by finding an 'ultimate foundation' in Dooyeweerd's philosophy? Would those who take Lyytinen's line have to reject Dooyeweerd?

What Weber hoped for as a general theory, and what Lyytinen disliked as an 'ultimate foundation' appear to be something different from what we have discussed here. Lyytinen was rejecting the presupposition that one single way can be found of making theory and one single language and logic for the field of IS. Clouser (2005) argues that any possible 'ultimate foundation' that arises from an Immanence Standpoint will be reductionist in some way, and it seems to be reductionism that Lyytinen's dislikes. What we have found, using Dooyeweerd's philosophy, is that no single logic is possible in any of the areas, let alone across the areas. This is not because of reasons that Lyytinen adduces, which are based on the presumed autonomy of reason, but because of its very opposite. As Dooyeweerd revealed, theoretical thought itself is non-autonomous and there are multiple, irreducibly distinct rationalities (§3-4.3). In each area, different things are meaningful in a myriad of ways, and none should be forced into a meaning-framework that is too narrow for it.

This is why, in this book, we have not sought any single over-arching conceptual framework that covers all areas, but instead have constructed frameworks for understanding in each area. Each is able to affirm the discourses ('theories') in its area, each is critically founded, and each can help to enrich the discourses of practice and research. It can enrich the area as a whole in that each provides a way of situating discourses, exploring the relationships among them and welcoming new discourses whey they arise.

Might this satisfy Weber's (2003) concern about importing theories (§8-2.4)? As argued in §8-6.3, if the lingual meaning-sphere is the core, we may import theories about other meaning-spheres without losing our dignity. It is not a single framework that will provide core and coherence but a primary aspect as understood by a single philosophy as sphere of meaningfulness and law.

What makes a single root philosophy important is our desire to be able to make some sense of the 'whole story' that is ICT and information systems. We might bring the areas together by exploring the relationships between the areas at all levels, as depicted in Figure 10.1. Dooyeweerd's aspects might help us identify such relationships at any level. To identify and explore these relationships requires a whole research movement.

The harmony among the areas cannot, however, be captured in discretely identified relationships, however nuanced. It is constituted rather in the concepts in the frameworks formulated for each area deriving from the same philosophical stance. This means that the frameworks are compatible with each other conceptually. When those working in one area (say, ICT infrastructure) want to 'reach into' another area (say, the shaping of ICT features or ICT use) then there is a chance that they can do so without either denigration or misunderstanding.

Probably the main reason Dooyeweerd's philosophy has been able to do this is its recognition of oceanic meaningfulness and law, which transcends all the areas, and the everyday perspective that has been taken in each. Instead of seeking relationships, the next section discusses several concerns that cut across all areas.

10-2 Cross-Cutting Concerns

We discuss concerns that cut across all areas because these are things on which harmony among the foundational frameworks can be founded. The four most striking concerns that cut across all areas are that in all areas we have taken an everyday perspective rather than depending wholly on theory, we have treated meaningfulness as primary, we have tried to avoid separating normativity from understanding and we have been relatively independent of extant philosophies, employing Dooyeweerd's philosophy instead. Those are the main starting-points of Dooyeweerd's philosophy.

It might be tempting to treat Dooyeweerd's attempts to find a philosophical approach that was commensurate with his Christian beliefs but which could properly dialog with others, as a cross-cutting concern. Though that motivation certainly affected his philosophical ideas, it was not a primarily philosophical issue, and I have explained in §4-1.1 why I have not treated it as a starting-point.

10-2.1 Starting with Everyday Experience

Dooyeweerd started from everyday experience (§3-1.1). Not only did he deem it worth studying, but he believed that theoretical thought needs to be understood by reference to everyday experience (or as he called it, the pre-theoretical attitude of thought). He thus first explored the nature of, and conditions for, theoretical thought, before using this to understand everyday experience in its complexity, and indeed the nature of reality itself.

Likewise, we have sought to establish foundations in each of the areas of the field of information systems, by 'listening' to everyday experience as well as to theory. Everyday experience is treated as diverse and yet coherent in its meaningfulness and normativity (see next section). This makes the philosophical foundations that were created adequate to understand and guide not only research that properly understands everyday experience, but also everyday practice itself.

Theoretical thought is not denigrated, but rather seen in the context of everyday experience both of ICT itself and also of the research practice by which theoretical bodies of knowledge are generated and developed. Our everyday stance encourages us to situate ourselves 'outside' all extant theories, with some skepticism about their foundations; see §10-2.4. Extant theories are not rejected, but rather treated as offering some useful insights but flawed in their execution of those insights.

So, in each area, we have examined a number of discourses and sought to listen to, affirm, critique and enrich their theoretical approaches alongside their everyday experience. It is Dooyeweerd's philosophy that has made it possible, to avoid either acquiescing to extant theories without question or reacting against them, because it provides a foundation for seeing theoretical and pre-theoretical thought as part of the same reality. Instead, doors have been opened up, revealing paths to fruitful integrations towards a more humane ICT.

Everyday experience pervades all areas. The everyday experience of *ICT use*, discussed in Chapter 6, reveals that the human user engages with at least three things in different ways and with differing norms: with interface and technology (EIT: §6-3.4), with meaningful content (EMC, §6-3.5) and in life with ICT (ELI, §6-3.6), and each is diverse. The conceptual framework proposed in §6-3.2 covers both work and non-work domains of life, and enables us to think about functioning and repercussions, beneficial and detrimental, including unexpected ones, that are meaningful in every aspect.

The everyday experience of *ICT features*, discussed in Chapter 7, is largely in the proximal engagement that users have with them as they use ICT. This is best understood as a (Dooyeweerdian) law-subject-object relationship, in which features afford the user possibilities that are meaningful in various aspects. In each feature, several affordances might function simultaneously, especially among the different engagements that is ICT use.

The everyday experience of *ICT and society*, discussed in Chapter 8, is found in two ways, that widespread use of ICT in everyday life impacts society and the global environment, and that ICT as infrastructure impacts people's everyday experience. Both directions of this cyclical structuration process may be understood using Dooyeweerd's aspects.

The everyday experience of *ICT development*, discussed in Chapter 9, is found in the fulfilment of multi-aspectual responsibilities that constitute the development project. It includes, for example the joy of programming (Knuth 2001) or of getting to know domain experts intimately.

The discourses on the *nature of ICT*, discussed in Chapter 5, are largely conceptual, but everyday experience of information and computers involves and is based on our assumptions about what they are.

The everyday experience of *information systems research*, discussed in §4-3, are that research is not just an analytical process but involves all aspects of personalities, power relationships, attitudes and beliefs.

10-2.2 Starting With Meaningfulness and its Diversity and Coherence

One might expect that one of the cross-cutting concerns would be the ICT artefact (or system), or the human activity around it in use or development, or human or societal interpretation of it. But each of these is limited in its outlook and cannot properly accommodate the others. Moreover, each is amorphous; what does the artefact include: the hardware, software, purpose, documentation, users, its situation of use? Instead of trying to define this precisely, we focus on meaningfulness.

In making meaningfulness his starting-point (§3-1.2), Dooyeweerd was able to accommodate and account for being, activity, interpretation, as well as normativity, possibility and rationality, in ways that are philosophically sound (§3-7 to §3-9). Meaningfulness is like an 'ocean' in which all 'dwells' rather than something we add to things, and the same *ocean of meaningfulness* is shared by all things. Dooyeweerd called it the law-side. This oceanic meaningfulness is diverse and yet coherent, in that aspects of it may be delineated by theoretical analysis, but cannot be pulled apart in reality, and each aspect relates to the others in fundamental ways.

This meaningfulness pervades all areas of ICT or information systems. The *nature of ICT*, discussed in Chapter 5, is seen as a question of meaningfulness rather than substance, process or existential relating. Both information and computers are understood as multi-levelled being, each level qualified by a different aspect. Meaningfulness coheres in the being that is information, computer, program, etc.

ICT use is treated as meaningful in the lives of people, and its content conveys meaningfulness via signification (§6-3.2). Seeing meaningfulness as 'oceanic' (§6-3.3) offers a new way to understand cross-cultural use and unexpected and indirect repercussions of use, and also brings under one banner personal, organizational and societal use, along with pre-human impacts like climate-change emissions. It is Dooyeweerd's aspects that enable us to accept and address the diversity of all this. Meaningfulness coheres as the situation of use.

The idea of oceanic meaningfulness offers a way to understand how it can be that *ICT features*, which operate 'in-themselves' only in the physical or other early aspects can afford meaningfulness that is in the later aspects. Dooyeweerd's aspects offer a new way of understanding affordance (§7-3.3). They also provide a basis for understanding and judging appropriateness of features, in their user interfaces, innards and protocols (§7-4). Meaningfulness coheres in each feature and in the artefact comprising the features.

In *ICT and society*, a meaningfulness that transcends society and ICT alike provides destiny, dignity and responsibility, which, I have argued in §8-6.3, should be at the core of understanding the information systems field and enable us to understand progress as aspectual opening. It helps us understand the disparate widespread impacts of ICT (§8-4.2) and to clarify our approach to such issues as surveillance and e-government and of challenging usual assumptions about the digital divide (§8-4.3), and the multi-aspectual nature of structuration and infrastructure (§8-4.5, §8-5.3). Meaningfulness coheres in the historical-societal-religious phenomenon that is ICT.

ICT development, discussed in Chapter 9, is seen as anticipating future meaningful possibilities, and this implies responsibility. Meaningfulness pervades both the lives of developers and the impacts on stakeholders in their widest sense. Meaningfulness coheres around the ICT project and the artefact being produced.

Information systems research, discussed in Chapter 4, is grounded in meaningfulness in at least three ways: in its selection of what it is meaningful to study, in the rationalities (sense-making) that occur, and as origin of meaning, to which reference is made during critique of research and especially its paradigms. Meaningfulness coheres around the research aim and project. There is also a presupposition of a broader coherence among research approaches, such as social and technical, or positivist and interpretivist.

Inter-framework consistency is assured because all areas refer to the oceanic meaningfulness that transcends them.

10-2.3 Incorporating Normativity

Meaningfulness implies normativity, a difference between good and evil, beneficial and detrimental. As with meaningfulness, an understanding of the diversity of normativity, especially via Dooyeweerd's aspects (§3-7.5), enables us to separate out concerns that are normative or ethical in distinct ways, and free us, both in practice and research, from the tendency to either eulogise or demonise things. No longer need we be enslaved to technological or sociological fashions.

Normativity is easy to understand in ICT use as beneficiality, in ICT and society as opening, and in ICT development as responsibility for eventual functioning and repercussions that occur (in Chapters 6, 8, 9); see Figure 10.1. In ICT features normativity is most clearly located in appropriateness. Though it might expected that the *nature of ICT* is a-normative, there is an overall normativity of ICT to be meaningful, and the innate normativity of the aspects that make its multi-aspectual beings meaningful must not be neglected. The normativity of information is tied to the idea that information works well as information should, i.e., to inform, and it is multi-aspectual (§5-3.5). Similarly with the normativity of the computer (§5-4.3). What makes an information system 'good' is its ushering in of *shalom* (§3-8.5).

10-2.4 Independence From Conventional Philosophies

Dooyeweerd argued that most philosophy over the past centuries has taken an Immanence Standpoint, which has had a number of deleterious effects on philosophy itself (see §3-2.1), of which three that affect us are:

- Immanence philosophy has divorced meaningfulness from reality, and thus made it inherently difficult to explore the nature of meaningfulness.
- Immanence philosophy has prevented a truly sensitive approach to understanding everyday experience.

- Immanence philosophy has tended always to elevate one aspect of reality and ignore others, thus forming itself into warring factions and preventing a truly sensitive, interdisciplinary approach.

The Immanence Standpoint often generates dualistic ground-motives, which cause philosophy to swing between two poles and shut out half of reality at any one time, and breeds fruitless conflict.

Dooyeweerd eschewed the Immanence Standpoint and adopted a pluralistic ground-motive (§3-2.4) that was entirely comfortable with making everyday experience and meaningfulness the philosophical starting-points. It enabled him to understand theoretical thought in a new way and delineate his suite of aspects, which has proven so helpful in providing foundational understanding in all five areas in Part II.

He exercised an independence from extant philosophies of all kinds, which enabled him to uncover both their strengths and their deep flaws and not adhere to any. He was able to engage with such thinkers as Aristotle, Aquinas, Kant and Heidegger, neither acquiescing to their pronouncements nor rejecting them, but treating them as impaired insight.

In discussing ICT nature, use, features, society and development, occasional reference has been made to philosophers like these, as well as to more recent ones like Habermas, Bourdieu, Foucault, Bhaskar and others, which have been treated as Dooyeweerd would. The critique of individual philosophers that Dooyeweerd encourages is not at the level of internecine warfare between supporters of each, but at a deeper level of finding things we can jointly understand even though we disagree. He does this via his notion of Ground Idea, which, he argued, is relevant to all philosophies. An example of how this can bring apparently incommensurable approaches together is found in Section 4-2, which enables integration between them.

This is because of the approach we have tried to adopt across all areas, of listening, affirming, critiquing and enriching, as described in §4-1.3.

10-2.5 Listening, Affirming, Critiquing, Enriching

In all areas, our approach has been not to reject extant paradigms or theories but to listen immanently to the discourses, in order to discern issues that are centrally important (meaningful) to each, affirm what is most important, critique their presuppositions and suggest enrichments. This is discussed in the next chapter.

10-3 Extending the Frameworks

No claim has been made that the five areas explored here are the only ones. Instead, the discussion in Part II demonstrates how discourses may be identified in an area and laid alongside each other, how foundations of an area may be explored and how frameworks for understanding may be constructed. Other areas may be treated in a similar manner.

Might the discussion also offer something substantial to other fields? The discussion of ICT use might be extendable to any field where artefacts are employed in life. With pre-lingual technologies, engagement with meaningful content does not occur, but only engagement with technology and in life. The discussion of ICT development might be extendable to any activity of planning and development: seek to identify the multi-aspectual responsibilities therein and translate the intrinsic normativity of the aspects into guidance. The discussion of ICT features might be extendable to any kind of technology, for example in the construction industry. The discussion of ICT and society might be extendable to any societal issue, for example to mobility, by considering (a) whether it has a valid destiny, (b) the multi-aspectual nature of the circular structurational relationship, (c) idolatry. The discussion of 'What is ICT?' might be extendable to discussion of any kind of thing.

Example: They could be extended to that of sustainability—and indeed has been so extended by Brandon and Lombardi (2005), to provide an evaluative and guiding framework for urban sustainability, and Gunton et al. (2017), to extend the framework of ecosystem services. It has been employed in practice in agriculture on the Dutch farm, Eemlandhoeve, which tries to organise its life according to Dooyeweerd's aspects.

Whether this approach is possible without Dooyeweerd's philosophy, I cannot tell. Others must discover. However, I know that Dooyeweerd has worked, and worked well, so I recommend him.

10-4 Conclusion

The only way to find out the value of these frameworks, either in ICT or elsewhere, is for a wide range of researchers and practitioners to explore it further and act on the ideas suggested here. They might fail, or some might succeed. The next chapter will discuss the potential value ("So what?") of the application of Dooyeweerd's thought in the five areas of interest, and of Dooyeweerd's thought itself, and the limitations of our discussion.

References

Basden A. 2010. On using spheres of meaning to define and dignify the IS discipline. *International Journal of Information Management*, 30, 13–20.

Baskerville RL, Myers MD. 2002. Information systems as a reference discipline. *MIS Quarterly*, 26(1), 1–14.

Benbasat I, Weber R. 1996. Research commentary: Rethinking 'diversity' in information systems research. *Information Systems Research*, 7(4), 389–399.

Brandon PS, Lombardi P. 2005. *Evaluating Sustainable Development in the Built Environment*. Blackwell Science, Oxford, UK.

Clouser R. 2005. *The Myth of Religious Neutrality: An Essay on the Hidden Role of Religious Belief in Theories*. University of Notre Dame Press, Notre Dame, IN.

Dooyeweerd H. 1955. *A New Critique of Theoretical Thought* (Vols. I–IV, 1975 ed.). Paideia Press, Jordan Station, Ontario, Canada.

Gunton RM, van Asperen E, Basden A, Bookless D, Araya Y, Hanson DR, Goddard MA, Otieno G, Jones GO. 2017. Beyond ecosystem services: Valuing the invaluable. *Trends in Ecology and Evolution*, 32(4), 249-57.

Jones M. 2000. Mission impossible: Pluralism and 'multi-paradigm' IS research. *Information Systems Review*, 1(1), 217–232.

Knuth D. 2001. *Things a Computer Scientist Rarely Talks About*. CSLI, Stanford, CA.

Lyytinen KJ. 2003. Information systems and philosophy: The hopeless search for ultimate foundations. In JI DeGross (Ed.), *Proceedings of the Americas Conference on Information Systems: AMCIS 2003*. Association for Information Systems, Atlanta, GA.

Weber R. 2003. Editor's comments: Still desperately seeking the IT artifact. *MIS Quarterly*, 27(2), iii–xi.

11 Contributions and Limitations

Water, water everywhere
Nor any drop to drink

—Coleridge, *The Rime of the Ancient Mariner*

Aspects, aspects everywhere—but do we stop to think? Dooyeweerd's aspects are like an ocean, surrounding us (see §3-1.2.3)—over 20 tables with aspects in five chapters! As with Coleridge's mariner, might this ocean bring refreshment or be a torment?

The reason for using Dooyeweerd's aspects so much is precisely because they are, Dooyeweerd claimed, a best guess at understanding the diverse structure of reality that enables all to Be, Occur and Become. They are a best guess at the ways in which things may be meaningful at a fundamental level that pertains for all, regardless of culture, time or identity.

We should not look to aspects for answers, nor even for ready-made questions, but rather (to change our metaphor) to open up spaces for discourse. Aspects provide a view of where all the spaces are and help us situate extant discourses and issues that we find important, and to produce new ones.

Aspects, though the main portion of Dooyeweerd's thought to be employed in these discussions, are not the only portion. This chapter discusses the contributions that our discussions might make, and some of their limitations, before making recommendations in the next chapter.

11-1 Contributions to the Information Systems Field

The discussions in Part II offer contributions of relevance for each of the five areas of interest. However, before discussing those, it is useful to discuss the relevance of both Chapters 3 and 4 and Part II more generally, for the entire field of information systems and partially that of computer science, for research methods and for philosophy in various ways.

In Mingers and Willcocks' (2004) *Social Theory and Philosophy for Information Systems*, each chapter is devoted to a single philosophical approach, each written by an advocate thereof. Each chapter seems to tackle one main issue or area, as summarised in Table 2.1 in Chapter 2. Though this does not mean that each philosopher can only deal with one issue or area, it is perhaps an indication of their strengths and limitations. By contrast, as shown in the five main chapters here, Dooyeweerd is able to address all the issues that are meaningful in the wide range of discourses reviewed therein.

He does so by offering a philosophy that is different from, but not incommensurable with, conventional philosophies, and so is able to engage with them. Dooyeweerd is, perhaps, a meta-philosopher. (This ability to engage has been indicated in the text but will be discussed more fully in a forthcoming work.)

Whereas in the information systems field, social and technical have been brought together as a duality, which always threatens to become a dualism, Dooyeweerd's aspects provide a pluralistic view that some, such as Lee (2004), have recognised as necessary.

Dooyeweerd gives us a basis for affirming the dignity, destiny and responsibility of the IS field (§8-6.3). It can therefore resist being either isolated or submerged into other fields like business or organizational or computer science, and can interact with those fields with confidence. Perhaps this provides a basis for reinvigorating dialogue with the fields of human-computer interaction, computer science and software engineering and starting dialogue with artificial intelligence (see §6-4.1 and Chapters 7, 9 and 5).

Dooyeweerd has enabled us to bring five major areas together, those that treat ICT as a black box alongside those that try to understand ICT in its 'materiality'. The discourses in these areas can now be situated in relation to each other, with mutual benefit, by reference to the 'ocean of meaningfulness' within which all exist and occur (§3-1.2.3).

In each area, Dooyeweerd has helped us escape the straitjacket of dualistic ground-motives that incite unnecessary conflict between perspectives that work well together in everyday experience—especially those of determinism versus freedom and sacred versus secular. He encourages us not only to value everyday experience as something worth studying but, making the pre-theoretical attitude of thought the starting point (§3-1.1), to give theory a more healthy role, as servant rather than master. His view incorporates normativity and plurality and coherence right from the start, making it easy to generate or critically refine practical principles in a way that practice finds natural, rich and helpful. His view of time and progress (§3-3.2), especially as developed by Schuurman (§8-6.2), links past, present and future, and innovation with responsibility.

It has been shown how wide the range of discourses is, or could potentially be, in each area, and how they may be situated and, perhaps even integrated, in a wider landscape and engage in cross-discourse dialogue. Discourses that have traditionally been isolated from, or overlooked by, mainstream information systems thought can be affirmed in their importance—e.g., materiality of ICT (§7-2.2), computer games (§6-2.6; §6-4.6, §9-2.6) or religion, idolatry and ideology (§8-4.3). Pre-human, human,

Table 11.1 Summary of How Dooyeweerd's Philosophy Has Been Employed to Affirm, Critique, and Enrich Each Area

Area	*Affirmation*	*Critique*	*Enrichment*
Nature of ICT	1. Being of ICT as meaningfulness. 2. Data, information, knowledge: different aspects of same thing. 3. Program is virtual law-side. It might also be like performance art. 4. Computers, documents are multi-level beings, with many aspects. 5. "Computer = Human?" refer to Dooyeweerdian subject and object functioning in each aspect.	1. Most "What is?" discourse presumes primacy of being, which leads to antinomies. 2. Discourse on data, information, knowledge presumes substance idea or subject-object conflation, rather than aspects of one thing. 3. Little discussion on what a program is. 4. Too much focus on certain aspects. 5. AI question unresolvable under dualistic ground-motives. Use CFR ground-motive.	1. Being as multi-aspectual. 2,3,4. Aspects everywhere! Think about law-subject-object relation, especially in aspects not usually considered. 5. AI question has two answers: subject functioning, any functioning. ICT functions as subject-by-proxy in lingual aspect.
ICT Use	1. ICT use as meaningful everyday experience. 2. All discourses part of wider picture. 3. Aspectual engagements framework: three intertwined multi-aspectual human engagements with ICT, each a Dooyeweerdian subject-object relationship. 4. Each discourse is around selected engagements, aspects.	1. Over-theorizing isolates discourses into silos, e.g. ethics, games, GIS. 2. Some discourses missing from academia. 3. Nature-freedom ground-motive generates problematic dichotomies and reactions. EMC under-researched; few discourses recognise all three engagements. 4. Narrow focus on certain aspects (esp. formative, social, economic), little integration.	1,2. Dooyeweerd's everyday perspective reveals wider picture; use the aspectual engagements framework to facilitate inter-discourse discourse. With aspectual normativity, integrate ethics into all discourses. 3,4. Consider EMC alongside EIT, ELI: all three. Widen the range of aspects that are meaningful in each discourse.

ICT Features	1. Ocean of meaningfulness common to both users and features ('materiality'). 2. Features are seen in light of Dooyeweerdian subject-object relationship. 3. Two important issues: affordance, appropriateness. Understood by Dooyeweerd's aspects. 4. Materiality (physical analogy): directly understood as encapsulation of aspectual laws in three elements (interaction possibilities, innards, protocols).	1. Nature-freedom ground-motive has led IS scholars to oppose social/human to materiality of ICT. 2. Cartesian, Heideggerian subject-object ideas cannot explain affordance as in everyday experience. 3a. No basis for bringing different kinds and types of affordance together. 3b. Normativity (quality, appropriateness) of features is only weakly understood. 4. Materiality: too much reliance on metaphors.	1,2. Oceanic view of meaningfulness brings human and materiality together, understood as Dooyeweerdian proximal subject-object relationship in many aspects. 3a. Kinds, types of affordance: understood and situated as aspect triples. 3b. Normativity = norms of each aspect. 4. This can help design of good features and their elements, and of software libraries. 5. This can link information systems field with computer science.
ICT and Society See Table 8.5.	1. Impact of widespread ICT use: multiplied functioning in each aspect, with innate normativity. 2. Infrastructures: *Umwelten* constituted in correlative enkapsis, in which juridical, ethical, pistic aspect are important; examples: digital divide, surveillance, e-government. 3. ICT-society relationship: inter-*Umwelt* relationship, each functioning in a different range of aspects. 4. IS field: define by mandate to open up lingual aspect and thereby open up other aspects. 5. Technological progress: aspectual opening.	1. Narrow range of aspects considered. 2. Infrastructure issues are viewed through narrow lens of economic, formative, juridical aspects. Ethical, pistic not understood, esp. re. values, idolatry. 3. Dualistic ground-motive traps theories (e.g. TD-SCOT-SST); Immanence Standpoint isolates thinking from everyday experience and hinders agency-structure understanding; lack of understanding of *Umwelt*. 4. Approaches to IS field look to past, ignore lingual aspect and meaningfulness. 5. Progress is unquestioningly either rejected or accepted.	1. Recognise all aspects of widespread use, and their normativity. 2. Recognise importance of pistic, ethical aspects of ICT infrastructure, and its multi-aspectual normativity. 3. Offer plurality of aspects to widen extant theories and understand structure-agency nexus, and bring theories closer to everyday experience. 4. See IS field as centring on lingual aspect with neighbouring aspects, with mandate to open up all aspects (Schuurman's liberating vision). 5. Recognise both benefits of aspectual opening, and also dangers of hubris, self-interest and idolatry.

(*Continued*)

Table 11.1 (Continued)

Area	*Affirmation*	*Critique*	*Enrichment*
ICT Development	1. All development activity seen as multi-aspectual human functioning, oriented towards future possibility. 2. Four responsibilities, each of which involves every aspect and its normativity. 3. Extant discourses and most types of development activity seen oriented towards certain aspects / responsibilities. 4. Dooyeweerd's respect for everyday experience affirms ICT dev. as a practical endeavour that can be understood philosophically.	1,2. Nature-freedom ground-motive sets freedom v control; both neglect responsibility. 3. Theorizing tendency in academia hinders interaction of extant discourses. 4. ICT development has little philosophical foundation.	1. Seeing ICT development as responsibility for possibility invites us to consider every aspect of each, including overlooked ones. 2. Design-coding-testing becomes artefact-creation; user requirements analysis becomes use-anticipation and domain-understanding; project management becomes project-orchestration. All developers exercise all responsibilities (c.f. Agile). 3. Discourses may understand each other via aspects (common meaningfulness). 4. The everyday-oriented philosophical foundation offered here can be developed further by exploring other portions of Dooyeweerd's thought.

technical, organizational, societal and global issues are all brought together under one banner of an 'ocean of meaningfulness' that is diverse.

We have shown how it is possible to listen to, affirm, critique and enrich many discourses in each area. Listening has been by identifying actual or potential discourses and trying to immanently understand the issues they find important. Table 11.1 summarises affirmation, critique and enrichment for the five areas. The numbering in the cells sometimes matches that in neighbouring cells, but sometimes does not. Chapter 12 collects together the specific suggestions for research that have been mentioned in previous chapters.

A more elaborate summary of how various parts of Dooyeweerd's philosophy have been relevant, and their degree of importance, may be found in the tables in Chapter IX of Basden (2008).

11-2 Contributions to Information Systems Research

Research is seen, in its broadest sense, as contributing 'knowledge' to humanity's bodies of knowledge in various fields, where 'knowledge' is beliefs about the way that reality works, which are general and are worthy of being relied upon. 'Research' has been used here to cover both scientific and philosophical theoretical activity, even though philosophers might not normally consider what they do as research.

Contributions to IS research are discussed in Chapter 4. These include: disclosing the influence of the Nature-freedom ground-motive (§3-2.3) on the paradigms and lenses that guide our research, freeing us from the conflicts engendered by it, offering a way to affirm, critique and enrich extant paradigms by means of their Ground-Ideas (§3-5) and bring new ones to birth, understanding the lenses that are applied during research and the relationships between them and, most practical of all, providing methods of data collection and analysis that are open to down-to-earth issues and ways of analysing their plethoric complexity. These have been demonstrated in Chapters 5 to 9.

11-3 Possible Contributions to Philosophy?

Throughout our discussions, suggestions have been made that might indicate contributions to Dooyeweerd's philosophy, to philosophy of technology and to philosophy in general. Though this book is not primarily about philosophy itself, a few of them are listed in §12-7. Some are discussed in Basden (2008), and some possible contributions to philosophy of technology are discussed in §8-6.2 and §5-2. It is intended that contributions to philosophy will be discussed in a forthcoming work that discusses Dooyeweerd's philosophy in more detail in relation to others that researchers might encounter than was possible in Chapter 3, and are not discussed here. What is relevant here, however, is criticisms of Dooyeweerd, because those who apply his ideas need to be aware of these. So they are briefly discussed in the next section.

11-4 Limitations of This Discussion

This section briefly discusses some main limitations of this study.

11-4.1 Limitations in the Reviews of Discourses

In every area, a number of discourses have been selected for discussion. The selection, though informed by what others have said, is my own, based on my experience, over 50 years, of what seems important.

Some of the discussion is likely to be unbalanced or to have misunderstood. The depth with which discourses have been reviewed is variable and in most cases, too meagre to be taken as authoritative. In some, the cited work is dated. In every case, word count limits has prevented my discussing as deeply as I would like to.

Does this invalidate the arguments? The purposes of reviewing the discourses are three, and they do *not* include trying to obtain a comprehensive picture of any discourse that is authoritative. They are (a) to identify issues that are important in the area, so that we might gain a picture of the whole area, (b) to provide a backdrop against which we can suggest how discourses might be affirmed, critiqued and enriched; (c) to bring together discourses that are seldom brought side-by-side and draw attention to some that are overlooked. None of these purposes is completely undermined by the flaws in the treatment, even though fuller reviews might achieve the purposes more fully.

I invite readers who are more expert in the discourses than I am to redo the exercises here. I give them permission to use these ideas respectfully as though their own.

In addition, some discourses are likely to have been neglected. For the neglected discourses, I invite readers to adopt the approach taken here in order to offer contributions.

For example, I have not covered ubiquitous computing and the Internet of Things, where computing power is embedded in kettles, fridges, cars, etc. While I was writing this book, a major denial-of-service attack was launched by harnessing the computing power of these devices. Nor have I discussed digital marketing. Though it has recently become important, it is still in its infancy of both understanding and practice; it is too early to know whether it is a temporary fad or a change of historic proportions, so I have not commented on it. Topics like these might be investigated, as for example:

- Nature of ICT: What is the role of the lingual aspect in these? If none (e.g., embedded standalone controller), treat them as general technology.

Otherwise, treat them as a virtual law-side, and ask what aspectual laws are encapsulated within them.

- ICT use: What is the users' engagement with interface and technology, meaningful content, and in life? What is the meaningful content, and how might users engage in each aspect? In which aspects might there be repercussions in each? The denial-of-service attack depended on all this.
- ICT features: How appropriate are the interaction possibilities, innards and protocols? What are their affordances (of any kind)?
- ICT and society: Has the affluent cohort of the world taken such devices for granted? Where is e.g. digital marketing inappropriate?
- ICT development: How are developers fulfilling their four responsibilities? Most ubiquitous devices have meagre security protection.

11-4.2 My Interpretation of Dooyeweerd's Philosophy

My own interpretation of Dooyeweerd's ideas is partial and influenced by several desires and presuppositions. Here I outline some of the main ones, so readers might take them into account.

My emphasis on Dooyeweerd's starting points of everyday experience (§3-1.1) might extend somewhat his philosophical version of the pre-theoretical attitude of thought (he seldom uses the word 'everyday'). My emphasis is motivated by my having spent a dozen years outwith academic life in ICT, and my belief that ICT must be situated in 'everyday experience' in all life domains. I believe I am justified in my interpretation because of the many references to what I have called everyday experience throughout his writings.

My idea of 'ocean of meaningfulness' (§3-1.2) is an interpretation of Dooyeweerd's idea of law-side coupled with his clear statements at the start of his *magnum opus* (Dooyeweerd 1955) about Being rooted in Meaning. I have been told it is easier to understand than Dooyeweerd's own text because it tries to make more systematic what Dooyeweerd sometimes merely alluded to. It has proven useful throughout this book to point to new paradigms and possibilities for research and practice.

My understanding of the Immanence Standpoint and ground-motives is, I believe, fairly close to what Dooyeweerd intended, but perhaps has been oversimplified, especially in comparison with Dooyeweerd's (1979) discussion of them.

My understanding of Dooyeweerd's idea of law-subject-object relationships (§3-3.1) might be more systematic than Dooyeweerd intended, but I believe it is faithful to his ideas.

My interpretation of Dooyeweerd's idea of time (§3-3.2) might be awry. I have never found a clear exposition by Dooyeweerd of what he called "cosmic time", so I have had to work out what he meant. The view that time is constituted in the subject-object-side functioning-response to the law-side seems useful, but perhaps I am attracted by its radicality.

My understanding of Dooyeweerd's transcendental critique of theoretical thought (§3-4.3) and Ground-Idea (§3-5) is an interpretation of Dooyeweerd's convoluted presentations of it, applying it to science, whereas the bulk of Dooyeweerd's discussion was about philosophy. I have played down Dooyeweerd's discussion of the self, because it is tortuous and it seemed to suggest as transcendental something that is patently not so (while engaged in theoretical thought I am *not* always trying to analyse what 'self' is). Moreover, I found my interpretation of Ground Idea as world, rationalities and wider meaningfulness, has helped to understand all research approaches employed in the information systems field better than anyone else has been able to do (§4-2).

My understanding of Dooyeweerd's aspects, what they do and which ones there are (§3-6 to §3-8) is a systematic rendering of an understanding that has developed over 20 years from both theorizing, reflection and application. I would defend it as largely what Dooyeweerd had in mind.

My understanding of Dooyeweerd's theory of things, relationships and enkapsis (§3-9) is reasonably standard, but might include some imbalances.

11-4.3 Criticism of Dooyeweerd's Philosophy

There have been a number of critiques of Dooyeweerd over the years. Dooyeweerd himself welcomed criticism, and the criticism levelled at his first *magnum opus* (Dooyeweerd 1935) led to significant revision of his thought (Dooyeweerd 1955). But even after this, he was relatively modest about his philosophy, acknowledging that much of it stood in need of critique and refinement, and he was rather disappointed that it received so little good quality attention. The reason for his modesty is to be found partly in his Christian faith, which sees humility as a virtue, but is also to be found in his philosophy itself, which stresses that philosophy is not some avenue to absolute truth (see §3-4.1).

Unfortunately, the bulk of the criticism has been superficial. Some mainstream thinkers who are ideologically anti-essentialist mistake Dooyeweerd's idea of aspects that transcend us for essentialism, and reject it, without understanding Dooyeweerd's own anti-essentialist stance. Some of the criticisms are directed at how followers of Dooyeweerd have worked out his ideas, rather than of Dooyeweerd's ideas directly. Some Christian thinkers have criticised him for getting involved with philosophy rather than apologetics or theology, or have picked small holes around wording Dooyeweerd used.

Dooyeweerd's thought has been subjected to some more substantial critique, but not yet enough. Many have argued with his suite of aspects, redefining some or adding others. Dooyeweerd's emphasis on meaningfulness has been criticised as leaning too much towards the Linguistic Turn in philosophy. His transcendental critique of theoretical thought (§3-4.3) has been criticised for not being truly transcendental and in need of reinterpretation. His view of progress has been criticised as too conveniently close to Western progress. These criticisms have been referred to at various places in our discussions, and a more extensive discussion can be found in Basden (2008) and in the forthcoming work on Dooyeweerd.

All these critics, however, acknowledge the value of his ideas as providing radically fruitful avenues for philosophy. None yet has proposed a radical change in his thought and approach.

The main problem is that there have not been enough attempts to understand and employ Dooyeweerd in mainstream thought, so it is not yet clear wherein lie the real and important weaknesses of his thought. Though his ideas have begun to be applied in information systems and sustainability (see §3-8.5) and in technology teaching (Verkerk et al. 2015), they need much wider application in these fields and others and proper critique in philosophy, to provide proper critique on the basis of experience rather than philosophical stance. Only once this has happened will weaknesses emerge, and only when a serious, mainstream attempt has been made to overcome the weaknesses, will the most important weaknesses—the ones that cannot be overcome—be understood.

There has been very little if any critique of Dooyeweerd from mainstream philosophies. Though Dooyeweerd's mention of 'Christian philosophy' might alienate some who misunderstand Dooyeweerd's intention, it is probably also due to the characteristics of the current streams of philosophy themselves that limit their capacity to understand Dooyeweerd immanently. Analytic philosophy might find some issues he dealt with meaningless. Postmodernists might mistakenly dismiss his ideas as a 'grand narrative'. Neo-Kantians might be upset by Dooyeweerd's criticism. Phenomenology and existentialism might find his separation of law-side from subject-object-side confusing. Critical theory might feel threatened by the suggestion that emancipation and power are too limited in aspectual terms, despite Dooyeweerd being clearly commensurate with socio-critical theory (Basden 2002).

The challenge we face is that Dooyeweerd worked at a level deeper than the wars between Humanism and Scholasticism, between pre- and post-Kantian thought, between positivist, interpretivist and criticalist thought, between modernism and postmodernism. Until that is understood, no serious critique from mainstream philosophy is possible. I repeat:

> It will probably take someone of the calibre of Jürgen Habermas, who, like Dooyeweerd, has engaged in careful immanent critique of other thinkers and transcendental critique of issues, to sensitively yet powerfully get to grips with what Dooyeweerd was trying to do, understand it in its own terms, not get sidetracked by secondary issues with which Dooyeweerd's text is sprinkled, and on that basis make a real critique.
> (Basden 2008, 115)

I hope this book will stimulate (a) serious application in the information systems and related fields like computer science, software engineering, human-computer interaction and artificial intelligence, (b) serious consideration in other fields by taking this book as an exemplar of how Dooyeweerd's ideas might be applied there, and perhaps (c) interest among mainstream philosophers.

It might have seemed that Dooyeweerd's suite of aspects is almost a panacea. Could other suites of aspects be employed instead? It has been argued in §3-6.3 that Dooyeweerd's suite seems to be the best so far available, but that does not preclude the possibility of a better one appearing. However, before Dooyeweerd's suite is rejected, it must be properly understood and widely applied. For that to happen, we need practioners and especially researchers to adopt Dooyeweerd's ideas and run with them, discovering by practice what are their weaknesses.

11-5 Conclusion

This chapter has discussed the relevance and possible contributions that the Dooyeweerdian foundational understanding might make for practice and research, as well as some limitations. For these possibilities to be realised and tested, it is necessary that readers take action to employ Dooyeweerdian ideas in their practice and research. The next chapter discusses 'What Now?' It contains recommendations for actual of work that can be carried out.

References

Basden A. 2002. The critical theory of Herman Dooyeweerd? *Journal of Information Technology*, 17, 257–269.

Basden A. 2008. *Philosophical Frameworks for Understanding Information Systems*. IGI Global, Hershey, PA.

Dooyeweerd H. 1935. *De Wijsbegeerte der Wetsidee* (3 vols.). H.J. Paris, Amsterdam, the Netherlands.

Dooyeweerd H. 1955. *A New Critique of Theoretical Thought* (Vols. I–IV). Paideia Press, Jordan Station, Ontario, Canada.

Dooyeweerd H. 1979. *Roots of Western Culture: Pagan, Secular and Christian Options*. Wedge Publishing Company, Toronto, Ontario, Canada.

Lee AS. 2004. Thinking about social theory and philosophy in information systems. In J Mingers, LP Willcocks (Eds.), *Social Theory and Philosophy for Information Systems* (pp. 1–26). John Wiley & Sons, Chichester, UK.

Mingers J, Willcocks L. (Eds.). 2004. *Social Theory and Philosophy for Information Systems*. John Wiley & Sons, Chichester, UK.

Verkerk MJ, Hoogland J, van der Stoep J, de Vries MJ. 2015. *Philosophy of Technology: An Introduction for Technology and Business Students*. Routledge, London, UK.

12 Opportunities and Recommendations

Foundations have been laid; they need to be built on. Chapter 11 has discussed what contributions might be made and some of the limitations. The aim of this chapter is action.

Despite the arguments in this work sometimes being sketchy, they have yielded a plethora of suggestions. *Because* they are sketchy, readers are invited to take the arguments further. In this final chapter, some opportunities in research and practice are offered as specific recommendations. They are all in the light of Dooyeweerd's ideas and of the foundational frameworks constructed in Chapters 5 to 9 for understanding:

- the nature of ICT, as multi-aspectual things,
- ICT use, as three multi-aspectual engagements,
- ICT features, with triple-aspect affordance and appropriateness,
- ICT and society, as aspectual structuration, and
- ICT development, as four multi-aspectual responsibilities.

12-1 This Final Chapter

The bulk of this chapter consists of over a hundred specific suggestions for what might be done, drawn from the main chapters, in order that information systems (IS) practice and research might benefit from this unique approach.

Forming the bulk of this chapter are a number of lengthy tables containing the suggestions. They might seem overpowering and perhaps should be an appendix, yet hiding suggestions away does not encourage action. The decision to keep them as part of the main text was made when one person became excited just by reading through the tables! Readers might prefer to just browse them, or even to skip them altogether, over to the final part.

The final part is a brief discussion of how to take this work forward.

12-2 The Role of Foundations

This work has discussed foundations. Using the construction industry as a metaphor, foundations are laid, on foundations are built the frameworks and around frameworks buildings are constructed. These buildings are fitted out and then lived or worked in. In the soil of Dooyeweerd's philosophy foundational understandings have been laid, and five frameworks for understanding have been built. The buildings are perhaps discourses, and the fitting-out is perhaps the theories or general principles that have been added to our bodies of knowledge—which can then be used in life and work.

We might be tempted to suggest that on top of theories is built practice, but that is where the metaphor breaks down—for two reasons, known to Dooyeweerd. One is that much practice is carried out without explicit or even implicit reference to theories, but perhaps informed by some kind of paradigm (usually called a 'worldview') or presuppositions. Another is that the doing of theory, forming of paradigms and doing of philosophy are themselves practice. For practice, instead of paradigms and theories, we have scaffolding of principles and methodologies.

Foundational frameworks can provide recommendations in four ways: for principles and guidelines for *practice*, for *research* that advances the theoretical body of knowledge of our field, for *new ways of thinking* (paradigms?) about issues or perhaps suggesting how extant ways may be extended, and for sharpening themselves or each other by *philosophical reflection* on whole areas or the field as a whole. Suggestions for each are presented in the four tables.

This does not imply that the frameworks, paradigms or theories are in any way determined by the foundation; other factors come into play. Rather, the foundation provides philosophical understanding of what it is important to think about at all these levels.

12-3 Opportunities for Research and Practice

In each of the chapters, a framework for understanding an area related to ICT has been presented and applied to a range of issues in the area. From the ensuing discussions, suggestions have arisen for practical techniques and for research that ranges from individual, perhaps PhD-sized, projects to long-term research activities. The suggestions have been collected together on the website:

www.dooy.info/r/fisrp/

so that they can be updated as research is carried out or new suggestions emerge.

The next four sections summarise them: recommendations for practice, opportunities for research, new ways of seeing and philosophical suggestions. Readers might wish to use the sections either to find ideas for research that interests them and follow it, or to gain a broad view of the myriad of new research avenues that are opened up by the approach here. Either way,

I am happy if people take these ideas, run with them and receive the credit for any findings that emerge.

Each is presented in tabular form, so that readers can more easily scan and pick up opportunities that might interest them. In all tables, column 1 shows the opportunity, with a brief topic in bold, column 2 shows a type of opportunity, which is different for each table and is explained in the section. Column 3 indicates which portions of Dooyeweerd's thinking or the frameworks developed in the main chapters might be most relevant. Column 4 identifies sections where this opportunity is discussed, or which might inform it.

Column-3 abbreviations in all sections are:

- AEF = Aspectual Engagements Framework (Three multi-aspectual engagements in ICT use)
- Asp-x = Aspects with particular reference to x:
  - Asp-A = Inter-aspect analogy
  - Asp-C = The rich constellation of meaningfulness around an aspect
  - Asp-D = Inter-aspect dependency
  - Asp-F = Aspectual functioning and repercussions thereof
  - Asp-G = Gegenstand in various aspects
  - Asp-I = Irreducibility among aspects, categorization
  - Asp-K = Aspects or ways of knowing
  - Asp-L = Laws of aspects; aspectual law
  - Asp-M = Aspectual meaningfulness; kernel meanings
  - Asp-N = Aspectual normativity, responsibility; towards the Good
  - Asp-O = Overlooked aspects
  - Asp-P = Aspectual possibility
  - Asp-Q = Qualifying aspect and aspectual roles
  - Asp-R = Aspectual rationalities
  - Asp-S = Suite of aspects/Shalom/Salaam
  - Asp-T = Aspectual target
  - Asp-V = Levels of existence; multi-aspectual being
  - Asp-W = The whole suite of aspects taken together
  - Asp-X = Undefined: All the above
- Disc = Disciplines as centred on an aspect
- DivM = Diversity of meaning
- EDX = Everyday experience
- Enk = Enkaptic relationships between things
- FtC = Components of ICT features
- G-I = Ground-Ideas
- GMtv = Ground-motive
- Know = Dooyeweerd's theory of knowledge
- Law = Dooyeweerd's idea of law-side; c.f. Ocean

- LSO = Law-subject-object relation
- MAF = Multi-aspectual functioning
- Mng = Meaning, Meaningfulness
- Ocean = Meaningfulness as an 'ocean' within which all exist and occur
- Prog = Dooyeweerd's idea of progress
- T-C = Transcendental critique
- Thing = Dooyeweerd's theory of thingness, types and change
- Time = Dooyeweerd's idea of time
- Umw = *Umwelt*, correlative enkapsis

12-4 Opportunities to Enhance Practice

This work began with the case of Volkswagen's 'defeat device', a piece of software code that switched pollution controls off under normal driving conditions. All five areas of interest in ICT are exhibited in that episode. Can any of our discussion of Dooyeweerdian foundations for understanding ICT and information systems be useful in such practical cases, actual or potential?

- Defeat device use. Consider engagements of DD with users, as set out in Chapter 6: there is very little EIT or EMC except by engineers, but much ELI. Identify users (stakeholders) by reference to aspects: physical (releasing gases) affects planet; organic-biotic (pollution) affects people and communities and, indirectly, the health service; formative (technology), economic (lower costs), juridical (keeping within letter of law), ethical (cheating), pistic (vision of VW), are all the functioning of Volkswagen.
- Defeat device development. Consider all four responsibilities, in each aspect, and who should bear each. This helps us understand better what went wrong. If the inclusion of this defeat device was the work of "a couple of rogue programmers", as was claimed, then the analytic, formative, social and pistic (belief about their role in VW and in life) aspects were operative, in creating the artefact (programming), anticipating use (cheating), domain understanding (chemistry) and project orchestration (either hiding the idea from management, or colluding therewith). However, project orchestration implicates VW management. Either they sanctioned the deceit (VW developed several versions of the defeat device) or, if not, was there a company culture of control and fear (social, pistic), as some have claimed? Did ICT assume too much importance as a solution, and too little as a normative issue? Were employees seen, not as full human beings, nor even members of the VW family, but as items to control and use? Was it wrongly assumed that customers were uninterested in the level of pollution they caused when driving? All such social and pistic factors combined to lead to the decision to install cheat devices.
- Defeat device features. Volkswagen used lean nitrogen technology for pollution control rather than urea-based technology which others had used but LNT was less effective. Instead of analysing issues and engineering better

LNT or even turning to UBT, VW used its engineering prowess to cheat, it was claimed. The defeat device afforded more engine power (physical), cheating (juridical), and perhaps laziness in not developing better LNT (formative). It might have been appropriate physically but not juridically.

- Defeat device and Society. At another level comes the main shock we felt: a widely respected company was discovered cheating. Our belief (pistic aspect) was undermined. It is often the pistic aspect that engenders the deepest and longest-lasting reactions, whether positive or, as in this case, negative. The ethical aspect often accompanies the pistic, in that VW was revealed as no longer an upright, moral company whose primary interest was to serve its customers and the world, but as self-serving. Was the idea of ethical corporations itself seriously undermined, leading indirectly to worldwide reaction against the political-economic establishment?
- Nature of defeat device. Mainly embedded software and associated hardware, a virtual law-side that runs part of the car, in ways that are meaningful in several aspects. The encapsulated laws were not just physical but also analytic (whether in test mode) and juridical-ethical (self-serving deceit).

Thus we see how the frameworks and especially Dooyeweerd's aspects, can help us practically to understand more fully. They can also be used to act.

In Table 12.1 below is collected together various suggestions for how practice—including the practice of research—in ICT and IS in all areas might be enhanced. Some are relevant to other fields.

Key to Column 2 (How: the type of practical activity):

- Anal: Analysing, incl. in practice of research
- Attd: Changing attitudes
- Dsgn: Designing
- Eval: Evaluating things
- ISD: IS development
- Itvw: Interviewing
- Set: Setting parameters
- Writ: Writing up research

12-5 Opportunities for Research in Each Area of the IS Field

Table 12.2, on page 403, summarises some opportunities for research mentioned in each chapter. Some are about models, some more about paradigms or approaches. Some suggestions affirm, critique and enrich extant thought, while others suggest new ideas. This work has focused on the information systems field but has sometimes strayed towards HCI or computer science.

Table 12.1 Opportunities for Enhancing Practice

Enhancement	*How*	*Portions of Dooy*	*See*
The practice of analysis and research			
Informal aspectual analysis: In any situation or discussion, we can be aware of which aspects are being acted out or discussed, and which are being neglected, and can perhaps gently draw attention to absent aspects. Aspectual meanings are grasped intuitively, hence low cognitive load.	Anal	Asp-MS	§3-7.3 §4-4.2.1
Aspectual interview techniques: Interview participants can readily grasp Dooyeweerd's aspects intuitively, so they can be asked directly about what is meaningful. Winfield's MAKE and Kane's MAIT offer two methods.	Itvw	Asp-M Ocean	§4-4.2.2 §9-6.3 §9-5.3
Aspectual analysis: As intuitively-grasped meaningfulness, Dooyeweerd's aspects are useful for analysing issues in transcripts or texts, especially for 'down-to-earth' issues, often hidden. Particularly useful in **cross-cultural** situations.	Anal	Asp-M EDX	§4-4
Writing-up research in information systems, often expects PhD candidates and other authors to name philosophies underlying their work, but often they fit poorly. Instead, they might discuss the 3-part Ground-Idea (world, rationality, origin of meaning).	Writ	G-I	§3-5.1
Using ICT in Everyday Life			
Evaluating meaningful content with which we engage: To what extent does meaningful content express the laws of each aspect?	Eval	Asp-LM	§3-7.1 §6-3.5
Evaluating gameplay and quality of virtual worlds: To what extent does virtual world richly express the laws of each aspect, with suitable modifications?	Eval	Asp-L EMC	§6-3.5.2
Anticipating use of ICT (User Requirements Analysis) and its repercussions: Consider all three engagements (EIT, EMC, ELI), how they relate, and all the aspects of each.	ISD	ISD-WP AEF	§9-5 §6-3
IS evaluation: Evaluate all three engagements (EIT, EMC, ELI), how they relate, and all aspects of each, maybe as Fig. 4-f-3.	Eval	AEF Asp-N	§6-3
The practice of ICT development			
ICT development: All developers should be aware at all times of all four responsibilities even though specialising in one. Management should instil and maintain that attitude.	Attd	Asp-N Eth-Pis	§9-3

Designing content of applications: Use Dooyeweerd's aspects to guide design of the world, with laws of every relevant aspect richly represented.	Dsgn	Asp-LWC EMC	§9-6 §6-3.5.2
Design and evaluation for tacit knowledge: Refer to aspects of knowing, because each is tacit in different ways	Dsgn Eval	Asp-K Soc Asp	§3-8.4 §4-4.2.2
Designing content of games and virtual worlds: Design virtual world to richly express the laws of each aspect, with suitable modifications	Dsgn	Asp-LW EMC	§9-6 §6-3.5.2
User interface design: Remember forgotten aspects when designing.	Dsgn	Asp-ON	§6-3.4 §6-4.1
Systems maintenance: Remember all aspects of systems maintenance, not just technical.	Mthd	MAF	§9-4 §3-8.3
Refactoring of code: Aspectual retrocipation and antecipation can help separate out issues in the code.	Mthd	Asp-D	§7-4.2.2
ICT features in practice			
Malfunctions. Use Dooyeweerd's aspects to investigate malfunctions systematically.	Dsgn	Asp-N	§5-2.5
Affordance: Evaluate and design affordances using the triple-aspect model.	Eval Dsgn	Asp-MD LSO	§6-4.15 §7-3.3
File formats, protocols Design: Fundamental idea should be around primary aspect. Ensure this is richly catered for in notation and rules.	Eval Dsgn	Asp-ML	§7-4.3
Big data: Dooyeweerd's aspects can help setting Big Data parameters.	Set	Asp-M	§5-3.8
Digital preservation: Dooyeweerd's aspects can reveal specific issues in long-term preservation.	Anal	Asp-D	§5-3.7
Software libraries design: One aspect per module (family), inter-module links reflect inter-aspect dependency in both directions, with improved appropriateness, clarity and completeness to reduce inter-library interference.	Dsgn	Asp-DL FtC	§7-4.2 §3-7.4.4

Some suggestions might be time-limited, e.g., enriching TAM, in that the activity might soon been carried out; where this is so, ignore or modify the suggestion. Many opportunities that our discussion opens up are not mentioned, and of those that are, some might be more useful than others. Some might even have misjudged the state of extant discourse, but they are all offered as possible research projects or programmes or directions, and readers and others are invited to take them up and run with them.

Key to type of research (Column 2):

- Emp: Empirical research, often interviews
- Svy: Survey of literature, or of, e.g., software packages
- Des: Design research
- TDev: Theory (or model) development
- PhF: Philosophical foundations.

12-6 Some Opportunities for Changing the Way We See Things: Paradigm Development

Table 12.3 collects together suggestions for new ways of seeing things, or ways in which extant paradigms or approaches may be taken further, using Dooyeweerdian thought and our frameworks. The foundational understandings—of *ICT use* as three subject-object engagements, each of which exhibits every aspect, of *ICT development* as four interwoven, multi-aspectual, future-oriented responsibilities, of *ICT features* as encapsulating meaningfulness to offer generic possibility, of *ICT and society* as two *Umwelten* related to their denizens by multi-aspectual correlative enkapsis, and of the *nature of ICT* as a multi-aspectual, enkaptically bound thing, where its being is rooted in meaningfulness—can open up many new avenues for research. They also provide bases upon which to critically affirm extant ways of thinking (paradigms), reveal deep problems and then enrich or enhance them.

Most of these suggestions relate to suggestions in Table 12.2. Some might contribute to theories, some to whole discourses, some to groups of discourses.

Column 1 summarises the new way of seeing things. Column 2 indicates what kind of new way it is. Columns 3 and 4 are as above: relevant portions and relevant sections.

Key to Column 2 (Type):

- Extn: Extension of existing paradigm or way of thinking
- New: New paradigm or way of thinking

Most of the above are suggestions for existing topics. The foundational understanding in this book can also help us understand and perhaps develop ways of thinking for **emerging topics**, such as ubiquitous devices or digital marketing (see §11-4.1, where the five frameworks are applied).

Table 12.2 Possible Research Projects to Develop Theoretical Bodies of Knowledge

Possible research	*Type*	*Portions of Dooy*	*See*
Research mainly around the Nature of ICT (See also Table 12.3)			
Big data: Analyse factors of Big data with Dooyeweerd's aspects.	Svy	Asp-M	§5-3.8
Digital preservation: Analyse factors of digital preservation with Dooyeweerd's aspects.	Svy	Asp-D	§5-3.7
Research mainly around ICT Use			
HCI and ease of use: Forgotten aspects: Psychic to lingual aspects of HCI have been much researched since the 1980s, and the social; what is the importance of the pistic, ethical, juridical aspects, alongside the aesthetic and economic?	Svy Emp	Asp-OM	§6-3.4 §6-4.1
Holistic view of ICT use: Having explored how each aspect of engaging with the technology is important, investigate the dependency relationships among them.	TDev	Asp-WMD	§6-3.4 §6-4.1
Loyalties to technology: Dooyeweerd's aspects, esp. pistic, ethical offer fresh insights into brand and technology loyalties.	Svy Emp	Asp-I	Table 6.2
Engaging with meaningful content (EMC) has not been sufficiently recognised, and its difference from EIT, ELI needs to be understood. Dooyeweerd's law-subject-object idea can help.	PhF	LSO Asp-MP	§6-3.5
Aspects of meaningful content: satisfaction?: Study how the information satisfaction, fulfilment and usefulness of applications correlates with the inclusion or omission of relevant aspects in its meaningful content.	Emp	Asp-MN	§6-3.5 §6-4.7
Games and virtual worlds that satisfy: Hypothesis: Gameplay is better, VWs satisfy more if they encapsulate more aspects richly. Empirically investigate what users find meaningful in each aspect encapsulated in content of world.	Emp	Asp-WM EMC	§6-4.6 §6-3.5.2 § 9–6.4
Aspects of engaging with meaningful content: Empirically explore how each aspect is important for engaging with IS content, e.g. pistic for believability.	Emp	Asp-IM	§6-3.5

(*Continued*)

Table 12.2 (Continued)

Quality of engagement with games and virtual worlds: Use Aspectual Engagements Framework to analyse quality of engagement with games and virtual worlds. e.g. challenge (formative), generosity (ethical). Link with quality of *content* of world.	Emp	AEF Asp-N EMC	§6-4.6 §6-3.5.3 §9-6.4
Tacit knowledge in EMC: Which aspects of knowing are active in engaging with meaningful content, in games, in personal IS, in organizational IS, etc.	Emp	Know Asp-K	§6-3.5 §3-8.4
Tacit knowledge in organizations: Explore the aspects of tacit knowing (beyond psychic, social). Reinterpret extant taxonomies in aspectual terms. Differ by types of social relationship?	Emp	Asp-K	§6-4.4 §3-9.6.3
Social media at work: forgotten aspects: Which aspects of social media EIT, EMC, ELI have been overlooked, and what is their importance?	Emp	AEF EDX Asp-O	§6-4.2 §6-3.6
Unexpected, indirect impacts in ICT use cause problems in ICT use. Use aspects of functioning and repercussions to investigate types of repercussion and how they arise	Svy Emp	Asp-FO ELI	§6-3.6 §3-8.2
Understanding home computing: How is each aspect important in home computing? As part of life (ELI)? In EIT? In EMC?	Emp	AEF EDX	§6-4.6 §6-3.3
Computer procrastination is a complex, little-studied problem. Breems' initial work requires deepening, to understand the complex issues involved and the interplay among them.	Emp	AEF Asp-MN	§6-3.7 §6-4.13
Data/information quality would benefit from richer understanding, esp. of overlooked aspects. Dooyeweerd's aspects can expand and situate extant classifications (Wang & Strong).	TDev	Asp-N EMC	§6-4.7
Extending TAM: Given three engagements (EIT, EMC, ELI), add a construct about engaging with meaningful content alongside PEOU, PU.	TDev Emp	EMC	§6-4.8
Extending UTAUT: Why factors like age, gender and not e.g. faith, attitude? Bring in every aspect.	TDev Emp	Asp-M	§6-4.8
Extending Delone & McLean's ISSM: ISSM seems to overlook several aspects; example given of ethical.	TDev	Asp-MN	§6-4.9

Usefulness and ICT benefits are poorly conceptualized, especially for non-organizational use e.g. games. Aspectual normativity provides philosophical grounds for understanding this and tool for studying it. Reinterpet Yousafzai's factors and undertake empirical study.	Svy Emp	Asp-N	§6-4.10 §3-7.5
Intensive use of ICT: Clarify the various stages etc. by aspects; consider missing aspects (e.g. ethical: trust) and every engagement.	TDev Emp	Asp-F AEF	§6-4.12 §6-3.3 1
Innovative use of ICT: Study aspects of innovative use; conceptualize as aspectual possibility.	Emp	Asp-P	§6-4.12 §3-8.2
ICT use and climate change: Individual responsibility about ICT use, not just as power consumption but as how it changes our behaviour. The Aspectual Engagements Framework can take all such issues into account together.	Svy Emp	AEF Asp-F	§6-4.13 §8-2.1 §8-4.2
Ethics of ICT use: Various discourses may be grounded, situated and enriched, and also brought into contact with each other by Dooyeweerd's multi-aspectual normativity and Shalom Principle.	TDev	AEF Asp-N LSO	§6-4.13
Non-use of ICT; Resistance: Analyse reasons for non-use of ICT by Dooyeweerd's aspects, which allows for multiple and complex (multi-aspectual) reasons.	Emp	Asp-R	§6-4.14
Affordance is not properly understood: While reconceptualizing affordance as suggested under 'ICT features' (below): Reinterpret extant discourses and taxonomies of affordance using this. Enrich extant taxonomies with new aspectual affordances, incl empirically. Empirically investigate new kinds of affordance, e.g. games.	Svy Emp	Asp-MPD LSO	§6-4.15 §7-3.3 Table 7.1
Research mainly around ICT Features			
Reconceptualize Affordance: We must do more than classify affordances; must understand affordance. Ground affordance in 'oceanic' meaningfulness; triple-aspect 'model' as an expression of inter-aspect dependency and normativity of each affordance. Link with Aspectual Engagements Framework. Link with ICT use above.	TDev	Ocean LSO Asp-MDN AEF	§7-3.3 §6-4.15 §3-3.1 §3-1.2.3
Appropriateness is an important norm of ICT features (interaction possibilities, innards, protocols), but what is appropriateness? Develop the ideas in §7-3.4.	TDev	Asp-N	§7-3.4 §6-4.15

(*Continued*)

Table 12.2 (Continued)

Quality of ICT features: Survey literature on quality of ICT features through lens of aspectual appropriateness of interaction possibilities, innards and protocols.	Svy	Asp-N	§7-3 §6-4.15
Understanding Malfunctions. Use the idea of four aspectual dysfunctions.	TDev	Asp-N	§5-2
Software libraries: 1. Evaluate extant software libraries against aspectual appropriateness of innards. 2. Enrich extant. 3. Design ontologies for new aspects.	Des	Asp-ML	§7-4.2 §9-6.2 Table 7.3
File formats, protocols: Review protocols, file formats: how well their constructs cater for rich meaningfulness in each relevant aspect (primary, secondary).	Svy	Asp-M	§7-4.3 Table 7.5
Text-handling facilities currently inadequately cover full everyday experience of text-handling. Survey extant text protocols for suitability to handle this; Table 7.5 shows how, but needs developing. Design 'ideal' text-handling facility. Similarly with facilities meaningful in other aspects.	Svy Des	EDX Asp-M	§7-4.3.2 Table 7.5
Research mainly around ICT and Society			
Situating societal paradigms: Aspectually analyse ICT-and-society paradigms like TD, SCOT, SST to situate them in a wider picture. Empirically investigate the realities of work within these paradigms, to reveal which aspects are seen as important in each. Surprise us with grounds for dialogue, collaboration and mutual enrichment!	Svy Emp	Asp-M	§8-4.1
Analysis of widespread impacts of ICT using Table 8.1 (climate change) as example, on data from survey or empirical studies.	Svy Emp	Asp-F	§8-4.2.2 §6-4.13
Societal issues: Forgotten aspects: Among societal issues like surveillance or hacking, many aspects are overlooked; esp. aesthetic, ethical. Explore how all aspects important.	Svy TDev	Asp-O	§8-4.2.2
Life without ICT: Use aspects to study the life of those without ICT. Gain richer picture of what precisely is problematic about the **digital divide.**	Emp	Asp-NM	§8-4.3
Structuration theory: Overcome anomalies using Dooyeweerd's aspects and correlative enkapsis. Clarify, enrich Giddens' notion of values. Dooyeweerd's 'oceanic' view of meaningfulness and law subverts conventional macro-micro opposition.	TDev	Asp-M Umw Ocean	§8-4.5 §8-5.3 §8-5.4

Research mainly around ICT Development			
ICT development as multi-aspectual responsibilities: Develop the Four Responsibilities Framework by analysing extant advice/guidance on development of many kinds (e.g. games). Work to establish the framework in extant thought, then test its usefulness empirically. **Multiview** might be amenable to incorporating its ideas.	Svy	Asp-MN	§9-3 ff.
Views about ISD responsibilities. Explore e.g. C2's responsibilities of IS developers.	TDev	Asp-N	§9-4.2
Agile development: Critically analyse principles and practice of agile development; enrich for longevity and wider kinds of systems.	TDev Emp	Asp-N Asp-I	§9-7.2
Systems maintenance has little theoretical underpinning: Empirically investigate importance of each aspect in systems maintenance and upgrade, yielding better guidance. With this and Dooyeweerd's discussion of change, build theory.	Emp TDev	Asp-M Thing	§9-4.2
Aspectual interview techniques: Test, expand, develop *MAKE* for eliciting tacit knowledge, and *MAIT* for supportive interviewing. The 'oceanic' nature of Dooyeweerd's aspects makes aspectual analysis useful in **cross-cultural** situations.	Emp Svy	Asp-M Ocean	§9-6.3 §9-5.3 §4-4.2.2
Aspectual analysis: See Practice. Useful in Grounded Theory and interpretive field studies?		Asp-M	§4-4
Knowledge elicitation: Develop a knowledge elicitation technique combining both the Why and What Else questions with aspects	Emp	Asp-M	§9-6.3
Games development: Establish Bartle's theory of games development, enrich his principles — or those of others.	TDev	Asp-MN	§9-2.6 §9-6.4
Gamification of serious software: Dangers of inauthenticity might be addressed by understanding that games and gamified software are led by different aspects.	TDev	Asp-Q Asp-D	§9-2.6 §9-6.5

12-7 Opportunities for Direction, Philosophical Underpinnings or Philosophy Itself

Suggestions were made for new directions for the information systems field as a whole, for new frameworks for understanding areas of fields and for fresh thinking in philosophy itself—both mainstream and Dooyeweerdian philosophy. These are summarised further on in Table 12.4.

Key to Column 2 (Type):

- Dirn: Direction to be taken by the field of IS
- Dooy: Contributing to Dooyeweerd's philosophy
- PhF: Using philosophy to develop frameworks for understanding
- Phil: Contributing to philosophy itself

In addition to these, the very structure of the argument in the main chapters might indicate how such ideas might be worked out in other fields. Chapter 6, for example, starts with a few examples, reviews discourses in terms of what seems centrally meaningful to them or their *raison detre*, introduces a structure, then applies Dooyeweerd's philosophy to account for that and provide an understanding, then applies that back into the discourses. Other chapters demonstrate a different flow of argument. The attitude is to affirm, critique and enrich each discourse, not reject or undermine it, and also to show how they may all be situated in relation to each other and to the coherence of the field being addressed. Throughout, I have adopted an *everyday perspective*, and focused on *meaningfulness*. This implies working from the human towards the issues.

12-8 What Now?

This book offers three things:

- It has shown how Dooyeweerd's philosophy can be used to think about issues in information systems and ICT.
- It has developed foundational frameworks for understanding five main areas of ICT.
- It has offered suggestions for research that can be carried out, and how practice can be improved.

It is now the turn of the reader to carry on the work (see Preface). Readers may enter at any of these levels to benefit from Dooyeweerd's ideas. They will be considered in reverse order, since the last-mentioned is perhaps the easiest to enter.

12-8.1 How to Carry on This Work

To benefit from the suggestions for *practice* requires merely to understand the proposals (tool, technique, method), and use them. An internalised understanding of Dooyeweerd's aspects would help.

Table 12.3 Changing the Way We Think (Paradigms, etc.)

Research	*Type*	*Portions of Dooy*	*See*
Ways of Seeing the Nature of ICT			
Supervenience, emergence 'smuggle in' the meaningfulness of the aspect that is emerging. Dooyeweerd's notion of oceanic meaningfulness and aspects might account for them and open up new avenues of research.	New	Asp-M Ocean	§3-7.1
Data, Information, Knowledge may be understood as differentiated yet integrated with Dooyeweerd's aspects.	Extn	Asp-ML	§5-3
Artificial intelligence question ("Computer = Human?" generates fruitless conflict because of dualistic ground-motives. Question presuppositions about the "=", with Dooyeweerd's notion of Being-as-meaning. AI as multi-aspectual LSO relationship.	New	GMtv LSO	§5-6
Ways of Seeing ICT Use			
HCI, ease of use: Multi-aspectual: Give importance to every aspect, alongside those already considered.	Extn	Asp-M	§6-3.4 §6-4.1
Aspects of meaningful content: For quality of content, focus on spheres of meaningfulness (aspects) of content, not just methods. In both serious applications and games.	New	Asp-M	§6-3.5.2
Engaging with meaningful content: Recognise that EMC cannot be reduced to EIT or ELI. Understand links between them.	New	AEF	§6-3.5
Task-technology fit, User-system-task, as paradigms, contain ambiguities: Resolve these using Dooyeweerd's aspectual understanding of subject and objects (prior, generated), and the distinction between EIT, EMC, ELI.	Extn	LSO AEF Asp-M	§6-4.11 §3-3.1.2
Benefits as multi-aspectual normativity: Benefits and usefulness may be understood by Shalom Principle of multi-aspectual normativity.	New	Asp-MN	§6-4.10
Extending the Socio-technical approach: Socio-technical recognises formative, social aspects; Why not add lingual? Then all other aspects, of what is meaningful in IS?	New	Asp-M	§6-2.3 §6-4.3

(*Continued*)

Table 12.3 (Continued)

Research	*Type*	*Portions of Dooy*	*See*
Multi-aspectual tacit knowledge: Foundational understanding of tacit knowledge is weak, uncritically referring to few influential thinkers. Reinterpret as aspectual ways of knowing.	Extn	Asp-K	§6-4.4 §9-6
Systems as enkaptic wholes: Much systems thinking is weakened by part-whole presupposition. Use Dooyeweerd's notions of enkapsis and multi-aspectual things.	New	Enk Asp-V	§6-4.5
Multi-aspectual Actor Networks might benefit from separating out aspects of functioning, recognising Dooyeweerd's intimate subject-object functioning, subject-by-proxy and aspectual dependency.	Extn	Asp-D LSO	§6-4.5 §3-3.1 §5-4.4
Multi-aspectual Normativity (Ethics) of ICT Use: Fragmented discourse. Innate normativity of Dooyeweerd's aspects can integrate.	New?	Asp-N	§6-4.13 §3-7.5
ICT and climate change: Weak, limited discourse; strengthen and enrich with Aspectual Engagements Framework.	New?	AEF	§6-2.13 §8-4.2
Innovative use of ICT: Reconceptualize innovative use as aspectual potential, linked with affordance, rather than as either expression of freedom or something to measure.	New	Asp-P	§6-4.12 §6-2.12
Non-use of ICT ignored or reduced to resistance. Multi-levelled understandings of non-use may be grounded in aspects, aspectual possibility and inter-dependency, as offered by 'oceanic' views.	New	Asp-PD	§6-4.14
Down-to-earth issues in ICT use ('Meaningful Use'): Most IS literature on ICT use discusses issues meaningful to management, academics, etc., ignoring 'down-to-earth' issues meaningful to users. Dooyeweerd's respect for everyday experience offers philosophical grounding for this.	New	EDX DivM Asp-W	§6-2.16 §6-4.16 §3-1.1
Life domains of ICT use: relatively new paradigm in ICT use, poorly defined. Identify life domains by what is centrally meaningful in them (aspects), and suggest other domains.	Extn	Asp-I	§6-4.17

Virtual worlds: See VWs or games as virtual law-side and their quality as furnished by incorporating every aspect as meaningful content. Helps evaluation, design.	New	Asp-LM EMC	§6-4.6 §6-3.5.2 §9-2.6 §9-6.4
Ways of Seeing ICT Features			
Materiality of ICT: Analogy with the physical aspect from each aspect of ICT. How does each express some different important feature of materiality? Affirm, critique, ground, enrich the materiality analogy.	Extn	Asp-A	§7-3.2
Understanding ICT features in IS field: See ICT features as interaction possibilities, innards and protocols. Two main issues in each: affordance, appropriateness.	New	FtC	§7-3 §7-4
Software libraries: 1. On what basis may we soundly critique software libraries, especially in relation to future possibility? Instead of focusing on mere design-and-implementation, focus on what *aspectual meaningfulness* is encapsulated in libraries. 2. *Philosophical underpinning*: libraries as virtual law-sides, one per aspect, covering interaction possibilities, innards and protocols, and aspectual appropriateness.	New	Asp-ML Asp-DI FtC	§7-4.2 §9-6.2
Aspect-oriented File formats, protocols are not just sets of constructs and rules, but should be oriented to the meaningfulness of all relevant aspects (primary, secondary), according to 'real-life' use.	New	Asp-MI	§7-4.3
Ways of Seeing ICT and Society			
Values are ambiguous. Dooyeweerd's suite of aspects has been employed to introduce Ecosystem valuing; do something similar for IS, ICT.	New	Asp-NM	§8-4.3 §10-3
Aspects of Digital Divide: What actually is wrong about a digital divide? Reference aspectual normativity to clarify.	New	Asp-N	§8-4.3
Questioning Western culture: Opposing Western v. non-Western cultures, economic growth v. anti-capitalism too binary. Nuance with Dooyeweerd's aspectual idea of progress and importance of ethical and pistic aspects.	Extn	Prog Asp-MN	§8-5.4 §8-6.1.3

(*Continued*)

Table 12.3 (Continued)

Research	*Type*	*Portions of Dooy*	*See*
Progress, modernity, role of ICT: Humanity's opening up of each aspect should serve other aspects. ICT may be seen as contributing to the opening up of the lingual aspect, which then enables others to be opened up.	New	Prog	§5-3 §8-6.1
Philosophy of technology: Instead of 'technology' (formative aspect), consider 'information' (lingual), with three engagements, spanning personal and societal.	New	Lng Asp AEF	§5-2 §8-6.1
Ways of Seeing ICT Development			
ICT development as a human activity: Beyond 'socio-technical' and organizational IS, see ICT development as multi-aspectual responsibility of four kinds, which covers its everyday experience. Can enrich socio-technical approaches.	Extn	Asp-PFN EDX	Ch. 9
Aspect-oriented programming (AOP), philosophical foundation: Affirm, critique and enrich AOP with Dooyeweerd's aspects.	Extn	Asp-WM	§7-4.2.3

Table 12.4 Possible Research Directions or Philosophical Underpinnings

Research	*Type*	*Portions of Dooy*	*See*
Dooyeweerd-oriented research: Table 4.3 suggests where Dooyeweerd's ideas might be useful in research. Needs development by review or deliberate trial.	Dirn	All	§4-4.1 Table 4.3
Broaden reach of IS field beyond organizational contexts, to home computing, personal ICT use. Learn from silos of application. Aspects are applicable and normative to all ICT use (oceanic). Each kind finds an aspect primarily meaningful (organizational use is social).	Dirn	Ocean Asp-MN AEF	§6-4.6 §6-4.17
Relationships between areas of IS field: Relationships between the five areas in Part II occur at various levels, but have not been adequately discussed. Use aspects to analyse them and disclose hidden ones.	PhF	Five areas	Fig. 10-f-1
Research approaches in IS: Research approaches may be situated according to Dooyeweerd's notion of philosophical Ground-Idea, as in Table 4.1. Bring in other approaches, including Critical Realism.	Svy	G-I	§4-2.2
ICT as centred on lingual aspect): Develop implications of ICT being qualified by lingual aspect, not formative (technology). Gives **dignity and responsibility of the IS field.**	Dirn	Lng Asp	§5-2.5 §8-6.1
Computer system levels, e.g. Newell: Ground in Dooyeweerd's aspects.	PhF	Asp-V	§5-4.2
Four roles for computer: Computer-as-tool, computer-as-agent, computer-in-the-world, and computer-as-world views may be grounded and integrated in Dooyeweerd's understanding of existence.	PhF	LSO Umw	§5-4.1
What Is ICT Use? Undertake a philosophical transcendental critique of the universal and necessary conditions that make ICT use possible. Will require TC of ICT too.	PhF	T-C	§3-4.3 §6-3.2
Philosophy of information is still in development: (Floridi's 'open problems' are too cognitivist). Seeing information as lingually-qualified law-subject-object activity can assist this.	PhF	Asp-M	§5-3

(*Continued*)

Table 12.4 (Continued)

Research	*Type*	*Portions of Dooy*	*See*
Critical Realism: Like Dooyeweerd, CR maintains there is a reality behind phenomena. But it theorizes everdyay experience.	Phil	EDX Ocean	§3-4.1.1
Exploring the nature of meaning. Discuss how the kinds of (inter-)subjective meaning relate to oceanic meaningfulness.	Phil	Mng Ocean	§3-1.2 §3-8.2 §8-6.1.1
Testing, enriching Dooyeweerd's philosophy. Many suggestions have been made: Testing (§5-8) Meaning (§3-1.2.3, §6-4.15, §6-4.16, §8-6.1) CFR (§3-2.4) aspectual targets (§3-7.4.6) qualifying aspect (§3-9.4, §7-3.3) enkapsis (§3-9.6.2, §6-3.3, §9-3.3, §8-5) *Gegenstand* (§3-4.3.4) subject-object (§3-3.1.2, §5-4.4)	Dooy	Various	

To benefit from suggestions for *research projects*, readers may peruse the lists above and select research opportunities that interest them. Some of the suggestions are PhD-sized, a few are smaller, perhaps Masters-sized. A number are larger and might require multi-person, multi-project research activities. Opportunities exist for several research approaches, some being for testing hypotheses or ideas (positivist), some for gaining insight (interpretive), some for subverting prevailing assumptions, structures or attitudes (socio-critical), some for action research, some for design.

Read the referenced sections, and then the sections around them to gain context. All the references to sections of Chapter 3 (Dooyeweerd's Philosophy) should be followed up, in order to gain a grasp not only of the material of Dooyeweerd, but his mindset and the reasons he thought this way. Entering into Dooyeweerd's thought will be more fruitful than merely applying it. Then discuss and develop the research proposal and plan and carry out the research.

To benefit from the *foundational frameworks*, readers should thoroughly understand them, especially their motivations and how they try to relate to everyday experience. With the frameworks, examine extant ideas to see how those ideas might be affirmed, critiqued and enriched using the framework, perhaps following exemplars of doing this in each chapter—though readers might find better ways. Readers will then have begun to know the frameworks by use rather than just theory and may apply them to critique of paradigms or even the development of new paradigms.

The frameworks themselves need development. Those who have applied are in a good place to do that. I am quite happy if various versions emerge. I hope that some will become successful in mainstream thought—as long as they are reasonably faithful to Dooyeweerd's ideas.

Readers who wish to *apply Dooyeweerd's ideas* directly should first become familiar with relevant portions of his philosophy. I do not recommend reading Dooyeweerd's (1955) at first, because it is complex, tortuous and intended for philosophers. Instead, absorb the relevant sections of Chapter 3 and try to internalise it by seeing how the ideas relate in everyday life. For instance, if the reader wishes to apply Dooyeweerd's aspects, I recommend reading sections 3-6 to 3-8, then read around these, then read Chapter 4, which shows various ways of aspectual analysis. Then read through the chapters in Part II to see how aspects have been applied. While doing this, keep looking at aspects of your own life; this will help provide deeper intuitive understanding. At any stage, be ready to apply them in practice or research, but be modest about level of understanding; this author is still learning them.

Be aware, however, that my interpretation of Dooyeweerd might be disputed; I have tried to indicate, throughout, where this might be so (summary: §11-4.2). After understanding using this book, it is probably wise to read other material on Dooyeweerd, and even parts of Dooyeweerd's own *New Critique* (1955), which includes a good index.

Dooyeweerd's *New Critique* is available from the Dutch National Library for free download at:

Volume I, philosophy, transcendental critique and history: www.dbnl.org/tekst/dooy002newc05_01/
Volume II, aspects and epistemology: www.dbnl.org/tekst/dooy002newc05_02/
Volume III, things, relationships and the state: www.dbnl.org/tekst/dooy002newc05_03/
Volume IV, thematic index: www.dbnl.org/tekst/dooy002newc05_04/

The author's own *Dooyeweerd Pages* website (www.dooy.info/) discusses or explains many issues, some in a structured way, others ad-hoc. I hope to produce a work on Dooyeweerd in 2018 that is specifically aimed at researchers who need arguments and references, because I do not know of any such work extant.

Have fun! If you use Dooyeweerd's ideas, make them your own.

12-8.2 Attitudes and Approaches

Exposure to Dooyeweerd's ideas has had a profound effect on my way of viewing the world; indeed, it has made me a different person. I am not the only person to find this. An understanding of Dooyeweerd's aspects and a recognition of the groundedness of meaningfulness sensitises one to hidden issues and perspectives, for example, during discussions or when reading. More than an intellectual change, this calls for a change in attitude. I have found that my attitude towards ICT and towards Dooyeweerd and philosophy have changed.

My attitude towards ICT has become less compartmentalised, more aware of both global responsibilities and technical or human detail together, more concerned to benefit the world rather than just myself by my research and more open to harmonizing apparently disparate ideas. My attitude to philosophy has become more interested in the big picture, and also more gracious, valuing all kinds of philosophy, whether fashionable or not, but also more critical because Dooyeweerd's notion of three-part Ground-Idea (§3-5.1) offers a sound basis for critique than mere reaction is.

My attitude to Dooyeweerd has become more open. I can welcome critique of Dooyeweerd's ideas and explore it. Unfortunately there has been too little serious, immanent critique of his ideas and none yet from mainstream thinking.

Readers who are skeptical about Dooyeweerd should perhaps give his ideas a trial; then they can properly contribute to critique. Example: Once, early on, a colleague dismissed (my representation of) Dooyeweerd's aspects as, "It's too essentialist for me!" That remark did stimulate me to find out whether Dooyeweerd was in fact essentialist (he wasn't), and it raised the issue of what exactly is problematic about essentialism. Had I challenged him thus, he might then have been open to a more nuanced consideration of the non-essentialist Dooyeweerd, to critique and enrich his thought even if he did not adopt Dooyeweerd's ideas.

I have written this book to encourage engagement and dialogue between Dooyeweerd and mainstream thought in ways that are *interesting to the latter*. Dooyeweerd gave plenty of evidence that he respected mainstream thought, where it is good quality, and would himself try to engage with it.

What I have tried to do is to model use of Dooyeweerd to encourage this. I have been guided by a four-part approach: to listen, affirm, critique and enrich extant thought, which I can recommend. Listen from an everyday perspective, not just academic. Affirm rather than reject (however much my ego wishes to do the latter). Critique rather than uncritically accept (however hard this may be). Enrich rather than tinker (however much extra care this calls for).

- *Listen*. Listen to the discourses intently and immanently, to discern what is primarily meaningful in them, which explains the reason they occur and what their main contributions might be, and also to uncover their deepest assumptions and presuppositions. I have found Dooyeweerd's respect for pre-theoretical experience most encouraging.
- *Affirm*. Affirm what extant thought finds meaningful and good (to-be-aspired-to), where possible, and place it on a Dooyeweerdian foundation of what is meaningful in reality (usually Dooyeweerd's aspects). In *theories*, the concepts that constitute the theory are often affirmed by reference to aspects that make them meaningful. When new *paradigms* or approaches are introduced, what can be affirmed is often found in the identification of problems with previous thought. I have found Dooyeweerd's view of meaningfulness and his theories of aspects, the subject-object relationship and enkapsis most helpful (§3-1.2, §3-7, §3-8, §3-3.1.2, §3-9.6.2).
- *Critique*. Critique extant thought, not from the outside, where things meaningful to the critic are not meaningful to that which is being critiqued, but from the inside, in terms of what is important to that which is being critiqued (i.e., immanent critique). Critique of *theories* is often most fruitful when aimed at what is ignored. I have found Dooyeweerd's suite of aspects most useful here. Critique of *paradigms* should normally be aimed, not at what motivates them (which is likely to be affirmed) but at revealing presuppositions (meaning-context, Origin of Meaning) that prevent them from being worked out successfully. I have found Dooyeweerd's discussion of ground-motives and the Immanence Standpoint (§3-2) most useful here.
- *Enrich*. Enrich extant thought, by suggesting wider perspectives that it might adopt. Enriching the discourse around both *theories* and

paradigms might draw attention to aspects that have been overlooked; I have found Dooyeweerd's suite of aspects particularly useful for this.

So, let us take courage and move forward in exploring how Dooyeweerd's ideas can contribute to and engage with the mainstream discourses—discourses that are currently going on in research and practice in areas ranging across the individual and organizational, developmental, technological, societal and the philosophical. It may be that this can apply, not just in the information systems field and to ICT, but in any field—for example, urban sustainability (Brandon and Lombardi 2005; Gunton et al. 2017).

In his foreword to his *New Critique*, Dooyeweerd (1955, I, vii) wrote:

> I am strongly convinced that for the fruitful working out of this philosophy, in a genuinely scientific manner, there is needed a staff of fellow-labourers who would be in a position independently to think through its basic ideas in the special scientific fields.

That is what I have tried to do. If Dooyeweerd's are ideas are fundamentally flawed, then this needs to be discovered. However, it can only be discovered after mainstream thinkers have properly understood, employed and tried his ideas, discovered problems and then tried to fix the problems. Those not fixed indicate genuine flaws, with which Dooyeweerd himself would agree. I suspect, however, that we shall find his ideas very useful in both research and practice, and that Dooyeweerd is worthy of sitting alongside the great thinkers of the world.

References

Brandon PS, Lombardi P. 2005. *Evaluating Sustainable Development in the Built Environment*. Blackwell Science, Oxford, UK.

Dooyeweerd H. 1955. *A New Critique of Theoretical Thought* (Vols. I–IV, 1975 ed.). Paideia Press, Jordan Station, Ontario, Canada.

Gunton RM, vanAsperen E, Basden A, Bookless D, Araya Y, Hanson DR, Goddard MA, Otieno G, Jones GO. 2017. Beyond ecosystem services: Valuing the invaluable. *Trends in Ecology and Evolution*, 32(4), 249-57.

Index

The page numbers for tables are in **bold** and the page numbers for figures are in *italics*. Section numbers are preceded by §, with page numbers for the sections following in parentheses. Specific tables, figures, and chapters are identified with Figure, Table, and Chapter, followed by the number. Underlined references indicate key material.